OUR ETERNAL DESTINY

OUR ETERNAL DESTINY

A Chronology of Scriptural Prophecies from the Beginning to the End of the World

Greg Hammond

I want to thank my wife, Michelle, for the cover design and editing.

I am grateful for all of the incredible artists and photographers whose talents help bring the scriptures to life.

The inclusion of any artwork, figures, illustrations, photographs, charts, or other types of images in this book should not be construed as an endorsement of the subject matter contained in this book on the part of any copyright holders or creators of those images.

Also, the arrangement of scriptures and commentary in this book is solely my own and has not been endorsed in any way by The Church of Jesus Christ of Latter-day Saints.

Cover Designed by Michelle Hammond

Cover Image – Portrait of Christ, by Heinrich Hoffman

Our Eternal Destiny, ***A Chronology of Scriptural Prophecies from the Beginning to the End of the World.***

Colonel Dudley Publishing

Library of Congress Cataloging-in-Publication Data is available upon request.

ISBN 978-1-63972-538-0 (hardback)

ISBN 978-0-578-25177-6 (paperback)

To my wife Michelle,

And my children Cheyenne, Brant, Sienna, Charlotte,

Everett, Marlowe, and Gwen

Always remember who you are...and what you are becoming.

Surely the Lord GOD will do nothing, until he revealeth his secret unto his servants the prophets.

Amos 3:7

Table of Contents

Introduction

And the king said that a seer is greater than a prophet.

And Ammon said that a seer is a revelator and a prophet also; and a gift which is greater can no man have, except he should possess the power of God, which no man can; yet a man may have great power given him from God.

But a seer can know of things which are past, and also of things which are to come, and by them shall all things be revealed, or, rather, shall secret things be made manifest, and hidden things shall come to light, and things which are not known shall be made known by them, and also things shall be made known by them which otherwise could not be known.

Thus God has provided a means that man, through faith, might work mighty miracles; therefore he becometh a great benefit to his fellow beings.

Mosiah 8:15-18

The Book of Mormon

I have always been fascinated by the accounts of prophesies and visions found in the scriptures. Some seers, like Moses and Abraham, were shown the Creation of the Earth and the events of the Garden of Eden and the Fall of Adam and Eve. Other seers were given visions wherein they saw the events of Jesus Christ's life and His mission. While others, like John the Revelator, witnessed the events leading up to the Second Coming of Christ.

Upwards of sixty different seers and prophets in the scriptures saw visions that detailed what would be the history of God's children here on Earth. These accounts are scattered throughout thousands of pages of scripture, and in no particular order.

The purpose of this book is to arrange these scriptural prophecies and visions in chronological order, the result being one grand narrative of our history on Earth. Beginning with our preexistence and the War in Heaven, each chapter in this book addresses a different prophesied, historical event. Many prophesies have already been fulfilled, while others are still to come. When read in chronological order, the story the Lord is telling jumps off the page, and it becomes clear how and why one event leads to the next. It is stunning how prophets from different time periods and on different continents consistently describe the same future events – often using identical words and phrases.

It is difficult to conceive of a more exciting and personally meaningful story. Contained herein are prophesies and visions, given by the Lord Jesus Christ to His prophets and seers, that reveal our eternal destiny as children of God.

It is the ultimate story of good triumphing over evil. It is the story of the Lord's great plan of salvation for his children. It is the story of...

- Our pre-Earth life
- The Creation
- The origin of life
- Our relationship with God
- The Fall of Adam and Eve
- The purpose of life
- The life, ministry, and Atonement of Jesus Christ
- The growth of his church on two continents 2,000 years ago
- A worldwide Apostasy
- The Restoration of the gospel in the latter-days
- The gathering of Israel prior to the Second Coming of Christ
- The covenant people of God
- The destruction of the wicked prior to the Millennial reign of Christ
- What happens to us all after we die

Organizing this book was like piecing together a massive puzzle. For example, to get the full account of the Battle of Armageddon one must not only read John's Revelation, but also the accounts recorded by Joel, Ezekiel, Jeremiah, Nephi, Zechariah, Isaiah, and Joseph Smith (from multiple sections in the Doctrine and Covenants). Other events involve even more prophetic witnesses and even more page turning. Having to jump from source to source diminishes the momentum that can be gained from reading the revelations consecutively. Also, when read straight through, details stand out and the Lord's mission for us comes front and center, clear and unmistakable.

I had many instances along the way where the Spirit helped me understand and make sense of different parts of the gospel story. Such as, why was it so important for the gospel to be preached to the Gentiles? Why was it so important for the saints to build a temple when the church was restored in 1830? Why was the restored Church commanded to practice plural marriage? How many different Resurrections are there, when do they occur, and why? How will the living survive the Second Coming when the wicked will be burned as stubble? As you read the prophetic story in this book, the answers to these and many other questions will be revealed to you.

I have added commentary and historical background at the beginning of each chapter and throughout the book to guide the reader. I do not, however, want the book to be about me or what I think. The intent is to focus on the words of the prophets. There is tremendous power and authority in the scriptures you are about to read.

The sources used here include the Old and New Testaments of the Bible, the Book of Mormon, the Doctrine and Covenants, and the Pearl of Great Price. For those who are unfamiliar with the Church of Jesus Christ of Latter-Day Saints, let me first provide an explanation of the Book of Mormon, Doctrine and Covenants, and Pearl of Great Price.

The Book of Mormon contains the writings of ancient prophets who inhabited the American continent between 2000 BC to 400 AD. Their writings were ultimately compiled into one book by an ancient prophet named Mormon. Just as the Bible describes God's dealings with his people in Israel, Egypt, and Europe, the Book of Mormon tells the story of his people who lived in ancient America. It teaches the gospel and testifies of our Savior, Jesus Christ.

The Book of Mormon is unique among scriptures in that it was not written for the people of ancient America. It was written and then buried in the ground by a prophet who knew the only people who would ever read it were the people in our day. Isaiah and Ezekiel foresaw this latter-day event where truth would spring forth out of the

Earth allowing those ancient prophets of the Americas to whisper from the dust to testify of the Lord Jesus Christ.

The Book of Mormon was preserved by the Lord to come forth in the last days to usher in the Restoration of the gospel by the prophet Joseph Smith, who was able to translate the Book of Mormon by the miraculous gift and power of God. It was published in 1830. The coming forth of the Book of Mormon is the sign given that the gathering of Israel would begin prior to the Second Coming of Jesus Christ.

The Doctrine and Covenants is a volume of scripture that is comprised of direct revelations and visions received mainly by the prophet Joseph Smith. It is not a translation of ancient records. It is modern revelation – the voice of the Lord Jesus Christ speaking to us in our day. Joseph Smith said that the Doctrine and Covenants is "the foundation of the Church in these last days, and a benefit to the world, showing that the keys of the mysteries of the kingdom of our Savior are again entrusted to man." (section heading for Doctrine and Covenants Section 70).

For the biblical prophesies, I use the Joseph Smith Translation of the King James Version of the Bible. Joseph Smith was called upon to provide a translation of the Bible. Using a copy of the King James Bible as his starting point, he restored many parts of the Bible that had been lost or corrupted over the centuries. Selections from the Bible where the prophet Joseph Smith was inspired to translate differently than the King James Version are written in italics and labeled [JST] (Joseph Smith Translation) for reference.

Some of the more lengthy passages of scripture from Joseph Smith's Translation of the Bible were published in 1850 as The Pearl of Great Price. This volume of scripture contains the visions of Moses and Abraham, and the Olivet Discourse from the Book of Matthew, as well Joseph Smith's record of his First Vision and his account of receiving the gold plates, which contained the Book of Mormon, from the angel Moroni.

In addition, I reference the King Follett Discourse, which was a sermon given by Joseph Smith to a gathering of some 10,000 saints at the funeral of a fellow church member named King Follett. The sermon is significant as Joseph lends his understanding of many of the doctrines described in this book such as the nature of God and man. While not considered scripture, Joseph Smith's insights into these topics are of great interest.

I also included the dedication of the Holy Land for the return of the Jewish people by an early church apostle, Elder Orson Hyde. This dedication and prophecy, given in 1841, would be fulfilled, in dramatic fashion, in the 190 years that followed.

For each scriptural citation, I list the name of the book of scripture (i.e., Isaiah), the chapter number, the prophet's name, and approximate year the prophecy was given. I have used the Bible Dictionary for the approximate dates of Old Testament prophecies, and I have relied on the currently accepted dates of New Testament writings. Many of these dates are estimates and should not be considered exact. The purpose of adding the dates is simply to give the reader some perspective on when the prophecy was originally given.

Prophecies of historical events in between the Fall of Adam and the birth of Christ are not included in this book. I wanted to tie the Fall of Adam to the Redemption of Christ and then pick up the historical narrative from there. Ancient events such as the Flood, the Exodus, the fall of the Kingdoms of Israel and Judah, while important, are less relevant in our day. The focus of this book is primarily on the mission of Jesus Christ and on the latter-day events leading up to the Second Coming of Christ.

At times it was difficult to attribute the prophetic source of a certain prophecy. For example, when compiling his inspired translation of the Bible, Joseph Smith received divine revelation that restored many of the original writings of Moses, which are now found in the Pearl of Great Price. In some of those scriptural passages, Moses quoted older prophets, such as Enoch. Enoch's prophecy, from 3000 BC, was lost to history until the Lord revealed it to Moses. Then the account of Moses was lost to history and restored by Joseph Smith. Should credit for the prophecy, then, be given to Enoch, Moses, or Joseph Smith? All had a role to play, but in most instances, I gave credit to the original author of the prophecy, in this case Enoch.

While the scriptures referenced here are attributed to specific prophets and seers, it is with the understanding that the words therein were given by Jesus Christ. Quite often, the prophecies are direct quotes from Christ himself. This is particularly true with respect to the visions and revelations recorded by Joseph Smith in the Doctrine and Covenants. These revelations almost always beginning with phrases such as: "Thus saith the Lord…" "Hearken O ye people of my Church…" "I am Alpha and Omega, the beginning and the end, the redeemer of the world…" "Hearken unto the voice of the Lord your God…" I give Joseph Smith credit with receiving the revelation, but the words are the Lord's.

In organizing this book, I gained a new appreciation for the contributions made to the prophetic vision of our Earthly existence by the prophet Joseph Smith. In comparing the sheer output of scripture, no other prophet, seer, or revelator comes close to Joseph Smith. For example, Moses is credited with the first five books of the Old Testament – just over 308 pages. The writings of Isaiah comprise about 80 pages. Joseph Smith, by comparison, received 135 revelations recorded in the Doctrine and Covenants – about 280 pages. He also recorded his First Vision and his visions with the Angel Moroni. And he would also translate the entire 531 pages of the Book of Mormon by pure prophetic inspiration. None other than Isaiah himself described the miraculous coming forth of the Book of Mormon as a "marvelous work and wonder" and a miracle on the level of "the Lord making bare his arm in the eyes of all nations" (Isa 52:10). Joseph Smith also wrote an inspired translation of the Bible in which many of the plain and precious truths of the gospel were restored. He was a remarkable seer.

This book tells the story of our past, present and future as the Lord has revealed it to his prophets. Most of the prophecies in this book have already been fulfilled. It's 2021 – we are 21 years into the seventh thousand-year period, or 7th seal as John describes it. The gospel has been restored; the Book of Mormon has gone forth throughout the Earth, ushering in the gathering of Israel; and temples dot the Earth. What an exciting time to be alive! Prophets throughout history have described our times – but we get to live them! We get to experience the gathering of Israel, the sacred ordinances of the restored gospel, and the saving of souls from both sides of the veil.

Of greatest importance, perhaps, are the prophecies that lie ahead. History has borne witness that the prophecies up to the current day have been fulfilled, thus the prophecies of future events will certainly also be fulfilled. Soon the remaining events will unfold: the Jews will embrace the gospel, a temple will be built in Jerusalem, Christ will appear and save his people at the Battle of Armageddon, the saints will be resurrected, Christ will return, the Earth will be purified, the wicked and rebellious will be consumed and cast out from the presence of Christ, and the kingdom of God will be established on Earth.

I am grateful for my testimony of God the Father, his Son Jesus Christ, and of the truthfulness of the gospel as taught in the Church of Jesus Christ of Latter-day Saints. Writing and organizing this book has strengthened my faith immeasurably, and helped me understand many aspects of the gospel.

I believe that your faith will be strengthened by reading this book. I believe that you will see where you fit into the Lord's grand plan of salvation. I hope that you choose the side of faith, repentance, and happiness that awaits those who are saved by the Atonement of Jesus Christ. In doing so you will have joy and live with confidence, knowing who you are and who you are becoming. Our sacred responsibility is to be prepared for what is surely to come. After reading the prophecies in this book, we will not be able to claim ignorance. Our time is short, and the end is near. The Lord has given us the full story; we know how it will end. What course will we choose? Our eternal destiny awaits.

Part 1

PROPHECIES OF THE CREATION, THE WAR IN HEAVEN, AND THE FALL OF ADAM AND EVE

1

WORLDS WITHOUT NUMBER

+++

Abraham, Moses, and Joseph Smith each receive visions wherein they converse with the Lord face-to-face and are shown the expanse of the universe and magnitude of God's creations. God reveals that he has created worlds without number, but that he will only reveal the details about the Creation of the Earth. God does not address the question of the origin and Creation of the universe.

DOCTRINE AND COVENANTS 76

Joseph Smith — *February 1832*

11 We, Joseph Smith, Jun., and Sidney
Rigdon, being in the Spirit on the six-
teenth day of February, in the year of our
Lord one thousand eight hundred and
thirty-two—
12 By the power of the Spirit our eyes
were opened and our understandings
were enlightened, so as to see and under-
stand the things of God—
13 Even those things which were from the
beginning before the world was, which
were ordained of the Father, through his
Only Begotten Son, who was in the bosom
of the Father, even from the beginning;
14 Of whom we bear record; and the
record which we bear is the fulness of the
gospel of Jesus Christ, who is the Son,
whom we saw and with whom we
conversed in the heavenly vision.
15 For while we were doing the work of
translation, which the Lord had appointed
unto us, we came to the twenty-ninth
verse of the fifth chapter of John, which
was given unto us as follows—
16 Speaking of the resurrection of the
dead, concerning those who shall hear the
voice of the Son of Man:
17 And shall come forth; they who have
done good, in the resurrection of the just;
and they who have done evil, in the
resurrection of the unjust.
18 Now this caused us to marvel, for it was
given unto us of the Spirit.
19 And while we meditated upon these
things, the Lord touched the eyes of our
understandings and they were opened,
and the glory of the Lord shone round
about.
20 And we beheld the glory of the Son, on
the right hand of the Father, and received
of his fulness;
21 And saw the holy angels, and them
who are sanctified before his throne,
worshiping God, and the Lamb, who wor-
ship him forever and ever.
22 And now, after the many testimonies
which have been given of him, this is the
testimony, last of all, which we give of
him: That he lives!
23 For we saw him, even on the right hand
of God; and we heard the voice bearing
record that he is the Only Begotten of the
Father—
24 That by him, and through him, and of
him, the worlds are and were created, and
the inhabitants thereof are begotten sons
and daughters unto God.

ABRAHAM 3

Abraham — *1950 BC*

1 And I, Abraham, had the Urim and
Thummim, which the Lord my God had
given unto me, in Ur of the Chaldees;
2 And I saw the stars, that they were very
great, and that one of them was nearest
unto the throne of God; and there were
many great ones which were near unto it;
3 And the Lord said unto me: These are
the governing ones; and the name of the
great one is Kolob, because it is near unto
me, for I am the Lord thy God: I have set
this one to govern all those which belong
to the same order as that upon which thou
standest.
4 And the Lord said unto me, by the Urim
and Thummim, that Kolob was after the
manner of the Lord, according to its times
and seasons in the revolutions thereof;
that one revolution was a day unto the
Lord, after his manner of reckoning, it

being one thousand years according to the
time appointed unto that whereon thou
standest. This is the reckoning of the
Lord's time, according to the reckoning of
Kolob.
5 And the Lord said unto me: The planet
which is the lesser light, lesser than that
which is to rule the day, even the night, is
above or greater than that upon which
thou standest in point of reckoning, for it
moveth in order more slow; this is in order
because it standeth above the Earth upon
which thou standest, therefore the
reckoning of its time is not so many as to
its number of days, and of months, and of
years.
6 And the Lord said unto me: Now,
Abraham, these two facts exist, behold
thine eyes see it; it is given unto thee to
know the times of reckoning, and the set
time, yea, the set time of the Earth upon
which thou standest, and the set time of
the greater light which is set to rule the
day, and the set time of the lesser light
which is set to rule the night.
7 Now the set time of the lesser light is a
longer time as to its reckoning than the
reckoning of the time of the Earth upon
which thou standest.
8 And where these two facts exist, there
shall be another fact above them, that is,
there shall be another planet whose
reckoning of time shall be longer still;
9 And thus there shall be the reckoning of
the time of one planet above another,
until thou come nigh unto Kolob, which
Kolob is after the reckoning of the Lord's
time; which Kolob is set nigh unto the
throne of God, to govern all those planets
which belong to the same order as that
upon which thou standest.
10 And it is given unto thee to know the
set time of all the stars that are set to give
light, until thou come near unto the
throne of God.
11 Thus I, Abraham, talked with the Lord,
face to face, as one man talketh with
another; and he told me of the works
which his hands had made;
12 And he said unto me: My son, my son
(and his hand was stretched out), behold I
will show you all these. And he put his
hand upon mine eyes, and I saw those
things which his hands had made, which
were many; and they multiplied before
mine eyes, and I could not see the end
thereof.
13 And he said unto me: This is Shinehah,
which is the sun. And he said unto me:
Kokob, which is star. And he said unto me:
Olea, which is the moon. And he said unto
me: Kokaubeam, which signifies stars, or
all the great lights, which were in the
firmament of heaven.
14 And it was in the night time when the
Lord spake these words unto me: I will
multiply thee, and thy seed after thee, like
unto these; and if thou canst count the
number of sands, so shall be the number
of thy seeds.
15 And the Lord said unto me: Abraham,
I show these things unto thee before ye go
into Egypt, that ye may declare all these
words.
16 If two things exist, and there be one
above the other, there shall be greater
things above them; therefore Kolob is the
greatest of all the Kokaubeam that thou
hast seen, because it is nearest unto me.
17 Now, if there be two things, one above
the other, and the moon be above the
Earth, then it may be that a planet or a star
may exist above it; and there is nothing
that the Lord thy God shall take in his
heart to do but what he will do it.
18 Howbeit that he made the greater star;
as, also, if there be two spirits, and one
shall be more intelligent than the other,
yet these two spirits, notwithstanding one
is more intelligent than the other, have no
beginning; they existed before, they shall
have no end, they shall exist after, for they
are gnolaum, or eternal.
19 And the Lord said unto me: These two
facts do exist, that there are two spirits,
one being more intelligent than the other;
there shall be another more intelligent
than they; I am the Lord thy God, I am
more intelligent than they all.
20 The Lord thy God sent his angel to
deliver thee from the hands of the priest
of Elkenah.
21 I dwell in the midst of them all; I now,
therefore, have come down unto thee to
declare unto thee the works which my
hands have made, wherein my wisdom
excelleth them all, for I rule in the
heavens above, and in the Earth beneath,
in all wisdom and prudence, over all the

Hubble telescope ultra-deep field image, courtesy NASA. In 2003-2004 the Hubble space telescope focused on a tiny speck of deep space in the constellation of Fornax known for its absence of visible light. The resulting image stunned astronomers. Over 10,000 objects, most of which are galaxies, are seen in the image from an area of space the size of 1 square mm held 1 meter away from your eyes. In this image there are about 100 galaxies that are calculated to be 13.1 billion light-years from Earth. This makes them the most distant objects ever viewed by man. The origin of the universe itself dates to 13.7 billion years ago.

intelligences thine eyes have seen from the beginning; I came down in the beginning in the midst of all the intelligences thou hast seen.

MOSES 1

Moses — *1475 BC*

1 The words of God, which he spake unto Moses at a time when Moses was caught up into an exceedingly high mountain,
2 And he saw God face to face, and he talked with him, and the glory of God was upon Moses; therefore Moses could endure his presence.
3 And God spake unto Moses, saying: Behold, I am the Lord God Almighty, and Endless is my name; for I am without beginning of days or end of years; and is not this endless?
4 And, behold, thou art my son; wherefore look, and I will show thee the workmanship of mine hands; but not all, for my works are without end, and also my words, for they never cease.
5 Wherefore, no man can behold all my works, except he behold all my glory; and no man can behold all my glory, and

afterwards remain in the flesh on the Earth.

6 And I have a work for thee, Moses, my son; and thou art in the similitude of mine Only Begotten; and mine Only Begotten is and shall be the Savior, for he is full of grace and truth; but there is no God beside me, and all things are present with me, for I know them all.

7 And now, behold, this one thing I show unto thee, Moses, my son, for thou art in the world, and now I show it unto thee.

8 And it came to pass that Moses looked, and beheld the world upon which he was created; and Moses beheld the world and the ends thereof, and all the children of men which are, and which were created; of the same he greatly marveled and wondered.

9 And the presence of God withdrew from Moses, that his glory was not upon Moses; and Moses was left unto himself. And as he was left unto himself, he fell unto the Earth.

10 And it came to pass that it was for the space of many hours before Moses did again receive his natural strength like unto man; and he said unto himself: Now, for this cause I know that man is nothing, which thing I never had supposed.

11 But now mine own eyes have beheld God; but not my natural, but my spiritual eyes, for my natural eyes could not have beheld; for I should have withered and died in his presence; but his glory was upon me; and I beheld his face, for I was transfigured before him.

12 And it came to pass that when Moses had said these words, behold, Satan came tempting him, saying: Moses, son of man, worship me.

13 And it came to pass that Moses looked upon Satan and said: Who art thou? For behold, I am a son of God, in the similitude of his Only Begotten; and where is thy glory, that I should worship thee?

14 For behold, I could not look upon God, except his glory should come upon me, and I were transfigured before him. But I can look upon thee in the natural man. Is it not so, surely?

15 Blessed be the name of my God, for his Spirit hath not altogether withdrawn from me, or else where is thy glory, for it is darkness unto me? And I can judge between thee and God; for God said unto me: Worship God, for him only shalt thou serve.

16 Get thee hence, Satan; deceive me not; for God said unto me: Thou art after the similitude of mine Only Begotten.

17 And he also gave me commandments when he called unto me out of the burning bush, saying: Call upon God in the name of mine Only Begotten, and worship me.

18 And again Moses said: I will not cease to call upon God, I have other things to inquire of him: for his glory has been upon me, wherefore I can judge between him and thee. Depart hence, Satan.

19 And now, when Moses had said these words, Satan cried with a loud voice, and ranted upon the Earth, and commanded, saying: I am the Only Begotten, worship me.

20 And it came to pass that Moses began to afear exceedingly; and as he began to fear, he saw the bitterness of hell. Nevertheless, calling upon God, he received strength, and he commanded, saying: Depart from me, Satan, for this one God only will I worship, which is the God of glory.

21 And now Satan began to tremble, and the Earth shook; and Moses received strength, and called upon God, saying: In the name of the Only Begotten, depart hence, Satan.

22 And it came to pass that Satan cried with a loud voice, with weeping, and wailing, and gnashing of teeth; and he departed hence, even from the presence of Moses, that he beheld him not.

23 And now of this thing Moses bore record; but because of wickedness it is not had among the children of men.

24 And it came to pass that when Satan had departed from the presence of Moses, that Moses lifted up his eyes unto heaven, being filled with the Holy Ghost, which beareth record of the Father and the Son;

25 And calling upon the name of God, he beheld his glory again, for it was upon him; and he heard a voice, saying: Blessed art thou, Moses, for I, the Almighty, have chosen thee, and thou shalt be made stronger than many waters; for they shall obey thy command as if thou wert God.

26 And lo, I am with thee, even unto the end of thy days; for thou shalt deliver my

people from bondage, even Israel my
chosen.
27 And it came to pass, as the voice was
still speaking, Moses cast his eyes and
beheld the Earth, yea, even all of it; and
there was not a particle of it which he did
not behold, discerning it by the Spirit of
God.
28 And he beheld also the inhabitants
thereof, and there was not a soul which he
beheld not; and he discerned them by the
Spirit of God; and their numbers were
great, even numberless as the sand upon
the sea shore.
29 And he beheld many lands; and each
land was called Earth, and there were
inhabitants on the face thereof.
30 And it came to pass that Moses called
upon God, saying: Tell me, I pray thee,
why these things are so, and by what thou
madest them?
31 And behold, the glory of the Lord was
upon Moses, so that Moses stood in the
presence of God, and talked with him face
to face. And the Lord God said unto
Moses: For mine own purpose have I made
these things. Here is wisdom and it
remaineth in me.
32 And by the word of my power, have I
created them, which is mine Only
Begotten Son, who is full of grace and
truth.
33 And worlds without number have I
created; and I also created them for mine
own purpose; and by the Son I created
them, which is mine Only Begotten.
34 And the first man of all men have I
called Adam, which is many.
35 But only an account of this Earth, and
the inhabitants thereof, give I unto you.
For behold, there are many worlds that
have passed away by the word of my
power. And there are many that now
stand, and innumerable are they unto
man; but all things are numbered unto me,
for they are mine and I know them.
36 And it came to pass that Moses spake
unto the Lord, saying: Be merciful unto
thy servant, O God, and tell me concern-
ing this Earth, and the inhabitants thereof,
and also the heavens, and then thy servant
will be content.
37 And the Lord God spake unto Moses,
saying: The heavens, they are many, and
they cannot be numbered unto man; but
they are numbered unto me, for they are
mine.
38 And as one Earth shall pass away, and
the heavens thereof even so shall another
come; and there is no end to my works,
neither to my words.
39 For behold, this is my work and my
glory—to bring to pass the immortality
and eternal life of man.
40 And now, Moses, my son, I will speak
unto thee concerning this Earth upon
which thou standest; and thou shalt write
the things which I shall speak.
41 And in a day when the children of men
shall esteem my words as naught and take
many of them from the book which thou
shalt write, behold, I will raise up another
like unto thee; and they shall be had again
among the children of men—among as
many as shall believe.

THE KING FOLLETT DISCOURSE

Joseph Smith — *April 7, 1844*

I shall comment on the very first Hebrew word in the Bible; I will make a comment on the very first sentence of the history of creation in the Bible—Berosheit. I want to analyze the word. Baith—in, by, through, and everything else. Rosh—the head, Sheit—grammatical termination. When the inspired man wrote it, he did not put the baith there. An old Jew without any authority added the word; he thought it too bad to begin to talk about the head! It read first, "The head one of the Gods brought forth the Gods." That is the true meaning of the words. Baurau signifies to bring forth. If you do not believe it, you do not believe the learned man of God. Learned men can teach you no more than what I have told you. Thus the head God brought forth the Gods in the grand council...

The head God called together the Gods and sat in grand council to bring forth the world. The grand councilors sat at the head in yonder heavens and contemplated the creation of the worlds which were created at the time...

In the beginning, the head of the Gods called a council of the Gods; and they came together and prepared a plan to create the world and people it. When we begin to learn this way, we begin to learn the only true God, and what kind of a being we have got to worship. Having a knowledge of God, we begin to know how to approach Him, and how to ask so as to receive an answer.

When we understand the character of God, and know how to come to Him, he begins to unfold the heavens to us, and to tell us all about it. When we are ready to come to him, he is ready to come to us.

Now, I ask all who hear me, why the learned men who are preaching salvation, say that God created the heavens and the Earth out of nothing? The reason is, that they are unlearned in the things of God, and have not the gift of the Holy Ghost; they account it blasphemy in any one to contradict their idea. If you tell them that God made the world out of something, they will call you a fool. But I am learned, and know more than all the world put together. The Holy Ghost does, anyhow, and he is within me, and comprehends more than all the world; and I will associate myself with him.

You ask the learned doctors why they say the world was made out of nothing, and they will answer, "Doesn't the Bible say he created the world?" And they infer, from the word create, that it must have been made out of nothing. Now, the word create came from the word baurau, which does not mean to create out of nothing; it means to organize; the same as a man would organize materials and build a ship. Hence we infer that God had materials to organize the world out of chaos—chaotic matter, which is element, and in which dwells all the glory. Element had an existence from the time He had. The pure principles of element are principles which can never be destroyed; they may be organized and re-organized, but not destroyed. They had no beginning and can have no end.

2

THE CREATION

The scriptures teach us that before anything was created physically it was first designed spiritually. Once the design was complete all the Lord had to do was utter the command and the elements obeyed to complete the design.

The prophet Lehi in the Book of Mormon taught that in life there are things that act and things that are acted upon. (2 Ne 2:13) Things that act are beings with agency – God and his children. Things that are acted upon are everything else – animals, plants, and all nonliving matter. "Things that are acted upon" obey the commands of the Lord without fail. "Things that act" are another story, as we routinely disobey the commands of God.

The Lord reveals that Lucifer rebelled against God saying, "Give me thine Honor" and the Lord then adds, "which is my power." (D&C 29:36) God is so good and so perfectly follows the eternal laws governing right and wrong that he commands the honor and obedience of all creatures and all elements and intelligence in the universe. This honor gives God his power. He gives a command and his word is obeyed without fail. By his word the Earth was created and filled with life.

The following prophetic accounts of the Creation come to us from glorious visions received by the prophets Abraham and Moses. Included here is Joseph Smith's inspired account of Moses's vision which restores many details that had been lost. These accounts show God engaged throughout the Creation process. It took God six "days" or time periods to perform the work—not a single instant. Science affirms this as different species of life suddenly appear fully-formed in the fossil record throughout history.

There is what looks like a discrepancy in the two accounts of Creation with respect to the creator with Moses saying "God" and Abraham referring to "the Gods." The difference is due to the nature of the visions each man received. Moses conversed with God the Father face-to-face and was commanded to "write the words which I speak." (Mos 2:1). Abraham also conversed with the Lord face-to-face but then was taken back in vision to the premortal Council in Heaven where God the Father, Jesus Christ and a myriad of other noble and great spirits planned the Creation. This is who Abraham is referring to as "the Gods." Abraham witnessed this event and described the conversations and actions that took place there. Moses also refers to multiple "gods" when Adam and Eve partook of the forbidden fruit. He records that God said: "Behold the man is become as one of us, to know good and evil." (Gen 3:22)

+++

Through the power of God's word all things are created. The children of God, as free agents or "things that act," choose whether or not they will obey the commands of God.

DOCTRINE AND COVENANTS 38
Joseph Smith *January 1831*
1 Thus saith the Lord your God, even Jesus Christ, the Great I Am, Alpha and Omega, the beginning and the end, the same which looked upon the wide expanse of eternity, and all the seraphic hosts of heaven, before the world was made;
2 The same which knoweth all things, for all things are present before mine eyes;
3 I am the same which spake, and the world was made, and all things came by me.

COLOSSIANS 1
Paul *60 AD*
16 For by him were all things created, that are in heaven, and that are in Earth, visible and invisible, whether they be thrones, or dominions, or principalities, or powers: all things were created by him, and for him:
17 And he is before all things, and by him all things consist.
18 And he is the head of the body, the church: who is the beginning, the firstborn from the dead; that in all things he might have the preeminence.
19 For it pleased the Father that in him should all fulness dwell;

DOCTRINE AND COVENANTS 29
Joseph Smith *September 1830*
30 But remember that all my judgments are not given unto men; and as the words have gone forth out of my mouth even so shall they be fulfilled, that the first shall be last, and that the last shall be first in all things whatsoever I have created by the word of my power, which is the power of my Spirit.
31 For by the power of my Spirit created I them; yea, all things both spiritual and temporal—
32 First spiritual, secondly temporal, which is the beginning of my work; and again, first temporal, and secondly spiritual, which is the last of my work—
33 Speaking unto you that you may naturally understand; but unto myself my works have no end, neither beginning; but it is given unto you that ye may understand, because ye have asked it of me and are agreed.

PSALM 33
David *1000 BC*
6 By the word of the Lord were the heavens made; and all the host of them by the breath of his mouth.

JACOB 4
Jacob, Son of Lehi *500 BC*
9 For behold, by the power of his word man came upon the face of the Earth, which Earth was created by the power of his word. Wherefore, if God being able to speak and the world was, and to speak and man was created, O then, why not able to command the Earth, or the workmanship of his hands upon the face of it, according to his will and pleasure?

HEBREWS 1
Paul *68 AD*
1 God, who at sundry times and in divers manners spake in time past unto the fathers by the prophets,
2 Hath in these last days spoken unto us by his Son, whom he hath appointed heir of all things, by whom also he made the worlds;

HELAMAN 12
Mormon *350 AD*
4 O how foolish, and how vain, and how evil, and devilish, and how quick to do iniquity, and how slow to do good, are the children of men; yea, how quick to hearken unto the words of the evil one, and to set their hearts upon the vain things of the world!
5 Yea, how quick to be lifted up in pride; yea, how quick to boast, and do all manner of that which is iniquity; and how slow are they to remember the Lord their God, and to give ear unto his counsels, yea, how slow to walk in wisdom's paths!
6 Behold, they do not desire that the Lord their God, who hath created them, should rule and reign over them; notwithstanding his great goodness and his mercy towards them, they do set at naught his

Artist impression of the Hadean Eon, the earliest period of Earth's history.

counsels, and they will not that he should
be their guide.
7 O how great is the nothingness of the
children of men; yea, even they are less
than the dust of the Earth.
8 For behold, the dust of the Earth moveth
hither and thither, to the dividing asunder, at the command of our great and
everlasting God.
9 Yea, behold at his voice do the hills and
the mountains tremble and quake.
10 And by the power of his voice they are
broken up, and become smooth, yea, even
like unto a valley.
11 Yea, by the power of his voice doth the
whole Earth shake;
12 Yea, by the power of his voice, do the
foundations rock, even to the very center.
13 Yea, and if he say unto the Earth—
Move—it is moved.
14 Yea, if he say unto the Earth—Thou
shalt go back, that it lengthen out the day
for many hours—it is done;
15 And thus, according to his word the
Earth goeth back, and it appeareth unto
man that the sun standeth still; yea, and
behold, this is so; for surely it is the Earth
that moveth and not the sun.
16 And behold, also, if he say unto the
waters of the great deep—Be thou dried
up—it is done.
17 Behold, if he say unto this mountain—
Be thou raised up, and come over and fall
upon that city, that it be buried up—
behold it is done.

FIRST DAY

The Earth is empty and covered with water. Its rotation is set forth, beginning regular night and day intervals.

The latest scientific advancements in estimating the age of rocks, not only from Earth but also from the Moon, Mars, and meteorites, place the formation of the Earth and the rest of the solar system between 4.58 to 4.53 billion years ago.

Scientists have described the earliest history of the Earth as a period of intense heat, volcanic activity, and meteor strikes. Scientists estimate that the earliest formation of water occurred between 4.4 to 4.0 billion years ago.

ABRAHAM 4

Abraham 1950 BC

1 And then the Lord said: Let us go down.
And they went down at the beginning,
and they, that is the Gods, organized and
formed the heavens and the Earth.
2 And the Earth, after it was formed, was
empty and desolate, because they had not
formed anything but the Earth; and
darkness reigned upon the face of the
deep, and the Spirit of the Gods was
brooding upon the face of the waters.
3 And they (the Gods) said: Let there be
light; and there was light.
4 And they (the Gods) comprehended the
light, for it was bright; and they divided

the light, or caused it to be divided, from the darkness.
5 And the Gods called the light Day, and the darkness they called Night. And it came to pass that from the evening until morning they called night; and from the morning until the evening they called day; and this was the first, or the beginning, of that which they called day and night.

MOSES 2

Moses 1475 BC

1 And it came to pass that the Lord spake unto Moses, saying: Behold, I reveal unto you concerning this heaven, and this Earth; write the words which I speak. I am the Beginning and the End, the Almighty God; by mine Only Begotten I created these things; yea, in the beginning I created the heaven, and the Earth upon which thou standest.
2 And the Earth was without form, and void; and I caused darkness to come up upon the face of the deep; and my Spirit moved upon the face of the water; for I am God.
3 And I, God, said: Let there be light; and there was light.
4 And I, God, saw the light; and that light was good. And I, God, divided the light from the darkness.
5 And I, God, called the light Day; and the darkness, I called Night; and this I did by the word of my power, and it was done as I spake; and the evening and the morning were the first day.

GENESIS 1

Moses 1475 BC

1 In the beginning God created the heaven and the Earth.
2 And the Earth was without form, and void; and darkness was upon the face of the deep. And the Spirit of God moved upon the face of the waters.
3 And God said, Let there be light: and there was light.
4 And God saw the light, that it was good: and God divided the light from the darkness.
5 And God called the light Day, and the darkness he called Night. And the evening and the morning were the first day.

SECOND DAY

The Earth's atmosphere is created. The Earth's magnetic field became well-established approximately 3.5 billion years ago. The magnetic field is critical because it protects the atmosphere from being swept away by intense solar winds. Initially, the Earth did not have an atmosphere. But as the Earth cooled, an atmosphere began to form that was comprised primarily of volcanic gases, such as hydrogen sulfide, methane, and carbon dioxide, but little oxygen. Around 2.7 billion years ago, cyanobacteria was created in the ocean. These organisms produce oxygen through photosynthesis. Around 2 billion years ago, there was enough free oxygen to turn the sky blue, and clear, for the first time. By 600 million years ago, the oxygen levels in the atmosphere reached 20%. By 350 million years ago, the oxygen levels in the atmosphere would be the same as today (21%).

ABRAHAM 4

Abraham 1950 BC

6 And the Gods also said: Let there be an expanse in the midst of the waters, and it shall divide the waters from the waters.
7 And the Gods ordered the expanse, so that it divided the waters which were under the expanse from the waters which were above the expanse; and it was so, even as they ordered.
8 And the Gods called the expanse, Heaven. And it came to pass that it was from evening until morning that they called night; and it came to pass that it was from morning until evening that they called day; and this was the second time that they called night and day.

MOSES 2

Moses 1475 BC

6 And again, I, God, said: Let there be a firmament in the midst of the water, and it was so, even as I spake; and I said: Let it divide the waters from the waters; and it was done;
7 And I, God, made the firmament and divided the waters, yea, the great waters under the firmament from the waters which were above the firmament, and it was so even as I spake.

The Earth's atmosphere or firmament. Photograph taken by NASA astronauts of multiple thunderstorms in the Pacific Ocean, 1994.

8 And I, God, called the firmament Heaven; and the evening and the morning were the second day.

GENESIS 1

Moses *1475 BC*

6 And God said, Let there be a firmament in the midst of the waters, and let it divide the waters from the waters.
7 And God made the firmament, and divided the waters which were under the firmament from the waters which were above the firmament: and it was so.
8 And God called the firmament Heaven. And the evening and the morning were the second day.

THIRD DAY

God commands dry land to appear. The Earth is prepared to bring forth plant life with the capacity to reproduce. Charles Darwin's theory of evolution postulates that, once created, life then evolved from a single organism to the great diversity of life on Earth through an unguided and random process of mutation and natural selection. In these accounts, God includes a key detail that refutes Darwinian evolution: plants, and later animals, may only reproduce after their own likeness and kind. They do not "evolve" from one kind of plant or animal into another.

There is evidence of dry land first appearing around 1.0 billion years ago. It is believed that the early continents came together and broke apart at least three times after that. The last supercontinent, referred to as Pangea, formed 335 million years ago and broke up by 180 million years ago with continents moving via plate tectonic forces to the positions they are in now.

The earliest appearance of vascular land plants was 430 million years ago. The first seed bearing plants appeared 360 million years ago. Flowering plants and grasses appear 200 and 40 million years ago respectively.

ABRAHAM 4

Abraham *1950 BC*

9 And the Gods ordered, saying: Let the waters under the heaven be gathered together unto one place, and let the Earth come up dry; and it was so as they ordered;
10 And the Gods pronounced the dry land, Earth; and the gathering together of the waters, pronounced they, Great Waters; and the Gods saw that they were obeyed.
11 And the Gods said: Let us prepare the Earth to bring forth grass; the herb yielding seed; the fruit tree yielding fruit, after his kind, whose seed in itself yieldeth its own likeness upon the Earth; and it was so, even as they ordered.
12 And the Gods organized the Earth to bring forth grass from its own seed, and the herb to bring forth herb from its own seed, yielding seed after his kind; and the Earth to bring forth the tree from its own seed, yielding fruit, whose seed could only bring forth the same in itself, after his kind; and the Gods saw that they were obeyed.
13 And it came to pass that they numbered the days; from the evening until the morning they called night; and it came to pass, from the morning until the evening they called day; and it was the third time.

MOSES 2

Moses *1475 BC*

9 And I, God, said: Let the waters under the heaven be gathered together unto one place, and it was so; and I, God, said: Let there be dry land; and it was so.

10 And I, God, called the dry land Earth; and the gathering together of the waters, called I the Sea; and I, God, saw that all things which I had made were good.
11 And I, God, said: Let the Earth bring forth grass, the herb yielding seed, the fruit tree yielding fruit, after his kind, and the tree yielding fruit, whose seed should be in itself upon the Earth, and it was so even as I spake.
12 And the Earth brought forth grass, every herb yielding seed after his kind, and the tree yielding fruit, whose seed should be in itself, after his kind; and I, God, saw that all things which I had made were good;
13 And the evening and the morning were the third day.

GENESIS 1

Moses — *1475 BC*

9 And God said, Let the waters under the heaven be gathered together unto one place, and let the dry land appear: and it was so.
10 And God called the dry land Earth; and the gathering together of the waters called he Seas: and God saw that it was good.

Fossil of plant leaf Fagus Sylvatica Pliocenica which dates back to 3.6-2.5 million years ago.

11 And God said, Let the Earth bring forth grass, the herb yielding seed, and the fruit tree yielding fruit after his kind, whose seed is in itself, upon the Earth: and it was so.
12 And the Earth brought forth grass, and herb yielding seed after his kind, and the tree yielding fruit, whose seed was in itself, after his kind: and God saw that it was good.
13 And the evening and the morning were the third day.

FOURTH DAY

The Sun, Moon, stars and planets are organized to provide means for man to calculate times and seasons, and to provide light during the day and night. This would only be possible after the formation of the atmosphere and dry land and plants had been created.

The improbable formation of the Moon is evidence of the hand of God at work. The giant-impact hypothesis of the Moon's creation postulates that about 4.5 billion years ago, a Mars-sized object collided with the newly formed Earth at the perfect speed and angle, and the resulting debris coalesced to form the Moon. The Moon happens to be the perfect size and location in relation to the Earth to stabilize the Earth's rotation and control the tides. Incredibly, the Moon and the Sun are the only bodies in the solar system that are perfectly round. Additionally, the Sun is exactly 400 times larger than the Moon, and exactly 400 times farther away from the Earth than the Moon. This makes the Sun and Moon appear the same size when viewed from Earth, allowing for perfect solar eclipses. The Earth is the only planet in the solar system where this is possible. Significant scientific discoveries have been made during solar eclipses, including the discovery of helium.

ABRAHAM 4

Abraham — *1950 BC*

14 And the Gods organized the lights in the expanse of the heaven, and caused them to divide the day from the night; and organized them to be for signs and for seasons, and for days and for years;

15 And organized them to be for lights in the expanse of the heaven to give light upon the Earth; and it was so.
16 And the Gods organized the two great lights, the greater light to rule the day, and the lesser light to rule the night; with the lesser light they set the stars also;
17 And the Gods set them in the expanse of the heavens, to give light upon the Earth, and to rule over the day and over the night, and to cause to divide the light from the darkness.
18 And the Gods watched those things which they had ordered until they obeyed.
19 And it came to pass that it was from evening until morning that it was night; and it came to pass that it was from morning until evening that it was day; and it was the fourth time.

MOSES 2

Moses *1475 BC*

14 And I, God, said: Let there be lights in the firmament of the heaven, to divide the day from the night, and let them be for signs, and for seasons, and for days, and for years;
15 And let them be for lights in the firmament of the heaven to give light upon the Earth; and it was so.
16 And I, God, made two great lights; the greater light to rule the day, and the lesser light to rule the night, and the greater light was the sun, and the lesser light was the moon; and the stars also were made even according to my word.
17 And I, God, set them in the firmament of the heaven to give light upon the Earth,
18 And the sun to rule over the day, and the moon to rule over the night, and to divide the light from the darkness; and I, God, saw that all things which I had made were good;
19 And the evening and the morning were the fourth day.

GENESIS 1

Moses *1475 BC*

14 And God said, Let there be lights in the firmament of the heaven to divide the day from the night; and let them be for signs, and for seasons, and for days, and years:
15 And let them be for lights in the firmament of the heaven to give light upon the Earth: and it was so.
16 And God made two great lights; the greater light to rule the day, and the lesser light to rule the night: he made the stars also.
17 And God set them in the firmament of the heaven to give light upon the Earth,
18 And to rule over the day and over the night, and to divide the light from the darkness: and God saw that it was good.
19 And the evening and the morning were the fourth day.

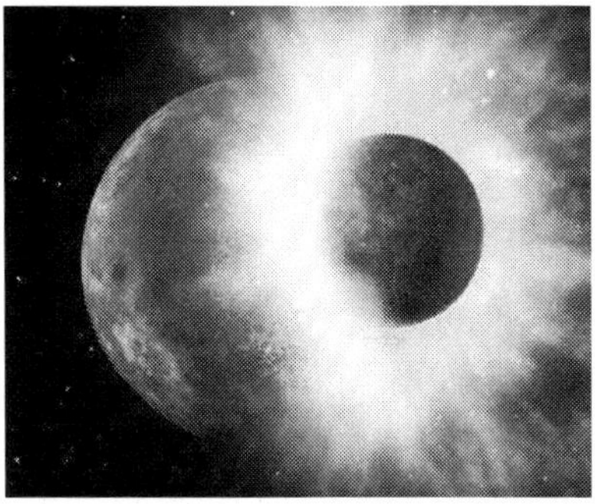

Artist rendering of the giant-impact hypothesis of the formation of the moon.

DOCTRINE AND COVENANTS 88

Joseph Smith *December 1832*

42 And again, verily I say unto you, he hath given a law unto all things, by which they move in their times and their seasons;
43 And their courses are fixed, even the courses of the heavens and the Earth, which comprehend the Earth and all the planets.
44 And they give light to each other in their times and in their seasons, in their minutes, in their hours, in their days, in their weeks, in their months, in their years—all these are one year with God, but not with man.
45 The Earth rolls upon her wings, and the sun giveth his light by day, and the moon giveth her light by night, and the stars also give their light, as they roll upon their wings in their glory, in the midst of the power of God.
46 Unto what shall I liken these kingdoms, that ye may understand?
47 Behold, all these are kingdoms, and any man who hath seen any or the least of

these hath seen God moving in his majesty
and power.
48 I say unto you, he hath seen him;
nevertheless, he who came unto his own
was not comprehended.
49 The light shineth in darkness, and the
darkness comprehendeth it not;
nevertheless, the day shall come when
you shall comprehend even God, being
quickened in him and by him.
50 Then shall ye know that ye have seen
me, that I am, and that I am the true light
that is in you, and that you are in me;
otherwise ye could not abound.

FIFTH DAY

God prepares the waters to be in a position to support life. Marine life and birds are created and set to reproduce only after their kind.

Prior to 541 million years ago, animal life in the primitive oceans was minimal and microscopic. Between 541 and 530 million years ago, the Cambrian explosion of life occurred in the ancient ocean. During this short window of time animals from 20 of the 27 animal phyla (broad categories of animals based on unique body plans) found in the fossil record suddenly appear, fully-formed and with no precursor species. These include arthropods, mollusks, sponges, worms, fish and other animals with spinal cords, and starfish.

From there, new species entered the fossil record at various times, demonstrating that the Creation was not a single event. God's creative work was ongoing.

Whales and fowl first appear about 150 and 50 million years ago, respectively.

ABRAHAM 4

Abraham — *1950 BC*

20 And the Gods said: Let us prepare the
waters to bring forth abundantly the
moving creatures that have life; and the
fowl, that they may fly above the Earth in
the open expanse of heaven.
21 And the Gods prepared the waters that
they might bring forth great whales, and
every living creature that moveth, which
the waters were to bring forth abundantly
after their kind; and every winged fowl
after their kind. And the Gods saw that
they would be obeyed, and that their plan
was good.
22 And the Gods said: We will bless them,
and cause them to be fruitful and multiply,
and fill the waters in the seas or great
waters; and cause the fowl to multiply in
the Earth.
23 And it came to pass that it was from
evening until morning that they called
night; and it came to pass that it was from
morning until evening that they called
day; and it was the fifth time.

MOSES 2

Moses — *1475 BC*

20 And I, God, said: Let the waters bring
forth abundantly the moving creature that
hath life, and fowl which may fly above
the Earth in the open firmament of
heaven.
21 And I, God, created great whales, and
every living creature that moveth, which
the waters brought forth abundantly, after
their kind, and every winged fowl after his
kind; and I, God, saw that all things which
I had created were good.
22 And I, God, blessed them, saying: Be
fruitful, and multiply, and fill the waters
in the sea; and let fowl multiply in the
Earth;
23 And the evening and the morning were
the fifth day.

Trilobite fossil, Cheirurus Ingricus, discovered in Russia in 1845. This particular trilobite species lived from 500 to 390 million years ago.

GENESIS 1

Moses — *1475 BC*

20 And God said, Let the waters bring
forth abundantly the moving creature that

The Garden of Eden with the Creation of Eve, by Jan Brueghel the Younger, ca 1630s.

hath life, and fowl that may fly above the Earth in the open firmament of heaven.
21 And God created great whales, and every living creature that moveth, which the waters brought forth abundantly, after their kind, and every winged fowl after his kind: and God saw that it was good.
22 And God blessed them, saying, Be fruitful, and multiply, and fill the waters in the seas, and let fowl multiply in the Earth.
23 And the evening and the morning were the fifth day.

SIXTH DAY

God prepares and organizes the Earth to bring forth animal life. Man is formed in the image of the Gods and is given dominion over all life on Earth. All of God's creations are obedient to his word.

The earliest evidence of an air breathing organism is a fossilized type of millipede that dates to approximately 430 million years ago (mya). Other animals created at various times: insects (400 mya), amphibians (360 mya), crocodiles (250 mya), turtles (220 mya), snakes (200 mya), dinosaurs (313-66 mya), flowering plants and pollinating insects (130-90 mya), and mammals 167 (mya). There were at least 5 major mass extinction events in history; the last of which wiped out the dinosaurs 66 million years ago and paved the way for the proliferation of mammals.

Man and woman, the last of God's creations, are created. The fossil record supports this with the earliest evidence of what would appear to be homo sapiens, or anatomically modern humans, dating to the relatively recent period of 300,000 years ago or less. Bones, primitive tools, and cave paintings indicate that a people existed who lived a hunter-gatherer life-style up until the emergence of modern civilization around 4,000 BC. This date, not coincidentally, is the time Adam and Eve were cast out of the Garden of Eden. We don't know who these people or creatures were who lived prior to 4,000 BC, but we do know that Adam and Eve were the first of the spiritual sons and daughters of God to become mortal. And their appearance coincides with the beginning of modern civilization.

ABRAHAM 4

Abraham — *1950 BC*

24 And the Gods prepared the Earth to bring forth the living creature after his kind, cattle and creeping things, and

beasts of the Earth after their kind; and it was so, as they had said.
25 And the Gods organized the Earth to bring forth the beasts after their kind, and cattle after their kind, and everything that creepeth upon the Earth after its kind; and the Gods saw they would obey.
26 And the Gods took counsel among themselves and said: Let us go down and form man in our image, after our likeness; and we will give them dominion over the fish of the sea, and over the fowl of the air, and over the cattle, and over all the Earth, and over every creeping thing that creepeth upon the Earth.
27 So the Gods went down to organize man in their own image, in the image of the Gods to form they him, male and female to form they them.
28 And the Gods said: We will bless them. And the Gods said: We will cause them to be fruitful and multiply, and replenish the Earth, and subdue it, and to have dominion over the fish of the sea, and over the fowl of the air, and over every living thing that moveth upon the Earth.
29 And the Gods said: Behold, we will give them every herb bearing seed that shall come upon the face of all the Earth, and every tree which shall have fruit upon it; yea, the fruit of the tree yielding seed to them we will give it; it shall be for their meat.
30 And to every beast of the Earth, and to every fowl of the air, and to everything that creepeth upon the Earth, behold, we will give them life, and also we will give to them every green herb for meat, and all these things shall be thus organized.
31 And the Gods said: We will do everything that we have said, and organize them; and behold, they shall be very obedient. And it came to pass that it was from evening until morning they called night; and it came to pass that it was from morning until evening that they called day; and they numbered the sixth time.

MOSES 2

Moses 1475 BC

24 And I, God, said: Let the Earth bring forth the living creature after his kind, cattle, and creeping things, and beasts of the Earth after their kind, and it was so;
25 And I, God, made the beasts of the Earth after their kind, and cattle after their kind, and everything which creepeth upon the Earth after his kind; and I, God, saw that all these things were good.
26 And I, God, said unto mine Only Begotten, which was with me from the beginning: Let us make man in our image, after our likeness; and it was so. And I, God, said: Let them have dominion over the fishes of the sea, and over the fowl of the air, and over the cattle, and over all the Earth, and over every creeping thing that creepeth upon the Earth.
27 And I, God, created man in mine own image, in the image of mine Only Begotten created I him; male and female created I them.
28 And I, God, blessed them, and said unto them: Be fruitful, and multiply, and replenish the Earth, and subdue it, and have dominion over the fish of the sea, and over the fowl of the air, and over every living thing that moveth upon the Earth.
29 And I, God, said unto man: Behold, I have given you every herb bearing seed, which is upon the face of all the Earth, and every tree in the which shall be the fruit of a tree yielding seed; to you it shall be for meat.
30 And to every beast of the Earth, and to every fowl of the air, and to everything that creepeth upon the Earth, wherein I grant life, there shall be given every clean herb for meat; and it was so, even as I spake.
31 And I, God, saw everything that I had made, and, behold, all things which I had made were very good; and the evening and the morning were the sixth day.

GENESIS 1

Moses 1475 BC

24 And God said, Let the Earth bring forth the living creature after his kind, cattle, and creeping thing, and beast of the Earth after his kind: and it was so.
25 And God made the beast of the Earth after his kind, and cattle after their kind, and everything that creepeth upon the Earth after his kind: and God saw that it was good.
26 And God said, Let us make man in our image, after our likeness: and let them

have dominion over the fish of the sea, and over the fowl of the air, and over the cattle, and over all the Earth, and over every creeping thing that creepeth upon the Earth.
27 So God created man in his own image, in the image of God created he him; male and female created he them.
28 And God blessed them, and God said unto them, Be fruitful, and multiply, and replenish the Earth, and subdue it: and have dominion over the fish of the sea, and over the fowl of the air, and over every living thing that moveth upon the Earth.
29 And God said, Behold, I have given you every herb bearing seed, which is upon the face of all the Earth, and every tree, in the which is the fruit of a tree yielding seed; to you it shall be for meat.
30 And to every beast of the Earth, and to every fowl of the air, and to everything that creepeth upon the Earth, wherein there is life, I have given every green herb for meat: and it was so.
31 And God saw everything that he had made, and, behold, it was very good. And the evening and the morning were the sixth day.

DOCTRINE AND COVENANTS 59

Joseph Smith — *August 1831*

16 Verily I say, that inasmuch as ye do this, the fulness of the Earth is yours, the beasts of the field and the fowls of the air, and that which climbeth upon the trees and walketh upon the Earth;
17 Yea, and the herb, and the good things which come of the Earth, whether for food or for raiment, or for houses, or for barns, or for orchards, or for gardens, or for vineyards;
18 Yea, all things which come of the Earth, in the season thereof, are made for the benefit and the use of man, both to please the eye and to gladden the heart;
19 Yea, for food and for raiment, for taste and for smell, to strengthen the body and to enliven the soul.
20 And it pleaseth God that he hath given all these things unto man; for unto this end were they made to be used, with judgment, not to excess, neither by extortion.

SEVENTH DAY

The seventh day (or "time" as Abraham notes). The work of Creation comes to an end. The Gods rest.

ABRAHAM 5

Abraham — *1950 BC*

1 And thus we will finish the heavens and the Earth, and all the hosts of them.
2 And the Gods said among themselves: On the seventh time we will end our work, which we have counseled; and we will rest on the seventh time from all our work which we have counseled.
3 And the Gods concluded upon the seventh time, because that on the seventh time they would rest from all their works which they (the Gods) counseled among themselves to form; and sanctified it. And thus were their decisions at the time that they counseled among themselves to form the heavens and the Earth.

MOSES 3

Moses — *1475 BC*

1 Thus the heaven and the Earth were finished, and all the host of them.
2 And on the seventh day I, God, ended my work, and all things which I had made; and I rested on the seventh day from all my work, and all things which I had made were finished, and I, God, saw that they were good;
3 And I, God, blessed the seventh day, and sanctified it; because that in it I had rested from all my work which I, God, had created and made.

GENESIS 2

Moses — *1475 BC*

1 Thus the heavens and the Earth were finished, and all the host of them.
2 And on the seventh day God ended his work which he had made; and he rested on the seventh day from all his work which he had made.
3 And God blessed the seventh day, and sanctified it: because that in it he had rested from all his work which God created and made.

3

THE WAR IN HEAVEN

+++

The pre-existence of man and the War in Heaven are described. The spirits of men and women (intelligent agents) were not created but were in the beginning with God. Jesus Christ and Lucifer present competing visions of agency and the salvation of man; Lucifer and his followers are cast out; he becomes Satan and seeks the destruction and misery of man. The remaining spirits choose to follow Jesus Christ and God and become, in essence, his children, and await their mortal time on Earth.

ABRAHAM 3

Abraham — *1950 BC*

22 Now the Lord had shown unto me, Abraham, the intelligences that were organized before the world was; and among all these there were many of the noble and great ones;
23 And God saw these souls that they were good, and he stood in the midst of them, and he said: These I will make my rulers; for he stood among those that were spirits, and he saw that they were good; and he said unto me: Abraham, thou art one of them; thou wast chosen before thou wast born.
24 And there stood one among them that was like unto God, and he said unto those who were with him: We will go down, for there is space there, and we will take of these materials, and we will make an Earth whereon these may dwell;
25 And we will prove them herewith, to see if they will do all things whatsoever the Lord their God shall command them;
26 And they who keep their first estate shall be added upon; and they who keep not their first estate shall not have glory in the same kingdom with those who keep their first estate; and they who keep their second estate shall have glory added upon their heads for ever and ever.
27 And the Lord said: Whom shall I send? And one answered like unto the Son of Man: Here am I, send me. And another answered and said: Here am I, send me. And the Lord said: I will send the first.
28 And the second was angry, and kept not his first estate; and, at that day, many followed after him.

MOSES 4

Moses — *1475 BC*

1 And I, the Lord God, spake unto Moses, saying: That Satan, whom thou hast commanded in the name of mine Only Begotten, is the same which was from the beginning, and he came before me, saying—Behold, here am I, send me, I will be thy son, and I will redeem all mankind, that one soul shall not be lost, and surely I will do it; wherefore give me thine honor.
2 But, behold, my Beloved Son, which was my Beloved and Chosen from the beginning, said unto me—Father, thy will be done, and the glory be thine forever.
3 Wherefore, because that Satan rebelled against me, and sought to destroy the agency of man, which I, the Lord God, had given him, and also, that I should give unto him mine own power; by the power of mine Only Begotten, I caused that he should be cast down;
4 And he became Satan, yea, even the devil, the father of all lies, to deceive and to blind men, and to lead them captive at his will, even as many as would not hearken unto my voice.

DOCTRINE AND COVENANTS 29

Joseph Smith — *September 1830*

36 And it came to pass that Adam, being tempted of the devil—for, behold, the devil was before Adam, for he rebelled against me, saying, Give me thine honor, which is my power; and also a third part of the hosts of heaven turned he away from me because of their agency;

Satan, by Gustave Dore, 1866.

37 And they were thrust down, and thus came the devil and his angels;
38 And, behold, there is a place prepared for them from the beginning, which place is hell.
39 And it must needs be that the devil should tempt the children of men, or they could not be agents unto themselves; for if they never should have bitter they could not know the sweet.

LUKE 10

Jesus Christ *32 AD*

18 And he [Jesus] said unto them, I beheld Satan as lightning fall from heaven.

ISAIAH 14

Isaiah *740 BC*

12 How art thou fallen from heaven, O Lucifer, son of the morning! how art thou cut down to the ground, which didst weaken the nations!
13 For thou hast said in thine heart, I will ascend into heaven, I will exalt my throne above the stars of God: I will sit also upon the mount of the congregation, in the sides of the north:
14 I will ascend above the heights of the clouds; I will be like the most High.
15 Yet thou shalt be brought down to hell, to the sides of the pit.

JOB 38

Job *600 BC*

4 Where wast thou when I laid the foundations of the Earth? declare, if thou hast understanding.

5 Who hath laid the measures thereof, if thou knowest? or who hath stretched the line upon it?

6 Whereupon are the foundations thereof fastened? or who laid the corner stone thereof;

7 When the morning stars sang together, and all the sons of God shouted for joy?

DOCTRINE AND COVENANTS 76

Joseph Smith *February 1832*

25 And this we saw also, and bear record, that an angel of God who was in authority in the presence of God, who rebelled against the Only Begotten Son whom the Father loved and who was in the bosom of the Father, was thrust down from the presence of God and the Son,

26 And was called Perdition, for the heavens wept over him—he was Lucifer, a son of the morning.

27 And we beheld, and lo, he is fallen! is fallen, even a son of the morning!

28 And while we were yet in the Spirit, the Lord commanded us that we should write the vision; for we beheld Satan, that old serpent, even the devil, who rebelled against God, and sought to take the kingdom of our God and his Christ—

29 Wherefore, he maketh war with the saints of God, and encompasseth them round about.

2 NEPHI 2

Lehi *580 BC*

17 And I, Lehi, according to the things which I have read, must needs suppose that an angel of God, according to that which is written, had fallen from heaven; wherefore, he became a devil, having sought that which was evil before God.

18 And because he had fallen from heaven, and had become miserable forever, he sought also the misery of all mankind.

JOHN 1

John *30 AD*

1 In the beginning was the *gospel preached through the Son. And the gospel was the word,* and the *word* was with *the Son, and the Son was with God,* and the *Son* was *of* God.

2 The same was in the beginning with God.

3 All things were made by him; and without him was not anything made which was made.

4 In him was *the gospel,* and *the gospel was the life,* and the life was the light of men;

5 And the light shineth *in the world,* and the *world perceiveth* it not.

16 *For in the beginning was the Word, even the Son, who is made flesh, and sent unto us by the will of the Father. And as many as believe on his name shall receive of his fullness.* And of his fullness have all we received, *even immortality and eternal life, through his* grace. [JST]

DOCTRINE AND COVENANTS 93

Joseph Smith *May 1833*

1 Verily, thus saith the Lord: It shall come to pass that every soul who forsaketh his sins and cometh unto me, and calleth on my name, and obeyeth my voice, and keepeth my commandments, shall see my face and know that I am;

2 And that I am the true light that lighteth every man that cometh into the world;

3 And that I am in the Father, and the Father in me, and the Father and I are one—

4 The Father because he gave me of his fulness, and the Son because I was in the world and made flesh my tabernacle, and dwelt among the sons of men.

5 I was in the world and received of my Father, and the works of him were plainly manifest.

6 And John saw and bore record of the fulness of my glory, and the fulness of John's record is hereafter to be revealed.

7 And he bore record, saying: I saw his glory, that he was in the beginning, before the world was;

8 Therefore, in the beginning the Word was, for he was the Word, even the messenger of salvation—

9 The light and the Redeemer of the world; the Spirit of truth, who came into the world, because the world was made by him, and in him was the life of men and the light of men.

10 The worlds were made by him; men were made by him; all things were made by him, and through him, and of him.
11 And I, John, bear record that I beheld his glory, as the glory of the Only Begotten of the Father, full of grace and truth, even the Spirit of truth, which came and dwelt in the flesh, and dwelt among us.
12 And I, John, saw that he received not of the fulness at the first, but received grace for grace;
13 And he received not of the fulness at first, but continued from grace to grace, until he received a fulness;
14 And thus he was called the Son of God, because he received not of the fulness at the first.
15 And I, John, bear record, and lo, the heavens were opened, and the Holy Ghost descended upon him in the form of a dove, and sat upon him, and there came a voice out of heaven saying: This is my beloved Son.
16 And I, John, bear record that he received a fulness of the glory of the Father;
17 And he received all power, both in heaven and on Earth, and the glory of the Father was with him, for he dwelt in him.
18 And it shall come to pass, that if you are faithful you shall receive the fulness of the record of John.
19 I give unto you these sayings that you may understand and know how to worship, and know what you worship, that you may come unto the Father in my name, and in due time receive of his fulness.
20 For if you keep my commandments you shall receive of his fulness, and be glorified in me as I am in the Father; therefore, I say unto you, you shall receive grace for grace.
21 And now, verily I say unto you, I was in the beginning with the Father, and am the Firstborn;
22 And all those who are begotten through me are partakers of the glory of the same, and are the church of the Firstborn.
23 Ye were also in the beginning with the Father; that which is Spirit, even the Spirit of truth;
24 And truth is knowledge of things as they are, and as they were, and as they are to come;
25 And whatsoever is more or less than this is the spirit of that wicked one who was a liar from the beginning.
26 The Spirit of truth is of God. I am the Spirit of truth, and John bore record of me, saying: He received a fulness of truth, yea, even of all truth;
27 And no man receiveth a fulness unless he keepeth his commandments.
28 He that keepeth his commandments receiveth truth and light, until he is glorified in truth and knoweth all things.
29 Man was also in the beginning with God. Intelligence, or the light of truth, was not created or made, neither indeed can be.
30 All truth is independent in that sphere in which God has placed it, to act for itself, as all intelligence also; otherwise there is no existence.
31 Behold, here is the agency of man, and here is the condemnation of man; because that which was from the beginning is plainly manifest unto them, and they receive not the light.
32 And every man whose spirit receiveth not the light is under condemnation.
33 For man is spirit. The elements are eternal, and spirit and element, inseparably connected, receive a fulness of joy;
34 And when separated, man cannot receive a fulness of joy.
35 The elements are the tabernacle of God; yea, man is the tabernacle of God, even temples; and whatsoever temple is defiled, God shall destroy that temple.
36 The glory of God is intelligence, or, in other words, light and truth.
37 Light and truth forsake that evil one.
38 Every spirit of man was innocent in the beginning; and God having redeemed man from the fall, men became again, in their infant state, innocent before God.
39 And that wicked one cometh and taketh away light and truth, through disobedience, from the children of men, and because of the tradition of their fathers.
40 But I have commanded you to bring up your children in light and truth.

REVELATION 12
John 95 AD
6 And there was war in heaven; Michael and his angels fought against the dragon; and the dragon and his angels *fought against Michael;*
7 And *the dragon* prevailed not *against Michael, neither the child, nor the woman which was the church of God, who had been delivered of her pains, and brought forth the kingdom of our God and his Christ.*
8 Neither was *there* place found in heaven *for* the great dragon, *who* was cast out; that old serpent called the devil, and *also called* Satan, which deceiveth the whole world; he was cast out into the Earth; and his angels were cast out with him.
9 And I heard a loud voice saying in heaven, Now is come salvation, and strength, and the kingdom of our God, and the power of his Christ;
10 For the accuser of our brethren is cast down, which accused them before our God day and night.
12 *And after these things I heard another voice saying,* Woe to the inhabiters of the Earth, *yea,* and *they who dwell upon the islands* of the sea! for the devil is come down unto you, having great wrath, because he knoweth that he hath but a short time.

1 And there appeared a great *sign* in heaven, *in the likeness of things on the Earth;* a woman clothed with the sun, and the moon under her feet, and upon her head a crown of twelve stars.
2 And *the woman* being with child, cried, travailing in birth, and pained to be delivered.
3 *And she brought forth a man child, who was to rule all nations with a rod of iron; and her child was caught up unto God and his throne.*
4 And there appeared another *sign* in heaven; and behold, a great red dragon, having seven heads and ten horns, and seven crowns upon his heads. And his tail drew the third part of the stars of heaven, and did cast them to the Earth. And the dragon stood before the woman which was delivered, *ready* to devour her child *after* it was born.
11 *For* they *have overcome* him by the blood of the Lamb, and by the word of their testimony; *for* they loved not their own lives, *but kept the testimony even* unto death. Therefore, rejoice O heavens, and ye that dwell in them. [JST]

The Spiritual Descent of Lucifer into Satan, by Gustave Dore, 1866.

4

THE GARDEN OF EDEN

+++

THE FIRST MAN

All things are created (designed) spiritually before being created physically. The physical body of man is created from the dust of the Earth and joined with man's eternal spirit.

ABRAHAM 5

Abraham 1950 BC

4 And the Gods came down and formed these the generations of the heavens and of the Earth, when they were formed in the day that the Gods formed the Earth and the heavens,
5 According to all that which they had said concerning every plant of the field before it was in the Earth, and every herb of the field before it grew; for the Gods had not caused it to rain upon the Earth when they counseled to do them, and had not formed a man to till the ground.
6 But there went up a mist from the Earth, and watered the whole face of the ground.
7 And the Gods formed man from the dust of the ground, and took his spirit (that is, the man's spirit), and put it into him; and breathed into his nostrils the breath of life, and man became a living soul.

MOSES 3

Moses 1475 BC

4 And now, behold, I say unto you, that these are the generations of the heaven and of the Earth, when they were created, in the day that I, the Lord God, made the heaven and the Earth,
5 And every plant of the field before it was in the Earth, and every herb of the field before it grew. For I, the Lord God, created all things, of which I have spoken, spiritually, before they were naturally upon the face of the Earth. For I, the Lord God, had not caused it to rain upon the face of the Earth. And I, the Lord God, had created all the children of men; and not yet a man to till the ground; for in heaven created I them; and there was not yet flesh upon the Earth, neither in the water, neither in the air;
6 But I, the Lord God, spake, and there went up a mist from the Earth, and watered the whole face of the ground.
7 And I, the Lord God, formed man from the dust of the ground, and breathed into his nostrils the breath of life; and man became a living soul, the first flesh upon the Earth, the first man also; nevertheless, all things were before created; but spiritually were they created and made according to my word.

GENESIS 2

Moses 1475 BC

4 These are the generations of the heavens and of the Earth when they were created, in the day that the Lord God made the Earth and the heavens,
5 And every plant of the field before it was in the Earth, and every herb of the field before it grew: for the Lord God had not caused it to rain upon the Earth, and there was not a man to till the ground.
6 But there went up a mist from the Earth, and watered the whole face of the ground.
7 And the Lord God formed man of the dust of the ground, and breathed into his nostrils the breath of life; and man became a living soul.

THE GARDEN OF EDEN

Man is placed in the Garden of Eden with the commandment to eat of all the trees of the garden except the tree of the knowledge of good and evil. Eating this fruit will cause man to die.

A popular false doctrine purports that the story of the Garden of Eden is metaphorical and not actual history, and that Adam and Eve were not real people. To show Moses that the Garden of Eden was a real place, the Lord gives some geo-

graphical locations that Moses would recognize – some of which are known to this day – such as Ethiopia, Assyria, and the Euphrates river. In addition, in the books of Genesis, Chronicles, Matthew and Luke, the Lord provides genealogies of the descendants of Adam and Eve to show that everyone on Earth was related to them. Furthermore, if Adam and Eve are fictional, then there was no Fall, no need for redemption, and no need for Jesus Christ. The Lord wants us to know that the Garden of Eden was a real place and that Adam and Eve were the first man and woman to live on Earth.

ABRAHAM 5

Abraham — *1950 BC*

8 And the Gods planted a garden, eastward in Eden, and there they put the man, whose spirit they had put into the body which they had formed.
9 And out of the ground made the Gods to grow every tree that is pleasant to the sight and good for food; the tree of life, also, in the midst of the garden, and the tree of knowledge of good and evil.
10 There was a river running out of Eden, to water the garden, and from thence it was parted and became into four heads.
11 And the Gods took the man and put him in the Garden of Eden, to dress it and to keep it.
12 And the Gods commanded the man, saying: Of every tree of the garden thou mayest freely eat,
13 But of the tree of knowledge of good and evil, thou shalt not eat of it; for in the time that thou eatest thereof, thou shalt surely die. Now I, Abraham, saw that it was after the Lord's time, which was after the time of Kolob; for as yet the Gods had not appointed unto Adam his reckoning.

MOSES 3

Moses — *1475 BC*

8 And I, the Lord God, planted a garden eastward in Eden, and there I put the man whom I had formed.
9 And out of the ground made I, the Lord God, to grow every tree, naturally, that is pleasant to the sight of man; and man could behold it. And it became also a living soul. For it was spiritual in the day that I created it; for it remaineth in the sphere in which I, God, created it, yea, even all things which I prepared for the use of man; and man saw that it was good for food. And I, the Lord God, planted the tree of life also in the midst of the garden, and also the tree of knowledge of good and evil.
10 And I, the Lord God, caused a river to go out of Eden to water the garden; and from thence it was parted, and became into four heads.
11 And I, the Lord God, called the name of the first Pison, and it compasseth the whole land of Havilah, where I, the Lord God, created much gold;
12 And the gold of that land was good, and there was bdellium and the onyx stone.
13 And the name of the second river was called Gihon; the same that compasseth the whole land of Ethiopia.
14 And the name of the third river was Hiddekel; that which goeth toward the east of Assyria. And the fourth river was the Euphrates.
15 And I, the Lord God, took the man, and put him into the Garden of Eden, to dress it, and to keep it.
16 And I, the Lord God, commanded the man, saying: Of every tree of the garden thou mayest freely eat,
17 But of the tree of the knowledge of good and evil, thou shalt not eat of it, nevertheless, thou mayest choose for thyself, for it is given unto thee; but, remember that I forbid it, for in the day thou eatest thereof thou shalt surely die.

GENESIS 2

Moses — *1475 BC*

8 And the Lord God planted a garden eastward in Eden; and there he put the man whom he had formed.
9 And out of the ground made the Lord God to grow every tree that is pleasant to the sight, and good for food; the tree of life also in the midst of the garden, and the tree of knowledge of good and evil.
10 And a river went out of Eden to water the garden; and from thence it was parted, and became into four heads.
11 The name of the first is Pison: that is it which compasseth the whole land of Havilah, where there is gold;
12 And the gold of that land is good: there is bdellium and the onyx stone.

Adam names the animals in the Garden of Eden.

13 And the name of the second river is Gihon: the same is it that compasseth the whole land of Ethiopia.
14 And the name of the third river is Hiddekel: that is it which goeth toward the east of Assyria. And the fourth river is Euphrates.
15 And the Lord God took the man, and put him into the garden of Eden to dress it and to keep it.
16 And the Lord God commanded the man, saying, Of every tree of the garden thou mayest freely eat:
17 But of the tree of the knowledge of good and evil, thou shalt not eat of it: for in the day that thou eatest thereof thou shalt surely die.

THE FIRST WOMAN

Woman is formed from Adam's rib. Adam and his wife are naked and not ashamed. Adam gives names to all the animals.

ABRAHAM 5

Abraham *1950 BC*

14 And the Gods said: Let us make an help meet for the man, for it is not good that the man should be alone, therefore we will form an help meet for him.
15 And the Gods caused a deep sleep to fall upon Adam; and he slept, and they took one of his ribs, and closed up the flesh in the stead thereof;
16 And of the rib which the Gods had taken from man, formed they a woman, and brought her unto the man.
17 And Adam said: This was bone of my bones, and flesh of my flesh; now she shall be called Woman, because she was taken out of man;
18 Therefore shall a man leave his father and his mother, and shall cleave unto his wife, and they shall be one flesh.
19 And they were both naked, the man and his wife, and were not ashamed.
20 And out of the ground the Gods formed every beast of the field, and every fowl of the air, and brought them unto Adam to see what he would call them; and whatsoever Adam called every living creature, that should be the name thereof.
21 And Adam gave names to all cattle, to the fowl of the air, to every beast of the field; and for Adam, there was found an help meet for him.

MOSES 3

Moses *1475 BC*

18 And I, the Lord God, said unto mine Only Begotten, that it was not good that the man should be alone; wherefore, I will make an help meet for him.
19 And out of the ground I, the Lord God, formed every beast of the field, and every fowl of the air; and commanded that they should come unto Adam, to see what he would call them; and they were also living souls; for I, God, breathed into them the breath of life, and commanded that whatsoever Adam called every living creature, that should be the name thereof.
20 And Adam gave names to all cattle, and to the fowl of the air, and to every beast of the field; but as for Adam, there was not found an help meet for him.
21 And I, the Lord God, caused a deep sleep to fall upon Adam; and he slept, and I took one of his ribs and closed up the flesh in the stead thereof;
22 And the rib which I, the Lord God, had taken from man, made I a woman, and brought her unto the man.
23 And Adam said: This I know now is bone of my bones, and flesh of my flesh; she shall be called Woman, because she was taken out of man.
24 Therefore shall a man leave his father and his mother, and shall cleave unto his wife; and they shall be one flesh.
25 And they were both naked, the man and his wife, and were not ashamed.

GENESIS 2

Moses *1475 BC*

18 And the Lord God said, It is not good that the man should be alone; I will make him an help meet for him.
19 And out of the ground the Lord God formed every beast of the field, and every fowl of the air; and brought them unto Adam to see what he would call them: and whatsoever Adam called every living creature, that was the name thereof.
20 And Adam gave names to all cattle, and to the fowl of the air, and to every beast of the field; but for Adam there was not found an help meet for him.
21 And the Lord God caused a deep sleep to fall upon Adam, and he slept: and he took one of his ribs, and closed up the flesh instead thereof;
22 And the rib, which the Lord God had taken from man, made he a woman, and brought her unto the man.
23 And Adam said, This is now bone of my bones, and flesh of my flesh: she shall be called Woman, because she was taken out of Man.
24 Therefore shall a man leave his father and his mother, and shall cleave unto his wife: and they shall be one flesh.
25 And they were both naked, the man and his wife, and were not ashamed.

5

THE FALL OF ADAM AND EVE

+++

Satan tempts Eve to eat of the fruit of the tree of knowledge of good and evil. Satan lies, telling her that she will not die, but he also tells the truth, saying she and Adam will become as the Gods, knowing good and evil. Eve recognizes that she and Adam cannot obey God's commandment to have children without first partaking of the tree of knowledge of good and evil. Eve and Adam decide to eat the fruit and face the consequences.

MOSES 4

Moses 1475 BC

5 And now the serpent was more subtle than any beast of the field which I, the Lord God, had made.
6 And Satan put it into the heart of the serpent, (for he had drawn away many after him,) and he sought also to beguile Eve, for he knew not the mind of God, wherefore he sought to destroy the world.
7 And he said unto the woman: Yea, hath God said—Ye shall not eat of every tree of the garden? (And he spake by the mouth of the serpent.)
8 And the woman said unto the serpent: We may eat of the fruit of the trees of the garden;
9 But of the fruit of the tree which thou beholdest in the midst of the garden, God hath said—Ye shall not eat of it, neither shall ye touch it, lest ye die.
10 And the serpent said unto the woman: Ye shall not surely die;
11 For God doth know that in the day ye eat thereof, then your eyes shall be opened, and ye shall be as gods, knowing good and evil.
12 And when the woman saw that the tree was good for food, and that it became pleasant to the eyes, and a tree to be desired to make her wise, she took of the fruit thereof, and did eat, and also gave unto her husband with her, and he did eat.

GENESIS 3

Moses 1475 BC

1 Now the serpent was more subtle than any beast of the field which the Lord God had made. And he said unto the woman, Yea, hath God said, Ye shall not eat of every tree of the garden?
2 And the woman said unto the serpent, We may eat of the fruit of the trees of the garden:
3 But of the fruit of the tree which is in the midst of the garden, God hath said, Ye shall not eat of it, neither shall ye touch it, lest ye die.
4 And the serpent said unto the woman, Ye shall not surely die:
5 For God doth know that in the day ye eat thereof, then your eyes shall be opened, and ye shall be as gods, knowing good and evil.
6 And when the woman saw that the tree was good for food, and that it was pleasant to the eyes, and a tree to be desired to make one wise, she took of the fruit thereof, and did eat, and gave also unto her husband with her; and he did eat.

Adam and Eve cover their nakedness and are questioned by God.

MOSES 4

Moses 1475 BC

13 And the eyes of them both were opened, and they knew that they had been naked. And they sewed fig leaves together and made themselves aprons.
14 And they heard the voice of the Lord God, as they were walking in the garden, in the cool of the day; and Adam and his wife went to hide themselves from the presence of the Lord God amongst the trees of the garden.
15 And I, the Lord God, called unto Adam, and said unto him: Where goest thou?

16 And he said: I heard thy voice in the garden, and I was afraid, because I beheld that I was naked, and I hid myself.
17 And I, the Lord God, said unto Adam: Who told thee thou wast naked? Hast thou eaten of the tree whereof I commanded thee that thou shouldst not eat, if so thou shouldst surely die?
18 And the man said: The woman thou gavest me, and commandest that she should remain with me, she gave me of the fruit of the tree and I did eat.
19 And I, the Lord God, said unto the woman: What is this thing which thou hast done? And the woman said: The serpent beguiled me, and I did eat.

GENESIS 3
Moses *1475 BC*

7 And the eyes of them both were opened, and they knew that they were naked; and they sewed fig leaves together, and made themselves aprons.
8 And they heard the voice of the Lord God walking in the garden in the cool of the day: and Adam and his wife hid themselves from the presence of the Lord God amongst the trees of the garden.
9 And the Lord God called unto Adam, and said unto him, Where art thou?
10 And he said, I heard thy voice in the garden, and I was afraid, because I was naked; and I hid myself.
11 And he said, Who told thee that thou wast naked? Hast thou eaten of the tree, whereof I commanded thee that thou shouldest not eat?
12 And the man said, The woman whom thou gavest to be with me, she gave me of the tree, and I did eat.
13 And the Lord God said unto the woman, What is this that thou hast done? And the woman said, The serpent beguiled me, and I did eat.

Consequences for the serpent: it will lose its legs and be able to bite a man's heel, but man will have power to bruise its head. In other words, Satan will have power to tempt the children of Adam and Eve to sin, but Christ (the seed of Adam and Eve) will have power to overcome Satan and the effects of sin and death.

MOSES 4
Moses *1475 BC*

20 And I, the Lord God, said unto the serpent: Because thou hast done this thou shalt be cursed above all cattle, and above every beast of the field; upon thy belly shalt thou go, and dust shalt thou eat all the days of thy life;
21 And I will put enmity between thee and the woman, between thy seed and her seed; and he shall bruise thy head, and thou shalt bruise his heel.

GENESIS 3
Moses *1475 BC*

14 And the Lord God said unto the serpent, Because thou hast done this, thou art cursed above all cattle, and above every beast of the field; upon thy belly shalt thou go, and dust shalt thou eat all the days of thy life:
15 And I will put enmity between thee and the woman, and between thy seed and her seed; it shall bruise thy head, and thou shalt bruise his heel.

Consequences for Eve.

MOSES 4
Moses *1475 BC*

22 Unto the woman, I, the Lord God, said: I will greatly multiply thy sorrow and thy conception. In sorrow thou shalt bring forth children, and thy desire shall be to thy husband, and he shall rule over thee.

GENESIS 3
Moses *1475 BC*

16 Unto the woman he said, I will greatly multiply thy sorrow and thy conception; in sorrow thou shalt bring forth children; and thy desire shall be to thy husband, and he shall rule over thee.

Consequences for Adam.

MOSES 4
Moses *1475 BC*

23 And unto Adam, I, the Lord God, said: Because thou hast hearkened unto the voice of thy wife, and hast eaten of the fruit of the tree of which I commanded thee, saying—Thou shalt not eat of it, cursed shall be the ground for thy sake; in

The Expulsion of Adam and Eve from Paradise, by Benjamin West, 1791.

sorrow shalt thou eat of it all the days of thy life.
24 Thorns also, and thistles shall it bring forth to thee, and thou shalt eat the herb of the field.
25 By the sweat of thy face shalt thou eat bread, until thou shalt return unto the ground—for thou shalt surely die—for out of it wast thou taken: for dust thou wast, and unto dust shalt thou return.

GENESIS 3

Moses 1475 BC

17 And unto Adam he said, Because thou hast hearkened unto the voice of thy wife, and hast eaten of the tree, of which I commanded thee, saying, Thou shalt not eat of it: cursed is the ground for thy sake; in sorrow shalt thou eat of it all the days of thy life;
18 Thorns also and thistles shall it bring forth to thee; and thou shalt eat the herb of the field;
19 In the sweat of thy face shalt thou eat bread, till thou return unto the ground; for out of it wast thou taken: for dust thou art, and unto dust shalt thou return

God clothes Adam and Eve in coats of skins as they prepare to exit the Garden of Eden. Perhaps they were lamb skins, pointing to the sacrifice of Christ, the Lamb of God, who will overcome sin and death. The couple, now knowing good and evil and being agents to act for themselves, are cast out of the Garden.

MOSES 4

Moses 1475 BC

26 And Adam called his wife's name Eve, because she was the mother of all living; for thus have I, the Lord God, called the first of all women, which are many.
27 Unto Adam, and also unto his wife, did I, the Lord God, make coats of skins, and clothed them.
28 And I, the Lord God, said unto mine Only Begotten: Behold, the man is become as one of us to know good and evil; and now lest he put forth his hand and partake also of the tree of life, and eat and live forever,
29 Therefore I, the Lord God, will send him forth from the Garden of Eden, to till the ground from whence he was taken;
30 For as I, the Lord God, liveth, even so my words cannot return void, for as they go forth out of my mouth they must be fulfilled.
31 So I drove out the man, and I placed at the east of the Garden of Eden, cherubim and a flaming sword, which turned every way to keep the way of the tree of life.
32 (And these are the words which I spake unto my servant Moses, and they are true

Adam and Eve are Driven Out of Eden, by Gustave Dore.

even as I will; and I have spoken them unto you. See thou show them unto no man, until I command you, except to them that believe. Amen.)

GENESIS 3

Moses *1475 BC*

20 And Adam called his wife's name Eve;
because she was the mother of all living.
21 Unto Adam also and to his wife did the
Lord God make coats of skins, and clothed
them.
22 And the Lord God said, Behold, the
man is become as one of us, to know good
and evil: and now, lest he put forth his
hand, and take also of the tree of life, and
eat, and live forever:
23 Therefore the Lord God sent him forth
from the garden of Eden, to till the ground
from whence he was taken.
24 So he drove out the man; and he placed
at the east of the garden of Eden
Cherubims, and a flaming sword which
turned every way, to keep the way of the
tree of life.

6

THE PURPOSE OF LIFE

The Fall brings sin and death into the world, thus separating mankind both physically and spiritually from the presence of God. Jesus Christ will come into the world to overcome both sin and death. Adam and Eve's posterity may return to God's presence on conditions of repentance. Thus, our life on Earth is a time to repent and to prepare to meet God.

ALMA 12

Alma the Younger — *82 BC*

22 ...Now we see that Adam did fall by the partaking of the forbidden fruit, according to the word of God; and thus we see, that by his fall, all mankind became a lost and fallen people.

23 And now behold, I say unto you that if it had been possible for Adam to have partaken of the fruit of the tree of life at that time, there would have been no death, and the word would have been void, making God a liar, for he said: If thou eat thou shalt surely die.

24 And we see that death comes upon mankind, yea, the death which has been spoken of by Amulek, which is the temporal death; nevertheless there was a space granted unto man in which he might repent; therefore this life became a probationary state; a time to prepare to meet God; a time to prepare for that endless state which has been spoken of by us, which is after the resurrection of the dead.

25 Now, if it had not been for the plan of redemption, which was laid from the foundation of the world, there could have been no resurrection of the dead; but there was a plan of redemption laid, which shall bring to pass the resurrection of the dead, of which has been spoken.

26 And now behold, if it were possible that our first parents could have gone forth and partaken of the tree of life they would have been forever miserable, having no preparatory state; and thus the plan of redemption would have been frustrated, and the word of God would have been void, taking none effect.

27 But behold, it was not so; but it was appointed unto men that they must die; and after death, they must come to judgment, even that same judgment of which we have spoken, which is the end.

2 NEPHI 2

Lehi — *580 BC*

11 For it must needs be, that there is an opposition in all things. If not so, my firstborn in the wilderness, righteousness could not be brought to pass, neither wickedness, neither holiness nor misery, neither good nor bad. Wherefore, all things must needs be a compound in one; wherefore, if it should be one body it must needs remain as dead, having no life neither death, nor corruption nor incorruption, happiness nor misery, neither sense nor insensibility.

12 Wherefore, it must needs have been created for a thing of naught; wherefore there would have been no purpose in the end of its creation. Wherefore, this thing must needs destroy the wisdom of God and his eternal purposes, and also the power, and the mercy, and the justice of God.

13 And if ye shall say there is no law, ye shall also say there is no sin. If ye shall say there is no sin, ye shall also say there is no righteousness. And if there be no righteousness there be no happiness. And if there be no righteousness nor happiness there be no punishment nor misery. And if these things are not there is no God. And if there is no God we are not, neither the Earth; for there could have been no creation of things, neither to act nor to be acted upon; wherefore, all things must have vanished away.

14 And now, my sons, I speak unto you these things for your profit and learning; for there is a God, and he hath created all things, both the heavens and the Earth, and all things that in them are, both things to act and things to be acted upon.

15 And to bring about his eternal purposes in the end of man, after he had created our first parents, and the beasts of the field and the fowls of the air, and in fine, all things which are created, it must needs be that there was an opposition; even the forbidden fruit in opposition to the tree of life; the one being sweet and the other bitter.

16 Wherefore, the Lord God gave unto man that he should act for himself. Wherefore, man could not act for himself save it should be that he was enticed by the one or the other.

17 And I, Lehi, according to the things which I have read, must needs suppose that an angel of God, according to that which is written, had fallen from heaven; wherefore, he became a devil, having sought that which was evil before God.

18 And because he had fallen from heaven, and had become miserable forever, he sought also the misery of all mankind. Wherefore, he said unto Eve, yea, even that old serpent, who is the devil, who is the father of all lies, wherefore he said: Partake of the forbidden fruit, and ye shall not die, but ye shall be as God, knowing good and evil.

19 And after Adam and Eve had partaken of the forbidden fruit they were driven out of the garden of Eden, to till the Earth.

20 And they have brought forth children; yea, even the family of all the Earth.

21 And the days of the children of men were prolonged, according to the will of God, that they might repent while in the flesh; wherefore, their state became a state of probation, and their time was lengthened, according to the commandments which the Lord God gave unto the children of men. For he gave commandment that all men must repent; for he showed unto all men that they were lost, because of the transgression of their parents.

22 And now, behold, if Adam had not transgressed he would not have fallen, but he would have remained in the garden of Eden. And all things which were created must have remained in the same state in which they were after they were created; and they must have remained forever, and had no end.

23 And they would have had no children; wherefore they would have remained in a state of innocence, having no joy, for they knew no misery; doing no good, for they knew no sin.

24 But behold, all things have been done in the wisdom of him who knoweth all things.

25 Adam fell that men might be; and men are, that they might have joy.

26 And the Messiah cometh in the fulness of time, that he may redeem the children of men from the fall. And because that they are redeemed from the fall they have become free forever, knowing good from evil; to act for themselves and not to be acted upon, save it be by the punishment of the law at the great and last day, according to the commandments which God hath given.

27 Wherefore, men are free according to the flesh; and all things are given them which are expedient unto man. And they are free to choose liberty and eternal life, through the great Mediator of all men, or to choose captivity and death, according to the captivity and power of the devil; for he seeketh that all men might be miserable like unto himself.

28 And now, my sons, I would that ye should look to the great Mediator, and hearken unto his great commandments; and be faithful unto his words, and choose eternal life, according to the will of his Holy Spirit;

29 And not choose eternal death, according to the will of the flesh and the evil which is therein, which giveth the spirit of the devil power to captivate, to bring you down to hell, that he may reign over you in his own kingdom.

ALMA 42

Alma the Younger *73 BC*

2 ...For behold, after the Lord God sent our first parents forth from the garden of Eden, to till the ground, from whence they were taken—yea, he drew out the man, and he placed at the east end of the garden of Eden, cherubim, and a flaming sword which turned every way, to keep the tree of life—

3 Now, we see that the man had become as God, knowing good and evil; and lest he should put forth his hand, and take also of the tree of life, and eat and live forever, the Lord God placed cherubim and the flaming sword, that he should not partake of the fruit—
4 And thus we see, that there was a time granted unto man to repent, yea, a probationary time, a time to repent and serve God.
5 For behold, if Adam had put forth his hand immediately, and partaken of the tree of life, he would have lived forever, according to the word of God, having no space for repentance; yea, and also the word of God would have been void, and the great plan of salvation would have been frustrated.
6 But behold, it was appointed unto man to die—therefore, as they were cut off from the tree of life they should be cut off from the face of the Earth—and man became lost forever, yea, they became fallen man.
7 And now, ye see by this that our first parents were cut off both temporally and spiritually from the presence of the Lord; and thus we see they became subjects to follow after their own will.
8 Now behold, it was not expedient that man should be reclaimed from this temporal death, for that would destroy the great plan of happiness.
9 Therefore, as the soul could never die, and the fall had brought upon all mankind a spiritual death as well as a temporal, that is, they were cut off from the presence of the Lord, it was expedient that mankind should be reclaimed from this spiritual death.
10 Therefore, as they had become carnal, sensual, and devilish, by nature, this probationary state became a state for them to prepare; it became a preparatory state.

DOCTRINE AND COVENANTS 29

Joseph Smith *September 1830*

40 Wherefore, it came to pass that the devil tempted Adam, and he partook of the forbidden fruit and transgressed the commandment, wherein he became subject to the will of the devil, because he yielded unto temptation.
41 Wherefore, I, the Lord God, caused that he should be cast out from the Garden of Eden, from my presence, because of his transgression, wherein he became spiritually dead, which is the first death, even that same death which is the last death, which is spiritual, which shall be pronounced upon the wicked when I shall say: Depart, ye cursed.

7

THE CHILDREN OF ADAM ARE TAUGHT THE GOSPEL OF JESUS CHRIST

+++

The Lord teaches Adam and his posterity the commandments and to believe in the Son of God. Satan tempts the children of Adam to sin and disobey God.

MOSES 5

Moses *1475 BC*

1 And it came to pass that after I, the Lord God, had driven them out, that Adam began to till the Earth, and to have dominion over all the beasts of the field, and to eat his bread by the sweat of his brow, as I the Lord had commanded him. And Eve, also, his wife, did labor with him.

2 And Adam knew his wife, and she bare unto him sons and daughters, and they began to multiply and to replenish the Earth.

3 And from that time forth, the sons and daughters of Adam began to divide two and two in the land, and to till the land, and to tend flocks, and they also begat sons and daughters.

4 And Adam and Eve, his wife, called upon the name of the Lord, and they heard the voice of the Lord from the way toward the Garden of Eden, speaking unto them, and they saw him not; for they were shut out from his presence.

5 And he gave unto them commandments, that they should worship the Lord their God, and should offer the firstlings of their flocks, for an offering unto the Lord. And Adam was obedient unto the commandments of the Lord.

6 And after many days an angel of the Lord appeared unto Adam, saying: Why dost thou offer sacrifices unto the Lord? And Adam said unto him: I know not, save the Lord commanded me.

7 And then the angel spake, saying: This thing is a similitude of the sacrifice of the Only Begotten of the Father, which is full of grace and truth.

8 Wherefore, thou shalt do all that thou doest in the name of the Son, and thou shalt repent and call upon God in the name of the Son forevermore.

9 And in that day the Holy Ghost fell upon Adam, which beareth record of the Father and the Son, saying: I am the Only Begotten of the Father from the beginning, henceforth and forever, that as thou hast fallen thou mayest be redeemed, and all mankind, even as many as will.

10 And in that day Adam blessed God and was filled, and began to prophesy concerning all the families of the Earth, saying: Blessed be the name of God, for because of my transgression my eyes are opened, and in this life I shall have joy, and again in the flesh I shall see God.

11 And Eve, his wife, heard all these things and was glad, saying: Were it not for our transgression we never should have had seed, and never should have known good and evil, and the joy of our redemption, and the eternal life which God giveth unto all the obedient.

12 And Adam and Eve blessed the name of God, and they made all things known unto their sons and their daughters.

13 And Satan came among them, saying: I am also a son of God; and he commanded them, saying: Believe it not; and they believed it not, and they loved Satan more than God. And men began from that time forth to be carnal, sensual, and devilish.

14 And the Lord God called upon men by the Holy Ghost everywhere and commanded them that they should repent;

15 And as many as believed in the Son, and repented of their sins, should be saved; and as many as believed not and repented not, should be damned; and the words went forth out of the mouth of God in a firm decree; wherefore they must be fulfilled...

55 And thus the works of darkness began
to prevail among all the sons of men.
56 And God cursed the Earth with a sore
curse, and was angry with the wicked,
with all the sons of men whom he had
made;
57 For they would not hearken unto his
voice, nor believe on his Only Begotten
Son, even him whom he declared should
come in the meridian of time, who was
prepared from before the foundation of
the world.
58 And thus the Gospel began to be
preached, from the beginning, being
declared by holy angels sent forth from
the presence of God, and by his own voice,
and by the gift of the Holy Ghost.
59 And thus all things were confirmed
unto Adam, by an holy ordinance, and the
Gospel preached, and a decree sent forth,
that it should be in the world, until the
end thereof; and thus it was. Amen.

MOSES 6

Adam *1475 BC*

50 But God hath made known unto our
fathers that all men must repent.
51 And he called upon our father Adam by
his own voice, saying: I am God; I made
the world, and men before they were in
the flesh.
52 And he also said unto him: If thou wilt
turn unto me, and hearken unto my voice,
and believe, and repent of all thy trans-
gressions, and be baptized, even in water,
in the name of mine Only Begotten Son,
who is full of grace and truth, which is
Jesus Christ, the only name which shall be
given under heaven, whereby salvation
shall come unto the children of men, ye
shall receive the gift of the Holy Ghost,
asking all things in his name, and
whatsoever ye shall ask, it shall be given
you.
53 And our father Adam spake unto the
Lord, and said: Why is it that men must
repent and be baptized in water? And the
Lord said unto Adam: Behold I have
forgiven thee thy transgression in the
Garden of Eden.
54 Hence came the saying abroad among
the people, that the Son of God hath
atoned for original guilt, wherein the sins
of the parents cannot be answered upon
the heads of the children, for they are
whole from the foundation of the world.
55 And the Lord spake unto Adam, saying:
Inasmuch as thy children are conceived in
sin, even so when they begin to grow up,
sin conceiveth in their hearts, and they
taste the bitter, that they may know to
prize the good.
56 And it is given unto them to know good
from evil; wherefore they are agents unto
themselves, and I have given unto you
another law and commandment.
57 Wherefore teach it unto your children,
that all men, everywhere, must repent, or
they can in nowise inherit the kingdom of
God, for no unclean thing can dwell there,
or dwell in his presence; for, in the
language of Adam, Man of Holiness is his
name, and the name of his Only Begotten
is the Son of Man, even Jesus Christ, a
righteous Judge, who shall come in the
meridian of time.
58 Therefore I give unto you a command-
ment, to teach these things freely unto
your children, saying:
59 That by reason of transgression cometh
the fall, which fall bringeth death, and
inasmuch as ye were born into the world
by water, and blood, and the spirit, which
I have made, and so became of dust a
living soul, even so ye must be born again
into the kingdom of heaven, of water, and
of the Spirit, and be cleansed by blood,
even the blood of mine Only Begotten;
that ye might be sanctified from all sin,
and enjoy the words of eternal life in this
world, and eternal life in the world to
come, even immortal glory;
60 For by the water ye keep the com-
mandment; by the Spirit ye are justified,
and by the blood ye are sanctified;
61 Therefore it is given to abide in you;
the record of heaven; the Comforter; the
peaceable things of immortal glory; the
truth of all things; that which quickeneth
all things, which maketh alive all things;
that which knoweth all things, and hath
all power according to wisdom, mercy,
truth, justice, and judgment.
62 And now, behold, I say unto you: This
is the plan of salvation unto all men,
through the blood of mine Only Begotten,
who shall come in the meridian of time.
63 And behold, all things have their like-
ness, and all things are created and made
to bear record of me, both things which
are temporal, and things which are
spiritual; things which are in the heavens

above, and things which are on the Earth,
and things which are in the Earth, and
things which are under the Earth, both
above and beneath: all things bear record
of me.
64 And it came to pass, when the Lord had
spoken with Adam, our father, that Adam
cried unto the Lord, and he was caught
away by the Spirit of the Lord, and was
carried down into the water, and was laid
under the water, and was brought forth
out of the water.
65 And thus he was baptized, and the
Spirit of God descended upon him, and
thus he was born of the Spirit, and became
quickened in the inner man.
66 And he heard a voice out of heaven,
saying: Thou art baptized with fire, and
with the Holy Ghost. This is the record of
the Father, and the Son, from henceforth
and forever;
67 And thou art after the order of him
who was without beginning of days or end
of years, from all eternity to all eternity.
68 Behold, thou art one in me, a son of
God; and thus may all become my sons.
Amen.

ALMA 12

Alma the Younger — *82 BC*

28 And after God had appointed that these
things should come unto man, behold,
then he saw that it was expedient that
man should know concerning the things
whereof he had appointed unto them;
29 Therefore he sent angels to converse
with them, who caused men to behold of
his glory.
30 And they began from that time forth to
call on his name; therefore God conversed
with men, and made known unto them
the plan of redemption, which had been
prepared from the foundation of the
world; and this he made known unto them
according to their faith and repentance
and their holy works.
31 Wherefore, he gave commandments
unto men, they having first transgressed
the first commandments as to things
which were temporal, and becoming as
gods, knowing good from evil, placing
themselves in a state to act, or being
placed in a state to act according to their
wills and pleasures, whether to do evil or
to do good—
32 Therefore God gave unto them com-
mandments, after having made known
unto them the plan of redemption, that
they should not do evil, the penalty
thereof being a second death, which was
an everlasting death as to things pertain-
ing unto righteousness; for on such the
plan of redemption could have no power,
for the works of justice could not be
destroyed, according to the supreme
goodness of God.
33 But God did call on men, in the name
of his Son, (this being the plan of
redemption which was laid) saying: If ye
will repent, and harden not your hearts,
then will I have mercy upon you, through
mine Only Begotten Son;
34 Therefore, whosoever repenteth, and
hardeneth not his heart, he shall have
claim on mercy through mine Only
Begotten Son, unto a remission of his sins;
and these shall enter into my rest.

2 NEPHI 2

Lehi — *580 BC*

4 ...And the way is prepared from the fall
of man, and salvation is free.
5 And men are instructed sufficiently that
they know good from evil. And the law is
given unto men. And by the law no flesh
is justified; or, by the law men are cut off.
Yea, by the temporal law they were cut
off; and also, by the spiritual law they
perish from that which is good, and
become miserable forever.
6 Wherefore, redemption cometh in and
through the Holy Messiah; for he is full of
grace and truth.
7 Behold, he offereth himself a sacrifice
for sin, to answer the ends of the law, unto
all those who have a broken heart and a
contrite spirit; and unto none else can the
ends of the law be answered.
8 Wherefore, how great the importance to
make these things known unto the inhab-
itants of the Earth, that they may know
that there is no flesh that can dwell in the
presence of God, save it be through the
merits, and mercy, and grace of the Holy
Messiah, who layeth down his life
according to the flesh, and taketh it again
by the power of the Spirit, that he may
bring to pass the resurrection of the dead,
being the first that should rise.
9 Wherefore, he is the first fruits unto
God, inasmuch as he shall make inter-

cession for all the children of men; and they that believe in him shall be saved.
10 And because of the intercession for all, all men come unto God; wherefore, they stand in the presence of him, to be judged of him according to the truth and holiness which is in him. Wherefore, the ends of the law which the Holy One hath given, unto the inflicting of the punishment which is affixed, which punishment that is affixed is in opposition to that of the happiness which is affixed, to answer the ends of the atonement—

DOCTRINE AND COVENANTS 29

Joseph Smith *September 1830*

42 But, behold, I say unto you that I, the Lord God, gave unto Adam and unto his seed, that they should not die as to the temporal death, until I, the Lord God, should send forth angels to declare unto them repentance and redemption, through faith on the name of mine Only Begotten Son.
43 And thus did I, the Lord God, appoint unto man the days of his probation—that by his natural death he might be raised in immortality unto eternal life, even as many as would believe;
44 And they that believe not unto eternal damnation; for they cannot be redeemed from their spiritual fall, because they repent not;
45 For they love darkness rather than light, and their deeds are evil, and they receive their wages of whom they list to obey.

DOCTRINE AND COVENANTS 58

Joseph Smith *August 1831*

26 For behold, it is not meet that I should command in all things; for he that is compelled in all things, the same is a slothful and not a wise servant; wherefore he receiveth no reward.
27 Verily I say, men should be anxiously engaged in a good cause, and do many things of their own free will, and bring to pass much righteousness;
28 For the power is in them, wherein they are agents unto themselves. And inasmuch as men do good they shall in nowise lose their reward.

8

ALL PROPHETS TESTIFY OF CHRIST

+++

Ancient prophets on two continents foresee the life, Atonement, and Resurrection of Jesus Christ.

ALMA 39

Alma the Younger — *73 BC*

15 And now, my son, I would say somewhat unto you concerning the coming of Christ. Behold, I say unto you, that it is he that surely shall come to take away the sins of the world; yea, he cometh to declare glad tidings of salvation unto his people.
16 And now, my son, this was the ministry unto which ye were called, to declare these glad tidings unto this people, to prepare their minds; or rather that salvation might come unto them, that they may prepare the minds of their children to hear the word at the time of his coming.
17 And now I will ease your mind somewhat on this subject. Behold, you marvel why these things should be known so long beforehand. Behold, I say unto you, is not a soul at this time as precious unto God as a soul will be at the time of his coming?
18 Is it not as necessary that the plan of redemption should be made known unto this people as well as unto their children?
19 Is it not as easy at this time for the Lord to send his angel to declare these glad tidings unto us as unto our children, or as after the time of his coming?

DEUTERONOMONY 18

Moses — *1475 BC*

15 The Lord thy God will raise up unto thee a Prophet from the midst of thee, of thy brethren, like unto me; unto him ye shall hearken;
16 According to all that thou desiredst of the Lord thy God in Horeb in the day of the assembly, saying, Let me not hear again the voice of the Lord my God, neither let me see this great fire any more, that I die not.
17 And the Lord said unto me, They have well-spoken that which they have spoken.
18 I will raise them up a Prophet from among their brethren, like unto thee, and will put my words in his mouth; and he shall speak unto them all that I shall command him.
19 And it shall come to pass, that whosoever will not hearken unto my words which he shall speak in my name, I will require it of him.
20 But the prophet, which shall presume to speak a word in my name, which I have not commanded him to speak, or that shall speak in the name of other gods, even that prophet shall die.

ALMA 22

Aaron — *85 BC*

13 And Aaron did expound unto him the scriptures from the creation of Adam, laying the fall of man before him, and their carnal state and also the plan of redemption, which was prepared from the foundation of the world, through Christ, for all whosoever would believe on his name.
14 And since man had fallen he could not merit anything of himself; but the sufferings and death of Christ atone for their sins, through faith and repentance, and so forth; and that he breaketh the bands of death, that the grave shall have no victory, and that the sting of death should be swallowed up in the hopes of glory; and Aaron did expound all these things unto the king.

MOSIAH 27

Alma the Younger — *100 BC*

30 I rejected my Redeemer, and denied that which had been spoken of by our fathers; but now that they may foresee that he will come, and that he remem-

Moses raises up the brazen serpent, a type and a shadow of Jesus Christ. An illustration from the 1890 Holman Bible.

bereth every creature of his creating, he will make himself manifest unto all.

NUMBERS 21

Moses *1500 BC*

4 And they journeyed from mount Hor by the way of the Red sea, to compass the land of Edom: and the soul of the people was much discouraged because of the way.
5 And the people spake against God, and against Moses, Wherefore have ye brought us up out of Egypt to die in the wilderness? for there is no bread, neither is there any water; and our soul loatheth this light bread.
6 And the Lord sent fiery serpents among the people, and they bit the people; and much people of Israel died.
7 Therefore the people came to Moses, and said, We have sinned, for we have spoken against the Lord, and against thee; pray unto the Lord, that he take away the serpents from us. And Moses prayed for the people.
8 And the Lord said unto Moses, Make thee a fiery serpent, and set it upon a pole: and it shall come to pass, that every one that is bitten, when he looketh upon it, shall live.
9 And Moses made a serpent of brass, and put it upon a pole, and it came to pass, that if a serpent had bitten any man, when he beheld the serpent of brass, he lived.

HELAMAN 8

Nephi, Son of Helaman *20 BC*

11 Therefore he was constrained to speak more unto them saying: Behold, my brethren, have ye not read that God gave power unto one man, even Moses, to smite upon the waters of the Red Sea, and they parted hither and thither, insomuch that the Israelites, who were our fathers, came through upon dry ground, and the waters closed upon the armies of the Egyptians and swallowed them up?
12 And now behold, if God gave unto this man such power, then why should ye dispute among yourselves, and say that he hath given unto me no power whereby I may know concerning the judgments that shall come upon you except ye repent?
13 But, behold, ye not only deny my words, but ye also deny all the words

which have been spoken by our fathers, and also the words which were spoken by this man, Moses, who had such great power given unto him, yea, the words which he hath spoken concerning the coming of the Messiah.

14 Yea, did he not bear record that the Son of God should come? And as he lifted up the brazen serpent in the wilderness, even so shall he be lifted up who should come.

15 And as many as should look upon that serpent should live, even so as many as should look upon the Son of God with faith, having a contrite spirit, might live, even unto that life which is eternal.

16 And now behold, Moses did not only testify of these things, but also all the holy prophets, from his days even to the days of Abraham.

17 Yea, and behold, Abraham saw of his coming, and was filled with gladness and did rejoice.

18 Yea, and behold I say unto you, that Abraham not only knew of these things, but there were many before the days of Abraham who were called by the order of God; yea, even after the order of his Son; and this that it should be shown unto the people, a great many thousand years before his coming, that even redemption should come unto them.

19 And now I would that ye should know, that even since the days of Abraham there have been many prophets that have testified these things; yea, behold, the prophet Zenos did testify boldly; for the which he was slain.

20 And behold, also Zenock, and also Ezias, and also Isaiah, and Jeremiah, (Jeremiah being that same prophet who testified of the destruction of Jerusalem) and now we know that Jerusalem was destroyed according to the words of Jeremiah. O then why not the Son of God come, according to his prophecy?

21 And now will you dispute that Jerusalem was destroyed? Will ye say that the sons of Zedekiah were not slain, all except it were Mulek? Yea, and do ye not behold that the seed of Zedekiah are with us, and they were driven out of the land of Jerusalem? But behold, this is not all—

22 Our father Lehi was driven out of Jerusalem because he testified of these things. Nephi also testified of these things, and also almost all of our fathers, even down to this time; yea, they have testified of the coming of Christ, and have looked forward, and have rejoiced in his day which is to come.

23 And behold, he is God, and he is with them, and he did manifest himself unto them, that they were redeemed by him; and they gave unto him glory, because of that which is to come.

24 And now, seeing ye know these things and cannot deny them except ye shall lie, therefore in this ye have sinned, for ye have rejected all these things, notwithstanding so many evidences which ye have received; yea, even ye have received all things, both things in heaven, and all things which are in the Earth, as a witness that they are true.

2 NEPHI 25

Nephi, Son of Lehi *550 BC*

20 And now, my brethren, I have spoken plainly that ye cannot err. And as the Lord God liveth that brought Israel up out of the land of Egypt, and gave unto Moses power that he should heal the nations after they had been bitten by the poisonous serpents, if they would cast their eyes unto the serpent which he did raise up before them, and also gave him power that he should smite the rock and the water should come forth; yea, behold I say unto you, that as these things are true, and as the Lord God liveth, there is none other name given under heaven save it be this Jesus Christ, of which I have spoken, whereby man can be saved.

JEREMIAH 23

Jeremiah *628 BC*

5 Behold, the days come, saith the LORD, that I will raise unto David a righteous Branch, and a King shall reign and prosper, and shall execute judgment and justice in the Earth.

6 In his days Judah shall be saved, and Israel shall dwell safely: and this is his name whereby he shall be called, THE LORD OUR RIGHTEOUSNESS.

ALMA 33

Alma the Younger *74 BC*

12 And now Alma said unto them: Do ye believe those scriptures which have been written by them of old?

13 Behold, if ye do, ye must believe what Zenos said; for, behold he said: Thou hast turned away thy judgments because of thy Son.

14 Now behold, my brethren, I would ask if ye have read the scriptures? If ye have, how can ye disbelieve on the Son of God?

15 For it is not written that Zenos alone spake of these things, but Zenock also spake of these things—

16 For behold, he said: Thou art angry, O Lord, with this people, because they will not understand thy mercies which thou hast bestowed upon them because of thy Son.

17 And now, my brethren, ye see that a second prophet of old has testified of the Son of God, and because the people would not understand his words they stoned him to death.

18 But behold, this is not all; these are not the only ones who have spoken concerning the Son of God.

19 Behold, he was spoken of by Moses; yea, and behold a type was raised up in the wilderness, that whosoever would look upon it might live. And many did look and live.

20 But few understood the meaning of those things, and this because of the hardness of their hearts. But there were many who were so hardened that they would not look, therefore they perished. Now the reason they would not look is because they did not believe that it would heal them.

21 O my brethren, if ye could be healed by merely casting about your eyes that ye might be healed, would ye not behold quickly, or would ye rather harden your hearts in unbelief, and be slothful, that ye would not cast about your eyes, that ye might perish?

22 If so, wo shall come upon you; but if not so, then cast about your eyes and begin to believe in the Son of God, that he will come to redeem his people, and that he shall suffer and die to atone for their sins; and that he shall rise again from the dead, which shall bring to pass the resurrection, that all men shall stand before him, to be judged at the last and judgment day, according to their works.

23 And now, my brethren, I desire that ye shall plant this word in your hearts, and as it beginneth to swell even so nourish it by your faith. And behold, it will become a tree, springing up in you unto everlasting life. And then may God grant unto you that your burdens may be light, through the joy of his Son. And even all this can ye do if ye will. Amen.

1 NEPHI 1

Nephi, Son of Lehi *600 BC*

19 And it came to pass that the Jews did mock him [Lehi] because of the things which he testified of them; for he truly testified of their wickedness and their abominations; and he testified that the things which he saw and heard, and also the things which he read in the book, manifested plainly of the coming of a Messiah, and also the redemption of the world.

2 NEPHI 11

Nephi, Son of Lehi *550 BC*

2 And now I, Nephi, write more of the words of Isaiah, for my soul delighteth in his words. For I will liken his words unto my people, and I will send them forth unto all my children, for he verily saw my Redeemer, even as I have seen him.

3 And my brother, Jacob, also has seen him as I have seen him; wherefore, I will send their words forth unto my children to prove unto them that my words are true. Wherefore, by the words of three, God hath said, I will establish my word. Nevertheless, God sendeth more witnessses, and he proveth all his words.

4 Behold, my soul delighteth in proving unto my people the truth of the coming of Christ; for, for this end hath the law of Moses been given; and all things which have been given of God from the beginning of the world, unto man, are the typifying of him.

5 And also my soul delighteth in the covenants of the Lord which he hath made to our fathers; yea, my soul delighteth in his grace, and in his justice, and power, and mercy in the great and eternal plan of deliverance from death.

6 And my soul delighteth in proving unto my people that save Christ should come all men must perish.

7 For if there be no Christ there be no God; and if there be no God we are not, for there could have been no creation. But

there is a God, and he is Christ, and he cometh in the fulness of his own time.

2 NEPHI 25

Nephi, Son of Lehi — *550 BC*

23 For we labor diligently to write, to persuade our children, and also our brethren, to believe in Christ, and to be reconciled to God; for we know that it is by grace that we are saved, after all we can do.
24 And, notwithstanding we believe in Christ, we keep the law of Moses, and look forward with steadfastness unto Christ, until the law shall be fulfilled.
25 For, for this end was the law given; wherefore the law hath become dead unto us, and we are made alive in Christ because of our faith; yet we keep the law because of the commandments.
26 And we talk of Christ, we rejoice in Christ, we preach of Christ, we prophesy of Christ, and we write according to our prophecies, that our children may know to what source they may look for a remission of their sins.
27 Wherefore, we speak concerning the law that our children may know the deadness of the law; and they, by knowing the deadness of the law, may look forward unto that life which is in Christ, and know for what end the law was given. And after the law is fulfilled in Christ, that they need not harden their hearts against him when the law ought to be done away.
28 And now behold, my people, ye are a stiffnecked people; wherefore, I have spoken plainly unto you, that ye cannot misunderstand. And the words which I have spoken shall stand as a testimony against you; for they are sufficient to teach any man the right way; for the right way is to believe in Christ and deny him not; for by denying him ye also deny the prophets and the law.
29 And now behold, I say unto you that the right way is to believe in Christ, and deny him not; and Christ is the Holy One of Israel; wherefore ye must bow down before him, and worship him with all your might, mind, and strength, and your whole soul; and if ye do this ye shall in nowise be cast out.

Face of Jesus, Reconstructed from the Shroud of Turin image.

MOSIAH 13

Abinadi — *148 BC*

28 And moreover, I say unto you, that salvation doth not come by the law alone; and were it not for the atonement, which God himself shall make for the sins and iniquities of his people, that they must unavoidably perish, notwithstanding the law of Moses.
32 And now, did they understand the law? I say unto you, Nay, they did not all understand the law; and this because of the hardness of their hearts; for they understood not that there could not any man be saved except it were through the redemption of God.
33 For behold, did not Moses prophesy unto them concerning the coming of the Messiah, and that God should redeem his people? Yea, and even all the prophets who have prophesied ever since the world began—have they not spoken more or less concerning these things?
34 Have they not said that God himself should come down among the children of men, and take upon him the form of man, and go forth in mighty power upon the face of the Earth?

35 Yea, and have they not said also that he should bring to pass the resurrection of the dead, and that he, himself, should be oppressed and afflicted?

2 NEPHI 32

Nephi, Son of Lehi *550 BC*

3 Angels speak by the power of the Holy Ghost; wherefore, they speak the words of Christ. Wherefore, I said unto you, feast upon the words of Christ; for behold, the words of Christ will tell you all things what ye should do.

6 Behold, this is the doctrine of Christ, and there will be no more doctrine given until after he shall manifest himself unto you in the flesh. And when he shall manifest himself unto you in the flesh, the things which he shall say unto you shall ye observe to do.

2 NEPHI 33

Nephi, Son of Lehi *550 BC*

4 And I know that the Lord God will consecrate my prayers for the gain of my people. And the words which I have written in weakness will be made strong unto them; for it persuadeth them to do good; it maketh known unto them of their fathers; and it speaketh of Jesus, and persuadeth them to believe in him, and to endure to the end, which is life eternal.

5 And it speaketh harshly against sin, according to the plainness of the truth; wherefore, no man will be angry at the words which I have written save he shall be of the spirit of the devil.

6 I glory in plainness; I glory in truth; I glory in my Jesus, for he hath redeemed my soul from hell.

7 I have charity for my people, and great faith in Christ that I shall meet many souls spotless at his judgment-seat.

8 I have charity for the Jew—I say Jew, because I mean them from whence I came.

9 I also have charity for the Gentiles. But behold, for none of these can I hope except they shall be reconciled unto Christ, and enter into the narrow gate, and walk in the strait path which leads to life, and continue in the path until the end of the day of probation.

10 And now, my beloved brethren, and also Jew, and all ye ends of the Earth, hearken unto these words and believe in Christ; and if ye believe not in these words believe in Christ. And if ye shall believe in Christ ye will believe in these words, for they are the words of Christ, and he hath given them unto me; and they teach all men that they should do good.

11 And if they are not the words of Christ, judge ye—for Christ will show unto you, with power and great glory, that they are his words, at the last day; and you and I shall stand face to face before his bar; and ye shall know that I have been commanded of him to write these things, notwithstanding my weakness.

12 And I pray the Father in the name of Christ that many of us, if not all, may be saved in his kingdom at that great and last day.

Daniel prophesies of the Atonement of Jesus Christ. In his prophecies, a day equals a year, and a week equals seven years. Thus seventy weeks, or 70 times 7 days, would equal 490 years. The statement: "from the time of the going forth of the commandment to restore and build Jerusalem" is understood as the 457 BC decree of Persian King Artaxerxes to allow the Jews to rebuild Jerusalem and the temple. From this date, Daniel says it would be 490 years to "finish the transgression, and to make an end of sins, and to make reconciliation for iniquity, and to bring everlasting righteousness..." This event, the Atonement of Jesus Christ in 33 AD, would occur in exactly 490 years.

DANIEL 9

Daniel *606 BC*

20 And whiles I was speaking, and praying, and confessing my sin and the sin of my people Israel, and presenting my supplication before the LORD my God for the holy mountain of my God;

21 Yea, whiles I was speaking in prayer, even the man Gabriel, whom I had seen in the vision at the beginning, being caused to fly swiftly, touched me about the time of the evening oblation.

22 And he informed me, and talked with me, and said, O Daniel, I am now come forth to give thee skill and understanding.

23 At the beginning of thy supplications the commandment came forth, and I am come to shew thee; for thou art greatly

beloved: therefore understand the matter, and consider the vision.
24 Seventy weeks are determined upon thy people and upon thy holy city, to finish the transgression, and to make an end of sins, and to make reconciliation for iniquity, and to bring in everlasting righteousness, and to seal up the vision and prophecy, and to anoint the most Holy.
25 Know therefore and understand, that from the going forth of the commandment to restore and to build Jerusalem unto the Messiah the Prince shall be seven weeks, and threescore and two weeks: the street shall be built again, and the wall, even in troublous times.
26 And after threescore and two weeks shall Messiah be cut off, but not for himself: and the people of the prince that shall come shall destroy the city and the sanctuary; and the end thereof shall be with a flood, and unto the end of the war desolations are determined.
27 And he shall confirm the covenant with many for one week: and in the midst of the week he shall cause the sacrifice and the oblation to cease, and for the overspreading of abominations he shall make it desolate, even until the consummation, and that determined shall be poured upon the desolate.

JACOB 1

Jacob, Son of Lehi — *545 BC*

6 And we also had many revelations, and the spirit of much prophecy; wherefore, we knew of Christ and his kingdom, which should come.
7 Wherefore we labored diligently among our people, that we might persuade them to come unto Christ, and partake of the goodness of God, that they might enter into his rest, lest by any means he should swear in his wrath they should not enter in, as in the provocation in the days of temptation while the children of Israel were in the wilderness.
8 Wherefore, we would to God that we could persuade all men not to rebel against God, to provoke him to anger, but that all men would believe in Christ, and view his death, and suffer his cross and bear the shame of the world; wherefore, I, Jacob, take it upon me to fulfil the commandment of my brother Nephi.

JACOB 4

Jacob, Son of Lehi — *545 BC*

4 For, for this intent have we written these things, that they may know that we knew of Christ, and we had a hope of his glory many hundred years before his coming; and not only we ourselves had a hope of his glory, but also all the holy prophets which were before us.
5 Behold, they believed in Christ and worshiped the Father in his name, and also we worship the Father in his name. And for this intent we keep the law of Moses, it pointing our souls to him; and for this cause it is sanctified unto us for righteousness, even as it was accounted unto Abraham in the wilderness to be obedient unto the commands of God in offering up his son Isaac, which is a similitude of God and his Only Begotten Son.
6 Wherefore, we search the prophets, and we have many revelations and the spirit of prophecy; and having all these witnesses we obtain a hope, and our faith becometh unshaken, insomuch that we truly can command in the name of Jesus and the very trees obey us, or the mountains, or the waves of the sea.
7 Nevertheless, the Lord God showeth us our weakness that we may know that it is by his grace, and his great condescensions unto the children of men, that we have power to do these things.
11 Wherefore, beloved brethren, be reconciled unto him through the atonement of Christ, his Only Begotten Son, and ye may obtain a resurrection, according to the power of the resurrection which is in Christ, and be presented as the first-fruits of Christ unto God, having faith, and obtained a good hope of glory in him before he manifesteth himself in the flesh.
12 And now, beloved, marvel not that I tell you these things; for why not speak of the atonement of Christ, and attain to a perfect knowledge of him, as to attain to the knowledge of a resurrection and the world to come?
13 Behold, my brethren, he that prophesieth, let him prophesy to the understanding of men; for the Spirit speaketh the truth and lieth not. Wherefore, it speaketh of things as they really care, and of things as they really will be; wherefore, these things are manifested unto us

Abraham's sacrifice of his only son, Isaac, was a similitude of God the Father's sacrifice of his only-begotten son, Jesus Christ. Le Sacrifice d'Isaac, by Philippe de Champaigne (1602-1674).

plainly, for the salvation of our souls. But behold, we are not witnesses alone in these things; for God also spake them unto prophets of old.

ACTS 3

Peter 34 AD

19 Repent ye therefore, and be converted, that your sins may be blotted out, when the times of refreshing shall come from the presence of the Lord;
20 And he shall send Jesus Christ, which before was preached unto you:
21 Whom the heaven must receive until the times of restitution of all things, which God hath spoken by the mouth of all his holy prophets since the world began.
22 For Moses truly said unto the fathers, A prophet shall the Lord your God raise up unto you of your brethren, like unto me; him shall ye hear in all things whatsoever he shall say unto you.
23 And it shall come to pass, that every soul, which will not hear that prophet, shall be destroyed from among the people.
24 Yea, and all the prophets from Samuel and those that follow after, as many as have spoken, have likewise foretold of these days.
25 Ye are the children of the prophets, and of the covenant which God made with our fathers, saying unto Abraham, And in thy seed shall all the kindreds of the Earth be blessed.
26 Unto you first God, having raised up his Son Jesus, sent him to bless you, in turning away every one of you from his iniquities.

ALMA 37

Alma the Younger 73 BC

33 Preach unto them repentance, and faith on the Lord Jesus Christ; teach them to humble themselves and to be meek and lowly in heart; teach them to withstand every temptation of the devil, with their faith on the Lord Jesus Christ.
44 For behold, it is as easy to give heed to the word of Christ, which will point to you a straight course to eternal bliss, as it was for our fathers to give heed to this compass, which would point unto them a straight course to the promised land.
45 And now I say, is there not a type in this thing? For just as surely as this director did bring our fathers, by following its course, to the promised land, shall the words of Christ, if we follow their course, carry us beyond this vale of sorrow into a far better land of promise.

ETHER 3

The Brother of Jared 2200 BC

4 And I know, O Lord, that thou hast all power, and can do whatsoever thou wilt for the benefit of man; therefore touch these stones, O Lord, with thy finger, and prepare them that they may shine forth in darkness; and they shall shine forth unto us in the vessels which we have prepared, that we may have light while we shall cross the sea.
5 Behold, O Lord, thou canst do this. We know that thou art able to show forth

great power, which looks small unto the understanding of men.
6 And it came to pass that when the brother of Jared had said these words, behold, the Lord stretched forth his hand and touched the stones one by one with his finger. And the veil was taken from off the eyes of the brother of Jared, and he saw the finger of the Lord; and it was as the finger of a man, like unto flesh and blood; and the brother of Jared fell down before the Lord, for he was struck with fear.
7 And the Lord saw that the brother of Jared had fallen to the Earth; and the Lord said unto him: Arise, why hast thou fallen?
8 And he saith unto the Lord: I saw the finger of the Lord, and I feared lest he should smite me; for I knew not that the Lord had flesh and blood.
9 And the Lord said unto him: Because of thy faith thou hast seen that I shall take upon me flesh and blood; and never has man come before me with such exceeding faith as thou hast; for were it not so ye could not have seen my finger. Sawest thou more than this?
10 And he answered: Nay; Lord, show thyself unto me.
11 And the Lord said unto him: Believest thou the words which I shall speak?
12 And he answered: Yea, Lord, I know that thou speakest the truth, for thou art a God of truth, and canst not lie.
13 And when he had said these words, behold, the Lord showed himself unto him, and said: Because thou knowest these things ye are redeemed from the fall; therefore ye are brought back into my presence; therefore I show myself unto you.
14 Behold, I am he who was prepared from the foundation of the world to redeem my people. Behold, I am Jesus Christ. I am the Father and the Son. In me shall all mankind have life, and that eternally, even they who shall believe on my name; and they shall become my sons and my daughters.
15 And never have I showed myself unto man whom I have created, for never has man believed in me as thou hast. Seest thou that ye are created after mine own image? Yea, even all men were created in the beginning after mine own image.
16 Behold, this body, which ye now behold, is the body of my spirit; and man have I created after the body of my spirit; and even as I appear unto thee to be in the spirit will I appear unto my people in the flesh.

ETHER 12

Moroni — *425 AD*

38 And now I, Moroni, bid farewell unto the Gentiles, yea, and also unto my brethren whom I love, until we shall meet before the judgment-seat of Christ, where all men shall know that my garments are not spotted with your blood.
39 And then shall ye know that I have seen Jesus, and that he hath talked with me face to face, and that he told me in plain humility, even as a man telleth another in mine own language, concerning these things;
40 And only a few have I written, because of my weakness in writing.
41 And now, I would commend you to seek this Jesus of whom the prophets and apostles have written, that the grace of God the Father, and also the Lord Jesus Christ, and the Holy Ghost, which beareth record of them, may be and abide in you forever. Amen.

Part 2

PROPHECIES OF EVENTS FROM 1 – 1000 AD

9

THE SIGNS OF CHRIST'S BIRTH

+++

Ancient American prophets prophesy of the signs of Christ's birth: a full night with no darkness and the appearance of a new star in the heavens.

HELAMAN 14

Samuel the Lamanite — *6 BC*

1 And now it came to pass that Samuel, the Lamanite, did prophesy a great many more things which cannot be written.
2 And behold, he said unto them: Behold, I give unto you a sign; for five years more cometh, and behold, then cometh the Son of God to redeem all those who shall believe on his name.
3 And behold, this will I give unto you for a sign at the time of his coming; for behold, there shall be great lights in heaven, insomuch that in the night before he cometh there shall be no darkness, insomuch that it shall appear unto man as if it was day.
4 Therefore, there shall be one day and a night and a day, as if it were one day and there were no night; and this shall be unto you for a sign; for ye shall know of the rising of the sun and also of its setting; therefore they shall know of a surety that there shall be two days and a night; nevertheless the night shall not be darkened; and it shall be the night before he is born.
5 And behold, there shall a new star arise, such an one as ye never have beheld; and this also shall be a sign unto you.
6 And behold this is not all, there shall be many signs and wonders in heaven.
7 And it shall come to pass that ye shall all be amazed, and wonder, insomuch that ye shall fall to the Earth.
8 And it shall come to pass that whosoever shall believe on the Son of God, the same shall have everlasting life.

HELAMAN 16

Mormon — *2 BC*

13 But it came to pass in the ninetieth year of the reign of the judges, there were great signs given unto the people, and wonders; and the words of the prophets began to be fulfilled.
14 And angels did appear unto men, wise men, and did declare unto them glad tidings of great joy; thus in this year the scriptures began to be fulfilled.
15 Nevertheless, the people began to harden their hearts, all save it were the most believing part of them, both of the Nephites and also of the Lamanites, and began to depend upon their own strength and upon their own wisdom, saying:
16 Some things they may have guessed right, among so many; but behold, we know that all these great and marvelous works cannot come to pass, of which has been spoken.
17 And they began to reason and to contend among themselves, saying:
18 That it is not reasonable that such a being as a Christ shall come; if so, and he be the Son of God, the Father of heaven and of Earth, as it has been spoken, why will he not show himself unto us as well as unto them who shall be at Jerusalem?
19 Yea, why will he not show himself in this land as well as in the land of Jerusalem?
20 But behold, we know that this is a wicked tradition, which has been handed down unto us by our fathers, to cause us that we should believe in some great and marvelous thing which should come to pass, but not among us, but in a land which is far distant, a land which we know not; therefore they can keep us in ignorance, for we cannot witness with our own eyes that they are true.
21 And they will, by the cunning and the mysterious arts of the evil one, work some great mystery which we cannot understand, which will keep us down to be servants to their words, and also new

servants unto them, for we depend upon them to teach us the word; and thus will they keep us in ignorance if we will yield ourselves unto them, all the days of our lives.
22 And many more things did the people imagine up in their hearts, which were foolish and vain; and they were much disturbed, for Satan did stir them up to do iniquity continually; yea, he did go about spreading rumors and contentions upon all the face of the land, that he might harden the hearts of the people against that which was good and against that which should come.
23 And notwithstanding the signs and the wonders which were wrought among the people of the Lord, and the many miracles which they did, Satan did get great hold upon the hearts of the people upon all the face of the land.

3 NEPHI 1

Nephi, Son of Nephi *1 AD*

4 And it came to pass that in the commencement of the ninety and second year, behold, the prophecies of the prophets began to be fulfilled more fully; for there began to be greater signs and greater miracles wrought among the people.
5 But there were some who began to say that the time was past for the words to be fulfilled, which were spoken by Samuel, the Lamanite.
6 And they began to rejoice over their brethren, saying: Behold the time is past, and the words of Samuel are not fulfilled; therefore, your joy and your faith concerning this thing hath been vain.
7 And it came to pass that they did make a great uproar throughout the land; and the people who believed began to be very sorrowful, lest by any means those things which had been spoken might not come to pass.
8 But behold, they did watch steadfastly for that day and that night and that day which should be as one day as if there were no night, that they might know that their faith had not been vain.
9 Now it came to pass that there was a day set apart by the unbelievers, that all those who believed in those traditions should be put to death except the sign should come to pass, which had been given by Samuel the prophet.
10 Now it came to pass that when Nephi, the son of Nephi, saw this wickedness of his people, his heart was exceedingly sorrowful.
11 And it came to pass that he went out and bowed himself down upon the Earth, and cried mightily to his God in behalf of his people, yea, those who were about to be destroyed because of their faith in the tradition of their fathers.
12 And it came to pass that he cried mightily unto the Lord all that day; and behold, the voice of the Lord came unto him, saying:
13 Lift up your head and be of good cheer; for behold, the time is at hand, and on this night shall the sign be given, and on the morrow come I into the world, to show unto the world that I will fulfil all that which I have caused to be spoken by the mouth of my holy prophets.
14 Behold, I come unto my own, to fulfil all things which I have made known unto the children of men from the foundation of the world, and to do the will, both of the Father and of the Son—of the Father because of me, and of the Son because of my flesh. And behold, the time is at hand, and this night shall the sign be given.
15 And it came to pass that the words which came unto Nephi were fulfilled, according as they had been spoken; for behold, at the going down of the sun there was no darkness; and the people began to be astonished because there was no darkness when the night came.
16 And there were many, who had not believed the words of the prophets, who fell to the Earth and became as if they were dead, for they knew that the great plan of destruction which they had laid for those who believed in the words of the prophets had been frustrated; for the sign which had been given was already at hand.
17 And they began to know that the Son of God must shortly appear; yea, in fine, all the people upon the face of the whole Earth from the west to the east, both in the land north and in the land south, were so exceedingly astonished that they fell to the Earth.
18 For they knew that the prophets had testified of these things for many years, and that the sign which had been given was already at hand; and they began to

fear because of their iniquity and their
unbelief.
19 And it came to pass that there was no
darkness in all that night, but it was as
light as though it was mid-day. And it
came to pass that the sun did rise in the
morning again, according to its proper
order; and they knew that it was the day
that the Lord should be born, because of
the sign which had been given.
20 And it had come to pass, yea, all things,
every whit, according to the words of the
prophets.
21 And it came to pass also that a new star
did appear, according to the word.
22 And it came to pass that from this time
forth there began to be lyings sent forth
among the people, by Satan, to harden
their hearts, to the intent that they might
not believe in those signs and wonders
which they had seen; but notwithstanding
these lyings and deceivings the more part
of the people did believe, and were
converted unto the Lord.
23 And it came to pass that Nephi went
forth among the people, and also many
others, baptizing unto repentance, in the
which there was a great remission of sins.
And thus, the people began again to have
peace in the land.
24 And there were no contentions, save it
were a few that began to preach,
endeavoring to prove by the scriptures
that it was no more expedient to observe
the law of Moses. Now in this thing they
did err, having not understood the
scriptures.
25 But it came to pass that they soon
became converted, and were convinced of
the error which they were in, for it was
made known unto them that the law was
not yet fulfilled, and that it must be
fulfilled in every whit; yea, the word came
unto them that it must be fulfilled; yea,
that one jot or tittle should not pass away
till it should all be fulfilled; therefore in
this same year were they brought to a
knowledge of their error and did confess
their faults.
26 And thus the ninety and second year
did pass away, bringing glad tidings unto
the people because of the signs which did
come to pass, according to the words of
the prophecy of all the holy prophets.

The New Star in China

Ancient Chinese astronomers kept meticulous records of astronomical events. In 5 BC, the year many modern scholars believe best fits the year of Christ's birth, the following was recorded:

"In the second month of the second year of Jian Ping (March 9-April 6, 5 BC) a comet came out from Altair for more than 70 days. It is said that comets appear to signify the old being replaced by the new. Altair, the sun, the moon, and the five stars are in movement to signify the beginning of a new epoch, the beginning of a new year, a new month, and a new day. The appearance of this comet undoubtedly symbolized change, the extended appearance of this comet indicates that this is of great importance. The primary meaning of Altair: the key supporting pillar of the Heavens, is the perfect sacrifice."

Historical Records, Vol. 27, Book of Astronomy of Han Dynasty

10

THE BIRTH OF JESUS CHRIST

The Nativity, attributed to Jacobo Bassano, 1510-1592.

+++

The conception and birth of Jesus Christ; he would be born of Judah from the lineage of David, in Bethlehem, and his mother, Mary, would be a virgin.

1 CHRONICLES 5

Moses 1475 BC

2 For Judah prevailed above his brethren, and of him came the chief ruler; but the birthright was Joseph's...

MICAH 5

Micah 722 BC

2 But thou, Bethlehem Ephratah, though thou be little among the thousands of Judah, yet out of thee shall he come forth unto me that is to be ruler in Israel; whose goings forth have been from of old, from everlasting.

JEREMIAH 23

Jeremiah 628 BC

5 Behold, the days come, saith the Lord, that I will raise unto David a righteous Branch, and a King shall reign and prosper, and shall execute judgment and justice in the Earth.

1 NEPHI 11

Nephi, Son of Lehi 595 BC

13 And it came to pass that I looked and beheld the great city of Jerusalem, and also other cities. And I beheld the city of Nazareth; and in the city of Nazareth I beheld a virgin, and she was exceedingly fair and white.
14 And it came to pass that I saw the heavens open; and an angel came down and stood before me; and he said unto me: Nephi, what beholdest thou?
15 And I said unto him: A virgin, most beautiful and fair above all other virgins.

16 And he said unto me: Knowest thou the condescension of God?
17 And I said unto him: I know that he loveth his children; nevertheless, I do not know the meaning of all things.
18 And he said unto me: Behold, the virgin whom thou seest is the mother of the Son of God, after the manner of the flesh.
19 And it came to pass that I beheld that she was carried away in the Spirit; and after she had been carried away in the Spirit for the space of a time the angel spake unto me, saying: Look!
20 And I looked and beheld the virgin again, bearing a child in her arms.
21 And the angel said unto me: Behold the Lamb of God, yea, even the Son of the Eternal Father! Knowest thou the meaning of the tree which thy father saw?
22 And I answered him, saying: Yea, it is the love of God, which sheddeth itself abroad in the hearts of the children of men; wherefore, it is the most desirable above all things.
23 And he spake unto me, saying: Yea, and the most joyous to the soul.

2 NEPHI 17 (see also ISAIAH 7)

Isaiah 740 BC

14 Therefore, the Lord himself shall give you a sign—Behold, a virgin shall conceive, and shall bear a son, and shall call his name Immanuel.
15 Butter and honey shall he eat, that he may know to refuse the evil and to choose the good.
16 For before the child shall know to refuse the evil and choose the good, the land that thou abhorrest shall be forsaken of both her kings.

2 NEPHI 19 (see also ISAIAH 9)

Isaiah 740 BC

2 The people that walked in darkness have seen a great light; they that dwell in the land of the shadow of death, upon them hath the light shined.
3 Thou hast multiplied the nation, and increased the joy—they joy before thee according to the joy in harvest, and as men rejoice when they divide the spoil.
4 For thou hast broken the yoke of his burden, and the staff of his shoulder, the rod of his oppressor.

The Prophet Isaiah, by Raphael, 1511.

5 For every battle of the warrior is with confused noise, and garments rolled in blood; but this shall be with burning and fuel of fire.
6 For unto us a child is born, unto us a son is given; and the government shall be upon his shoulder; and his name shall be called, Wonderful, Counselor, The Mighty God, The Everlasting Father, The Prince of Peace.
7 Of the increase of government and peace there is no end, upon the throne of David, and upon his kingdom to order it, and to establish it with judgment and with justice from henceforth, even forever. The zeal of the Lord of Hosts will perform this.

1 NEPHI 10

Nephi, Son of Lehi 595 BC

4 Yea, even six hundred years from the time that my father left Jerusalem, a prophet would the Lord God raise up among the Jews—even a Messiah, or, in other words, a Savior of the world.
5 And he [Lehi] also spake concerning the prophets, how great a number had testified of these things, concerning this Messiah, of whom he had spoken, or this Redeemer of the world.
6 Wherefore, all mankind were in a lost and in a fallen state, and ever would be save they should rely on this Redeemer.

The Nativity with the infant Jesus, John the Baptist and Shepherds, by follower of Il Sodoma, ca 1550.

ALMA 7

Alma the Younger — *83 BC*

7 For behold, I say unto you there be many things to come; and behold, there is one thing which is of more importance than they all—for behold, the time is not far distant that the Redeemer liveth and cometh among his people.
8 Behold, I do not say that he will come among us at the time of his dwelling in his mortal tabernacle; for behold, the Spirit hath not said unto me that this should be the case. Now as to this thing I do not know; but this much I do know, that the Lord God hath power to do all things which are according to his word.
9 But behold, the Spirit hath said this much unto me, saying: Cry unto this people, saying—Repent ye, and prepare the way of the Lord, and walk in his paths, which are straight; for behold, the kingdom of heaven is at hand, and the Son of God cometh upon the face of the Earth.
10 And behold, he shall be born of Mary, at Jerusalem which is the land of our forefathers, she being a virgin, a precious and chosen vessel, who shall be overshadowed and conceive by the power of the Holy Ghost, and bring forth a son, yea, even the Son of God.
11 And he shall go forth, suffering pains and afflictions and temptations of every kind; and this that the word might be fulfilled which saith he will take upon him the pains and the sicknesses of his people.
12 And he will take upon him death, that he may loose the bands of death which bind his people; and he will take upon him their infirmities, that his bowels may be filled with mercy, according to the flesh, that he may know according to the flesh how to succor his people according to their infirmities.
13 Now the Spirit knoweth all things; nevertheless the Son of God suffereth according to the flesh that he might take upon him the sins of his people, that he might blot out their transgressions according to the power of his deliverance; and now behold, this is the testimony which is in me.

GENESIS 15

Moses — *1475 BC*

12 *And it came to pass, that Abram looked forth and saw the days of the Son of Man, and was glad, and his soul found rest*, and he believed in the Lord; and *the Lord* counted it unto him for righteousness. [JST]

ALMA 19

King Lamoni — *90 BC*

12 And it came to pass that he [King Lamoni] arose, according to the words of Ammon; and as he arose, he stretched forth his hand unto the woman [his wife, the Queen], and said: Blessed be the name of God, and blessed art thou.
13 For as sure as thou livest, behold, I have seen my Redeemer; and he shall come forth, and be born of a woman, and he shall redeem all mankind who believe on his name. Now, when he had said these words, his heart was swollen within him, and he sunk again with joy; and the queen also sunk down, being overpowered by the Spirit.

11

THE BAPTISM OF JESUS CHRIST

St. John the Baptist Bearing Witness, by Annibale Carracci, ca 1600.

+++

The preparatory ministry of John the Baptist (Elias) and the baptism of Jesus Christ.

ISAIAH 40

Isaiah *740 BC*

3 The voice of him that crieth in the wilderness, Prepare ye the way of the LORD, make straight in the desert a highway for our God.

4 Every valley shall be exalted, and every mountain and hill shall be made low: and the crooked shall be made straight, and the rough places plain:

5 And the glory of the LORD shall be revealed, and all flesh shall see it together: for the mouth of the LORD hath spoken it.

6 The voice said, Cry. And he said, What shall I cry? All flesh is grass, and all the goodliness thereof is as the flower of the field:

7 The grass withereth, the flower fadeth: because the spirit of the LORD bloweth upon it: surely the people is grass.
8 The grass withereth, the flower fadeth: but the word of our God shall stand for ever.

MATTHEW 3

Matthew — *30 AD*

1 In those days came John the Baptist, preaching in the wilderness of Judæa,
2 And saying, Repent ye: for the kingdom of heaven is at hand.
3 For this is he that was spoken of by the prophet Esaias, saying, The voice of one crying in the wilderness, Prepare ye the way of the Lord, make his paths straight.
4 And the same John had his raiment of camel's hair, and a leathern girdle about his loins; and his meat was locusts and wild honey.
5 Then went out to him Jerusalem, and all Judæa, and all the region round about Jordan,
6 And were baptized of him in Jordan, confessing their sins.
7 But when he saw many of the Pharisees and Sadducees come to his baptism, he said unto them, O generation of vipers, who hath warned you to flee from the wrath to come?
8 *Why is it that ye receive not the preaching of him whom God hath sent? If ye receive not this in your hearts, ye receive not me; and if ye receive not me, ye receive not him of whom I am sent to bear record; and for your sins ye have no cloak.*
9 *Repent therefore, and* bring forth therefore fruits meet for repentance:
10 And think not to say within yourselves, *We are the children of Abraham, and we only have power to bring seed unto our father Abraham*; for I say unto you, that God is able of these stones to raise up children *into* Abraham.
11 And now also the axe is laid unto the root of the trees: therefore every tree which bringeth not forth good fruit is hewn down, and cast into the fire.
12 I indeed baptize you with water, *upon your* repentance; *and when he of whom I bear record cometh, who is* mightier than I, whose shoes I am not worthy to bear, *(or whose place I am not able to fill,) as I said, I indeed baptize you before he cometh, that when he cometh he may* baptize you with the Holy Ghost and fire.
13 *And it is he of whom I shall bear record*, whose fan *shall be* in his hand, and he will thoroughly purge his floor, and gather his wheat into the garner; but *in the fullness of his own time* will burn up the chaff with unquenchable fire.
14 *Thus came John, preaching and baptizing in the river of Jordan; bearing record, that he who was coming after him had power to baptize with the Holy Ghost and fire.*
15 Then cometh Jesus from Galilee to Jordan unto John, to be baptized of him.
16 But John forbad him, saying, I have need to be baptized of thee, and comest thou to me?
17 And Jesus, answering, said unto him, Suffer *me to be baptized of thee*, for thus it becometh us to fulfill all righteousness. Then he suffered him.
18 *And John went down into the water and baptized him.*
19 And Jesus when he was baptized, went up straightway out of the water; *and John saw*, and lo, the heavens were opened unto him, and he saw the Spirit of God descending like a dove and lighting upon *Jesus.*
20 And lo, *he heard* a voice from heaven, saying, This is my beloved Son, in whom I am well pleased. *Hear ye him.* [JST]

LUKE 3

Luke — *30 AD*

4 As it is written in the book of the *prophet* Esaias; *and these are the words*, saying, The voice of one crying in the wilderness, Prepare ye the way of the Lord, and make his paths straight.
5 *For behold, and lo, he shall come, as it is written in the book of the prophets, to take away the sins of the world, and to bring salvation unto the heathen nations, to gather together those who are lost, who are of the sheepfold of Israel;*
6 *Yea, even the dispersed and afflicted; and also to prepare the way, and make possible the preaching of the gospel unto the Gentiles;*
7 *And to be a light unto all who sit in darkness, unto the uttermost parts of the Earth; to bring to pass the resurrection from the dead, and to ascend up on high, to dwell on the right hand of the Father,*

8 *Until the fullness of time, and the law*
and the testimony shall be sealed, and the
keys of the kingdom shall be delivered up
again unto the Father;
9 *To administer justice unto all; to come*
down in judgment upon all, and to con-
vince all the ungodly of their ungodly
deeds, which they have committed; and
all this in the day that he shall come;
10 *For it is a day of power; yea, every*
valley shall be filled, and every mountain
and hill shall be brought low; the crooked
shall be made straight, and the rough ways
made smooth;
11 *And all flesh shall see the salvation of*
God. [JST]

1 NEPHI 10

Nephi, Son of Lehi — *595 BC*

7 And he [Lehi] spake also concerning a
prophet who should come before the
Messiah, to prepare the way of the Lord—
8 Yea, even he should go forth and cry in
the wilderness: Prepare ye the way of the
Lord, and make his paths straight; for
there standeth one among you whom ye
know not; and he is mightier than I,
whose shoe's latchet I am not worthy to
unloose. And much spake my father
concerning this thing.
9 And my father said he should baptize in
Bethabara, beyond Jordan; and he also said
he should baptize with water; even that he
should baptize the Messiah with water.
10 And after he had baptized the Messiah
with water, he should behold and bear
record that he had baptized the Lamb of
God, who should take away the sins of the
world.

JOHN 1

John — *30 AD*

1 In the beginning was the *gospel*
preached through the Son. And the gospel
was the word, and the *word* was with *the*
Son, and the Son was with God, and
the *Son* was *of* God.
2 The same was in the beginning with
God.
3 All things were made by him; and
without him was not anything made
which was made.
4 In him was *the gospel,* and *the gospel*
was the life, and the life was the light of
men;
5 And the light shineth *in the world,* and
the *world perceiveth* it not.
6 There was a man sent from God, whose
name was John.
7 The same came *into the world* for a
witness, to bear witness of the *light, to*
bear record of the gospel through the Son,
unto all, that through him *men* might
believe.
8 He was not that *light,* but *came* to bear
witness of that *light,*
9 Which was the true *light,* which light-
eth every man *who* cometh into the
world;
10 *Even the Son of God.* He *who* was in
the world, and the world was made by
him, and the world knew him not.
11 He came unto his own, and his own
received him not.
12 But as many as received him, to them
gave he power to become the sons of
God; *only* to them who believe on his
name.
13 *He was* born, not of blood, nor of the
will of the flesh, nor of the will of man,
but of God.
14 And the *same word* was made flesh,
and dwelt among us, and we beheld his
glory, the glory as of the Only Begotten of
the Father, full of grace and truth.
15 John *bear* witness of him, and cried,
saying, This *is* he of whom I spake; He
who cometh after me, is preferred before
me; for he was before me.
16 *For in the beginning was the Word,*
even the Son, who is made flesh, and sent
unto us by the will of the Father. And as
many as believe on his name shall receive
of his fullness. And of his fullness have all
we received, *even immortality and eternal*
life, through his grace.
17 For the law was given *through* Moses,
but *life* and truth came *through* Jesus
Christ.
18 *For the law was after a carnal com-*
mandment, to the administration of death;
but the gospel was after the power of an
endless life, through Jesus Christ, the Only
Begotten Son, who is in the bosom of the
Father.
19 *And* no man hath seen God at any
time, *except he hath borne record of the*
Son; for except it is through him no man
can be saved.

John the Baptist Baptizing Jesus, from the Life on Earth of our Blessed Lord, by Grace Wallace Doonan, 1913.

20 And this is the record of John, when the Jews sent priests and Levites from Jerusalem, to ask him; Who art thou?
21 And he confessed, and denied not *that he was Elias;* but confessed, *saying;* I am not the Christ.
22 And they asked him, *saying; How then art thou Elias?* And he said, I am not *that Elias who was to restore all things. And they asked him, saying,* Art thou that prophet? And he answered, No.
23 Then said they unto him, Who art thou? that we may give an answer to them that sent us. What sayest thou of thyself?
24 He said, I am the voice of one crying in the wilderness, Make straight the way of the Lord, as saith the prophet Esaias.
25 And they who were sent were of the Pharisees.
26 And they asked him, and said unto him; Why baptizest thou then, if thou be not the Christ, nor Elias *who was to restore all things,* neither that prophet?
27 John answered them, saying; I baptize with water, but there standeth one among you, whom ye know not;
28 He it is *of whom I bear record. He is that prophet, even Elias,* who, coming after me, is preferred before me, whose shoe's latchet I am not worthy to unloose, *or whose place I am not able to fill; for he shall baptize, not only with water, but with fire, and with the Holy Ghost.*

29 The next day John seeth Jesus coming
unto him, and said; Behold the Lamb of
God, who taketh away the sin of the
world!
30 *And John bare record of him unto the
people, saying,* This is he of whom I said;
After me cometh a man who is preferred
before me; for he was before me, and I
knew him, *and* that he should be made
manifest to Israel; therefore am I come
baptizing with water.
31 And John bare record, saying; *When
he was baptized of me,* I saw the Spirit
descending from heaven like a dove, and
it abode upon him.
32 And I knew him; *for* he who sent me to
baptize with water, the same said unto me;
Upon whom thou shalt see the Spirit
descending, and remaining on him, the
same is he who baptizeth with the Holy
Ghost.
33 And I saw, and bare record that this is
the Son of God.
34 *These things were done in Bethabara,
beyond Jordan, where John was baptizing.*
[JST]

DOCTRINE AND COVENANTS 84

Joseph Smith — *December 1832*

19 And this greater priesthood admin-
istereth the gospel and holdeth the key of
the mysteries of the kingdom, even the
key of the knowledge of God.
20 Therefore, in the ordinances thereof,
the power of godliness is manifest.
21 And without the ordinances thereof,
and the authority of the priesthood, the
power of godliness is not manifest unto
men in the flesh;
22 For without this no man can see the
face of God, even the Father, and live.
23 Now this Moses plainly taught to the
children of Israel in the wilderness, and
sought diligently to sanctify his people
that they might behold the face of God;
24 But they hardened their hearts and
could not endure his presence; therefore,
the Lord in his wrath, for his anger was
kindled against them, swore that they
should not enter into his rest while in the
wilderness, which rest is the fulness of his
glory.
25 Therefore, he took Moses out of their
midst, and the Holy Priesthood also;
26 And the lesser priesthood continued,
which priesthood holdeth the key of the
ministering of angels and the preparatory
gospel;
27 Which gospel is the gospel of repent-
ance and of baptism, and the remission of
sins, and the law of carnal command-
ments, which the Lord in his wrath caused
to continue with the house of Aaron
among the children of Israel until John,
whom God raised up, being filled with the
Holy Ghost from his mother's womb.
28 For he was baptized while he was yet
in his childhood, and was ordained by the
angel of God at the time he was eight days
old unto this power, to overthrow the
kingdom of the Jews, and to make straight
the way of the Lord before the face of his
people, to prepare them for the coming of
the Lord, in whose hand is given all
power.

2 NEPHI 31

Nephi, Son of Lehi — *550 BC*

4 Wherefore, I would that ye should
remember that I have spoken unto you
concerning that prophet which the Lord
showed unto me, that should baptize the
Lamb of God, which should take away the
sins of the world.
5 And now, if the Lamb of God, he being
holy, should have need to be baptized by
water, to fulfil all righteousness, O then,
how much more need have we, being
unholy, to be baptized, yea, even by
water!
6 And now, I would ask of you, my
beloved brethren, wherein the Lamb of
God did fulfil all righteousness in being
baptized by water?
7 Know ye not that he was holy? But not-
withstanding he being holy, he showeth
unto the children of men that, according
to the flesh he humbleth himself before
the Father, and witnesseth unto the
Father that he would be obedient unto
him in keeping his commandments.
8 Wherefore, after he was baptized with
water the Holy Ghost descended upon
him in the form of a dove.
9 And again, it showeth unto the children
of men the strait-ness of the path, and the
narrowness of the gate, by which they
should enter, he having set the example
before them.
10 And he said unto the children of men:
Follow thou me. Wherefore, my beloved
brethren, can we follow Jesus save we

The Baptism of Christ, by Grigory Gagarin, ca. 1840-50.

shall be willing to keep the command-
ments of the Father?
11 And the Father said: Repent ye, repent
ye, and be baptized in the name of my
Beloved Son.
12 And also, the voice of the Son came
unto me, saying: He that is baptized in my
name, to him will the Father give the Holy
Ghost, like unto me; wherefore, follow
me, and do the things which ye have seen
me do.

1 NEPHI 11

Nephi, Son of Lehi *595 BC*

26 And the angel said unto me again: Look
and behold the condescension of God!
27 And I looked and beheld the Redeemer
of the world, of whom my father had
spoken; and I also beheld the prophet who
should prepare the way before him. And
the Lamb of God went forth and was
baptized of him; and after he was baptized,
I beheld the heavens open, and the Holy
Ghost come down out of heaven and abide
upon him in the form of a dove.

12

CHRIST'S MINISTRY AND ATONEMENT

Christ and the Rich Young Ruler, by Heinrich Hoffman, 1889.

+++

The events in the life and ministry of Jesus Christ. His sufferings, death, and resurrection are foretold.

1 NEPHI 1

Nephi, Son of Lehi — *600 BC*

8 And being thus overcome with the
Spirit, he [Lehi] was carried away in a
vision, even that he saw the heavens open,
and he thought he saw God sitting upon
his throne, surrounded with numberless
concourses of angels in the attitude of
singing and praising their God.
9 And it came to pass that he saw One
descending out of the midst of heaven,
and he beheld that his luster was above
that of the sun at noon-day.
10 And he also saw twelve others follow-
ing him, and their brightness did exceed
that of the stars in the firmament.
11 And they came down and went forth
upon the face of the Earth;

1 NEPHI 11

Nephi, Son of Lehi — *595 BC*

24 And after he had said these words, he
said unto me: Look! And I looked, and I
beheld the Son of God going forth among
the children of men; and I saw many fall
down at his feet and worship him.
25 And it came to pass that I beheld that
the rod of iron, which my father had seen,
was the word of God, which led to the
fountain of living waters, or to the tree of
life; which waters are a representation of
the love of God; and I also beheld that the
tree of life was a representation of the love
of God.
28 And I beheld that he went forth
ministering unto the people, in power and
great glory; and the multitudes were
gathered together to hear him; and I
beheld that they cast him out from among
them.
29 And I also beheld twelve others
following him. And it came to pass that
they were carried away in the Spirit from
before my face, and I saw them not.

30 And it came to pass that the angel spake unto me again, saying: Look! And I looked, and I beheld the heavens open again, and I saw angels descending upon the children of men; and they did minister unto them.
31 And he spake unto me again, saying: Look! And I looked, and I beheld the Lamb of God going forth among the children of men. And I beheld multitudes of people who were sick, and who were afflicted with all manner of diseases, and with devils and unclean spirits; and the angel spake and showed all these things unto me. And they were healed by the power of the Lamb of God; and the devils and the unclean spirits were cast out.
32 And it came to pass that the angel spake unto me again, saying: Look! And I looked and beheld the Lamb of God, that he was taken by the people; yea, the Son of the everlasting God was judged of the world; and I saw and bear record.
33 And I, Nephi, saw that he was lifted up upon the cross and slain for the sins of the world.

ZECHARIAH 9

Zechariah — *520 BC*

9 Rejoice greatly, O daughter of Zion; shout, O daughter of Jerusalem: behold, thy King cometh unto thee: he is just, and having salvation; lowly, and riding upon an ass, and upon a colt the foal of an ass.

ZECHARIAH 11

Zechariah — *520 BC*

12 And I said unto them, If ye think good, give me my price; and if not, forbear. So they weighed for my price thirty pieces of silver.
13 And the LORD said unto me, Cast it unto the potter: a goodly price that I was prised at of them. And I took the thirty pieces of silver, and cast them to the potter in the house of the LORD.

2 NEPHI 7 (see also ISAIAH 50)

Isaiah — *740 BC*

1 Yea, for thus saith the Lord: Have I put thee away, or have I cast thee off forever? For thus saith the Lord: Where is the bill of your mother's divorcement? To whom

Christ Healing the Sick at Bethesda, by Carl Bloch, 1883.

have I put thee away, or to which of my creditors have I sold you? Yea, to whom have I sold you? Behold, for your iniquities have ye sold yourselves, and for your transgressions is your mother put away.
2 Wherefore, when I came, there was no man; when I called, yea, there was none to answer. O house of Israel, is my hand shortened at all that it cannot redeem, or have I no power to deliver? Behold, at my rebuke I dry up the sea, I make their rivers a wilderness and their fish to stink because the waters are dried up, and they die because of thirst.
3 I clothe the heavens with blackness, and I make sackcloth their covering.
4 The Lord God hath given me the tongue of the learned, that I should know how to speak a word in season unto thee, O house of Israel. When ye are weary he waketh morning by morning. He waketh mine ear to hear as the learned.
5 The Lord God hath opened mine ear, and I was not rebellious, neither turned away back.
6 I gave my back to the smiter, and my cheeks to them that plucked off the hair. I hid not my face from shame and spitting.

The Mocking of Christ, by Carl Bloch, 1880.

7 For the Lord God will help me, therefore shall I not be confounded. Therefore have I set my face like a flint, and I know that I shall not be ashamed.

1 NEPHI 19

Nephi, Son of Lehi 580 BC

8 And behold he cometh, according to the words of the angel, in six hundred years from the time my father left Jerusalem.
9 And the world, because of their iniquity, shall judge him to be a thing of naught; wherefore they scourge him, and he suffereth it; and they smite him, and he suffereth it. Yea, they spit upon him, and he suffereth it, because of his loving kindness and his long-suffering towards the children of men.

MOSIAH 3

King Benjamin 124 BC

2 And the things which I shall tell you are made known unto me by an angel from God. And he said unto me: Awake; and I awoke, and behold he stood before me.
3 And he said unto me: Awake, and hear the words which I shall tell thee; for behold, I am come to declare unto you the glad tidings of great joy.
4 For the Lord hath heard thy prayers, and hath judged of thy righteousness, and hath sent me to declare unto thee that thou mayest rejoice; and that thou mayest declare unto thy people, that they may also be filled with joy.
5 For behold, the time cometh, and is not far distant, that with power, the Lord Omnipotent who reigneth, who was, and is from all eternity to all eternity, shall come down from heaven among the children of men, and shall dwell in a tabernacle of clay, and shall go forth amongst men, working mighty miracles, such as healing the sick, raising the dead, causing the lame to walk, the blind to receive their sight, and the deaf to hear, and curing all manner of diseases.
6 And he shall cast out devils, or the evil spirits which dwell in the hearts of the children of men.
7 And lo, he shall suffer temptations, and pain of body, hunger, thirst, and fatigue, even more than man can suffer, except it be unto death; for behold, blood cometh from every pore, so great shall be his

anguish for the wickedness and the
abominations of his people.
8 And he shall be called Jesus Christ, the
Son of God, the Father of heaven and
Earth, the Creator of all things from the
beginning; and his mother shall be called
Mary.
9 And lo, he cometh unto his own, that
salvation might come unto the children of
men even through faith on his name; and
even after all this they shall consider him
a man, and say that he hath a devil, and
shall scourge him, and shall crucify him.
10 And he shall rise the third day from the
dead; and behold, he standeth to judge the
world; and behold, all these things are
done that a righteous judgment might
come upon the children of men.
11 For behold, and also his blood atoneth
for the sins of those who have fallen by the
transgression of Adam, who have died not
knowing the will of God concerning
them, or who have ignorantly sinned.
12 But wo, wo unto him who knoweth
that he rebelleth against God! For salva-
tion cometh to none such except it be
through repentance and faith on the Lord
Jesus Christ.
13 And the Lord God hath sent his holy
prophets among all the children of men, to
declare these things to every kindred,
nation, and tongue, that thereby who-
soever should believe that Christ should
come, the same might receive remission of
their sins, and rejoice with exceedingly
great joy, even as though he had already
come among them.
14 Yet the Lord God saw that his people
were a stiff-necked people, and he
appointed unto them a law, even the law
of Moses.
15 And many signs, and wonders, and
types, and shadows showed he unto them,
concerning his coming; and also holy
prophets spake unto them concerning his
coming; and yet they hardened their
hearts, and understood not that the law of
Moses availeth nothing except it were
through the atonement of his blood.
16 And even if it were possible that little
children could sin they could not be saved;
but I say unto you they are blessed; for
behold, as in Adam, or by nature, they fall,
even so the blood of Christ atoneth for
their sins.
17 And moreover, I say unto you, that
there shall be no other name given nor
any other way nor means whereby
salvation can come unto the children of
men, only in and through the name of
Christ, the Lord Omnipotent.
18 For behold he judgeth, and his judg-
ment is just; and the infant perisheth not
that dieth in his infancy; but men drink
damnation to their own souls except they
humble themselves and become as little
children, and believe that salvation was,
and is, and is to come, in and through the
atoning blood of Christ, the Lord
Omnipotent.
19 For the natural man is an enemy to
God, and has been from the fall of Adam,
and will be, forever and ever, unless he
yields to the enticings of the Holy Spirit,
and putteth off the natural man and
becometh a saint through the atonement
of Christ the Lord, and becometh as a
child, submissive, meek, humble, patient,
full of love, willing to submit to all things
which the Lord seeth fit to inflict upon
him, even as a child doth submit to his
father.

HELAMAN 5

Helaman *30 BC*

9 O remember, remember, my sons, the
words which king Benjamin spake unto
his people; yea, remember that there is no
other way nor means whereby man can be
saved, only through the atoning blood of
Jesus Christ, who shall come; yea,
remember that he cometh to redeem the
world.
10 And remember also the words which
Amulek spake unto Zeezrom, in the city
of Ammonihah; for he said unto him that
the Lord surely should come to redeem his
people, but that he should not come to
redeem them in their sins, but to redeem
them from their sins.
11 And he hath power given unto him
from the Father to redeem them from
their sins because of repentance; therefore
he hath sent his angels to declare the
tidings of the conditions of repentance,
which bringeth unto the power of the
Redeemer, unto the salvation of their
souls.
12 And now, my sons, remember,
remember that it is upon the rock of our
Redeemer, who is Christ, the Son of God,

that ye must build your foundation; that when the devil shall send forth his mighty winds, yea, his shafts in the whirlwind, yea, when all his hail and his mighty storm shall beat upon you, it shall have no power over you to drag you down to the gulf of misery and endless wo, because of the rock upon which ye are built, which is a sure foundation, a foundation whereon if men build they cannot fall.

ALMA 11

Amulek *82 BC*

38 Now Zeezrom saith again unto him: Is the Son of God the very Eternal Father?
39 And Amulek said unto him: Yea, he is the very Eternal Father of heaven and of Earth, and all things which in them are; he is the beginning and the end, the first and the last;
40 And he shall come into the world to redeem his people; and he shall take upon him the transgressions of those who believe on his name; and these are they that shall have eternal life, and salvation cometh to none else.

ALMA 9

Alma the Younger *82 BC*

25 And now for this cause, that ye may not be destroyed, the Lord has sent his angel to visit many of his people, declaring unto them that they must go forth and cry mightily unto this people, saying: Repent ye, for the kingdom of heaven is nigh at hand;
26 And not many days hence the Son of God shall come in his glory; and his glory shall be the glory of the Only Begotten of the Father, full of grace, equity, and truth, full of patience, mercy, and long-suffering, quick to hear the cries of his people and to answer their prayers.
27 And behold, he cometh to redeem those who will be baptized unto repentance, through faith on his name.

MOSIAH 7

Limhi *121 BC*

26 And a prophet of the Lord [Abinadi] have they slain; yea, a chosen man of God, who told them of their wickedness and abominations, and prophesied of many things which are to come, yea, even the coming of Christ.
27 And because he said unto them that Christ was the God, the Father of all things, and said that he should take upon him the image of man, and it should be the image after which man was created in the beginning; or in other words, he said that man was created after the image of God, and that God should come down among the children of men, and take upon him flesh and blood, and go forth upon the face of the Earth—
28 And now, because he said this, they did put him to death;

MOSIAH 14 (see also ISAIAH 53)

Isaiah / Abinadi *740 BC*

1 Yea, even doth not Isaiah say: Who hath believed our report, and to whom is the arm of the Lord revealed?
2 For he shall grow up before him as a tender plant, and as a root out of dry ground; he hath no form nor comeliness; and when we shall see him there is no beauty that we should desire him.
3 He is despised and rejected of men; a man of sorrows, and acquainted with grief; and we hid as it were our faces from him; he was despised, and we esteemed him not.
4 Surely he has borne our griefs, and carried our sorrows; yet we did esteem him stricken, smitten of God, and afflicted.
5 But he was wounded for our transgressions, he was bruised for our iniquities; the chastisement of our peace was upon him; and with his stripes we are healed.
6 All we, like sheep, have gone astray; we have turned everyone to his own way; and the Lord hath laid on him the iniquities of us all.
7 He was oppressed, and he was afflicted, yet he opened not his mouth; he is brought as a lamb to the slaughter, and as a sheep before her shearers is dumb so he opened not his mouth.
8 He was taken from prison and from judgment; and who shall declare his generation? For he was cut off out of the land of the living; for the transgressions of my people was he stricken.
9 And he made his grave with the wicked, and with the rich in his death; because he had done no evil, neither was any deceit in his mouth.

10 Yet it pleased the Lord to bruise him;
he hath put him to grief; when thou shalt make his soul an offering for sin he shall see his seed, he shall prolong his days, and the pleasure of the Lord shall prosper in his hand.
11 He shall see the travail of his soul, and shall be satisfied; by his knowledge shall my righteous servant justify many; for he shall bear their iniquities.
12 Therefore will I divide him a portion with the great, and he shall divide the spoil with the strong; because he hath poured out his soul unto death; and he was numbered with the transgressors; and he bore the sins of many, and made intercession for the transgressors.

MOSIAH 15

Abinadi — *148 BC*

1 And now Abinadi said unto them: I would that ye should understand that God himself shall come down among the children of men, and shall redeem his people.
2 And because he dwelleth in flesh he shall be called the Son of God, and having subjected the flesh to the will of the Father, being the Father and the Son—
3 The Father, because he was conceived by the power of God; and the Son, because of the flesh; thus becoming the Father and Son—
4 And they are one God, yea, the very Eternal Father of heaven and of Earth.
5 And thus the flesh becoming subject to the Spirit, or the Son to the Father, being one God, suffereth temptation, and yieldeth not to the temptation, but suffereth himself to be mocked, and scourged, and cast out, and disowned by his people.
6 And after all this, after working many mighty miracles among the children of men, he shall be led, yea, even as Isaiah said, as a sheep before the shearer is dumb, so he opened not his mouth.
7 Yea, even so he shall be led, crucified, and slain, the flesh becoming subject even unto death, the will of the Son being swallowed up in the will of the Father.
8 And thus God breaketh the bands of death, having gained the victory over death; giving the Son power to make intercession for the children of men—
9 Having ascended into heaven, having the bowels of mercy; being filled with compassion towards the children of men; standing betwixt them and justice; having broken the bands of death, taken upon himself their iniquity and their transgressions, having redeemed them, and satisfied the demands of justice.

ALMA 34

Amulek — *74 BC*

8 And now, behold, I will testify unto you of myself that these things are true. Behold, I say unto you, that I do know that Christ shall come among the children of men, to take upon him the transgressions of his people, and that he shall atone for the sins of the world; for the Lord God hath spoken it.
9 For it is expedient that an atonement should be made; for according to the great plan of the Eternal God there must be an atonement made, or else all mankind must unavoidably perish; yea, all are hardened; yea, all are fallen and are lost, and must perish except it be through the atonement which it is expedient should be made.
10 For it is expedient that there should be a great and last sacrifice; yea, not a sacrifice of man, neither of beast, neither of any manner of fowl; for it shall not be a human sacrifice; but it must be an infinite and eternal sacrifice.
11 Now there is not any man that can sacrifice his own blood which will atone for the sins of another. Now, if a man murdereth, behold will our law, which is just, take the life of his brother? I say unto you, Nay.
12 But the law requireth the life of him who hath murdered; therefore there can be nothing which is short of an infinite atonement which will suffice for the sins of the world.
13 Therefore, it is expedient that there should be a great and last sacrifice, and then shall there be, or it is expedient there should be, a stop to the shedding of blood; then shall the law of Moses be fulfilled; yea, it shall be all fulfilled, every jot and tittle, and none shall have passed away.
14 And behold, this is the whole meaning of the law, every whit pointing to that great and last sacrifice; and that great and last sacrifice will be the Son of God, yea, infinite and eternal.
15 And thus he shall bring salva-tion to all those who shall believe on his name; this being the intent of this last sacrifice, to

bring about the bowels of mercy, which overpowereth justice, and bringeth about means unto men that they may have faith unto repentance.
16 And thus mercy can satisfy the demands of justice, and encircles them in the arms of safety, while he that exercises no faith unto repentance is exposed to the whole law of the demands of justice; therefore only unto him that has faith unto repentance is brought about the great and eternal plan of redemption.
17 Therefore may God grant unto you, my brethren, that ye may begin to exercise your faith unto repentance, that ye begin to call upon his holy name, that he would have mercy upon you;

Christ in Gethsemane, by Carl Bloch, 1873.

DOCTRINE AND COVENANTS 18

Joseph Smith *June 1829*

10 Remember the worth of souls is great in the sight of God;
11 For, behold, the Lord your Redeemer suffered death in the flesh; wherefore he suffered the pain of all men, that all men might repent and come unto him.
12 And he hath arisen again from the dead, that he might bring all men unto him, on conditions of repentance.
13 And how great is his joy in the soul that repenteth!

ALMA 42

Alma the Younger *73 BC*

11 And now remember, my son, if it were not for the plan of redemption, (laying it aside) as soon as they were dead their souls were miserable, being cut off from the presence of the Lord.
12 And now, there was no means to reclaim men from this fallen state, which man had brought upon himself because of his own disobedience;
13 Therefore, according to justice, the plan of redemption could not be brought about, only on conditions of repentance of men in this probationary state, yea, this preparatory state; for except it were for these conditions, mercy could not take effect except it should destroy the work of justice. Now the work of justice could not be destroyed; if so, God would cease to be God.
14 And thus we see that all mankind were fallen, and they were in the grasp of justice; yea, the justice of God, which consigned them forever to be cut off from his presence.
15 And now, the plan of mercy could not be brought about except an atonement should be made; therefore God himself atoneth for the sins of the world, to bring about the plan of mercy, to appease the demands of justice, that God might be a perfect, just God, and a merciful God also.
16 Now, repentance could not come unto men except there were a punishment, which also was eternal as the life of the soul should be, affixed opposite to the plan of happiness, which was as eternal also as the life of the soul.
17 Now, how could a man repent except he should sin? How could he sin if there was no law? How could there be a law save there was a punishment?

18 Now, there was a punishment affixed, and a just law given, which brought remorse of conscience unto man.

19 Now, if there was no law given—if a man murdered he should die—would he be afraid he would die if he should murder?

20 And also, if there was no law given against sin men would not be afraid to sin.

21 And if there was no law given, if men sinned what could justice do, or mercy either, for they would have no claim upon the creature?

22 But there is a law given, and a punishment affixed, and a repentance granted; which repentance, mercy claimeth; otherwise, justice claimeth the creature and executeth the law, and the law inflicteth the punishment; if not so, the works of justice would be destroyed, and God would cease to be God.

23 But God ceaseth not to be God, and mercy claimeth the penitent, and mercy cometh because of the atonement; and the atonement bringeth to pass the resurrection of the dead; and the resurrection of the dead bringeth back men into the presence of God; and thus they are restored into his presence, to be judged according to their works, according to the law and justice.

24 For behold, justice exerciseth all his demands, and also mercy claimeth all which is her own; and thus, none but the truly penitent are saved.

25 What, do ye suppose that mercy can rob justice? I say unto you, Nay; not one whit. If so, God would cease to be God.

26 And thus God bringeth about his great and eternal purposes, which were prepared from the foundation of the world. And thus cometh about the salvation and the redemption of men, and also their destruction and misery.

ALMA 36

Alma the Younger — *73 BC*

17 And it came to pass that as I was thus racked with torment, while I was harrowed up by the memory of my many sins, behold, I remembered also to have heard my father prophesy unto the people concerning the coming of one Jesus Christ, a Son of God, to atone for the sins of the world.

18 Now, as my mind caught hold upon this thought, I cried within my heart: O Jesus, thou Son of God, have mercy on me, who am in the gall of bitterness, and am encircled about by the everlasting chains of death.

19 And now, behold, when I thought this, I could remember my pains no more; yea, I was harrowed up by the memory of my sins no more.

20 And oh, what joy, and what marvelous light I did behold; yea, my soul was filled with joy as exceeding as was my pain!

21 Yea, I say unto you, my son, that there could be nothing so exquisite and so bitter as were my pains. Yea, and again I say unto you, my son, that on the other hand, there can be nothing so exquisite and sweet as was my joy.

22 Yea, methought I saw, even as our father Lehi saw, God sitting upon his throne, surrounded with numberless concourses of angels, in the attitude of singing and praising their God; yea, and my soul did long to be there.

23 But behold, my limbs did receive their strength again, and I stood upon my feet, and did manifest unto the people that I had been born of God.

24 Yea, and from that time even until now, I have labored without ceasing, that I might bring souls unto repentance; that I might bring them to taste of the exceeding joy of which I did taste; that they might also be born of God, and be filled with the Holy Ghost.

ALMA 37

Alma the Younger — *73 BC*

8 And it came to pass that I was three days and three nights in the most bitter pain and anguish of soul; and never, until I did cry out unto the Lord Jesus Christ for mercy, did I receive a remission of my sins. But behold, I did cry unto him and I did find peace to my soul.

9 And now, my son, I have told you this that ye may learn wisdom, that ye may learn of me that there is no other way or means whereby man can be saved, only in and through Christ. Behold, he is the life and the light of the world. Behold, he is the word of truth and righteousness.

Christ at the Cross, by Carl Bloch, 1870.

2 NEPHI 6

Jacob, Son of Lehi — *550 BC*

9 ...And he also has shown unto me that
the Lord God, the Holy One of Israel,
should manifest himself unto them in the
flesh; and after he should manifest himself
they should scourge him and crucify him,
according to the words of the angel who
spake it unto me.

PSALM 22

David — *1000 BC*

1 My God, my God, why hast thou
forsaken me? why art thou so far from
helping me, and from the words of my
roaring?
6 But I am a worm, and no man; a
reproach of men, and despised of the
people.
7 All they that see me laugh me to scorn:
they shoot out the lip, they shake the
head, saying,
8 He trusted on the Lord that he would
deliver him: let him deliver him, seeing he
delighted in him.
16 For dogs have compassed me: the
assembly of the wicked have inclosed me:
they pierced my hands and my feet.
17 I may tell all my bones: they look and
stare upon me.
18 They part my garments among them,
and cast lots upon my vesture.

PSALM 69

David — *1000 BC*

20 Reproach hath broken my heart; and I
am full of heaviness: and I looked for some
to take pity, but there was none; and for
comforters, but I found none.
21 They gave me also gall for my meat; and
in my thirst they gave me vinegar to
drink.

PSALM 34

David *1000 AD*

15 The eyes of the Lord are upon the righteous, and his ears are open unto their cry.
16 The face of the Lord is against them that do evil, to cut off the remembrance of them from the Earth.
17 The righteous cry, and the Lord heareth, and delivereth them out of all their troubles.
18 The Lord is nigh unto them that are of a broken heart; and saveth such as be of a contrite spirit.
19 Many are the afflictions of the righteous: but the Lord delivereth him out of them all.
20 He keepeth all his bones: not one of them is broken.
21 Evil shall slay the wicked: and they that hate the righteous shall be desolate.
22 The Lord redeemeth the soul of his servants: and none of them that trust in him shall be desolate.

PSALM 31

David *1000 BC*

5 Into thine hand I commit my spirit: thou hast redeemed me, O Lord God of truth.

ALMA 40

Alma the Younger *73 BC*

1 Now my son, here is somewhat more I would say unto thee; for I perceive that thy mind is worried concerning the resurrection of the dead.
2 Behold, I say unto you, that there is no resurrection—or, I would say, in other words, that this mortal does not put on immortality, this corruption does not put on incorruption—until after the coming of Christ.
3 Behold, he bringeth to pass the resurrection of the dead. But behold, my son, the resurrection is not yet.

MATTHEW 27

Matthew *33 AD*

50 Jesus, when he had cried again with a loud voice, yielded up the ghost.
51 And, behold, the veil of the temple was rent in twain from the top to the bottom; and the Earth did quake, and the rocks rent;
52 And the graves were opened; and many bodies of the saints which slept arose,
53 And came out of the graves after his resurrection, and went into the holy city, and appeared unto many.
54 Now when the centurion, and they that were with him, watching Jesus, saw the earthquake, and those things that were done, they feared greatly, saying, Truly this was the Son of God.

2 NEPHI 25

Nephi, Son of Lehi *550 BC*

19 For according to the words of the prophets, the Messiah cometh in six hundred years from the time that my father left Jerusalem; and according to the words of the prophets, and also the word of the angel of God, his name shall be Jesus Christ, the Son of God.
12 ...and when the day cometh that the Only Begotten of the Father, yea, even the Father of heaven and of Earth, shall manifest himself unto them in the flesh, behold, they will reject him, because of their iniquities, and the hardness of their hearts, and the stiffness of their necks.
13 Behold, they will crucify him; and after he is laid in a sepulchre for the space of three days he shall rise from the dead, with healing in his wings; and all those who shall believe on his name shall be saved in the kingdom of God. Wherefore, my soul delighteth to prophesy concerning him, for I have seen his day, and my heart doth magnify his holy name.

MOSES 7

Enoch *3000 BC*

45 And it came to pass that Enoch looked; and from Noah, he beheld all the families of the Earth; and he cried unto the Lord, saying: When shall the day of the Lord come? When shall the blood of the Righteous be shed, that all they that mourn may be sanctified and have eternal life?
46 And the Lord said: It shall be in the meridian of time, in the days of wickedness and vengeance.
47 And behold, Enoch saw the day of the coming of the Son of Man, even in the flesh; and his soul rejoiced, saying: The Righteous is lifted up, and the Lamb is slain from the foundation of the world; and through faith I am in the bosom of the Father, and behold, Zion is with me.

The Resurrection, by Carl Bloch, 1881.

48 And it came to pass that Enoch looked upon the Earth; and he heard a voice from the bowels thereof, saying: Wo, wo is me, the mother of men; I am pained, I am weary, because of the wickedness of my children. When shall I rest, and be cleansed from the filthiness which is gone forth out of me? When will my Creator sanctify me, that I may rest, and righteousness for a season abide upon my face?
49 And when Enoch heard the Earth mourn, he wept, and cried unto the Lord, saying: O Lord, wilt thou not have compassion upon the Earth? Wilt thou not bless the children of Noah?
50 And it came to pass that Enoch continued his cry unto the Lord, saying: I ask thee, O Lord, in the name of thine Only Begotten, even Jesus Christ, that thou wilt have mercy upon Noah and his seed, that the Earth might never more be covered by the floods.
51 And the Lord could not withhold; and he covenanted with Enoch, and sware unto him with an oath, that he would stay the floods; that he would call upon the children of Noah;
52 And he sent forth an unalterable decree, that a remnant of his seed should always be found among all nations, while the Earth should stand;
53 And the Lord said: Blessed is he through whose seed Messiah shall come; for he saith—I am Messiah, the King of Zion, the Rock of Heaven, which is broad as eternity; whoso cometh in at the gate and climbeth up by me shall never fall; wherefore, blessed are they of whom I have spoken, for they shall come forth with songs of everlasting joy.
54 And it came to pass that Enoch cried unto the Lord, saying: When the Son of Man cometh in the flesh, shall the Earth rest? I pray thee, show me these things.
55 And the Lord said unto Enoch: Look, and he looked and beheld the Son of Man lifted up on the cross, after the manner of men;
56 And he heard a loud voice; and the heavens were veiled; and all the creations of God mourned; and the Earth groaned; and the rocks were rent; and the saints arose, and were crowned at the right hand of the Son of Man, with crowns of glory;
57 And as many of the spirits as were in prison came forth, and stood on the right hand of God; and the remainder were reserved in chains of darkness until the judgment of the great day.
58 And again Enoch wept and cried unto the Lord, saying: When shall the Earth rest?
59 And Enoch beheld the Son of Man ascend up unto the Father; and he called unto the Lord, saying: Wilt thou not come again upon the Earth? Forasmuch as thou

art God, and I know thee, and thou hast sworn unto me, and commanded me that I should ask in the name of thine Only Begotten; thou hast made me, and given unto me a right to thy throne, and not of myself, but through thine own grace; wherefore, I ask thee if thou wilt not come again on the Earth.

ALMA 21

Aaron — *85 BC*

9 Now Aaron began to open the scriptures unto them concerning the coming of Christ, and also concerning the resurrection of the dead, and that there could be no redemption for mankind save it were through the death and sufferings of Christ, and the atonement of his blood.

HELAMAN 14

Samuel the Lamanite — *6 BC*

11 And ye shall hear my words, for, for this intent have I come up upon the walls of this city, that ye might hear and know of the judgments of God which do await you because of your iniquities, and also that ye might know the conditions of repentance;
12 And also that ye might know of the coming of Jesus Christ, the Son of God, the Father of heaven and of Earth, the Creator of all things from the beginning; and that ye might know of the signs of his coming, to the intent that ye might believe on his name.
13 And if ye believe on his name ye will repent of all your sins, that thereby ye may have a remission of them through his merits.
14 And behold, again, another sign I give unto you, yea, a sign of his death.
15 For behold, he surely must die that salvation may come; yea, it behooveth him and becometh expedient that he dieth, to bring to pass the resurrection of the dead, that thereby men may be brought into the presence of the Lord.
16 Yea, behold, this death bringeth to pass the resurrection, and redeemeth all mankind from the first death—that spiritual death; for all mankind, by the fall of Adam being cut off from the presence of the Lord, are considered as dead, both as to things temporal and to things spiritual.
17 But behold, the resurrection of Christ redeemeth mankind, yea, even all mankind, and bringeth them back into the presence of the Lord.
18 Yea, and it bringeth to pass the condition of repentance, that whosoever repenteth the same is not hewn down and cast into the fire; but whosoever repenteth not is hewn down and cast into the fire; and there cometh upon them again a spiritual death, yea, a second death, for they are cut off again as to things pertaining to righteousness.
19 Therefore repent ye, repent ye, lest by knowing these things and not doing them ye shall suffer yourselves to come under condemnation, and ye are brought down unto this second death.

2 NEPHI 9

Jacob, Son of Lehi — *550 BC*

4 For I know that ye have searched much, many of you, to know of things to come; wherefore I know that ye know that our flesh must waste away and die; nevertheless, in our bodies we shall see God.
5 Yea, I know that ye know that in the body he shall show himself unto those at Jerusalem, from whence we came; for it is expedient that it should be among them; for it behooveth the great Creator that he suffereth himself to become subject unto man in the flesh, and die for all men, that all men might become subject unto him.
6 For as death hath passed upon all men, to fulfil the merciful plan of the great Creator, there must needs be a power of resurrection, and the resurrection must needs come unto man by reason of the fall; and the fall came by reason of transgression; and because man became fallen they were cut off from the presence of the Lord.
7 Wherefore, it must needs be an infinite atonement—save it should be an infinite atonement this corruption could not put on incorruption. Wherefore, the first judgment which came upon man must needs have remained to an endless duration. And if so, this flesh must have laid down to rot and to crumble to its mother Earth, to rise no more.
8 O the wisdom of God, his mercy and grace! For behold, if the flesh should rise no more our spirits must become subject to that angel who fell from before the presence of the Eternal God, and became the devil, to rise no more.

9 And our spirits must have become like unto him, and we become devils, angels to a devil, to be shut out from the presence of our God, and to remain with the father of lies, in misery, like unto himself; yea, to that being who beguiled our first parents, who transformeth himself nigh unto an angel of light, and stirreth up the children of men unto secret combinations of murder and all manner of secret works of darkness.
10 O how great the goodness of our God, who prepareth a way for our escape from the grasp of this awful monster; yea, that monster, death and hell, which I call the death of the body, and also the death of the spirit.
20 O how great the holiness of our God! For he knoweth all things, and there is not anything save he knows it.
21 And he cometh into the world that he may save all men if they will hearken unto his voice; for behold, he suffereth the pains of all men, yea, the pains of every living creature, both men, women, and children, who belong to the family of Adam.
22 And he suffereth this that the resurrection might pass upon all men, that all might stand before him at the great and judgment day.
23 And he commandeth all men that they must repent, and be baptized in his name, having perfect faith in the Holy One of Israel, or they cannot be saved in the kingdom of God.
24 And if they will not repent and believe in his name, and be baptized in his name, and endure to the end, they must be damned; for the Lord God, the Holy One of Israel, has spoken it.

MOSIAH 15

Abinadi — *148 BC*

19 For were it not for the redemption which he hath made for his people, which was prepared from the foundation of the world, I say unto you, were it not for this, all mankind must have perished.
20 But behold, the bands of death shall be broken, and the Son reigneth, and hath power over the dead; therefore, he bringeth to pass the resurrection of the dead.
21 And there cometh a resurrection, even a first resurrection; yea, even a resurrection of those that have been, and who are, and who shall be, even until the resurrection of Christ—for so shall he be called.
22 And now, the resurrection of all the prophets, and all those that have believed in their words, or all those that have kept the commandments of God, shall come forth in the first resurrection; therefore, they are the first resurrection.

PSALM 49

David — *1000 BC*

15 But God will redeem my soul from the power of the grave: for he shall receive me. Selah.

ALMA 40

Alma the Younger — *73 BC*

16 And behold, again it hath been spoken, that there is a first resurrection, a resurrection of all those who have been, or who are, or who shall be, down to the resurrection of Christ from the dead.
17 Now, we do not suppose that this first resurrection, which is spoken of in this manner, can be the resurrection of the souls and their consignation to happiness or misery. Ye cannot suppose that this is what it meaneth.
18 Behold, I say unto you, Nay; but it meaneth the reuniting of the soul with the body, of those from the days of Adam down to the resurrection of Christ.
19 Now, whether the souls and the bodies of those of whom has been spoken shall all be reunited at once, the wicked as well as the righteous, I do not say; let it suffice, that I say that they all come forth; or in other words, their resurrection cometh to pass before the resurrection of those who die after the resurrection of Christ.
20 Now, my son, I do not say that their resurrection cometh at the resurrection of Christ; but behold, I give it as my opinion, that the souls and the bodies are reunited, of the righteous, at the resurrection of Christ, and his ascension into heaven.
21 But whether it be at his resurrection or after, I do not say; but this much I say, that there is a space between death and the resurrection of the body, and a state of the soul in happiness or in misery until the time which is appointed of God that the dead shall come forth, and be reunited, both soul and body, and be brought to

Christ's Appearance to Mary Magdalene After the Resurrection, by Alexander Ivanov, 1835.

stand before God, and be judged according to their works.
22 Yea, this bringeth about the restoration of those things of which has been spoken by the mouths of the prophets.
23 The soul shall be restored to the body, and the body to the soul; yea, and every limb and joint shall be restored to its body; yea, even a hair of the head shall not be lost; but all things shall be restored to their proper and perfect frame.
24 And now, my son, this is the restoration of which has been spoken by the mouths of the prophets—
25 And then shall the righteous shine forth in the kingdom of God.

JOHN 10

Jesus Christ 32 AD

16 And other sheep I have, which are not of this fold: them also I must bring, and they shall hear my voice; and there shall be one fold, and one shepherd.

ACTS 1

Luke 33 AD

6 When they therefore were come together, they asked of him, saying, Lord, wilt thou at this time restore again the kingdom to Israel?
7 And he said unto them, It is not for you to know the times or the seasons, which the Father hath put in his own power.
8 But ye shall receive power, after that the Holy Ghost is come upon you: and ye shall be witnesses unto me both in Jerusalem, and in all Judæa, and in Samaria, and unto the uttermost part of the Earth.
9 And when he had spoken these things, while they beheld, he was taken up; and a cloud received him out of their sight.
10 And while they looked steadfastly toward heaven as he went up, behold, two men stood by them in white apparel;
11 Which also said, Ye men of Galilee, why stand ye gazing up into heaven? this same Jesus, which is taken up from you into heaven, shall so come in like manner as ye have seen him go into heaven.

1 CORINTHIANS 15

Paul *54 AD*

3 For I delivered unto you first of all that which I also received, how that Christ died for our sins according to the scriptures;
4 And that he was buried, and that he rose again the third day according to the scriptures:
5 And that he was seen of Cephas, then of the twelve:
6 After that, he was seen of above five hundred brethren at once; of whom the greater part remain unto this present, but some are fallen asleep.
7 After that, he was seen of James; then of all the apostles.
8 And last of all he was seen of me also, as of one born out of due time.
20 But now is Christ risen from the dead, and become the first fruits of them that slept.
21 For since by man came death, by man came also the resurrection of the dead.
22 For as in Adam all die, even so in Christ shall all be made alive.
23 But every man in his own order: Christ the first fruits; afterward they that are Christ's at his coming.

DOCTRINE AND COVENANTS 20

Joseph Smith *April 1830*

20 But by the transgression of these holy laws man became sensual and devilish, and became fallen man.
21 Wherefore, the Almighty God gave his Only Begotten Son, as it is written in those scriptures which have been given of him.
22 He suffered temptations but gave no heed unto them.
23 He was crucified, died, and rose again the third day;
24 And ascended into heaven, to sit down on the right hand of the Father, to reign with almighty power according to the will of the Father;
25 That as many as would believe and be baptized in his holy name, and endure in faith to the end, should be saved—
26 Not only those who believed after he came in the meridian of time, in the flesh, but all those from the beginning, even as many as were before he came, who believed in the words of the holy prophets, who spake as they were inspired by the gift of the Holy Ghost, who truly testified of him in all things, should have eternal life,
27 As well as those who should come after, who should believe in the gifts and callings of God by the Holy Ghost, which beareth record of the Father and of the Son;
28 Which Father, Son, and Holy Ghost are one God, infinite and eternal, without end. Amen.
29 And we know that all men must repent and believe on the name of Jesus Christ, and worship the Father in his name, and endure in faith on his name to the end, or they cannot be saved in the kingdom of God.
30 And we know that justification through the grace of our Lord and Savior Jesus Christ is just and true;
31 And we know also, that sanctification through the grace of our Lord and Savior Jesus Christ is just and true, to all those who love and serve God with all their mights, minds, and strength.

13

JESUS CHRIST'S MINISTRY IN ANCIENT AMERICA

Temple of the Feathered Serpent, Teotihuacan, Mexico. The feathered serpent is a common symbol in ancient America. It is a symbol of the Savior Jesus Christ from the story of Moses, who lifted up a brazen serpent on a pole and that whomever looked at it would be healed of a poisonous snake bite. The feathers show the serpent is flying or up high.

+++

Prophets in ancient America prophesy that the resurrected Christ will descend from heaven and minister to their people. This marvelous event would be preceded by great darkness and destruction, which was a sign of his death in Jerusalem. These were the people Christ referred to in John 10:16 as the other sheep he must visit.

During his ministry among the righteous Nephites and Lamanites, Christ revealed that he must visit still other sheep – other scattered remnants of the House of Israel.

An event as momentous as the Lord descending from heaven and ministering to the people would be very unlikely to be lost to history. Indeed, many legends of this event were preserved by the native Americans. Their legends describe a white, bearded man, born of a virgin, who came down from heaven and taught his people wisdom and great knowledge.[1] He taught them to build temples. He taught them that through sacrifice they could be purified and that only the pure would gain immortality. He was the God of Creation and linked to fertility and resurrection. The Mayas, Toltecs, Aztecs, Incas, Olmecs and many others talk of this great fair-skinned God and his promise to return and visit them in the future. They called him the Feathered Serpent, Quetzalcoatl, the God of Goodness and Wisdom, Viracocha,

[1] Garcilaso de la Vega, The Royal Commentaries of the Incas (written in 1609), trans. Maria Jolas (New York: Orion Press, 1961), book 5, p. 137.

and the Maize God (the Bread of Life). The similarities with Christ are significant.

There are, however, many aspects of the legend that bear little resemblance to Christ, which would be expected as the story was embellished and retold for generations. The core points of the legend do support the Book of Mormon account of Christ's personal ministry to the Nephites and Lamanites 2000 years ago. Also, the wide range of ancient societies throughout North and South America and Polynesia that all share this same legend is evidence that Christ visited other groups of people, just as the Book of Mormon account said he would.

ALMA 16

Alma the Younger — *78 BC*

18 Now those priests who did go forth
among the people did preach against all
lyings, and deceivings, and envyings, and
strifes, and malice, and revilings, and
stealing, robbing, plundering, murdering,
committing adultery, and all manner of
lasciviousness, crying that these things
ought not so to be—
19 Holding forth things which must
shortly come; yea, holding forth the
coming of the Son of God, his sufferings
and death, and also the resurrection of the
dead.
20 And many of the people did inquire
concerning the place where the Son of
God should come; and they were taught
that he would appear unto them after his
resurrection; and this the people did hear
with great joy and gladness.

1 NEPHI 12

Nephi, Son of Lehi — *600 BC*

1 And it came to pass that the angel said
unto me: Look, and behold thy seed, and
also the seed of thy brethren. And I looked
and beheld the land of promise; and I
beheld multitudes of people, yea, even as
it were in number as many as the sand of
the sea.
2 And it came to pass that I beheld
multitudes gathered together to battle,
one against the other; and I beheld wars,
and rumors of wars, and great slaughters
with the sword among my people.
3 And it came to pass that I beheld many
generations pass away, after the manner of
wars and contentions in the land; and I
beheld many cities, yea, even that I did
not number them.
4 And it came to pass that I saw a mist of
darkness on the face of the land of
promise; and I saw lightnings, and I heard
thunderings, and earthquakes, and all
manner of tumultuous noises; and I saw
the Earth and the rocks, that they rent;
and I saw mountains tumbling into pieces;
and I saw the plains of the Earth, that they
were broken up; and I saw many cities
that they were sunk; and I saw many that
they were burned with fire; and I saw
many that did tumble to the Earth,
because of the quaking thereof.
5 And it came to pass after I saw these
things, I saw the vapor of darkness, that it
passed from off the face of the Earth; and
behold, I saw multitudes who had not
fallen because of the great and terrible
judgments of the Lord.
6 And I saw the heavens open, and the
Lamb of God descending out of heaven;
and he came down and showed himself
unto them.
7 And I also saw and bear record that the
Holy Ghost fell upon twelve others; and
they were ordained of God, and chosen.
8 And the angel spake unto me, saying:
Behold the twelve disciples of the Lamb,
who are chosen to minister unto thy seed.
9 And he said unto me: Thou rememberest
the twelve apostles of the Lamb? Behold
they are they who shall judge the twelve
tribes of Israel; wherefore, the twelve
ministers of thy seed shall be judged of
them; for ye are of the house of Israel.
10 And these twelve ministers whom thou
beholdest shall judge thy seed. And,
behold, they are righteous forever; for
because of their faith in the Lamb of God
their garments are made white in his
blood.
11 And the angel said unto me: Look! And
I looked, and beheld three generations
pass away in righteousness; and their gar-
ments were white even like unto the
Lamb of God. And the angel said unto me:
These are made white in the blood of the
Lamb, because of their faith in him.
12 And I, Nephi, also saw many of the
fourth generation who passed away in
righteousness.

1 NEPHI 19

Nephi, Son of Lehi — *580 BC*

10 And the God of our fathers, who were led out of Egypt, out of bondage, and also were preserved in the wilderness by him, yea, the God of Abraham, and of Isaac, and the God of Jacob, yieldeth himself, according to the words of the angel, as a man, into the hands of wicked men, to be lifted up, according to the words of Zenock, and to be crucified, according to the words of Neum, and to be buried in a sepulchre, according to the words of Zenos, which he spake concerning the three days of darkness, which should be a sign given of his death unto those who should inhabit the isles of the sea, more especially given unto those who are of the house of Israel.

11 For thus spake the prophet: The Lord God surely shall visit all the house of Israel at that day, some with his voice, because of their righteousness, unto their great joy and salvation, and others with the thunderings and the lightnings of his power, by tempest, by fire, and by smoke, and vapor of darkness, and by the opening of the Earth, and by mountains which shall be carried up.

12 And all these things must surely come, saith the prophet Zenos. And the rocks of the Earth must rend; and because of the groanings of the Earth, many of the kings of the isles of the sea shall be wrought upon by the Spirit of God, to exclaim: The God of nature suffers.

2 NEPHI 26

Nephi, Son of Lehi — *550 BC*

1 And after Christ shall have risen from the dead he shall show himself unto you, my children, and my beloved brethren; and the words which he shall speak unto you shall be the law which ye shall do.

2 For behold, I say unto you that I have beheld that many generations shall pass away, and there shall be great wars and contentions among my people.

3 And after the Messiah shall come there shall be signs given unto my people of his birth, and also of his death and resurrection; and great and terrible shall that day be unto the wicked, for they shall perish; and they perish because they cast out the prophets, and the saints, and stone them, and slay them; wherefore the cry of the blood of the saints shall ascend up to God from the ground against them.

4 Wherefore, all those who are proud, and that do wickedly, the day that cometh shall burn them up, saith the Lord of Hosts, for they shall be as stubble.

5 And they that kill the prophets, and the saints, the depths of the Earth shall swallow them up, saith the Lord of Hosts; and mountains shall cover them, and whirlwinds shall carry them away, and buildings shall fall upon them and crush them to pieces and grind them to powder.

6 And they shall be visited with thunderings, and lightnings, and earthquakes, and all manner of destructions, for the fire of the anger of the Lord shall be kindled against them, and they shall be as stubble, and the day that cometh shall consume them, saith the Lord of Hosts.

7 O the pain, and the anguish of my soul for the loss of the slain of my people! For I, Nephi, have seen it, and it well nigh consumeth me before the presence of the Lord; but I must cry unto my God: Thy ways are just.

8 But behold, the righteous that hearken unto the words of the prophets, and destroy them not, but look forward unto Christ with steadfastness for the signs which are given, notwithstanding all persecution—behold, they are they which shall not perish.

9 But the Son of Righteousness shall appear unto them; and he shall heal them, and they shall have peace with him, until three generations shall have passed away, and many of the fourth generation shall have passed away in righteousness.

HELAMAN 14

Samuel the Lamanite — *6 BC*

20 But behold, as I said unto you concerning another sign, a sign of his death, behold, in that day that he shall suffer death the sun shall be darkened and refuse to give his light unto you; and also the moon and the stars; and there shall be no light upon the face of this land, even from the time that he shall suffer death, for the space of three days, to the time that he shall rise again from the dead.

21 Yea, at the time that he shall yield up the ghost there shall be thunderings and lightnings for the space of many hours, and the Earth shall shake and tremble; and

the rocks which are upon the face of this
Earth, which are both above the Earth and
beneath, which ye know at this time are
solid, or the more part of it is one solid
mass, shall be broken up;
22 Yea, they shall be rent in twain, and
shall ever after be found in seams and in
cracks, and in broken fragments upon the
face of the whole Earth, yea, both above
the Earth and beneath.
23 And behold, there shall be great tem-
pests, and there shall be many mountains
laid low, like unto a valley, and there shall
be many places which are now called
valleys which shall become mountains,
whose height is great.
24 And many highways shall be broken
up, and many cities shall become desolate.
25 And many graves shall be opened, and
shall yield up many of their dead; and
many saints shall appear unto many.
26 And behold, thus hath the angel
spoken unto me; for he said unto me that
there should be thunderings and light-
nings for the space of many hours.
27 And he said unto me that while the
thunder and the lightning lasted, and the
tempest, that these things should be, and
that darkness should cover the face of the
whole Earth for the space of three days.
28 And the angel said unto me that many
shall see greater things than these, to the
intent that they might believe that these
signs and these wonders should come to
pass upon all the face of this land, to the
intent that there should be no cause for
unbelief among the children of men—
29 And this to the intent that whosoever
will believe might be saved, and that
whosoever will not believe, a righteous
judgment might come upon them; and
also if they are condemned they bring
upon themselves their own condem-
nation.

3 NEPHI 9

Jesus Christ — *34 AD*

12 And many great destructions have I
caused to come upon this land, and upon
this people, because of their wickedness
and their abominations.
13 O all ye that are spared because ye were
more righteous than they, will ye not now
return unto me, and repent of your sins,
and be converted, that I may heal you?
14 Yea, verily I say unto you, if ye will
come unto me ye shall have eternal life.
Behold, mine arm of mercy is extended
towards you, and whosoever will come,
him will I receive; and blessed are those
who come unto me.
15 Behold, I am Jesus Christ the Son of
God. I created the heavens and the Earth,
and all things that in them are. I was with
the Father from the beginning. I am in the
Father, and the Father in me; and in me
hath the Father glorified his name.
16 I came unto my own, and my own
received me not. And the scriptures con-
cerning my coming are fulfilled.
17 And as many as have received me, to
them have I given to become the sons of
God; and even so will I to as many as shall
believe on my name, for behold, by me
redemption cometh, and in me is the law
of Moses fulfilled.
18 I am the light and the life of the world.
I am Alpha and Omega, the beginning and
the end.
19 And ye shall offer up unto me no more
the shedding of blood; yea, your sacrifices
and your burnt offerings shall be done
away, for I will accept none of your sacri-
fices and your burnt offerings.
20 And ye shall offer for a sacrifice unto
me a broken heart and a contrite spirit.
And whoso cometh unto me with a
broken heart and a contrite spirit, him will
I baptize with fire and with the Holy
Ghost, even as the Lamanites, because of
their faith in me at the time of their con-
version, were baptized with fire and with
the Holy Ghost, and they knew it not.
21 Behold, I have come unto the world to
bring redemption unto the world, to save
the world from sin.
22 Therefore, whoso repenteth and
cometh unto me as a little child, him will
I receive, for of such is the kingdom of
God. Behold, for such I have laid down my
life, and have taken it up again; therefore
repent, and come unto me ye ends of the
Earth, and be saved.

3 NEPHI 11

Jesus Christ — *34 AD*

6 And behold, the third time they did
understand the voice which they heard;
and it said unto them:

7 Behold my Beloved Son, in whom I am
well pleased, in whom I have glorified my
name—hear ye him.
8 And it came to pass, as they understood
they cast their eyes up again towards
heaven; and behold, they saw a Man
descending out of heaven; and he was
clothed in a white robe; and he came
down and stood in the midst of them; and
the eyes of the whole multitude were
turned upon him, and they durst not open
their mouths, even one to another, and
wist not what it meant, for they thought it
was an angel that had appeared unto them.
9 And it came to pass that he stretched
forth his hand and spake unto the people,
saying:
10 Behold, I am Jesus Christ, whom the
prophets testified shall come into the
world.
11 And behold, I am the light and the life
of the world; and I have drunk out of that
bitter cup which the Father hath given
me, and have glorified the Father in taking
upon me the sins of the world, in the
which I have suffered the will of the
Father in all things from the beginning.
12 And it came to pass that when Jesus had
spoken these words the whole multitude
fell to the Earth; for they remembered that
it had been prophesied among them that
Christ should show himself unto them
after his ascension into heaven.
13 And it came to pass that the Lord spake
unto them saying:
14 Arise and come forth unto me, that ye
may thrust your hands into my side, and
also that ye may feel the prints of the nails
in my hands and in my feet, that ye may
know that I am the God of Israel, and the
God of the whole Earth, and have been
slain for the sins of the world.
15 And it came to pass that the multitude
went forth, and thrust their hands into his
side, and did feel the prints of the nails in
his hands and in his feet; and this they did
do, going forth one by one until they had
all gone forth, and did see with their eyes
and did feel with their hands, and did
know of a surety and did bear record, that
it was he, of whom it was written by the
prophets, that should come.
16 And when they had all gone forth and
had witnessed for themselves, they did cry
out with one accord, saying:

Christ in the Land Bountiful, by Simon Dewey, 2010.

17 Hosanna! Blessed be the name of the
Most High God! And they did fall down at
the feet of Jesus, and did worship him.

3 NEPHI 11

Jesus Christ *34 AD*

31 Behold, verily, verily, I say unto you, I
will declare unto you my doctrine.
32 And this is my doctrine, and it is the
doctrine which the Father hath given
unto me; and I bear record of the Father,
and the Father beareth record of me, and
the Holy Ghost beareth record of the
Father and me; and I bear record that the
Father commandeth all men, every-
where, to repent and believe in me.
33 And whoso believeth in me, and is
baptized, the same shall be saved; and they
are they who shall inherit the kingdom of
God.
34 And whoso believeth not in me, and is
not baptized, shall be damned.
37 And again I say unto you, ye must
repent, and become as a little child, and be
baptized in my name, or ye can in nowise
receive these things.
38 And again I say unto you, ye must
repent, and be baptized in my name, and

become as a little child, or ye can in nowise inherit the kingdom of God.

3 NEPHI 15

Jesus Christ 34 AD

11 And now it came to pass that when Jesus had spoken these words, he said unto those twelve whom he had chosen:
12 Ye are my disciples; and ye are a light unto this people, who are a remnant of the house of Joseph.
13 And behold, this is the land of your inheritance; and the Father hath given it unto you.
14 And not at any time hath the Father given me commandment that I should tell it unto your brethren at Jerusalem.
15 Neither at any time hath the Father given me commandment that I should tell unto them concerning the other tribes of the house of Israel, whom the Father hath led away out of the land.
16 This much did the Father command me, that I should tell unto them:
17 That other sheep I have which are not of this fold; them also I must bring, and they shall hear my voice; and there shall be one fold, and one shepherd.
18 And now, because of stiffneckedness and unbelief they understood not my word; therefore I was commanded to say no more of the Father concerning this thing unto them.
19 But, verily, I say unto you that the Father hath commanded me, and I tell it unto you, that ye were separated from among them because of their iniquity; therefore it is because of their iniquity that they know not of you.
20 And verily, I say unto you again that the other tribes hath the Father separated from them; and it is because of their iniquity that they know not of them.
21 And verily I say unto you, that ye are they of whom I said: Other sheep I have which are not of this fold; them also I must bring, and they shall hear my voice; and there shall be one fold, and one shepherd.
22 And they understood me not, for they supposed it had been the Gentiles; for they understood not that the Gentiles should be converted through their preaching.
23 And they understood me not that I said they shall hear my voice; and they understood me not that the Gentiles should not at any time hear my voice—that I should not manifest myself unto them save it were by the Holy Ghost.
24 But behold, ye have both heard my voice, and seen me; and ye are my sheep, and ye are numbered among those whom the Father hath given me.

3 NEPHI 16

Jesus Christ 34 AD

1 And verily, verily, I say unto you that I have other sheep, which are not of this land, neither of the land of Jerusalem, neither in any parts of that land round about whither I have been to minister.
2 For they of whom I speak are they who have not as yet heard my voice; neither have I at any time manifested myself unto them.
3 But I have received a commandment of the Father that I shall go unto them, and that they shall hear my voice, and shall be numbered among my sheep, that there may be one fold and one shepherd; therefore I go to show myself unto them.

Christ Appears to the Nephites, from The Story of the Book of Mormon, by George Reynolds, 1888.

14

THE APOSTASY OF THE JEWS

+++

The first to receive the gospel of Jesus Christ, the Jews, are the first to reject it. As a result, the Lord instructs Peter to direct the missionary efforts of the early church to the Gentiles, who embrace the gospel. The following prophecies detail the Apostasy and destruction of the Jews by the Roman Emperor Vespasian and his son Titus in the first century. The siege of Jerusalem in 70 AD, which lasted about five months, resulted in an estimated 1.1 million dead and the annihilation of the city and the temple. The Jews would be despised and scattered among nations.

2 NEPHI 10
Jacob, Son of Lehi — *550 BC*

3 Wherefore, as I said unto you, it must needs be expedient that Christ—for in the last night the angel spake unto me that this should be his name—should come among the Jews, among those who are the more wicked part of the world; and they shall crucify him—for thus it behooveth our God, and there is none other nation on Earth that would crucify their God.
4 For should the mighty miracles be wrought among other nations they would repent, and know that he be their God.
5 But because of priestcrafts and iniquities, they at Jerusalem will stiffen their necks against him, that he be crucified.
6 Wherefore, because of their iniquities, destructions, famines, pestilences, and bloodshed shall come upon them; and they who shall not be destroyed shall be scattered among all nations.

MATTHEW 21
Jesus Christ — *33 AD*

42 Jesus saith unto them, Did ye never read in the scriptures, The stone which the builders rejected, the same is become the head of the corner: this is the Lord's doing, and it is marvellous in our eyes?
43 Therefore say I unto you, The kingdom of God shall be taken from you, and given to a nation bringing forth the fruits thereof.
44 And whosoever shall fall on this stone shall be broken: but on whomsoever it shall fall, it will grind him to powder.

LUKE 21
Jesus Christ — *32 AD*

12 But before all these, they shall lay their hands on you, and persecute you, delivering you up to the synagogues, and into prisons, being brought before kings and rulers for my name's sake.
13 And it shall turn to you for a testimony.
14 Settle it therefore in your hearts, not to meditate before what ye shall answer:
15 For I will give you a mouth and wisdom, which all your adversaries shall not be able to gainsay nor resist.
16 And ye shall be betrayed both by parents, and brethren, and kinsfolks, and friends; and some of you shall they cause to be put to death.
17 And ye shall be hated of all men for my name's sake.
18 But there shall not an hair of your head perish.
19 In your patience possess ye your souls.
20 And when ye shall see Jerusalem compassed with armies, then know that the desolation thereof is nigh.
21 Then let them which are in Judæa flee to the mountains; and let them which are in the midst of it depart out; and let not them that are in the countries enter thereinto.
22 For these be the days of vengeance, that all things which are written may be fulfilled.
23 But woe unto them that are with child, and to them that give suck, in those days! for there shall be great distress in the land, and wrath upon this people.
24 And they shall fall by the edge of the sword, and shall be led away captive into all nations: and Jerusalem shall be trodden

The Destruction of the Temple of Jerusalem, (70 AD), by Francesco Hayez, 1867.

down of the Gentiles, until the times of the Gentiles be fulfilled. *Now these things he spake unto the, concerning the destruction of Jerusalem.* [JST]

DOCTRINE AND COVENANTS 45

Joseph Smith *March 1831*

15 Wherefore, hearken and I will reason with you, and I will speak unto you and prophesy, as unto men in days of old.
16 And I will show it plainly as I showed it unto my disciples as I stood before them in the flesh, and spake unto them, saying: As ye have asked of me concerning the signs of my coming, in the day when I shall come in my glory in the clouds of heaven, to fulfil the promises that I have made unto your fathers,
17 For as ye have looked upon the long absence of your spirits from your bodies to be a bondage, I will show unto you how the day of redemption shall come, and also the restoration of the scattered Israel.
18 And now ye behold this temple, which is in Jerusalem, which ye call the house of God, and your enemies say that this house shall never fall.
19 But, verily I say unto you, that desolation shall come upon this generation as a thief in the night, and this people shall be destroyed and scattered among all nations.
20 And this temple which ye now see shall be thrown down that there shall not be left one stone upon another.
21 And it shall come to pass, that this generation of Jews shall not pass away until every desolation which I have told you concerning them shall come to pass.
22 Ye say that ye know that the end of the world cometh; ye say also that ye know that the heavens and the Earth shall pass away;
23 And in this ye say truly, for so it is; but these things which I have told you shall not pass away until all shall be fulfilled.
24 And this I have told you concerning Jerusalem; and when that day shall come, shall a remnant be scattered among all nations;

2 NEPHI 25

Nephi, Son of Lehi *550 BC*

14 And behold it shall come to pass that after the Messiah hath risen from the dead, and hath manifested himself unto his people, unto as many as will believe on his name, behold, Jerusalem shall be destroyed again; for wo unto them that fight against God and the people of his church.
15 Wherefore, the Jews shall be scattered among all nations; yea, and also Babylon shall be destroyed; wherefore, the Jews shall be scattered by other nations.

ISAIAH 22

Isaiah *740 BC*

21 And I will clothe him with thy robe, and strengthen him with thy girdle, and I will commit thy government into his hand: and he shall be a father to the inhabitants of Jerusalem, and to the house of Judah.
22 And the key of the house of David will I lay upon his shoulder; so he shall open, and none shall shut; and he shall shut, and none shall open.
23 And I will fasten him as a nail in a sure place; and he shall be for a glorious throne to his father's house.
24 And they shall hang upon him all the glory of his father's house, the offspring and the issue, all vessels of small quantity, from the vessels of cups, even to all the vessels of flagons.
25 In that day, saith the LORD of hosts, shall the nail that is fastened in the sure place be removed, and be cut down, and fall; and the burden that was upon it shall be cut off: for the LORD hath spoken it.

1 NEPHI 19

Nephi, Son of Lehi *580 BC*

13 And as for those who are at Jerusalem, saith the prophet, they shall be scourged by all people, because they crucify the God of Israel, and turn their hearts aside, rejecting signs and wonders, and the power and glory of the God of Israel.
14 And because they turn their hearts aside, saith the prophet, and have despised the Holy One of Israel, they shall wander in the flesh, and perish, and become a hiss and a byword, and be hated among all nations.

2 NEPHI 6

Jacob, Son of Lehi *550 BC*

10 And after they have hardened their hearts and stiffened their necks against the Holy One of Israel, behold, the judgments of the Holy One of Israel shall come upon them. And the day cometh that they shall be smitten and afflicted.

1 THESSALONIANS 2

Paul *51 AD*

14 For ye, brethren, became followers of the churches of God which in Judæa are in Christ Jesus: for ye also have suffered like things of your own countrymen, even as they have of the Jews:
15 Who both killed the Lord Jesus, and their own prophets, and have persecuted us; and they please not God, and are contrary to all men:
16 Forbidding us to speak to the Gentiles that they might be saved, to fill up their sins alway: for the wrath is come upon them to the uttermost.

HOSEA 4

Hosea *826 BC*

1 Hear the word of the LORD, ye children of Israel: for the LORD hath a controversy with the inhabitants of the land, because there is no truth, nor mercy, nor knowledge of God in the land.
2 By swearing, and lying, and killing, and stealing, and committing adultery, they break out, and blood toucheth blood.
3 Therefore shall the land mourn, and every one that dwelleth therein shall languish, with the beasts of the field, and with the fowls of heaven; yea, the fishes of the sea also shall be taken away.
4 Yet let no man strive, nor reprove another: for thy people are as they that strive with the priest.
5 Therefore shalt thou fall in the day, and the prophet also shall fall with thee in the night, and I will destroy thy mother.
6 My people are destroyed for lack of knowledge: because thou hast rejected knowledge, I will also reject thee, that thou shalt be no priest to me: seeing thou hast forgotten the law of thy God, I will also forget thy children.
7 As they were increased, so they sinned against me: therefore will I change their glory into shame.

8 They eat up the sin of my people, and
they set their heart on their iniquity.
9 And there shall be, like people, like
priest: and I will punish them for their
ways, and reward them their doings.
10 For they shall eat, and not have
enough: they shall commit whoredom,
and shall not increase: because they have
left off to take heed to the LORD.
11 Whoredom and wine and new wine
take away the heart.
12 My people ask counsel at their stocks,
and their staff declareth unto them: for
the spirit of whoredoms hath caused them
to err, and they have gone a whoring from
under their God.
13 They sacrifice upon the tops of the
mountains, and burn incense upon the
hills, under oaks and poplars and elms,
because the shadow thereof is good: therefore your daughters shall commit whoredom, and your spouses shall commit
adultery.
14 I will not punish your daughters when
they commit whoredom, nor your spouses
when they commit adultery: for themselves are separated with whores, and they
sacrifice with harlots: therefore the people
that doth not understand shall fall.
15 Though thou, Israel, play the harlot,
yet let not Judah offend; and come not ye
unto Gilgal, neither go ye up to Beth-aven,
nor swear, The LORD liveth.
16 For Israel slideth back as a backsliding
heifer: now the LORD will feed them as a
lamb in a large place.
17 Ephraim is joined to idols: let him
alone.
18 Their drink is sour: they have committed whoredom continually: her rulers
with shame do love, Give ye.
19 The wind hath bound her up in her
wings, and they shall be ashamed because
of their sacrifices.

HOSEA 5

Hosea *826 BC*

3 I know Ephraim, and Israel is not hid
from me: for now, O Ephraim, thou
committest whoredom, and Israel is
defiled.
4 They will not frame their doings to turn
unto their God: for the spirit of whoredoms is in the midst of them, and they
have not known the LORD.
5 And the pride of Israel doth testify to his
face: therefore shall Israel and Ephraim
fall in their iniquity; Judah also shall fall
with them.
6 They shall go with their flocks and with
their herds to seek the LORD; but they
shall not find him; he hath withdrawn
himself from them.
7 They have dealt treacherously against
the LORD: for they have begotten strange
children: now shall a month devour them
with their portions.
8 Blow ye the cornet in Gibeah, and the
trumpet in Ramah: cry aloud at Beth-aven, after thee, O Benjamin.
9 Ephraim shall be desolate in the day of
rebuke: among the tribes of Israel have I
made known that which shall surely be.
10 The princes of Judah were like them
that remove the abound: therefore I will
pour out my wrath upon them like water.
11 Ephraim is oppressed and broken in
judgment, because he willingly walked
after the commandment.
12 Therefore will I be unto Ephraim as a
moth, and to the house of Judah as
rottenness.
13 When Ephraim saw his sickness, and
Judah saw his wound, then went Ephraim
to the Assyrian, and sent to king Jareb: yet
could he not heal you, nor cure you of
your wound.
14 For I will be unto Ephraim as a lion,
and as a young lion to the house of Judah:
I, even I, will tear and go away; I will take
away, and none shall rescue him.
15 I will go and return to my place, till
they acknowledge their offence, and seek
my face: in their affliction they will seek
me early.

HOSEA 6

Hosea *826 BC*

4 O Ephraim, what shall I do unto thee? O
Judah, what shall I do unto thee? for your
goodness is as a morning cloud, and as the
early dew it goeth away.
5 Therefore have I hewed them by the
prophets; I have slain them by the words
of my mouth: and thy judgments are as the
light that goeth forth.
6 For I desired mercy, and not sacrifice;
and the knowledge of God more than
burnt offerings.

South inner panel of the Arch of Titus, which still stands in Rome, commemorating the Roman victory at Jerusalem, 70 AD. The relief depicts the Romans parading with the spoils of the temple.

7 But they like men have transgressed the covenant: there have they dealt treacherously against me.
8 Gilead is a city of them that work iniquity, and is polluted with blood.
9 And as troops of robbers wait for a man, so the company of priests murder in the way by consent: for they commit lewdness.
10 I have seen an horrible thing in the house of Israel: there is the whoredom of Ephraim, Israel is defiled.
11 Also, O Judah, he hath set an harvest for thee, when I returned the captivity of my people.

HOSEA 8

Hosea — *826 BC*

1 Set the trumpet to thy mouth. He shall come as an eagle against the house of the LORD, because they have transgressed my covenant, and trespassed against my law.
2 Israel shall cry unto me, My God, we know thee.
3 Israel hath cast off the thing that is good: the enemy shall pursue him.
4 They have set up kings, but not by me: they have made princes, and I knew it not: of their silver and their gold have they made them idols, that they may be cut off.
5 Thy calf, O Samaria, hath cast thee off; mine anger is kindled against them: how long will it be ere they attain to innocency?
6 For from Israel was it also: the workman made it; therefore it is not God: but the calf of Samaria shall be broken in pieces.
7 For they have sown the wind, and they shall reap the whirlwind: it hath no stalk: the bud shall yield no meal: if so be it yield, the strangers shall swallow it up.
8 Israel is swallowed up: now shall they be among the Gentiles as a vessel wherein is no pleasure.
9 For they are gone up to Assyria, a wild ass alone by himself: Ephraim hath hired lovers.
10 Yea, though they have hired among the nations, now will I gather them, and they shall sorrow a little for the burden of the king of princes.

11 Because Ephraim hath made many altars to sin, altars shall be unto him to sin.
12 I have written to him the great things of my law, but they were counted as a strange thing.
13 They sacrifice flesh for the sacrifices of mine offerings, and eat it; but the LORD accepteth them not; now will he remember their iniquity, and visit their sins: they shall return to Egypt.
14 For Israel hath forgotten his Maker, and buildeth temples; and Judah hath multiplied fenced cities: but I will send a fire upon his cities, and it shall devour the palaces thereof.

HOSEA 9

Hosea 826 BC

1 Rejoice not, O Israel, for joy, as other people: for thou hast gone a whoring from thy God, thou hast loved a reward upon every corn floor.
3 They shall not dwell in the LORD's land; but Ephraim shall return to Egypt, and they shall eat unclean things in Assyria.
15 All their wickedness is in Gilgal: for there I hated them: for the wickedness of their doings I will drive them out of mine house, I will love them no more: all their princes are revolters.
16 Ephraim is smitten, their root is dried up, they shall bear no fruit: yea, though they bring forth, yet will I slay even the beloved fruit of their womb.
17 My God will cast them away, because they did not hearken unto him: and they shall be wanderers among the nations.

3 NEPHI 24 (see also MALACHI 3)

Malachi 432 BC

7 Even from the days of your fathers ye are gone away from mine ordinances, and have not kept them. Return unto me and I will return unto you, saith the Lord of Hosts. But ye say: Wherein shall we return?
8 Will a man rob God? Yet ye have robbed me. But ye say: Wherein have we robbed thee? In tithes and offerings.
9 Ye are cursed with a curse, for ye have robbed me, even this whole nation.
10 Bring ye all the tithes into the storehouse, that there may be meat in my house; and prove me now herewith, saith the Lord of Hosts, if I will not open you the windows of heaven, and pour you out a blessing that there shall not be room enough to receive it.

ISAIAH 65

Isaiah 740 BC

1 I am sought of them that asked not for me; I am found of them that sought me not: I said, Behold me, behold me, unto a nation that was not called by my name.
2 I have spread out my hands all the day unto a rebellious people, which walketh in a way that was not good, after their own thoughts;
3 A people that provoketh me to anger continually to my face; that sacrificeth in gardens, and burneth incense upon altars of brick;
4 Which remain among the graves, and lodge in the monuments, which eat swine's flesh, and broth of abominable things is in their vessels;
5 Which say, Stand by thyself, come not near to me; for I am holier than thou. These are a smoke in my nose, a fire that burneth all the day.
6 Behold, it is written before me: I will not keep silence, but will recompense, even recompense into their bosom,
7 Your iniquities, and the iniquities of your fathers together, saith the LORD, which have burned incense upon the mountains, and blasphemed me upon the hills: therefore will I measure their former work into their bosom.

AMOS 9

Amos 792 AD

8 Behold, the eyes of the Lord GOD are upon the sinful kingdom, and I will destroy it from off the face of the Earth; saving that I will not utterly destroy the house of Jacob, saith the LORD.
9 For, lo, I will command, and I will sift the house of Israel among all nations, like as corn is sifted in a sieve, yet shall not the least grain fall upon the Earth.
10 All the sinners of my people shall die by the sword, which say, The evil shall not overtake nor prevent us.

ISAIAH 59

Isaiah 740 BC

1 Behold, the LORD's hand is not shortened, that it cannot save; neither his ear heavy, that it cannot hear:

2 But your iniquities have separated between you and your God, and your sins have hid his face from you, that he will not hear.
3 For your hands are defiled with blood, and your fingers with iniquity; your lips have spoken lies, your tongue hath muttered perverseness.
4 None calleth for justice, nor any pleadeth for truth: they trust in vanity, and speak lies; they conceive mischief, and bring forth iniquity.
5 They hatch cockatrice' eggs, and weave the spider's web: he that eateth of their eggs dieth, and that which is crushed breaketh out into a viper.
6 Their webs shall not become garments, neither shall they cover themselves with their works: their works are works of iniquity, and the act of violence is in their hands.
7 Their feet run to evil, and they make haste to shed innocent blood: their thoughts are thoughts of iniquity; wasting and destruction are in their paths.
8 The way of peace they know not; and there is no judgment in their goings: they have made them crooked paths: whosoever goeth therein shall not know peace.
9 Therefore is judgment far from us, neither doth justice overtake us: we wait for light, but behold obscurity; for brightness, but we walk in darkness.
10 We grope for the wall like the blind, and we grope as if we had no eyes: we stumble at noonday as in the night; we are in desolate places as dead men.
11 We roar all like bears, and mourn sore like doves: we look for judgment, but there is none; for salvation, but it is far off from us.
12 For our transgressions are multiplied before thee, and our sins testify against us: for our transgressions are with us; and as for our iniquities, we know them;
13 In transgressing and lying against the LORD, and departing away from our God, speaking oppression and revolt, conceiving and uttering from the heart words of falsehood.

EZEKIEL 12

Ezekiel 598 BC

14 And I will scatter toward every wind all that are about him to help him, and all his bands; and I will draw out the sword after them.
15 And they shall know that I am the LORD, when I shall scatter them among the nations, and disperse them in the countries.
16 But I will leave a few men of them from the sword, from the famine, and from the pestilence; that they may declare all their abominations among the heathen whither they come; and they shall know that I am the LORD.

EZEKIEL 39

Ezekiel 598 BC

23 And the heathen shall know that the house of Israel went into captivity for their iniquity: because they trespassed against me, therefore hid I my face from them, and gave them into the hand of their enemies: so fell they all by the sword.
24 According to their uncleanness and according to their transgressions have I done unto them, and hid my face from them.

15

THE GENTILES RECEIVE THE GOSPEL

+++

The gospel is taught to the Gentiles. Up until this point in history, the Lord's covenant people were limited to those who could trace their genealogy to the patriarch Jacob. The Apostle Peter, shortly after the Crucifixion, was commanded by the Lord to preach the gospel to the Gentiles, who quickly embraced it. This proved a critical moment in history, because of all the peoples of the Earth in ancient times who believed in Jesus Christ, only the Gentile Christians of Europe and the Middle East would preserve a recognizable belief in Christ to the present day. These Gentile Christians would play a key role in the Restoration of the gospel in the latter-days and in the gathering of the scattered remnants of the House of Israel from the four quarters of the Earth prior to the Second Coming.

1 NEPHI 10

Nephi, Son of Lehi — *600 BC*

11 And it came to pass after my father had spoken these words he spake unto my brethren concerning the gospel which should be preached among the Jews, and also concerning the dwindling of the Jews in unbelief. And after they had slain the Messiah, who should come, and after he had been slain he should rise from the dead, and should make himself manifest, by the Holy Ghost, unto the Gentiles.

2 NEPHI 26

Nephi, Son of Lehi — *550 BC*

12 And as I spake concerning the convincing of the Jews, that Jesus is the very Christ, it must needs be that the Gentiles be convinced also that Jesus is the Christ, the Eternal God;

13 And that he manifesteth himself unto all those who believe in him, by the power of the Holy Ghost; yea, unto every nation, kindred, tongue, and people, working mighty miracles, signs, and wonders, among the children of men according to their faith.

3 NEPHI 15

Jesus Christ — *34 AD*

21 And verily I say unto you, that ye are they of whom I said: Other sheep I have which are not of this fold; them also I must bring, and they shall hear my voice; and there shall be one fold, and one shepherd.

22 And they [Jews] understood me not, for they supposed it had been the Gentiles; for they understood not that the Gentiles should be converted through their preaching.

23 And they understood me not that I said they shall hear my voice; and they understood me not that the Gentiles should not at any time hear my voice—that I should not manifest myself unto them save it were by the Holy Ghost.

ACTS 9

Luke — *37 AD*

15 But the Lord said unto him [Ananias], Go thy way: for he [Saul] is a chosen vessel unto me, to bear my name before the Gentiles, and kings, and the children of Israel:

16 For I will shew him how great things he must suffer for my name's sake.

ACTS 10

Peter — *40 AD*

1 There was a certain man in Cæsarea called Cornelius, a centurion of the band called the Italian band,

2 A devout man, and one that feared God with all his house, which gave much alms to the people, and prayed to God alway.

3 He saw in a vision evidently about the ninth hour of the day an angel of God coming into him, and saying unto him, Cornelius.

4 And when he looked on him, he was afraid, and said, What is it, Lord? And he

Vision of Cornelius the Centurion, by Gerbrand van den Eeckhout, 1664.

said unto him, Thy prayers and thine alms
are come up for a memorial before God.
5 And now send men to Joppa, and call for
one Simon, whose surname is Peter:
6 He lodgeth with one Simon a tanner,
whose house is by the sea side: he shall tell
thee what thou oughtest to do.
7 And when the angel which spake unto
Cornelius was departed, he called two of
his household servants, and a devout
soldier of them that waited on him
continually;
8 And when he had declared all these
things unto them, he sent them to Joppa.
9 On the morrow, as they went on their
journey, and drew nigh unto the city,
Peter went up upon the housetop to pray
about the sixth hour:
10 And he became very hungry, and
would have eaten: but while they made
ready, he fell into a trance,
11 And saw heaven opened, and a certain
vessel descending unto him, as it had been
a great sheet knit at the four corners, and
let down to the Earth:
12 Wherein were all manner of fourfooted
beasts of the Earth, and wild beasts, and
creeping things, and fowls of the air.
13 And there came a voice to him, Rise,
Peter; kill, and eat.
14 But Peter said, Not so, Lord; for I have
never eaten anything that is common or
unclean.
15 And the voice spake unto him again the
second time, What God hath cleansed,
that call not thou common.
16 This was done thrice: and the vessel
was received up again into heaven.
17 Now while Peter doubted in himself
what this vision which he had seen should
mean, behold, the men which were sent
from Cornelius had made inquiry for
Simon's house, and stood before the gate,
18 And called, and asked whether Simon,
which was surnamed Peter, were lodged
there.
19 While Peter thought on the vision, the
Spirit said unto him, Behold, three men
seek thee.

20 Arise therefore, and get thee down, and
ago with them, doubting nothing: for I
have sent them.
21 Then Peter went down to the men
which were sent unto him from
Cornelius; and said, Behold, I am he
whom ye seek: what is the cause where-
fore ye are come?
22 And they said, Cornelius the centurion,
a just man, and one that feareth God, and
of good report among all the nation of the
Jews, was warned from God by an holy
angel to send for thee into his house, and
to hear words of thee.
23 Then called he them in, and lodged
them. And on the morrow Peter went
away with them, and certain brethren
from Joppa accompanied him.
24 And the morrow after they entered
into Cæsarea. And Cornelius waited for
them, and had called together his kinsmen
and near friends.
25 And as Peter was coming in, Cornelius
met him, and fell down at his feet, and
worshipped him.
26 But Peter took him up, saying, Stand
up; I myself also am a aman.
27 And as he talked with him, he went in,
and found many that were come together.
28 And he said unto them, Ye know how
that it is an unlawful thing for a man that
is a Jew to keep company, or come unto
one of another nation; but God hath
shewed me that I should not call any man
common or unclean.
29 Therefore came I unto you without
gainsaying, as soon as I was sent for: I ask
therefore for what intent ye have sent for
me?
30 And Cornelius said, Four days ago I was
fasting until this hour; and at the ninth
hour I prayed in my house, and, behold, a
man stood before me in bright clothing,
31 And said, Cornelius, thy prayer is
heard, and thine alms are had in remem-
brance in the sight of God.
32 Send therefore to Joppa, and call hither
Simon, whose surname is Peter; he is
lodged in the house of one Simon a tanner
by the sea side: who, when he cometh,
shall speak unto thee.
33 Immediately therefore I sent to thee;
and thou hast well done that thou art
come. Now therefore are we all here
present before God, to hear all things that
are commanded thee of God.
34 Then Peter opened his mouth, and said,
Of a truth I perceive that God is no
respecter of persons:
35 But in every nation he that feareth him,
and worketh righteousness, is accepted
with him.
36 The word which God sent unto the
children of Israel, preaching peace by
Jesus Christ: (he is Lord of all:)
37 That word, I say, ye know, which was
published throughout all Judæa, and
began from Galilee, after the baptism
which John preached;
38 How God anointed Jesus of Nazareth
with the Holy Ghost and with power: who
went about doing good, and healing all
that were oppressed of the devil; for God
was with him.
39 And we are witnesses of all things
which he did both in the land of the Jews,
and in Jerusalem; whom they slew and
hanged on a tree:
40 Him God raised up the third day, and
shewed him openly;
41 Not to all the people, but unto
witnesses chosen before of God, even to
us, who did eat and drink with him after
he rose from the dead.
42 And he commanded us to preach unto
the people, and to testify that it is he
which was ordained of God to be the
Judge of quick and dead.
43 To him give all the prophets witness,
that through his name whosoever believe-
eth in him shall receive remission of sins.
44 While Peter yet spake these words, the
Holy Ghost fell on all them which heard
the word.
45 And they of the circumcision which
believed were astonished, as many as
came with Peter, because that on the
Gentiles also was poured out the gift of the
Holy Ghost.
46 For they heard them speak with
tongues, and magnify God. Then
answered Peter,
47 Can any man forbid water, that these
should not be baptized, which have
received the Holy Ghost as well as we?
48 And he commanded them to be
baptized in the name of the Lord. Then
prayed they him to tarry certain days.

ACTS 13

Paul *48 AD*

46 Then Paul and Barnabas waxed bold, and said, It was necessary that the word of God should first have been spoken to you: but seeing ye put it from you, and judge yourselves unworthy of everlasting life, lo, we turn to the Gentiles.
47 For so hath the Lord commanded us, saying, I have set thee to be a light of the Gentiles, that thou shouldest be for salvation unto the ends of the Earth.
48 And when the Gentiles heard this, they were glad, and glorified the word of the Lord: and as many as were ordained to eternal life believed.

ACTS 26

Paul *37 AD*

12 Whereupon as I went to Damascus with authority and commission from the chief priests,
13 At midday, O king, I saw in the way a light from heaven, above the brightness of the sun, shining round about me and them which journeyed with me.
14 And when we were all fallen to the Earth, I heard a voice speaking unto me, and saying in the Hebrew tongue, Saul, Saul, why persecutest thou me? it is hard for thee to kick against the pricks.
15 And I said, Who art thou, Lord? And he said, I am Jesus whom thou persecutest.
16 But rise, and stand upon thy feet: for I have appeared unto thee for this purpose, to make thee a minister and a witness both of these things which thou hast seen, and of those things in the which I will appear unto thee;
17 Delivering thee from the people, and from the Gentiles, unto whom now I send thee,
18 To open their eyes, and to turn them from darkness to light, an from the power of Satan unto God, that they may receive forgiveness of sins, and inheritance among them which are sanctified by faith that is in me.
19 Whereupon, O King Agrippa, I was not disobedient unto the heavenly vision:
20 But shewed first unto them of Damascus, and at Jerusalem, and through-

The Conversion of Saint Paul, who sees an angel, falls off his horse, and is blinded by the light.

out all the coasts of Judæa, and then to the Gentiles, that they should repent and turn to God, and do works meet for repentance.
21 For these causes the Jews caught me in the temple, and went about to kill me.
22 Having therefore obtained help of God, I continue unto this day, witnessing both to small and great, saying none other things than those which the prophets and Moses did say should come:
23 That Christ should suffer, and that he should be the first that should brise from the dead, and should shew light unto the people, and to the Gentiles.

GALATIANS 2

Paul — *54 AD*

7 But contrariwise, when they saw that the gospel of the uncircumcision was committed unto me, as the gospel of the circumcision was unto Peter;
8 (For he that wrought effectually in Peter to the apostleship of the circumcision, the same was mighty in me toward the Gentiles:)
9 And when James, Cephas, and John, who seemed to be pillars, perceived the grace that was given unto me, they gave to me and Barnabas the right hands of fellowship; that we should go unto the heathen, and they unto the circumcision.

ROMANS 9

Paul — *57 AD*

23 And that he might make known the riches of his glory on the vessels of mercy, which he had afore prepared unto glory,
24 Even us, whom he hath called, not of the Jews only, but also of the Gentiles?
25 As he saith also in Hosea, I will call them my people, which were not my people; and her beloved, which was not beloved.
26 And it shall come to pass, that in the place where it was said unto them, Ye are not my people; there shall they be called the children of the living God.
27 Esaias also crieth concerning Israel, Though the number of the children of Israel be as the sand of the sea, a remnant shall be saved:
28 For he will finish the work, and cut it short in righteousness: because a short work will the Lord make upon the Earth.
29 And as Esaias said before, Except the Lord of Sabaoth had left us a seed, we had been as Sodoma, and been made like unto Gomorrha.
30 What shall we say then? That the Gentiles, which followed not after righteousness, have attained to righteousness, even the righteousness which is of faith.
31 But Israel, which followed after the law of righteousness, hath not attained to the law of righteousness.
32 Wherefore? Because they sought it not by faith, but as it were by the works of the law. For they stumbled at that stumbling stone;
33 As it is written, Behold, I lay in Sion a stumbling stone and rock of offence: and whosoever believeth on him shall not be ashamed.

1 NEPHI 10

Nephi, Son of Lehi — *600 BC*

12 Yea, even my father [Lehi] spake much concerning the Gentiles, and also concerning the house of Israel, that they should be compared like unto an olive tree, whose branches should be broken off and should be scattered upon all the face of the Earth.
13 Wherefore, he said it must needs be that we should be led with one accord into the land of promise, unto the fulfilling of the word of the Lord, that we should be scattered upon all the face of the Earth.

JACOB 4

Jacob, Son of Lehi — *500 BC*

14 But behold, the Jews were a stiff-necked people; and they despised the words of plainness, and killed the prophets, and sought for things that they could not understand. Wherefore, because of their blindness, which blindness came by looking beyond the mark, they must needs fall; for God hath taken away his plainness from them, and delivered unto them many things which they cannot understand, because they desired it. And because they desired it God hath done it, that they may stumble.
15 And now I, Jacob, am led on by the Spirit unto prophesying; for I perceive by the workings of the Spirit which is in me, that by the stumbling of the Jews they will reject the stone upon which they might build and have safe foundation.
16 But behold, according to the scriptures, this stone shall become the great, and the

last, and the only sure foundation, upon which the Jews can build.

17 And now, my beloved, how is it possible that these, after having rejected the sure foundation, can ever build upon it, that it may become the head of their corner?

18 Behold, my beloved brethren, I will unfold this mystery unto you; if I do not, by any means, get shaken from my firmness in the Spirit, and stumble because of my over anxiety for you.

JACOB 5

Zenos *750 BC?*

1 Behold, my brethren, do ye not remember to have read the words of the prophet Zenos, which he spake unto the house of Israel, saying:

2 Hearken, O ye house of Israel, and hear the words of me, a prophet of the Lord.

3 For behold, thus saith the Lord, I will liken thee, O house of Israel, like unto a tame olive tree, which a man took and nourished in his vineyard; and it grew, and waxed old, and began to decay.

4 And it came to pass that the master of the vineyard went forth, and he saw that his olive tree began to decay; and he said: I will prune it, and dig about it, and nourish it, that perhaps it may shoot forth young and tender branches, and it perish not.

5 And it came to pass that he pruned it, and digged about it, and nourished it according to his word.

6 And it came to pass that after many days it began to put forth somewhat a little, young and tender branches; but behold, the main top thereof began to perish.

The Lord's Plan to Save the Tree

About 1000 BC to 100 AD
Lehi, Ishmael, Mulek, and other "natural branches" leave Israel and settle in ancient America and other parts of the world. Due to the wickedness of, and in an effort to save, the House of Israel (the olive tree), the Gentiles (the wild olive tree) are adopted into the House of Israel after Christ's Resurrection.

7 And it came to pass that the master of the vineyard saw it, and he said unto his servant: It grieveth me that I should lose this tree; wherefore, go and pluck the branches from a wild olive tree, and bring them hither unto me; and we will pluck off those main branches which are beginning to wither away, and we will cast them into the fire that they may be burned.

8 And behold, saith the Lord of the vineyard, I take away many of these young and tender branches, and I will graft them whithersoever I will; and it mattereth not that if it so be that the root of this tree will perish, I may preserve the fruit thereof unto myself; wherefore, I will take these young and tender branches, and I will graft them whithersoever I will.

9 Take thou the branches of the wild olive tree, and graft them in, in the stead thereof; and these which I have plucked off I will cast into the fire and burn them, that they may not cumber the ground of my vineyard.

Lord's Servant Carries Out the Plan

10 And it came to pass that the servant of the Lord of the vineyard did according to the word of the Lord of the vineyard and grafted in the branches of the wild olive tree.

11 And the Lord of the vineyard caused that it should be digged about, and pruned, and nourished, saying unto his servant: It grieveth me that I should lose this tree; wherefore, that perhaps I might preserve the roots thereof that they perish not, that I might preserve them unto myself, I have done this thing.

12 Wherefore, go thy way; watch the tree, and nourish it, according to my words.

13 And these will I place in the nethermost part of my vineyard, whithersoever I will, it mattereth not unto thee; and I do it that I may preserve unto myself the natural branches of the tree; and also, that I may lay up fruit thereof against the season, unto myself; for it grieveth me that I should lose this tree and the fruit thereof.

14 And it came to pass that the Lord of the vineyard went his way, and hid the natural branches of the tame olive tree in the nethermost parts of the vineyard, some in one and some in another, according to his will and pleasure.

Circa 40 AD – 200 AD
In the Roman Empire, the Gentiles thrive in the gospel up until 100 AD; three other groups in unknown locations also thrive (China? India? Africa?); in ancient America, by about 200-250 AD the people are split, half being righteous and half being wicked.

15 And it came to pass that a long time passed away, and the Lord of the vineyard said unto his servant: Come, let us go down into the vineyard, that we may labor in the vineyard.

16 And it came to pass that the Lord of the vineyard, and also the servant, went down into the vineyard to labor. And it came to pass that the servant said unto his master: Behold, look here; behold the tree.

17 And it came to pass that the Lord of the vineyard looked and beheld the tree in the which the wild olive branches had been grafted; and it had sprung forth and begun to bear fruit. And he beheld that it was good; and the fruit thereof was like unto the natural fruit.

18 And he said unto the servant: Behold, the branches of the wild tree have taken hold of the moisture of the root thereof, that the root thereof hath brought forth much strength; and because of the much strength of the root thereof the wild branches have brought forth tame fruit. Now, if we had not grafted in these branches, the tree thereof would have perished. And now, behold, I shall lay up much fruit, which the tree thereof hath brought forth; and the fruit thereof I shall lay up against the season, unto mine own self.

19 And it came to pass that the Lord of the vineyard said unto the servant: Come, let us go to the nethermost part of the vineyard, and behold if the natural branches of the tree have not brought forth much fruit also, that I may lay up of the fruit thereof against the season, unto mine own self.

20 And it came to pass that they went forth whither the master had hid the natural branches of the tree, and he said unto the servant: Behold these; and he beheld the first that it had brought forth much fruit; and he beheld also that it was good. And he said unto the servant: Take of the fruit thereof, and lay it up against the season, that I may preserve it unto mine own self; for behold, said he, this long time have I nourished it, and it hath brought forth much fruit.

21 And it came to pass that the servant said unto his master: How comest thou hither to plant this tree, or this branch of the tree? For behold, it was the poorest spot in all the land of thy vineyard.

22 And the Lord of the vineyard said unto him: Counsel me not; I knew that it was a poor spot of ground; wherefore, I said unto thee, I have nourished it this long time, and thou beholdest that it hath brought forth much fruit.

23 And it came to pass that the Lord of the vineyard said unto his servant: Look hither; behold I have planted another branch of the tree also; and thou knowest that this spot of ground was poorer than the first. But, behold the tree. I have nourished it this long time, and it hath brought forth much fruit; therefore, gather it, and lay it up against the season, that I may preserve it unto mine own self.

24 And it came to pass that the Lord of the vineyard said again unto his servant: Look hither, and behold another branch also, which I have planted; behold that I have nourished it also, and it hath brought forth fruit.

25 And he said unto the servant: Look hither and behold the last. Behold, this have I planted in a good spot of ground; and I have nourished it this long time, and only a part of the tree hath brought forth tame fruit, and the other part of the tree hath brought forth wild fruit; behold, I have nourished this tree like unto the others.

26 And it came to pass that the Lord of the vineyard said unto the servant: Pluck off the branches that have not brought forth good fruit, and cast them into the fire.

27 But behold, the servant said unto him: Let us prune it, and dig about it, and nourish it a little longer, that perhaps it may bring forth good fruit unto thee, that thou canst lay it up against the season.

28 And it came to pass that the Lord of the vineyard and the servant of the Lord of the vineyard did nourish all the fruit of the vineyard.

Paul also compares the Gentiles receiving the gospel to the branches of a wild olive tree being grafted into the tame olive tree. Did Paul have access to Zenos's allegory of the olive tree, or did the Lord inspire him to make the exact same comparison?

ROMANS 11

Paul *57 AD*

1 I say then, Hath God cast away his people? God forbid. For I also am an Israelite, of the seed of Abraham, of the tribe of Benjamin.
2 God hath not cast away his people which he foreknew. Wot ye not what the scripture saith of Elias? how he maketh intercession to God against Israel, saying,
3 Lord, they have killed thy prophets, and digged down thine altars; and I am left alone, and they seek my life.
4 But what saith the answer of God unto him? I have reserved to myself seven thousand men, who have not bowed the knee to the image of Baal.
5 Even so then at this present time also there is a remnant according to the election of grace.
6 And if by grace, then is it no more of works: otherwise grace is no more grace. But if it be of works, then is it no more grace: otherwise work is no more work.
7 What then? Israel hath not obtained that which he seeketh for; but the election hath obtained it, and the rest were blinded
8 (According as it is written, God hath given them the spirit of slumber, eyes that they should not see, and ears that they should not hear;) unto this day.
9 And David saith, Let their table be made a snare, and a trap, and a stumbling block, and a recompence unto them:
10 Let their eyes be darkened, that they may not see, and bow down their back alway.
11 I say then, Have they stumbled that they should fall? God forbid: but rather through their fall salvation is come unto the Gentiles, for to provoke them to jealousy.
12 Now if the fall of them be the riches of the world, and the diminishing of them the riches of the Gentiles; how much more their fulness?
13 For I speak to you Gentiles, inasmuch as I am the apostle of the Gentiles, I magnify mine office:
14 If by any means I may provoke to emulation them which are my flesh, and might save some of them.
15 For if the casting away of them be the reconciling of the world, what shall the receiving of them be, but life from the dead?
16 For if the first fruit be holy, the lump is also holy: and if the root be holy, so are the branches.
17 And if some of the branches be broken off, and thou, being a wild olive tree, wert grafted in among them, and with them partakest of the root and fatness of the olive tree;
18 Boast not against the branches. But if thou boast, thou bearest not the root, but the root thee.
19 Thou wilt say then, The branches were broken off, that I might be grafted in.
20 Well; because of unbelief they were broken off, and thou standest by faith. Be not highminded, but fear:
21 For if God spared not the natural branches, take heed lest he also spare not thee.
22 Behold therefore the goodness and severity of God: on them which fell, severity; but toward thee, goodness, if thou continue in his goodness: otherwise thou also shalt be cut off.
23 And they also, if they abide not still in unbelief, shall be grafted in: for God is able to graft them in again.
24 For if thou wert cut out of the olive tree which is wild by nature, and wert grafted contrary to nature into a good olive tree: how much more shall these, which be the natural branches, be grafted into their own olive tree?
25 For I would not, brethren, that ye should be ignorant of this mystery, lest ye should be wise in your own conceits; that blindness in part is happened to Israel, until the fulness of the Gentiles be come in.
26 And so all Israel shall be saved: as it is written, There shall come out of Sion the Deliverer, and shall turn away ungodliness from Jacob:
27 For this is my covenant unto them, when I shall take away their sins.

ROMANS 15
Paul *57 AD*
9 And that the Gentiles might glorify God for his mercy; as it is written, For this cause I will confess to thee among the Gentiles, and sing unto thy name.
10 And again he saith, Rejoice, ye Gentiles, with his people.
11 And again, Praise the Lord, all ye Gentiles; and laud him, all ye people.
12 And again, Esaias saith, There shall be a root of Jesse, and he that shall rise to reign over the Gentiles; in him shall the Gentiles trust.
13 Now the God of hope fill you with all joy and peace in believing, that ye may abound in hope, through the power of the Holy Ghost.
14 And I myself also am persuaded of you, my brethren, that ye also are full of goodness, filled with all knowledge, able also to admonish one another.
15 Nevertheless, brethren, I have written the more boldly unto you in some sort, as putting you in mind, because of the grace that is given to me of God,
16 That I should be the minister of Jesus Christ to the Gentiles, ministering the gospel of God, that the offering up of the Gentiles might be acceptable, being sanctified by the Holy Ghost.
17 I have therefore whereof I may glory through Jesus Christ in those things which pertain to God.
18 For I will not dare to speak of any of those things which Christ hath not wrought by me, to make the Gentiles obedient, by word and deed,
19 Through mighty signs and wonders, by the power of the Spirit of God; so that from Jerusalem, and round about unto Illyricum, I have fully preached the gospel of Christ.
20 Yea, so have I strived to preach the gospel, not where Christ was named, lest I should build upon another man's foundation:
21 But as it is written, To whom he was not spoken of, they shall see: and they that have not heard shall understand.

EPHESIANS 3
Paul *62 AD*
1 For this cause I Paul, the prisoner of Jesus Christ for you Gentiles,
2 If ye have heard of the dispensation of the grace of God which is given me to you-ward:
3 How that by revelation he made known unto me the mystery; (as I wrote afore in few words,
4 Whereby, when ye read, ye may understand my knowledge in the mystery of Christ)
5 Which in other ages was not made known unto the sons of men, as it is now revealed unto his holy apostles and prophets by the Spirit;
6 That the Gentiles should be fellow heirs, and of the same body, and partakers of his promise in Christ by the gospel:
7 Whereof I was made a minister, according to the gift of the grace of God given unto me by the effectual working of his power.
8 Unto me, who am less than the least of all saints, is this grace given, that I should preach among the Gentiles the unsearchable riches of Christ;
9 And to make all men see what is the fellowship of the mystery, which from the beginning of the world hath been hid in God, who created all things by Jesus Christ:
10 To the intent that now unto the principalities and powers in heavenly places might be known by the church the manifold wisdom of God,
11 According to the eternal purpose which he purposed in Christ Jesus our Lord:
12 In whom we have boldness and access with confidence by the faith of him.

1 NEPHI 11
Nephi, Son of Lehi *595 BC*
33 And I, Nephi, saw that he was lifted up upon the cross and slain for the sins of the world.
34 And after he was slain I saw the multitudes of the Earth, that they were gathered together to fight against the apostles of the Lamb; for thus were the twelve called by the angel of the Lord.
35 And the multitude of the Earth was gathered together; and I beheld that they were in a large and spacious building, like unto the building which my father saw. And the angel of the Lord spake unto me again, saying: Behold the world and the wisdom thereof; yea, behold the house of

Israel hath gathered together to fight against the twelve apostles of the Lamb.
36 And it came to pass that I saw and bear record, that the great and spacious building was the pride of the world;

DOCTRINE AND COVENANTS 77

Joseph Smith *1832*

7 Q. What are we to understand by the seven seals with which it was sealed? A. We are to understand that the first seal contains the things of the first thousand years, and the second also of the second thousand years, and so on until the seventh.

REVELATION 6

John *95 AD*

9 And when he had opened the fifth seal, I saw under the altar the souls of them that were slain for the word of God, and for the testimony which they held:
10 And they cried with a loud voice, saying, How long, O Lord, holy and true, dost thou not judge and avenge our blood on them that dwell on the Earth?
11 And white robes were given unto every one of them; and it was said unto them, that they should rest yet for a little season, until their fellow servants also and their brethren, that should be killed as they were, should be fulfilled.

Triumph of Faith, Christian Martyrs in the Time of Nero, by Eugene Thirion, 1800s.

16

THE APOSTASY OF THE CHRISTIAN CHURCH

+++

The first century witnessed the organization and rapid growth of the Church of Jesus Christ on at least two continents. This was due, in large part, to the outpouring of the Holy Ghost and the many witnesses of the miracle of Christ's resurrection. The early church in the east faced intense persecution from both Jewish and Roman authorities, which cost the lives of many saints, including all of the Apostles. Church leaders faced a constant barrage of false doctrines from Jewish and pagan converts, as well as from popular Greek philosophy. The Apostles repeatedly warned the saints against heretical doctrines and other false teachings from within the church. With the deaths of the Apostles in the mid to late 1st *century, the church lost its leadership and its connection to divine revelation and priesthood authority. In this rudderless state, the church was infected with many false teachings. The pure doctrine taught by Jesus Christ and the Apostles became more and more corrupted. The Apostles repeatedly prophesied of this coming Apostasy throughout the New Testament.*

2 THESSALONIANS 2

Paul — 52 AD

1 Now we beseech you, brethren, by the coming of our Lord Jesus Christ, and by our gathering together unto him,
2 That ye be not soon shaken in mind, or be troubled *by letter, except ye receive it from us*; neither by spirit, nor by word, as that the day of Christ is at hand. [JST]
3 Let no man deceive you by any means: for *there shall come a falling away first*, and that man of sin be revealed, the son of perdition; [JST]
4 Who opposeth and exalteth himself above all that is called God, or that is worshipped; so that he as God sitteth in the temple of God, shewing himself that he is God.
5 Remember ye not, that, when I was yet with you, I told you these things?
6 And now ye know what withholdeth that he might be revealed in his time.
7 For the mystery of iniquity doth already work: *and he it is who now worketh, and Christ suffereth him to work, until the time is fulfilled that he shall* be taken out of the way. [JST]
9 *Yea, the Lord, even Jesus,* whose coming is *not until after there cometh a falling away, by* the working of Satan with all power, and signs and lying wonders. [JST]

Pope Boniface VIII (1294-1303) was among the most wicked of popes. In a fulfillment of Paul's prophecy in 2 Thessalonians, in 1302, he issued a Papal Bull decreeing it "absolutely necessary for salvation that every human creature be subject to the Roman pontiff." Like many popes before him, he held immense unchecked temporal and spiritual power. Italian poet Dante Alighieri placed him in the 8th circle of hell for his depravity and many heinous sins.

GALATIANS 1

Paul *54 AD*

6 I marvel that ye are so soon removed from him that called you into the grace of Christ unto another gospel:

7 Which is not another; but there be some that trouble you, and would pervert the gospel of Christ.

8 But though we, or an angel from heaven, preach any other gospel unto you than that which we have preached unto you, let him be accursed.

9 As we said before, so say I now again, If any man preach any other gospel unto you than that ye have received, let him be accursed.

GALATIANS 2

Paul *54 AD*

11 But when Peter was come to Antioch, I withstood him to the face, because he was to be blamed.

12 For before that certain came from James, he did eat with the Gentiles: but when they were come, he withdrew and separated himself, fearing them which were of the circumcision.

13 And the other Jews dissembled likewise with him; insomuch that Barnabas also was carried away with their dissimulation.

14 But when I saw that they walked not uprightly according to the truth of the gospel, I said unto Peter before them all, If thou, being a Jew, livest after the manner of Gentiles, and not as do the Jews, why compellest thou the Gentiles to live as do the Jews?

15 We who are Jews by nature, and not sinners of the Gentiles,

16 Knowing that a man is not justified by the works of the law, but by the faith of Jesus Christ, even we have believed in Jesus Christ, that we might be justified by the faith of Christ, and not by the works of the law: for by the works of the law shall no flesh be justified.

17 But if, while we seek to be justified by Christ, we ourselves also are found sinners, is therefore Christ the minister of sin? God forbid.

18 For if I build again the things which I destroyed, I make myself a transgressor.

19 For I through the law am dead to the law, that I might live unto God.

20 I am crucified with Christ: nevertheless I live; yet not I, but Christ liveth in me: and the life which I now live in the flesh I live by the faith of the Son of God, who loved me, and gave himself for me.

21 I do not frustrate the grace of God: for if righteousness come by the law, then Christ is dead in vain.

GALATIANS 3

Paul *54 AD*

1 O foolish Galatians, who hath bewitched you, that ye should not obey the truth, before whose eyes Jesus Christ hath been evidently set forth, crucified among you?

2 This only would I learn of you, Received ye the Spirit by the works of the law, or by the hearing of faith?

GALATIANS 4

Paul *54 AD*

8 Howbeit then, when ye knew not God, ye did service unto them which by nature are no gods.

9 But now, after that ye have known God, or rather are known of God, how turn ye again to the weak and beggarly elements, whereunto ye desire again to be in bondage?

10 Ye observe days, and months, and times, and years.

11 I am afraid of you, lest I have bestowed upon you labour in vain.

16 Am I therefore become your enemy, because I tell you the truth?

19 My little children, of whom I travail in birth again until Christ be formed in you,

20 I desire to be present with you now, and to change my voice; for I stand in doubt of you.

1 CORINTHIANS 1

Paul *54 AD*

10 Now I beseech you, brethren, by the name of our Lord Jesus Christ, that ye all speak the same thing, and that there be no divisions among you; but that ye be perfectly joined together in the same mind and in the same judgment.

11 For it hath been declared unto me of you, my brethren, by them which are of the house of Chloe, that there are contentions among you.

12 Now this I say, that every one of you saith, I am of Paul; and I of Apollos; and I of Cephas; and I of Christ.

13 Is Christ divided? was Paul crucified for you? or were ye baptized in the name of Paul?
14 I thank God that I baptized none of you, but Crispus and Gaius;
15 Lest any should say that I had baptized in mine own name.
16 And I baptized also the household of Stephanas: besides, I know not whether I baptized any other.
17 For Christ sent me not to baptize, but to preach the gospel: not with wisdom of words, lest the cross of Christ should be made of none effect.
18 For the preaching of the cross is to them that perish foolishness; but unto us which are saved it is the power of God.
19 For it is written, I will destroy the wisdom of the wise, and will bring to nothing the understanding of the prudent.
20 Where is the wise? where is the scribe? where is the disputer of this world? hath not God made foolish the wisdom of this world?
21 For after that in the wisdom of God the world by wisdom knew not God, it pleased God by the foolishness of preaching to save them that believe.
22 For the Jews require a sign, and the Greeks seek after wisdom:
23 But we preach Christ crucified, unto the Jews a stumbling block, and unto the Greeks foolishness;
24 But unto them *who believe*, both Jews and Greeks, Christ the power of God, and the wisdom of God. [JST]

1 CORINTHIANS 5

Paul — *54 AD*

1 It is reported commonly that there is fornication among you, and such fornication as is not so much as named among the Gentiles, that one should have his father's wife.
2 And ye are puffed up, and have not rather mourned, that he that hath done this deed might be taken away from among you.
3 For I verily, as absent in body, but present in spirit, have judged already, as though I were present, concerning him that hath so done this deed,
4 In the name of our Lord Jesus Christ, when ye are gathered together, and *have the* spirit, with the power of our Lord Jesus Christ, [JST]
5 To deliver such an one unto Satan for the destruction of the flesh, that the spirit may be saved in the day of the Lord Jesus.
9 I wrote unto you in an epistle not to company with fornicators:
10 Yet not altogether with the fornicators of this world, or with the covetous, or extortioners, or with idolaters; for then must ye needs go out of the world.
11 But now I have written unto you not to keep company, if any man that is called a brother be a fornicator, or covetous, or an idolater, or a railer, or a drunkard, or an extortioner; with such an one no not to eat.
12 For what have I to do to judge them also that are without? do not ye judge them that are within?
13 But them that are without God judgeth. Therefore put away from among yourselves that wicked person.

2 CORINTHIANS 11

Paul — *57 AD*

2 For I am jealous over you with godly jealousy: for I have espoused you to one husband, that I may present you as a chaste virgin to Christ.
3 But I fear, lest by any means, as the serpent beguiled Eve through his subtilty, so your minds should be corrupted from the simplicity that is in Christ.
4 For if he that cometh preacheth another Jesus, whom we have not preached, or if ye receive another spirit, which ye have not received, or another gospel, which ye have not accepted, ye might well bear with him.
13 For such are false apostles, deceitful workers, transforming themselves into the apostles of Christ.
14 And no marvel; for Satan himself is transformed into an angel of light.
15 Therefore it is no great thing if his ministers also be transformed as the ministers of righteousness; whose end shall be according to their works.

2 CORINTHIANS 12

Paul — *57 AD*

20 For I fear, lest, when I come, I shall not find you such as I would, and that I shall be found unto you such as ye would not: lest there be debates, envyings, wraths, strifes, backbitings, whisperings, swellings, tumults:

21 And lest, when I come again, my God will humble me among you, and that I shall bewail many which have sinned already, and have not repented of the uncleanness and fornication and lasciviousness which they have committed.

ACTS 20

Paul *57 AD*

28 Take heed therefore unto yourselves, and to all the flock, over the which the Holy Ghost hath made you overseers, to feed the church of God, which he hath purchased with his own blood.
29 For I know this, that after my departing shall grievous wolves enter in among you, not sparing the flock.
30 Also of your own selves shall men arise, speaking perverse things, to draw away disciples after them.
31 Therefore watch, and remember, that by the space of three years I ceased not to warn every one night and day with tears.

Saint Paul, by Bartolomeo Montagna, 1482.

ROMANS 16

Paul *57 AD*

17 Now I beseech you, brethren, mark them which cause divisions and offences contrary to the doctrine which ye have learned; and avoid them.
18 For they that are such serve not our Lord Jesus Christ, but their own belly; and by good words and fair speeches deceive the hearts of the simple.

COLOSSIANS 2

Paul *62 AD*

4 And this I say, lest any man should beguile you with enticing words.
8 Beware lest any man spoil you through philosophy and vain deceit, after the tradition of men, after the rudiments of the world, and not after Christ.
18 Let no man beguile you of your reward in a voluntary humility and worshipping of angels, intruding into those things which he hath not seen, vainly puffed up by his fleshly mind,

1 TIMOTHY 1

Paul *63 AD*

3 As I besought thee to abide still at Ephesus, when I went into Macedonia, that thou mightest charge some that they teach no other doctrine,
4 Neither give heed to fables and endless genealogies, which minister questions, rather than godly edifying which is in faith: so do.
5 Now the end of the commandment is charity out of a pure heart, and of a good conscience, and of faith unfeigned:
6 From which some having swerved have turned aside unto vain jangling;
7 Desiring to be teachers of the law; understanding neither what they say, nor whereof they affirm.
18 This charge I commit unto thee, son Timothy, according to the prophecies which went before on thee, that thou by them mightest war a good warfare;

19 Holding faith, and a good conscience; which some having put away concerning faith have made shipwreck:
20 Of whom is Hymenæus and Alexander; whom I have delivered unto Satan, that they may learn not to blaspheme.

1 TIMOTHY 4
Paul *63 AD*
1 Now the Spirit speaketh expressly, that in the latter-times some shall depart from the faith, giving heed to seducing spirits, and doctrines of devils;
2 Speaking lies in hypocrisy; having their conscience seared with a hot iron;
3 Forbidding to marry, and commanding to abstain from meats, which God hath created to be received with thanksgiving of them which believe and know the truth.
7 But refuse profane and old wives' fables, and exercise thyself rather unto godliness.

TITUS 1
Paul *66 AD*
10 For there are many unruly and vain talkers and deceivers, specially they of the circumcision:
11 Whose mouths must be stopped, who subvert whole houses, teaching things which they ought not, for filthy lucre's sake.
12 One of themselves, even a prophet of their own, said, The Cretians are alway liars, evil beasts, slow bellies.
13 This witness is true. Wherefore rebuke them sharply, that they may be sound in the faith;
14 Not giving heed to Jewish fables, and commandments of men, that turn from the truth.
15 Unto the pure, let all things be pure: but unto them that are defiled and unbelieving is nothing pure; but even their mind and conscience is defiled.
16 They profess that they know God; but in works they deny him, being abominable, and disobedient, and unto every good work reprobate.

HEBREWS 13
Paul *68 AD*
8 Jesus Christ the same yesterday, and today, and forever.
9 Be not carried about with divers and strange doctrines...

TITUS 3
Paul *66 AD*
9 But avoid foolish questions, and genealogies, and contentions, and strivings about the law; for they are unprofitable and vain.
10 A man that is an heretick after the first and second admonition reject;
11 Knowing that he that is such is subverted, and sinneth, being condemned of himself.

2 PETER 1
Peter *67 AD*
16 For we have not followed cunningly devised fables, when we made known unto you the power and coming of our Lord Jesus Christ, but were eyewitnesses of his majesty.

2 PETER 2
Peter *67 AD*
1 But there were false prophets also among the people, even as there shall be false teachers among you, who privily shall bring in damnable heresies, even denying the Lord that bought them, and bring upon themselves swift destruction.
2 And many shall follow their pernicious ways; by reason of whom the way of truth shall be evil spoken of.
3 And through covetousness shall they with feigned words make merchandise of you: whose judgment now of a long time lingereth not, and their damnation slumbereth not.

2 PETER 3
Peter *67 AD*
17 Ye therefore, beloved, seeing ye know before *the things which are coming*, beware lest ye also, being led away with the error of the wicked, fall from your own steadfastness. [JST]

2 TIMOTHY 1
Paul *67 AD*
15 This thou knowest, that all they which are in Asia be turned away from me; of whom are Phygellus and Hermogenes.

2 TIMOTHY 2
Paul *67 AD*
16 But shun profane and vain babblings: for they will increase unto more ungodliness.

17 And their word will eat as doth a canker: of whom is Hymenæus and Philetus;
18 Who concerning the truth have erred, saying that the resurrection is past already; and overthrow the faith of some.
23 But foolish and unlearned questions avoid, knowing that they do gender strifes.
24 And the servant of the Lord must not strive; but be gentle unto all men, apt to teach, patient,
25 In meekness instructing those that oppose themselves; if God peradventure will give them repentance to the acknowledging of the truth;
26 And that they may recover themselves out of the snare of the devil, who are taken captive by him at his will.

JOHN 16

John *32 AD*

2 They shall put you out of the synagogues: yea, the time cometh, that whosoever killeth you will think that he doeth God service.
3 And these things will they do unto you, because they have not known the Father, nor me.

2 TIMOTHY 4

Paul *67 AD*

3 For the time will come when they will not endure sound doctrine; but after their own lusts shall they heap to themselves teachers, having itching ears;
4 And they shall turn away their ears from the truth, and shall be turned unto fables.
5 But watch thou in all things, endure afflictions, do the work of an evangelist, make full proof of thy ministry.
6 For I am now ready to be offered, and the time of my departure is at hand.
7 I have fought a good fight, I have finished my course, I have kept the faith:
8 Henceforth there is laid up for me a crown of righteousness, which the Lord, the righteous judge, shall give me at that day: and not to me only, but unto all them also that love his appearing.
9 Do thy diligence to come shortly unto me:
10 For Demas hath forsaken me, having loved this present world, and is departed unto Thessalonica; Crescens to Galatia, Titus unto Dalmatia.
11 Only Luke is with me. Take Mark, and bring him with thee: for he is profitable to me for the ministry.

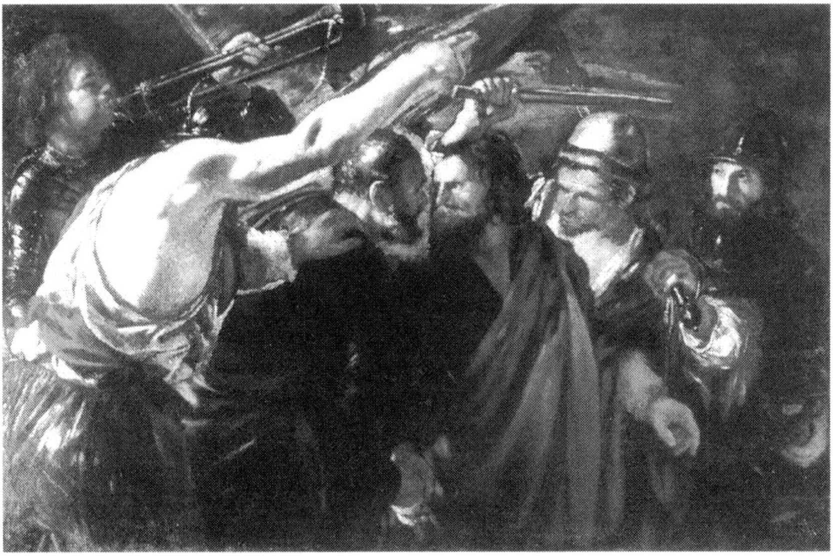

Parting of St Peter and Paul – Being Led to Martyrdom, by Giovanni Serodine, 1625.

12 And Tychicus have I sent to Ephesus.
13 The cloak that I left at Troas with
Carpus, when thou comest, bring with
thee, and the books, but especially the
parchments.
14 Alexander the coppersmith did me
much evil: the Lord reward him according
to his works:
15 Of whom be thou ware also; for he hath
greatly withstood our words.
16 At my first answer no man stood with
me, but all men forsook me: I pray God
that it may not be laid to their charge.
17 Notwithstanding the Lord stood with
me, and strengthened me; that by me the
preaching might be fully known, and that
all the Gentiles might hear: and I was
delivered out of the mouth of the lion.
18 And the Lord shall deliver me from
every evil work, and will preserve me
unto his heavenly kingdom: to whom be
glory for ever and ever. Amen.

JUDE 1

Jude — *68 AD*

3 Beloved, when I gave all diligence to
write unto you of the common salvation,
it was needful for me to write unto you,
and exhort you that ye should earnestly
contend for the faith which was once
delivered unto the saints.
4 For there are certain men crept in
unawares, who were before of old
ordained to this condemnation, ungodly
men, turning the grace of our God into
lasciviousness, and denying the only Lord
God, and our Lord Jesus Christ.
5 I will therefore put you in remem-
brance, though ye once knew this, how
that the Lord, having saved the people out
of the land of Egypt, afterward destroyed
them that believed not.
6 And the angels which kept not their first
estate, but left their own habitation, he
hath reserved in everlasting chains under
darkness unto the judgment of the great
day.
7 Even as Sodom and Gomorrha, and the
cities about them in like manner, giving
themselves over to fornication, and going
after strange flesh, are set forth for an
example, suffering the vengeance of
eternal fire.
8 Likewise also these filthy dreamers
defile the flesh, despise dominion, and
speak evil of dignities.
9 Yet Michael the archangel, when
contending with the devil he disputed
about the body of Moses, durst not bring
against him a railing accusation, but said,
The Lord rebuke thee.
10 But these speak evil of those things
which they know not: but what they
know naturally, as brute beasts, in those
things they corrupt themselves.
11 Woe unto them! for they have gone in
the way of Cain, and ran greedily after the
error of Balaam for reward, and *shall
perish* in the gainsaying of Core. [JST]
12 These are spots in your feasts of charity,
when they feast with you, feeding them-
selves without fear: clouds they are with-
out water, carried about of winds; trees
whose fruit withereth, without fruit,
twice dead, plucked up by the roots;
13 Raging waves of the sea, foaming out
their own shame; wandering stars, to
whom is reserved the blackness of dark-
ness forever.
14 And Enoch also, the seventh from
Adam, prophesied of these, saying,
Behold, the Lord cometh with ten thou-
sands of his saints,
15 To execute judgment upon all, and to
convince all that are ungodly among them
of all their ungodly deeds which they have
ungodly committed, and of all their hard
speeches which ungodly sinners have
spoken against him.
16 These are murmurers, complainers,
walking after their own lusts; and their
mouth speaketh great swelling words,
having men's persons in admiration
because of advantage.
17 But, beloved, remember ye the words
which were spoken before of the apostles
of our Lord Jesus Christ;
18 How that they told you there should be
mockers in the last time, who should walk
after their own ungodly lusts.
19 These be they who separate
themselves, sensual, having not the Spirit.

REVELATION 2

John — *95 AD*

1 Unto the *servant* of the church of
Ephesus write; These things saith he that
holdeth the seven stars in his right hand,
who walketh in the midst of the seven
golden candlesticks; [JST}
2 I know thy works, and thy labour, and
thy patience, and how thou canst not bear

them which are evil: and thou hast tried them which say they are apostles, and are not, and hast found them liars:
3 And hast borne, and hast patience, and for my name's sake hast laboured, and hast not fainted.
4 Nevertheless I have somewhat against thee, because thou hast left thy first love.
5 Remember therefore from whence thou art fallen, and repent, and do the first works; or else I will come unto thee quickly, and will remove thy candlestick out of his place, except thou repent.
6 But this thou hast, that thou hatest the deeds of the Nicolaitans, which I also hate.
8 And unto the *servant* of the church in Smyrna write; These things saith the first and the last, which was dead, and is alive; [JST]
9 I know thy works, and tribulation, and poverty, (but thou art rich) and I know the blasphemy of them which say they are Jews, and are not, but are the synagogue of Satan.
10 Fear none of those things which thou shalt suffer: behold, the devil shall cast some of you into prison, that ye may be tried; and ye shall have tribulation ten days: be thou faithful unto death, and I will give thee a crown of life.
12 And to the *servant* of the church in Pergamos write; These things saith he which hath the sharp sword with two edges; [JST]
13 I know thy works, and where thou dwellest, even where Satan's seat is: and thou holdest fast my name, and hast not denied my faith, even in those days wherein Antipas was my faithful martyr, who was slain among you, where Satan dwelleth.
14 But I have a few things against thee, because thou hast there them that hold the doctrine of Balaam, who taught Balac to cast a stumbling block before the children of Israel, to eat things sacrificed unto idols, and to commit fornication.
15 So hast thou also them that hold the doctrine of the Nicolaitans, which thing I hate.
16 Repent; or else I will come unto thee quickly, and will fight against them with the sword of my mouth.
18 And unto the *servant* of the church in Thyatira write; These things saith the Son of God, who hath his eyes like unto a flame of fire, and his feet are like fine brass; [JST]
19 I know thy works, and charity, and service, and faith, and thy patience, and thy works; and the last to be more than the first.
20 Notwithstanding I have a few things against thee, because thou sufferest that woman Jezebel, which calleth herself a prophetess, to teach and to seduce my servants to commit fornication, and to eat things sacrificed unto idols.
21 And I gave her space to repent of her fornication; and she repented not.
22 Behold, I will cast her into a bed, and them that commit adultery with her into great tribulation, except they repent of their deeds.
23 And I will kill her children with death; and all the churches shall know that I am he which searcheth the reins and hearts: and I will give unto every one of you according to your works.

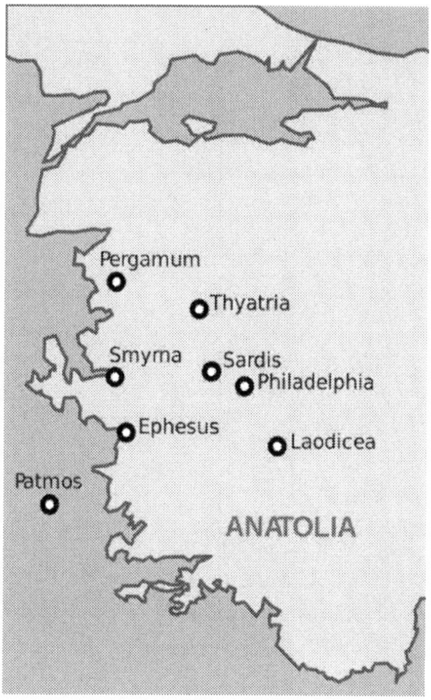

Map of western Anatolia (Turkey) showing the locations of the seven churches of Asia referenced in the Book of Revelation.

24 But unto you I say, and unto the rest in Thyatira, as many as have not this doctrine, and which have not known the depths of Satan, as they speak; I will put upon you none other burden.
25 But that which ye have already ahold fast till I come.

REVELATION 3
John *95 AD*

1 And unto the *servant* of the church in Sardis write; These things saith he *who* hath the seven *stars, which are* the seven *servants of God*; I know thy works, that thou hast a name that thou livest, and art dead.
2 Be watchful *therefore*, and strengthen *those who* remain, *who* are ready to die: for I have not found thy works perfect before God. [JST]
3 Remember *therefore* how thou hast received and heard, and hold fast, and repent. If therefore thou shalt not watch, I will come on thee as a thief, and thou shalt not know what hour I will come upon thee.
4 Thou hast a few names even in Sardis which have not defiled their garments; and they shall walk with me in white: for they are worthy.
7 And to the *servant* of the church in Philadelphia write; These things saith he that is holy, he that is true, he that hath the key of David, he that openeth, and no man shutteth; and shutteth, and no man openeth; [JST]
8 I know thy works: behold, I have set before thee an open door, and no man can shut it: for thou hast a little strength, and hast kept my word, and hast not denied my name.
9 Behold, I will make them of the synagogue of Satan, which say they are Jews, and are not, but do lie; behold, I will make them to come and worship before thy feet, and to know that I have loved thee.
10 Because thou hast kept the word of my patience, I also will keep thee from the hour of temptation, which shall come upon all the world, to try them that dwell upon the Earth.
11 Behold, I come quickly: hold that fast which thou hast, that no man take thy crown.
14 And unto the *servant* of the church of the Laodiceans write; These things saith the Amen, the faithful and true witness, the beginning of the creation of God; [JST]
15 I know thy works, that thou art neither cold nor hot: I would thou wert cold or hot.
16 So then because thou art lukewarm, and neither cold nor hot, I will spue thee out of my mouth.
17 Because thou sayest, I am rich, and increased with goods, and have need of nothing; and knowest not that thou art wretched, and miserable, and poor, and blind, and naked:
18 I counsel thee to buy of me gold tried in the fire, that thou mayest be rich; and white raiment, that thou mayest be clothed, and that the shame of thy nakedness do not appear; and anoint thine eyes with eyesalve, that thou mayest see.
19 As many as I love, I rebuke and chasten: be zealous therefore, and repent.
20 Behold, I stand at the door, and knock: if any man hear my voice, and open the door, I will come in to him, and will sup with him, and he with me.

1 JOHN 2
John *90 AD*

18 Little children, it is the last time: and as ye have heard that antichrist shall come, even now are there many antichrists; whereby we know that it is the last time.
19 They went out from us, but they were not of us; for if they had been of us, they would no doubt have continued with us: but they went out, that they might be made manifest that they were not all of us.
20 But ye have an unction from the Holy One, and ye know all things.
21 I have not written unto you because ye know not the truth, but because ye know it, and that no lie is of the truth.
22 Who is a liar but he that denieth that Jesus is the Christ? He is antichrist, that denieth the Father and the Son.
23 Whosoever denieth the Son, the same hath not the Father: [but] he that acknowledgeth the Son hath the Father also.
24 Let that therefore abide in you, which ye have heard from the beginning. If that which ye have heard from the beginning shall remain in you, ye also shall continue in the Son, and in the Father.
25 And this is the promise that he hath promised us, even eternal life.

26 These things have I written unto you concerning them that seduce you.
27 But the anointing which ye have received of him abideth in you, and ye need not that any man teach you: but as the same anointing teacheth you of all things, and is truth, and is no lie, and even as it hath taught you, ye shall abide in him.
28 And now, little children, abide in him; that, when he shall appear, we may have confidence, and not be ashamed before him at his coming.
29 If ye know that he is righteous, ye know that everyone that doeth righteousness is born of him.

1 JOHN 4
John — *90 AD*

1 Beloved, believe not every spirit, but try the spirits whether they are of God: because many false prophets are gone out into the world.
2 Hereby know ye the Spirit of God: Every spirit that confesseth that Jesus Christ is come in the flesh is of God:
3 And every spirit that confesseth not that Jesus Christ is come in the flesh is not of God: and this is that spirit of antichrist, whereof ye have heard that it should come; and even now already is it in the world.

2 JOHN 1
John — *92 AD*

4 I rejoiced greatly that I found of thy children walking in truth, as we have received a commandment from the Father.
5 And now I beseech thee, lady, not as though I wrote a new commandment unto thee, but that which we had from the beginning, that we love one another.
6 And this is love, that we walk after his commandments. This is the commandment, That, as ye have heard from the beginning, ye should walk in it.
7 For many deceivers are entered into the world, who confess not that Jesus Christ is come in the flesh. This is a deceiver and an antichrist.
8 Look to yourselves, that we lose not those things which we have wrought, but that we receive a full reward.
9 Whosoever transgresseth, and abideth not in the doctrine of Christ, hath not God. He that abideth in the doctrine of Christ, he hath both the Father and the Son.
10 If there come any unto you, and bring not this doctrine, receive him not into your house, neither bid him God speed:
11 For he that biddeth him God speed is partaker of his evil deeds.

3 JOHN 1
John — *95 AD*

9 I wrote unto the church: but Diotrephes, who loveth to have the preeminence among them, receiveth us not.
10 Wherefore, if I come, I will remember his deeds which he doeth, prating against us with malicious words: and not content therewith, neither doth he himself receive the brethren, and forbiddeth them that would, and casteth them out of the church.
11 Beloved, follow not that which is evil, but that which is good. He that doeth good is of God: but he that doeth evil hath not seen God.

17

THE APOSTASY OF THE NEPHITES

Classic Period (250 AD) Mayan mural of a high-status man being painted red via bloodletting. Bonampak, Mexico.

+++

Prophecies concerning the Apostasy and destruction of the Christians living in ancient America, among the Nephites and Lamanites. After Christ's visit and ministry there, the prophet Mormon confirms that the peace and righteousness of the people lasted only through the first and second generations. Similar to the apostasy that occurred with the Christians in the Old World, by 200 AD wickedness prevailed among the Nephites and Lamanites. Ancient prophets foresaw wars and a final battle that completely destroyed the Nephite people in 385 AD.

2 NEPHI 26

<u>*Nephi, Son of Lehi* *550 BC*</u>

9 But the Son of Righteousness shall
appear unto them; and he shall heal them,
and they shall have peace with him, until
three generations shall have passed away,
and many of the fourth generation shall
have passed away in righteousness.
10 And when these things have passed
away a speedy destruction cometh unto
my people; for, notwithstanding the pains
of my soul, I have seen it; wherefore, I
know that it shall come to pass; and they
sell themselves for naught; for, for the
reward of their pride and their foolishness
they shall reap destruction; for because
they yield unto the devil and choose
works of darkness rather than light, therefore they must go down to hell.
11 For the Spirit of the Lord will not
always strive with man. And when the
Spirit ceaseth to strive with man then
cometh speedy destruction, and this
grieveth my soul.

2 NEPHI 26

Nephi, Son of Lehi 550 BC

18 Wherefore, as those who have been
destroyed have been destroyed speedily;
and the multitude of their terrible ones
shall be as chaff that passeth away—yea,
thus saith the Lord God: It shall be at an
instant, suddenly—

1 NEPHI 15

Nephi, Son of Lehi 595 BC

4 And now I, Nephi, was grieved because
of the hardness of their hearts, and also,
because of the things which I had seen,
and knew they must unavoidably come to
pass because of the great wickedness of the
children of men.
5 And it came to pass that I was overcome
because of my afflictions, for I considered
that mine afflictions were great above all,
because of the destruction of my people,
for I had beheld their fall.

2 NEPHI 1

Lehi 580 BC

10 But behold, when the time cometh that
they shall dwindle in unbelief, after they
have received so great blessings from the
hand of the Lord—having a knowledge of
the creation of the Earth, and all men,
knowing the great and marvelous works
of the Lord from the creation of the world;
having power given them to do all things
by faith; having all the commandments
from the beginning, and having been
brought by his infinite goodness into this
precious land of promise—behold, I say, if
the day shall come that they will reject the
Holy One of Israel, the true Messiah, their
Redeemer and their God, behold, the
judgments of him that is just shall rest
upon them.
12 Yea, as one generation passeth to
another there shall be bloodsheds, and
great visitations among them; wherefore,
my sons, I would that ye would remem-
ber; yea, I would that ye would hearken
unto my words.

ALMA 9

Alma the Younger 82 BC

18 But behold, I say unto you that if ye
persist in your wickedness that your days
shall not be prolonged in the land, for the
Lamanites shall be sent upon you; and if
ye repent not they shall come in a time
when you know not, and ye shall be
visited with utter destruction; and it shall
be according to the fierce anger of the
Lord.
19 For he will not suffer you that ye shall
live in your iniquities, to destroy his
people. I say unto you, Nay; he would
rather suffer that the Lamanites might
destroy all his people who are called the
people of Nephi, if it were possible that
they could fall into sins and trans-
gressions, after having had so much light
and so much knowledge given unto them
of the Lord their God;
20 Yea, after having been such a highly
favored people of the Lord; yea, after
having been favored above every other
nation, kindred, tongue, or people; after
having had all things made known unto
them, according to their desires, and their
faith, and prayers, of that which has been,
and which is, and which is to come;
21 Having been visited by the Spirit of
God; having conversed with angels, and
having been spoken unto by the voice of
the Lord; and having the spirit of
prophecy, and the spirit of revelation, and
also many gifts, the gift of speaking with
tongues, and the gift of preaching, and the
gift of the Holy Ghost, and the gift of
translation;
22 Yea, and after having been delivered of
God out of the land of Jerusalem, by the
hand of the Lord; having been saved from
famine, and from sickness, and all manner
of diseases of every kind; and they having
waxed strong in battle, that they might
not be destroyed; having been brought out
of bondage time after time, and having
been kept and preserved until now; and
they have been prospered until they are
rich in all manner of things—
23 And now behold I say unto you, that if
this people, who have received so many
blessings from the hand of the Lord,
should transgress contrary to the light and
knowledge which they do have, I say unto
you that if this be the case, that if they
should fall into transgression, it would be
far more tolerable for the Lamanites than
for them.
24 For behold, the promises of the Lord
are extended to the Lamanites, but they
are not unto you if ye transgress; for has
not the Lord expressly promised and
firmly decreed, that if ye will rebel against

War Scene, from a vase depicting warfare between two Maya forces.

him that ye shall utterly be destroyed from off the face of the Earth?

ALMA 45

Helaman, Son of Alma *73 BC*

9 But behold, I have somewhat to prophesy unto thee; but what I prophesy unto thee ye shall not make known; yea, what I prophesy unto thee shall not be made known, even until the prophecy is fulfilled; therefore write the words which I shall say.

10 And these are the words: Behold, I perceive that this very people, the Nephites, according to the spirit of revelation which is in me, in four hundred years from the time that Jesus Christ shall manifest himself unto them, shall dwindle in unbelief.

11 Yea, and then shall they see wars and pestilences, yea, famines and bloodshed, even until the people of Nephi shall become extinct—

12 Yea, and this because they shall dwindle in unbelief and fall into the works of darkness, and lasciviousness, and all manner of iniquities; yea, I say unto you, that because they shall sin against so great light and knowledge, yea, I say unto you, that from that day, even the fourth generation shall not all pass away before this great iniquity shall come.

13 And when that great day cometh, behold, the time very soon cometh that those who are now, or the seed of those who are now numbered among the people of Nephi, shall no more be numbered among the people of Nephi.

14 But whosoever remaineth, and is not destroyed in that great and dreadful day, shall be numbered among the Lamanites, and shall become like unto them, all, save it be a few who shall be called the disciples of the Lord; and them shall the Lamanites pursue even until they shall become extinct. And now, because of iniquity, this prophecy shall be fulfilled.

HELAMAN 13

Samuel the Lamanite *6 BC*

5 And he said unto them: Behold, I, Samuel, a Lamanite, do speak the words of the Lord which he doth put into my heart; and behold he hath put it into my heart to say unto this people that the sword of justice hangeth over this people; and four hundred years pass not away save the sword of justice falleth upon this people.

6 Yea, heavy destruction awaiteth this people, and it surely cometh unto this people, and nothing can save this people save it be repentance and faith on the Lord Jesus Christ, who surely shall come into the world, and shall suffer many things and shall be slain for his people.

7 And behold, an angel of the Lord hath declared it unto me, and he did bring glad tidings to my soul. And behold, I was sent unto you to declare it unto you also, that ye might have glad tidings; but behold ye would not receive me.

8 Therefore, thus saith the Lord: Because of the hardness of the hearts of the people of the Nephites, except they repent I will take away my word from them, and I will withdraw my Spirit from them, and I will

suffer them no longer, and I will turn the
hearts of their brethren against them.
9 And four hundred years shall not pass
away before I will cause that they shall be
smitten; yea, I will visit them with the
sword and with famine and with
pestilence.
10 Yea, I will visit them in my fierce
anger, and there shall be those of the
fourth generation who shall live, of your
enemies, to behold your utter destruction;
and this shall surely come except ye
repent, saith the Lord; and those of the
fourth generation shall visit your
destruction.
11 But if ye will repent and return unto
the Lord your God I will turn away mine
anger, saith the Lord; yea, thus saith the
Lord, blessed are they who will repent and
turn unto me, but wo unto him that
repenteth not.
12 Yea, wo unto this great city of
Zarahemla; for behold, it is because of
those who are righteous that it is saved;
yea, wo unto this great city, for I perceive,
saith the Lord, that there are many, yea,
even the more part of this great city, that
will harden their hearts against me, saith
the Lord.
13 But blessed are they who will repent,
for them will I spare. But behold, if it were
not for the righteous who are in this great
city, behold, I would cause that fire should
come down out of heaven and destroy it.
14 But behold, it is for the righteous' sake
that it is spared. But behold, the time
cometh, saith the Lord, that when ye shall
cast out the righteous from among you,
then shall ye be ripe for destruction; yea,
wo be unto this great city, because of the
wickedness and abominations which are
in her.
15 Yea, and wo be unto the city of Gideon,
for the wickedness and abominations
which are in her.
16 Yea, and wo be unto all the cities which
are in the land round about, which are
possessed by the Nephites, because of the
wickedness and abominations which are
in them.
17 And behold, a curse shall come upon
the land, saith the Lord of Hosts, because
of the people's sake who are upon the
land, yea, because of their wickedness and
their abominations.
18 And it shall come to pass, saith the Lord
of Hosts, yea, our great and true God, that
whoso shall hide up treasures in the Earth
shall find them again no more, because of
the great curse of the land, save he be a
righteous man and shall hide it up unto
the Lord.
19 For I will, saith the Lord, that they shall
hide up their treasures unto me; and
cursed be they who hide not up their
treasures unto me; for none hideth up
their treasures unto me save it be the
righteous; and he that hideth not up his
treasures unto me, cursed is he, and also
the treasure, and none shall redeem it
because of the curse of the land.
20 And the day shall come that they shall
hide up their treasures, because they have
set their hearts upon riches; and because
they have set their hearts upon their
riches, and will hide up their treasures
when they shall flee before their enemies;
because they will not hide them up unto
me, cursed be they and also their
treasures; and in that day shall they be
smitten, saith the Lord.
21 Behold ye, the people of this great city,
and hearken unto my words; yea, hearken
unto the words which the Lord saith; for
behold, he saith that ye are cursed because
of your riches, and also are your riches
cursed because ye have set your hearts
upon them, and have not hearkened unto
the words of him who gave them unto
you.
22 Ye do not remember the Lord your God
in the things with which he hath blessed
you, but ye do always remember your
riches, not to thank the Lord your God for
them; yea, your hearts are not drawn out
unto the Lord, but they do swell with
great pride, unto boasting, and unto great
swelling, envyings, strifes, malice, per-
secutions, and murders, and all manner of
iniquities.
23 For this cause hath the Lord God
caused that a curse should come upon the
land, and also upon your riches, and this
because of your iniquities.
24 Yea, wo unto this people, because of
this time which has arrived, that ye do cast
out the prophets, and do mock them, and
cast stones at them, and do slay them, and
do all manner of iniquity unto them, even
as they did of old time.

25 And now when ye talk, ye say: If our days had been in the days of our fathers of old, we would not have slain the prophets; we would not have stoned them, and cast them out.

26 Behold ye are worse than they; for as the Lord liveth, if a prophet come among you and declareth unto you the word of the Lord, which testifieth of your sins and iniquities, ye are angry with him, and cast him out and seek all manner of ways to destroy him; yea, you will say that he is a false prophet, and that he is a sinner, and of the devil, because he testifieth that your deeds are evil.

27 But behold, if a man shall come among you and shall say: Do this, and there is no iniquity; do that and ye shall not suffer; yea, he will say: Walk after the pride of your own hearts; yea, walk after the pride of your eyes, and do whatsoever your heart desireth—and if a man shall come among you and say this, ye will receive him, and say that he is a prophet.

28 Yea, ye will lift him up, and ye will give unto him of your substance; ye will give unto him of your gold, and of your silver, and ye will clothe him with costly apparel; and because he speaketh flattering words unto you, and he saith that all is well, then ye will not find fault with him.

29 O ye wicked and ye perverse generation; ye hardened and ye stiffnecked people, how long will ye suppose that the Lord will suffer you? Yea, how long will ye suffer yourselves to be led by foolish and blind guides? Yea, how long will ye choose darkness rather than light?

30 Yea, behold, the anger of the Lord is already kindled against you; behold, he hath cursed the land because of your iniquity.

31 And behold, the time cometh that he curseth your riches, that they become slippery, that ye cannot hold them; and in the days of your poverty ye cannot retain them.

32 And in the days of your poverty ye shall cry unto the Lord; and in vain shall ye cry, for your desolation is already come upon you, and your destruction is made sure; and then shall ye weep and howl in that day, saith the Lord of Hosts. And then shall ye lament, and say:

33 O that I had repented, and had not killed the prophets, and stoned them, and cast them out. Yea, in that day ye shall say: O that we had remembered the Lord our God in the day that he gave us our riches, and then they would not have become slippery that we should lose them; for behold, our riches are gone from us.

34 Behold, we lay a tool here and on the morrow it is gone; and behold, our swords are taken from us in the day we have sought them for battle.

35 Yea, we have hid up our treasures and they have slipped away from us, because of the curse of the land.

36 O that we had repented in the day that the word of the Lord came unto us; for behold the land is cursed, and all things are become slippery, and we cannot hold them.

37 Behold, we are surrounded by demons, yea, we are encircled about by the angels of him who hath sought to destroy our souls. Behold, our iniquities are great. O Lord, canst thou not turn away thine anger from us? And this shall be your language in those days.

38 But behold, your days of probation are past; ye have procrastinated the day of your salvation until it is everlastingly too late, and your destruction is made sure; yea, for ye have sought all the days of your lives for that which ye could not obtain; and ye have sought for happiness in doing iniquity, which thing is contrary to the nature of that righteousness which is in our great and Eternal Head.

39 O ye people of the land, that ye would hear my words! And I pray that the anger of the Lord be turned away from you, and that ye would repent and be saved.

HELAMAN 15

Samuel the Lamanite — 6 BC

1 And now, my beloved brethren, behold, I declare unto you that except ye shall repent your houses shall be left unto you desolate.

2 Yea, except ye repent, your women shall have great cause to mourn in the day that they shall give suck; for ye shall attempt to flee and there shall be no place for refuge; yea, and wo unto them which are with child, for they shall be heavy and cannot flee; therefore, they shall be trodden down and shall be left to perish.

17 And now behold, saith the Lord, concerning the people of the Nephites: If

they will not repent, and observe to do my will, I will utterly destroy them, saith the Lord, because of their unbelief notwithstanding the many mighty works which I have done among them; and as surely as the Lord liveth shall these things be, saith the Lord.

3 NEPHI 27

Jesus Christ — *34 AD*

32 But behold, it sorroweth me because of the fourth generation from this generation, for they are led away captive by him even as was the son of perdition; for they will sell me for silver and for gold, and for that which moth doth corrupt and which thieves can break through and steal. And in that day will I visit them, even in turning their works upon their own heads.

1 NEPHI 12

Nephi, Son of Lehi — *595 BC*

14 And the angel said unto me: Behold thy seed, and also the seed of thy brethren.
15 And it came to pass that I looked and beheld the people of my seed gathered together in multitudes against the seed of my brethren; and they were gathered together to battle.
16 And the angel spake unto me, saying: Behold the fountain of filthy water which thy father saw; yea, even the river of which he spake; and the depths thereof are the depths of hell.
17 And the mists of darkness are the temptations of the devil, which blindeth the eyes, and hardeneth the hearts of the children of men, and leadeth them away into broad roads, that they perish and are lost.
18 And the large and spacious building, which thy father saw, is vain imaginations and the pride of the children of men. And a great and a terrible gulf divideth them; yea, even the word of the justice of the Eternal God, and the Messiah who is the Lamb of God, of whom the Holy Ghost beareth record, from the beginning of the world until this time, and from this time henceforth and forever.
19 And while the angel spake these words, I beheld and saw that the seed of my brethren did contend against my seed, according to the word of the angel; and because of the pride of my seed, and the temptations of the devil, I beheld that the seed of my brethren did overpower the people of my seed.
20 And it came to pass that I beheld, and saw the people of the seed of my brethren that they had overcome my seed; and they went forth in multitudes upon the face of the land.
21 And I saw them gathered together in multitudes; and I saw wars and rumors of wars among them; and in wars and rumors of wars I saw many generations pass away.
22 And the angel said unto me: Behold these shall dwindle in unbelief.
23 And it came to pass that I beheld, after they had dwindled in unbelief they became a dark, and loathsome, and a filthy people, full of idleness and all manner of abominations.

MORMON 5

Mormon — *380 AD*

15 ...for this people shall be scattered, and shall become a dark, a filthy, and a loathsome people, beyond the description of that whichever hath been amongst us, yea, even that which hath been among the Lamanites, and this because of their unbelief and idolatry.
16 For behold, the Spirit of the Lord hath already ceased to strive with their fathers; and they are without Christ and God in the world; and they are driven about as chaff before the wind.
17 They were once a delightsome people, and they had Christ for their shepherd; yea, they were led even by God the Father.
18 But now, behold, they are led about by Satan, even as chaff is driven before the wind, or as a vessel is tossed about upon the waves, without sail or anchor, or without anything wherewith to steer her; and even as she is, so are they.

1 NEPHI 22

Nephi, Son of Lehi — *580 BC*

1 And now it came to pass that after I, Nephi, had read these things which were engraven upon the plates of brass, my brethren came unto me and said unto me: What meaneth these things which ye have read? Behold, are they to be understood according to things which are spiritual, which shall come to pass according to the spirit and not the flesh?

2 And I, Nephi, said unto them: Behold
they were manifest unto the prophet by
the voice of the Spirit; for by the Spirit are
all things made known unto the prophets,
which shall come upon the children of
men according to the flesh.
3 Wherefore, the things of which I have
read are things pertaining to things both
temporal and spiritual; for it appears that
the house of Israel, sooner or later, will be
scattered upon all the face of the Earth,
and also among all nations.
4 And behold, there are many who are
already lost from the knowledge of those
who are at Jerusalem. Yea, the more part
of all the tribes have been led away; and
they are scattered to and fro upon the isles
of the sea; and whither they are none of us
knoweth, save that we know that they
have been led away.
5 And since they have been led away,
these things have been prophesied con-
cerning them, and also concerning all
those who shall hereafter be scattered and
be confounded, because of the Holy One
of Israel; for against him will they harden
their hearts; wherefore, they shall be
scattered among all nations and shall be
hated of all men.

Mayan Ruins, Yucatan; by Robert Scott Duncanson, 1848.

18

THE GREAT APOSTASY

+++

A worldwide Apostasy from the truths of the gospel of Jesus Christ resulted in a long period of darkness where Satan ruled the Earth. The church is described as having fled into the wilderness. This was a period without priesthood leadership, without an organized church, without saving ordinances, without revelation, nor gifts of the spirit that come after baptism. How long would this Apostasy last? Daniel and John described it as lasting 42 months, 1,260 days, or as a time, times, and a dividing of time. Forty-two months equals 1,260 days in the 30 day Jewish calendar. And "a time, times, and half a time" equals 1+2+.5 = 3.5. If 360 days are in a Jewish calendar year, then 3.5 x 360 equals 1,260 days. Joseph Smith interpreted the word "days" to mean "years". A possible interpretation could place this period of Apostasy from the demise of the Nephite civilization in around 360 AD to the arrival of the Mayflower pilgrims in America in 1620. Whatever the case, this Apostasy was to last a long time, at least 1,260 years, and span the Dark Ages and Medieval period in world history.

AMOS 8

Amos — *792 BC*

11 Behold, the days come, saith the Lord GOD, that I will send a famine in the land, not a famine of bread, nor a thirst for water, but of hearing the words of the LORD:
12 And they shall wander from sea to sea, and from the north even to the east, they shall run to and fro to seek the word of the LORD, and shall not find it.

PSALM 14

David — *1000 BC*

1 The fool hath said in his heart, *There is no man that has seen God. Because he showeth himself not unto us, therefore* there is no God. *Behold,* they are corrupt, they have done abominable works, *and none of them* doeth good.
2 The Lord looked down from heaven upon the children of men, *and by his voice said unto his servant, Seek ye among the children of men,* to see if there *are* any that *do* understand God. *And he opened his mouth unto the Lord, and said, Behold, all these who say they are thine.*
3 *The Lord answered and said,* They are all gone aside, they are together become filthy, *thou canst behold* none of them that *are doing good,* no, not one.
4 *All they have for their teachers are* workers of iniquity, *and there is* no knowledge *in them. They are they* who eat up my people. They eat bread and call not upon the Lord.
5 They *are* in great fear, for God *dwells* in the generation of the righteous. *He is the counsel of the poor, because they are ashamed of the wicked, and flee unto the Lord, for their refuge.*
6 *They are ashamed of* the counsel of the poor because the Lord is his refuge.
7 Oh that *Zion were established out of heaven,* the salvation of Israel. *O Lord, when wilt thou establish Zion?* When the Lord bringeth back the captivity of his people, Jacob shall rejoice, Israel shall be glad. [JST]

ISAIAH 29

Isaiah — *740 BC*

10 For the LORD hath poured out upon you the spirit of deep sleep, and hath closed your eyes: the prophets and your rulers, the seers hath he covered.

Hosea likens the House of Israel's relationship to God like a marriage; the House of Israel has been adulterous in worshipping other Gods or has worshipped none at all.

HOSEA 2

Hosea *790 BC*

1 Say ye unto your brethren, Ammi; and to your sisters, Ruhamah.
2 Plead with your mother, plead: for she is not my wife, neither am I her husband: let her therefore put away her whoredoms out of her sight, and her adulteries from between her breasts;
3 Lest I strip her naked, and set her as in the day that she was born, and make her as a wilderness, and set her like a dry land, and slay her with thirst.
4 And I will not have mercy upon her children; for they be the children of whoredoms.
5 For their mother hath played the harlot: she that conceived them hath done shamefully: for she said, I will go after my lovers, that give me my bread and my water, my wool and my flax, mine oil and my drink.
6 Therefore, behold, I will hedge up thy way with thorns, and make a wall, that she shall not find her paths.
7 And she shall follow after her lovers, but she shall not overtake them; and she shall seek them, but shall not find them: then shall she say, I will go and return to my first husband; for then was it better with me than now.

Parable of the Olive Tree

The House of Israel has become apostate in every part of the world. The original church, including the "adopted in" Gentiles, is the only group on Earth with a recognizable belief in Jesus Christ. Every other Christian group on Earth has become either corrupt or, in the case of the Nephites, has "withered away and died."

JACOB 5

Zenos *~700-800 BC*

29 And it came to pass that a long time had passed away, and the Lord of the vineyard said unto his servant: Come, let us go down into the vineyard, that we may labor again in the vineyard. For behold, the time draweth near, and the end soon cometh; wherefore, I must lay up fruit against the season, unto mine own self.
30 And it came to pass that the Lord of the vineyard and the servant went down into the vineyard; and they came to the tree whose natural branches had been broken off, and the wild branches had been grafted in; and behold all sorts of fruit did cumber the tree.
31 And it came to pass that the Lord of the vineyard did taste of the fruit, every sort according to its number. And the Lord of the vineyard said: Behold, this long time have we nourished this tree, and I have laid up unto myself against the season much fruit.
32 But behold, this time it hath brought forth much fruit, and there is none of it which is good. And behold, there are all kinds of bad fruit; and it profiteth me nothing, notwithstanding all our labor; and now it grieveth me that I should lose this tree.
33 And the Lord of the vineyard said unto the servant: What shall we do unto the tree, that I may preserve again good fruit thereof unto mine own self?
34 And the servant said unto his master: Behold, because thou didst graft in the branches of the wild olive tree they have nourished the roots, that they are alive and they have not perished; wherefore thou beholdest that they are yet good.
35 And it came to pass that the Lord of the vineyard said unto his servant: The tree profiteth me nothing, and the roots thereof profit me nothing so long as it shall bring forth evil fruit.
36 Nevertheless, I know that the roots are good, and for mine own purpose I have preserved them; and because of their much strength they have hitherto brought forth, from the wild branches, good fruit.
37 But behold, the wild branches have grown and have overrun the roots thereof; and because that the wild branches have overcome the roots thereof it hath brought forth much evil fruit; and because that it hath brought forth so much evil fruit thou beholdest that it beginneth to perish; and it will soon become ripened, that it may be cast into the fire, except we should do something for it to preserve it.
38 And it came to pass that the Lord of the vineyard said unto his servant: Let us go down into the nethermost parts of the vineyard, and behold if the natural branches have also brought forth evil fruit.

39 And it came to pass that they went down into the nethermost parts of the vineyard. And it came to pass that they beheld that the fruit of the natural branches had become corrupt also; yea, the first and the second and also the last; and they had all become corrupt.
40 And the wild fruit of the last had overcome that part of the tree which brought forth good fruit, even that the branch had withered away and died.
41 And it came to pass that the Lord of the vineyard wept, and said unto the servant: What could I have done more for my vineyard?
42 Behold, I knew that all the fruit of the vineyard, save it were these, had become corrupted. And now these which have once brought forth good fruit have also become corrupted; and now all the trees of my vineyard are good for nothing save it be to be hewn down and cast into the fire.
43 And behold this last, whose branch hath withered away, I did plant in a good spot of ground; yea, even that which was choice unto me above all other parts of the land of my vineyard.
44 And thou beheldest that I also cut down that which cumbered this spot of ground, that I might plant this tree in the stead thereof.
45 And thou beheldest that a part thereof brought forth good fruit, and a part thereof brought forth wild fruit; and because I plucked not the branches thereof and cast them into the fire, behold, they have overcome the good branch that it hath withered away.
46 And now, behold, notwithstanding all the care which we have taken of my vineyard, the trees thereof have become corrupted, that they bring forth no good fruit; and these I had hoped to preserve, to have laid up fruit thereof against the season, unto mine own self. But, behold, they have become like unto the wild olive tree, and they are of no worth but to be hewn down and cast into the fire; and it grieveth me that I should lose them.
47 But what could I have done more in my vineyard? Have I slackened mine hand, that I have not nourished it? Nay, I have nourished it, and I have digged about it, and I have pruned it, and I have dunged it; and I have stretched forth mine hand almost all the day long, and the end draweth nigh. And it grieveth me that I should hew down all the trees of my vineyard and cast them into the fire that they should be burned. Who is it that has corrupted my vineyard?
48 And it came to pass that the servant said unto his master: Is it not the loftiness of thy vineyard—have not the branches thereof overcome the roots which are good? And because the branches have overcome the roots thereof, behold they grew faster than the strength of the roots, taking strength unto themselves. Behold, I say, is not this the cause that the trees of thy vineyard have become corrupted?
49 And it came to pass that the Lord of the vineyard said unto the servant: Let us go to and hew down the trees of the vineyard and cast them into the fire, that they shall not cumber the ground of my vineyard, for I have done all. What could I have done more for my vineyard?
50 But, behold, the servant said unto the Lord of the vineyard: Spare it a little longer.
51 And the Lord said: Yea, I will spare it a little longer, for it grieveth me that I should lose the trees of my vineyard.

The changes made to the ordinance of baptism highlight the apostate nature of the Church after the loss of the Apostles. By 200 AD church leaders in both the Roman Empire and in ancient America would corrupt this sacred ordinance by introducing the baptism of infants. The prophet Mormon warned his son about this misguided and wicked practice.

MORONI 8

Mormon *370 BC*

4 And now, my son, I speak unto you concerning that which grieveth me exceedingly; for it grieveth me that there should disputations rise among you.
5 For, if I have learned the truth, there have been disputations among you concerning the baptism of your little children.
6 And now, my son, I desire that ye should labor diligently, that this gross error should be removed from among you; for, for this intent I have written this epistle.
7 For immediately after I had learned these things of you I inquired of the Lord

The Baptism, by Pietro Longhi, 1755.

concerning the matter. And the word of
the Lord came to me by the power of the
Holy Ghost, saying:
8 Listen to the words of Christ, your
Redeemer, your Lord and your God.
Behold, I came into the world not to call
the righteous but sinners to repentance;
the whole need no physician, but they
that are sick; wherefore, little children are
whole, for they are not capable of com-
mitting sin; wherefore the curse of Adam
is taken from them in me, that it hath no
power over them; and the law of circum-
cision is done away in me.
9 And after this manner did the Holy
Ghost manifest the word of God unto me;
wherefore, my beloved son, I know that it
is solemn mockery before God, that ye
should baptize little children.
10 Behold I say unto you that this thing
shall ye teach—repentance and baptism
unto those who are accountable and
capable of committing sin; yea, teach
parents that they must repent and be
baptized, and humble themselves as their
little children, and they shall all be saved
with their little children.
11 And their little children need no
repentance, neither baptism. Behold, bap-
tism is unto repentance to the fulfilling
the commandments unto the remission of
sins.
12 But little children are alive in Christ,
even from the foundation of the world; if
not so, God is a partial God, and also a
changeable God, and a respecter to
persons; for how many little children have
died without baptism!

13 Wherefore, if little children could not be saved without baptism, these must have gone to an endless hell.

14 Behold I say unto you, that he that supposeth that little children need baptism is in the gall of bitterness and in the bonds of iniquity; for he hath neither faith, hope, nor charity; wherefore, should he be cut off while in the thought, he must go down to hell.

15 For awful is the wickedness to suppose that God saveth one child because of baptism, and the other must perish because he hath no baptism.

16 Wo be unto them that shall pervert the ways of the Lord after this manner, for they shall perish except they repent. Behold, I speak with boldness, having authority from God; and I fear not what man can do; for perfect love casteth out all fear.

17 And I am filled with charity, which is everlasting love; wherefore, all children are alike unto me; wherefore, I love little children with a perfect love; and they are all alike and partakers of salvation.

18 For I know that God is not a partial God, neither a changeable being; but he is unchangeable from all eternity to all eternity.

19 Little children cannot repent; wherefore, it is awful wickedness to deny the pure mercies of God unto them, for they are all alive in him because of his mercy.

20 And he that saith that little children need baptism denieth the mercies of Christ, and setteth at naught the atonement of him and the power of his redemption.

21 Wo unto such, for they are in danger of death, hell, and an endless torment. I speak it boldly; God hath commanded me. Listen unto them and give heed, or they stand against you at the judgment-seat of Christ.

22 For behold that all little children are alive in Christ, and also all they that are without the law. For the power of redemption cometh on all them that have no law; wherefore, he that is not condemned, or he that is under no condemnation, cannot repent; and unto such baptism availeth nothing—

23 But it is mockery before God, denying the mercies of Christ, and the power of his Holy Spirit, and putting trust in dead works.

24 Behold, my son, this thing ought not to be; for repentance is unto them that are under condemnation and under the curse of a broken law.

25 And the first fruits of repentance is baptism; and baptism cometh by faith unto the fulfilling the commandments; and the fulfilling the commandments bringeth remission of sins;

26 And the remission of sins bringeth meekness, and lowliness of heart; and because of meekness and lowliness of heart cometh the visitation of the Holy Ghost, which Comforter filleth with hope and perfect love, which love endureth by diligence unto prayer, until the end shall come, when all the saints shall dwell with God.

2 NEPHI 15 (see also ISAIAH 5)

Isaiah *740 BC*

1 And then will I sing to my well-beloved a song of my beloved, touching his vineyard. My well-beloved hath a vineyard in a very fruitful hill.

2 And he fenced it, and gathered out the stones thereof, and planted it with the choicest vine, and built a tower in the midst of it, and also made a wine-press therein; and he looked that it should bring forth grapes, and it brought forth wild grapes.

3 And now, O inhabitants of Jerusalem, and men of Judah, judge, I pray you, betwixt me and my vineyard.

4 What could have been done more to my vineyard that I have not done in it? Wherefore, when I looked that it should bring forth grapes it brought forth wild grapes.

5 And now go to; I will tell you what I will do to my vineyard—I will take away the hedge thereof, and it shall be eaten up; and I will break down the wall thereof, and it shall be trodden down;

6 And I will lay it waste; it shall not be pruned nor digged; but there shall come up briers and thorns; I will also command the clouds that they rain no rain upon it.

7 For the vineyard of the Lord of Hosts is the house of Israel, and the men of Judah his pleasant plant; and he looked for judgment, and behold, oppression; for righteousness, but behold, a cry.

8 Wo unto them that join house to house,
till there can be no place, that they may be
placed alone in the midst of the Earth!
9 In mine ears, said the Lord of Hosts, of a
truth many houses shall be desolate, and
great and fair cities without inhabitant.
10 Yea, ten acres of vineyard shall yield
one bath, and the seed of a homer shall
yield an ephah.
11 Wo unto them that rise up early in the
morning, that they may follow strong
drink, that continue until night, and wine
inflame them!
12 And the harp, and the viol, the tabret,
and pipe, and wine are in their feasts; but
they regard not the work of the Lord,
neither consider the operation of his
hands.
13 Therefore, my people are gone into
captivity, because they have no knowledge; and their honorable men are
famished, and their multitude dried up
with thirst.
14 Therefore, hell hath enlarged herself,
and opened her mouth without measure;
and their glory, and their multitude, and
their pomp, and he that rejoiceth, shall
descend into it.
15 And the mean man shall be brought
down, and the mighty man shall be
humbled, and the eyes of the lofty shall be
humbled.

HOSEA 3

Hosea — *790 BC*

4 For the children of Israel shall abide
many days without a king, and without a
prince, and without a sacrifice, and without an image, and without an ephod, and
without teraphim:

2 NEPHI 16 (see also ISAIAH 6)

Isaiah — *740 BC*

11 Then said I: Lord, how long? And he
said: Until the cities be wasted without
inhabitant, and the houses without man,
and the land be utterly desolate;
12 And the Lord have removed men far
away, for there shall be a great forsaking
in the midst of the land.

DOCTRINE AND COVENANTS 86

Joseph Smith — *December 1832*

1 Verily, thus saith the Lord unto you my
servants, concerning the parable of the
wheat and of the tares:
2 Behold, verily I say, the field was the
world, and the apostles were the sowers of
the seed;
3 And after they have fallen asleep the
great persecutor of the church, the
apostate, the whore, even Babylon, that
maketh all nations to drink of her cup, in
whose hearts the enemy, even Satan,
sitteth to reign—behold he soweth the
tares; wherefore, the tares choke the
wheat and drive the church into the
wilderness.

REVELATION 12

John — *95 AD*

13 *For* when the dragon saw that he was
cast unto the Earth, he persecuted the
woman which brought forth the man
child.
5 And the woman fled into the wilderness,
where she *had* a place prepared of God,
that they should feed her there a thousand
two hundred and threescore *years*.
14 *Therefore*, to the woman were given
two wings of a great eagle, that she might
flee into the wilderness, into her place,
where she is nourished for a time, and
times, and half a time, from the face of the
serpent.
15 And the serpent casteth out of his
mouth water as a flood after the woman,
that he might cause her to be carried away
of the flood.
16 And the Earth *helpeth* the woman, and
the Earth *openeth* her mouth, and
swalloweth up the flood which the dragon
casteth out of his mouth.
17 *Therefore*, the dragon was wroth with
the woman, and went to make war with
the remnant of her seed, which keep the
commandments of God, and have the
testimony of Jesus Christ. [JST]

DANIEL 12

Daniel — *600 BC*

5 Then I Daniel looked, and behold, there
stood other two, the one on this side of the
bank of the river, and the other on that
side of the bank of the river.
6 And one said to the man clothed in
linen, which was upon the waters of the
river, How long shall it be to the end of
these wonders?
7 And I heard the man clothed in linen,
which was upon the waters of the river,
when he held up his right hand and his

left hand unto heaven, and sware by him that liveth for ever that it shall be for a time, times, and an half; and when he shall have accomplished to scatter the power of the holy people, all these things shall be finished.
8 And I heard, but I understood not: then said I, O my Lord, what shall be the end of these things?
9 And he said, Go thy way, Daniel: for the words are closed up and sealed till the time of the end.
10 Many shall be purified, and made white, and tried; but the wicked shall do wickedly: and none of the wicked shall understand; but the wise shall understand.
11 And from the time that the daily sacrifice shall be taken away, and the abomination that maketh desolate set up, there shall be a thousand two hundred and ninety days.
12 Blessed is he that waiteth, and cometh to the thousand three hundred and five and thirty days.
13 But go thou thy way till the end be: for thou shalt rest, and stand in thy lot at the end of the days.

DANIEL 7

Daniel *600 BC*

8 I considered the horns, and, behold, there came up among them another little horn, before whom there were three of the first horns plucked up by the roots: and, behold, in this horn were eyes like the eyes of man, and a mouth speaking great things.
20 And of the ten horns that were in his head, and of the other which came up, and before whom three fell; even of that horn that had eyes, and a mouth that spake very great things, whose look was more stout than his fellows.
24 And the ten horns out of this kingdom are ten kings that shall arise: and another shall rise after them; and he shall be diverse from the first, and he shall subdue three kings.
21 I beheld, and the same horn made war with the saints, and prevailed against them;
25 And he shall speak great words against the most High, and shall wear out the saints of the most High, and think to change times and laws: and they shall be given into his hand until a time and times and the dividing of time.

REVELATION 13

John *95 AD*

1 And I *saw another sign, in the likeness of the kingdoms of the Earth;* a beast rise up out of the sea, *and he stood upon the sand of the sea,* having seven heads and ten horns, and upon his horns ten crowns, and upon his heads the name of blasphemy. [JST]
2 And the beast which I saw was like unto a leopard, and his feet were as the feet of a bear, and his mouth as the mouth of a lion: and the dragon gave him his power, and his seat, and great authority.
3 And I saw one of his heads as it were wounded to death; and his deadly wound was healed: and all the world wondered after the beast.
4 And they worshipped the dragon which gave power unto the beast: and they worshipped the beast, saying, Who is like unto the beast? who is able to make war with him?
5 And there was given unto him a mouth speaking great things and blasphemies; and power was given unto him to continue forty and two months.
6 And he opened his mouth in blasphemy against God, to blaspheme his name, and his tabernacle, and them that dwell in heaven.
7 And it was given unto him to make war with the saints, and to overcome them: and power was given him over all kindreds, and tongues, and nations.
8 And all that dwell upon the Earth shall worship him, whose names are not written in the book of life of the Lamb slain from the foundation of the world.
9 If any man have an ear, let him hear.
10 He that leadeth into captivity shall go into captivity: he that killeth with the sword must be killed with the sword. Here is the patience and the faith of the saints.
11 And I beheld another beast coming up out of the Earth; and he had two horns like a lamb, and he spake as a dragon.
12 And he exerciseth all the power of the first beast before him, and causeth the Earth and them which dwell therein to worship the first beast, whose deadly wound was healed.

13 And he doeth great wonders, so that he maketh fire come down from heaven on the Earth in the sight of men,
14 And deceiveth them that dwell on the Earth by the means of those miracles which he had power to do in the sight of the beast; saying to them that dwell on the Earth, that they should make an image to the beast, which had the wound by a sword, and did live.
15 And he had power to give life unto the image of the beast, that the image of the beast should both speak, and cause that as many as would not worship the image of the beast should be killed.
16 And he causeth all, both small and great, rich and poor, free and bond, to receive a mark in their right hand, or in their foreheads:
17 And that no man might buy or sell, save he that had the mark, or the name of the beast, or the number of his name.
18 Here is wisdom. Let him that hath understanding count the number of the beast: for it is the number of a man; and his number is Six hundred threescore and six.

DANIEL 8

Daniel — *600 BC*

9 And out of one of them came forth a little horn, which waxed exceeding great, toward the south, and toward the east, and toward the pleasant land.
10 And it waxed great, even to the host of heaven; and it cast down some of the host and of the stars to the ground, and stamped upon them.
23 And in the latter-time of their kingdom, when the transgressors are come to the full, a king of fierce countenance, and understanding dark sentences, shall stand up.
24 And his power shall be mighty, but not by his own power: and he shall destroy wonderfully, and shall prosper, and practise, and shall destroy the mighty and the holy people.
25 And through his policy also he shall cause craft to prosper in his hand; and he shall magnify himself in his heart, and by peace shall destroy many: he shall also stand up against the Prince of princes; but he shall be broken without hand.

The Whore of Babylon, Woodcut by Lucas Cranach (1472-1553).

DEUTERONOMY 4

Moses *1635 BC*

23 Take heed unto yourselves, lest ye forget the covenant of the Lord your God, which he made with you, and make you a graven image, or the likeness of anything, which the Lord thy God hath forbidden thee.

24 For the Lord thy God is a consuming fire, even a jealous God.

25 When thou shalt beget children, and children's children, and ye shall have remained long in the land, and shall corrupt yourselves, and make a graven image, or the likeness of anything, and shall do evil in the sight of the Lord thy God, to provoke him to anger:

26 I call heaven and Earth to witness against you this day, that ye shall soon utterly perish from off the land whereunto ye go over Jordan to possess it; ye shall not prolong your days upon it, but shall utterly be destroyed.

27 And the Lord shall scatter you among the nations, and ye shall be left few in number among the heathen, whither the Lord shall lead you.

28 And there ye shall serve gods, the work of men's hands, wood and stone, which neither see, nor hear, nor eat, nor smell.

REVELATION 17

John *95 AD*

1 And there came one of the seven angels which had the seven vials, and talked with me, saying unto me, Come hither; I will shew unto thee the judgment of the great whore that sitteth upon many waters:

2 With whom the kings of the Earth have committed fornication, and the inhabitants of the Earth have been made drunk with the wine of her fornication.

3 So he carried me away in the spirit into the wilderness: and I saw a woman sit upon a scarlet-coloured beast, full of names of blasphemy, having seven heads and ten horns.

4 And the woman was arrayed in purple and scarlet colour, and decked with gold and precious stones and pearls, having a golden cup in her hand full of abominations and filthiness of her fornication:

5 And upon her forehead was a name written, MYSTERY, BABYLON THE GREAT, THE MOTHER OF HARLOTS AND ABOMINATIONS OF THE EARTH.

6 And I saw the woman drunken with the blood of the saints, and with the blood of the martyrs of Jesus: and when I saw her, I wondered with great admiration.

Part 3

PROPHECIES OF EVENTS FROM 1000 -2000 AD

19

EARTHQUAKE AND WICKEDNESS

+++

Prophecy of a tremendous earthquake at the opening of the sixth seal. On May 20, 1202, an estimated magnitude 7.6+ Earthquake hit the Dead Sea Transform in Syria reportedly killing as many as 1.1 million people. Wickedness continues to prevail in the nations and kingdoms of the Earth.

REVELATION 6

John 95 AD

12 And I beheld when he had opened the sixth seal, and, lo, there was a great earthquake; and the sun became black as sackcloth of hair, and the moon became as blood;
13 And the stars of heaven fell unto the Earth, even as a fig tree casteth her untimely figs, when she is shaken of a mighty wind.
14 And the *heavens opened* as a *scroll is opened* when it is rolled together; and every mountain, and island, *was* moved out of *its place*. [JST]
15 And the kings of the Earth, and the great men, and the rich men, and the chief captains, and the mighty men, and every bondman, and every free man, hid themselves in the dens and in the rocks of the mountains;
16 And said to the mountains and rocks, Fall on us, and hide us from the face of him that sitteth on the throne, and from the wrath of the Lamb:
17 For the great day of his wrath is come; and who shall be able to stand?

1 NEPHI 13

Nephi, Son of Lehi 595 BC

1 And it came to pass that the angel spake unto me, saying: Look! And I looked and beheld many nations and kingdoms.
2 And the angel said unto me: What beholdest thou? And I said: I behold many nations and kingdoms.
3 And he said unto me: These are the nations and kingdoms of the Gentiles.
4 And it came to pass that I saw among the nations of the Gentiles the formation of a great church.
5 And the angel said unto me: Behold the formation of a church which is most abominable above all other churches, which slayeth the saints of God, yea, and tortureth them and bindeth them down, and yoketh them with a yoke of iron, and bringeth them down into captivity.
6 And it came to pass that I beheld this great and abominable church; and I saw the devil that he was the founder of it.
7 And I also saw gold, and silver, and silks, and scarlets, and fine-twined linen, and all manner of precious clothing; and I saw many harlots.
8 And the angel spake unto me, saying: Behold the gold, and the silver, and the silks, and the scarlets, and the fine-twined linen, and the precious clothing, and the harlots, are the desires of this great and abominable church.
9 And also for the praise of the world do they destroy the saints of God, and bring them down into captivity.

2 NEPHI 27 (see also ISAIAH 29)

Isaiah 740 BC

1 But, behold, in the last days, or in the days of the Gentiles—yea, behold all the nations of the Gentiles and also the Jews, both those who shall come upon this land and those who shall be upon other lands, yea, even upon all the lands of the Earth, behold, they will be drunken with iniquity and all manner of abominations—
2 And when that day shall come they shall be visited of the Lord of Hosts, with thunder and with earthquake, and with a great noise, and with storm, and with tempest, and with the flame of devouring fire.
3 And all the nations that fight against Zion, and that distress her, shall be as a dream of a night vision; yea, it shall be

Taking of Jerusalem by the Crusaders, 15th July 1099; by Emile Signol, 1847.

unto them, even as unto a hungry man which dreameth, and behold he eateth but he awaketh and his soul is empty; or like unto a thirsty man which dreameth, and behold he drinketh but he awaketh and behold he is faint, and his soul hath appetite; yea, even so shall the multitude of all the nations be that fight against Mount Zion.
4 For behold, all ye that doeth iniquity, stay yourselves and wonder, for ye shall cry out, and cry; yea, ye shall be drunken but not with wine, ye shall stagger but not with strong drink.
5 For behold, the Lord hath poured out upon you the spirit of deep sleep. For behold, ye have closed your eyes, and ye have rejected the prophets; and your rulers, and the seers hath he covered because of your iniquity.

2 TIMOTHY 3

Paul *67 AD*

1 This know also, that in the last days perilous times shall come.
2 For men shall be lovers of their own selves, covetous, boasters, proud, blasphemers, disobedient to parents, unthankful, unholy,
3 Without natural affection, truce breakers, false accusers, incontinent, fierce, despisers of those that are good,
4 Traitors, heady, highminded, lovers of pleasures more than lovers of God;
5 Having a form of godliness, but denying the power thereof: from such turn away.
6 For of this sort are they which creep into houses, and lead captive silly women laden with sins, led away with divers lusts,
7 Ever learning, and never able to come to the knowledge of the truth.
8 Now as Jannes and Jambres withstood Moses, so do these also resist the truth: men of corrupt minds, reprobate concerning the faith.
13 But evil men and seducers shall wax worse and worse, deceiving, and being deceived.

20

GENTILE CHRISTIANS SPREAD THE GOSPEL TO THE WORLD

+++

Light begins to break through the darkness as the Renaissance, Reformation and the Age of Discovery begin to prepare the children of Adam for the eventual Restoration of the gospel in 1830.

Beginning around 1500 AD, Christopher Columbus and other European explorers, missionaries, and colonists would convert much of the world to Christianity. Nephi prophesies that these men would carry a book with them (the Bible). The Guttenberg Bible was printed in 1455 and was among the first books printed on the newly invented printing press. The widespread availability of books, notably the Bible, would trigger an explosion of missionary work worldwide.

Catholic missionaries (Jesuits, Dominicans, Franciscans) from Spain, Portugal and Italy preach the gospel to the "heathen" nations of the Earth and convert many, oftentimes by force.

As a consequence of their wickedness, it is prophesied that the native American peoples would be decimated and brutalized by their European conquerors.

Bishop Diego de Landa arrived in the Yucatan, Mexico in 1549 and earnestly began work in converting the Mayan people. The Mayans and many other American tribes found the story of Jesus Christ very similar to their God Quetzalcoatl and the Maize God. Scholars suggest that these three are all the same God.[2] *Although their outward manifestation of beliefs were nothing like Christianity, the "root" or foundation of Mayan beliefs, as mentioned in Zenos's parable, was still "good" and compatible with the Christian faith.*

Waves of missionaries from Protestant Christian countries in Europe and North America would spread the gospel message to the four corners of the Earth in the 1600s-1900s, gaining millions of converts.

David Brainerd, an early American missionary, led successful missions to the native Delaware, Susquehanna, and Stockbridge tribes in New York, New Jersey, and Massachusetts. Of this experience, he said in 1745, "They soon came in, one after another; with tears in their eyes, to know what they should do to be saved ... It was an amazing season of power among them, and seemed as if God had bowed the heavens and come down ... and that God was about to convert the whole world."[3]

Many of these missionaries would be murdered by the native populations they attempted to minister to. Their bravery and courage in spreading the gospel of Jesus Christ was remarkable. Like John the Baptist, these Christian missionaries fulfilled the prophecies, listed below, related to gathering the scattered remnants of the house of Israel. And in doing so, they converted them to a belief in Jesus Christ, thus preparing the way for the Restoration of the fulness of the gospel through the prophet Joseph Smith. The Lord does not forget his covenant people.

---

[2] Wirth, Diane E., *Quetzalcoatl, the Maya Maize God and Jesus Christ,* Journal of Book of Mormon Studies, 11/1 (2002): 4-15, 107

[3] Tucker, Ruth (2004) *From Jerusalem to Irian Jaya: A Biographical History of Christian Missions,* 55

DOCTRINE AND COVENANTS 77

Joseph Smith *March 1832*

14 Q. What are we to understand by the little book, which was eaten by John, as mentioned in the 10th chapter of Revelation?
A. We are to understand that it was a mission, and an ordinance, for him to gather the tribes of Israel; behold, this is Elias, who, as it is written, must come and restore all things.

REVELATION 10

John *95 AD*

8 And the voice which I heard from heaven spake unto me again, and said, Go and take the little book which is open in the hand of the angel which standeth upon the sea and upon the Earth.
9 And I went unto the angel, and said unto him, Give me the little book. And he said unto me, Take it, and eat it up; and it shall make thy belly bitter, but it shall be in thy mouth sweet as honey.
10 And I took the little book out of the angel's hand, and ate it up; and it was in my mouth sweet as honey: and as soon as I had eaten it, my belly was bitter.
11 And he said unto me, Thou must prophesy again before many peoples, and nations, and tongues, and kings.

JACOB 5

Zenos *~700-800 BC*

52 Wherefore, let us take of the branches of these which I have planted in the nethermost parts of my vineyard, and let us graft them into the tree from whence they came; and let us pluck from the tree those branches whose fruit is most bitter, and graft in the natural branches of the tree in the stead thereof.
53 And this will I do that the tree may not perish, that, perhaps, I may preserve unto myself the roots thereof for mine own purpose.
54 And, behold, the roots of the natural branches of the tree which I planted whithersoever I would are yet alive; wherefore, that I may preserve them also for mine own purpose, I will take of the branches of this tree, and I will graft them in unto them. Yea, I will graft in unto them the branches of their mother tree, that I may preserve the roots also unto mine own self, that when they shall be sufficiently strong perhaps they may bring forth good fruit unto me, and I may yet have glory in the fruit of my vineyard.
55 And it came to pass that they took from the natural tree which had become wild, and grafted in unto the natural trees, which also had become wild.
56 And they also took of the natural trees which had become wild, and grafted into their mother tree.
57 And the Lord of the vineyard said unto the servant: Pluck not the wild branches from the trees, save it be those which are most bitter; and in them ye shall graft according to that which I have said.
58 And we will nourish again the trees of the vineyard, and we will trim up the branches thereof; and we will pluck from the trees those branches which are ripened, that must perish, and cast them into the fire.
59 And this I do that, perhaps, the roots thereof may take strength because of their goodness; and because of the change of the branches, that the good may overcome the evil.
60 And because that I have preserved the natural branches and the roots thereof, and that I have grafted in the natural branches again into their mother tree, and have preserved the roots of their mother tree, that, perhaps, the trees of my vineyard may bring forth again good fruit; and that I may have joy again in the fruit of my vineyard, and, perhaps, that I may rejoice exceedingly that I have preserved the roots and the branches of the first fruit—

MORMON 5

Mormon *384 AD*

20 But behold, it shall come to pass that they [Lamanites] shall be driven and scattered by the Gentiles…

DOCTRINE AND COVENANTS 45

Joseph Smith *March 1831*

24 And this I have told you concerning Jerusalem; and when that day shall come, shall a remnant be scattered among all nations;
25 But they shall be gathered again; but they shall remain until the times of the Gentiles be fulfilled.
26 And in that day shall be heard of wars and rumors of wars, and the whole Earth

shall be in commotion, and men's hearts shall fail them, and they shall say that Christ delayeth his coming until the end of the Earth.

27 And the love of men shall wax cold, and iniquity shall abound.

2 NEPHI 1

Lehi *580 BC*

11 Yea, he will bring other nations unto them [Lamanites], and he will give unto them [other nations] power, and he will take away from them [Lamanites] the lands of their possessions, and he will cause them [Lamanites] to be scattered and smitten.

1 NEPHI 13

Nephi, Son of Lehi *595 BC*

10 And it came to pass that I looked and beheld many waters; and they divided the Gentiles from the seed of my brethren.

11 And it came to pass that the angel said unto me: Behold the wrath of God is upon the seed of thy brethren.

12 And I looked and beheld a man among the Gentiles, who was separated from the seed of my brethren by the many waters; and I beheld the Spirit of God, that it came down and wrought upon the man; and he went forth upon the many waters, even unto the seed of my brethren, who were in the promised land.

Christopher Columbus, by Sebastiano del Piombo 1519.

13 And it came to pass that I beheld the Spirit of God, that it wrought upon other Gentiles; and they went forth out of captivity, upon the many waters.

14 And it came to pass that I beheld many multitudes of the Gentiles upon the land of promise; and I beheld the wrath of God, that it was upon the seed of my brethren; and they were scattered before the Gentiles and were smitten.

20 And it came to pass that I, Nephi, beheld that they [Gentiles] did prosper in the land; and I beheld a book, and it was carried forth among them.

21 And the angel said unto me: Knowest thou the meaning of the book?

22 And I said unto him: I know not.

23 And he said: Behold it proceedeth out of the mouth of a Jew. And I, Nephi, beheld it; and he said unto me: The book that thou beholdest is a record of the Jews, which contains the covenants of the Lord, which he hath made unto the house of Israel; and it also containeth many of the prophecies of the holy prophets; and it is a record like unto the engravings which are upon the plates of brass, save there are not so many; nevertheless, they contain the covenants of the Lord, which he hath made unto the house of Israel; wherefore, they are of great worth unto the Gentiles.

24 And the angel of the Lord said unto me: Thou hast beheld that the book proceeded forth from the mouth of a Jew; and when it proceeded forth from the mouth of a Jew it contained the fulness of the gospel of the Lord, of whom the twelve apostles bear record; and they bear record according to the truth which is in the Lamb of God.

25 Wherefore, these things go forth from the Jews in purity unto the Gentiles, according to the truth which is in God.

26 And after they go forth by the hand of the twelve apostles of the Lamb, from the Jews unto the Gentiles, thou seest the formation of that great and abominable church, which is most abominable above all other churches; for behold, they have taken away from the gospel of the Lamb many parts which are plain and most precious; and also many covenants of the Lord have they taken away.

John Wesley (1703-1791), founder of Methodism, preaching to native American Indians.

27 And all this have they done that they
might pervert the right ways of the Lord,
that they might blind the eyes and harden
the hearts of the children of men.
28 Wherefore, thou seest that after the
book hath gone forth through the hands
of the great and abominable church, that
there are many plain and precious things
taken away from the book, which is the
book of the Lamb of God.
29 And after these plain and precious
things were taken away it goeth forth
unto all the nations of the Gentiles; and
after it goeth forth unto all the nations of
the Gentiles, yea, even across the many
waters which thou hast seen with the
Gentiles which have gone forth out of
captivity, thou seest—because of the
many plain and precious things which
have been taken out of the book, which
were plain unto the understanding of the
children of men, according to the plain-
ness which is in the Lamb of God—
because of these things which are taken
away out of the gospel of the Lamb, an
exceedingly great many do stumble, yea,
insomuch that Satan hath great power
over them.

2 NEPHI 26

Nephi, Son of Lehi — *550 BC*

19 And it shall come to pass, that those
who have dwindled in unbelief shall be
smitten by the hand of the Gentiles.
20 And the Gentiles are lifted up in the
pride of their eyes, and have stumbled,
because of the greatness of their stumbling
block, that they have built up many
churches; nevertheless, they put down the
power and miracles of God, and preach up
unto themselves their own wisdom and
their own learning, that they may get gain
and grind upon the face of the poor.
21 And there are many churches built up
which cause envyings, and strifes, and
malice.

3 NEPHI 16

Jesus Christ — *34 AD*

8 But wo, saith the Father, unto the
unbelieving of the Gentiles—for notwith-
standing they have come forth upon the
face of this land, and have scattered my
people who are of the house of Israel; and
my people who are of the house of Israel
have been cast out from among them, and
have been trodden under feet by them;
9 And because of the mercies of the Father
unto the Gentiles, and also the judgments
of the Father upon my people who are of
the house of Israel, verily, verily, I say
unto you, that after all this, and I have
caused my people who are of the house of
Israel to be smitten, and to be afflicted,
and to be slain, and to be cast out from
among them, and to become hated by
them, and to become a hiss and a byword
among them—

1 NEPHI 19

Nephi, Son of Lehi *585 BC*

15 Nevertheless, when that day cometh, saith the prophet, that they no more turn aside their hearts against the Holy One of Israel, then will he remember the covenants which he made to their fathers.

16 Yea, then will he remember the aisles of the sea; yea, and all the people who are of the house of Israel, will I gather in, saith the Lord, according to the words of the prophet Zenos, from the four quarters of the Earth.

17 Yea, and all the Earth shall see the salvation of the Lord, saith the prophet; every nation, kindred, tongue and people shall be blessed.

18 And I, Nephi, have written these things unto my people, that perhaps I might persuade them that they would remember the Lord their Redeemer.

19 Wherefore, I speak unto all the house of Israel, if it so be that they should obtain these things.

1 NEPHI 21 (see also ISAIAH 49)

Isaiah *740 BC*

1 And again: Hearken, O ye house of Israel, all ye that are broken off and are driven out because of the wickedness of the pastors of my people; yea, all ye that are broken off, that are scattered abroad, who are of my people, O house of Israel. Listen, O isles, unto me, and hearken ye people from far; the Lord hath called me from the womb; from the bowels of my mother hath he made mention of my name.

5 And now, saith the Lord—that formed me from the womb that I should be his servant, to bring Jacob again to him—though Israel be not gathered, yet shall I be glorious in the eyes of the Lord, and my God shall be my strength.

6 And he said: It is a light thing that thou shouldst be my servant to raise up the tribes of Jacob, and to restore the preserved of Israel. I will also give thee for a light to the Gentiles, that thou mayest be my salvation unto the ends of the Earth.

7 Thus saith the Lord, the Redeemer of Israel, his Holy One, to him whom man despiseth, to him whom the nations abhorreth, to servant of rulers: Kings shall see and arise, princes also shall worship, because of the Lord that is faithful.

8 Thus saith the Lord: In an acceptable time have I heard thee, O isles of the sea, and in a day of salvation have I helped thee; and I will preserve thee, and give thee my servant for a covenant of the people, to establish the Earth, to cause to inherit the desolate heritages;

9 That thou mayest say to the prisoners: Go forth; to them that sit in darkness: Show yourselves. They shall feed in the ways, and their pastures shall be in all high places.

10 They shall not hunger nor thirst, neither shall the heat nor the sun smite them; for he that hath mercy on them shall lead them, even by the springs of water shall he guide them.

11 And I will make all my mountains a way, and my highways shall be exalted.

12 And then, O house of Israel, behold, these shall come from far; and lo, these from the north and from the west; and these from the land of Sinim.

13 Sing, O heavens; and be joyful, O Earth; for the feet of those who are in the east shall be established; and break forth into singing, O mountains; for they shall be smitten no more; for the Lord hath comforted his people, and will have mercy upon his afflicted.

14 But, behold, Zion hath said: The Lord hath forsaken me, and my Lord hath forgotten me—but he will show that he hath not.

15 For can a woman forget her sucking child, that she should not have compassion on the son of her womb? Yea, they may forget, yet will I not forget thee, O house of Israel.

16 Behold, I have graven thee upon the palms of my hands; thy walls are continually before me.

17 Thy children shall make haste against thy destroyers; and they that made thee waste shall go forth of thee.

18 Lift up thine eyes round about and behold; all these gather themselves together, and they shall come to thee. And as I live, saith the Lord, thou shalt surely clothe thee with them all, as with an ornament, and bind them on even as a bride.

21

THE UNITED STATES OF AMERICA

AN ENSIGN TO ALL NATIONS

Surrender of Lord Cornwallis at Yorktown, October 19, 1781, By John Trumbull 1820.

+++

Prophecies of the Revolutionary War and of the divinely inspired foundation of the United States of America, which becomes a beacon of freedom and hope to the scattered tribes of Israel. Millions of freedom-seeking Protestant and Catholic Christians are drawn to the United States seeking a better life. One way to bring the gospel to the world is to bring the world to the gospel...or to the country where the gospel would be restored.

1 NEPHI 13

Nephi, Son of Lehi *595 BC*

15 And I beheld the Spirit of the Lord, that
it was upon the Gentiles, and they did
prosper and obtain the land for their
inheritance; and I beheld that they were
white, and exceedingly fair and beautiful,
like unto my people before they were
slain.
16 And it came to pass that I, Nephi,
beheld that the Gentiles who had gone
forth out of captivity did humble them-
selves before the Lord; and the power of
the Lord was with them.
17 And I beheld that their mother Gen-
tiles were gathered together upon the
waters, and upon the land also, to battle
against them.
18 And I beheld that the power of God
was with them, and also that the wrath of
God was upon all those that were gathered
together against them to battle.
19 And I, Nephi, beheld that the Gentiles
that had gone out of captivity were
delivered by the power of God out of the
hands of all other nations.

3 NEPHI 16
Jesus Christ *34 AD*
6 And blessed are the Gentiles, because of their belief in me, in and of the Holy Ghost, which witnesses unto them of me and of the Father.

3 NEPHI 21
Jesus Christ *34 AD*
4 For it is wisdom in the Father that they should be established in this land, and be set up as a free people by the power of the Father, that these things [The Book of Mormon] might come forth from them unto a remnant of your seed, that the covenant of the Father may be fulfilled which he hath covenanted with his people, O house of Israel;

MORMON 5
Mormon *385 AD*
19 And behold, the Lord hath reserved their [Lamanites] blessings, which they might have received in the land, for the Gentiles who shall possess the land.

2 NEPHI 10
Jacob, Son of Lehi *550 BC*
10 But behold, this land, said God, shall be a land of thine inheritance, and the Gentiles shall be blessed upon the land.
11 And this land shall be a land of liberty unto the Gentiles, and there shall be no kings upon the land, who shall raise up unto the Gentiles.
12 And I will fortify this land against all other nations.
13 And he that fighteth against Zion shall perish, saith God.
14 For he that raiseth up a king against me shall perish, for I, the Lord, the king of heaven, will be their king, and I will be a light unto them forever, that hear my words.

3 NEPHI 20
Jesus Christ *34 AD*
21 And it shall come to pass that I will establish my people, O house of Israel.
22 And behold, this people will I establish in this land, unto the fulfilling of the covenant which I made with your father Jacob; and it shall be a New Jerusalem. And the powers of heaven shall be in the midst of this people; yea, even I will be in the midst of you.
23 Behold, I am he of whom Moses spake, saying: A prophet shall the Lord your God raise up unto you of your brethren, like unto me; him shall ye hear in all things whatsoever he shall say unto you. And it shall come to pass that every soul who will not hear that prophet shall be cut off from among the people.
24 Verily I say unto you, yea, and all the prophets from Samuel and those that follow after, as many as have spoken, have testified of me.
25 And behold, ye are the children of the prophets; and ye are of the house of Israel; and ye are of the covenant which the Father made with your fathers, saying unto Abraham: And in thy seed shall all the kindreds of the Earth be blessed.
26 The Father having raised me up unto you first, and sent me to bless you in turning away every one of you from his iniquities; and this because ye are the children of the covenant—
27 And after that ye were blessed then fulfilleth the Father the covenant which he made with Abraham, saying: In thy seed shall all the kindreds of the Earth be blessed—unto the pouring out of the Holy Ghost through me upon the Gentiles, which blessing upon the Gentiles shall make them mighty above all, unto the scattering of my people, O house of Israel.
28 And they shall be a scourge unto the people of this land.

2 NEPHI 21 (see also ISAIAH 11)
Isaiah *740 BC*
10 And in that day there shall be a root of Jesse, which shall stand for an ensign of the people; to it shall the Gentiles seek; and his crest shall be glorious.
11 And it shall come to pass in that day that the Lord shall set his hand again the second time to recover the remnant of his people which shall be left, from Assyria, and from Egypt, and from Pathros, and from Cush, and from Elam, and from Shinar, and from Hamath, and from the islands of the sea.
12 And he shall set up an ensign for the nations, and shall assemble the outcasts of Israel, and gather together the dispersed of Judah from the four corners of the Earth.

George Washington at the Constitutional Convention on September 17, 1787, Signing of United States Constitution, by Junius Brutus Stearns, 1856.

13 The envy of Ephraim also shall depart,
and the adversaries of Judah shall be cut
off; Ephraim shall not envy Judah, and
Judah shall not vex Ephraim.
14 But they shall fly upon the shoulders of
the Philistines towards the west; they
shall spoil them of the east together; they
shall lay their hand upon Edom and Moab;
and the children of Ammon shall obey
them.
15 And the Lord shall utterly destroy the
tongue of the Egyptian sea; and with his
mighty wind he shall shake his hand over
the river, and shall smite it in the seven
streams, and make men go over dry shod.
16 And there shall be a highway for the
remnant of his people which shall be left,
from Assyria, like as it was to Israel in the
day that he came up out of the land of
Egypt.

1 NEPHI 21 (see also ISAIAH 49)

Isaiah 740 BC

6 And he said: It is a light thing that thou
shouldst be my servant to raise up the
tribes of Jacob, and to restore the pre-
served of Israel. I will also give thee for a
light to the Gentiles, that thou mayest be
my salvation unto the ends of the Earth.
22 Thus saith the Lord God: Behold, I will
lift up mine hand to the Gentiles, and set
up my standard to the people; and they
shall bring thy sons in their arms, and thy
daughters shall be carried upon their
shoulders.
23 And kings shall be thy nursing fathers,
and their queens thy nursing mothers;
they shall bow down to thee with their
face towards the Earth, and lick up the
dust of thy feet; and thou shalt know that
I am the Lord; for they shall not be
ashamed that wait for me.

1 NEPHI 22

Nephi, Son of Lehi 580 BC

6 Nevertheless, after they shall be nursed
by the Gentiles, and the Lord has lifted up
his hand upon the Gentiles and set them
up for a standard, and their children have
been carried in their arms, and their
daughters have been carried upon their
shoulders, behold these things of which
are spoken are temporal; for thus are the
covenants of the Lord with our fathers;
and it meaneth us in the days to come, and

also all our brethren who are of the house
of Israel.
7 And it meaneth that the time cometh
that after all the house of Israel have been
scattered and confounded, that the Lord
God will raise up a mighty nation among
the Gentiles, yea, even upon the face of
this land; and by them shall our seed be
scattered.

2 NEPHI 10

Jacob, Son of Lehi — *550 BC*

7 But behold, thus saith the Lord God:
When the day cometh that they shall
believe in me, that I am Christ, then have
I covenanted with their fathers that they
shall be restored in the flesh, upon the
Earth, unto the lands of their inheritance.
8 And it shall come to pass that they shall
be gathered in from their long dispersion,
from the isles of the sea, and from the four
parts of the Earth; and the nations of the
Gentiles shall be great in the eyes of me,
saith God, in carrying them forth to the
lands of their inheritance.
9 Yea, the kings of the Gentiles shall be
nursing fathers unto them, and their
queens shall become nursing mothers;
wherefore, the promises of the Lord are
great unto the Gentiles, for he hath
spoken it, and who can dispute?

2 NEPHI 6

Jacob, Son of Lehi — *550 BC*

11 Wherefore, after they are driven to and
fro, for thus saith the angel, many shall be
afflicted in the flesh, and shall not be
suffered to perish, because of the prayers
of the faithful; they shall be scattered, and
smitten, and hated; nevertheless, the Lord
will be merciful unto them, that when
they shall come to the knowledge of their
Redeemer, they shall be gathered together
again to the lands of their inheritance.
12 And blessed are the Gentiles, they of
whom the prophet has written; for
behold, if it so be that they shall repent
and fight not against Zion, and do not
unite themselves to that great and
abominable church, they shall be saved;
for the Lord God will fulfil his covenants
which he has made unto his children; and
for this cause the prophet has written
these things.
13 Wherefore, they that fight against Zion
and the covenant people of the Lord shall
lick up the dust of their feet; and the
people of the Lord shall not be ashamed.
For the people of the Lord are they who
wait for him; for they still wait for the
coming of the Messiah.

DOCTRINE AND COVENANTS 101

Joseph Smith — *December 1833*

76 And again I say unto you, those who
have been scattered by their enemies, it is
my will that they should continue to
importune for redress, and redemption, by
the hands of those who are placed as rulers
and are in authority over you—
77 According to the laws and constitution
of the people, which I have suffered to be
established, and should be maintained for
the rights and protection of all flesh,
according to just and holy principles;
78 That every man may act in doctrine
and principle pertaining to futurity,
according to the moral agency which I
have given unto him, that every man may
be accountable for his own sins in the day
of judgment.
79 Therefore, it is not right that any man
should be in bondage one to another.
80 And for this purpose have I established
the Constitution of this land, by the hands
of wise men whom I raised up unto this
very purpose, and redeemed the land by
the shedding of blood.

DOCTRINE AND COVENANTS 98

Joseph Smith — *August 1833*

4 And now, verily I say unto you con-
cerning the laws of the land, it is my will
that my people should observe to do all
things whatsoever I command them.
5 And that law of the land which is
constitutional, supporting that principle
of freedom in maintaining rights and
privileges, belongs to all mankind, and is
justifiable before me.
6 Therefore, I, the Lord, justify you, and
your brethren of my church, in befriend-
ing that law which is the constitutional
law of the land;
7 And as pertaining to law of man, what-
soever is more or less than this, cometh of
evil.
8 I, the Lord God, make you free, there-
fore ye are free indeed; and the law also
maketh you free.
9 Nevertheless, when the wicked rule the
people mourn.

10 Wherefore, honest men and wise men should be sought for diligently, and good men and wise men ye should observe to uphold; otherwise whatsoever is less than these cometh of evil.

DOCTRINE AND COVENANTS 109

Joseph Smith *March 1836*

54 Have mercy, O Lord, upon all the nations of the Earth; have mercy upon the rulers of our land; may those principles, which were so honorably and nobly defended, namely, the Constitution of our land, by our fathers, be established forever.

2 NEPHI 10

Jacob, Son of Lehi *550 BC*

17 For I will fulfil my promises which I have made unto the children of men, that I will do unto them while they are in the flesh—
18 Wherefore, my beloved brethren, thus saith our God: I will afflict thy seed by the hand of the Gentiles; nevertheless, I will soften the hearts of the Gentiles, that they shall be like unto a father to them; wherefore, the Gentiles shall be blessed and numbered among the house of Israel.
19 Wherefore, I will consecrate this land unto thy seed, and them who shall be numbered among thy seed, forever, for the land of their inheritance; for it is a choice land, saith God unto me, above all other lands, wherefore I will have all men that dwell thereon that they shall worship me, saith God.
20 And now, my beloved brethren, seeing that our merciful God has given us so great knowledge concerning these things, let us remember him, and lay aside our sins, and not hang down our heads, for we are not cast off; nevertheless, we have been driven out of the land of our inheritance; but we have been led to a better land, for the Lord has made the sea our path, and we are upon an isle of the sea.
21 But great are the promises of the Lord unto them who are upon the aisles of the sea; wherefore as it says isles, there must needs be more than this, and they are inhabited also by our brethren.
22 For behold, the Lord God has led away from time to time from the house of Israel, according to his will and pleasure. And now behold, the Lord remembereth all them who have been broken off, wherefore he remembereth us also.

2 NEPHI 1

Lehi *580 BC*

5 But, said he [Lehi], notwithstanding our afflictions, we have obtained a land of promise, a land which is choice above all other lands; a land which the Lord God hath covenanted with me should be a land for the inheritance of my seed. Yea, the Lord hath covenanted this land unto me, and to my children forever, and also all those who should be led out of other countries by the hand of the Lord.
6 Wherefore, I, Lehi, prophesy according to the workings of the Spirit which is in me, that there shall none come into this land save they shall be brought by the hand of the Lord.
7 Wherefore, this land is consecrated unto him whom he shall bring. And if it so be that they shall serve him according to the commandments which he hath given, it shall be a land of liberty unto them; wherefore, they shall never be brought down into captivity; if so, it shall be because of iniquity; for if iniquity shall abound cursed shall be the land for their sakes, but unto the righteous it shall be blessed forever.
8 And behold, it is wisdom that this land should be kept as yet from the knowledge of other nations; for behold, many nations would overrun the land, that there would be no place for an inheritance.
9 Wherefore, I, Lehi, have obtained a promise, that inasmuch as those whom the Lord God shall bring out of the land of Jerusalem shall keep his commandments, they shall prosper upon the face of this land; and they shall be kept from all other nations, that they may possess this land unto themselves. And if it so be that they shall keep his commandments they shall be blessed upon the face of this land, and there shall be none to molest them, nor to take away the land of their inheritance; and they shall dwell safely forever.

ETHER 2

Moroni *420 AD*

7 And the Lord would not suffer that they should stop beyond the sea in the wilderness, but he would that they should come forth even unto the land of promise,

The Statue of Liberty National Monument. A symbol of liberty, freedom, and the hope of a better life to oppressed people all over the world

which was choice above all other lands, which the Lord God had preserved for a righteous people.
8 And he had sworn in his wrath unto the brother of Jared, that whoso should possess this land of promise, from that time henceforth and forever, should serve him, the true and only God, or they should be swept off when the fulness of his wrath should come upon them.
9 And now, we can behold the decrees of God concerning this land, that it is a land of promise; and whatsoever nation shall possess it shall serve God, or they shall be swept off when the fulness of his wrath shall come upon them. And the fulness of his wrath cometh upon them when they are ripened in iniquity.
10 For behold, this is a land which is choice above all other lands; wherefore he that doth possess it shall serve God or shall be swept off; for it is the everlasting decree of God. And it is not until the fulness of iniquity among the children of the land, that they are swept off.
11 And this cometh unto you, O ye Gentiles, that ye may know the decrees of God—that ye may repent, and not continue in your iniquities until the fulness come, that ye may not bring down the fulness of the wrath of God upon you as the inhabitants of the land have hitherto done.
12 Behold, this is a choice land, and whatsoever nation shall possess it shall be free from bondage, and from captivity, and from all other nations under heaven, if they will but serve the God of the land, who is Jesus Christ, who hath been manifested by the things which we have written.

22

THE RESTORATION OF THE GOSPEL OF JESUS CHRIST

+++

By 1820, the Lamanites had been scattered and smitten by the Gentiles. Much of the Earth was converted to a belief in Jesus Christ. A powerful nation, the United States of America, was formed on the principles of religious liberty. The Reformation, Renaissance, and Age of Discovery had opened the minds of God's children; and the elect of God were gathering to the United States. The groundwork had thus been laid for the Restoration of the fulness of the gospel of Jesus Christ to the Earth.

1 NEPHI 13

Nephi, Son of Lehi — *595 BC*

30 Nevertheless, thou beholdest that the Gentiles who have gone forth out of captivity, and have been lifted up by the power of God above all other nations, upon the face of the land which is choice above all other lands, which is the land that the Lord God hath covenanted with thy father that his seed should have for the land of their inheritance; wherefore, thou seest that the Lord God will not suffer that the Gentiles will utterly destroy the mixture of thy seed, which are among thy brethren.
31 Neither will he suffer that the Gentiles shall destroy the seed of thy brethren.
32 Neither will the Lord God suffer that the Gentiles shall forever remain in that awful state of blindness, which thou beholdest they are in, because of the plain and most precious parts of the gospel of the Lamb which have been kept back by that abominable church, whose formation thou hast seen.
33 Wherefore saith the Lamb of God: I will be merciful unto the Gentiles, unto the visiting of the remnant of the house of Israel in great judgment.
34 And it came to pass that the angel of the Lord spake unto me, saying: Behold, saith the Lamb of God, after I have visited the remnant of the house of Israel—and this remnant of whom I speak is the seed of thy father—wherefore, after I have visited them in judgment, and smitten them by the hand of the Gentiles, and after the Gentiles do stumble exceedingly, because of the most plain and precious parts of the gospel of the Lamb which have been kept back by that abominable church, which is the mother of harlots, saith the Lamb—I will be merciful unto the Gentiles in that day, insomuch that I will bring forth unto them, in mine own power, much of my gospel, which shall be plain and precious, saith the Lamb.

DANIEL 2

Daniel — *600 BC*

44 And in the days of these kings shall the God of heaven set up a kingdom, which shall never be destroyed: and the kingdom shall not be left to other people, but it shall break in pieces and consume all these kingdoms, and it shall stand for ever.
45 Forasmuch as thou sawest that the stone was cut out of the mountain without hands, and that it brake in pieces the iron, the brass, the clay, the silver, and the gold; the great God hath made known to the king what shall come to pass hereafter: and the dream is certain, and the interpretation thereof sure.

GENESIS 48

Jacob (Israel) — *1690 BC*

7 And Jacob said unto Joseph, When the God of my fathers appeared unto me in Luz, in the land of Canaan; he sware unto me, that he would give unto me, and unto my seed, the land for an everlasting possession.

8 Therefore, O my son, he hath blessed me in raising thee up to be a servant unto me, in saving my house from death;
9 In delivering my people, thy brethren, from famine which was sore in the land; wherefore the God of thy fathers shall bless thee, and the fruit of thy loins, that they shall be blessed above thy brethren, and above thy father's house;
10 For thou hast prevailed, and thy father's house hath bowed down unto thee, even as it was shown unto thee, before thou wast sold into Egypt by the hands of thy brethren; wherefore thy brethren shall bow down unto thee, from generation to generation, unto the fruit of thy loins forever;
11 For thou shalt be a light unto my people, to deliver them in the days of their captivity, from bondage; and to bring salvation unto them, when they are altogether bowed down under sin. [JST]

JACOB 5

Zenos — *~700-800 BC*

61 Wherefore, go to, and call servants, that we may labor diligently with our might in the vineyard, that we may prepare the way, that I may bring forth again the natural fruit, which natural fruit is good and the most precious above all other fruit.
62 Wherefore, let us go to and labor with our might this last time, for behold the end draweth nigh, and this is for the last time that I shall prune my vineyard.
63 Graft in the branches; begin at the last that they may be first, and that the first may be blast, and dig about the trees, both old and young, the first and the last; and the last and the first, that all may be nourished once again for the last time.
64 Wherefore, dig about them, and prune them, and dung them once more, for the last time, for the end draweth nigh. And if it be so that these last grafts shall grow, and bring forth the natural fruit, then shall ye prepare the way for them, that they may grow.
65 And as they begin to grow ye shall clear away the branches which bring forth bitter fruit, according to the strength of the good and the size thereof; and ye shall not clear away the bad thereof all at once, lest the roots thereof should be too strong for the graft, and the graft thereof shall perish, and I lose the trees of my vineyard.
66 For it grieveth me that I should lose the trees of my vineyard; wherefore ye shall clear away the bad according as the good shall grow, that the root and the top may be equal in strength, until the good shall overcome the bad, and the bad be hewn down and cast into the fire, that they cumber not the ground of my vineyard; and thus will I sweep away the bad out of my vineyard.
67 And the branches of the natural tree will I graft in again into the natural tree;
68 And the branches of the natural tree will I graft into the natural branches of the tree; and thus will I bring them together again, that they shall bring forth the natural fruit, and they shall be one.
69 And the bad shall be cast away, yea, even out of all the land of my vineyard; for behold, only this once will I prune my vineyard.

ACTS 3

Peter — *34 AD*

19 Repent ye therefore, and be converted, that your sins may be blotted out, when the times of refreshing shall come from the presence of the Lord;
20 And he shall send Jesus Christ, *whom ye have crucified*, which before was preached unto you: [JST]
21 Whom the heaven must receive until the times of restitution of all things, which God hath spoken by the mouth of all his holy prophets since the world began.

DOCTRINE AND COVENANTS 88

Joseph Smith — *December 1832*

66 Behold, that which you hear is as the voice of one crying in the wilderness—in the wilderness, because you cannot see him—my voice, because my voice is Spirit; my Spirit is truth; truth abideth and hath no end; and if it be in you it shall abound.

DOCTRINE AND COVENANTS 45

Joseph Smith — *March 1831*

28 And when the times of the Gentiles is come in, a light shall break forth among them that sit in darkness, and it shall be the fulness of my gospel;
29 But they receive it not; for they perceive not the light, and they turn their

hearts from me because of the precepts of men.
30 And in that generation shall the times of the Gentiles be fulfilled.
31 And there shall be men standing in that generation, that shall not pass until they shall see an overflowing scourge; for a desolating sickness shall cover the land.
32 But my disciples shall stand in holy places, and shall not be moved; but among the wicked, men shall lift up their voices and curse God and die.
33 And there shall be earthquakes also in divers places, and many desolations; yet men will harden their hearts against me, and they will take up the sword, one against another, and they will kill one another.
34 And now, when I the Lord had spoken these words unto my disciples, they were troubled.
35 And I said unto them: Be not troubled, for, when all these things shall come to pass, ye may know that the promises which have been made unto you shall be fulfilled.
36 And when the light shall begin to break forth, it shall be with them like unto a parable which I will show you—
37 Ye look and behold the fig trees, and ye see them with your eyes, and ye say when they begin to shoot forth, and their leaves are yet tender, that summer is now nigh at hand;
38 Even so it shall be in that day when they shall see all these things, then shall they know that the hour is nigh.

ISAIAH 44

Isaiah — *740 BC*

21 Remember these, O Jacob and Israel; for thou art my servant: I have formed thee; thou art my servant: O Israel, thou shalt not be forgotten of me.
22 I have blotted out, as a thick cloud, thy transgressions, and, as a cloud, thy sins: return unto me; for I have redeemed thee.
23 Sing, O ye heavens; for the Lord hath done it: shout, ye lower parts of the Earth: break forth into singing, ye mountains, O forest, and every tree therein: for the Lord hath redeemed Jacob, and glorified himself in Israel.
24 Thus saith the Lord, thy redeemer, and he that formed thee from the womb, I am the Lord that maketh all things; that stretcheth forth the heavens alone; that spreadeth abroad the Earth by myself;
25 That frustrateth the tokens of the liars, and maketh diviners mad; that turneth wise men backward, and maketh their knowledge foolish;
26 That confirmeth the word of his servant, and performeth the counsel of his messengers; that saith to Jerusalem, Thou shalt be inhabited; and to the cities of Judah, Ye shall be built, and I will raise up the decayed places thereof:
27 That saith to the deep, Be dry, and I will dry up thy rivers:
28 That saith of Cyrus, He is my shepherd, and shall perform all my pleasure: even saying to Jerusalem, Thou shalt be built; and to the temple, Thy foundation shall be laid.

ISAIAH 42

Isaiah — *740 BC*

1 Behold my servant, whom I uphold; mine elect, in whom my soul delighteth; I have put my spirit upon him: he shall bring forth judgment to the Gentiles.
6 I the LORD have called thee in righteousness, and will hold thine hand, and will keep thee, and give thee for a covenant of the people, for a light of the Gentiles;
7 To open the blind eyes, to bring out the prisoners from the prison, and them that sit in darkness out of the prison house.

ISAIAH 43

Isaiah — *740 BC*

5 Fear not: for I am with thee: I will bring thy seed from the east, and gather thee from the west;
6 I will say to the north, Give up; and to the south, Keep not back: bring my sons from far, and my daughters from the ends of the Earth;
7 Even every one that is called by my name: for I have created him for my glory, I have formed him; yea, I have made him.
8 Bring forth the blind people that have eyes, and the deaf that have ears.
9 Let all the nations be gathered together, and let the people be assembled: who among them can declare this, and shew us former things? let them bring forth their witnesses, that they may be justified: or let them hear, and say, It is truth.

10 Ye are my witnesses, saith the LORD, and my servant whom I have chosen: that ye may know and believe me, and understand that I am he: before me there was no God formed, neither shall there be after me.
11 I, even I, am the LORD; and beside me there is no saviour.
25 I, even I, am he that blotteth out thy transgressions for mine own sake, and will not remember thy sins.

EZEKIEL 16

Ezekiel — *598 BC*

60 Nevertheless I will remember my covenant with thee in the days of thy youth, and I will establish unto thee an everlasting covenant.
61 Then thou shalt remember thy ways, and be ashamed, when thou shalt receive thy sisters, thine elder and thy younger: and I will give them unto thee for daughters, but not by thy covenant.
62 And I will establish my covenant with thee; and thou shalt know that I am the LORD:
63 That thou mayest remember, and be confounded, and never open thy mouth anymore because of thy shame, when I am pacified toward thee for all that thou hast done, saith the Lord GOD.

DOCTRINE AND COVENANTS 65

Joseph Smith — *October 1831*

1 Hearken, and lo, a voice as of one sent down from on high, who is mighty and powerful, whose going forth is unto the ends of the Earth, yea, whose voice is unto men—Prepare ye the way of the Lord, make his paths straight.
2 The keys of the kingdom of God are committed unto man on the Earth, and from thence shall the gospel roll forth unto the ends of the Earth, as the stone which is cut out of the mountain without hands shall roll forth, until it has filled the whole Earth.
3 Yea, a voice crying—Prepare ye the way of the Lord, prepare ye the supper of the Lamb, make ready for the Bridegroom.
4 Pray unto the Lord, call upon his holy name, make known his wonderful works among the people.
5 Call upon the Lord, that his kingdom may go forth upon the Earth, that the inhabitants thereof may receive it, and be prepared for the days to come, in the which the Son of Man shall come down in heaven, clothed in the brightness of his glory, to meet the kingdom of God which is set up on the Earth.
6 Wherefore, may the kingdom of God go forth, that the kingdom of heaven may come, that thou, O God, mayest be glorified in heaven so on Earth, that thine enemies may be subdued; for thine is the honor, power and glory, forever and ever. Amen.

23

JOSEPH SMITH – A MODERN MOSES

Joseph Smith's First Vision, Unknown Artist, 1913.

+++

Joseph Smith will be a great prophet, compared to Moses. He will restore the fulness of the gospel in the latter-days, will bring forth the Book of Mormon, will restore many lost plain and precious truths to the Bible, and will receive 135 revelations recorded in the Doctrine and Covenants.

MOSES 1

Moses — *1475 BC*

40 And now, Moses, my son, I will speak unto thee concerning this Earth upon which thou standest; and thou shalt write the things which I shall speak.
41 And in a day when the children of men shall esteem my words as naught and take many of them from the book which thou shalt write, behold, I will raise up another like unto thee; and they shall be had again among the children of men—among as many as shall believe.

2 NEPHI 3

Lehi — *580 BC*

3 And now, Joseph, my last-born, whom I have brought out of the wilderness of mine afflictions, may the Lord bless thee forever, for thy seed shall not utterly be destroyed.
4 For behold, thou art the fruit of my loins; and I am a descendant of Joseph who was carried captive into Egypt. And great were the covenants of the Lord which he made unto Joseph.
5 Wherefore, Joseph truly saw our day. And he obtained a promise of the Lord, that out of the fruit of his loins the Lord God would raise up a righteous branch unto the house of Israel; not the Messiah, but a branch which was to be broken off, nevertheless, to be remembered in the covenants of the Lord that the Messiah should be made manifest unto them in the latter-days, in the spirit of power, unto the bringing of them out of darkness unto light—yea, out of hidden darkness and out of captivity unto freedom.
6 For Joseph truly testified, saying: A seer shall the Lord my God raise up, who shall be a choice seer unto the fruit of my loins.
7 Yea, Joseph truly said: Thus saith the Lord unto me: A choice seer will I raise up out of the fruit of thy loins; and he shall be esteemed highly among the fruit of thy loins. And unto him will I give commandment that he shall do a work for the fruit of thy loins, his brethren, which shall be of great worth unto them, even to the bringing of them to the knowledge of the covenants which I have made with thy fathers.

8 And I will give unto him a commandment that he shall do none other work, save the work which I shall command him. And I will make him great in mine eyes; for he shall do my work.
9 And he shall be great like unto Moses, whom I have said I would raise up unto you, to deliver my people, O house of Israel.
10 And Moses will I raise up, to deliver thy people out of the land of Egypt.
11 But a seer will I raise up out of the fruit of thy loins; and unto him will I give power to bring forth my word unto the seed of thy loins—and not to the bringing forth my word only, saith the Lord, but to the convincing them of my word, which shall have already gone forth among them.
12 Wherefore, the fruit of thy loins shall write; and the fruit of the loins of Judah shall write; and that which shall be written by the fruit of thy loins, and also that which shall be written by the fruit of the loins of Judah, shall grow together, unto the confounding of false doctrines and laying down of contentions, and establishing peace among the fruit of thy loins, and bringing them to the knowledge of their fathers in the latter-days, and also to the knowledge of my covenants, saith the Lord.
13 And out of weakness he shall be made strong, in that day when my work shall commence among all my people, unto the restoring thee, O house of Israel, saith the Lord.
14 And thus prophesied Joseph, saying: Behold, that seer will the Lord bless; and they that seek to destroy him shall be confounded; for this promise, which I have obtained of the Lord, of the fruit of my loins, shall be fulfilled. Behold, I am sure of the fulfilling of this promise;
15 And his name shall be called after me; and it shall be after the name of his father. And he shall be like unto me; for the thing, which the Lord shall bring forth by his hand, by the power of the Lord shall bring my people unto salvation.
16 Yea, thus prophesied Joseph: I am sure of this thing, even as I am sure of the promise of Moses; for the Lord hath said unto me, I will preserve thy seed forever.
17 And the Lord hath said: I will raise up a Moses; and I will give power unto him in a rod; and I will give judgment unto him in writing. Yet I will not loose his tongue, that he shall speak much, for I will not make him mighty in speaking. But I will write unto him my law, by the finger of mine own hand; and I will make a spokesman for him.
18 And the Lord said unto me also: I will raise up unto the fruit of thy loins; and I will make for him a spokesman. And I, behold, I will give unto him that he shall write the writing of the fruit of thy loins, unto the fruit of thy loins; and the spokesman of thy loins shall declare it.
19 And the words which he shall write shall be the words which are expedient in my wisdom should go forth unto the fruit of thy loins. And it shall be as if the fruit of thy loins had cried unto them from the dust; for I know their faith.
20 And they shall cry from the dust; yea, even repentance unto their brethren, even after many generations have gone by them. And it shall come to pass that their cry shall go, even according to the simpleness of their words.
21 Because of their faith their words shall proceed forth out of my mouth unto their brethren who are the fruit of thy loins; and the weakness of their words will I make strong in their faith, unto the remembering of my covenant which I made unto thy fathers.
22 And now, behold, my son Joseph, after this manner did my father of old prophesy.
23 Wherefore, because of this covenant thou art blessed; for thy seed shall not be destroyed, for they shall hearken unto the words of the book.
24 And there shall rise up one mighty among them, who shall do much good, both in word and in deed, being an instrument in the hands of God, with exceeding faith, to work mighty wonders, and do that thing which is great in the sight of God, unto the bringing to pass much restoration unto the house of Israel, and unto the seed of thy brethren.
25 And now, blessed art thou, Joseph. Behold, thou art little; wherefore hearken unto the words of thy brother, Nephi, and it shall be done unto thee even according to the words which I have spoken. Remember the words of thy dying father. Amen.

Joseph Smith, painted circa 1842 by unknown artist.

GENESIS 50
Joseph, Son of Israel 1635 BC
24 And Joseph said unto his brethren, *I die, and go unto my fathers; and I go down to my grave with joy. The God of my father Jacob be with you, to deliver you out of affliction in the days of your bondage; for the Lord hath visited me, and I have obtained a promise of the Lord, that out of the fruit of my loins, the Lord God will raise up a righteous branch out of my loins; and unto thee, whom my father Jacob hath named Israel, a prophet; (not the Messiah who is called Shilo;) and this prophet shall deliver my people out of Egypt in the days of thy bondage.*
25 *And it shall come to pass that they shall be scattered again; and a branch shall be broken off, and shall be carried into a far country; nevertheless they shall be remembered in the covenants of the Lord, when the Messiah cometh; for he shall be made manifest unto them in the latter-days, in the Spirit of power; and shall bring them out of darkness into light; out of hidden darkness, and out of captivity unto freedom.*
26 *A seer shall the Lord my God raise up, who shall be a choice seer unto the fruit of my loins.*
27 *Thus saith the Lord God of my fathers unto me, A choice seer will I raise up out of the fruit of thy loins, and he shall be esteemed highly among the fruit of thy loins; and unto him will I give commandment that he shall do a work for the fruit of thy loins, his brethren.*
28 *And he shall bring them to the knowledge of the covenants which I have made with thy fathers; and he shall do whatsoever work I shall command him.*
29 *And I will make him great in mine eyes, for he shall do my work; and he shall be great like unto him whom I have said I would raise up unto you, to deliver my people, O house of Israel, out of the land of Egypt; for a seer will I raise up to deliver my people out of the land of Egypt; and he shall be called Moses. And by this name he shall know that he is of thy house; for he shall be nursed by the king's daughter, and shall be called her son.*
30 *And again, a seer will I raise up out of the fruit of thy loins, and unto him will I give power to bring forth my word unto the seed of thy loins; and not to the bringing forth of my word only, saith the Lord, but to the convincing them of my word, which shall have already gone forth among them in the last days;*
31 *Wherefore the fruit of thy loins shall write, and the fruit of the loins of Judah shall write; and that which shall be written by the fruit of thy loins, and also that which shall be written by the fruit of the loins of Judah, shall grow together unto the confounding of false doctrines, and laying down of contentions, and establishing peace among the fruit of thy loins, and bringing them to a knowledge of their fathers in the latter-days; and also to the knowledge of my covenants, saith the Lord.*
32 *And out of weakness shall he be made strong, in that day when my work shall go forth among all my people, which shall restore them, who are of the house of Israel, in the last days.*
33 *And that seer will I bless, and they that seek to destroy him shall be confounded; for this promise I give unto you; for I will remember you from generation to generation; and his name shall be called Joseph, and it shall be after the name of his father; and he shall be like unto you; for the thing*

which the Lord shall bring forth by his hand shall bring my people unto salvation.
34 *And the Lord sware unto Joseph that he would preserve his seed forever, saying, I will raise up Moses, and a rod shall be in his hand, and he shall gather together my people, and he shall lead them as a flock, and he shall smite the waters of the Red Sea with his rod.*
35 *And he shall have judgment and shall write the word of the Lord. And he shall not speak many words, for I will write unto him my law by the finger of mine own hand. And I will make a spokesman for him, and his name shall be called Aaron.*
36 *And it shall be done unto thee in the last days also, even as I have sworn. Therefore,* Joseph said unto his brethren, God will surely visit you, and bring you out of this land, unto the land which he sware unto Abraham, and unto Isaac, and to Jacob. [JST]

DOCTRINE AND COVENANTS 103

Joseph Smith — *February 1834*

15 Behold, I say unto you, the redemption of Zion must needs come by power;
16 Therefore, I will raise up unto my people a man, who shall lead them like as Moses led the children of Israel.
17 For ye are the children of Israel, and of the seed of Abraham, and ye must needs be led out of bondage by power, and with a stretched-out arm.
18 And as your fathers were led at the first, even so shall the redemption of Zion be.
19 Therefore, let not your hearts faint, for I say not unto you as I said unto your fathers: Mine angel shall go up before you, but not my presence.
20 But I say unto you: Mine angels shall go up before you, and also my presence, and in time ye shall possess the goodly land.
21 Verily, verily I say unto you, that my servant Joseph Smith, Jun., is the man to whom I likened the servant to whom the Lord of the vineyard spake in the parable which I have given unto you.
22 Therefore let my servant Joseph Smith, Jun., say unto the strength of my house, my young men and the middle aged—Gather yourselves together unto the land of Zion, upon the land which I have bought with money that has been consecrated unto me.

DOCTRINE AND COVENANTS 135

John Taylor — *June 1844*

3 Joseph Smith, the Prophet and Seer of the Lord, has done more, save Jesus only, for the salvation of men in this world, than any other man that ever lived in it. In the short space of twenty years, he has brought forth the Book of Mormon, which he translated by the gift and power of God, and has been the means of publishing it on two continents; has sent the fulness of the everlasting gospel, which it contained, to the four quarters of the Earth; has brought forth the revela-tions and commandments which compose this book of Doctrine and Covenants, and many other wise documents and instructions for the benefit of the children of men; gathered many thousands of the Latter-day Saints, founded a great city, and left a fame and name that cannot be slain. He lived great, and he died great in the eyes of God and his people; and like most of the Lord's anointed in ancient times, has sealed his mission and his works with his own blood; and so has his brother Hyrum. In life they were not divided, and in death they were not separated!

24

THE BOOK OF MORMON COMES FORTH

+++

The miraculous coming forth of the Book of Mormon is foretold.

MOSES 7

Enoch *3000 BC*

62 And righteousness will I send down out of heaven; and truth will I send forth out of the Earth, to bear testimony of mine Only Begotten; his Resurrection from the dead; yea, and also the Resurrection of all men; and righteousness and truth will I cause to sweep the Earth as with a flood, to gather out mine elect from the four quarters of the Earth, unto a place which I shall prepare, an Holy City, that my people may gird up their loins, and be looking forth for the time of my coming; for there shall be my tabernacle, and it shall be called Zion, a New Jerusalem.

MORMON 8

Moroni *400 AD*

14 And I am the same who hideth up this record unto the Lord; the plates thereof are of no worth, because of the commandment of the Lord. For he truly saith that no one shall have them to get gain; but the record thereof is of great worth; and whoso shall bring it to light, him will the Lord bless.
15 For none can have power to bring it to light save it be given him of God; for God wills that it shall be done with an eye single to his glory, or the welfare of the ancient and long dispersed covenant people of the Lord.
16 And blessed be he that shall bring this thing to light; for it shall be brought out of darkness unto light, according to the word of God; yea, it shall be brought out of the Earth, and it shall shine forth out of darkness, and come unto the knowledge of the people; and it shall be done by the power of God.

2 NEPHI 27 (see also ISAIAH 29)

Isaiah *740 BC*

23 For behold, I am God; and I am a God of miracles; and I will show unto the world that I am the same yesterday, today, and forever; and I work not among the children of men save it be according to their faith.
24 And again it shall come to pass that the Lord shall say unto him that shall read the words that shall be delivered him:
25 Forasmuch as this people draw near unto me with their mouth, and with their lips do honor me, but have removed their hearts far from me, and their fear towards me is taught by the precepts of men—
26 Therefore, I will proceed to do a marvelous work among this people, yea, a marvelous work and a wonder, for the wisdom of their wise and learned shall perish, and the understanding of their prudent shall be hid.
27 And wo unto them that seek deep to hide their counsel from the Lord! And their works are in the dark; and they say: Who seeth us, and who knoweth us? And they also say: Surely, your turning of things upside down shall be esteemed as the potter's clay. But behold, I will show unto them, saith the Lord of Hosts, that I know all their works. For shall the work say of him that made it, he made me not? Or shall the thing framed say of him that framed it, he had no understanding?
28 But behold, saith the Lord of Hosts: I will show unto the children of men that it is yet a very little while and Lebanon shall be turned into a fruitful field; and the fruitful field shall be esteemed as a forest.
29 And in that day shall the deaf hear the words of the book, and the eyes of the blind shall see out of obscurity and out of darkness.
30 And the meek also shall increase, and their joy shall be in the Lord, and the poor

The Angel Moroni Delivering the Plates of the Book of Mormon to Joseph Smith, Jun., artwork from 1886.

among men shall rejoice in the Holy One of Israel.
31 For assuredly as the Lord liveth they shall see that the terrible one is brought to naught, and the scorner is consumed, and all that watch for iniquity are cut off;
32 And they that make a man an offender for a word, and lay a snare for him that reproveth in the gate, and turn aside the just for a thing of naught.
33 Therefore, thus saith the Lord, who redeemed Abraham, concerning the house of Jacob: Jacob shall not now be ashamed, neither shall his face now wax pale.
34 But when he seeth his children, the work of my hands, in the midst of him, they shall sanctify my name, and sanctify the Holy One of Jacob, and shall fear the God of Israel.
35 They also that erred in spirit shall come to understanding, and they that murmured shall learn doctrine.

ISAIAH 29

Isaiah 740 BC

4 And thou shalt be brought down, and shalt speak out of the ground, and thy speech shall be low out of the dust, and thy voice shall be, as of one that hath a

familiar spirit, out of the ground, and thy speech shall whisper out of the dust.

PSALM 85

David *1000 BC*

1 Lord, thou hast been favourable unto thy land: thou hast brought back the captivity of Jacob.
2 Thou hast forgiven the iniquity of thy people, thou hast covered all their sin. Selah.
3 Thou hast taken away all thy wrath: thou hast turned thyself from the fierceness of thine anger.
4 Turn us, O God of our salvation, and cause thine anger toward us to cease.
5 Wilt thou be angry with us forever? wilt thou draw out thine anger to all generations?
6 Wilt thou not revive us again: that thy people may rejoice in thee?
7 Shew us thy mercy, O Lord, and grant us thy salvation.
8 I will hear what God the Lord will speak: for he will speak peace unto his people, and to his saints: but let them not turn again to folly.
9 Surely his salvation is nigh them that fear him; that glory may dwell in our land.
10 Mercy and truth are met together; righteousness and peace have kissed each other.
11 Truth shall spring out of the Earth; and righteousness shall look down from heaven.
12 Yea, the Lord shall give that which is good; and our land shall yield her increase.
13 Righteousness shall go before him; and shall set us in the way of his steps.

2 NEPHI 26

Nephi, Son of Lehi *550 BC*

15 ...yet the words of the righteous shall be written, and the prayers of the faithful shall be heard, and all those who have dwindled in unbelief shall not be forgotten.
16 For those who shall be destroyed shall speak unto them out of the ground, and their speech shall be low out of the dust, and their voice shall be as one that hath a familiar spirit; for the Lord God will give unto him power, that he may whisper concerning them, even as it were out of the ground; and their speech shall whisper out of the dust.
17 For thus saith the Lord God: They shall write the things which shall be done among them, and they shall be written and sealed up in a book, and those who have dwindled in unbelief shall not have them, for they seek to destroy the things of God.

AMOS 5

Amos *792 BC*

15 Hate the evil, and love the good, and establish judgment in the gate: it may be that the LORD God of hosts will be gracious unto the remnant of Joseph.

MORMON 9

Moroni *421 AD*

34 But the Lord knoweth the things which we have written, and also that none other people knoweth our language; and because that none other people knoweth our language, therefore he hath prepared means for the interpretation thereof.
35 And these things are written that we may rid our garments of the blood of our brethren, who have dwindled in unbelief.
36 And behold, these things which we have desired concerning our brethren, yea, even their restoration to the knowledge of Christ, are according to the prayers of all the saints who have dwelt in the land.
37 And may the Lord Jesus Christ grant that their prayers may be answered according to their faith; and may God the Father remember the covenant which he hath made with the house of Israel; and may he bless them forever, through faith on the name of Jesus Christ. Amen.

25

MORONI'S APPEARANCES TO JOSEPH SMITH

+++

The account of the visitation and prophecies of the angel Moroni to Joseph Smith September 21st, 1823. Joseph receives the gold plates.

JOSEPH SMITH – HISTORY 1

Joseph Smith *September 1823*

29 In consequence of these things, I often felt condemned for my weakness and imperfections; when, on the evening of the above-mentioned twenty-first of September, after I had retired to my bed for the night, I betook myself to prayer and supplication to Almighty God for forgiveness of all my sins and follies, and also for a manifestation to me, that I might know of my state and standing before him; for I had full confidence in obtaining a divine manifestation, as I previously had one.

30 While I was thus in the act of calling upon God, I discovered a light appearing in my room, which continued to increase until the room was lighter than at noonday, when immediately a personage appeared at my bedside, standing in the air, for his feet did not touch the floor.

31 He had on a loose robe of most exquisite whiteness. It was a whiteness beyond anything Earthly I had ever seen; nor do I believe that any Earthly thing could be made to appear so exceedingly white and brilliant. His hands were naked, and his arms also, a little above the wrist; so, also, were his feet naked, as were his legs, a little above the ankles. His head and neck were also bare. I could discover that he had no other clothing on but this robe, as it was open, so that I could see into his bosom.

32 Not only was his robe exceedingly white, but his whole person was glorious beyond description, and his countenance truly like lightning. The room was exceedingly light, but not so very bright as immediately around his person. When I first looked upon him, I was afraid; but the fear soon left me.

33 He called me by name, and said unto me that he was a messenger sent from the presence of God to me, and that his name was Moroni; that God had a work for me to do; and that my name should be had for good and evil among all nations, kindreds, and tongues, or that it should be both good and evil spoken of among all people.

34 He said there was a book deposited, written upon gold plates, giving an account of the former inhabitants of this continent, and the source from whence they sprang. He also said that the fulness of the everlasting Gospel was contained in it, as delivered by the Savior to the ancient inhabitants;

35 Also, that there were two stones in silver bows—and these stones, fastened to a breastplate, constituted what is called the Urim and Thummim—deposited with the plates; and the possession and use of these stones were what constituted "seers" in ancient or former times; and that God had prepared them for the purpose of translating the book.

36 After telling me these things, he commenced quoting the prophecies of the Old Testament. He first quoted part of the third chapter of Malachi; and he quoted also the fourth or last chapter of the same prophecy, though with a little variation from the way it reads in our Bibles. Instead of quoting the first verse as it reads in our books, he quoted it thus:

37 For behold, the day cometh that shall burn as an oven, and all the proud, yea, and all that do wickedly shall burn as stubble; for they that come shall burn them, saith the Lord of Hosts, that it shall leave them neither root nor branch.

Joseph Smith Receiving the Golden Plates, by Edward Stevenson, 1893.

38 And again, he quoted the fifth verse
thus: Behold, I will reveal unto you the
Priesthood, by the hand of Elijah the
prophet, before the coming of the great
and dreadful day of the Lord.
39 He also quoted the next verse
differently: And he shall plant in the
hearts of the children the promises made
to the fathers, and the hearts of the
children shall turn to their fathers. If it
were not so, the whole Earth would be
utterly wasted at his coming.
40 In addition to these, he quoted the
eleventh chapter of Isaiah, saying that it
was about to be fulfilled. He quoted also
the third chapter of Acts, twenty-second
and twenty-third verses, precisely as they
stand in our New Testament. He said that
that prophet was Christ; but the day had
not yet come when "they who would not
hear his voice should be cut off from
among the people," but soon would come.
41 He also quoted the second chapter of
Joel, from the twenty-eighth verse to the

last. He also said that this was not yet fulfilled, but was soon to be. And he further stated that the fulness of the Gentiles was soon to come in. He quoted many other passages of scripture, and offered many explanations which cannot be mentioned here.
42 Again, he told me, that when I got those plates of which he had spoken—for the time that they should be obtained was not yet fulfilled—I should not show them to any person; neither the breastplate with the Urim and Thummim; only to those to whom I should be commanded to show them; if I did I should be destroyed. While he was conversing with me about the plates, the vision was opened to my mind that I could see the place where the plates were deposited, and that so clearly and distinctly that I knew the place again when I visited it.
43 After this communication, I saw the light in the room begin to gather immediately around the person of him who had been speaking to me, and it continued to do so until the room was again left dark, except just around him; when, instantly I saw, as it were, a conduit open right up into heaven, and he ascended till he entirely disappeared, and the room was left as it had been before this heavenly light had made its appearance.
44 I lay musing on the singularity of the scene, and marveling greatly at what had been told to me by this extraordinary messenger; when, in the midst of my meditation, I suddenly discovered that my room was again beginning to get lighted, and in an instant, as it were, the same heavenly messenger was again by my bedside.
45 He commenced, and again related the very same things which he had done at his first visit, without the least variation; which having done, he informed me of great judgments which were coming upon the Earth, with great desolations by famine, sword, and pestilence; and that these grievous judgments would come on the Earth in this generation. Having related these things, he again ascended as he had done before.
46 By this time, so deep were the impressions made on my mind, that sleep had fled from my eyes, and I lay overwhelmed in astonishment at what I had both seen and heard. But what was my surprise when again I beheld the same messenger at my bedside, and heard him rehearse or repeat over again to me the same things as before; and added a caution to me, telling me that Satan would try to tempt me (in consequence of the indigent circumstances of my father's family), to get the plates for the purpose of getting rich. This he forbade me, saying that I must have no other object in view in getting the plates but to glorify God, and must not be influenced by any other motive than that of building his kingdom; otherwise I could not get them.
47 After this third visit, he again ascended into heaven as before, and I was again left to ponder on the strangeness of what I had just experienced; when almost immediately after the heavenly messenger had ascended from me for the third time, the cock crowed, and I found that day was approaching, so that our interviews must have occupied the whole of that night.
48 I shortly after arose from my bed, and, as usual, went to the necessary labors of the day; but, in attempting to work as at other times, I found my strength so exhausted as to render me entirely unable. My father, who was laboring along with me, discovered something to be wrong with me, and told me to go home. I started with the intention of going to the house; but, in attempting to cross the fence out of the field where we were, my strength entirely failed me, and I fell helpless on the ground, and for a time was quite unconscious of anything.
49 The first thing that I can recollect was a voice speaking unto me, calling me by name. I looked up, and beheld the same messenger standing over my head, surrounded by light as before. He then again related unto me all that he had related to me the previous night, and commanded me to go to my father and tell him of the vision and commandments which I had received.
50 I obeyed; I returned to my father in the field, and rehearsed the whole matter to him. He replied to me that it was of God, and told me to go and do as commanded by the messenger. I left the field, and went to the place where the messenger had told me the plates were deposited; and owing to the distinctness of the vision which I

had had concerning it, I knew the place the instant that I arrived there.
51 Convenient to the village of Manchester, Ontario county, New York, stands a hill of considerable size, and the most elevated of any in the neighborhood. On the west side of this hill, not far from the top, under a stone of considerable size, lay the plates, deposited in a stone box. This stone was thick and rounding in the middle on the upper side, and thinner towards the edges, so that the middle part of it was visible above the ground, but the edge all around was covered with Earth.
52 Having removed the Earth, I obtained a lever, which I got fixed under the edge of the stone, and with a little exertion raised it up. I looked in, and there indeed did I behold the plates, the Urim and Thum-mim, and the breastplate, as stated by the messenger. The box in which they lay was formed by laying stones together in some kind of cement. In the bottom of the box were laid two stones crossways of the box, and on these stones lay the plates and the other things with them.
53 I made an attempt to take them out, but was forbidden by the messenger, and was again informed that the time for bringing them forth had not yet arrived, neither would it, until four years from that time; but he told me that I should come to that place precisely in one year from that time, and that he would there meet with me, and that I should continue to do so until the time should come for obtaining the plates.
54 Accordingly, as I had been commanded, I went at the end of each year, and at each time I found the same messenger there, and received instruction and intelligence from him at each of our interviews, respecting what the Lord was going to do, and how and in what manner his kingdom was to be conducted in the last days.
59 At length the time arrived for obtaining the plates, the Urim and Thummim, and the breastplate. On the twenty-second day of September, one thousand eight hundred and twenty-seven, having gone as usual at the end of another year to the place where they were deposited, the same heavenly messenger delivered them up to me with this charge: that I should be responsible for them; that if I should let them go carelessly, or through any neglect of mine, I should be cut off; but that if I would use all my endeavors to preserve them, until he, the messenger, should call for them, they should be protected.

The Hill Cumorah, by C.C.A. Christensen, 19th century.

26

A MARVELOUS WORK AND A WONDER

+++

The gold plates are delivered to Joseph Smith. A portion of the record is sealed. Joseph is commanded to translate only the unsealed portion. Characters copied from the plates are delivered to Dr. Charles Anthon of Columbia College, NY, who declares that the characters appear authentic, but that he cannot read a sealed book.

DOCTRINE AND COVENANTS 4

Joseph Smith *February 1829*

1 Now behold, a marvelous work is about
to come forth among the children of men.
2 Therefore, O ye that embark in the
service of God, see that ye serve him with
all your heart, might, mind and strength,
that ye may stand blameless before God at
the last day.
3 Therefore, if ye have desires to serve
God ye are called to the work;
4 For behold the field is white already to
harvest; and lo, he that thrusteth in his
sickle with his might, the same layeth up
in store that he perisheth not, but
bringeth salvation to his soul;
5 And faith, hope, charity and love, with
an eye single to the glory of God, qualify
him for the work.
6 Remember faith, virtue, knowledge,
temperance, patience, brotherly kindness,
godliness, charity, humility, diligence.
7 Ask, and ye shall receive; knock, and it
shall be opened unto you. Amen.

2 NEPHI 27 (see also ISAIAH 29)

Isaiah *550 BC*

6 And it shall come to pass that the Lord
God shall bring forth unto you the words
of a book, and they shall be the words of
them which have slumbered.
7 And behold the book shall be sealed; and
in the book shall be a revelation from God,
from the beginning of the world to the
ending thereof.
8 Wherefore, because of the things which
are sealed up, the things which are sealed
shall not be delivered in the day of the
wickedness and abominations of the
people. Wherefore the book shall be kept
from them.
9 But the book shall be delivered unto a
man, and he shall deliver the words of the
book, which are the words of those who
have slumbered in the dust, and he shall
deliver these words unto another;
10 But the words which are sealed he shall
not deliver, neither shall he deliver the
book. For the book shall be sealed by the
power of God, and the revelation which
was sealed shall be kept in the book until
the own due time of the Lord, that they
may come forth; for behold, they reveal all
things from the foundation of the world
unto the end thereof.
11 And the day cometh that the words of
the book which were sealed shall be read
upon the house tops; and they shall be
read by the power of Christ; and all things
shall be revealed unto the children of men
which ever have been among the children
of men, and which ever will be even unto
the end of the Earth.
12 Wherefore, at that day when the book
shall be delivered unto the man of whom
I have spoken…
15 But behold, it shall come to pass that
the Lord God shall say unto him to whom
he shall deliver the book: Take these
words which are not sealed and deliver
them to another, that he may show them
unto the learned, saying: Read this, I pray
thee. And the learned shall say: Bring
hither the book, and I will read them.
16 And now, because of the glory of the
world and to get again will they say this,
and not for the glory of God.
17 And the man shall say: I cannot bring
the book, for it is sealed.

Dr. Charles Anthon

Dr. Samuel Latham Mitchill

18 Then shall the learned say: I cannot read it.
19 Wherefore it shall come to pass, that the Lord God will deliver again the book and the words thereof to him that is not learned; and the man that is not learned shall say: I am not learned.
20 Then shall the Lord God say unto him: The learned shall not read them, for they have rejected them, and I am able to do mine own work; wherefore thou shalt read the words which I shall give unto thee.
21 Touch not the things which are sealed, for I will bring them forth in mine own due time; for I will show unto the children of men that I am able to do mine own work.
22 Wherefore, when thou hast read the words which I have commanded thee, and obtained the witnesses which I have promised unto thee, then shalt thou seal up the book again, and hide it up unto me, that I may preserve the words which thou hast not read, until I shall see fit in mine own wisdom to reveal all things unto the children of men.

ETHER 5

Moroni — *400 AD*

1 And now I, Moroni, have written the words which were commanded me, according to my memory; and I have told you the things which I have sealed up; therefore touch them not in order that ye may translate; for that thing is forbidden you, except by and by it shall be wisdom in God.

ISAIAH 29

Isaiah — *740 BC*

11 And the vision of all is become unto you as the words of a book that is sealed, which men deliver to one that is learned, saying, Read this, I pray thee: and he saith, I cannot; for it is sealed:
12 And the book is delivered to him that is not learned, saying, Read this, I pray thee: and he saith, I am not learned.

JOSEPH SMITH - HISTORY 1

Joseph Smith — *1828*

62 By this timely aid was I enabled to reach the place of my destination in Pennsylvania; and immediately after my arrival there I commenced copying the characters off the plates. I copied a considerable number of them, and by means of the Urim and Thummim I translated some of them, which I did between the time I arrived at the house of my wife's father, in the month of December, and the February following.

63 Sometime in this month of February, the aforementioned Mr. Martin Harris came to our place, got the characters which I had drawn off the plates, and started with them to the city of New York. For what took place relative to him and the characters, I refer to his own account of the circumstances, as he related them to me after his return, which was as follows:
64 "I went to the city of New York, and presented the characters which had been translated, with the translation thereof, to Professor Charles Anthon, a gentleman celebrated for his literary attainments. Professor Anthon stated that the translation was correct, more so than any he had before seen translated from the Egyptian. I then showed him those which were not yet translated, and he said that they were Egyptian, Chaldaic, Assyriac, and Arabic; and he said they were true characters. He gave me a certificate, certifying to the people of Palmyra that they were true characters, and that the translation of such of them as had been translated was also correct. I took the certificate and put it into my pocket, and was just leaving the house, when Mr. Anthon called me back, and asked me how the young man found out that there were gold plates in the place where he found them. I answered that an angel of God had revealed it unto him.
65 "He then said to me, 'Let me see that certificate.' I accordingly took it out of my pocket and gave it to him, when he took it and tore it to pieces, saying that there was no such thing now as ministering of angels, and that if I would bring the plates to him he would translate them. I informed him that part of the plates were sealed, and that I was forbidden to bring them. He replied, 'I cannot read a sealed book.' I left him and went to Dr. Mitchell, who sanctioned what Professor Anthon had said respecting both the characters and the translation."

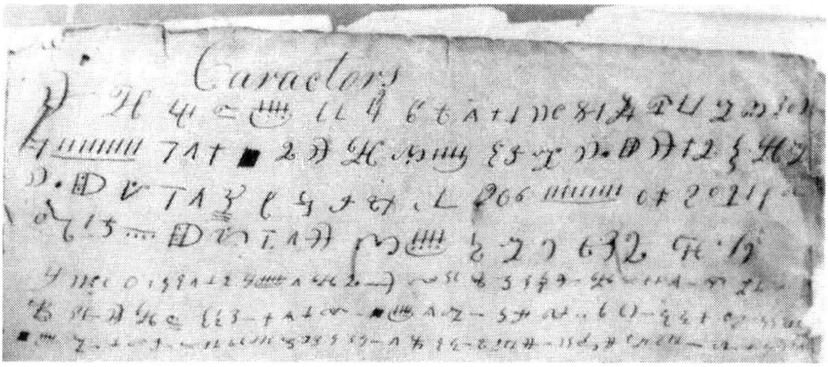

"Caractors Document" believed to be what was presented to, or was at least similar to, what was presented to Dr. Anthon and Dr. Mitchill by Martin Harris in 1828. Characters copied by John Whitmer, circa 1829–1831.

27

WITNESSES OF THE GOLD PLATES

✦✦✦

Prophecies relating to witnesses of the gold plates. There were twelve official witnesses of the gold plates and a handful of others. None ever denied their witness.

2 NEPHI 27

Isaiah — *550 BC*

12...the book shall be hid from the eyes of the world, that the eyes of none shall behold it save it be that three witnesses shall behold it, by the power of God, besides him to whom the book shall be delivered; and they shall testify to the truth of the book and the things therein.
13 And there is none other which shall view it, save it be a few according to the will of God, to bear testimony of his word unto the children of men; for the Lord God hath said that the words of the faithful should speak as if it were from the dead.
14 Wherefore, the Lord God will proceed to bring forth the words of the book; and in the mouth of as many witnesses as seemeth him good will he establish his word; and wo be unto him that rejecteth the word of God!

ETHER 5

Moroni — *400 AD*

2 And behold, ye may be privileged that ye may show the plates unto those who shall assist to bring forth this work;
3 And unto three shall they be shown by the power of God; wherefore they shall know of a surety that these things are true.
4 And in the mouth of three witnesses shall these things be established; and the testimony of three, and this work, in the which shall be shown forth the power of God and also his word, of which the Father, and the Son, and the Holy Ghost bear record—and all this shall stand as a testimony against the world at the last day.
5 And if it so be that they repent and come unto the Father in the name of Jesus, they shall be received into the kingdom of God.

DOCTRINE AND COVENANTS 5

Joseph Smith — *March 1829*

1 Behold, I say unto you, that as my servant Martin Harris has desired a witness at my hand, that you, my servant Joseph Smith, Jun., have got the plates of which you have testified and borne record that you have received of me;
2 And now, behold, this shall you say unto him—he who spake unto you, said unto you: I, the Lord, am God, and have given these things unto you, my servant Joseph Smith, Jun., and have commanded you that you should stand as a witness of these things;
3 And I have caused you that you should enter into a covenant with me, that you should not show them except to those persons to whom I commanded you; and you have no power over them except I grant it unto you.
4 And you have a gift to translate the plates; and this is the first gift that I bestowed upon you; and I have commanded that you should pretend to no other gift until my purpose is fulfilled in this; for I will grant unto you no other gift until it is finished.
5 Verily, I say unto you, that woe shall come unto the inhabitants of the Earth if they will not hearken unto my words;
6 For hereafter you shall be ordained and go forth and deliver my words unto the children of men.
7 Behold, if they will not believe my words, they would not believe you, my servant Joseph, if it were possible that you should show them all these things which I have committed unto you.
8 Oh, this unbelieving and stiffnecked generation—mine anger is kindled against them.
9 Behold, verily I say unto you, I have reserved those things which I have

entrusted unto you, my servant Joseph, for
a wise purpose in me, and it shall be made
known unto future generations;
10 But this generation shall have my word
through you;
11 And in addition to your testimony, the
testimony of three of my servants, whom
I shall call and ordain, unto whom I will
show these things, and they shall go forth
with my words that are given through
you.
12 Yea, they shall know of a surety that
these things are true, for from heaven will
I declare it unto them.
13 I will give them power that they may
behold and view these things as they are;
14 And to none else will I grant this
power, to receive this same testimony
among this generation, in this the begin-
ning of the rising up and the coming forth
of my church out of the wilderness—clear
as the moon, and fair as the sun, and
terrible as an army with banners.
15 And the testimony of three witnesses
will I send forth of my word.
16 And behold, whosoever believeth on
my words, them will I visit with the man-
ifestation of my Spirit; and they shall be
born of me, even of water and of the
Spirit—
17 And you must wait yet a little while,
for ye are not yet ordained—
18 And their testimony shall also go forth
unto the condemnation of this generation
if they harden their hearts against them;
23 And now, again, I speak unto you, my
servant Joseph, concerning the man that
desires the witness—
24 Behold, I say unto him, he exalts
himself and does not humble himself
sufficiently before me; but if he will bow
down before me, and humble himself in
mighty prayer and faith, in the sincerity of
his heart, then will I grant unto him a
view of the things which he desires to see.
25 And then he shall say unto the people
of this generation: Behold, I have seen the
things which the Lord hath shown unto
Joseph Smith, Jun., and I know of a surety
that they are true, for I have seen them,
for they have been shown unto me by the
power of God and not of man.
26 And I the Lord command him, my
servant Martin Harris, that he shall say no
more unto them concerning these things,
except he shall say: I have seen them, and
they have been shown unto me by the
power of God; and these are the words
which he shall say.
27 But if he deny this he will break the
covenant which he has before covenanted
with me, and behold, he is condemned.
28 And now, except he humble himself
and acknowledge unto me the things that
he has done which are wrong, and
covenant with me that he will keep my
commandments, and exercise faith in me,
behold, I say unto him, he shall have no
such views, for I will grant unto him no
views of the things of which I have
spoken.
29 And if this be the case, I command you,
my servant Joseph, that you shall say unto
him, that he shall do no more, nor trouble
me any more concerning this matter.

DOCTRINE AND COVENANTS 17

Joseph Smith *June 1829*

1 Behold, I say unto you, that you must
rely upon my word, which if you do with
full purpose of heart, you shall have a view
of the plates, and also of the breastplate,
the sword of Laban, the Urim and Thum-
mim, which were given to the brother of
Jared upon the mount, when he talked
with the Lord face to face, and the mira-
culous directors which were given to Lehi
while in the wilderness, on the borders of
the Red Sea.
2 And it is by your faith that you shall
obtain a view of them, even by that faith
which was had by the prophets of old.
3 And after that you have obtained faith,
and have seen them with your eyes, you
shall testify of them, by the power of God;
4 And this you shall do that my servant
Joseph Smith, Jun., may not be destroyed,
that I may bring about my righteous
purposes unto the children of men in this
work.
5 And ye shall testify that you have seen
them, even as my servant Joseph Smith,
Jun., has seen them; for it is by my power
that he has seen them, and it is because he
had faith.
6 And he has translated the book, even
that part which I have commanded him,
and as your Lord and your God liveth it is
true.
7 Wherefore, you have received the same
power, and the same faith, and the same
gift like unto him;

The three witnesses of the Book of Mormon.

8 And if you do these last commandments of mine, which I have given you, the gates of hell shall not prevail against you; for my grace is sufficient for you, and you shall be lifted up at the last day.
9 And I, Jesus Christ, your Lord and your God, have spoken it unto you, that I might bring about my righteous purposes unto the children of men. Amen.

THE TESTIMONY OF THREE WITNESSES

1830

Be it known unto all nations, kindreds, tongues, and people, unto whom this work shall come: That we, through the grace of God the Father, and our Lord Jesus Christ, have seen the plates which contain this record, which is a record of the people of Nephi, and also of the Lamanites, their brethren, and also of the people of Jared, who came from the tower of which hath been spoken. And we also know that they have been translated by the gift and power of God, for his voice hath declared it unto us; wherefore we know of a surety that the work is true. And we also testify that we have seen the engravings which are upon the plates; and they have been shown unto us by the power of God, and not of man. And we declare with words of soberness, that an angel of God came down from heaven, and he brought and laid before our eyes, that we beheld and saw the plates, and the engravings thereon; and we know that it is by the grace of God the Father, and our Lord Jesus Christ, that we beheld and bear record that these things are true. And it is marvelous in our eyes. Nevertheless, the voice of the Lord commanded us that we should bear record of it; wherefore, to be obedient unto the commandments of God, we bear testimony of these things. And we know that if we are faithful in Christ, we shall rid our garments of the blood of all men, and be found spotless before the judgment-seat of Christ, and shall dwell with him eternally in the heavens. And the honor be to the Father, and to the Son, and to the Holy Ghost, which is one God. Amen.

Oliver Cowdery
David Whitmer
Martin Harris

THE TESTIMONY OF EIGHT WITNESSES

1830

Be it known unto all nations, kindreds, tongues, and people, unto whom this work shall come: That Joseph Smith, Jun., the translator of this work, has shown unto us the plates of which hath been spoken, which have the appearance of gold; and as many of the leaves as the said Smith has translated we did handle with our hands; and we also saw the engravings thereon, all of which has the appearance of ancient work, and of curious workmanship. And this we bear record with words of soberness, that the said Smith has shown unto us, for we have seen and hefted, and know of a surety that the said Smith has got the plates of which we have spoken. And we give our names unto the world, to witness unto the world that which we have seen. And we lie not, God bearing witness of it.

Hyrum Smith

Jacob Whitmer

Joseph Smith, Sen.

John Whitmer

Samuel H. Smith

Not pictured:

Christian Whitmer

Peter Whitmer, Jun.

Hiram Page

28

THE REACTION TO THE BOOK OF MORMON

+++

Prophecies describing the state of Christianity at the time the Book of Mormon is published. Also related are prophecies of the worldly reaction to the Book of Mormon.

2 NEPHI 28

Nephi, Son of Lehi *550 BC*

1 And now, behold, my brethren, I have spoken unto you, according as the Spirit hath constrained me; wherefore, I know that they must surely come to pass.

2 And the things which shall be written out of the book shall be of great worth unto the children of men, and especially unto our seed, which is a remnant of the house of Israel.

3 For it shall come to pass in that day that the churches which are built up, and not unto the Lord, when the one shall say unto the other: Behold, I, I am the Lord's; and the others shall say: I, I am the Lord's; and thus shall everyone say that hath built up churches, and not unto the Lord—

4 And they shall contend one with another; and their priests shall contend one with another, and they shall teach with their learning, and deny the Holy Ghost, which giveth utterance.

5 And they deny the power of God, the Holy One of Israel; and they say unto the people: Hearken unto us, and hear ye our precept; for behold there is no God today, for the Lord and the Redeemer hath done his work, and he hath given his power unto men;

6 Behold, hearken ye unto my precept; if they shall say there is a miracle wrought by the hand of the Lord, believe it not; for this day he is not a God of miracles; he hath done his work.

7 Yea, and there shall be many which shall say: Eat, drink, and be merry, for tomorrow we die; and it shall be well with us.

8 And there shall also be many which shall say: Eat, drink, and be merry; nevertheless, fear God—he will justify in committing a little sin; yea, lie a little, take the advantage of one because of his words, dig a pit for thy neighbor; there is no harm in this; and do all these things, for tomorrow we die; and if it so be that we are guilty, God will beat us with a few stripes, and at last we shall be saved in the kingdom of God.

9 Yea, and there shall be many which shall teach after this manner, false and vain and foolish doctrines, and shall be puffed up in their hearts, and shall seek deep to hide

John Calvin (1509-1564), French reformer who developed a system of theology adhered to by various Congregational, Reformed, and Presbyterian churches. Originally as a reaction to claims of Roman Catholic miracles, he formulated the doctrine of cessationism – that spiritual gifts and miracles had ceased with the Apostolic age.

their counsels from the Lord; and their
works shall be in the dark.
10 And the blood of the saints shall cry
from the ground against them.
11 Yea, they have all gone out of the way;
they have become corrupted.
12 Because of pride, and because of false
teachers, and false doctrine, their
churches have become corrupted, and
their churches are lifted up; because of
pride they are puffed up.
13 They rob the poor because of their fine
sanctuaries; they rob the poor because of
their fine clothing; and they persecute the
meek and the poor in heart, because in
their pride they are puffed up.
14 They wear stiff necks and high heads;
yea, and because of pride, and wickedness,
and abominations, and whoredoms, they
have all gone astray save it be a few, who
are the humble followers of Christ; never-
theless, they are led, that in many
instances they do err because they are
taught by the precepts of men.
15 O the wise, and the learned, and the
rich, that are puffed up in the pride of
their hearts, and all those who preach false
doctrines, and all those who commit
whoredoms, and pervert the right way of
the Lord, wo, wo, wo be unto them, saith
the Lord God Almighty, for they shall be
thrust down to hell!
16 Wo unto them that turn aside the just
for a thing of naught and revile against
that which is good, and say that it is of no
worth! For the day shall come that the
Lord God will speedily visit the inhab-
itants of the Earth; and in that day that
they are fully ripe in iniquity they shall
perish.
17 But behold, if the inhabitants of the
Earth shall repent of their wickedness and
abominations they shall not be destroyed,
saith the Lord of Hosts.
18 But behold, that great and abominable
church, the whore of all the Earth, must
tumble to the Earth, and great must be the
fall thereof.
19 For the kingdom of the devil must
shake, and they which belong to it must
needs be stirred up unto repentance, or
the devil will grasp them with his ever-
lasting chains, and they be stirred up to
anger, and perish;
20 For behold, at that day shall he rage in
the hearts of the children of men, and stir
them up to anger against that which is
good.
21 And others will he pacify, and lull them
away into carnal security, that they will
say: All is well in Zion; yea, Zion
prospereth, all is well—and thus the devil
cheateth their souls, and leadeth them
away carefully down to hell.
22 And behold, others he flattereth away,
and telleth them there is no hell; and he
saith unto them: I am no devil, for there is
none—and thus he whispereth in their
ears, until he grasps them with his awful
chains, from whence there is no
deliverance.
23 Yea, they are grasped with death, and
hell; and death, and hell, and the devil,
and all that have been seized therewith
must stand before the throne of God, and
be judged according to their works, from
whence they must go into the place pre-
pared for them, even a lake of fire and
brimstone, which is endless torment.
24 Therefore, wo be unto him that is at
ease in Zion!
25 Wo be unto him that crieth: All is well!
26 Yea, wo be unto him that hearkeneth
unto the precepts of men, and denieth the
power of God, and the gift of the Holy
Ghost!
27 Yea, wo be unto him that saith: We
have received, and we need no more!
28 And in fine, wo unto all those who
tremble, and are angry because of the
truth of God! For behold, he that is built
upon the rock receiveth it with gladness;
and he that is built upon a sandy found-
ation trembleth lest he shall fall.
29 Wo be unto him that shall say: We
have received the word of God, and we
need no more of the word of God, for we
have enough!
30 For behold, thus saith the Lord God: I
will give unto the children of men line
upon line, precept upon precept, here a
little and there a little; and blessed are
those who hearken unto my precepts, and
lend an ear unto my counsel, for they shall
learn wisdom; for unto him that receiveth
I will give more; and from them that shall
say, We have enough, from them shall be
taken away even that which they have.
31 Cursed is he that putteth his trust in
man, or maketh flesh his arm, or shall
hearken unto the precepts of men, save

The Westminster Assembly of Divines crafted the Westminster Confession of Faith in 1647, which remains the standard doctrine of many Presbyterian churches to this day. Contained therein is the doctrine of Sufficiency of Scripture which holds that, "The whole counsel of God, concerning all things necessary for His own glory, man's salvation, faith, and life, is either expressly set down in Scripture, or by good and necessary consequence may be deduced from Scripture: unto which nothing at any time is to be added, whether by new revelations of the Spirit, or traditions of men."

their precepts shall be given by the power
of the Holy Ghost.
32 Wo be unto the Gentiles, saith the Lord
God of Hosts! For notwithstanding I shall
lengthen out mine arm unto them from
day to day, they will deny me; neverthe-
less, I will be merciful unto them, saith the
Lord God, if they will repent and come
unto me; for mine arm is lengthened out
all the day long, saith the Lord God of
Hosts.

MORMON 8

Moroni 400 AD

17 And if there be faults they be the faults
of a man. But behold, we know no fault;
nevertheless God knoweth all things;
therefore, he that condemneth, let him be
aware lest he shall be in danger of hell fire.
18 And he that saith: Show unto me, or ye
shall be smitten—let him beware lest he
commandeth that which is forbidden of
the Lord.
19 For behold, the same that judgeth
rashly shall be judged rashly again; for
according to his works shall his wages be;
therefore, he that smiteth shall be smitten
again, of the Lord.
20 Behold what the scripture says—man
shall not smite, neither shall he judge; for
judgment is mine, saith the Lord, and ven-
geance is mine also, and I will repay.
21 And he that shall breathe out wrath
and strifes against the work of the Lord,
and against the covenant people of the
Lord who are the house of Israel, and shall
say: We will destroy the work of the Lord,
and the Lord will not remember his
covenant which he hath made unto the
house of Israel—the same is in danger to
be hewn down and cast into the fire;
22 For the eternal purposes of the Lord
shall roll on, until all his promises shall be
fulfilled.
23 Search the prophecies of Isaiah.
Behold, I cannot write them. Yea, behold
I say unto you, that those saints who have
gone before me, who have possessed this
land, shall cry, yea, even from the dust
will they cry unto the Lord; and as the

Lord liveth he will remember the
covenant which he hath made with them.
24 And he knoweth their prayers, that
they were in behalf of their brethren. And
he knoweth their faith, for in his name
could they remove mountains; and in his
name could they cause the Earth to shake;
and by the power of his word did they
cause prisons to tumble to the Earth; yea,
even the fiery furnace could not harm
them, neither wild beasts nor poisonous
serpents, because of the power of his
word.
25 And behold, their prayers were also in
behalf of him that the Lord should suffer
to bring these things forth.
26 And no one need say they shall not
come, for they surely shall, for the Lord
hath spoken it; for out of the Earth shall
they come, by the hand of the Lord, and
none can stay it; and it shall come in a day
when it shall be said that miracles are
done away; and it shall come even as if one
should speak from the dead.
27 And it shall come in a day when the
blood of saints shall cry unto the Lord,
because of secret combinations and the
works of darkness.
28 Yea, it shall come in a day when the
power of God shall be denied, and
churches become defiled and be lifted up
in the pride of their hearts; yea, even in a
day when leaders of churches and
teachers shall rise in the pride of their
hearts, even to the envying of them who
belong to their churches.
29 Yea, it shall come in a day when there
shall be heard of fires, and tempests, and
vapors of smoke in foreign lands;
30 And there shall also be heard of wars,
rumors of wars, and earthquakes in divers
places.
31 Yea, it shall come in a day when there
shall be great pollutions upon the face of
the Earth; there shall be murders, and
robbing, and lying, and deceivings, and
whoredoms, and all manner of abomina-
tions; when there shall be many who will
say, Do this, or do that, and it mattereth
not, for the Lord will uphold such at the
last day. But wo unto such, for they are in
the gall of bitterness and in the bonds of
iniquity.
32 Yea, it shall come in a day when there
shall be churches built up that shall say:
Come unto me, and for your money you
shall be forgiven of your sins.
33 O ye wicked and perverse and stiff-
necked people, why have ye built up
churches unto yourselves to get gain?
Why have ye transfigured the holy word
of God, that ye might bring damnation
upon your souls? Behold, look ye unto the
revelations of God; for behold, the time
cometh at that day when all these things
must be fulfilled.
34 Behold, the Lord hath shown unto me
great and marvelous things concerning
that which must shortly come, at that day
when these things shall come forth among
you.
35 Behold, I speak unto you as if ye were
present, and yet ye are not. But behold,
Jesus Christ hath shown you unto me, and
I know your doing.
36 And I know that ye do walk in the
pride of your hearts; and there are none
save a few only who do not lift themselves
up in the pride of their hearts, unto the
wearing of very fine apparel, unto envy-
ing, and strifes, and malice, and persecu-
tions, and all manner of iniquities; and
your churches, yea, even everyone, have
become polluted because of the pride of
your hearts.
37 For behold, ye do love money, and your
substance, and your fine apparel, and the
adorning of your churches, more than ye
love the poor and the needy, the sick and
the afflicted.
38 O ye pollutions, ye hypocrites, ye
teachers, who sell yourselves for that
which will canker, why have ye polluted
the holy church of God? Why are ye
ashamed to take upon you the name of
Christ? Why do ye not think that greater
is the value of an endless happiness than
that misery which never dies—because of
the praise of the world?
39 Why do ye adorn yourselves with that
which hath no life, and yet suffer the
hungry, and the needy, and the naked,
and the sick and the afflicted to pass by
you, and notice them not?
40 Yea, why do ye build up your secret
abominations to get gain, and cause that
widows should mourn before the Lord,
and also orphans to mourn before the
Lord, and also the blood of their fathers
and their husbands to cry unto the Lord

from the ground, for vengeance upon your
heads?
41 Behold, the sword of vengeance hang-
eth over you; and the time soon cometh
that he avengeth the blood of the saints
upon you, for he will not suffer their cries
any longer.

2 NEPHI 29

Nephi, Son of Lehi — *550 BC*

1 But behold, there shall be many—at that
day when I shall proceed to do a marvel-
ous work among them, that I may remem-
ber my covenants which I have made unto
the children of men, that I may set my
hand again the second time to recover my
people, which are of the house of Israel;
2 And also, that I may remember the
promises which I have made unto thee,
Nephi, and also unto thy father, that I
would remember your seed; and that the
words of your seed should proceed forth
out of my mouth unto your seed; and my
words shall hiss forth unto the ends of the
Earth, for a standard unto my people,
which are of the house of Israel;
3 And because my words shall hiss forth—
many of the Gentiles shall say: A Bible! A
Bible! We have got a Bible, and there
cannot be any more Bible.
4 But thus saith the Lord God: O fools,
they shall have a Bible; and it shall pro-
ceed forth from the Jews, mine ancient
covenant people. And what thank they
the Jews for the Bible which they receive
from them? Yea, what do the Gentiles
mean? Do they remember the travails, and
the labors, and the pains of the Jews, and
their diligence unto me, in bringing forth
salvation unto the Gentiles?
5 O ye Gentiles, have ye remembered the
Jews, mine ancient covenant people? Nay;
but ye have cursed them, and have hated
them, and have not sought to recover
them. But behold, I will return all these
things upon your own heads; for I the
Lord have not forgotten my people.
6 Thou fool, that shall say: A Bible, we
have got a Bible, and we need no more
Bible. Have ye obtained a Bible save it
were by the Jews?
7 Know ye not that there are more nations
than one? Know ye not that I, the Lord
your God, have created all men, and that I
remember those who are upon the isles of
the sea; and that I rule in the heavens

"BLASPHEMY.—*Book of Mormon*, alias *The Golden Bible*.—The 'Book of Mormon' has been placed in our hands. A viler imposition was never practiced. It is an evidence of fraud, blasphemy and credulity, shocking to the Christian and moralist. The author and propriotor is one Joseph Smith, jr. a fellow who, by some hocus pocus, acquired such an influence over a wealthy farmer of Wayne county, that the latter mortgaged his farm for $3000, which he paid for printing and binding 5000 copies of this blasphemous work. The volume consists of about 600 pages, and is divided into the book of Nephi, of Jacob, of Mosiah, of Alma, of Mormon, of Ether, and of Helaman—'copy right secured."

A typical reaction to the Book of Mormon. Sentinel and Democrat; Burlington, VT, 4 June 1830, page 1

above and in the Earth beneath; and I
bring forth my word unto the children of
men, yea, even upon all the nations of the
Earth?

2 NEPHI 15 (see also ISAIAH 5)

Isaiah — *740 BC*

24 Therefore, as the fire devoureth the
stubble, and the flame consumeth the
chaff, their root shall be rottenness, and
their blossoms shall go up as dust; because
they have cast away the law of the Lord of
Hosts, and despised the word of the Holy
One of Israel.
25 Therefore, is the anger of the Lord
kindled against his people, and he hath
stretched forth his hand against them, and
hath smitten them; and the hills did
tremble, and their carcasses were torn in
the midst of the streets. For all this his
anger is not turned away, but his hand is
stretched out still.
26 And he will lift up an ensign to the
nations from far, and will hiss unto them
from the end of the Earth; and behold,
they shall come with speed swiftly; none
shall be weary nor stumble among them.

29

THE PURPOSE OF THE BOOK OF MORMON

+++

The purpose of the Book of Mormon is to prove the Bible is true. It confounds false doctrines, eliminates contentions, and establishes peace. It proves that the American Indians are of the House of Israel. It convinces the Jews that Jesus is the Christ. It contains the fullness of the gospel of Jesus Christ. And, it proves that God speaks to man today by inspiration and revelation, just as he has in the past.

TITLE PAGE – BOOK OF MORMON

Moroni — *421 AD*

Which is to show unto the remnant of the house of Israel what great things the Lord hath done for their fathers; and that they may know the covenants of the Lord, that they are not cast off forever—And also to the convincing of the Jew and Gentile that Jesus is the Christ, the Eternal God, manifesting himself unto all nations.

2 NEPHI 29

Nephi, Son of Lehi — *550 BC*

8 Wherefore murmur ye, because that ye shall receive more of my word? Know ye not that the testimony of two nations is a witness unto you that I am God, that I remember one nation like unto another? Wherefore, I speak the same words unto one nation like unto another. And when the two nations shall run together the testimony of the two nations shall run together also.

9 And I do this that I may prove unto many that I am the same yesterday, today, and forever; and that I speak forth my words according to mine own pleasure. And because that I have spoken one word ye need not suppose that I cannot speak another; for my work is not yet finished; neither shall it be until the end of man, neither from that time henceforth and forever.

10 Wherefore, because that ye have a Bible ye need not suppose that it contains all my words; neither need ye suppose that I have not caused more to be written.

11 For I command all men, both in the east and in the west, and in the north, and in the south, and in the islands of the sea, that they shall write the words which I speak unto them; for out of the books which shall be written I will judge the world, every man according to their works, according to that which is written.

12 For behold, I shall speak unto the Jews and they shall write it; and I shall also speak unto the Nephites and they shall write it; and I shall also speak unto the other tribes of the house of Israel, which I have led away, and they shall write it; and I shall also speak unto all nations of the Earth and they shall write it.

13 And it shall come to pass that the Jews shall have the words of the Nephites, and the Nephites shall have the words of the Jews; and the Nephites and the Jews shall have the words of the lost tribes of Israel; and the lost tribes of Israel shall have the words of the Nephites and the Jews.

14 And it shall come to pass that my people, which are of the house of Israel, shall be gathered home unto the lands of their possessions; and my word also shall be gathered in one. And I will show unto them that fight against my word and against my people, who are of the house of Israel, that I am God, and that I covenanted with Abraham that I would remember his seed forever.

MORMON 5

Mormon — *385 AD*

12 Now these things are written unto the remnant of the house of Jacob; and they are written after this manner, because it is known of God that wickedness will not bring them forth unto them; and they are to be hid up unto the Lord that they may come forth in his own due time.

13 And this is the commandment which I
have received; and behold, they shall
come forth according to the command-
ment of the Lord, when he shall see fit, in
his wisdom.
14 And behold, they shall go unto the
unbelieving of the Jews; and for this intent
shall they go—that they may be persuaded
that Jesus is the Christ, the Son of the
living God; that the Father may bring
about, through his most Beloved, his great
and eternal purpose, in restoring the Jews,
or all the house of Israel, to the land of
their inheritance, which the Lord their
God hath given them, unto the fulfilling
of his covenant;
15 And also that the seed of this people
may more fully believe his gospel, which
shall go forth unto them from the
Gentiles;

DOCTRINE AND COVENANTS 19

Joseph Smith — March 1830

26 And again, I command thee that thou
shalt not covet thine own property, but
impart it freely to the printing of the Book
of Mormon, which contains the truth and
the word of God—
27 Which is my word to the Gentile, that
soon it may go to the Jew, of whom the
Lamanites are a remnant, that they may
believe the gospel, and look not for a
Messiah to come who has already come.

MORMON 7

Mormon — 385 AD

8 Therefore repent, and be baptized in the
name of Jesus, and lay hold upon the
gospel of Christ, which shall be set before
you, not only in this record but also in the
record which shall come unto the Gentiles
from the Jews, which record shall come
from the Gentiles unto you.
9 For behold, this is written for the intent
that ye may believe that; and if ye believe
that ye will believe this also; and if ye
believe this ye will know concerning your
fathers, and also the marvelous works
which were wrought by the power of God
among them.
10 And ye will also know that ye are a
remnant of the seed of Jacob; therefore ye
are numbered among the people of the
first covenant; and if it so be that ye
believe in Christ, and are baptized, first
with water, then with fire and with the
Holy Ghost, following the example of our
Savior, according to that which he hath
commanded us, it shall be well with you
in the day of judgment. Amen.

1 NEPHI 13

Nephi, Son of Lehi — 595 BC

35 For, behold, saith the Lamb: I will
manifest myself unto thy seed, that they
shall write many things which I shall
minister unto them, which shall be plain
and precious; and after thy seed shall be
destroyed, and dwindle in unbelief, and
also the seed of thy brethren, behold,
these things shall be hid up, to come forth
unto the Gentiles, by the gift and power of
the Lamb.
36 And in them shall be written my
gospel, saith the Lamb, and my rock and
my salvation.
37 And blessed are they who shall seek to
bring forth my Zion at that day, for they
shall have the gift and the power of the
Holy Ghost; and if they endure unto the
end they shall be lifted up at the last day,
and shall be saved in the everlasting king-
dom of the Lamb; and whoso shall publish
peace, yea, tidings of great joy, how beaut-
iful upon the mountains shall they be.
38 And it came to pass that I beheld the
remnant of the seed of my brethren, and
also the book of the Lamb of God, which
had proceeded forth from the mouth of
the Jew, that it came forth from the Gen-
tiles unto the remnant of the seed of my
brethren.
39 And after it had come forth unto them
I beheld other books, which came forth by
the power of the Lamb, from the Gentiles
unto them, unto the convincing of the
Gentiles and the remnant of the seed of
my brethren, and also the Jews who were
scattered upon all the face of the Earth,
that the records of the prophets and of the
twelve apostles of the Lamb are true.
40 And the angel spake unto me, saying:
These last records, which thou hast seen
among the Gentiles, shall establish the
truth of the first, which are of the twelve
apostles of the Lamb, and shall make
known the plain and precious things
which have been taken away from them;
and shall make known to all kindreds,
tongues, and people, that the Lamb of God
is the Son of the Eternal Father, and the

Savior of the world; and that all men must
come unto him, or they cannot be saved.
41 And they must come according to the
words which shall be established by the
mouth of the Lamb; and the words of the
Lamb shall be made known in the records
of thy seed, as well as in the records of the
twelve apostles of the Lamb; wherefore
they both shall be established in one; for
there is one God and one Shepherd over
all the Earth.
42 And the time cometh that he shall
manifest himself unto all nations, both
unto the Jews and also unto the Gentiles;
and after he has manifested himself unto
the Jews and also unto the Gentiles, then
he shall manifest himself unto the Gen-
tiles and also unto the Jews, and the last
shall be first, and the first shall be last.

GENESIS 50

Joseph, Son of Israel — *1635 BC*

30 *And again, a seer will I raise up out of*
the fruit of thy loins, and unto him will I
give power to bring forth my word unto
the seed of thy loins; and not to the bring-
ing forth of my word only, saith the Lord,
but to the convincing them of my word,
which shall have already gone forth
among them in the last days;
31 *Wherefore the fruit of thy loins shall*
write, and the fruit of the loins of Judah
shall write; and that which shall be writ-
ten by the fruit of thy loins, and also that
which shall be written by the fruit of the
loins of Judah, shall grow together unto
the confounding of false doctrines, and
laying down of contentions, and establish-
ing peace among the fruit of thy loins, and
bringing them to a knowledge of their
fathers in the latter-days; and also to the
knowledge of my covenants, saith the
Lord. [JST]

EZEKIEL 37

Ezekiel — *598 BC*

15 The word of the LORD came again
unto me, saying,
16 Moreover, thou son of man, take thee
one stick, and write upon it, For Judah,
and for the children of Israel his compan-
ions: then take another stick, and write
upon it, For Joseph, the stick of Ephraim,
and for all the house of Israel his
companions:
17 And join them one to another into one
stick; and they shall become one in thine
hand.
18 And when the children of thy people
shall speak unto thee, saying, Wilt thou
not shew us what thou meanest by these?
19 Say unto them, Thus saith the Lord
GOD; Behold, I will take the stick of
Joseph, which is in the hand of Ephraim,
and the tribes of Israel his fellows, and will
put them with him, even with the stick of
Judah, and make them one stick, and they
shall be one in mine hand.
20 And the sticks whereon thou writest
shall be in thine hand before their eyes.

DOCTRINE AND COVENANTS 3

Joseph Smith — *July 1828*

16 Nevertheless, my work shall go forth,
for inasmuch as the knowledge of a Savior
has come unto the world, through the
testimony of the Jews, even so shall the

The prophecy of Ezekiel that the stick of Judah (Bible) and stick of Ephraim (Book of Mormon) will be joined together into one stick (book) is literally fulfilled in the last days.

knowledge of a Savior come unto my
people—
17 And to the Nephites, and the Jacobites,
and the Josephites, and the Zoramites,
through the testimony of their fathers—
18 And this testimony shall come to the
knowledge of the Lamanites, and the
Lemuelites, and the Ishmaelites, who
dwindled in unbelief because of the
iniquity of their fathers, whom the Lord
has suffered to destroy their brethren the
Nephites, because of their iniquities and
their abominations.
19 And for this very purpose are these
plates preserved, which contain these
records—that the promises of the Lord
might be fulfilled, which he made to his
people;
20 And that the Lamanites might come to
the knowledge of their fathers, and that
they might know the promises of the
Lord, and that they may believe the gospel
and rely upon the merits of Jesus Christ,
and be glorified through faith in his name,
and that through their repentance they
might be saved. Amen.

DOCTRINE AND COVENANTS 10

Joseph Smith *April 1829*

57 Behold, I am Jesus Christ, the Son of
God. I came unto mine own, and mine
own received me not.
58 I am the light which shineth in dark-
ness, and the darkness comprehendeth it
not.
59 I am he who said—Other sheep have I
which are not of this fold—unto my
disciples, and many there were that
understood me not.
60 And I will show unto this people that I
had other sheep, and that they were a
branch of the house of Jacob;
61 And I will bring to light their mar-
velous works, which they did in my name;
62 Yea, and I will also bring to light my
gospel which was ministered unto them,
and, behold, they shall not deny that
which you have received, but they shall
build it up, and shall bring to light the true
points of my doctrine, yea, and the only
doctrine which is in me.
63 And this I do that I may establish my
gospel, that there may not be so much
contention; yea, Satan doth stir up the
hearts of the people to contention con-
cerning the points of my doctrine; and in
these things they do err, for they do wrest
the scriptures and do not understand
them.
64 Therefore, I will unfold unto them this
great mystery;
65 For, behold, I will gather them as a hen
gathereth her chickens under her wings, if
they will not harden their hearts;
66 Yea, if they will come, they may, and
partake of the waters of life freely.
67 Behold, this is my doctrine—whoso-
ever repenteth and cometh unto me, the
same is my church.
68 Whosoever declareth more or less than
this, the same is not of me, but is against
me; therefore he is not of my church.
69 And now, behold, whosoever is of my
church, and endureth of my church to the
end, him will I establish upon my rock,
and the gates of hell shall not prevail
against them.
70 And now, remember the words of him
who is the life and light of the world, your
Redeemer, your Lord and your God.
Amen.

DOCTRINE AND COVENANTS 20

Joseph Smith *April 1830*

1 The rise of the Church of Christ in these
last days, being one thousand eight hun-
dred and thirty years since the coming of
our Lord and Savior Jesus Christ in the
flesh, it being regularly organized and
established agreeable to the laws of our
country, by the will and commandments
of God, in the fourth month, and on the
sixth day of the month which is called
April—
2 Which commandments were given to
Joseph Smith, Jun., who was called of God,
and ordained an apostle of Jesus Christ, to
be the first elder of this church;
3 And to Oliver Cowdery, who was also
called of God, an apostle of Jesus Christ, to
be the second elder of this church, and
ordained under his hand;
4 And this according to the grace of our
Lord and Savior Jesus Christ, to whom be
all glory, both now and forever. Amen.
5 After it was truly manifested unto this
first elder that he had received a remission
of his sins, he was entangled again in the
vanities of the world;
6 But after repenting, and humbling him-
self sincerely, through faith, God min-
istered unto him by an holy angel, whose

countenance was as lightning, and whose
garments were pure and white above all
other whiteness;
7 And gave unto him commandments
which inspired him;
8 And gave him power from on high, by
the means which were before prepared, to
translate the Book of Mormon;
9 Which contains a record of a fallen
people, and the fulness of the gospel of
Jesus Christ to the Gentiles and to the Jews
also;
10 Which was given by inspiration, and is
confirmed to others by the ministering of
angels, and is declared unto the world by
them—
11 Proving to the world that the holy
scriptures are true, and that God does
inspire men and call them to his holy
work in this age and generation, as well as
in generations of old;
12 Thereby showing that he is the same
God yesterday, today, and forever. Amen.
13 Therefore, having so great witnesses,
by them shall the world be judged, even as
many as shall hereafter come to a know-
ledge of this work.
14 And those who receive it in faith, and
work righteousness, shall receive a crown
of eternal life;
15 But those who harden their hearts in
unbelief, and reject it, it shall turn to their
own condemnation—
16 For the Lord God has spoken it; and we,
the elders of the church, have heard and
bear witness to the words of the glorious
Majesty on high, to whom be glory for-
ever and ever. Amen.

30

THE HOLY PRIESTHOOD IS RESTORED

+++

Twelve apostles are called on February 14, 1835. The keys of the holy priesthood are restored and conferred upon man by resurrected saints from all dispensations.

DOCTRINE AND COVENANTS 18

Joseph Smith *June 1829*

26 And now, behold, there are others who are called to declare my gospel, both unto Gentile and unto Jew;
27 Yea, even twelve; and the Twelve shall be my disciples, and they shall take upon them my name; and the Twelve are they who shall desire to take upon them my name with full purpose of heart.
28 And if they desire to take upon them my name with full purpose of heart, they are called to go into all the world to preach my gospel unto every creature.
29 And they are they who are ordained of me to baptize in my name, according to that which is written;
30 And you have that which is written before you; wherefore, you must perform it according to the words which are written.
31 And now I speak unto you, the Twelve—Behold, my grace is sufficient for you; you must walk uprightly before me and sin not.
32 And, behold, you are they who are ordained of me to ordain priests and teachers; to declare my gospel, according to the power of the Holy Ghost which is in you, and according to the callings and gifts of God unto men;
33 And I, Jesus Christ, your Lord and your God, have spoken it.

DOCTRINE AND COVENANTS 13

John the Baptist *May 1829*

1 Upon you my fellow servants, in the name of Messiah I confer the Priesthood of Aaron, which holds the keys of the ministering of angels, and of the gospel of repentance, and of baptism by immersion for the remission of sins; and this shall never be taken again from the Earth, until the sons of Levi do offer again an offering unto the Lord in righteousness.

DOCTRINE AND COVENANTS 27

Joseph Smith *May 1829*

5 Behold, this is wisdom in me; wherefore, marvel not, for the hour cometh that I will drink of the fruit of the vine with you on the Earth, and with Moroni, whom I have sent unto you to reveal the Book of Mormon, containing the fulness of my everlasting gospel, to whom I have committed the keys of the record of the stick of Ephraim;
6 And also with Elias, to whom I have committed the keys of bringing to pass the restoration of all things spoken by the mouth of all the holy prophets since the world began, concerning the last days;
7 And also John the son of Zacharias, which Zacharias he (Elias) visited and gave promise that he should have a son, and his name should be John, and he should be filled with the spirit of Elias;
8 Which John I have sent unto you, my servants, Joseph Smith, Jun., and Oliver Cowdery, to ordain you unto the first priesthood which you have received, that you might be called and ordained even as Aaron;
9 And also Elijah, unto whom I have committed the keys of the power of turning the hearts of the fathers to the children, and the hearts of the children to the fathers, that the whole Earth may not be smitten with a curse;
10 And also with Joseph and Jacob, and Isaac, and Abraham, your fathers, by whom the promises remain;
11 And also with Michael, or Adam, the father of all, the prince of all, the ancient of days;
12 And also with Peter, and James, and John, whom I have sent unto you, by whom I have ordained you and confirmed

you to be apostles, and especial witnesses
of my name, and bear the keys of your
ministry and of the same things which I
revealed unto them;
13 Unto whom I have committed the keys
of my kingdom, and a dispensation of the
gospel for the last times; and for the ful-
ness of times, in the which I will gather
together in gone all things, both which are
in heaven, and which are on Earth;
14 And also with all those whom my
Father hath given me out of the world.
15 Wherefore, lift up your hearts and
rejoice, and gird up your loins, and take
upon you my whole armor, that ye may be
able to withstand the evil day, having
done all, that ye may be able to stand.
16 Stand, therefore, having your loins girt
about with truth, having on the breast-
plate of righteousness, and your feet shod
with the preparation of the gospel of
peace, which I have sent mine angels to
commit unto you;
17 Taking the shield of faith wherewith ye
shall be able to quench all the fiery darts
of the wicked;
18 And take the helmet of salvation, and
the sword of my Spirit, which I will pour
out upon you, and my word which I reveal
unto you, and be agreed as touching all
things whatsoever ye ask of me, and be
faithful until I come, and ye shall be
caught up, that where I am ye shall be
also. Amen.

The Priesthood Restoration, by George Crocheron, 1898.

31

THE BOOK OF MORMON USHERS IN THE GATHERING OF ISRAEL

✦✦✦

The Book of Mormon is the sign given that the great gathering of Israel prior to the Second Coming of Jesus Christ has begun. Not since the Resurrection has such an obvious and unexplainable miracle been wrought by God. Ancient prophets referred to the coming of the Book of Mormon as a "marvelous work and a wonder." The Restoration of the power of the priesthood is likened unto "the Lord making bare his holy arm in the eyes of all the nations."

The purpose of the gathering is to fulfill the covenants made to the House of Israel – that the Lord would remember his covenant with them – and gather them into a belief in Jesus Christ. Through the power of the priesthood, they would enter into sacred covenants such as baptism and the sacred ordinances of the temple, which would protect them against the great day of burning. The Bride (the church) is preparing to meet the Bridegroom (Christ) for the great wedding (the Second Coming and arrival of the Kingdom of God on Earth.)

3 NEPHI 21

<u>*Jesus Christ* *34 AD*</u>

1 And verily I say unto you, I give unto
you a sign, that ye may know the time
when these things shall be about to take
place—that I shall gather in, from their
long dispersion, my people, O house of
Israel, and shall establish again among
them my Zion;
2 And behold, this is the thing which I
will give unto you for a sign—for verily I
say unto you that when these things
which I declare unto you, and which I
shall declare unto you hereafter of myself,
and by the power of the Holy Ghost
which shall be given unto you of the
Father, shall be made known unto the
Gentiles that they may know concerning
this people who are a remnant of the
house of Jacob, and concerning this my
people who shall be scattered by them;
3 Verily, verily, I say unto you, when
these things shall be made known unto
them of the Father, and shall come forth
of the Father, from them unto you;
4 For it is wisdom in the Father that they
should be established in this land, and be
set up as a free people by the power of the
Father, that these things might come forth
from them unto a remnant of your seed,
that the covenant of the Father may be
fulfilled which he hath covenanted with
his people, O house of Israel;
5 Therefore, when these works and the
works which shall be wrought among you
hereafter shall come forth from the Gen-

1830 Edition of the Book of Mormon.

tiles, unto your seed which shall dwindle
in unbelief because of iniquity;
6 For thus it behooveth the Father that it
should come forth from the Gentiles, that
he may show forth his power unto the
Gentiles, for this cause that the Gentiles, if
they will not harden their hearts, that
they may repent and come unto me and be
baptized in my name and know of the true
points of my doctrine, that they may be
numbered among my people, O house of
Israel;
7 And when these things come to pass that
thy seed shall begin to know these
things—it shall be a sign unto them, that
they may know that the work of the
Father hath already commenced unto the
fulfilling of the covenant which he hath
made unto the people who are of the
house of Israel.
8 And when that day shall come, it shall
come to pass that kings shall shut their
mouths; for that which had not been told
them shall they see; and that which they
had not heard shall they consider.
9 For in that day, for my sake shall the
Father work a work, which shall be a great
and a marvelous work among them; and
there shall be among them those who will
not believe it, although a man shall
declare it unto them.
10 But behold, the life of my servant shall
be in my hand; therefore they shall not
hurt him, although he shall be marred
because of them. Yet I will heal him, for I
will show unto them that my wisdom is
greater than the cunning of the devil.
11 Therefore it shall come to pass that
whosoever will not believe in my words,
who am Jesus Christ, which the Father
shall cause him to bring forth unto the
Gentiles, and shall give unto him power
that he shall bring them forth unto the
Gentiles, (it shall be done even as Moses
said) they shall be cut off from among my
people who are of the covenant.
12 And my people who are a remnant of
Jacob shall be among the Gentiles, yea, in
the midst of them as a lion among the
beasts of the forest, as a young lion among
the flocks of sheep, who, if he go through
both treadeth down and teareth in pieces,
and none can deliver.
13 Their hand shall be lifted up upon their
adversaries, and all their enemies shall be
cut off.
14 Yea, wo be unto the Gentiles except
they repent; for it shall come to pass in
that day, saith the Father, that I will cut
off thy horses out of the midst of thee, and
I will destroy thy chariots;
15 And I will cut off the cities of thy land,
and throw down all thy strongholds;
16 And I will cut off witchcrafts out of thy
land, and thou shalt have no more sooth-
sayers;
17 Thy graven images I will also cut off,
and thy standing images out of the midst
of thee, and thou shalt no more worship
the works of thy hands;
18 And I will pluck up thy groves out of
the midst of thee; so will I destroy thy
cities.
19 And it shall come to pass that all lyings,
and deceivings, and envyings, and strifes,
and priestcrafts, and whoredoms, shall be
done away.
20 For it shall come to pass, saith the
Father, that at that day whosoever will not
repent and come unto my Beloved Son,
them will I cut off from among my people,
O house of Israel;
21 And I will execute vengeance and fury
upon them, even as upon the heathen,
such as they have not heard.
22 But if they will repent and hearken
unto my words, and harden not their
hearts, I will establish my church among
them, and they shall come in unto the
covenant and be numbered among this the
remnant of Jacob, unto whom I have given
this land for their inheritance;
23 And they shall assist my people, the
remnant of Jacob, and also as many of the
house of Israel as shall come, that they
may build a city, which shall be called the
New Jerusalem.
24 And then shall they assist my people
that they may be gathered in, who are
scattered upon all the face of the land, in
unto the New Jerusalem.
25 And then shall the power of heaven
come down among them; and I also will
be in the midst.
26 And then shall the work of the Father
commence at that day, even when this
gospel shall be preached among the rem-
nant of this people. Verily I say unto you,
at that day shall the work of the Father
commence among all the dispersed of my
people, yea, even the tribes which have

been lost, which the Father hath led away out of Jerusalem.
27 Yea, the work shall commence among all the dispersed of my people, with the Father to prepare the way whereby they may come unto me, that they may call on the Father in my name.
28 Yea, and then shall the work commence, with the Father among all nations in preparing the way whereby his people may be gathered home to the land of their inheritance.
29 And they shall go out from all nations; and they shall not go out in haste, nor go by flight, for I will go before them, saith the Father, and I will be their rearward.

3 NEPHI 29

Mormon — *385 AD*

1 And now behold, I say unto you that when the Lord shall see fit, in his wisdom, that these sayings shall come unto the Gentiles according to his word, then ye may know that the covenant which the Father hath made with the children of Israel, concerning their restoration to the lands of their inheritance, is already beginning to be fulfilled.
2 And ye may know that the words of the Lord, which have been spoken by the holy prophets, shall all be fulfilled; and ye need not say that the Lord delays his coming unto the children of Israel.
3 And ye need not imagine in your hearts that the words which have been spoken are vain, for behold, the Lord will remember his covenant which he hath made unto his people of the house of Israel.
4 And when ye shall see these sayings coming forth among you, then ye need not any longer spurn at the doings of the Lord, for the sword of his justice is in his right hand; and behold, at that day, if ye shall spurn at his doings he will cause that it shall soon overtake you.
5 Wo unto him that spurneth at the doings of the Lord; yea, wo unto him that shall deny the Christ and his works!
6 Yea, wo unto him that shall deny the revelations of the Lord, and that shall say the Lord no longer worketh by revelation, or by prophecy, or by gifts, or by tongues, or by healings, or by the power of the Holy Ghost!
7 Yea, and wo unto him that shall say at that day, to get gain, that there can be no miracle wrought by Jesus Christ; for he that doeth this shall become like unto the son of perdition, for whom there was no mercy, according to the word of Christ!
8 Yea, and ye need not any longer hiss, nor spurn, nor make game of the Jews, nor any of the remnant of the house of Israel; for behold, the Lord remembereth his covenant unto them, and he will do unto them according to that which he hath sworn.
9 Therefore ye need not suppose that ye can turn the right hand of the Lord unto the left, that he may not execute judgment unto the fulfilling of the covenant which he hath made unto the house of Israel.

3 NEPHI 16

Jesus Christ — *34 AD*

4 And I command you that ye shall write these sayings after I am gone, that if it so be that my people at Jerusalem, they who have seen me and been with me in my ministry, do not ask the Father in my name, that they may receive a knowledge of you by the Holy Ghost, and also of the other tribes whom they know not of, that these sayings which ye shall write shall be kept and shall be manifested unto the Gentiles, that through the fulness of the Gentiles, the remnant of their seed, who shall be scattered forth upon the face of the Earth because of their unbelief, may be brought in, or may be brought to a knowledge of me, their Redeemer.
5 And then will I gather them in from the four quarters of the Earth; and then will I fulfil the covenant which the Father hath made unto all the people of the house of Israel.
7 Behold, because of their [Gentiles] belief in me, saith the Father, and because of the unbelief of you, O house of Israel, in the latter-day shall the truth come unto the Gentiles, that the fulness of these things shall be made known unto them.

1 NEPHI 22

Nephi, Son of Lehi — *580 BC*

8 And after our seed is scattered the Lord God will proceed to do a marvelous work among the Gentiles, which shall be of great worth unto our seed; wherefore, it is likened unto their being nourished by the Gentiles and being carried in their arms and upon their shoulders.

9 And it shall also be of worth unto the
Gentiles; and not only unto the Gentiles
but unto all the house of Israel, unto the
making known of the covenants of the
Father of heaven unto Abraham, saying:
In thy seed shall all the kindreds of the
Earth be blessed.
10 And I would, my brethren, that ye
should know that all the kindreds of the
Earth cannot be blessed unless he shall
make bare his arm in the eyes of the
nations.
11 Wherefore, the Lord God will proceed
to make bare his arm in the eyes of all the
nations, in bringing about his covenants
and his gospel unto those who are of the
house of Israel.
12 Wherefore, he will bring them again
out of captivity, and they shall be gathered
together to the lands of their inheritance;
and they shall be brought out of obscurity
and out of darkness; and they shall know
that the Lord is their Savior and their
Redeemer, the Mighty One of Israel.

MOSIAH 15

Abinadi — *148 BC*

28 And now I say unto you that the time
shall come that the salvation of the Lord
shall be declared to every nation, kindred,
tongue, and people.
29 Yea, Lord, thy watchmen shall lift up
their voice; with the voice together shall
they sing; for they shall see eye to eye,
when the Lord shall bring again Zion.
30 Break forth into joy, sing together, ye
waste places of Jerusalem; for the Lord
hath comforted his people, he hath
redeemed Jerusalem.
31 The Lord hath made bare his holy arm
in the eyes of all the nations; and all the
ends of the Earth shall see the salvation of
our God.

DOCTRINE AND COVENANTS 133

Joseph Smith — *November 1831*

1 Hearken, O ye people of my church,
saith the Lord your God, and hear the
word of the Lord concerning you—
2 The Lord who shall suddenly come to his
temple; the Lord who shall come down
upon the world with a curse to judgment;
yea, upon all the nations that forget God,
and upon all the ungodly among you.
3 For he shall make bare his holy arm in
the eyes of all the nations, and all the ends
of the Earth shall see the salvation of their
God.
4 Wherefore, prepare ye, prepare ye, O
my people; sanctify yourselves; gather ye
together, O ye people of my church, upon
the land of Zion, all you that have not
been commanded to tarry.
5 Go ye out from Babylon. Be ye clean that
bear the vessels of the Lord.
6 Call your solemn assemblies, and speak
often one to another. And let every man
call upon the name of the Lord.
7 Yea, verily I say unto you again, the time
has come when the voice of the Lord is
unto you: Go ye out of Babylon; gather ye
out from among the nations, from the four
winds, from one end of heaven to the
other.
8 Send forth the elders of my church unto
the nations which are afar off; unto the
islands of the sea; send forth unto foreign
lands; call upon all nations, first upon the
Gentiles, and then upon the Jews.
9 And behold, and lo, this shall be their
cry, and the voice of the Lord unto all
people: Go ye forth unto the land of Zion,
that the borders of my people may be
enlarged, and that her stakes may be
strengthened, and that Zion may go forth
unto the regions round about.

Dan Jones (1810-1862). In his two missions to Wales, he was responsible for the baptisms of over 5,600 people. He is considered to be one of the most successful missionaries in church history.

10 Yea, let the cry go forth among all people: Awake and arise and go forth to meet the Bridegroom; behold and lo, the Bridegroom cometh; go ye out to meet him. Prepare yourselves for the great day of the Lord.

11 Watch, therefore, for ye know neither the day nor the hour.

12 Let them, therefore, who are among the Gentiles flee unto Zion.

13 And let them who be of Judah flee unto Jerusalem, unto the mountains of the Lord's house.

14 Go ye out from among the nations, even from Babylon, from the midst of wickedness, which is spiritual Babylon.

15 But verily, thus saith the Lord, let not your flight be in haste, but let all things be prepared before you; and he that goeth, let him not look back lest sudden destruction shall come upon him.

16 Hearken and hear, O ye inhabitants of the Earth. Listen, ye elders of my church together, and hear the voice of the Lord; for he calleth upon all men, and he commandeth all men everywhere to repent.

ISAIAH 52

Isaiah 740 BC

1 Awake, awake; put on thy strength, O Zion; put on thy beautiful garments, O Jerusalem, the holy city: for henceforth there shall no more come into thee the uncircumcised and the unclean.

2 Shake thyself from the dust; arise, and sit down, O Jerusalem: loose thyself from the bands of thy neck, O captive daughter of Zion.

3 For thus saith the LORD, Ye have sold yourselves for nought; and ye shall be redeemed without money.

4 For thus saith the Lord GOD, My people went down aforetime into Egypt to sojourn there; and the Assyrian oppressed them without cause.

5 Now therefore, what have I here, saith the LORD, that my people is taken away for nought? they that rule over them make them to howl, saith the LORD; and my name continually every day is blasphemed.

6 Therefore my people shall know my name: therefore they shall know in that day that I am he that doth speak: behold, it is I.

7 How beautiful upon the mountains are the feet of him that bringeth good tidings, that publisheth peace; that bringeth good tidings of good, that publisheth salvation; that saith unto Zion, Thy God reigneth!

8 Thy watchmen shall lift up the voice; with the voice together shall they sing: for they shall see eye to eye, when the LORD shall bring again Zion.

9 Break forth into joy, sing together, ye waste places of Jerusalem: for the LORD hath comforted his people, he hath redeemed Jerusalem.

10 The LORD hath made bare his holy arm in the eyes of all the nations; and all the ends of the Earth shall see the salvation of our God.

11 Depart ye, depart ye, go ye out from thence, touch no unclean thing; go ye out of the midst of her; be ye clean, that bear the vessels of the LORD.

12 For ye shall not go out with haste, nor go by flight: for the LORD will go before you; and the God of Israel will be your rearward.

13 Behold, my servant shall deal prudently, he shall be exalted and extolled, and be very high.

14 As many were astonied at thee; his visage was so marred more than any man, and his form more than the sons of men:

15 So shall he sprinkle many nations; the kings shall shut their mouths at him: for that which had not been told them shall they see; and that which they had not heard shall they consider.

DOCTRINE AND COVENANTS 113

Joseph Smith *April 1838*

7 What is meant by the command in Isaiah, 52d chapter, 1st verse, which saith: Put on thy strength, O Zion—and what people had Isaiah reference to?

8 He had reference to those whom God should call in the last days, who should hold the power of priesthood to bring again Zion, and the redemption of Israel; and to put on her strength is to put on the authority of the priesthood, which she, Zion, has a right to by lineage; also to return to that power which she had lost.

9 What are we to understand by Zion loosing herself from the bands of her neck; 2d verse?

10 We are to understand that the scattered remnants are exhorted to return to the

Lord from whence they have fallen; which if they do, the promise of the Lord is that he will speak to them, or give them revelation. See the 6th, 7th, and 8th verses. The bands of her neck are the curses of God upon her, or the remnants of Israel in their scattered condition among the Gentiles.

32

THE TEMPLE ENDOWMENT WILL EMPOWER THE SAINTS TO GATHER ISRAEL

+++

Prophecies concerning the construction of the temple of the Lord for the purpose of endowing the saints with the power of God to preach the gospel in all the world. The original command from the Lord was for the saints to build a temple in Jackson County, MO. However, this command was revoked by the Lord due to mob violence and Governor Boggs' Extermination Order of 1838, which forced the saints to flee the state.

DOCTRINE AND COVENANTS 22

Joseph Smith *April 1830*

1 Behold, I say unto you that all old covenants have I caused to be done away in this thing; and this is a new and an everlasting covenant, even that which was from the beginning.
2 Wherefore, although a man should be baptized an hundred times it availeth him nothing, for you cannot enter in at the strait gate by the law of Moses, neither by your dead works.
3 For it is because of your dead works that I have caused this last covenant and this church to be built up unto me, even as in days of old.
4 Wherefore, enter ye in at the gate, as I have commanded, and seek not to counsel your God. Amen.

DOCTRINE AND COVENANTS 29

Joseph Smith *September 1830*

1 Listen to the voice of Jesus Christ, your Redeemer, the Great I AM, whose arm of mercy hath atoned for your sins;
2 Who will gather his people even as a hen gathereth her chickens under her wings, even as many as will hearken to my voice and humble themselves before me, and call upon me in mighty prayer.
3 Behold, verily, verily, I say unto you, that at this time your sins are forgiven you, therefore ye receive these things; but remember to sin no more, lest perils shall come upon you.
4 Verily, I say unto you that ye are chosen out of the world to declare my gospel with the sound of rejoicing, as with the voice of a trump.
5 Lift up your hearts and be glad, for I am in your midst, and am your advocate with the Father; and it is his good will to give you the kingdom.
6 And, as it is written—Whatsoever ye shall ask in faith, being united in prayer according to my command, ye shall receive.
7 And ye are called to bring to pass the gathering of mine elect; for mine elect hear my voice and harden not their hearts;
8 Wherefore the decree hath gone forth from the Father that they shall be gathered in unto one place upon the face of this land, to prepare their hearts and be prepared in all things against the day when tribulation and desolation are sent forth upon the wicked.

DOCTRINE AND COVENANTS 33

Joseph Smith *October 1830*

1 Behold, I say unto you, my servants Ezra and Northrop, open ye your ears and hearken to the voice of the Lord your God, whose word is quick and powerful, sharper than a two-edged sword, to the dividing asunder of the joints and marrow, soul and spirit; and is a discerner of the thoughts and intents of the heart.
2 For verily, verily, I say unto you that ye are called to lift up your voices as with the

sound of a trump, to declare my gospel
unto a crooked and perverse generation.
3 For behold, the field is white already to
harvest; and it is the eleventh hour, and
the last time that I shall call laborers into
my vineyard.
4 And my vineyard has become corrupted
every whit; and there is none which doeth
good save it be a few; and they err in many
instances because of priestcrafts, all
having corrupt minds.
5 And verily, verily, I say unto you, that
this church have I established and called
forth out of the wilderness.
6 And even so will I gather mine elect
from the four quarters of the Earth, even
as many as will believe in me, and hearken
unto my voice.
7 Yea, verily, verily, I say unto you, that
the field is white already to harvest;
wherefore, thrust in your sickles, and reap
with all your might, mind, and strength.
8 Open your mouths and they shall be
filled, and you shall become even as Nephi
of old, who journeyed from Jerusalem in
the wilderness.
9 Yea, open your mouths and spare not,
and you shall be laden with sheaves upon
your backs, for lo, I am with you.
10 Yea, open your mouths and they shall
be filled, saying: Repent, repent, and pre-
pare ye the way of the Lord, and make his
paths straight; for the kingdom of heaven
is at hand;
11 Yea, repent and be baptized, every one
of you, for a remission of your sins; yea, be
baptized even by water, and then cometh
the baptism of fire and of the Holy Ghost.
12 Behold, verily, verily, I say unto you,
this is my gospel; and remember that they
shall have faith in me or they can in
nowise be saved;
13 And upon this rock I will build my
church; yea, upon this rock ye are built,
and if ye continue, the gates of hell shall
not prevail against you.
14 And ye shall remember the church
articles and covenants to keep them.
15 And whoso having faith you shall
confirm in my church, by the laying on of
the hands, and I will bestow the gift of the
Holy Ghost upon them.
16 And the Book of Mormon and the holy
scriptures are given of me for your
instruction; and the power of my Spirit
quickeneth all things.
17 Wherefore, be faithful, praying always,
having your lamps trimmed and burning,
and oil with you, that you may be ready at
the coming of the Bridegroom—
18 For behold, verily, verily, I say unto
you, that I come quickly. Even so. Amen.

DOCTRINE AND COVENANTS 38

Joseph Smith *January 1831*

29 Ye hear of wars in far countries, and
you say that there will soon be great wars
in far countries, but ye know not the
hearts of men in your own land.
30 I tell you these things because of your
prayers; wherefore, treasure up wisdom in
your bosoms, lest the wickedness of men
reveal these things unto you by their
wickedness, in a manner which shall
speak in your ears with a voice louder than
that which shall shake the Earth; but if ye
are prepared ye shall not fear.
31 And that ye might escape the power of
the enemy, and be gathered unto me a
righteous people, without spot and blame-
less—
32 Wherefore, for this cause I gave unto
you the commandment that ye should go
to the Ohio; and there I will give unto you
my claw; and there you shall be endowed
with power from on high;
33 And from thence, whosoever I will
shall go forth among all nations, and it
shall be told them what they shall do; for
I have a great work laid up in store, for
Israel shall be saved, and I will lead them
whithersoever I will, and no power shall
stay my hand.

DOCTRINE AND COVENANTS 39

Joseph Smith *January 1831*

1 Hearken and listen to the voice of him
who is from all eternity to all eternity, the
Great I AM, even Jesus Christ—
2 The light and the life of the world; a
light which shineth in darkness and the
darkness comprehendeth it not;
3 The same which came in the meridian of
time unto mine own, and mine own
received me not;
4 But to as many as received me, gave I
power to become my sons; and even so
will I give unto as many as will receive me,
power to become my sons.
5 And verily, verily, I say unto you, he
that receiveth my gospel receiveth me;

and he that receiveth not my gospel receiveth not me.
6 And this is my gospel—repentance and baptism by water, and then cometh the baptism of fire and the Holy Ghost, even the Comforter, which showeth all things, and teacheth the peaceable things of the kingdom.
7 And now, behold, I say unto you, my servant James, I have looked upon thy works and I know thee.
8 And verily I say unto thee, thine heart is now right before me at this time; and, behold, I have bestowed great blessings upon thy head;
9 Nevertheless, thou hast seen great sorrow, for thou hast rejected me many times because of pride and the cares of the world.
10 But, behold, the days of thy deliverance are come, if thou wilt hearken to my voice, which saith unto thee: Arise and be baptized, and wash away your sins, calling on my name, and you shall receive my Spirit, and a blessing so great as you never have known.
11 And if thou do this, I have prepared thee for a greater work. Thou shalt preach the fulness of my gospel, which I have sent forth in these last days, the covenant which I have sent forth to recover my people, which are of the house of Israel.
12 And it shall come to pass that power shall rest upon thee; thou shalt have great faith, and I will be with thee and go before thy face.
13 Thou art called to labor in my vineyard, and to build up my church, and to bring forth Zion, that it may rejoice upon the hills and flourish.
14 Behold, verily, verily, I say unto thee, thou art not called to go into the eastern countries, but thou art called to go to the Ohio.
15 And inasmuch as my people shall assemble themselves at the Ohio, I have kept in store a blessing such as is not known among the children of men, and it shall be poured forth upon their heads. And from thence men shall go forth into all nations.
16 Behold, verily, verily, I say unto you, that the people in Ohio call upon me in much faith, thinking I will stay my hand in judgment upon the nations, but I cannot deny my word.
17 Wherefore lay to with your might and call faithful laborers into my vineyard, that it may be pruned for the last time.
18 And inasmuch as they do repent and receive the fulness of my gospel, and become sanctified, I will stay mine hand in judgment.
19 Wherefore, go forth, crying with a loud voice, saying: The kingdom of heaven is at hand; crying: Hosanna! blessed be the name of the Most High God.
20 Go forth baptizing with water, preparing the way before my face for the time of my coming;
21 For the time is at hand; the day or the hour no man knoweth; but it surely shall come.
22 And he that receiveth these things receiveth me; and they shall be gathered unto me in time and in eternity.
23 And again, it shall come to pass that on as many as ye shall baptize with water, ye shall lay your hands, and they shall receive the gift of the Holy Ghost, and shall be looking forth for the signs of my coming, and shall know me.
24 Behold, I come quickly. Even so. Amen.

ETHER 13

Moroni *400 AD*

2 For behold, they rejected all the words of Ether; for he truly told them of all things, from the beginning of man; and that after the waters had receded from off the face of this land it became a choice land above all other lands, a chosen land of the Lord; wherefore the Lord would have that all men should serve him who dwell upon the face thereof;
3 And that it was the place of the New Jerusalem, which should come down out of heaven, and the holy sanctuary of the Lord.
4 Behold, Ether saw the days of Christ, and he spake concerning a New Jerusalem upon this land.
6 And that a New Jerusalem should be built up upon this land, unto the remnant of the seed of Joseph, for which things there has been a type.
7 For as Joseph brought his father down into the land of Egypt, even so he died there; wherefore, the Lord brought a remnant of the seed of Joseph out of the land of Jerusalem, that he might be

merciful unto the seed of Joseph that they
should perish not, even as he was merciful
unto the father of Joseph that he should
perish not.
8 Wherefore, the remnant of the house of
Joseph shall be built upon this land; and it
shall be a land of their inheritance; and
they shall build up a holy city unto the
Lord, like unto the Jerusalem of old; and
they shall no more be confounded, until
the end come when the Earth shall pass
away.

DOCTRINE AND COVENANTS 28

Joseph Smith *September 1830*

9 And now, behold, I say unto you that it
is not revealed, and no man knoweth
where the city Zion shall be built, but it
shall be given hereafter. Behold, I say unto
you that it shall be on the borders by the
Lamanites.

DOCTRINE AND COVENANTS 42

Joseph Smith *February 1831*

8 And from this place ye shall go forth into
the regions westward; and inasmuch as ye
shall find them that will receive you ye
shall build up my church in every
region—
9 Until the time shall come when it shall
be revealed unto you from on high, when
the city of the New Jerusalem shall be
prepared, that ye may be gathered in one,
that ye may be my people and I will be
your God.
34 Therefore, the residue shall be kept in
my storehouse, to administer to the poor
and the needy, as shall be appointed by the
high council of the church, and the bishop
and his council;
35 And for the purpose of purchasing
lands for the public benefit of the church,
and building houses of worship, and
building up of the New Jerusalem which
is hereafter to be revealed—
36 That my covenant people may be
gathered in one in that day when I shall
come to my temple. And this I do for the
salvation of my people.
61 If thou shalt ask, thou shalt receive
revelation upon revelation, knowledge
upon knowledge, that thou mayest know
the mysteries and peaceable things—that
which bringeth joy, that which bringeth
life eternal.
62 Thou shalt ask, and it shall be revealed
unto you in mine own due time where the
New Jerusalem shall be built.
63 And behold, it shall come to pass that
my servants shall be sent forth to the east
and to the west, to the north and to the
south.
64 And even now, let him that goeth to
the east teach them that shall be con-
verted to flee to the west, and this in
consequence of that which is coming on
the Earth, and of secret combinations.
65 Behold, thou shalt observe all these
things, and great shall be thy reward; for
unto you it is given to know the mysteries
of the kingdom, but unto the world it is
not given to know them.
66 Ye shall observe the laws which ye
have received and be faithful.
67 And ye shall hereafter receive church
covenants, such as shall be sufficient to
establish you, both here and in the New
Jerusalem.

DOCTRINE AND COVENANTS 43

Joseph Smith *February 1831*

8 And now, behold, I give unto you a com-
mandment, that when ye are assembled
together ye shall instruct and edify each
other, that ye may know how to act and
direct my church, how to act upon the
points of my law and commandments,
which I have given.
9 And thus ye shall become instructed in
the law of my church, and be sanctified by
that which ye have received, and ye shall
bind yourselves to act in all holiness
before me—
10 That inasmuch as ye do this, glory shall
be added to the kingdom which ye have
received. Inasmuch as ye do it not, it shall
be taken, even that which ye have
received.
11 Purge ye out the iniquity which is
among you; sanctify yourselves before me;
12 And if ye desire the glories of the
kingdom, appoint ye my servant Joseph
Smith, Jun., and uphold him before me by
the prayer of faith.
13 And again, I say unto you, that if ye
desire the mysteries of the kingdom,
provide for him food and raiment, and
whatsoever thing he needeth to
accomplish the work wherewith I have
commanded him;

14 And if ye do it not he shall remain unto them that have received him, that I may reserve unto myself a pure people before me.

15 Again I say, hearken ye elders of my church, whom I have appointed: Ye are not sent forth to be taught, but to teach the children of men the things which I have put into your hands by the power of my Spirit;

16 And ye are to be taught from on high. Sanctify yourselves and ye shall be endowed with power, that ye may give even as I have spoken.

17 Hearken ye, for, behold, the great day of the Lord is nigh at hand.

18 For the day cometh that the Lord shall utter his voice out of heaven; the heavens shall shake and the Earth shall tremble, and the trump of God shall sound both long and loud, and shall say to the sleeping nations: Ye saints arise and live; ye sinners stay and sleep until I shall call again.

19 Wherefore gird up your loins lest ye be found among the wicked.

20 Lift up your voices and spare not. Call upon the nations to repent, both old and young, both bond and free, saying: Prepare yourselves for the great day of the Lord;

21 For if I, who am a man, do lift up my voice and call upon you to repent, and ye hate me, what will ye say when the day cometh when the thunders shall utter their voices from the ends of the Earth, speaking to the ears of all that live, saying—Repent, and prepare for the great day of the Lord?

22 Yea, and again, when the lightnings shall streak forth from the east unto the west, and shall utter forth their voices unto all that live, and make the ears of all tingle that hear, saying these words—Repent ye, for the great day of the Lord is come?

23 And again, the Lord shall utter his voice out of heaven, saying: Hearken, O ye nations of the Earth, and hear the words of that God who made you.

24 O, ye nations of the Earth, how often would I have gathered you together as a hen gathereth her chickens under her wings, but ye would not!

25 How oft have I called upon you by the mouth of my servants, and by the ministering of angels, and by mine own voice, and by the voice of thunderings, and by the voice of lightnings, and by the voice of tempests, and by the voice of earthquakes, and great hailstorms, and by the voice of famines and pestilences of every kind, and by the great sound of a trump, and by the voice of judgment, and by the voice of mercy all the day long, and by the voice of glory and honor and the riches of eternal life, and would have saved you with an everlasting salvation, but ye would not!

26 Behold, the day has come, when the cup of the wrath of mine indignation is full.

27 Behold, verily I say unto you, that these are the words of the Lord your God.

28 Wherefore, labor ye, labor ye in my vineyard for the last time—for the last time call upon the inhabitants of the Earth.

DOCTRINE AND COVENANTS 45

Joseph Smith — *March 1831*

63 Ye hear of wars in foreign lands; but, behold, I say unto you, they are nigh, even at your doors, and not many years hence ye shall hear of wars in your own lands.

64 Wherefore I, the Lord, have said, gather ye out from the eastern lands, assemble ye yourselves together ye elders of my church; go ye forth into the western countries, call upon the inhabitants to repent, and inasmuch as they do repent, build up churches unto me.

65 And with one heart and with one mind, gather up your riches that ye may purchase an inheritance which shall hereafter be appointed unto you.

66 And it shall be called the New Jerusalem, a land of peace, a city of refuge, a place of safety for the saints of the Most High God;

67 And the glory of the Lord shall be there, and the terror of the Lord also shall be there, insomuch that the wicked will not come unto it, and it shall be called Zion.

68 And it shall come to pass among the wicked, that every man that will not take his sword against his neighbor must needs flee unto Zion for safety.

69 And there shall be gathered unto it out of every nation under heaven; and it shall be the only people that shall not be at war one with another.

70 And it shall be said among the wicked: Let us not go up to battle against Zion, for the inhabitants of Zion are terrible; wherefore we cannot stand.
71 And it shall come to pass that the righteous shall be gathered out from among all nations, and shall come to Zion, singing with songs of everlasting joy.

DOCTRINE AND COVENANTS 49

Joseph Smith — *March 1831*

24 But before the great day of the Lord shall come, Jacob shall flourish in the wilderness, and the Lamanites shall blossom as the rose.
25 Zion shall flourish upon the hills and rejoice upon the mountains, and shall be assembled together unto the place which I have appointed.

DOCTRINE AND COVENANTS 52

Joseph Smith — *June 1831*

2 Saying: I, the Lord, will make known unto you what I will that ye shall do from this time until the next conference, which shall be held in Missouri, upon the land which I will consecrate unto my people, which are a remnant of Jacob, and those who are heirs according to the covenant.
3 Wherefore, verily I say unto you, let my servants Joseph Smith, Jun., and Sidney Rigdon take their journey as soon as preparations can be made to leave their homes, and journey to the land of Missouri.
5 And it shall also, inasmuch as they are faithful, be made known unto them the bland of your inheritance.
6 And inasmuch as they are not faithful, they shall be cut off, even as I will, as seemeth me good.
42 And thus, even as I have said, if ye are faithful ye shall assemble yourselves together to rejoice upon the land of Missouri, which is the land of your inheritance, which is now the land of your enemies.
43 But, behold, I, the Lord, will hasten the city in its time, and will crown the faithful with joy and with rejoicing.
44 Behold, I am Jesus Christ, the Son of God, and I will lift them up at the last day. Even so. Amen.

DOCTRINE AND COVENANTS 57

Joseph Smith — *July 1831*

1 Hearken, O ye elders of my church, saith the Lord your God, who have assembled yourselves together, according to my commandments, in this land, which is the land of Missouri, which is the land which I have appointed and consecrated for the gathering of the saints.
2 Wherefore, this is the land of promise, and the place for the city of Zion.
3 And thus saith the Lord your God, if you will receive wisdom here is wisdom. Behold, the place which is now called Independence is the center place; and a spot for the temple is lying westward, upon a lot which is not far from the court-house.
4 Wherefore, it is wisdom that the land should be purchased by the saints, and also every tract lying westward, even unto the line running directly between Jew and Gentile;
5 And also every tract bordering by the prairies, inasmuch as my disciples are enabled to buy lands. Behold, this is wisdom, that they may obtain it for an everlasting inheritance.

DOCTRINE AND COVENANTS 58

Joseph Smith — *August 1831*

1 Hearken, O ye elders of my church, and give ear to my word, and learn of me what I will concerning you, and also concerning this land unto which I have sent you.
2 For verily I say unto you, blessed is he that keepeth my commandments, whether in life or in death; and he that is faithful in tribulation, the reward of the same is greater in the kingdom of heaven.
3 Ye cannot behold with your natural eyes, for the present time, the design of your God concerning those things which shall come hereafter, and the glory which shall follow after much tribulation.
4 For after much tribulation come the blessings. Wherefore the day cometh that ye shall be crowned with much glory; the hour is not yet, but is nigh at hand.
5 Remember this, which I tell you before, that you may lay it to heart, and receive that which is to follow.
6 Behold, verily I say unto you, for this cause I have sent you—that you might be obedient, and that your hearts might be

View (looking northeast) of the 2.5-acre temple lot (grassy area) in Independence, MO. This was part of the 63 acres purchased by Bishop Edward Partridge in December 1831. The saints were expelled from Independence in 1833, and from Missouri in 1839. In 1848, as the main body of Saints were heading west to the Utah territory, Brigham Young and other church leaders decided to give up their claim to the land in Independence. Groups that separated from the Church of Jesus Christ of Latter-day Saints, not wanting to make the trek to Utah, returned to Independence. The Church of Christ (Temple Lot) currently owns the 2.5-acre lot originally designated as the temple site and, to date, are unwilling to sell it. The Community of Christ owns the remainder of the 63 acres. From left to right are the Community of Christ Stone Church, the Church of Christ (Temple Lot) headquarters, and the spiral-shaped Community of Christ Independence Temple.

prepared to bear testimony of the things which are to come;
7 And also that you might be honored in laying the foundation, and in bearing record of the land upon which the Zion of God shall stand;
8 And also that a feast of fat things might be prepared for the poor; yea, a feast of fat things, of wine on the lees well refined, that the Earth may know that the mouths of the prophets shall not fail;
9 Yea, a supper of the house of the Lord, well prepared, unto which all nations shall be invited.
10 First, the rich and the learned, the wise and the noble;
11 And after that cometh the day of my power; then shall the poor, the lame, and the blind, and the deaf, come in unto the marriage of the Lamb, and partake of the supper of the Lord, prepared for the great day to come.
12 Behold, I, the Lord, have spoken it.
13 And that the testimony might go forth from Zion, yea, from the mouth of the city of the heritage of God—

44 And now, verily, I say concerning the residue of the elders of my church, the time has not yet come, for many years, for them to receive their inheritance in this land, except they desire it through the prayer of faith, only as it shall be appointed unto them of the Lord.
45 For, behold, they shall push the people together from the ends of the Earth.
46 Wherefore, assemble yourselves together; and they who are not appointed to stay in this land, let them preach the gospel in the regions round about; and after that let them return to their homes.
47 Let them preach by the way, and bear testimony of the truth in all places, and call upon the rich, the high and the low, and the poor to repent.
48 And let them build up churches, inasmuch as the inhabitants of the Earth will repent.
49 And let there be an agent appointed by the voice of the church, unto the church in Ohio, to receive moneys to purchase lands in Zion.

50 And I give unto my servant Sidney
Rigdon a commandment, that he shall
write a description of the land of Zion, and
a statement of the will of God, as it shall
be made known by the Spirit unto him;
51 And an epistle and subscription, to be
presented unto all the churches to obtain
moneys, to be put into the hands of the
bishop, of himself or the agent, as seemeth
him good or as he shall direct, to purchase
lands for an inheritance for the children of
God.
52 For, behold, verily I say unto you, the
Lord willeth that the disciples and the
children of men should open their hearts,
even to purchase this whole region of
country, as soon as time will permit.
53 Behold, here is wisdom. Let them do
this lest they receive none inheritance,
save it be by the shedding of blood.
54 And again, inasmuch as there is land
obtained, let there be workmen sent forth
of all kinds unto this land, to labor for the
saints of God.
55 Let all these things be done in order;
and let the privileges of the lands be made
known from time to time, by the bishop
or the agent of the church.
56 And let the work of the gathering be
not in haste, nor by flight; but let it be
done as it shall be counseled by the elders
of the church at the conferences, accord-
ing to the knowledge which they receive
from time to time.
57 And let my servant Sidney Rigdon
consecrate and dedicate this land, and the
spot for the temple, unto the Lord.
64 For, verily, the sound must go forth
from this place into all the world, and
unto the uttermost parts of the Earth—the
gospel must be preached unto every
creature, with signs following them that
believe.
65 And behold the Son of Man cometh.
Amen.

DOCTRINE AND COVENANTS 84

Joseph Smith September 1832

2 Yea, the word of the Lord concerning his
church, established in the last days for the
restoration of his people, as he has spoken
by the mouth of his prophets, and for the
gathering of his saints to stand upon
Mount Zion, which shall be the city of
New Jerusalem.
3 Which city shall be built, beginning at
the temple lot, which is appointed by the
finger of the Lord, in the western bound-
aries of the State of Missouri, and dedi-
cated by the hand of Joseph Smith, Jun.,
and others with whom the Lord was well
pleased.
4 Verily this is the word of the Lord, that
the city New Jerusalem shall be built by
the gathering of the saints, beginning at
this place, even the place of the temple,
which temple shall be reared in this
generation.
5 For verily this generation shall not all
pass away until an house shall be built
unto the Lord, and a cloud shall rest upon
it, which cloud shall be even the glory of
the Lord, which shall fill the house.

DOCTRINE AND COVENANTS 95

Joseph Smith June 1833

8 Yea, verily I say unto you, I gave unto
you a commandment that you should
build a house, in the which house I design
to endow those whom I have chosen with
power from on high;
4 For the preparation wherewith I design
to prepare mine apostles to prune my
vineyard for the last time, that I may bring
to pass my strange act, that I may pour out
my Spirit upon all flesh.

DOCTRINE AND COVENANTS 97

Joseph Smith August 1833

10 Verily I say unto you, that it is my will
that a house should be built unto me in the
land of Zion, like unto the pattern which
I have given you.
11 Yea, let it be built speedily, by the
tithing of my people.
12 Behold, this is the tithing and the
sacrifice which I, the Lord, require at their
hands, that there may be a chouse built
unto me for the salvation of Zion—
13 For a place of thanksgiving for all
saints, and for a place of instruction for all
those who are called to the work of the
ministry in all their several callings and
offices;
14 That they may be perfected in the
understanding of their ministry, in
theory, in principle, and in doctrine, in all
things pertaining to the kingdom of God
on the Earth, the keys of which kingdom
have been conferred upon you.

15 And inasmuch as my people build a house unto me in the name of the Lord, and do not suffer any unclean thing to come into it, that it be not defiled, my glory shall rest upon it;
16 Yea, and my presence shall be there, for I will come into it, and all the pure in heart that shall come into it shall see God.
17 But if it be defiled I will not come into it, and my glory shall not be there; for I will not come into unholy temples.
18 And, now, behold, if Zion do these things she shall prosper, and spread herself and become very glorious, very great, and very terrible.
19 And the nations of the Earth shall honor her, and shall say: Surely Zion is the city of our God, and surely Zion cannot fall, neither be moved out of her place, for God is there, and the hand of the Lord is there;
20 And he hath sworn by the power of his might to be her salvation and her high tower.
21 Therefore, verily, thus saith the Lord, let Zion rejoice, for this is Zion—THE PURE IN HEART; therefore, let Zion rejoice, while all the wicked shall mourn.

DOCTRINE AND COVENANTS 105

Joseph Smith — *June 1834*

5 And Zion cannot be built up unless it is by the principles of the law of the celestial kingdom; otherwise I cannot receive her unto myself.
11 And this cannot be brought to pass until mine elders are endowed with power from on high.
12 For behold, I have prepared a great endowment and blessing to be poured out upon them, inasmuch as they are faithful and continue in humility before me.
31 But first let my army become very great, and let it be sanctified before me, that it may become fair as the sun, and clear as the moon, and that her banners may be terrible unto all nations;
32 That the kingdoms of this world may be constrained to acknowledge that the kingdom of Zion is in very deed the kingdom of our God and his Christ; therefore, let us become subject unto her laws.
33 Verily I say unto you, it is expedient in me that the first elders of my church should receive their endowment from on high in my house, which I have commanded to be built unto my name in the land of Kirtland.
34 And let those commandments which I have given concerning Zion and her law be executed and fulfilled, after her redemption.
35 There has been a day of calling, but the time has come for a day of choosing; and let those be chosen that are worthy.
36 And it shall be manifest unto my servant, by the voice of the Spirit, those that are chosen; and they shall be sanctified;
37 And inasmuch as they follow the counsel which they receive, they shall have power after many days to accomplish all things pertaining to Zion.

DOCTRINE AND COVENANTS 124

Joseph Smith — *January 1841*

49 Verily, verily, I say unto you, that when I give a commandment to any of the sons of men to do a work unto my name, and those sons of men go with all their might and with all they have to perform that work, and cease not their diligence, and their enemies come upon them and hinder them from performing that work, behold, it behooveth me to require that work no more at the hands of those sons of men, but to accept of their offerings.
50 And the iniquity and transgression of my holy laws and commandments I will visit upon the heads of those who hindered my work, unto the third and fourth generation, so long as they repent not, and hate me, saith the Lord God.
51 Therefore, for this cause have I accepted the offerings of those whom I commanded to build up a city and a house unto my name, in Jackson county, Missouri, and were hindered by their enemies, saith the Lord your God.
52 And I will answer judgment, wrath, and indignation, wailing, and anguish, and gnashing of teeth upon their heads, unto the third and fourth generation, so long as they repent not, and hate me, saith the Lord your God.
53 And this I make an example unto you, for your consolation concerning all those who have been commanded to do a work and have been hindered by the hands of their enemies, and by oppression, saith the Lord your God.

54 For I am the Lord your God, and will
save all those of your brethren who have
been pure in heart, and have been slain in
the land of Missouri, saith the Lord.

The saints are driven from Jackson County, Missouri by mobs with the backing of Governor Lilburn Boggs's 1838 Extermination Order, which forced the saints to move the gathering place to Nauvoo, IL. Painting by C.A.A. Christensen.

33

THE COMING OF MOSES AND ELIJAH

+++

Prophecies concerning the building of the Kirtland Temple and the coming of Moses and Elijah to restore the keys to the gathering of Israel and to the sealing power. The restoration of these keys, covenants, and ordinances are what will prepare the saints to withstand the great and dreadful day of the Lord where the wicked and rebellious will be burned. The completion of the Nauvoo Temple in 1846 fulfilled the prophecies relating to Elijah and the sealing power and turning the hearts of the children to their fathers. Ordinance work for the dead began in the Kirtland Temple in 1836.

REVELATION 7

John — *95 AD*

1 And after these things I saw four angels standing on the four corners of the Earth, holding the four winds of the Earth, that the wind should not blow on the Earth, nor on the sea, nor on any tree.

2 And I saw another angel ascending from the east, having the seal of the living God: and he cried with a loud voice to the four angels, to whom it was given to hurt the Earth and the sea,

3 Saying, Hurt not the Earth, neither the sea, nor the trees, till we have sealed the servants of our God in their foreheads.

4 And I heard the number of them which were sealed: and there were sealed an hundred and forty and four thousand of all the tribes of the children of Israel.

5 Of the tribe of Juda were sealed twelve thousand. Of the tribe of Reuben were sealed twelve thousand. Of the tribe of Gad were sealed twelve thousand.

6 Of the tribe of Asher were sealed twelve thousand. Of the tribe of Naphtali were sealed twelve thousand. Of the tribe of Manasseh were sealed twelve thousand.

7 Of the tribe of Simeon were sealed twelve thousand. Of the tribe of Levi were sealed twelve thousand. Of the tribe of Issachar were sealed twelve thousand.

8 Of the tribe of Zebulon were sealed twelve thousand. Of the tribe of Joseph were sealed twelve thousand. Of the tribe of Benjamin were sealed twelve thousand.

DOCTRINE AND COVENANTS 77

Joseph Smith — *March 1832*

8 Q. What are we to understand by the four angels, spoken of in the 7th chapter and 1st verse of Revelation?

A. We are to understand that they are four angels sent forth from God, to whom is given power over the four parts of the Earth, to save life and to destroy; these are they who have the everlasting gospel to commit to every nation, kindred, tongue, and people; having power to shut up the heavens, to seal up unto life, or to cast down to the regions of darkness.

9 Q. What are we to understand by the angel ascending from the east, Revelation 7th chapter and 2nd verse?

A. We are to understand that the angel ascending from the east is he to whom is given the seal of the living God over the twelve tribes of Israel; wherefore, he crieth unto the four angels having the everlasting gospel, saying: Hurt not the Earth, neither the sea, nor the trees, till we have sealed the servants of our God in their foreheads. And, if you will receive it, this is Elias which was to come to gather together the tribes of Israel and restore all things.

10 Q. What time are the things spoken of in this chapter to be accomplished?

A. They are to be accomplished in the sixth thousand years, or the opening of the sixth seal.

11 Q. What are we to understand by sealing the one hundred and forty-four thousand, out of all the tribes of Israel—twelve thousand out of every tribe?

A. We are to understand that those who are sealed are high priests, ordained unto the holy order of God, to administer the everlasting gospel; for they are they who are ordained out of every nation, kindred, tongue, and people, by the angels to whom is given power over the nations of the Earth, to bring as many as will come to the church of the Firstborn.

DOCTRINE AND COVENANTS 88

Joseph Smith *December 1832*

103 And another trump shall sound, which is the fifth trump, which is the fifth angel who committeth the everlasting gospel—flying through the midst of heaven, unto all nations, kindreds, tongues, and people;
104 And this shall be the sound of his trump, saying to all people, both in heaven and in Earth, and that are under the Earth—for every ear shall hear it, and every knee shall bow, and every tongue shall confess, while they hear the sound of the trump, saying: Fear God, and give glory to him who sitteth upon the throne, forever and ever; for the hour of his judgment is come.

2 NEPHI 12 (see also ISAIAH 2)

Isaiah *740 BC*

1 The word that Isaiah, the son of Amoz, saw concerning Judah and Jerusalem:
2 And it shall come to pass in the last days, when the mountain of the Lord's house shall be established in the top of the mountains, and shall be exalted above the hills, and all nations shall flow unto it.
3 And many people shall go and say, Come ye, and let us go up to the mountain of the Lord, to the house of the God of Jacob; and he will teach us of his ways, and we will walk in his paths; for out of Zion shall go forth the law, and the word of the Lord from Jerusalem.
4 And he shall judge among the nations, and shall rebuke many people: and they shall beat their swords into plow-shares, and their spears into pruning-hooks—nation shall not lift up sword against nation, neither shall they learn war any more.
5 O house of Jacob, come ye and let us walk in the light of the Lord; yea, come, for ye have all agone astray, everyone to his wicked ways.

MICAH 4

Micah *722 BC*

1 But in the last days it shall come to pass, that the mountain of the house of the LORD shall be established in the top of the mountains, and it shall be exalted above the hills; and people shall flow unto it.
2 And many nations shall come, and say, Come, and let us go up to the mountain of the LORD, and to the house of the God of Jacob; and he will teach us of his ways, and we will walk in his paths: for the law shall go forth of Zion, and the word of the LORD from Jerusalem.

DOCTRINE AND COVENANTS 36

Joseph Smith *December 1830*

8 I am Jesus Christ, the Son of God; wherefore, gird up your loins and I will suddenly come to my temple. Even so. Amen.

DOCTRINE AND COVENANTS 109 KIRTLAND TEMPLE DEDICATORY PRAYER

Joseph Smith *April 1836*

1 Thanks be to thy name, O Lord God of Israel, who keepest covenant and showest mercy unto thy servants who walk uprightly before thee, with all their hearts—
2 Thou who hast commanded thy servants to build a house to thy name in this place [Kirtland].
3 And now thou beholdest, O Lord, that thy servants have done according to thy commandment.
4 And now we ask thee, Holy Father, in the name of Jesus Christ, the Son of thy bosom, in whose name alone salvation can be administered to the children of men, we ask thee, O Lord, to accept of this house, the workmanship of the hands of us, thy servants, which thou didst command us to build.
5 For thou knowest that we have done this work through great tribulation; and out of our poverty we have given of our substance to build a house to thy name, that the Son of Man might have a place to manifest himself to his people.
6 And as thou hast said in a revelation, given to us, calling us thy friends, saying—Call your solemn assembly, as I have commanded you;
7 And as all have not faith, seek ye diligently and teach one another words of

1912 photograph of the Kirtland Temple. Dedicated in April 1836.

wisdom; yea, seek ye out of the best books
words of wisdom, seek learning even by
study and also by faith;
8 Organize yourselves; prepare every
needful thing, and establish a house, even
a house of prayer, a house of fasting, a
house of faith, a house of learning, a house
of glory, a house of order, a house of God;
9 That your incomings may be in the name
of the Lord, that your outgoings may be in
the name of the Lord, that all your salu-
tations may be in the name of the Lord,
with uplifted hands unto the Most High—
10 And now, Holy Father, we ask thee to
assist us, thy people, with thy grace, in
calling our solemn assembly, that it may
be done to thine honor and to thy divine
acceptance;
11 And in a manner that we may be found
worthy, in thy sight, to secure a fulfilment
of the promises which thou hast made
unto us, thy people, in the revelations
given unto us;
12 That thy glory may rest down upon thy
people, and upon this thy house, which
we now dedicate to thee, that it may be
sanctified and consecrated to be holy, and
that thy holy presence may be continually
in this house;
13 And that all people who shall enter
upon the threshold of the Lord's house
may feel thy power, and feel constrained
to acknowledge that thou hast sanctified
it, and that it is thy house, a place of thy
holiness.
14 And do thou grant, Holy Father, that
all those who shall worship in this house
may be taught words of wisdom out of the
best books, and that they may seek
learning even by study, and also by faith,
as thou hast said;
15 And that they may grow up in thee,
and receive a fulness of the Holy Ghost,
and be organized according to thy laws,
and be prepared to obtain every needful
thing;
16 And that this house may be a house of
prayer, a house of fasting, a house of faith,
a house of glory and of God, even thy
house;
17 That all the incomings of thy people,
into this house, may be in the name of the
Lord;
18 That all their outgoings from this house
may be in the name of the Lord;
19 And that all their salutations may be in
the name of the Lord, with holy hands,
uplifted to the Most High;

20 And that no unclean thing shall be permitted to come into thy house to pollute it;
21 And when thy people transgress, any of them, they may speedily repent and return unto thee, and find favor in thy sight, and be restored to the blessings which thou hast ordained to be poured out upon those who shall reverence thee in thy house.
22 And we ask thee, Holy Father, that thy servants may go forth from this house armed with thy power, and that thy name may be upon them, and thy glory be round about them, and thine angels have charge over them;
23 And from this place they may bear exceedingly great and glorious tidings, in truth, unto the ends of the Earth, that they may know that this is thy work, and that thou hast put forth thy hand, to fulfil that which thou hast spoken by the mouths of the prophets, concerning the last days.
24 We ask thee, Holy Father, to establish the people that shall worship, and honorably hold a name and standing in this thy house, to all generations and for eternity;
25 That no weapon formed against them shall prosper; that he who diggeth a pit for them shall fall into the same himself;
26 That no combination of wickedness shall have power to rise up and prevail over thy people upon whom thy name shall be put in this house;
27 And if any people shall rise against this people, that thine anger be kindled against them;
28 And if they shall smite this people thou wilt smite them; thou wilt fight for thy people as thou didst in the day of battle, that they may be delivered from the hands of all their enemies.
29 We ask thee, Holy Father, to confound, and astonish, and to bring to shame and confusion, all those who have spread lying reports abroad, over the world, against thy servant or servants, if they will not repent, when the everlasting gospel shall be proclaimed in their ears;
30 And that all their works may be brought to naught, and be swept away by the hail, and by the judgments which thou wilt send upon them in thine anger, that there may be an end to lyings and slanders against thy people.
31 For thou knowest, O Lord, that thy servants have been innocent before thee in bearing record of thy name, for which they have suffered these things.
32 Therefore we plead before thee for a full and complete deliverance from under this yoke;
33 Break it off, O Lord; break it off from the necks of thy servants, by thy power, that we may rise up in the midst of this generation and do thy work.
34 O Jehovah, have mercy upon this people, and as all men sin, forgive the transgressions of thy people, and let them be blotted out forever.
35 Let the anointing of thy ministers be sealed upon them with power from on high.
36 Let it be fulfilled upon them, as upon those on the day of Pentecost; let the gift of tongues be poured out upon thy people, even cloven tongues as of fire, and the interpretation thereof.
37 And let thy house be filled, as with a rushing mighty wind, with thy glory.
38 Put upon thy servants the testimony of the covenant, that when they go out and proclaim thy word they may seal up the law, and prepare the hearts of thy saints for all those judgments thou art about to send, in thy wrath, upon the inhabitants of the Earth, because of their transgressions, that thy people may not faint in the day of trouble.
39 And whatsoever city thy servants shall enter, and the people of that city receive their testimony, let thy peace and thy salvation be upon that city; that they may gather out of that city the righteous, that they may come forth to Zion, or to her stakes, the places of thine appointment, with songs of everlasting joy;
40 And until this be accomplished, let not thy judgments fall upon that city.
41 And whatsoever city thy servants shall enter, and the people of that city receive not the testimony of thy servants, and thy servants warn them to save themselves from this untoward generation, let it be upon that city according to that which thou hast spoken by the mouths of thy prophets.
42 But deliver thou, O Jehovah, we beseech thee, thy servants from their hands, and cleanse them from their blood.

43 O Lord, we delight not in the destruction of our fellow men; their souls are precious before thee;

44 But thy word must be fulfilled. Help thy servants to say, with thy grace assisting them: Thy will be done, O Lord, and not ours.

45 We know that thou hast spoken by the mouth of thy prophets terrible things concerning the wicked, in the last days—that thou wilt pour out thy judgments, without measure;

46 Therefore, O Lord, deliver thy people from the calamity of the wicked; enable thy servants to seal up the law, and bind up the testimony, that they may be prepared against the day of burning.

47 We ask thee, Holy Father, to remember those who have been driven by the inhabitants of Jackson county, Missouri, from the lands of their inheritance, and break off, O Lord, this yoke of affliction that has been put upon them.

48 Thou knowest, O Lord, that they have been greatly oppressed and afflicted by wicked men; and our hearts flow out with sorrow because of their grievous burdens.

49 O Lord, how long wilt thou suffer this people to bear this affliction, and the cries of their innocent ones to ascend up in thine ears, and their blood come up in testimony before thee, and not make a display of thy testimony in their behalf?

50 Have mercy, O Lord, upon the wicked mob, who have driven thy people, that they may cease to spoil, that they may repent of their sins if repentance is to be found;

51 But if they will not, make bare thine arm, O Lord, and redeem that which thou didst appoint a Zion unto thy people.

52 And if it cannot be otherwise, that the cause of thy people may not fail before thee may thine anger be kindled, and thine indignation fall upon them, that they may be wasted away, both root and branch, from under heaven;

53 But inasmuch as they will repent, thou art gracious and merciful, and wilt turn away thy wrath when thou lookest upon the face of thine Anointed.

54 Have mercy, O Lord, upon all the nations of the Earth; have mercy upon the rulers of our land; may those principles, which were so honorably and nobly defended, namely, the Constitution of our land, by our fathers, be established forever.

55 Remember the kings, the princes, the nobles, and the great ones of the Earth, and all people, and the churches, all the poor, the needy, and afflicted ones of the Earth;

56 That their hearts may be softened when thy servants shall go out from thy house, O Jehovah, to bear testimony of thy name; that their prejudices may give way before the truth, and thy people may obtain favor in the sight of all;

57 That all the ends of the Earth may know that we, thy servants, have heard thy voice, and that thou hast sent us;

58 That from among all these, thy servants, the sons of Jacob, may gather out the righteous to build a holy city to thy name, as thou hast commanded them.

59 We ask thee to appoint unto Zion other stakes besides this one which thou hast appointed, that the gathering of thy people may roll on in great power and majesty, that thy work may be cut short in righteousness.

60 Now these words, O Lord, we have spoken before thee, concerning the revelations and commandments which thou hast given unto us, who are identified with the Gentiles.

61 But thou knowest that thou hast a great love for the children of Jacob, who have been scattered upon the mountains for a long time, in a cloudy and dark day.

62 We therefore ask thee to have mercy upon the children of Jacob, that Jerusalem, from this hour, may begin to be redeemed;

63 And the yoke of bondage may begin to be broken off from the house of David;

64 And the children of Judah may begin to return to the lands which thou didst give to Abraham, their father.

65 And cause that the remnants of Jacob, who have been cursed and smitten because of their transgression, be converted from their wild and savage condition to the fulness of the everlasting gospel;

66 That they may lay down their weapons of bloodshed, and cease their rebellions.

67 And may all the scattered remnants of Israel, who have been driven to the ends of the Earth, come to a knowledge of the truth, believe in the Messiah, and be

redeemed from oppression, and rejoice
before thee.
68 O Lord, remember thy servant, Joseph
Smith, Jun., and all his afflictions and
persecutions—how he has covenanted
with Jehovah, and vowed to thee, O
Mighty God of Jacob—and the command-
ments which thou hast given unto him,
and that he hath sincerely striven to do
thy will.
69 Have mercy, O Lord, upon his wife and
children, that they may be exalted in thy
presence, and preserved by thy fostering
hand.
70 Have mercy upon all their immediate
connections, that their prejudices may be
broken up and swept away as with a flood;
that they may be converted and redeemed
with Israel, and know that thou art God.
71 Remember, O Lord, the presidents,
even all the presidents of thy church, that
thy right hand may exalt them, with all
their families, and their immediate con-
nections, that their names may be perpet-
uated and had in everlasting remem-
brance from generation to generation.
72 Remember all thy church, O Lord, with
all their families, and all their immediate
connections, with all their sick and
afflicted ones, with all the poor and meek
of the Earth; that the kingdom, which
thou hast set up without hands, may
become a great mountain and fill the
whole Earth;
73 That thy church may come forth out of
the wilderness of darkness, and shine
forth fair as the moon, clear as the sun, and
terrible as an army with banners;
74 And be adorned as a bride for that day
when thou shalt unveil the heavens, and
cause the mountains to flow down at thy
presence, and the valleys to be exalted, the
rough places made smooth; that thy glory
may fill the Earth;
75 That when the trump shall sound for
the dead, we shall be caught up in the
cloud to meet thee, that we may ever be
with the Lord;
76 That our garments may be pure, that
we may be clothed upon with robes of
righteousness, with palms in our hands,
and crowns of glory upon our heads, and
reap eternal joy for all our sufferings.
77 O Lord God Almighty, hear us in these
our petitions, and answer us from heaven,
thy holy habitation, where thou sittest
enthroned, with glory, honor, power,
majesty, might, dominion, truth, justice,
judgment, mercy, and an infinity of
fulness, from everlasting to everlasting.
78 O hear, O hear, O hear us, O Lord! And
answer these petitions, and accept the
dedication of this house unto thee, the
work of our hands, which we have built
unto thy name;
79 And also this church, to put upon it thy
name. And help us by the power of thy
Spirit, that we may mingle our voices with
those bright, shining seraphs around thy
throne, with acclamations of praise,
singing Hosanna to God and the Lamb!
80 And let these, thine anointed ones, be
clothed with salvation, and thy saints
shout aloud for joy. Amen, and Amen.

3 NEPHI 24 (see also MALACHI 3)

Malachi — *432 AD*

1 And it came to pass that he commanded
them that they should write the words
which the Father had given unto Malachi,
which he should tell unto them. And it
came to pass that after they were written
he expounded them. And these are the
words which he did tell unto them,
saying: Thus said the Father unto
Malachi—Behold, I will send my messen-
ger, and he shall prepare the way before
me, and the Lord whom ye seek shall
suddenly come to his temple, even the
messenger of the covenant, whom ye
delight in; behold, he shall come, saith the
Lord of Hosts.

3 NEPHI 25

Jesus Christ — *34 AD*

5 Behold, I will send you Elijah the
prophet before the coming of the great
and dreadful day of the Lord;
6 And he shall turn the heart of the fathers
to the children, and the heart of the
children to their fathers, lest I come and
smite the Earth with a curse.

DOCTRINE AND COVENANTS 2

Moroni — *September 1823*

1 Behold, I will reveal unto you the Priest-
hood, by the hand of Elijah the prophet,
before the coming of the great and
dreadful day of the Lord.
2 And he shall plant in the hearts of the
children the promises made to the fathers,

Interior of Kirtland Temple, photo taken in 1934, where Jesus Christ, Elijah, Moses, and others appeared and delivered the keys of their dispensations to Joseph Smith in 1836.

and the hearts of the children shall turn to their fathers.

3 If it were not so, the whole Earth would be utterly wasted at his coming.

DOCTRINE AND COVENANTS 110

Joseph Smith *April 1836*

1 The veil was taken from our minds, and the eyes of our understanding were opened.

2 We saw the Lord standing upon the breastwork of the pulpit, before us; and under his feet was a paved work of pure gold, in color like amber.

3 His eyes were as a flame of fire; the hair of his head was white like the pure snow; his countenance shone above the brightness of the sun; and his voice was as the sound of the rushing of great waters, even the voice of Jehovah, saying:

4 I am the first and the last; I am he who liveth, I am he who was slain; I am your advocate with the Father.

5 Behold, your sins are forgiven you; you are clean before me; therefore, lift up your heads and rejoice.

6 Let the hearts of your brethren rejoice, and let the hearts of all my people rejoice, who have, with their might, built this house to my name.

7 For behold, I have accepted this house, and my name shall be here; and I will manifest myself to my people in mercy in this house.

8 Yea, I will appear unto my servants, and speak unto them with mine own voice, if my people will keep my commandments, and do not pollute this holy house.

9 Yea the hearts of thousands and tens of thousands shall greatly rejoice in consequence of the blessings which shall be poured out, and the endowment with which my servants have been endowed in this house.

10 And the fame of this house shall spread to foreign lands; and this is the beginning of the blessing which shall be poured out upon the heads of my people. Even so. Amen.

11 After this vision closed, the heavens were again opened unto us; and Moses appeared before us, and committed unto us the keys of the gathering of Israel from the four parts of the Earth, and the leading of the ten tribes from the land of the north.

12 After this, Elias appeared, and committed the dispensation of the gospel of Abraham, saying that in us and our seed all generations after us should be blessed.

13 After this vision had closed, another great and glorious vision burst upon us; for Elijah the prophet, who was taken to heaven without tasting death, stood before us, and said:

14 Behold, the time has fully come, which was spoken of by the mouth of Malachi—testifying that he [Elijah] should be sent, before the great and dreadful day of the Lord come—

15 To turn the hearts of the fathers to the children, and the children to the fathers, lest the whole Earth be smitten with a curse—

16 Therefore, the keys of this dispensation are committed into your hands; and by this ye may know that the great and dreadful day of the Lord is near, even at the doors.

Daniel says that the temple daily sacrifice would be trodden under foot for 2,300 days at which point it would be cleansed. Most scholars place the start date of Daniel's prophecy to 457 BC, which is the date Persian King Artaxerxes issued a decree to allow the Jews to rebuild Solomon's temple, which had been destroyed by the Babylonians. This smaller second temple was desecrated a number of times by the Greeks and finally destroyed by the Romans in 70 AD.

If the 2,300 days is interpreted as years, then the end date, or date when the temple ordinance work would be cleansed and restored, would be 1844. Many Christians incorrectly believed that 1844 would be the year of the Second Coming of Christ. But the prophecy relates to temple work.

The Nauvoo Temple was dedicated in early 1846, which was the first temple where eternal marriage sealings and baptisms for the dead were performed. These ordinances began in December 1845. This is certainly a fulfillment of Daniel's prophecy, of the sanctuary finally being cleansed and these essential ordinances of salvation for the living and the dead being restored to the Earth.

DANIEL 8

<u>*Daniel* 600 BC</u>

11 Yea, he magnified himself even to the prince of the host, and by him the daily sacrifice was taken away, and the place of his sanctuary was cast down.
12 And an host was given him against the daily sacrifice by reason of transgression, and it cast down the truth to the ground; and it practiced, and prospered.
13 Then I heard one saint speaking, and another saint said unto that certain saint which spake, How long shall be the vision concerning the daily sacrifice, and the transgression of desolation, to give both the sanctuary and the host to be trodden under foot?
14 And he said unto me, Unto two thousand and three hundred days; then shall the sanctuary be cleansed.

Nauvoo Temple, Daguerreotype photograph, by Louis R. Chaffin, 1847.

DOCTRINE AND COVENANTS 124

<u>*Joseph Smith* *January 1841*</u>

29 For a baptismal font there is not upon the Earth, that they, my saints, may be baptized for those who are dead—
30 For this ordinance belongeth to my house, and cannot be acceptable to me, only in the days of your poverty, wherein ye are not able to build a house unto me.
31 But I command you, all ye my saints, to build a house unto me; and I grant unto you a sufficient time to build a house unto me; and during this time your baptisms shall be acceptable unto me.
39 Therefore, verily I say unto you, that your anointings, and your washings, and your baptisms for the dead, and your solemn assemblies, and your memorials for your sacrifices by the sons of Levi, and for your oracles in your most holy places wherein you receive conversations, and your statutes and judgments, for the beginning of the revelations and foundation of Zion, and for the glory, honor, and endowment of all her municipals, are ordained by the ordinance of my holy house, which my people are always commanded to build unto my holy name.

Baptismal font in the Salt Lake Temple, circa 1909 by Charles Roscoe Savage.

40 And verily I say unto you, let this house be built unto my name, that I may reveal mine ordinances therein unto my people;
41 For I deign to reveal unto my church things which have been kept hid from before the foundation of the world, things that pertain to the dispensation of the fulness of times.
55 And again, verily I say unto you, I command you again to build a house to my name, even in this place, that you may prove yourselves unto me that ye are faithful in all things whatsoever I command you, that I may bless you, and crown you with honor, immortality, and eternal life.

DOCTRINE AND COVENANTS 128

Joseph Smith *September 1842*

5 You may think this order of things to be very particular; but let me tell you that it is only to answer the will of God, by conforming to the ordinance and preparation that the Lord ordained and prepared before the foundation of the world, for the salvation of the dead who should die without a knowledge of the gospel.
6 And further, I want you to remember that John the Revelator was contemplating this very subject in relation to the dead, when he declared, as you will find recorded in Revelation 20:12—And I saw the dead, small and great, stand before God; and the books were opened; and another book was opened, which is the book of life; and the dead were judged out of those things which were written in the books, according to their works.
7 You will discover in this quotation that the books were opened; and another book was opened, which was the book of life; but the dead were judged out of those things which were written in the books, according to their works; consequently, the books spoken of must be the books which contained the record of their works, and refer to the records which are kept on the Earth. And the book which was the book of life is the record which is kept in heaven; the principle agreeing precisely with the doctrine which is commanded you in the revelation contained in the letter which I wrote to you previous to my leaving my place—that in all your recordings it may be recorded in heaven.
8 Now, the nature of this ordinance consists in the power of the priesthood, by the revelation of Jesus Christ, wherein it is granted that whatsoever you bind on Earth shall be bound in heaven, and whatsoever you loose on Earth shall be loosed in heaven. Or, in other words, taking a different view of the translation, whatsoever you record on Earth shall be recorded in heaven, and whatsoever you do not record on Earth shall not be

recorded in heaven; for out of the books shall your dead be judged, according to their own works, whether they themselves have attended to the ordinances in their own propria persona, or by the means of their own agents, according to the ordinance which God has prepared for their salvation from before the foundation of the world, according to the records which they have kept concerning their dead.
9 It may seem to some to be a very bold doctrine that we talk of—a power which records or binds on Earth and binds in heaven. Nevertheless, in all ages of the world, whenever the Lord has given a dispensation of the priesthood to any man by actual revelation, or any set of men, this power has always been given. Hence, whatsoever those men did in authority, in the name of the Lord, and did it truly and faithfully, and kept a proper and faithful record of the same, it became a law on Earth and in heaven, and could not be annulled, according to the decrees of the great Jehovah. This is a faithful saying. Who can hear it?
10 And again, for the precedent, Matthew 16:18, 19: And I say also unto thee, That thou art Peter, and upon this rock I will build my church; and the gates of hell shall not prevail against it. And I will give unto thee the keys of the kingdom of heaven: and whatsoever thou shalt bind on Earth shall be bound in heaven; and whatsoever thou shalt loose on Earth shall be loosed in heaven.
11 Now the great and grand secret of the whole matter, and the summum bonum of the whole subject that is lying before us, consists in obtaining the powers of the Holy Priesthood. For him to whom these keys are given there is no difficulty in obtaining a knowledge of facts in relation to the salvation of the children of men, both as well for the dead as for the living.
12 Herein is glory and honor, and immortality and eternal life—The ordinance of baptism by water, to be immersed therein in order to answer to the likeness of the dead, that one principle might accord with the other; to be immersed in the water and come forth out of the water is in the likeness of the resurrection of the dead in coming forth out of their graves; hence, this ordinance was instituted to form a relationship with the ordinance of baptism for the dead, being in likeness of the dead.
13 Consequently, the baptismal font was instituted as a similitude of the grave, and was commanded to be in a place underneath where the living are wont to assemble, to show forth the living and the dead, and that all things may have their likeness, and that they may accord one with another—that which is Earthly conforming to that which is heavenly, as Paul hath declared, 1 Corinthians 15:46, 47, and 48:
14 Howbeit that was not first which is spiritual, but that which is natural; and afterward that which is spiritual. The first man is of the Earth, Earthy; the second man is the Lord from heaven. As is the Earthy, such are they also that are Earthy; and as is the heavenly, such are they also that are heavenly. And as are the records on the Earth in relation to your dead, which are truly made out, so also are the records in heaven. This, therefore, is the sealing and binding power, and, in one sense of the word, the keys of the kingdom, which consist in the key of knowledge.
15 And now, my dearly beloved brethren and sisters, let me assure you that these are principles in relation to the dead and the living that cannot be lightly passed over, as pertaining to our salvation. For their salvation is necessary and essential to our salvation, as Paul says concerning the fathers—that they without us cannot be made perfect—neither can we without our dead be made perfect.
16 And now, in relation to the baptism for the dead, I will give you another quotation of Paul, 1 Corinthians 15:29: Else what shall they do which are baptized for the dead, if the dead rise not at all? Why are they then baptized for the dead?
17 And again, in connection with this quotation I will give you a quotation from one of the prophets, who had his eye fixed on the restoration of the priesthood, the glories to be revealed in the last days, and in an especial manner this most glorious of all subjects belonging to the everlasting gospel, namely, the baptism for the dead; for Malachi says, last chapter, verses 5th and 6th: Behold, I will send you Elijah the prophet before the coming of the great

The Nauvoo Temple before it was destroyed by a tornado on May 27th, 1850

and dreadful day of the Lord: And he shall turn the heart of the fathers to the children, and the heart of the children to their fathers, lest I come and smite the Earth with a curse.

18 I might have rendered a plainer translation to this, but it is sufficiently plain to suit my purpose as it stands. It is sufficient to know, in this case, that the Earth will be smitten with a curse unless there is a welding link of some kind or other between the fathers and the children, upon some subject or other—and behold what is that subject? It is the baptism for the dead. For we without them cannot be made perfect; neither can they without us be made perfect. Neither can they nor we be made perfect without those who have died in the gospel also; for it is necessary in the ushering in of the dispensation of the fulness of times, which dispensation is now beginning to usher in, that a whole and complete and perfect union, and welding together of dispensations, and keys, and powers, and glories should take place, and be revealed from the days of Adam even to the present time. And not only this, but those things which never have been revealed from the foundation of the world, but have been kept hid from the wise and prudent, shall be revealed unto babes and sucklings in this, the dispensation of the fulness of times.

19 Now, what do we hear in the gospel which we have received? A voice of gladness! A voice of mercy from heaven; and a voice of truth out of the Earth; glad tidings for the dead; a voice of gladness for the living and the dead; glad tidings of great joy. How beautiful upon the mountains are the feet of those that bring glad tidings of good things, and that say unto Zion: Behold, thy God reigneth! As the dews of Carmel, so shall the know-ledge of God descend upon them!

20 And again, what do we hear? Glad tidings from Cumorah! Moroni, an angel from heaven, declaring the fulfilment of the prophets—the book to be revealed. A voice of the Lord in the wilderness of Fayette, Seneca county, declaring the three witnesses to bear record of the book! The voice of Michael on the banks of the Susquehanna, detecting the devil when he appeared as an angel of light! The voice of Peter, James, and John in the wilderness between Harmony, Susquehanna county, and Colesville, Broome county, on the Susquehanna river, declaring themselves as possessing the keys of the kingdom, and of the dispensation of the fulness of times!

21 And again, the voice of God in the chamber of old Father Whitmer, in Fayette, Seneca county, and at sundry times, and in divers places through all the travels and tribulations of this Church of

Jesus Christ of Latter-day Saints! And the voice of Michael, the archangel; the voice of Gabriel, and of Raphael, and of divers angels, from Michael or Adam down to the present time, all declaring their dispensation, their rights, their keys, their honors, their majesty and glory, and the power of their priesthood; giving line upon line, precept upon precept; here a little, and there a little; giving us consolation by holding forth that which is to come, confirming our hope!
22 Brethren, shall we not go on in so great a cause? Go forward and not backward. Courage, brethren; and on, on to the victory! Let your hearts rejoice, and be exceedingly glad. Let the Earth break forth into singing. Let the dead speak forth anthems of eternal praise to the King Immanuel, who hath ordained, before the world was, that which would enable us to redeem them out of their prison; for the prisoners shall go free.
23 Let the mountains shout for joy, and all ye valleys cry aloud; and all ye seas and dry lands tell the wonders of your Eternal King! And ye rivers, and brooks, and rills, flow down with gladness. Let the woods and all the trees of the field praise the Lord; and ye solid rocks weep for joy! And let the sun, moon, and the morning stars sing together, and let all the sons of God shout for joy! And let the eternal creations declare his name forever and ever! And again I say, how glorious is the voice we hear from heaven, proclaiming in our ears, glory, and salvation, and honor, and immortality, and eternal life; kingdoms, principalities, and powers!

THE KING FOLLETT DISCOURSE

Joseph Smith — *April 7, 1844*

I want to talk more of the relation of man to God. I will open your eyes in relation to the dead. All things whatsoever God in his infinite wisdom has seen fit and proper to reveal to us, while we are dwelling in mortality, in regard to our mortal bodies, are revealed to us in the abstract, and independent of affinity of this mortal tabernacle, but are revealed to our spirits precisely as though we had no bodies at all; and those revelations which will save our spirits will save our bodies. God reveals them to us in view of no eternal dissolution of the body, or tabernacle. Hence the responsibility, the awful responsibility, that rests upon us in relation to our dead; for all the spirits who have not obeyed the Gospel in the flesh must either obey it in the spirit or be damned. Solemn thought!—dreadful thought! Is there nothing to be done?—no preparation—no salvation for our fathers and friends who have died without having had the opportunity to obey the decrees of the Son of Man? Would to God that I had forty days and nights in which to tell you all! I would let you know that I am not a "fallen prophet."

What promises are made in relation to the subject of the salvation of the dead? and what kind of characters are those who can be saved, although their bodies are mouldering and decaying in the grave? When His commandments teach us, it is in view of eternity; for we are looked upon by God as though we were in eternity; God dwells in eternity, and does not view things as we do.

The greatest responsibility in this world that God has laid upon us is to seek after our dead. The apostle says, "They without us cannot be made perfect"; for it is necessary that the sealing power should be in our hands to seal our children and our dead for the fulness of the dispensation of times—a dispensation to meet the promises made by Jesus Christ before the foundation of the world for the salvation of man.

Now, I will speak of them. I will meet Paul half way. I say to you, Paul, you cannot be perfect without us. It is necessary that those who are going before and those who come after us should have salvation in common with us; and thus hath God made it obligatory upon man. Hence, God said, "I will send you Elijah the prophet before the coming of the great and dreadful day of the Lord: he shall turn the heart of the fathers to the children, and the heart of the children to their fathers, lest I come and smite the Earth with a curse…"

34

MULTIPLY AND REPLENISH THE EARTH

+++

Plural marriage, as a doctrine of the restored Church, was made public in 1852 but was taught and practiced privately as early as 1831 and continued until 1904. Considering that the Lord had a limited amount of time to gather Israel before the Second Coming of Christ, it is reasonable that God would bring back the doctrine of plural marriage to jump start the growth of the church. The following prophecies relate to plural marriage and some of the justification and rules regarding the practice.

JACOB 2

Jacob, Son of Lehi — *500 BC*

27 Wherefore, my brethren, hear me, and hearken to the word of the Lord: For there shall not any man among you have save it be one wife; and concubines he shall have none;
28 For I, the Lord God, delight in the chastity of women. And whoredoms are an abomination before me; thus saith the Lord of Hosts.
29 Wherefore, this people shall keep my commandments, saith the Lord of Hosts, or cursed be the land for their sakes.
30 For if I will, saith the Lord of Hosts, raise up seed unto me, I will command my people; otherwise they shall hearken unto these things.

2 NEPHI 14 (see also ISAIAH 4)

Isaiah — *740 BC*

1 And in that day, seven women shall take hold of one man, saying: We will eat our own bread, and wear our own apparel; only let us be called by thy name to take away our reproach.
2 In that day shall the branch of the Lord be beautiful and glorious; the fruit of the Earth excellent and comely to them that are escaped of Israel.

DOCTRINE AND COVENANTS 132

Joseph Smith — *July 1843*

1 Verily, thus saith the Lord unto you my servant Joseph, that inasmuch as you have inquired of my hand to know and understand wherein I, the Lord, justified my servants Abraham, Isaac, and Jacob, as also Moses, David and Solomon, my servants, as touching the principle and doctrine of their having many wives and concubines—
2 Behold, and lo, I am the Lord thy God, and will answer thee as touching this matter.
34 God commanded Abraham, and Sarah gave Hagar to Abraham to wife. And why did she do it? Because this was the law; and from Hagar sprang many people. This, therefore, was fulfilling, among other things, the promises.
35 Was Abraham, therefore, under condemnation? Verily I say unto you, Nay; for I, the Lord, commanded it.
36 Abraham was commanded to offer his son Isaac; nevertheless, it was written: Thou shalt not kill. Abraham, however, did not refuse, and it was accounted unto him for righteousness.
37 Abraham received concubines, and they bore him children; and it was accounted unto him for righteousness, because they were given unto him, and he abode in my law; as Isaac also and Jacob did none other things than that which they were commanded; and because they did none other things than that which they were commanded, they have entered into their exaltation, according to the promises, and sit upon thrones, and are not angels but are gods.
38 David also received many wives and concubines, and also Solomon and Moses my servants, as also many others of my servants, from the beginning of creation until this time; and in nothing did they sin

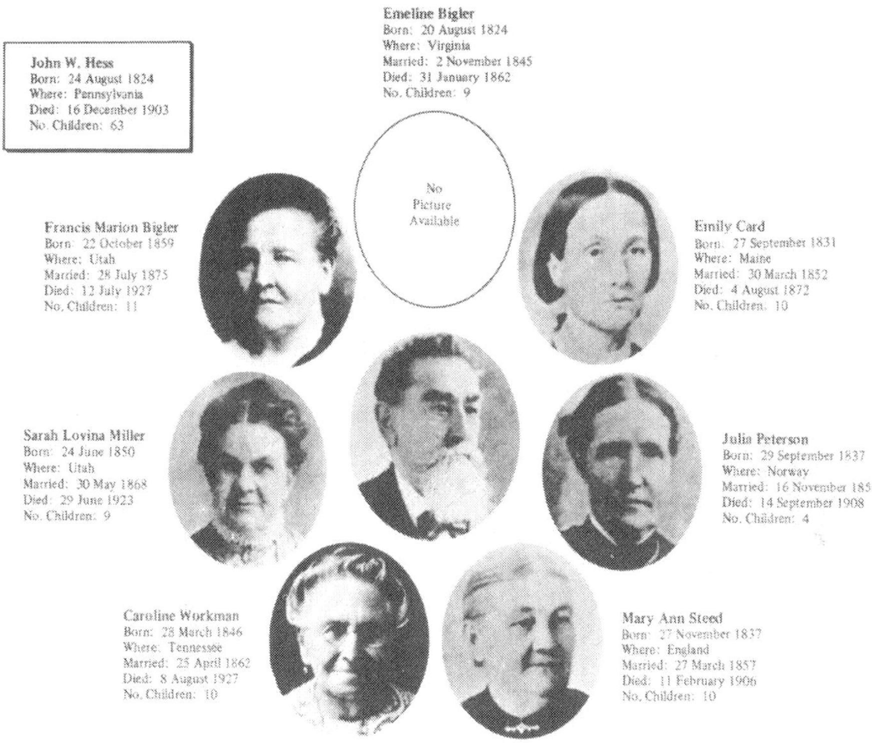

John W. Hess, my great-great grandfather, had seven wives and 63 children. It is interesting that the Lord called for the saints to practice plural marriage in an era when it was not uncommon for a couple to have 10 or more children. Allowing for multiple wives at this point in history would certainly accomplish the Lord's purpose in raising up numerous seed unto him in a short amount of time.

save in those things which they received
not of me.
39 David's wives and concubines were
given unto him of me, by the hand of
Nathan, my servant, and others of the
prophets who had the keys of this power;
and in none of these things did he sin
against me save in the case of Uriah and
his wife; and, therefore he hath fallen
from his exaltation, and received his
portion; and he shall not inherit them out
of the world, for I gave them unto
another, saith the Lord.
40 I am the Lord thy God, and I gave unto
thee, my servant Joseph, an appointment,
and restore all things. Ask what ye will,
and it shall be given unto you according to
my word.
41 And as ye have asked concerning
adultery, verily, verily, I say unto you, if a
man receiveth a wife in the new and ever-
lasting covenant, and if she be with
another man, and I have not appointed
unto her by the holy anointing, she hath
committed adultery and shall be
destroyed.
42 If she be not in the new and everlasting
covenant, and she be with another man,
she has committed adultery.
43 And if her husband be with another
woman, and he was under a vow, he hath
broken his vow and hath committed
adultery.
44 And if she hath not committed
adultery, but is innocent and hath not
broken her vow, and she knoweth it, and

I reveal it unto you, my servant Joseph, then shall you have power, by the power of my Holy Priesthood, to take her and give her unto him that hath not committed adultery but hath been faithful; for he shall be made ruler over many.

45 For I have conferred upon you the keys and power of the priesthood, wherein I restore all things, and make known unto you all things in due time.

46 And verily, verily, I say unto you, that whatsoever you seal on Earth shall be sealed in heaven; and whatsoever you bind on Earth, in my name and by my word, saith the Lord, it shall be eternally bound in the heavens; and whosesoever sins you remit on Earth shall be remitted eternally in the heavens; and whosesoever sins you retain on Earth shall be retained in heaven.

47 And again, verily I say, whomsoever you bless I will bless, and whomsoever you curse I will curse, saith the Lord; for I, the Lord, am thy God.

48 And again, verily I say unto you, my servant Joseph, that whatsoever you give on Earth, and to whomsoever you give any one on Earth, by my word and according to my law, it shall be visited with blessings and not cursings, and with my power, saith the Lord, and shall be without condemnation on Earth and in heaven.

49 For I am the Lord thy God, and will be with thee even unto the end of the world, and through all eternity; for verily I seal upon you your exaltation, and prepare a throne for you in the kingdom of my Father, with Abraham your father.

50 Behold, I have seen your sacrifices, and will forgive all your sins; I have seen your sacrifices in obedience to that which I have told you. Go, therefore, and I make a way for your escape, as I accepted the offering of Abraham of his son Isaac.

51 Verily, I say unto you: A commandment I give unto mine handmaid, Emma Smith, your wife, whom I have given unto you, that she stay herself and partake not of that which I commanded you to offer unto her; for I did it, saith the Lord, to prove you all, as I did Abraham, and that I might require an offering at your hand, by covenant and sacrifice.

52 And let mine handmaid, Emma Smith, receive all those that have been given unto my servant Joseph, and who are virtuous and pure before me; and those who are not pure, and have said they were pure, shall be destroyed, saith the Lord God.

53 For I am the Lord thy God, and ye shall obey my voice; and I give unto my servant Joseph that he shall be made ruler over many things; for he hath been faithful over a few things, and from henceforth I will strengthen him.

54 And I command mine handmaid, Emma Smith, to abide and cleave unto my servant Joseph, and to none else. But if she will not abide this commandment she shall be destroyed, saith the Lord; for I am the Lord thy God, and will destroy her if she abide not in my law.

55 But if she will not abide this commandment, then shall my servant Joseph do all things for her, even as he hath said; and I will bless him and multiply him and give unto him an hundredfold in this world, of fathers and mothers, brothers and sisters, houses and lands, wives and children, and crowns of eternal lives in the eternal worlds.

56 And again, verily I say, let mine handmaid forgive my servant Joseph his trespasses; and then shall she be forgiven her trespasses, wherein she has trespassed against me; and I, the Lord thy God, will bless her, and multiply her, and make her heart to rejoice.

57 And again, I say, let not my servant Joseph put his property out of his hands, lest an enemy come and destroy him; for Satan seeketh to destroy; for I am the Lord thy God, and he is my servant; and behold, and lo, I am with him, as I was with Abraham, thy father, even unto his exaltation and glory.

58 Now, as touching the law of the priesthood, there are many things pertaining thereunto.

59 Verily, if a man be called of my Father, as was Aaron, by mine own voice, and by the voice of him that sent me, and I have endowed him with the keys of the power of this priesthood, if he do anything in my name, and according to my law and by my word, he will not commit sin, and I will justify him.

60 Let no one, therefore, set on my servant Joseph; for I will justify him; for he shall do the sacrifice which I require at his

hands for his transgressions, saith the Lord your God.
61 And again, as pertaining to the law of the priesthood—if any man espouse a virgin, and desire to espouse another, and the first give her consent, and if he espouse the second, and they are virgins, and have vowed to no other man, then is he justified; he cannot commit adultery for they are given unto him; for he cannot commit adultery with that that belongeth unto him and to no one else.
62 And if he have ten virgins given unto him by this law, he cannot commit adultery, for they belong to him, and they are given unto him; therefore is he justified.
63 But if one or either of the ten virgins, after she is espoused, shall be with another man, she has committed adultery, and shall be destroyed; for they are given unto him to multiply and replenish the Earth, according to my commandment, and to fulfil the promise which was given by my Father before the foundation of the world, and for their exaltation in the eternal worlds, that they may bear the souls of men; for herein is the work of my Father continued, that he may be glorified.
64 And again, verily, verily, I say unto you, if any man have a wife, who holds the keys of this power, and he teaches unto her the law of my priesthood, as pertaining to these things, then shall she believe and administer unto him, or she shall be destroyed, saith the Lord your God; for I will destroy her; for I will magnify my name upon all those who receive and abide in my law.
65 Therefore, it shall be lawful in me, if she receive not this law, for him to receive all things whatsoever I, the Lord his God, will give unto him, because she did not believe and administer unto him according to my word; and she then becomes the transgressor; and he is exempt from the law of Sarah, who administered unto Abraham according to the law when I commanded Abraham to take Hagar to wife.
66 And now, as pertaining to this law, verily, verily, I say unto you, I will reveal more unto you, hereafter; therefore, let this suffice for the present. Behold, I am Alpha and Omega. Amen.

Ira Eldredge and his wives Nancy, Hannah, and Helvig. Ira was Bishop of the Sugar House Ward in Salt Lake City at the time this image was taken, 1864.

35

THE GATHERING OF ISRAEL

+++

The gathering of Israel and the growth of the Church of Jesus Christ in the latter-days is foreseen. After the house of Israel had been scattered and smitten, the Lord would remember his covenant and establish a new and everlasting covenant in the last days. He would send out his missionaries into all the world to gather the elect of Israel. The House of Israel would also be led out of oppressive countries to free countries where they could receive the gospel.

The initial growth of the church came from the northeastern United States and the British Isles. Later, growth came from the Protestant countries of Northern Europe: Holland, Denmark, Sweden, Norway, Germany. The prophets of old had foreseen many of the lost tribes of Israel returning from the north countries. In the 20th century, much of the growth would come from Latin America, the South Pacific Islands, Asia and Africa.

DOCTRINE AND COVENANTS 45
Joseph Smith *March 1831*
1 Hearken, O ye people of my church, to whom the kingdom has been given; hearken ye and give ear to him who laid the foundation of the Earth, who made the heavens and all the hosts thereof, and by whom all things were made which live, and move, and have a being.
2 And again I say, hearken unto my voice, lest death shall overtake you; in an hour when ye think not the summer shall be past, and the harvest ended, and your souls not saved.
9 And even so I have sent mine everlasting covenant into the world, to be a light to the world, and to be a standard for my people, and for the Gentiles to seek to it, and to be a messenger before my face to prepare the way before me.
10 Wherefore, come ye unto it, and with him that cometh I will reason as with men in days of old, and I will show unto you my strong reasoning.

DOCTRINE AND COVENANTS 14
Joseph Smith *June 1829*
9 Behold, I am Jesus Christ, the Son of the living God, who created the heavens and the Earth, a light which cannot be hid in darkness;
10 Wherefore, I must bring forth the fulness of my gospel from the Gentiles unto the house of Israel.

DEUTERONOMONY 33
Moses *1475 BC*
13 And of Joseph he said, Blessed of the Lord be his land, for the precious things of heaven, for the dew, and for the deep that coucheth beneath,
14 And for the precious fruits brought forth by the sun, and for the precious things put forth by the moon,
15 And for the chief things of the ancient mountains, and for the precious things of the lasting hills,
16 And for the precious things of the Earth and fulness thereof, and for the good will of him that dwelt in the bush: let the blessing come upon the head of Joseph, and upon the top of the head of him that was separated from his brethren.
17 His glory is like the firstling of his bullock, and his horns are like the horns of unicorns: with them he shall push the people together to the ends of the Earth: and they are the ten thousands of Ephraim, and they are the thousands of Manasseh.

MORMON 5
Mormon *385 AD*
20 ...and after they have been driven and scattered by the Gentiles, behold, then will the Lord remember the covenant

My father-in-law, James L. Ray, served in the Uruguay Mission. He is pictured here teaching the Incas of Peru (and a few interested llamas) while on his way home in 1967.

which he made unto Abraham and unto all the house of Israel.
21 And also the Lord will remember the prayers of the righteous, which have been put up unto him for them.

ALMA 9

Alma the Younger — *82 BC*

16 For there are many promises which are extended to the Lamanites; for it is because of the traditions of their fathers that caused them to remain in their state of ignorance; therefore the Lord will be merciful unto them and prolong their existence in the land.
17 And at some period of time they will be brought to believe in his word, and to know of the incorrectness of the traditions of their fathers; and many of them will be saved, for the Lord will be merciful unto all who call on his name.

DEUTERONOMONY 4

Moses — *1475 BC*

29 But if from thence thou shalt seek the Lord thy God, thou shalt find him, if thou seek him with all thy heart and with all thy soul.
30 When thou art in tribulation, and all these things are come upon thee, even in the latter-days, if thou turn to the Lord thy God, and shalt be obedient unto his voice;
31 (For the Lord thy God is a merciful God;) he will not forsake thee, neither destroy thee, nor forget the covenant of thy fathers which he sware unto them.

1 NEPHI 10

Nephi, Son of Lehi — *600 BC*

14 And after the house of Israel should be scattered they should be gathered together again; or, in fine, after the Gentiles had received the fulness of the Gospel, the natural branches of the olive tree, or the remnants of the house of Israel, should be grafted in, or come to the knowledge of the true Messiah, their Lord and their Redeemer.

2 NEPHI 9

Jacob, Son of Lehi — *550 BC*

53 And behold how great the covenants of the Lord, and how great his condescendsions unto the children of men; and because of his greatness, and his grace and mercy, he has promised unto us that our seed shall not utterly be destroyed, according to the flesh, but that he would preserve them; and in future generations they shall become a righteous branch unto the house of Israel.

2 NEPHI 10

Jacob, Son of Lehi — *550 BC*

2 For behold, the promises which we have obtained are promises unto us according to the flesh; wherefore, as it has been shown unto me that many of our children shall perish in the flesh because of unbelief, nevertheless, God will be merciful unto many; and our children shall be restored, that they may come to that which will give them the true knowledge of their Redeemer.

ISAIAH 61

Isaiah — *740 BC*

1 The Spirit of the Lord GOD is upon me; because the LORD hath anointed me to preach good tidings unto the meek; he hath sent me to bind up the brokenhearted, to proclaim liberty to the captives, and the opening of the prison to them that are bound;

2 To proclaim the acceptable year of the LORD, and the day of vengeance of our God; to comfort all that mourn;

3 To appoint unto them that mourn in Zion, to give unto them beauty for ashes, the oil of joy for mourning, the garment of praise for the spirit of heaviness; that they might be called trees of righteousness, the planting of the LORD, that he might be glorified.

4 And they shall build the old wastes, they shall raise up the former desolations, and they shall repair the waste cities, the desolations of many generations.

5 And strangers shall stand and feed your flocks, and the sons of the alien shall be your plowmen and your vinedressers.

6 But ye shall be named the Priests of the LORD: men shall call you the Ministers of our God: ye shall eat the riches of the Gentiles, and in their glory shall ye boast yourselves.

7 For your shame ye shall have double; and for confusion they shall rejoice in their portion: therefore in their land they shall possess the double: everlasting joy shall be unto them.

8 For I the LORD love judgment, I hate robbery for burnt offering; and I will direct their work in truth, and I will make an everlasting covenant with them.

9 And their seed shall be known among the Gentiles, and their offspring among the people: all that see them shall acknowledge them, that they are the seed which the LORD hath blessed.

10 I will greatly rejoice in the LORD, my soul shall be joyful in my God; for he hath clothed me with the garments of salvation, he hath covered me with the robe of righteousness, as a bridegroom decketh himself with ornaments, and as a bride adorneth herself with her jewels.

11 For as the Earth bringeth forth her bud, and as the garden causeth the things that are sown in it to spring forth; so the Lord GOD will cause righteousness and praise to spring forth before all the nations.

ISAIAH 55

Isaiah — *740 BC*

1 Ho, every one that thirsteth, come ye to the waters, and he that hath no money; come ye, buy, and eat; yea, come, buy wine and milk without money and without price.

2 Wherefore do ye spend money for that which is not bread? and your labour for that which satisfieth not? hearken diligently unto me, and eat ye that which is good, and let your soul delight itself in fatness.

3 Incline your ear, and come unto me: hear, and your soul shall live; and I will make an everlasting covenant with you, even the sure mercies of David.

6 Seek ye the LORD while he may be found, call ye upon him while he is near:

7 Let the wicked forsake his way, and the unrighteous man his thoughts: and let him return unto the LORD, and he will have mercy upon him; and to our God, for he will abundantly pardon.

JEREMIAH 31

Jeremiah *628 BC*

1 At the same time, saith the LORD, will I
be the God of all the families of Israel, and
they shall be my people.
2 Thus saith the LORD, the people which
were left of the sword found grace in the
wilderness; even Israel, when I went to
cause him to rest.
3 The LORD hath appeared of old unto
me, saying, Yea, I have loved thee with an
everlasting love: therefore, with loving
kindness have I drawn thee.
4 Again I will build thee, and thou shalt be
built, O virgin of Israel: thou shalt again
be adorned with thy tabrets, and shalt go
forth in the dances of them that make
merry.
5 Thou shalt yet plant vines upon the
mountains of Samaria: the planters shall
plant and shall eat them as common
things.
6 For there shall be a day, that the watch-
men upon the mount Ephraim shall cry,
arise ye, and let us go up to Zion unto the
LORD our God.
7 For thus saith the LORD; Sing with
gladness for Jacob, and shout among the
chief of the nations: publish ye, praise ye,
and say, O LORD, save thy people, the
remnant of Israel.
8 Behold, I will bring them from the north
country, and gather them from the coasts
of the Earth, and with them the blind and
the lame, the woman with child and her
that travaileth with child together: a great
company shall return thither.
9 They shall come with weeping, and with
supplications will I lead them: I will cause
them to walk by the rivers of waters in a
straight way, wherein they shall not
stumble: for I am a father to Israel, and
Ephraim is my firstborn.
10 Hear the word of the LORD, O ye
nations, and declare it in the isles afar off,
and say, He that scattered Israel will
gather him, and keep him, as a shepherd
doth his flock.
11 For the LORD hath redeemed Jacob
and ransomed him from the hand of him
that was stronger than he.
12 Therefore they shall come and sing in
the height of Zion and shall flow together
to the goodness of the LORD, for wheat,
and for wine, and for oil, and for the
young of the flock and of the herd: and
their soul shall be as a watered garden; and
they shall not sorrow any more at all.
13 Then shall the virgin rejoice in the
dance, both young men and old together:
for I will turn their mourning into joy, and
will comfort them, and make them rejoice
from their sorrow.
14 And I will satiate the soul of the priests
with fatness, and my people shall be
satisfied with my goodness, saith the
LORD.
15 Thus saith the LORD; A voice was
heard in Ramah, lamentation, and bitter
weeping; Rahel weeping for her children
refused to be comforted for her children,
because they were not.
16 Thus saith the LORD; Refrain thy voice
from weeping, and thine eyes from tears:
for thy work shall be rewarded, saith the
LORD; and they shall come again from the
land of the enemy.
17 And there is hope in thine bend, saith
the LORD, that thy children shall come
again to their own border.
18 I have surely heard Ephraim bemoan-
ing himself; thus, thou hast chastised me,
and I was chastised, as a bullock unaccust-
omed to the yoke: turn thou me, and I
shall be turned; for thou art the LORD my
God.
19 Surely after that I was turned, I
repented; and after that I was instructed, I
smote upon my thigh: I was ashamed, yea,
even confounded, because I did bear the
reproach of my youth.
20 Is Ephraim my dear son? Is he a
pleasant child? for since I spake against
him, I do earnestly remember him still:
therefore, my bowels are troubled for him;
I will surely have mercy upon him, saith
the LORD.
21 Set thee up waymarks, make thee high
heaps: set thine heart toward the high-
way, even the way which thou wentest:
turn again, O virgin of Israel, turn again to
these thy cities.
31 Behold, the days come, saith the
LORD, that I will make a new covenant
with the house of Israel, and with the
house of Judah:
32 Not according to the covenant that I
made with their fathers in the day that I
took them by the hand to bring them out
of the land of Egypt, which my covenant
they brake, although I was an husband
unto them, saith the LORD:

33 But this shall be the covenant that I will make with the house of Israel; After those days, saith the LORD, I will put my law in their inward parts, and write it in their hearts; and will be their God, and they shall be my people.

34 And they shall teach no more every man his neighbour, and every man his brother, saying, Know the LORD: for they shall all know me, from the least of them unto the greatest of them, saith the LORD: for I will forgive their iniquity, and I will remember their sin no more.

35 Thus saith the LORD, which giveth the sun for a light by day, and the ordinances of the moon and of the stars for a light by night, which divideth the sea when the waves thereof roar; The LORD of hosts is his name:

36 If those ordinances depart from before me, saith the LORD, then the seed of Israel also shall cease from being a nation before me forever.

37 Thus saith the LORD; If heaven above can be measured, and the foundations of the Earth searched out beneath, I will also cast off all the seed of Israel for all that they have done, saith the LORD.

3 NEPHI 22 (see also ISAIAH 54)

Isaiah *740 BC*

1 And then shall that which is written come to pass: Sing, O barren, thou that didst not bear; break forth into singing, and cry aloud, thou that didst not travail with child; for more are the children of the desolate than the children of the married wife, saith the Lord.

2 Enlarge the place of thy tent, and let them stretch forth the curtains of thy habitations; spare not, lengthen thy cords and strengthen thy stakes;

3 For thou shalt break forth on the right hand and on the left, and thy seed shall inherit the Gentiles and make the desolate cities to be inhabited.

4 Fear not, for thou shalt not be ashamed; neither be thou confounded, for thou shalt not be put to shame; for thou shalt forget the shame of thy youth, and shalt not remember the reproach of thy youth, and shalt not remember the reproach of thy widowhood anymore.

5 For thy maker, thy husband, the Lord of Hosts is his name; and thy Redeemer, the Holy One of Israel—the God of the whole Earth shall he be called.

6 For the Lord hath called thee as a woman forsaken and grieved in spirit, and a wife of youth, when thou wast refused, saith thy God.

7 For a small moment have I forsaken thee, but with great mercies will I gather thee.

8 In a little wrath I hid my face from thee for a moment, but with everlasting kindness will I have mercy on thee, saith the Lord thy Redeemer.

9 For this, the waters of Noah unto me, for as I have sworn that the waters of Noah should no more go over the Earth, so have I sworn that I would not be wroth with thee.

10 For the mountains shall depart and the hills be removed, but my kindness shall not depart from thee, neither shall the covenant of my peace be removed, saith the Lord that hath mercy on thee.

11 O thou afflicted, tossed with tempest, and not comforted! Behold, I will lay thy stones with fair colors, and lay thy foundations with sapphires.

12 And I will make thy windows of agates, and thy gates of carbuncles, and all thy borders of pleasant stones.

13 And all thy children shall be taught of the Lord; and great shall be the peace of thy children.

14 In righteousness shalt thou be established; thou shalt be far from oppression for thou shalt not fear, and from terror for it shall not come near thee.

15 Behold, they shall surely gather together against thee, not by me; whosoever shall gather together against thee shall fall for thy sake.

16 Behold, I have created the smith that bloweth the coals in the fire, and that bringeth forth an instrument for his work; and I have created the waster to destroy.

17 No weapon that is formed against thee shall prosper; and every tongue that shall revile against thee in judgment thou shalt condemn. This is the heritage of the servants of the Lord, and their righteousness is of me, saith the Lord.

HELAMAN 15

Samuel the Lamanite *6 BC*

11 Yea, even if they should dwindle in unbelief the Lord shall prolong their days,

until the time shall come which hath been spoken of by our fathers, and also by the prophet Zenos, and many other prophets, concerning the restoration of our brethren, the Lamanites, again to the knowledge of the truth—

12 Yea, I say unto you, that in the lattertimes the promises of the Lord have been extended to our brethren, the Lamanites; and notwithstanding the many afflictions which they shall have, and notwithstanding they shall be driven to and fro upon the face of the Earth, and be hunted, and shall be smitten and scattered abroad, having no place for refuge, the Lord shall be merciful unto them.

13 And this is according to the prophecy, that they shall again be brought to the true knowledge, which is the knowledge of their Redeemer, and their great and true shepherd, and be numbered among his sheep.

16 Therefore, saith the Lord: I will not utterly destroy them, but I will cause that in the day of my wisdom they shall return again unto me, saith the Lord.

3 NEPHI 5

Mormon — *385 AD*

23 Yea, and surely shall he again bring a remnant of the seed of Joseph to the knowledge of the Lord their God.

24 And as surely as the Lord liveth, will he gather in from the four quarters of the Earth all the remnant of the seed of Jacob, who are scattered abroad upon all the face of the Earth.

25 And as he hath covenanted with all the house of Jacob, even so shall the covenant wherewith he hath covenanted with the house of Jacob be fulfilled in his own due time, unto the restoring all the house of Jacob unto the knowledge of the covenant that he hath covenanted with them.

26 And then shall they know their Redeemer, who is Jesus Christ, the Son of God; and then shall they be gathered in from the four quarters of the Earth unto their own lands, from whence they have been dispersed; yea, as the Lord liveth so shall it be. Amen.

3 NEPHI 20

Jesus Christ — *34 AD*

11 Ye remember that I spake unto you, and said that when the words of Isaiah should be fulfilled—behold they are written, ye have them before you, therefore search them—

12 And verily, verily, I say unto you, that when they shall be fulfilled then is the fulfilling of the covenant which the Father hath made unto his people, O house of Israel.

13 And then shall the remnants, which shall be scattered abroad upon the face of the Earth, be gathered in from the east and from the west, and from the south and from the north; and they shall be brought to the knowledge of the Lord their God, who hath redeemed them.

PSALMS 14

David — *1000 BC*

7 Oh that the salvation of Israel were come out of Zion! when the Lord bringeth back the captivity of his people, Jacob shall rejoice, and Israel shall be glad.

DEUTERONOMONY 30

Moses — *1475 BC*

1 And it shall come to pass, when all these things [Israel scattered and smitten] are come upon thee, the blessing and the curse, which I have set before thee, and thou shalt call them to mind among all the nations, whither the Lord thy God hath driven thee,

2 And shalt return unto the Lord thy God, and shalt obey his voice according to all that I command thee this day, thou and thy children, with all thine heart, and with all thy soul;

3 That then the Lord thy God will turn thy captivity, and have compassion upon thee, and will return and gather thee from all the nations, whither the Lord thy God hath scattered thee.

4 If any of thine be driven out unto the outmost parts of heaven, from thence will the Lord thy God gather thee, and from thence will he fetch thee:

5 And the Lord thy God will bring thee into the land which thy fathers possessed, and thou shalt possess it; and he will do thee good, and multiply thee above thy fathers.

6 And the Lord thy God will circumcise thine heart, and the heart of thy seed, to love the Lord thy God with all thine heart, and with all thy soul, that thou mayest live.

7 And the Lord thy God will put all these
curses upon thine enemies, and on them
that hate thee, which persecuted thee.
8 And thou shalt return and obey the
voice of the Lord, and do all his command-
ments which I command thee this day.
9 And the Lord thy God will make thee
plenteous in every work of thine hand, in
the fruit of thy body, and in the fruit of
thy cattle, and in the fruit of thy land, for
good: for the Lord will again rejoice over
thee for good, as he rejoiced over thy
fathers:
10 If thou shalt hearken unto the voice of
the Lord thy God, to keep his command-
ments and his statutes which are written
in this book of the law, and if thou turn
unto the Lord thy God with all thine
heart, and with all thy soul.

JACOB 5

Zenos *~700-800 BC*

70 And it came to pass that the Lord of the
vineyard sent his servant; and the servant
went and did as the Lord had commanded
him, and brought other servants; and they
were few.
71 And the Lord of the vineyard said unto
them: Go to, and labor in the vineyard,
with your might. For behold, this is the
last time that I shall nourish my vineyard;
for the end is nigh at hand, and the season
speedily cometh; and if ye labor with your
might with me ye shall have joy in the
fruit which I shall lay up unto myself
against the time which will soon come.
72 And it came to pass that the servants
did go and labor with their mights; and
the Lord of the vineyard labored also with
them; and they did obey the command-
ments of the Lord of the vineyard in all
things.
73 And there began to be the natural fruit
again in the vineyard; and the natural
branches began to grow and thrive
exceedingly; and the wild branches began
to be plucked off and to be cast away; and
they did keep the root and the top thereof
equal, according to the strength thereof.

EZEKIEL 36

Ezekiel *598 BC*

8 But ye, O mountains of Israel, ye shall
shoot forth your branches, and yield your
fruit to my people of Israel; for they are at
hand to come.
9 For, behold, I am for you, and I will turn
unto you, and ye shall be tilled and sown:
10 And I will multiply men upon you, all
the house of Israel, even all of it: and the
cities shall be inhabited, and the wastes
shall be builded:
11 And I will multiply upon you man and
beast; and they shall increase and bring
fruit: and I will settle you after your old
estates and will do better unto you than at
your beginnings: and ye shall know that I
am the LORD.
12 Yea, I will cause men to walk upon you,
even my people Israel; and they shall
possess thee, and thou shalt be their
inheritance, and thou shalt no more
henceforth bereave them of men.
13 Thus saith the Lord GOD; Because they
say unto you, thou land devourest up men,
and hast bereaved thy nations.
14 Therefore thou shalt devour men no
more, neither bereave thy nations any-
more, saith the Lord GOD.
15 Neither will I cause men to hear in thee
the shame of the heathen anymore,
neither shalt thou bear the reproach of the
people anymore, neither shalt thou cause
thy nations to fall any more, saith the Lord
GOD.

1 NEPHI 15

Nephi, Son of Lehi *595 BC*

12 Behold, I say unto you, that the house
of Israel was compared unto an olive tree,
by the Spirit of the Lord which was in our
father; and behold are we not broken off
from the house of Israel, and are we not a
branch of the house of Israel?
13 And now, the thing which our father
meaneth concerning the grafting in of the
natural branches through the fulness of
the Gentiles, is, that in the latter-days,
when our seed shall have dwindled in
unbelief, yea, for the space of many years,
and many generations after the Messiah
shall be manifested in body unto the
children of men, then shall the fulness of
the gospel of the Messiah come unto the
Gentiles, and from the Gentiles unto the
remnant of our seed—
14 And at that day shall the remnant of
our seed know that they are of the house
of Israel, and that they are the covenant
people of the Lord; and then shall they
know and come to the knowledge of their
forefathers, and also to the knowledge of

the gospel of their Redeemer, which was
ministered unto their fathers by him;
wherefore, they shall come to the know-
ledge of their Redeemer and the very
points of his doctrine, that they may know
how to come unto him and be saved.
15 And then at that day will they not
rejoice and give praise unto their ever-
lasting God, their rock and their salvation?
Yea, at that day, will they not receive the
strength and nourishment from the true
vine? Yea, will they not come unto the
true fold of God?
16 Behold, I say unto you, Yea; they shall
be remembered again among the house of
Israel; they shall be grafted in, being a
natural branch of the olive tree, into the
true olive tree.
17 And this is what our father meaneth;
and he meaneth that it will not come to
pass until after they are scattered by the
Gentiles; and he meaneth that it shall
come by way of the Gentiles, that the Lord
may show his power unto the Gentiles, for
the very cause that he shall be rejected of
the Jews, or of the house of Israel.
18 Wherefore, our father hath not spoken
of our seed alone, but also of all the house
of Israel, pointing to the covenant which
should be fulfilled in the latter-days;
which covenant the Lord made to our
father Abraham, saying: In thy seed shall
all the kindreds of the Earth be blessed.

2 NEPHI 30

Nephi, Son of Lehi — *550 BC*

1 And now behold, my beloved brethren,
I would speak unto you; for I, Nephi,
would not suffer that ye should suppose
that ye are more righteous than the Gen-
tiles shall be. For behold, except ye shall
keep the commandments of God ye shall
all likewise perish; and because of the
words which have been spoken ye need
not suppose that the Gentiles are utterly
destroyed.
2 For behold, I say unto you that as many
of the Gentiles as will repent are the
covenant people of the Lord; and as many
of the Jews as will not repent shall be cast
off; for the Lord covenanteth with none
save it be with them that repent and
believe in his Son, who is the Holy One of
Israel.
3 And now, I would prophesy somewhat
more concerning the Jews and the Gen-
tiles. For after the book of which I have
spoken shall come forth, and be written
unto the Gentiles, and sealed up again
unto the Lord, there shall be many which
shall believe the words which are written;
and they shall carry them forth unto the
remnant of our seed.
4 And then shall the remnant of our seed
know concerning us, how that we came
out from Jerusalem, and that they are
descendants of the Jews.
5 And the gospel of Jesus Christ shall be
declared among them; wherefore, they
shall be restored unto the knowledge of
their fathers, and also to the knowledge of
Jesus Christ, which was had among their
fathers.
6 And then shall they rejoice; for they
shall know that it is a blessing unto them
from the hand of God; and their scales of
darkness shall begin to fall from their eyes;
and many generations shall not pass away
among them, save they shall be a pure and
a delightsome people.
8 And it shall come to pass that the Lord
God shall commence his work among all
nations, kindreds, tongues, and people, to
bring about the restoration of his people
upon the Earth.

ISAIAH 18

Isaiah — *740 BC*

1 Woe to the land shadowing with wings,
which is beyond the rivers of Ethiopia:
2 That sendeth ambassadors by the sea,
even in vessels of bulrushes upon the
waters, saying, Go, ye swift messengers, to
a nation scattered and peeled, to a people
terrible from their beginning hitherto; a
nation meted out and trodden down,
whose land the rivers have spoiled!
3 All ye inhabitants of the world, and
dwellers on the Earth, see ye, when he
lifteth up an ensign on the mountains; and
when he bloweth a trumpet, hear ye.
7 In that time shall the present be brought
unto the LORD of hosts of a people
scattered and peeled, and from a people
terrible from their beginning hitherto; a
nation meted out and trodden under foot,
whose land the rivers have spoiled, to the
place of the name of the LORD of hosts,
the mount Zion.

The baptism of Sister Desiraa Nkohla by Elder Clint Bennion (right) and Elder Christensen (left) September 26, 1993, in Daveyton Township, South Africa.

JACOB 6

Jacob, Son of Lehi *520 BC*

1 And now, behold, my brethren, as I said
unto you that I would prophesy, behold,
this is my prophecy—that the things
which this prophet Zenos spake, concern-
ing the house of Israel, in the which he
likened them unto a tame olive tree, must
surely come to pass.
2 And the day that he shall set his hand
again the second time to recover his
people, is the day, yea, even the last time,
that the servants of the Lord shall go forth
in his power, to nourish and prune his
vineyard; and after that the end soon
cometh.
3 And how blessed are they who have
labored diligently in his vineyard; and
how cursed are they who shall be cast out
into their own place! And the world shall
be burned with fire.
4 And how merciful is our God unto us,
for he remembereth the house of Israel,
both roots and branches; and he stretches
forth his hands unto them all the day long;
and they are a stiffnecked and a gainsaying
people; but as many as will not harden
their hearts shall be saved in the kingdom
of God.

DOCTRINE AND COVENANTS 84

Joseph Smith *December 1832*

61 For I will forgive you of your sins with
this commandment—that you remain
steadfast in your minds in solemnity and
the spirit of prayer, in bearing testimony
to all the world of those things which are
communicated unto you.
62 Therefore, go ye into all the world; and
unto whatsoever place ye cannot go ye
shall send, that the testimony may go from
you into all the world unto every creature.
63 And as I said unto mine apostles, even
so I say unto you, for you are mine
apostles, even God's high priests; ye are
they whom my Father hath given me; ye
are my friends;
64 Therefore, as I said unto mine apostles,
I say unto you again, that every soul who
believeth on your words, and is baptized
by water for the remission of sins, shall
receive the Holy Ghost.
65 And these signs shall follow them that
believe—
66 In my name they shall do many
wonderful works;
67 In my name they shall cast out devils;
68 In my name they shall heal the sick;

69 In my name they shall open the eyes of
the blind, and unstop the ears of the deaf;
70 And the tongue of the dumb shall
speak;
71 And if any man shall administer poison
unto them it shall not hurt them;
72 And the poison of a serpent shall not
have power to harm them.
73 But a commandment I give unto them,
that they shall not boast themselves of
these things, neither speak them before
the world; for these things are given unto
you for your profit and for salvation.
74 Verily, verily, I say unto you, they who
believe not on your words, and are not
baptized in water in my name, for the
remission of their sins, that they may
receive the Holy Ghost, shall be damned,
and shall not come into my Father's
kingdom where my Father and I am.
75 And this revelation unto you, and com-
mandment, is in force from this very hour
upon all the world, and the gospel is unto
all who have not received it.
76 But, verily I say unto all those to whom
the kingdom has been given—from you it
must be preached unto them, that they
shall repent of their former evil works; for
they are to be upbraided for their evil
hearts of unbelief, and your brethren in
Zion for their rebellion against you at the
time I sent you.
77 And again I say unto you, my friends,
for from henceforth I shall call you
friends, it is expedient that I give unto you
this commandment, that ye become even
as my friends in days when I was with
them, traveling to preach the gospel in my
power;
78 For I suffered them not to have purse
or scrip, neither two coats.
79 Behold, I send you out to prove the
world, and the laborer is worthy of his
hire.
80 And any man that shall go and preach
this gospel of the kingdom, and fail not to
continue faithful in all things, shall not be
weary in mind, neither darkened, neither
in body, limb, nor joint; and a hair of his
head shall not fall to the ground
unnoticed. And they shall not go hungry,
neither athirst.

DOCTRINE AND COVENANTS 88

Joseph Smith December 1832

69 Remember the great and last promise
which I have made unto you; cast away
your idle thoughts and your excess of
laughter far from you.
70 Tarry ye, tarry ye in this place, and call
a solemn assembly, even of those who are
the first laborers in this last kingdom.
71 And let those whom they have warned
in their traveling call on the Lord, and
ponder the warning in their hearts which
they have received, for a little season.
72 Behold, and lo, I will take care of your
flocks, and will raise up elders and send
unto them.
73 Behold, I will hasten my work in its
time.
74 And I give unto you, who are the first
laborers in this last kingdom, a command-
ment that you assemble yourselves
together, and organize yourselves, and
prepare yourselves, and sanctify your-
selves; yea, purify your hearts, and cleanse
your hands and your feet before me, that I
may make you clean;
75 That I may testify unto your Father,
and your God, and my God, that you are
clean from the blood of this wicked
generation; that I may fulfil this promise,
this great and last promise, which I have
made unto you, when I will.
76 Also, I give unto you a commandment
that ye shall continue in prayer and
fasting from this time forth.
77 And I give unto you a commandment
that you shall teach one another the
doctrine of the kingdom.
78 Teach ye diligently and my grace shall
attend you, that you may be instructed
more perfectly in theory, in principle, in
doctrine, in the law of the gospel, in all
things that pertain unto the kingdom of
God, that are expedient for you to
understand;
79 Of things both in heaven and in the
Earth, and under the Earth; things which
have been, things which are, things which
must shortly come to pass; things which
are at home, things which are abroad; the
wars and the perplexities of the nations,
and the judgments which are on the land;
and a knowledge also of countries and of
kingdoms—
80 That ye may be prepared in all things
when I shall send you again to magnify

the calling whereunto I have called you, and the mission with which I have commissioned you.

DOCTRINE AND COVENANTS 35

Joseph Smith *November 1830*

13 Wherefore, I call upon the weak things of the world, those who are unlearned and despised, to thresh the nations by the power of my Spirit;
14 And their arm shall be my arm, and I will be their shield and their buckler; and I will gird up their loins, and they shall fight manfully for me; and their enemies shall be under their feet; and I will let fall the sword in their behalf, and by the fire of mine indignation will I preserve them.
15 And the poor and the meek shall have the gospel preached unto them, and they shall be looking forth for the time of my coming, for it is nigh at hand –

3 NEPHI 28

Mormon *385 AD*

25 Behold, I was about to write the names of those who were never to taste of death, but the Lord forbade; therefore I write them not, for they are hid from the world.
26 But behold, I have seen them, and they have ministered unto me.
27 And behold they will be among the Gentiles, and the Gentiles shall know them not.
28 They will also be among the Jews, and the Jews shall know them not.
29 And it shall come to pass, when the Lord seeth fit in his wisdom that they shall minister unto all the scattered tribes of Israel, and unto all nations, kindreds, tongues and people, and shall bring out of them unto Jesus many souls, that their desire may be fulfilled, and also because of the convincing power of God which is in them.
30 And they are as the angels of God, and if they shall pray unto the Father in the name of Jesus they can show themselves unto whatsoever man it seemeth them good.
31 Therefore, great and marvelous works shall be wrought by them, before the great and coming day when all people must surely stand before the judgment-seat of Christ;
32 Yea even among the Gentiles shall there be a great and marvelous work wrought by them, before that judgment day.

ISAIAH 56

Isaiah *740 BC*

1 Thus saith the LORD, keep ye judgment, and do justice: for my salvation is near to come, and my righteousness to be revealed.
2 Blessed is the man that doeth this, and the son of man that layeth hold on it; that keepeth the sabbath from polluting it, and keepeth his hand from doing any evil.
3 Neither let the son of the stranger, that hath joined himself to the LORD, speak, saying, The LORD hath utterly separated me from his people: neither let the eunuch say, Behold, I am a dry tree.
4 For thus saith the LORD unto the eunuchs that keep my sabbaths, and choose the things that please me, and take hold of my covenant;
5 Even unto them will I give in mine house and within my walls a place and a name better than of sons and of daughters: I will give them an everlasting name, that shall not be cut off.
6 Also the sons of the stranger, that join themselves to the LORD, to serve him, and to love the name of the LORD, to be his servants, everyone that keepeth the sabbath from polluting it, and taketh hold of my covenant;
7 Even them will I bring to my holy mountain, and make them joyful in my house of prayer: their burnt offerings and their sacrifices shall be accepted upon mine altar; for mine house shall be called an house of prayer for all people.
8 The Lord GOD which gathereth the outcasts of Israel saith, Yet will I gather others to him, beside those that are gathered unto him.

ZECHARIAH 10

Zechariah *520 BC*

6 And I will strengthen the house of Judah, and I will save the house of Joseph, and I will bring them again to place them; for I have mercy upon them: and they shall be as though I had not cast them off: for I am the LORD their God, and will hear them.
7 And they of Ephraim shall be like a mighty man, and their heart shall rejoice as through wine: yea, their children shall

see it, and be glad; their heart shall rejoice
in the LORD.
8 I will hiss for them, and gather them; for
I have redeemed them: and they shall
increase as they have increased.
9 And I will sow them among the people:
and they shall remember me in far
countries; and they shall live with their
children, and turn again.
10 I will bring them again also out of the
land of Egypt, and gather them out of
Assyria; and I will bring them into the
land of Gilead and Lebanon; and place
shall not be found for them.
11 And he shall pass through the sea with
affliction, and shall smite the waves in the
sea, and all the deeps of the river shall dry
up: and the pride of Assyria shall be
brought down, and the sceptre of Egypt
shall depart away.
12 And I will strengthen them in the
LORD; and they shall walk up and down
in his name, saith the LORD.

JEREMIAH 3

Jeremiah *628 BC*

12 Go and proclaim these words toward
the north, and say, Return, thou back-
sliding Israel, saith the LORD; and I will
not cause mine anger to fall upon you: for
I am merciful, saith the LORD, and I will
not keep anger forever.
13 Only acknowledge thine iniquity, that
thou hast transgressed against the LORD
thy God, and hast scattered thy ways to
the strangers under every green tree, and
ye have not obeyed my voice, saith the
LORD.
14 Turn, O backsliding children, saith the
LORD; for I am married unto you: and I
will take you one of a city, and two of a
family, and I will bring you to Zion:
15 And I will give you pastors according
to mine heart, which shall feed you with
knowledge and understanding.
16 And it shall come to pass, when ye be
multiplied and increased in the land, in
those days, saith the LORD, they shall say
no more, the ark of the covenant of the
LORD: neither shall it come to mind:
neither shall they remember it; neither
shall they visit it; neither shall that be
done any more.

MICAH 2

Micah *722 BC*

12 I will surely assemble, O Jacob, all of
thee; I will surely gather the remnant of
Israel; I will put them together as the
sheep of Bozrah, as the flock in the midst
of their fold: they shall make great noise
by reason of the multitude of men.

HOSEA 3

Hosea *790 BC*

5 Afterward shall the children of Israel
return, and seek the LORD their God, and
David their king; and shall fear the LORD
and his goodness in the latter-days.

EPHESIANS 1

Paul *62 AD*

10 That in the dispensation of the fulness
of times he might gather together in one
all things in Christ, both which are in
heaven, and which are on Earth; even in
him:

ISAIAH 35

Isaiah *740 BC*

1 The wilderness and the solitary place
shall be glad for them; and the desert shall
rejoice, and blossom as the rose.
2 It shall blossom abundantly and rejoice
even with joy and singing: the glory of
Lebanon shall be given unto it, the excel-
lency of Carmel and Sharon, they shall see
the glory of the LORD, and the excellency
of our God.
3 Strengthen ye the weak hands and
confirm the feeble knees.
4 Say to them that are of a fearful heart, be
strong, fear not: behold, your God will
come with vengeance, even God with a
recompence; he will come and save you.
5 Then the eyes of the blind shall be
opened, and the ears of the deaf shall be
unstopped.
6 Then shall the lame man leap as an hart,
and the tongue of the dumb sing: for in the
wilderness shall waters break out, and
streams in the desert.
7 And the parched ground shall become a
pool, and the thirsty land springs of water:
in the habitation of dragons, where each
lay, shall be grass with reeds and rushes.
8 And an highway shall be there, and a
way, and it shall be called the way of
holiness; the unclean shall not pass over it;

A photo from my mission in Vermont, where I was blessed to participate first hand in the gathering of the scattered remnants of Israel. Refugees from Vietnam were arriving in Burlington at that time. They represented traditional Vietnamese ethnicities, as well as the Khmer people from southern Vietnam who spoke Cambodian. Some were baptized in refugee camps in the Philippines (the Lam family on the left not wearing white), while others were baptized once they arrived in the United States. Pictured here is Elder Doug Johnson on the left and myself in the center back. To my right are Se and Em Thai, and Sinh Kim on my far right. To my left are the five members of the Lam family (no relation to the other Lam family). About thirty Vietnamese and Khmer people were attending the Burlington Ward then (March 14, 1992).

but it shall be for those: the wayfaring
men, though fools, shall not err therein.
9 No lion shall be there, nor any ravenous
beast shall go up thereon, it shall not be
found there; but the redeemed shall walk
there:
10 And the ransomed of the LORD shall
return and come to Zion with songs and
everlasting joy upon their heads: they
shall obtain joy and gladness, and sorrow
and sighing shall flee away.

HOSEA 6

Hosea *790 BC*

1 Come and let us return unto the LORD:
for he hath torn, and he will heal us; he
hath smitten, and he will bind us up.
2 After two days will he revive us: in the
third day he will raise us up, and we shall
live in his sight.
3 Then shall we know, if we follow on to
know the LORD: his going forth is
prepared as the morning; and he shall
come unto us as the rain, as the latter and
former rain unto the Earth.

2 NEPHI 8 (see also ISAIAH 51)

Isaiah *740 BC*

11 Therefore, the redeemed of the Lord
shall return, and come with singing unto
Zion; and everlasting joy and holiness
shall be upon their heads; and they shall
obtain gladness and joy; sorrow and
mourning shall flee away.

DOCTRINE AND COVENANTS 1

Joseph Smith *November 1831*

17 Wherefore, I the Lord, knowing the
calamity which should come upon the
inhabitants of the Earth, called upon my
servant Joseph Smith, Jun., and spake unto
him from heaven, and gave him
commandments;

18 And also gave commandments to
others, that they should proclaim these
things unto the world; and all this that it
might be fulfilled, which was written by
the prophets—
19 The weak things of the world shall
come forth and break down the mighty
and strong ones, that man should not
counsel his fellow man, neither trust in
the arm of flesh—
20 But that every man might speak in the
name of God the Lord, even the Savior of
the world;
21 That faith also might increase in the
Earth;
22 That mine everlasting covenant might
be established;
23 That the fulness of my gospel might be
proclaimed by the weak and the simple
unto the ends of the world, and before
kings and rulers.
24 Behold, I am God and have spoken it;
these commandments are of me, and were
given unto my servants in their weakness,
after the manner of their language, that
they might come to understanding.
25 And inasmuch as they erred it might be
made known;
26 And inasmuch as they sought wisdom
they might be instructed;
27 And inasmuch as they sinned they
might be chastened, that they might
repent;
28 And inasmuch as they were humble
they might be made strong, and blessed
from on high, and receive knowledge
from time to time.
29 And after having received the record of
the Nephites, yea, even my servant Joseph
Smith, Jun., might have power to translate
through the mercy of God, by the power
of God, the Book of Mormon.
30 And also those to whom these com-
mandments were given, might have
power to lay the foundation of this
church, and to bring it forth out of
obscurity and out of darkness, the only
true and living church upon the face of the
whole Earth, with which I, the Lord, am
well pleased, speaking unto the church
collectively and not individually—
31 For I the Lord cannot look upon sin
with the least degree of allowance;
32 Nevertheless, he that repents and does
the commandments of the Lord shall be
forgiven;
33 And he that repents not, from him shall
be taken even the light which he has
received; for my Spirit shall not always
strive with man, saith the Lord of Hosts.
34 And again, verily I say unto you, O
inhabitants of the Earth: I the Lord am
willing to make these things known unto
all flesh;
35 For I am no respecter of persons, and
will that all men shall know that the day
speedily cometh; the hour is not yet, but
is nigh at hand, when peace shall be taken
from the Earth, and the devil shall have
power over his own dominion.
36 And also the Lord shall have power
over his saints, and shall reign in their
midst, and shall come down in judgment
upon Idumea, or the world.
37 Search these commandments, for they
are true and faithful, and the prophecies
and promises which are in them shall all
be fulfilled.
38 What I the Lord have spoken, I have
spoken, and I excuse not myself; and
though the heavens and the Earth pass
away, my word shall not pass away, but
shall all be fulfilled, whether by mine own
voice or by the voice of my servants, it is
the same.
39 For behold, and lo, the Lord is God, and
the Spirit beareth record, and the record is
true, and the truth abideth forever and
ever. Amen.

36

THE JEWS GATHER TO JERUSALEM

+++

The Jews will physically gather to Palestine in the last days to prepare them to receive the gospel of Jesus Christ prior to his coming. Jeremiah (accurately) prophecies that the Jews, like much of the scattered tribes of Israel, will come mainly from the north country.

JEREMIAH 23

Jeremiah — *620 BC*

7 Therefore, behold, the days come, saith the LORD, that they shall no more say, The LORD liveth, which brought up the children of Israel out of the land of Egypt;
8 But, The LORD liveth, which brought up and which led the seed of the house of Israel out of the north country, and from all countries whither I had driven them; and they shall dwell in their own land.

Immigrants to Israel 1882-2020

By Region	Total
Total	3,857,489
Europe	2,380,069
Africa	561,642
Asia	500,053
Americas and Oceania	272,373

By Country	
Russia (Europe)	1,301,479
Poland	343,718
Romania	317,691
Morocco	272,077
United States	135,394
Iraq	130,994
Ethiopia and Eritrea	96,691
France	90,384
Persia, Iran	84,107
Russia (Asia)	74,410

https://en.wikipedia.org/wiki/Aliyah#Historic_data

JEREMIAH 30

Jeremiah — *620 BC*

1 The word that came to Jeremiah from the LORD, saying,
2 Thus speaketh the LORD God of Israel, saying, Write thee all the words that I have spoken unto thee in a book.
3 For, lo, the days come, saith the LORD, that I will bring again the captivity of my people Israel and Judah, saith the LORD: and I will cause them to return to the land that I gave to their fathers, and they shall possess it.

AMOS 9

Amos — *792 BC*

14 And I will bring again the captivity of my people of Israel, and they shall build the waste cities, and inhabit them; and they shall plant vineyards, and drink the wine thereof; they shall also make gardens, and eat the fruit of them.
15 And I will plant them upon their land, and they shall no more be pulled up out of their land which I have given them, saith the Lord thy God.

3 NEPHI 20

Jesus Christ — *34 AD*

29 And I will remember the covenant which I have made with my people; and I have covenanted with them that I would gather them together in mine own due time, that I would give unto them again the land of their fathers for their inheritance, which is the land of Jerusalem, which is the promised land unto them forever, saith the Father.

ISAIAH 65

Isaiah — *740 BC*

8 Thus saith the LORD, As the new wine is found in the cluster, and one saith, destroy it not; for a blessing is in it: so will I do for my servants' sakes, that I may not destroy them all.
9 And I will bring forth a seed out of Jacob, and out of Judah an inheritor of my

mountains: and mine elect shall inherit it, and my servants shall dwell there.

ETHER 13

Ether *600 BC*

5 And he spake also concerning the house of Israel, and the Jerusalem from whence Lehi should come—after it should be destroyed it should be built up again, a holy city unto the Lord; wherefore, it could not be a new Jerusalem for it had been in a time of old; but it should be built up again, and become a holy city of the Lord; and it should be built unto the house of Israel—

DOCTRINE AND COVENANTS 109 KIRTLAND TEMPLE DEDICATORY PRAYER

Joseph Smith *April 1836*

61 But thou knowest that thou hast a great love for the children of Jacob, who have been scattered upon the mountains for a long time, in a cloudy and dark day.
62 We therefore ask thee to have mercy upon the children of Jacob, that Jerusalem, from this hour, may begin to be redeemed;
63 And the yoke of bondage may begin to be broken off from the house of David;
64 And the children of Judah may begin to return to the lands which thou didst give to Abraham, their father.
65 And cause that the remnants of Jacob, who have been cursed and smitten because of their transgression, be converted from their wild and savage condition to the fulness of the everlasting gospel;
66 That they may lay down their weapons of bloodshed, and cease their rebellions.
67 And may all the scattered remnants of Israel, who have been driven to the ends of the Earth, come to a knowledge of the truth, believe in the Messiah, and be redeemed from oppression, and rejoice before thee.

During the April 1840 conference of the church, Joseph Smith commissioned one of the apostles, Elder Orson Hyde, to travel to Jerusalem to dedicate the land for the return of the Jewish people.

GENERAL CONFERENCE ADDRESS

Joseph Smith *April 1840*

Be it known that we the constituted authorities of the Church of Jesus Christ of Latter-day Saints, assembled in conference, at Nauvoo, Hancock county and State of Illinois, on this, sixth day of April, in the year of our Lord, one thousand, eight hundred and forty, considering an important event at hand, an event involving the interest and fate of the Gentile nations throughout the world. From the signs of the times, and from declarations contained in the oracles of God, we are forced to come to this conclusion.

The Jewish nation have been scattered abroad among the Gentiles for a long period; and in our estimation, the time of the commencement of their return to the Holy land, has already arrived.

As this scattered and persecuted people are set among the Gentiles as a sign unto them of the Second Coming of the Messiah; and also, of the overthrow of the present kingdom's and Governments of the Earth, by the potency of his Almighty arm in scattering famine and pestilence like the frosts and snows of winter, and sending the sword, with nation against nation to bathe it in each other's blood: It is highly important, in our opinion, that the present views and movements of the Jewish people be sought after, and laid before the American people for their consideration, their profit and their learning; and feeling it to be our duty to employ the most efficient means in our power to save the children of men from the "abomination that maketh desolate."— We have, by the counsel of the Holy Spirit, appointed Elder Orson Hyde, the bearer of these presents, a faithful and worthy minister of Jesus Christ, to be our agent and representative in foreign lands, to visit the cities of London, Amsterdam, Constantinople and Jerusalem; and also other places that he may deem expedient, and converse with the priests, rulers and Elders of the Jews, and obtain from them all the information possible, and communicate the same to some principal paper for publication, that it may have a general circulation throughout the United States.

As Mr. Hyde has willingly and cheerfully accepted the appointment to become our servant, and the servant of the public in distant and foreign countries for Christs' sake, we do confidently recommend him to all religious and Christian people, and to gentlemen and ladies, making no profession, as a worthy member of society, possessing much zeal to promote the happiness of mankind, fully believing that they will be forward to render him all the pecuniary aid he needs, to accomplish this laborious and hazardous mission for the general good of the human family."

DEDICATION OF THE LAND OF JERUSALEM TO THE GATHERING OF THE JEWS

Orson Hyde *October 1841*

On Sunday morning, October 24, a good while before day, I arose from sleep, and went out of the city as soon as the gates were opened, crossed the brook Kedron, and went upon the Mount of Olives, and there, in solemn silence, with pen, ink, and paper, just as I saw in the vision, offered up the following prayer to Him who lives forever and ever.

Prayer of the Apostle of the Lord, Elder Orson Hyde, on the Mount of Olives:

"O Thou! who art from everlasting to everlasting, eternally and unchangeably the same, even the God who rules in the heavens above, and controls the destinies of men on the Earth, wilt Thou not condescend, through thine infinite goodness and royal favor, to listen to the prayer of Thy servant which he this day offers up unto Thee in the name of Thy holy child Jesus, upon this land, where the Son of Righteousness set in blood, and thine Anointed One expired.

Be pleased, O Lord, to forgive all the follies, weaknesses, vanities, and sins of Thy servant, and strengthen him to resist all future temptations. Give him prudence and discernment that he may avoid the evil, and a heart to choose the good; give him fortitude to bear up under trying and adverse circumstances, and grace to endure all things for Thy name's sake, until the end shall come, when all the Saints shall rest in peace.

Now, O Lord! Thy servant has been obedient to the heavenly vision which Thou gavest him in his native land; and under the shadow of Thine outstretched arm, he has safely arrived in this place to dedicate and consecrate this land unto Thee, for the gathering together of Judah's scattered remnants, according to the predictions of the holy Prophets — for the building up of Jerusalem again after it has been trodden down by the Gentiles so long, and for rearing a Temple in honor of Thy name. Everlasting thanks be ascribed unto Thee, O Father, Lord of heaven and Earth, that Thou hast preserved Thy servant from the dangers of the seas, and from the plague and pestilence which have caused the land to mourn. The violence of man has also been restrained, and Thy providential care by night and by day has been exercised over Thine unworthy servant. Accept, therefore, O Lord, the tribute of a grateful heart for all past favors, and be pleased to continue Thy kindness and mercy towards a needy worm of the dust.

O Thou, Who didst covenant with Abraham, Thy friend, and who didst renew that covenant with Isaac, and confirm the same with Jacob with an oath, that Thou wouldst not only give them this land for an everlasting inheritance, but that Thou wouldst also remember their seed forever. Abraham, Isaac, and Jacob have long since closed their eyes in death, and made the grave their mansion. Their children are scattered and dispersed abroad among the nations of the Gentiles like sheep that have no shepherd, and are still looking forward for the fulfillment of those promises which Thou didst make concerning them; and even this land, which once poured forth nature's richest bounty, and flowed, as it were, with milk and honey, has, to a certain extent, been smitten with barrenness and sterility since it drank from murderous hands the blood of Him who never sinned.

In 1947, 4,500 European Jews, many of which were holocaust survivors, arrived in Palestine from France aboard the SS Exodus, referred to as "the ship that launched a nation." The nation of Israel was officially recognized and admitted to the United Nations on 11 May, 1949. The Law of Return was passed in 1950, stating that all Jews have the right to return and live in Israel as Israeli citizens.

Grant, therefore, O Lord, in the name of Thy well-beloved Son, Jesus Christ, to remove the barrenness and sterility of this land, and let springs of living water break forth to water its thirsty soil. Let the vine and olive produce in their strength, and the fig-tree bloom and flourish. Let the land become abundantly fruitful when possessed by its rightful heirs; let it again flow with plenty to feed the returning prodigals who come home with a spirit of grace and supplication; upon it let the clouds distil virtue and richness, and let the fields smile with plenty. Let the flocks and the herds greatly increase and multiply upon the mountains and the hills; and let Thy great kindness conquer and subdue the unbelief of Thy people. Do Thou take from them their stony heart, and give them a heart of flesh; and may the Sun of Thy favor dispel the cold mists of darkness which have beclouded their atmosphere. Incline them to gather in upon this land according to Thy word. Let them come like clouds and like doves to their windows. Let the large ships of the nations bring them from the distant isles; and let kings become their nursing fathers, and queens with motherly fondness wipe the tear of sorrow from their eye.

Thou, O Lord, did once move upon the heart of Cyrus to show favor unto Jerusalem and her children. Do Thou now also be pleased to inspire the hearts of kings and the powers of the Earth to look with a friendly eye towards this place, and with a desire to see Thy righteous purposes executed in relation thereto. Let them know that it is Thy good pleasure to restore the kingdom unto Israel — raise up Jerusalem as its capital, and constitute her people a distinct nation and government, with David Thy servant, even a descendant from the loins of ancient David to be their king.

Let that nation or that people who shall take an active part in behalf of Abraham's

Orson Hyde, original member of the Quorum of the Twelve Apostles (1835-1878).

children, and in the raising up of Jerusalem, find favor in Thy sight. Let not their enemies prevail against them, neither let pestilence or famine overcome them, but let the glory of Israel overshadow them, and the power of the Highest protect them; while that nation or kingdom that will not serve Thee in this glorious work must perish, according to Thy word — Yea, those nations shall be utterly wasted.

Though Thy servant is now far from his home, and from the land bedewed with his earliest tear, yet he remembers, O Lord, his friend: who are there, and family, whom for Thy sake he has left. Though poverty and privation be our Earthly lot, yet ah! do Thou richly endow us with an inheritance where moth and rust do not corrupt, and where thieves do not break through and steal.

The hands that have fed, clothed, or shown favor unto the family of Thy servant in his absence, or that shall hereafter do so, let them not lose their reward, but let a special blessing rest upon them, and in Thy kingdom let them have an inheritance when Thou shalt come to be glorified in this society.

Do Thou also look with favor upon all those through whose liberality I have been enabled to come to this land; and in the day when Thou shalt reward all people according to their works, let these also not be passed by or forgotten, but in time let them be in readiness to enjoy the glory of those mansions which Jesus has gone to prepare. Particularly do Thou bless the stranger in Philadelphia, whom I never saw, but who sent me gold, with a request that I should pray for him in Jerusalem. Now, O Lord, let blessings come upon him from an unexpected quarter, and let his basket be filled, and his storehouse abound with plenty, and let not the good things of the Earth be his only portion, but let him be found among those to whom it shall be said, 'Thou hast been faithful over a few things, and I will make thee ruler over many.'

O my Father in heaven! I now ask Thee in the name of Jesus to remember Zion, with all her Stakes, and with all her assemblies. She has been grievously afflicted and smitten; she has mourned; she has wept; her enemies have triumphed, and have said, 'Ah, where is thy God?' Her Priests and Prophets have groaned in chains and fetters within the gloomy walls of prisons, while many were slain, and now sleep in the arms of death. How long, O Lord, shall iniquity triumph, and sin go unpunished?

Do Thou arise in the majesty of Thy strength, and make bare Thine arm in behalf of Thy people. Redress their wrongs, and turn their sorrow into joy. Pour the spirit of light and knowledge, grace and wisdom, into the hearts of her Prophets, and clothe her Priests with salvation. Let light and knowledge march forth through the empire of darkness, and may the honest in heart flow to their standard, and join in the march to go forth to meet the Bridegroom.

Let a peculiar blessing rest upon the Presidency of Thy Church, for at them are the arrows of the enemy directed. Be Thou to them a sun and a shield, their strong tower and hiding place; and in the time of distress or danger be Thou near to deliver. Also the quorum of the Twelve, do Thou be pleased to stand by them for Thou

Orson Hyde Memorial Park, Jerusalem, Israel.

knowest the obstacles which they have to encounter, the temptations to which they are exposed, and the privations which they must suffer. Give us, [the Twelve] therefore, strength according to our day, and help us to bear a faithful testimony of Jesus and His Gospel, to finish with fidelity and honor the work which Thou hast given us to do, and then give us a place in Thy glorious kingdom. And let this blessing rest upon every faithful officer and member in Thy Church. And all the glory and honor will we ascribe unto God and the Lamb forever and ever. Amen."

On the top of Mount Olives I erected a pile of stones as a witness according to ancient custom. On what was anciently called Mount Zion, [Moriah?] where the Temple stood, I erected another, and used the rod according to the prediction upon my head.

I have found many Jews who listened with intense interest. The idea of the Jews being restored to Palestine is gaining ground in Europe almost every day. Jerusalem is strongly fortified with many cannon upon its walls. The wall is ten feet thick on the sides that would be most exposed, and four or five feet where the descent from the wall is almost perpendicular. The number of inhabitants within the walls is about twenty thousand. About seven thousand of this number are Jews, the balance being mostly Turks and Armenians. Many of the Jews who are old go to this place to die, and many are coming from Europe into this eastern world. The great wheel is unquestionably in motion, and the word of the Almighty has declared that it shall roll.

As of 2021 the population of Israel was 8,790,140, of which 75% (6,593,000) are Jews. The prophecies of the Jews returning to their homeland have been fulfilled.

https://worldpopulationreview.com/countries/israel-population

37

THE GENTILES REJECT THE GOSPEL

+++

Increasing wickedness and the rise of secret combinations, evil ideologies, government corruption and vast criminal enterprises will destroy societies. As the Second Coming approaches, the once great Christian Gentile nations of the West begin to abandon Christianity and become more wicked, while the formerly "heathen" nations of the world embrace the gospel.

3 NEPHI 16

Jesus Christ *34 AD*

10 And thus commandeth the Father that
I should say unto you: At that day when
the Gentiles shall sin against my gospel,
and shall reject the fulness of my gospel,
and shall be lifted up in the pride of their
hearts above all nations, and above all the
people of the whole Earth, and shall be
filled with all manner of lyings, and of
deceits, and of mischiefs, and all manner
of hypocrisy, and murders, and priest-
crafts, and whoredoms, and of secret
abominations; and if they shall do all those
things, and shall reject the fulness of my
gospel, behold, saith the Father, I will
bring the fulness of my gospel from among
them.
11 And then will I remember my cove-
nant which I have made unto my people,
O house of Israel, and I will bring my
gospel unto them.
12 And I will show unto thee, O house of
Israel, that the Gentiles shall not have
power over you; but I will remember my
covenant unto you, O house of Israel, and
ye shall come unto the knowledge of the
fulness of my gospel.
13 But if the Gentiles will repent and
return unto me, saith the Father, behold
they shall be numbered among my people,
O house of Israel.
14 And I will not suffer my people, who
are of the house of Israel, to go through
among them, and tread them down, saith
the Father.
15 But if they will not turn unto me, and
hearken unto my voice, I will suffer them,
yea, I will suffer my people, O house of
Israel, that they shall go through among
them, and shall tread them down, and
they shall be as salt that hath lost its savor,
which is thenceforth good for nothing but
to be cast out, and to be trodden under
foot of my people, O house of Israel.
16 Verily, verily, I say unto you, thus hath
the Father commanded me—that I should
give unto this people this land for their
inheritance.
17 And then the words of the prophet
Isaiah shall be fulfilled, which say:
18 Thy watchmen shall lift up the voice;
with the voice together shall they sing, for
they shall see eye to eye when the Lord
shall bring again Zion.
19 Break forth into joy, sing together, ye
waste places of Jerusalem; for the Lord
hath comforted his people, he hath
redeemed Jerusalem.
20 The Lord hath made bare his holy arm
in the eyes of all the nations; and all the
ends of the Earth shall see the salvation of
God.

1 NEPHI 14

Nephi, Son of Lehi *595 BC*

1 And it shall come to pass, that if the
Gentiles shall hearken unto the Lamb of
God in that day that he shall manifest
himself unto them in word, and also in
power, in very deed, unto the taking away
of their stumbling blocks—
2 And harden not their hearts against the
Lamb of God, they shall be numbered
among the seed of thy father; yea, they
shall be numbered among the house of
Israel; and they shall be a blessed people
upon the promised land forever; they shall
be no more brought down into captivity;
and the house of Israel shall no more be
confounded.

Worldwide Statistics 2021 Church of Jesus Christ of Latter-day Saints

Area	Membership	Congregations	Missions	Temples
North America (30 countries)	9,419,307	18,256	173	110
South America (13 countries)	4,178,375	5,570	95	21
Asia (20 countries)	1,230,515	2,130	44	8
Africa - (31 countries)	666,508	2,327	35	4
Oceania (21 countries)	572,895	1,283	17	10
Europe (45 countries)	497,436	1,374	34	14
Total	**16,565,036**	**30,940**	**398**	**167**

https://newsroom.churchofjesuschrist.org/facts-and-statistics

5 And it came to pass that the angel spake unto me, Nephi, saying: Thou hast beheld that if the Gentiles repent it shall be well with them; and thou also knowest concerning the covenants of the Lord unto the house of Israel; and thou also hast heard that whoso repenteth not must perish.
6 Therefore, wo be unto the Gentiles if it so be that they harden their hearts against the Lamb of God.
7 For the time cometh, saith the Lamb of God, that I will work a great and a marvelous work among the children of men; a work which shall be everlasting, either on the one hand or on the other—either to the convincing of them unto peace and life eternal, or unto the deliverance of them to the hardness of their hearts and the blindness of their minds unto their being brought down into captivity, and also into destruction, both temporally and spiritually, according to the captivity of the devil, of which I have spoken.

MORMON 5

Mormon 385 AD

22 And then, O ye Gentiles, how can ye stand before the power of God, except ye shall repent and turn from your evil ways?
23 Know ye not that ye are in the hands of God? Know ye not that he hath all power, and at his great command the Earth shall be rolled together as a scroll?
24 Therefore, repent ye, and humble yourselves before him, lest he shall come out in justice against you—lest a remnant of the seed of Jacob shall go forth among you as a lion, and tear you in pieces, and there is none to deliver.

3 NEPHI 20

Jesus Christ 34 AD

14 And the Father hath commanded me that I should give unto you this land, for your inheritance.
15 And I say unto you, that if the Gentiles do not repent after the blessing which they shall receive, after they have scattered my people—
16 Then shall ye, who are a remnant of the house of Jacob, go forth among them; and ye shall be in the midst of them who shall be many; and ye shall be among them as a lion among the beasts of the forest, and as a young lion among the flocks of sheep, who, if he goeth through both treadeth down and teareth in pieces, and none can deliver.
17 Thy hand shall be lifted up upon thine adversaries, and all thine enemies shall be cut off.
18 And I will gather my people together as a man gathereth his sheaves into the floor.
19 For I will make my people with whom the Father hath covenanted, yea, I will make thy horn iron, and I will make thy hoofs brass. And thou shalt beat in pieces many people; and I will consecrate their gain unto the Lord, and their substance unto the Lord of the whole Earth. And behold, I am he who doeth it.
20 And it shall come to pass, saith the Father, that the sword of my justice shall

hang over them at that day; and except they repent it shall fall upon them, saith the Father, yea, even upon all the nations of the Gentiles.

MICAH 4

Micah *722 BC*

6 In that day, saith the LORD, will I assemble her that halteth, and I will gather her that is driven out, and her that I have afflicted;
7 And I will make her that halted a remnant, and her that was cast far off a strong nation: and the LORD shall reign over them in mount Zion from henceforth, even for ever.
11 Now also many nations are gathered against thee, that say, Let her be defiled, and let our eye look upon Zion.
12 But they know not the thoughts of the LORD, neither understand they his counsel: for he shall gather them as the sheaves into the floor.
13 Arise and thresh, O daughter of Zion: for I will make thine horn iron, and I will make thy hoofs brass: and thou shalt beat in pieces many people: and I will consecrate their gain unto the LORD, and their substance unto the Lord of the whole Earth.

MICAH 5

Micah *722 BC*

3 Therefore will he give them up, until the time that she which travaileth hath brought forth: then the remnant of his brethren shall return unto the children of Israel.
4 And he shall stand and feed in the strength of the LORD, in the majesty of the name of the LORD his God; and they shall abide: for now, shall he be great unto the ends of the Earth.
5 And this man shall be the peace...
7 And the remnant of Jacob shall be in the midst of many people as a dew from the LORD, as the showers upon the grass, that tarrieth not for man, nor waiteth for the sons of men.
8 And the remnant of Jacob shall be among the Gentiles in the midst of many people as a lion among the beasts of the forest, as a young lion among the flocks of sheep: who, if he go through, both treadeth down, and teareth in pieces, and none can deliver.
9 Thine hand shall be lifted up upon thine adversaries, and all thine enemies shall be cut off.
10 And it shall come to pass in that day, saith the LORD, that I will cut off thy horses out of the midst of thee, and I will destroy thy chariots:
11 And I will cut off the cities of thy land, and throw down all thy strong holds:
12 And I will cut off witchcrafts out of thine hand; and thou shalt have no more soothsayers:
13 Thy graven images also will I cut off, and thy standing images out of the midst of thee; and thou shalt no more worship the work of thine hands.
14 And I will pluck up thy groves out of the midst of thee: so will I destroy thy cities.
15 And I will execute vengeance in anger and fury upon the heathen, such as they have not heard.

3 NEPHI 20

Jesus Christ *34 AD*

28 ...Nevertheless, when they shall have received the fulness of my gospel, then if they shall harden their hearts against me I will return their iniquities upon their own heads, saith the Father.

3 NEPHI 30

Mormon/Jesus Christ *34 AD*

1 Hearken, O ye Gentiles, and hear the words of Jesus Christ, the Son of the living God, which he hath commanded me that I should speak concerning you, for, behold he commandeth me that I should write, saying:
2 Turn, all ye Gentiles, from your wicked ways; and repent of your evil doings, of your lyings and deceivings, and of your whoredoms, and of your secret abominations, and your idolatries, and of your murders, and your priestcrafts, and your envyings, and your strifes, and from all your wickedness and abominations, and come unto me, and be baptized in my name, that ye may receive a remission of your sins, and be filled with the Holy Ghost, that ye may be numbered with my people who are of the house of Israel.

ETHER 8
Moroni *400 AD*
19 For the Lord worketh not in secret
combinations, neither doth he will that
man should shed blood, but in all things
hath forbidden it, from the beginning of
man.
20 And now I, Moroni, do not write the
manner of their oaths and combinations,
for it hath been made known unto me that
they are had among all people, and they
are had among the Lamanites.
21 And they have caused the destruction
of this people of whom I am now speaking,
and also the destruction of the people of
Nephi.
22 And whatsoever nation shall uphold
such secret combinations, to get power
and gain, until they shall spread over the
nation, behold, they shall be destroyed;
for the Lord will not suffer that the blood
of his saints, which shall be shed by them,
shall always cry unto him from the ground
for vengeance upon them and yet he
avenge them not.
23 Wherefore, O ye Gentiles, it is wisdom
in God that these things should be shown
unto you, that thereby ye may repent of
your sins, and suffer not that these mur-
derous combinations shall get above you,
which are built up to get power and
gain—and the work, yea, even the work
of destruction come upon you, yea, even
the sword of the justice of the Eternal God
shall fall upon you, to your overthrow and
destruction if ye shall suffer these things
to be.
24 Wherefore, the Lord commandeth you,
when ye shall see these things come
among you that ye shall awake to a sense
of your awful situation, because of this
secret combination which shall be among
you; or wo be unto it, because of the blood
of them who have been slain; for they cry
from the dust for vengeance upon it, and
also upon those who built it up.
25 For it cometh to pass that whoso build-
eth it up seeketh to overthrow the free-
dom of all lands, nations, and countries;
and it bringeth to pass the destruction of
all people, for it is built up by the devil,
who is the father of all lies; even that same
liar who beguiled our first parents, yea,
even that same liar who hath caused man
to commit murder from the beginning;
who hath hardened the hearts of men that
they have murdered the prophets, and
stoned them, and cast them out from the
beginning.

Karl Marx (1818-1883) German-born philosopher, economist, socialist revolutionary. Author of The Communist Manifesto and Das Kapital. His theories attacking capitalism led to an explosion of socialist/communist revolutions in the developing world in the 20th century, most notably in Russia and China, that resulted in the death and misery of hundreds of millions. In arguing for forced equality at the expense of personal liberty, Marx articulated Lucifer's plan in the pre-existence – to deny man his agency and force him to obey God's commandments.

DOCTRINE AND COVENANTS 64
Joseph Smith *September 1831*
41 For, behold, I say unto you that Zion
shall flourish, and the glory of the Lord
shall be upon her;
42 And she shall be an ensign unto the
people, and there shall come unto her out
of every nation under heaven.
43 And the day shall come when the
nations of the Earth shall tremble because
of her, and shall fear because of her
terrible ones. The Lord hath spoken it.
Amen.

38

WARS PLAGUES NATURAL DISASTERS

+++

The US Civil War is foreseen, along with the unprecedented scale of wars and destruction among nations in the 19th and 20th centuries. The Gentile Christian nations of Europe and the United States grow more wicked, and ripen for destruction. As with the parable of the wheat and the tares, the righteous of the Earth are gathered out from among the wicked.

DOCTRINE AND COVENANTS 63

Joseph Smith — *August 1831*

32 I, the Lord, am angry with the wicked; I am holding my Spirit from the inhabitants of the Earth.

33 I have sworn in my wrath, and decreed wars upon the face of the Earth, and the wicked shall slay the wicked, and fear shall come upon every man;

34 And the saints also shall hardly escape;

37 And that every man should take righteousness in his hands and faithfulness upon his loins, and lift a warning voice unto the inhabitants of the Earth; and declare both by word and by flight that desolation shall come upon the wicked.

57 And again, verily I say unto you, those who desire in their hearts, in meekness, to warn sinners to repentance, let them be ordained unto this power.

58 For this is a day of warning, and not a day of many words. For I, the Lord, am not to be mocked in the last days.

59 Behold, I am from above, and my power lieth beneath. I am over all, and in all, and through all, and search all things, and the day cometh that all things shall be subject unto me.

60 Behold, I am Alpha and Omega, even Jesus Christ.

61 Wherefore, let all men beware how they take my name in their lips—

62 For behold, verily I say, that many there be who are under this condemnation, who use the name of the Lord, and use it in vain, having not authority.

DOCTRINE AND COVENANTS 87

Joseph Smith — *December 1832*

1 Verily, thus saith the Lord concerning the wars that will shortly come to pass, beginning at the rebellion of South Carolina, which will eventually terminate in the death and misery of many souls;

2 And the time will come that war will be poured out upon all nations, beginning at this place.

3 For behold, the Southern States shall be divided against the Northern States, and the Southern States will call on other nations, even the nation of Great Britain, as it is called, and they shall also call upon other nations, in order to defend themselves against other nations; and then war shall be poured out upon all nations.

4 And it shall come to pass, after many days, slaves shall rise up against their masters, who shall be marshaled and disciplined for war.

5 And it shall come to pass also that the remnants who are left of the land will marshal themselves, and shall become exceedingly angry, and shall vex the Gentiles with a sore vexation.

6 And thus, with the sword and by bloodshed the inhabitants of the Earth shall mourn; and with famine, and plague, and earthquake, and the thunder of heaven, and the fierce and vivid lightning also, shall the inhabitants of the Earth be made to feel the wrath, and indignation, and chastening hand of an Almighty God, until the consumption decreed hath made a full end of all nations;

7 That the cry of the saints, and of the blood of the saints, shall cease to come up into the ears of the Lord of Sabaoth, from the Earth, to be avenged of their enemies.

8 Wherefore, stand ye in holy places, and be not moved, until the day of the Lord come; for behold, it cometh quickly, saith the Lord. Amen.

Battle of Gettysburg, Showing Pickett's Charge, by Thure de Thulstrup, 1887, restoration by Adam Cuerden.

DOCTRINE AND COVENANTS 130

Joseph Smith — *December 1842*

12 I prophesy, in the name of the Lord God, that the commencement of the difficulties which will cause much bloodshed previous to the coming of the Son of Man will be in South Carolina.
13 It may probably arise through the slave question. This a voice declared to me, while I was praying earnestly on the subject, December 25th, 1832.

DOCTRINE AND COVENANTS 101

Joseph Smith — *December 1833*

85 Thus will I liken the children of Zion.
86 Let them importune at the feet of the judge;
87 And if he heed them not, let them importune at the feet of the governor;
88 And if the governor heed them not, let them importune at the feet of the president;
89 And if the president heed them not, then will the Lord arise and come forth out of his hiding place, and in his fury vex the nation;
90 And in his hot displeasure, and in his fierce anger, in his time, will cut off those wicked, unfaithful, and unjust stewards, and appoint them their portion among hypocrites, and unbelievers;
91 Even in outer darkness, where there is weeping, and wailing, and gnashing of teeth.

DOCTRINE AND COVENANTS 103

Joseph Smith — *February 1834*

1 Verily I say unto you, my friends, behold, I will give unto you a revelation and commandment, that you may know how to act in the discharge of your duties concerning the salvation and redemption of your brethren, who have been scattered on the land of Zion;
2 Being driven and smitten by the hands of mine enemies, on whom I will pour out my wrath without measure in mine own time.
3 For I have suffered them thus far, that they might fill up the measure of their iniquities, that their cup might be full;

DOCTRINE AND COVENANTS 124

Joseph Smith *January 1841*

2 Your prayers are acceptable before me; and in answer to them I say unto you, that you are now called immediately to make a solemn proclamation of my gospel, and of this stake which I have planted to be a cornerstone of Zion, which shall be polished with the refinement which is after the similitude of a palace.

3 This proclamation shall be made to all the kings of the world, to the four corners thereof, to the honorable president-elect, and the high-minded governors of the nation in which you live, and to all the nations of the Earth scattered abroad.

4 Let it be written in the spirit of meekness and by the power of the Holy Ghost, which shall be in you at the time of the writing of the same;

5 For it shall be given you by the Holy Ghost to know my will concerning those kings and authorities, even what shall befall them in a time to come.

6 For, behold, I am about to call upon them to give heed to the light and glory of Zion, for the set time has come to favor her.

7 Call ye, therefore, upon them with loud proclamation, and with your testimony, fearing them not, for they are as grass, and all their glory as the flower thereof which soon falleth, that they may be left also without excuse—

8 And that I may visit them in the day of visitation, when I shall unveil the face of my covering, to appoint the portion of the oppressor among hypocrites, where there is gnashing of teeth, if they reject my servants and my testimony which I have revealed unto them.

9 And again, I will visit and soften their hearts, many of them for your good, that ye may find grace in their eyes, that they may come to the light of truth, and the Gentiles to the exaltation or lifting up of Zion.

10 For the day of my visitation cometh speedily, in an hour when ye think not of; and where shall be the safety of my people, and refuge for those who shall be left of them?

11 Awake, O kings of the Earth! Come ye, O, come ye, with your gold and your silver, to the help of my people, to the house of the daughters of Zion.

DOCTRINE AND COVENANTS 136

Brigham Young *January 1847*

34 Thy brethren have rejected you and your testimony, even the nation that has driven you out;

35 And now cometh the day of their calamity, even the days of sorrow, like a woman that is taken in travail; and their sorrow shall be great unless they speedily repent, yea, very speedily.

36 For they killed the prophets, and them that were sent unto them; and they have shed innocent blood, which crieth from the ground against them.

After the assassination of the Prophet Joseph Smith in 1844, the Lord commanded the church to move west to the Utah Territory. This may have seemed an impossible task at the time, but in doing so, the fledgling new church avoided the Civil War which claimed 650,000+ lives.

Also, in the 1800s new converts were urged to come to Zion with haste. By 1900, as the following prophecy details, church leaders would no longer encourage members to gather to Utah, but rather to stay and build up the stakes of Zion in the states or countries in which they lived. By 1920, US immigration policy was changed to severely restrict immigration and would stay this way until the 1960s.

DOCTRINE AND COVENANTS 101

Joseph Smith *December 1833*

11 Mine indignation is soon to be poured out without measure upon all nations; and this will I do when the cup of their iniquity is full.

12 And in that day all who are found upon the watchtower, or in other words, all mine Israel, shall be saved.

13 And they that have been scattered shall be gathered.

14 And all they who have mourned shall be comforted.

15 And all they who have given their lives for my name shall be crowned.

16 Therefore, let your hearts be comforted concerning Zion; for all flesh is in mine hands; be still and know that I am God.

17 Zion shall not be moved out of her place, notwithstanding her children are scattered.

18 They that remain, and are pure in heart, shall return, and come to their inheritances, they and their children, with songs of everlasting joy, to build up the waste places of Zion—
19 And all these things that the prophets might be fulfilled.
20 And, behold, there is none other place appointed than that which I have appointed; neither shall there be any other place appointed than that which I have appointed, for the work of the gathering of my saints—
21 Until the day cometh when there is found no more room for them; and then I have other places which I will appoint unto them, and they shall be called stakes, for the curtains or the strength of Zion.
63 Again, verily I say unto you, I will show unto you wisdom in me concerning all the churches, inasmuch as they are willing to be guided in a right and proper way for their salvation—
64 That the work of the gathering together of my saints may continue, that I may build them up unto my name upon holy places; for the time of harvest is come, and my word must needs be fulfilled.
65 Therefore, I must gather together my people, according to the parable of the wheat and the tares, that the wheat may be secured in the garners to possess eternal life, and be crowned with celestial glory, when I shall come in the kingdom of my Father to reward every man according as his work shall be;
66 While the tares shall be bound in bundles, and their bands made strong, that they may be burned with unquenchable fire.

DOCTRINE AND COVENANTS 86

Joseph Smith — *December 1832*

4 But behold, in the last days, even now while the Lord is beginning to bring forth the word, and the blade is springing up and is yet tender—
5 Behold, verily I say unto you, the angels are crying unto the Lord day and night, who are ready and waiting to be sent forth to reap down the fields;
6 But the Lord saith unto them, pluck not up the tares while the blade is yet tender (for verily your faith is weak), lest you destroy the wheat also.
7 Therefore, let the wheat and the tares grow together until the harvest is fully ripe; then ye shall first gather out the wheat from among the tares, and after the gathering of the wheat, behold and lo, the tares are bound in bundles, and the field remaineth to be burned.

The previously strong Christian nations of Europe gradually lose their faith and turn to wickedness. As a result, the Gentiles turn on themselves as war after war of increasing magnitude occur in Europe and around the world, sending hundreds of millions to their deaths. As Christianity wanes in Europe, the gospel sees great growth in the USA, Latin America, and the South Pacific (the scattered remnants of Israel). The prophecy of two churches becomes more of a reality as the great and dreadful day of the Lord approaches. The righteous and the wicked are both being gathered – the righteous to the stakes of Zion and the wicked into bundles to be burned.

1 NEPHI 14

Nephi, Son of Lehi — *595 BC*

8 And it came to pass that when the angel had spoken these words, he said unto me: Rememberest thou the covenants of the Father unto the house of Israel? I said unto him, Yea.
9 And it came to pass that he said unto me: Look, and behold that great and abominable church, which is the mother of abominations, whose founder is the devil.
10 And he said unto me: Behold there are save two churches only; the one is the church of the Lamb of God, and the other is the church of the devil; wherefore, whoso belongeth not to the church of the Lamb of God belongeth to that great church, which is the mother of abominations; and she is the whore of all the Earth.
11 And it came to pass that I looked and beheld the whore of all the Earth, and she sat upon many waters; and she had dominion over all the Earth, among all nations, kindreds, tongues, and people.
12 And it came to pass that I beheld the church of the Lamb of God, and its numbers were few, because of the wickedness and abominations of the whore who

sat upon many waters; nevertheless, I beheld that the church of the Lamb, who were the saints of God, were also upon all the face of the Earth; and their dominions upon the face of the Earth were small, because of the wickedness of the great whore whom I saw.
13 And it came to pass that I beheld that the great mother of abominations did gather together multitudes upon the face of all the Earth, among all the nations of the Gentiles, to fight against the Lamb of God.
14 And it came to pass that I, Nephi, beheld the power of the Lamb of God, that it descended upon the saints of the church of the Lamb, and upon the covenant people of the Lord, who were scattered upon all the face of the Earth; and they were armed with righteousness and with the power of God in great glory.
15 And it came to pass that I beheld that the wrath of God was poured out upon that great and abominable church, insomuch that there were wars and rumors of wars among all the nations and kindreds of the Earth.
16 And as there began to be wars and rumors of wars among all the nations which belonged to the mother of abominations, the angel spake unto me, saying: Behold, the wrath of God is upon the mother of harlots; and behold, thou seest all these things—
17 And when the day cometh that the wrath of God is poured out upon the mother of harlots, which is the great and abominable church of all the Earth, whose founder is the devil, then, at that day, the work of the Father shall commence, in preparing the way for the fulfilling of his covenants, which he hath made to his people who are of the house of Israel.

2 NEPHI 10

Jacob, Son of Lehi *550 BC*

15 Wherefore, for this cause, that my covenants may be fulfilled which I have made unto the children of men, that I will do unto them while they are in the flesh, I must needs destroy the secret works of darkness, and of murders, and of abominations.
16 Wherefore, he that fighteth against Zion, both Jew and Gentile, both bond and free, both male and female, shall perish; for they are they who are the whore of all the Earth; for they who are not for me are against me, saith our God.

Major Wars in History

1300-1400 – 2 wars

1400-1500 – 4 wars

1500-1600 – 5 wars

1600-1700 – 11 wars

1700-1800 – 21 wars

1800-1900 – 36 wars

1900-2000 – 37 wars

https://www.britannica.com/topic/list-of-wars-2031197

DOCTRINE AND COVENANTS 97

Joseph Smith *August 1833*

22 For behold, and lo, vengeance cometh speedily upon the ungodly as the whirlwind; and who shall escape it?
23 The Lord's scourge shall pass over by night and by day, and the report thereof shall vex all people; yea, it shall not be stayed until the Lord come;
24 For the indignation of the Lord is kindled against their abominations and all their wicked works.
25 Nevertheless, Zion shall escape if she observe to do all things whatsoever I have commanded her.
26 But if she observe not to do whatsoever I have commanded her, I will visit her according to all her works, with sore affliction, with pestilence, with plague, with sword, with vengeance, with devouring fire.
27 Nevertheless, let it be read this once to her ears, that I, the Lord, have accepted of her offering; and if she sin no more none of these things shall come upon her;
28 And I will bless her with blessings, and multiply a multiplicity of blessings upon her, and upon her generations forever and ever, saith the Lord your God. Amen.

As the effectiveness in preaching the gospel declines in a wicked world, the Lord's voice of warning is increasingly heard through earthquakes, tempests, fires, tsunamis, famines, pandemics, and every other type of physical and natural disaster.

DOCTRINE AND COVENANTS 88
Joseph Smith *December 1832*
87 For not many days hence and the Earth shall tremble and reel to and fro as a drunken man; and the sun shall hide his face, and shall refuse to give light; and the moon shall be bathed in blood; and the stars shall become exceedingly angry, and shall cast themselves down as a fig that falleth from off a fig tree.
88 And after your testimony cometh wrath and indignation upon the people.
89 For after your testimony cometh the testimony of earthquakes, that shall cause groanings in the midst of her, and men shall fall upon the ground and shall not be able to stand.
90 And also cometh the testimony of the voice of thunderings, and the voice of lightnings, and the voice of tempests, and the voice of the waves of the sea heaving themselves beyond their bounds.
91 And all things shall be in commotion; and surely, men's hearts shall fail them; for fear shall come upon all people.

Nephi prophesies that John the Revelator will foresee and record the events of the end of the world.

1 NEPHI 14
Nephi, Son of Lehi *595 BC*
18 And it came to pass that the angel spake unto me, saying: Look!
19 And I looked and beheld a man, and he was dressed in a white robe.
20 And the angel said unto me: Behold one of the twelve apostles of the Lamb.
21 Behold, he shall see and write the remainder of these things; yea, and also many things which have been.
22 And he shall also write concerning the end of the world.
23 Wherefore, the things which he shall write are just and true; and behold they are written in the book which thou beheld proceeding out of the mouth of the Jew; and at the time they proceeded out of the mouth of the Jew, or, at the time the book proceeded out of the mouth of the Jew, the things which were written were plain and pure, and most precious and easy to the understanding of all men.
24 And behold, the things which this apostle of the Lamb shall write are many things which thou hast seen; and behold, the remainder shalt thou see.
25 But the things which thou shalt see hereafter thou shalt not write; for the Lord God hath ordained the apostle of the Lamb of God that he should write them.
26 And also others who have been, to them hath he shown all things, and they have written them; and they are sealed up to come forth in their purity, according to the truth which is in the Lamb, in the own due time of the Lord, unto the house of Israel.
27 And I, Nephi, heard and bear record, that the name of the apostle of the Lamb was John, according to the word of the angel.
28 And behold, I, Nephi, am forbidden that I should write the remainder of the things which I saw and heard; wherefore the things which I have written sufficeth me; and I have written but a small part of the things which I saw.
29 And I bear record that I saw the things which my father saw, and the angel of the Lord did make them known unto me.
30 And now I make an end of speaking concerning the things which I saw while I was carried away in the Spirit; and if all the things which I saw are not written, the things which I have written are true. And thus it is. Amen.

39

CALL A SOLEMN ASSEMBLY

+++

John records a prophecy of an event that would occur at the close of the sixth seal. The details are strikingly similar to those of a temple dedication.

On April 6th, 2000, the Palmyra Temple dedication was the first ever broadcast in North America reaching an audience of 1.5 million members. This was followed by the Winter Quarters Temple dedication in 2001, which was also broadcast in North America, and finally the Nauvoo Temple dedication, which was broadcast worldwide in 2002 to millions of saints. Church members had to be interviewed and found worthy to attend these temple dedications. A key moment in each temple dedication is the Hosanna Shout, where the saints in attendance stand and wave a white handkerchief (a symbol of the palms the ancient saints waved upon Jesus's triumphal entry into Jerusalem) and shout "Hosanna to God and the Lamb."

Hosanna means "save us." These temple dedications, broadcast to so many millions of saints worldwide, are symbolic of the midnight announcement at a Jewish wedding that the bridegroom was soon coming, typically within 30 minutes. Following the opening of the seventh seal, John prophesies that there will be silence in heaven for half an hour, or about 21 years in actual time. (If you equate a 24 hour day to the 1,000 year seal period, then half an hour equals about 21 years.) After the silence, the great tribulations and destructions preceding the Second Coming of Christ, the Bridegroom, will begin.

Speaking at the Palmyra Temple dedication, and perhaps recognizing the magnitude of the event both as a fulfillment of John's prophecy and as a monumental gathering of worthy saints, Church President Gordon B. Hinkley said, "There will never be another day quite like this..." He then paused, overcome with emotion, then continued, "...in the history of this work."

REVELATION 7

John 95 AD

9 After this I beheld, and, lo, a great multitude, which no man could number, of all nations, and kindreds, and people, and tongues, stood before the throne, and before the Lamb, clothed with white robes, and palms in their hands;
10 And cried with a loud voice, saying, Salvation to our God which sitteth upon the throne, and unto the Lamb.
11 And all the angels stood round about the throne, and about the elders and the four beasts, and fell before the throne on their faces, and worshipped God,
12 Saying, Amen: Blessing, and glory, and wisdom, and thanksgiving, and honour, and power, and might, be unto our God for ever and ever. Amen.
13 And one of the elders answered, saying unto me, What are these which are arrayed in white robes? and whence came they?
14 And I said unto him, Sir, thou knowest. And he said to me, These are they which came out of great tribulation, and have washed their robes, and made them white in the blood of the Lamb.
15 Therefore are they before the throne of God, and serve him day and night in his temple: and he that sitteth on the throne shall dwell among them.
16 They shall hunger no more, neither thirst anymore; neither shall the sun light on them, nor any heat.
17 For the Lamb which is in the midst of the throne shall feed them, and shall lead them unto living fountains of waters: and God shall wipe away all tears from their eyes.

Palmyra, New York Temple

JOEL 1

Joel *850 BC*

14 Sanctify ye a fast, call a solemn assembly, gather the elders and all the inhabitants of the land into the house of the LORD your God, and cry unto the LORD,
15 Alas for the day! for the day of the LORD is at hand, and as a destruction from the Almighty shall it come.

JOEL 2

Joel *850 BC*

1 Blow ye the trumpet in Zion, and sound an alarm in my holy mountain: let all the inhabitants of the land tremble: for the day of the LORD cometh, for it is nigh at hand;
11 And the LORD shall utter his voice before his army: for his camp is very great: for he is strong that executeth his word: for the day of the LORD is great and very terrible; and who can abide it?
12 Therefore also now, saith the LORD, turn ye even to me with all your heart, and with fasting, and with weeping, and with mourning:
13 And rend your heart, and not your garments, *and repent*, and turn unto the Lord your God; for he is gracious and merciful, slow to anger, and of great kindness, and *he will turn away the evil from you.* [JST]
14 *Therefore repent, and* who knoweth *but* he will return and leave a blessing behind him; *that you may offer* a meat offering and a drink offering unto the LORD your God? [JST]
15 Blow the trumpet in Zion, sanctify a fast, call a solemn assembly:
16 Gather the people, sanctify the congregation, assemble the elders, gather the children, and those that suck the breasts: let the bridegroom go forth of his chamber, and the bride out of her closet.
17 Let the priests, the ministers of the LORD, weep between the porch and the altar, and let them say, Spare thy people, O LORD, and give not thine heritage to reproach, that the heathen should rule over them: wherefore should they say among the people, Where is their God?
18 Then will the LORD be jealous for his land, and pity his people.

19 Yea, the LORD will answer and say
unto his people, Behold, I will send you
corn, and wine, and oil, and ye shall be
satisfied therewith: and I will no more
make you a reproach among the heathen:
20 But I will remove far off from you the
northern army, and will drive him into a
land barren and desolate, with his face
toward the east sea, and his hinder part
toward the utmost sea, and his stink shall
come up, and his ill savour shall come up,
because he hath done great things.
21 Fear not, O land; be glad and rejoice:
for the LORD will do great things.
22 Be not afraid, ye beasts of the field: for
the pastures of the wilderness do spring,
for the tree beareth her fruit, the fig tree
and the vine do yield their strength.
23 Be glad then, ye children of Zion, and
rejoice in the LORD your God: for he hath
given you the former rain moderately, and
he will cause to come down for you the
rain, the former rain, and the latter rain in
the first month.
24 And the floors shall be full of wheat,
and the fats shall overflow with wine and
oil.
25 And I will restore to you the years that
the locust hath eaten, the cankerworm,
and the caterpillar, and the palmerworm,
my great army which I sent among you.
26 And ye shall eat in plenty, and be
satisfied, and praise the name of the LORD
your God, that hath dealt wondrously
with you: and my people shall never be
ashamed.
27 And ye shall know that I am in the
amidst of Israel, and that I am the LORD
your God, and none else: and my people
shall never be ashamed.

MATTHEW 25

Jesus Christ *33 AD*

1 Then shall the kingdom of heaven be
likened unto ten virgins, which took their
lamps, and went forth to meet the bride-
groom.
2 And five of them were wise, and five
were foolish.
3 They that were foolish took their lamps,
and took no oil with them:
4 But the wise took oil in their vessels with
their lamps.
5 While the bridegroom tarried, they all
slumbered and slept.
6 And at midnight there was a cry made,
Behold, the bridegroom cometh; go ye out
to meet him.
7 Then all those virgins arose, and trim-
med their lamps.
8 And the foolish said unto the wise, Give
us of your oil; for our lamps are gone out.
9 But the wise answered, saying, Not so;
lest there be not enough for us and you:
but go ye rather to them that sell, and buy
for yourselves.
10 And while they went to buy, the bride-
groom came; and they that were ready
went in with him to the marriage: and the
door was shut.
11 Afterward came also the other virgins,
saying, Lord, Lord, open to us.
12 But he answered and said, Verily I say
unto you, I know you not.
13 Watch therefore, for ye know neither
the day nor the hour wherein the Son of
man cometh.

Parable of the 10 Virgins, by Ernst Friedrich von Liphart, 1886.

40

A GREAT SIGN IN THE HEAVENS

✦✦✦

Prophecy of a great sign in the heavens at the close of the sixth seal. In April 2000, Jupiter, Saturn, and the moon were all grouped closely together in the sky. In addition, just after the Palmyra Temple dedication, a massive aurora borealis display was visible in the northern hemisphere from as far south as Florida and Texas and lasted from April 6th to April 25th.

DOCTRINE AND COVENANTS 88

Joseph Smith December 1832

92 And angels shall fly through the midst of heaven, crying with a loud voice, sounding the trump of God, saying: Prepare ye, prepare ye, O inhabitants of the Earth; for the judgment of our God is come. Behold, and lo, the Bridegroom cometh; go ye out to meet him.
93 And immediately there shall appear a great sign in heaven, and all people shall see it together.
94 And another angel shall sound his trump, saying: That great church, the mother of abominations, that made all nations drink of the wine of the wrath of her fornication, that persecuteth the saints of God, that shed their blood—she who sitteth upon many waters, and upon the islands of the sea—behold, she is the tares of the Earth; she is bound in bundles; her bands are made strong, no man can loose them; therefore, she is ready to be burned. And he shall sound his trump both long and loud, and all nations shall hear it.
95 And there shall be silence in heaven for the space of half an hour…

Aurora borealis, or northern lights, above Bear Lake, Alaska.

Part 4

PROPHECIES OF THE EVENTS FROM 2000 – 3000 AD

41

SILENCE FOR HALF AN HOUR

+++

As the gathering of Israel nears completion and the wicked and the righteous are polarized into two groups, there will be silence in heaven for about half an hour. The silence is caused by the great wickedness among the children of men. The gospel will be preached in all the world. Great signs in the heavens will precede Christ's coming.

REVELATION 8

John 95 AD

1 And when he had opened the seventh seal, there was silence in heaven about the space of half an hour.
2 And I saw the seven angels which stood before God; and to them were given seven trumpets.
3 And another angel came and stood at the altar, having a golden censer; and there was given unto him much incense, that he should offer it with the prayers of all saints upon the golden altar which was before the throne.
4 And the smoke of the incense, which came with the prayers of the saints, ascended up before God out of the angel's hand.
5 And the angel took the censer, and filled it with fire of the altar, and cast it into the Earth: and there were voices, and thunderings, and lightnings, and an earthquake.
6 And the seven angels which had the seven trumpets prepared themselves to sound.

DOCTRINE AND COVENANTS 38

Joseph Smith January 1831

10 Verily I say unto you, ye are clean, but not all; and there is none else with whom I am well pleased;
11 For all flesh is corrupted before me; and the powers of darkness prevail upon the Earth, among the children of men, in the presence of all the hosts of heaven—
12 Which causeth silence to reign, and all eternity is pained, and the angels are waiting the great command to reap down the Earth, to gather the tares that they may be burned; and behold, the enemy is combined.

DOCTRINE AND COVENANTS 82

Joseph Smith April 1832

5 Therefore, what I say unto one I say unto all: Watch, for the adversary spreadeth his dominions, and darkness reigneth;
6 And the anger of God kindleth against the inhabitants of the Earth; and none doeth good, for all have gone out of the way.

DOCTRINE AND COVENANTS 88

Joseph Smith December 1832

81 Behold, I sent you out to testify and warn the people, and it becometh every man who hath been warned to warn his neighbor.
82 Therefore, they are left without excuse, and their sins are upon their own heads.
83 He that seeketh me early shall find me, and shall not be forsaken.
84 Therefore, tarry ye, and labor diligently, that you may be perfected in your ministry to go forth among the Gentiles for the last time, as many as the mouth of the Lord shall name, to bind up the law and seal up the testimony, and to prepare the saints for the hour of judgment which is to come;
85 That their souls may escape the wrath of God, the desolation of abomination which awaits the wicked, both in this world and in the world to come. Verily, I say unto you, let those who are not the first elders continue in the vineyard until the mouth of the Lord shall call them, for their time is not yet come; their garments are not clean from the blood of this generation.

86 Abide ye in the liberty wherewith ye are made free; entangle not yourselves in sin, but let your hands be clean, until the Lord comes.

JOSEPH SMITH – MATTHEW 24

Jesus Christ 33 AD

21 Behold, these things I have spoken unto you concerning the Jews; and again, after the tribulation of those days which shall come upon Jerusalem, if any man shall say unto you, Lo, here is Christ, or there, believe him not;
22 For in those days there shall also arise false Christs, and false prophets, and shall show great signs and wonders, insomuch, that, if possible, they shall deceive the very elect, who are the elect according to the covenant.
23 Behold, I speak these things unto you for the elect's sake; and you also shall hear of wars, and rumors of wars; see that ye be not troubled, for all I have told you must come to pass; but the end is not yet.
24 Behold, I have told you before;
25 Wherefore, if they shall say unto you: Behold, he is in the desert; go not forth: Behold, he is in the secret chambers; believe it not;
26 For as the light of the morning cometh out of the east, and shineth even unto the west, and covereth the whole Earth, so shall also the coming of the Son of Man be.
27 And now I show unto you a parable. Behold, wheresoever the carcass is, there will the eagles be gathered together; so likewise shall mine elect be gathered from the four quarters of the Earth.
28 And they shall hear of wars, and rumors of wars.
29 Behold I speak for mine elect's sake; for nation shall rise against nation, and kingdom against kingdom; there shall be famines, and pestilences, and earthquakes, in divers places.
30 And again, because iniquity shall abound, the love of men shall wax cold; but he that shall not be overcome, the same shall be saved.
31 And again, this Gospel of the Kingdom shall be preached in all the world, for a witness unto all nations, and then shall the end come, or the destruction of the wicked;
32 And again shall the abomination of desolation, spoken of by Daniel the prophet, be fulfilled.
33 And immediately after the tribulation of those days, the sun shall be darkened, and the moon shall not give her light, and the stars shall fall from heaven, and the powers of heaven shall be shaken.
34 Verily, I say unto you, this generation, in which these things shall be shown forth, shall not pass away until all I have told you shall be fulfilled.
35 Although, the days will come, that heaven and Earth shall pass away; yet my words shall not pass away, but all shall be fulfilled.

Total Solar Eclipse 21 August 2017 at Orin Junction, Wyoming.

MARK 13

Jesus Christ 33 AD

6 For many shall come in my name, saying, I am Christ; and shall deceive many.
7 And when ye shall hear of wars and rumours of wars, be ye not troubled: for such things must needs be; but the end shall not be yet.
8 For nation shall rise against nation, and kingdom against kingdom: and there shall be earthquakes in divers places, and there shall be famines and troubles: these are the beginnings of sorrows.
9 But take heed to yourselves: for they shall deliver you up to councils; and in the synagogues ye shall be beaten: and ye shall be brought before rulers and kings for my sake, for a testimony against them.
10 And the gospel must first be published among all nations.

11 But when they shall lead you, and deliver you up, take no thought beforehand what ye shall speak, neither do ye premeditate: but whatsoever shall be given you in that hour, that speak ye: for it is not ye that speak, but the Holy Ghost.
12 Now the brother shall betray the brother to death, and the father the son; and children shall rise up against their parents, and shall cause them to be put to death.
13 And ye shall be hated of all men for my name's sake: but he that shall endure unto the end, the same shall be saved.
14 But when ye shall see the abomination of desolation, spoken of by Daniel the prophet, standing where it ought not, (let him that readeth understand,) then let them that be in Judæa flee to the mountains:
15 And let him that is on the housetop not go down into the house, neither enter therein, to take any thing out of his house:
16 And let him that is in the field not turn back again for to take up his garment.
17 But woe to them that are with child, and to them that give suck in those days!
18 And pray ye that your flight be not in the winter.
19 For in those days shall be affliction, such as was not from the beginning of the creation which God created unto this time, neither shall be.
20 And except that the Lord had shortened those days, no flesh should be saved: but for the elect's sake, whom he hath chosen, he hath shortened the days.
21 And then if any man shall say to you, Lo, here is Christ; or, lo, he is there; believe him not:
22 For false Christs and false prophets shall rise, and shall shew signs and wonders, to seduce, if it were possible, even the elect.
23 But take ye heed: behold, I have foretold you all things.
24 But in those days, after that tribulation, the sun shall be darkened, and the moon shall not give her light,
25 And the stars of heaven shall fall, and the powers that are in heaven shall be shaken.
26 And then shall they see the Son of man coming in the clouds with great power and glory.
27 And then shall he send his angels, and shall gather together his elect from the four winds, from the uttermost part of the Earth to the uttermost part of heaven.
28 Now learn a parable of the fig tree; When her branch is yet tender, and putteth forth leaves, ye know that summer is near:
29 So ye in like manner, when ye shall see these things come to pass, know that it is nigh, even at the doors.
30 Verily I say unto you, that this generation shall not pass, till all these things be done.
31 Heaven and Earth shall pass away: but my words shall not pass away.
32 But of that day and that hour knoweth no man, no, not the angels which are in heaven, neither the Son, but the Father.
33 Take ye heed, watch and pray: for ye know not when the time is.
34 For the Son of man is as a man taking a far journey, who left his house, and gave authority to his servants, and to every man his work, and commanded the porter to watch.
35 Watch ye therefore: for ye know not when the master of the house cometh, at even, or at midnight, or at the cock-crowing, or in the morning:
36 Lest coming suddenly he find you sleeping.
37 And what I say unto you I say unto all, Watch.

LUKE 21

Jesus Christ *33 AD*

7 And they asked him, saying, Master, but when shall these things be? and what sign will there be when these things shall come to pass?
8 And he said, Take heed that ye be not deceived: for many shall come in my name, saying, I am Christ; and the time draweth near: go ye not therefore after them.
9 But when ye shall hear of wars and commotions, be not terrified: for these things must first come to pass; but the end is not by and by.
10 Then said he unto them, Nation shall rise against nation, and kingdom against kingdom:
11 And great earthquakes shall be in divers places, and famines, and pestil-

ences; and fearful sights and great signs shall there be from heaven.
24 *Now these things he spake unto them, concerning the destruction of Jerusalem. And then his disciples asked him, saying, Master, tell us concerning thy coming?*
25 *And he answered them, and said, In the generation in which the times of the Gentiles shall be fulfilled,* there shall be signs in the sun, and in the moon, and in the stars; and upon the Earth distress of nations with perplexity, *like* the sea and the waves roaring. *The Earth also shall be troubled, and the waters of the great deep*; [JST]
26 Men's hearts failing them for fear, and for looking after those things which are coming on the Earth: for the powers of heaven shall be shaken.

JOEL 2

Joel 856 BC

28 And it shall come to pass afterward, that I will pour out my spirit upon all flesh; and your sons and your daughters shall prophesy, your old men shall dream dreams, your young men shall see visions:
29 And also upon the servants and upon the handmaids in those days will I pour out my spirit.
30 And I will shew wonders in the heavens and in the Earth, blood, and fire, and pillars of smoke.
31 The sun shall be turned into darkness, and the moon into blood, before the great and the terrible day of the LORD come.
32 And it shall come to pass, that whosoever shall call on the name of the LORD shall be delivered: for in mount Zion and in Jerusalem shall be deliverance, as the LORD hath said, and in the remnant whom the LORD shall call.

DOCTRINE AND COVENANTS 29

Joseph Smith September 1830

14 But, behold, I say unto you that before this great day shall come the sun shall be darkened, and the moon shall be turned into blood, and the stars shall fall from

September 11, 2001, terrorist attack on New York City. Photo by Michael Foran. Blood, fire, pillars of smoke.

Blood Moon Eclipse over California, 28 September 2015.

heaven, and there shall be greater signs in heaven above and in the Earth beneath;

DOCTRINE AND COVENANTS 34

Joseph Smith *November 1830*

9 But before that great day shall come, the sun shall be darkened, and the moon be turned into blood; and the stars shall refuse their shining, and some shall fall, and great destructions await the wicked.

ACTS 2

Peter *33 AD*

19 And I will shew wonders in heaven above, and signs in the Earth beneath; blood, and fire, and vapour of smoke:
20 The sun shall be turned into darkness, and the moon into blood, before that great and notable day of the Lord come:

DOCTRINE AND COVENANTS 45

Joseph Smith *March 1831*

39 And it shall come to pass that he that feareth me shall be looking forth for the great day of the Lord to come, even for the signs of the coming of the Son of Man.
40 And they shall see signs and wonders, for they shall be shown forth in the heavens above, and in the Earth beneath.
41 And they shall behold blood, and fire, and vapors of smoke.
42 And before the day of the Lord shall come, the sun shall be darkened, and the moon be turned into blood, and the stars fall from heaven.

2 PETER 3

Peter *67 AD*

3 Knowing this first, that *in the last days* there shall come scoffers, walking after their own lusts.
4 *Denying the Lord Jesus Christ*, and saying, Where is the promise of his coming? for since the fathers fell asleep, all things *must* continue as they *are, and have continued as they are* from the beginning of the creation. [JST]

42

THE JEWS EMBRACE THE GOSPEL

The first to receive the gospel of Jesus Christ will be the last to accept it before the Second Coming. After the Jews are scattered, and after they have been reestablished in the land of Israel, they will be persuaded to believe in Jesus Christ. Subsequently, the Jews will believe in the Book of Mormon and the restored gospel as taught to them by ordained missionaries from the Church of Jesus Christ of Latter-day Saints. They will live safely in Israel.

2 NEPHI 9

Jacob, Son of Lehi — *550 BC*

1 And now, my beloved brethren, I have read these things that ye might know concerning the covenants of the Lord that he has covenanted with all the house of Israel—

2 That he has spoken unto the Jews, by the mouth of his holy prophets, even from the beginning down, from generation to generation, until the time comes that they shall be restored to the true church and fold of God; when they shall be gathered home to the lands of their inheritance, and shall be established in all their lands of promise.

DOCTRINE AND COVENANTS 112

Joseph Smith — *July 1837*

4 Let thy heart be of good cheer before my face; and thou shalt bear record of my name, not only unto the Gentiles, but also unto the Jews; and thou shalt send forth my word unto the ends of the Earth.

2 NEPHI 25

Nephi, Son of Lehi — *550 BC*

16 And after they have been scattered, and the Lord God hath scourged them by other nations for the space of many generations, yea, even down from generation to generation until they shall be persuaded to believe in Christ, the Son of God, and the atonement, which is infinite for all mankind—and when that day shall come that they shall believe in Christ, and worship the Father in his name, with pure hearts and clean hands, and look not forward any more for another Messiah, then, at that time, the day will come that it must needs be expedient that they should believe these things.

17 And the Lord will set his hand again the second time to restore his people from their lost and fallen state. Wherefore, he will proceed to do a marvelous work and a wonder among the children of men.

18 Wherefore, he shall bring forth his words unto them, which words shall judge them at the last day, for they shall be given them for the purpose of convincing them of the true Messiah, who was rejected by them; and unto the convincing of them that they need not look forward any more for a Messiah to come, for there should not any come, save it should be a false Messiah which should deceive the people; for there is save one Messiah spoken of by the prophets, and that Messiah is he who should be rejected of the Jews.

1 NEPHI 15

Nephi, Son of Lehi — *595 BC*

19 And it came to pass that I, Nephi, spake much unto them concerning these things; yea, I spake unto them concerning the restoration of the Jews in the latter-days.

20 And I did rehearse unto them the words of Isaiah, who spake concerning the restoration of the Jews, or of the house of Israel; and after they were restored they should no more be confounded, neither should they be scattered again. And it came to pass that I did speak many words unto my brethren, that they were pacified and did humble themselves before the Lord.

ISAIAH 27
Isaiah 740 BC
12 And it shall come to pass in that day, that the LORD shall beat off from the channel of the river unto the stream of Egypt, and ye shall be gathered one by one, O ye children of Israel.
13 And it shall come to pass in that day, that the great trumpet shall be blown, and they shall come which were ready to perish in the land of Assyria, and the outcasts in the land of Egypt, and shall worship the LORD in the holy mount at Jerusalem.

2 NEPHI 20 (see also ISAIAH 11)
Isaiah 740 BC
20 And it shall come to pass in that day, that the remnant of Israel, and such as are escaped of the house of Jacob, shall no more again stay upon him that smote them, but shall stay upon the Lord, the Holy One of Israel, in truth.
21 The remnant shall return, yea, even the remnant of Jacob, unto the mighty God.
22 For though thy people Israel be as the sand of the sea, yet a remnant of them shall return;

EZEKIEL 39
Ezekiel 600 BC
25 Therefore thus saith the Lord GOD; Now will I bring again the captivity of Jacob, and have mercy upon the whole house of Israel, and will be jealous for my holy name;
26 After that they have borne their shame, and all their trespasses whereby they have trespassed against me, when they dwelt safely in their land, and none made them afraid.
27 When I have brought them again from the people, and gathered them out of their

Jews Praying in the Synagogue on Yom Kippur, by Maurycy Gottlieb, 1878.

enemies' lands, and am sanctified in them in the sight of many nations;

28 Then shall they know that I am the LORD their God, which caused them to be led into captivity among the heathen: but I have gathered them unto their own land, and have left none of them anymore there.

29 Neither will I hide my face any more from them: for I have poured out my spirit upon the house of Israel, saith the Lord GOD.

MICAH 7

Micah — *722 BC*

18 Who is a God like unto thee, that pardoneth iniquity, and passeth by the transgression of the remnant of his heritage? he retaineth not his anger forever, because he delighteth in mercy.

19 He will turn again, he will have compassion upon us; he will subdue our iniquities; and thou wilt cast all their sins into the depths of the sea.

20 Thou wilt perform the truth to Jacob, and the mercy to Abraham, which thou hast sworn unto our fathers from the days of old.

JEREMIAH 30

Jeremiah — *620 BC*

4 And these are the words that the LORD spake concerning Israel and concerning Judah.

5 For thus saith the LORD; We have heard a voice of trembling, of fear, and not of peace.

6 Ask ye now, and see whether a man doth travail with child? wherefore do I see every man with his hands on his loins, as a woman in travail, and all faces are turned into paleness?

7 Alas! for that day is great, so that none is like it: it is even the time of Jacob's trouble; but he shall be saved out of it.

8 For it shall come to pass in that day, saith the LORD of hosts, that I will break his yoke from off thy neck, and will burst thy bonds, and strangers shall no more serve themselves of him:

9 But they shall serve the LORD their God, and David their king, whom I will raise up unto them.

10 Therefore fear thou not, O my servant Jacob, saith the LORD; neither be dismayed, O Israel: for, lo, I will save thee from afar, and thy seed from the land of their captivity; and Jacob shall return, and shall be in rest, and be quiet, and none shall make him afraid.

11 For I am with thee, saith the LORD, to save thee: though I make a full end of all nations whither I have scattered thee, yet will I not make a full end of thee: but I will correct thee in measure, and will not leave thee altogether unpunished.

12 For thus saith the LORD, Thy bruise is incurable, and thy wound is grievous.

13 There is none to plead thy cause, that thou mayest be bound up: thou hast no healing medicines.

14 All thy lovers have forgotten thee; they seek thee not; for I have wounded thee with the wound of an enemy, with the chastisement of a cruel one, for the multitude of thine iniquity; because thy sins were increased.

15 Why criest thou for thine affliction? thy sorrow is incurable for the multitude of thine iniquity: because thy sins were increased, I have done these things unto thee.

16 Therefore all they that devour thee shall be devoured; and all thine adversaries, every one of them, shall go into captivity; and they that spoil thee shall be a spoil, and all that prey upon thee will I give for a prey.

17 For I will restore health unto thee, and I will heal thee of thy wounds, saith the LORD; because they called thee an Outcast, saying, This is Zion, whom no man seeketh after.

18 Thus saith the LORD; Behold, I will bring again the captivity of Jacob's tents, and have mercy on his dwelling places; and the city shall be builded upon her own heap, and the palace shall remain after the manner thereof.

19 And out of them shall proceed thanksgiving and the voice of them that make merry: and I will multiply them, and they shall not be few; I will also glorify them, and they shall not be small.

20 Their children also shall be as aforetime, and their congregation shall be established before me, and I will punish all that oppress them.

21 And their nobles shall be of themselves, and their governor shall proceed from the midst of them; and I will cause him to draw near, and he shall approach unto me:

for who is this that engaged his heart to approach unto me? saith the LORD.
22 And ye shall be my people, and I will be your God.
23 Behold, the whirlwind of the LORD goeth forth with fury, a continuing whirlwind: it shall fall with pain upon the head of the wicked.
24 The fierce anger of the LORD shall not return, until he have done it, and until he have performed the intents of his heart: in the latter-days ye shall consider it.

HEBREWS 4

Paul *68 AD*

6 Seeing therefore it remaineth that some must enter therein, and they to whom it was first preached entered not in because of unbelief:
7 Again, he limiteth a certain day, saying in David, Today, after so long a time; as it is said, Today if ye will hear his voice, harden not your hearts.
8 For if Jesus had given them rest, then would he not afterward have spoken of another day.
9 There remaineth therefore a rest to the people of God.

2 NEPHI 30

Nephi, Son of Lehi *550 BC*

7 And it shall come to pass that the Jews which are scattered also shall begin to believe in Christ; and they shall begin to gather in upon the face of the land; and as many as shall believe in Christ shall also become a delightsome people.

3 NEPHI 20

Jesus Christ *34 AD*

29 And I will remember the covenant which I have made with my people; and I have covenanted with them that I would gather them together in mine own due time, that I would give unto them again the land of their fathers for their inheritance, which is the land of Jerusalem, which is the promised land unto them forever, saith the Father.
30 And it shall come to pass that the time cometh, when the fulness of my gospel shall be preached unto them;
31 And they shall believe in me, that I am Jesus Christ, the Son of God, and shall pray unto the Father in my name.
32 Then shall their watchmen lift up their voice, and with the voice together shall they sing; for they shall see eye to eye. [Isa 52:8]
33 Then will the Father gather them together again, and give unto them Jerusalem for the land of their inheritance.
34 Then shall they break forth into joy—Sing together, ye waste places of Jerusalem; for the Father hath comforted his people, he hath redeemed Jerusalem.
35 The Father hath made bare his holy arm in the eyes of all the nations; and all the ends of the Earth shall see the salvation of the Father; and the Father and I are one. [Isa 52:9,10]
36 And then shall be brought to pass that which is written: Awake, awake again, and put on thy strength, O Zion; put on thy beautiful garments, O Jerusalem, the holy city, for henceforth there shall no more come into thee the uncircumcised and the unclean.
37 Shake thyself from the dust; arise, sit down, O Jerusalem; loose thyself from the bands of thy neck, O captive daughter of Zion.
38 For thus saith the Lord: Ye have sold yourselves for naught, and ye shall be redeemed without money . [Isa 52:1-3]
39 Verily, verily, I say unto you, that my people shall know my name; yea, in that day they shall know that I am he that doth speak. [Isa 52: 6]
40 And then shall they say: How beautiful upon the mountains are the feet of him that bringeth good tidings unto them, that publisheth peace; that bringeth good tidings unto them of good, that publisheth salvation; that saith unto Zion: Thy God reigneth! [Isa 52:7]
41 And then shall a cry go forth: Depart ye, depart ye, go ye out from thence, touch not that which is unclean; go ye out of the midst of her; be ye clean that bear the vessels of the Lord.
42 For ye shall not go out with haste nor go by flight; for the Lord will go before you, and the God of Israel shall be your rearward.
43 Behold, my servant shall deal prudently; he shall be exalted and extolled and be very high.

44 As many were astonished at thee—his
visage was so marred, more than any man,
and his form more than the sons of men—
45 So shall he sprinkle many nations; the
kings shall shut their mouths at him, for
that which had not been told them shall
they see; and that which they had not
heard shall they consider. [Isa 52:11-15]
46 Verily, verily, I say unto you, all these
things shall surely come, even as the
Father hath commanded me. Then shall
this covenant which the Father hath
covenanted with his people be fulfilled;
and then shall Jerusalem be inhabited
again with my people, and it shall be the
land of their inheritance.

DOCTRINE AND COVENANTS 49

Joseph Smith — *March 1831*

24 But before the great day of the Lord
shall come, Jacob shall flourish in the
wilderness, and the Lamanites shall
blossom as the rose.

JEREMIAH 3

Jeremiah — *620 BC*

17 At that time they shall call Jerusalem
the throne of the LORD; and all the
nations shall be gathered unto it, to the
name of the LORD, to Jerusalem: neither
shall they walk any more after the
imagination of their evil heart.
18 In those days the house of Judah shall
walk with the house of Israel, and they
shall come together out of the land of the
north to the land that I have given for an
inheritance unto your fathers.
19 But I said, How shall I put thee among
the children, and give thee a pleasant land,
a goodly heritage of the hosts of nations?
and I said, Thou shalt call me, My father;
and shalt not turn away from me.

JEREMIAH 32

Jeremiah — *620 BC*

37 Behold, I will gather them out of all
countries, whither I have driven them in
mine anger, and in my fury, and in great
wrath; and I will bring them again unto
this place, and I will cause them to dwell
safely:
38 And they shall be my people, and I will
be their God:
39 And I will give them one heart, and one
way, that they may fear me forever, for
the good of them, and of their children
after them:
40 And I will make an everlasting
covenant with them, that I will not turn
away from them, to do them good; but I
will put my fear in their hearts, that they
shall not depart from me.
41 Yea, I will rejoice over them to do them
good, and I will plant them in this land
assuredly with my whole heart and with
my whole soul.
42 For thus saith the LORD; Like as I have
brought all this great evil upon this
people, so will I bring upon them all the
good that I have promised them.
43 And fields shall be bought in this land,
whereof ye say, It is desolate without man
or beast; it is given into the hand of the
Chaldeans.
44 Men shall buy fields for money, and
subscribe evidences, and seal them, and
take witnesses in the land of Benjamin,
and in the places about Jerusalem, and in
the cities of Judah, and in the cities of the
mountains, and in the cities of the valley,
and in the cities of the south: for I will
cause their captivity to return, saith the
LORD.

1 NEPHI 22

Nephi, Son of Lehi — *580 BC*

24 And the time cometh speedily that the
righteous must be led up as calves of the
stall, and the Holy One of Israel must
reign in dominion, and might, and power,
and great glory.
25 And he gathereth his children from the
four quarters of the Earth; and he number-
eth his sheep, and they know him; and
there shall be one fold and one shepherd;
and he shall feed his sheep, and in him
they shall find pasture.
27 And now behold, I, Nephi, say unto
you that all these things must come
according to the flesh.
28 But, behold, all nations, kindreds,
tongues, and people shall dwell safely in
the Holy One of Israel if it so be that they
will repent.

EZEKIEL 34

Ezekiel — *600 BC*

11 For thus saith the Lord GOD; Behold,
I, even I, will both search my sheep, and
seek them out.

12 As a shepherd seeketh out his flock in the day that he is among his sheep that are scattered; so will I seek out my sheep, and will deliver them out of all places where they have been scattered in the cloudy and dark day.

13 And I will bring them out from the people, and gather them from the countries, and will bring them to their own land, and feed them upon the mountains of Israel by the rivers, and in all the inhabited places of the country.

14 I will feed them in a good pasture, and upon the high mountains of Israel shall their fold be: there shall they lie in a good fold, and in a fat pasture shall they feed upon the mountains of Israel.

15 I will feed my flock, and I will cause them to lie down, saith the Lord GOD.

16 I will seek that which was lost, and bring again that which was driven away, and will bind up that which was broken, and will strengthen that which was sick: but I will destroy the fat and the strong; I will feed them with judgment.

22 Therefore will I save my flock, and they shall no more be a prey; and I will judge between cattle and cattle.

23 And I will set up one shepherd over them, and he shall feed them, even my servant David; he shall feed them, and he shall be their shepherd.

24 And I the LORD will be their God, and my servant David a prince among them; I the LORD have spoken it.

25 And I will make with them a covenant of peace, and will cause the evil beasts to cease out of the land: and they shall dwell safely in the wilderness, and sleep in the woods.

26 And I will make them and the places round about my hill a blessing; and I will cause the shower to come down in his season; there shall be showers of blessing.

27 And the tree of the field shall yield her fruit, and the Earth shall yield her increase, and they shall be safe in their land, and shall know that I am the LORD, when I have broken the bands of their yoke, and delivered them out of the hand of those that served themselves of them.

28 And they shall no more be a prey to the heathen, neither shall the beast of the land devour them; but they shall dwell safely, and none shall make them afraid.

29 And I will raise up for them a plant of renown, and they shall be no more consumed with hunger in the land, neither bear the shame of the heathen any more.

30 Thus shall they know that I the LORD their God am with them, and that they, even the house of Israel, are my people, saith the Lord GOD.

31 And ye my flock, the flock of my pasture, are men, and I am your God, saith the Lord GOD.

ETHER 13

Ether — *600 BC*

11 And then also cometh the Jerusalem of old; and the inhabitants thereof, blessed are they, for they have been washed in the blood of the Lamb; and they are they who were scattered and gathered in from the four quarters of the Earth, and from the north countries, and are partakers of the fulfilling of the covenant which God made with their father, Abraham.

JEREMIAH 31

Jeremiah — *620 BC*

38 Behold, the days come, saith the LORD, that the city shall be built to the LORD from the tower of Hananeel unto the gate of the corner.

39 And the measuring line shall yet go forth over against it upon the hill Gareb, and shall compass about to Goath.

40 And the whole valley of the dead bodies, and of the ashes, and all the fields unto the brook of Kidron, unto the corner of the horse gate toward the east, shall be holy unto the LORD; it shall not be plucked up, nor thrown down any more forever.

The leadership of the Church of Jesus Christ of Latter-day Saints, referred to by the prophets as "Gentiles" and "strangers," will teach the gospel to the new Jewish converts and train them in church administration. Prophets of old likened this to the Jews nursing from the Gentiles and being bounced on their knees like children. Church membership will grow quickly among the Jews.

DOCTRINE AND COVENANTS 90

Joseph Smith — *March 1833*

7 As also through your administration the keys of the school of the prophets, which I have commanded to be organized;
8 That thereby they may be perfected in their ministry for the salvation of Zion, and of the nations of Israel, and of the Gentiles, as many as will believe;
9 That through your administration they may receive the word, and through their administration the word may go forth unto the ends of the Earth, unto the Gentiles first, and then, behold, and lo, they shall turn unto the Jews.
10 And then cometh the day when the arm of the Lord shall be revealed in power in convincing the nations, the heathen nations, the house of Joseph, of the gospel of their salvation.
11 For it shall come to pass in that day, that every man shall hear the fulness of the gospel in his own tongue, and in his own language, through those who are ordained unto this power, by the administration of the Comforter, shed forth upon them for the revelation of Jesus Christ.

DOCTRINE AND COVENANTS 107

Joseph Smith — *March 1835*

33 The Twelve are a Traveling Presiding High Council, to officiate in the name of the Lord, under the direction of the Presidency of the Church, agreeable to the institution of heaven; to build up the church, and regulate all the affairs of the same in all nations, first unto the Gentiles and secondly unto the Jews.
34 The Seventy are to act in the name of the Lord, under the direction of the Twelve or the traveling high council, in building up the church and regulating all the affairs of the same in all nations, first unto the Gentiles and then to the Jews—
35 The Twelve being sent out, holding the keys, to open the door by the proclamation of the gospel of Jesus Christ, and first unto the Gentiles and then unto the Jews.
97 And these seventy are to be traveling ministers, unto the Gentiles first and also unto the Jews.

2 NEPHI 24 (see also ISAIAH 14)

Isaiah — *740 BC*

1 For the Lord will have mercy on Jacob, and will yet choose Israel, and set them in their own land; and the strangers shall be joined with them, and they shall cleave to the house of Jacob.
2 And the people shall take them and bring them to their place; yea, from far unto the ends of the Earth; and they shall return to their lands of promise. And the house of Israel shall possess them, and the land of the Lord shall be for servants and handmaids; and they shall take them captives unto whom they were captives; and they shall rule over their oppressors.
3 And it shall come to pass in that day that the Lord shall give thee rest, from thy sorrow, and from thy fear, and from the hard bondage wherein thou wast made to serve.
7 The whole Earth is at rest, and is quiet; they break forth into singing.
8 Yea, the fir trees rejoice at thee, and also the cedars of Lebanon, saying: Since thou art laid down no feller is come up against us.

ISAIAH 60

Isaiah — *740 BC*

1 Arise, shine; for thy light is come, and the glory of the LORD is risen upon thee.
2 For, behold, the darkness shall cover the Earth, and gross darkness the people: but the LORD shall arise upon thee, and his glory shall be seen upon thee.
3 And the Gentiles shall come to thy light, and kings to the brightness of thy rising.
4 Lift up thine eyes round about, and see: all they gather themselves together, they come to thee: thy sons shall come from far, and thy daughters shall be nursed at thy side.
5 Then thou shalt see, and flow together, and thine heart shall fear, and be enlarged; because the abundance of the sea shall be converted unto thee, the forces of the Gentiles shall come unto thee.
6 The multitude of camels shall cover thee, the dromedaries of Midian and Ephah; all they from Sheba shall come: they shall bring gold and incense; and they shall shew forth the praises of the LORD.
7 All the flocks of Kedar shall be gathered together unto thee, the rams of Nebaioth

shall minister unto thee: they shall come up with acceptance on mine altar, and I will glorify the house of my glory.
8 Who are these that fly as a cloud, and as the doves to their windows?
9 Surely the isles shall wait for me, and the ships of Tarshish first, to bring thy sons from far, their silver and their gold with them, unto the name of the LORD thy God, and to the Holy One of Israel, because he hath glorified thee.
10 And the sons of strangers shall build up thy walls, and their kings shall minister unto thee: for in my wrath I smote thee, but in my favour have I had mercy on thee.
11 Therefore thy gates shall be open continually; they shall not be shut day nor night; that men may bring unto thee the forces of the Gentiles, and that their kings may be brought.
12 For the nation and kingdom that will not serve thee shall perish; yea, those nations shall be utterly wasted.
13 The glory of Lebanon shall come unto thee, the fir tree, the pine tree, and the box together, to beautify the place of my sanctuary; and I will make the place of my feet glorious.
14 The sons also of them that afflicted thee shall come bending unto thee; and all they that despised thee shall bow themselves down at the soles of thy feet; and they shall call thee, The city of the LORD, The Zion of the Holy One of Israel.
15 Whereas thou hast been forsaken and hated, so that no man went through thee, I will make thee an eternal excellency, a joy of many generations.
16 Thou shalt also suck the milk of the Gentiles, and shalt suck the breast of kings: and thou shalt know that I the LORD am thy Saviour and thy Redeemer, the mighty One of Jacob.

ISAIAH 66

Isaiah *740 BC*

7 Before she travailed, she brought forth; before her pain came, she was delivered of a man child.
8 Who hath heard such a thing? who hath seen such things? Shall the Earth be made to bring forth in one day? or shall a nation be born at once? for as soon as Zion travailed, she brought forth her children.
9 Shall I bring to the birth, and not cause to bring forth? saith the LORD: shall I cause to bring forth, and shut the womb? saith thy God.
10 Rejoice ye with Jerusalem, and be glad with her, all ye that love her: rejoice for joy with her, all ye that mourn for her:
11 That ye may suck, and be satisfied with the breasts of her consolations; that ye may milk out, and be delighted with the abundance of her glory.
12 For thus saith the LORD, Behold, I will extend peace to her like a river, and the glory of the Gentiles like a flowing stream: then shall ye suck, ye shall be borne upon her sides, and be dandled upon her knees.
13 As one whom his mother comforteth, so will I comfort you; and ye shall be comforted in Jerusalem.
14 And when ye see this, your heart shall rejoice, and your bones shall flourish like an herb: and the hand of the LORD shall be known toward his servants, and his indignation toward his enemies.

Continued peace, safety, prosperity, and the glorious presence of the Lord attracts saints from all over the world to Israel.

EZEKIEL 28

Ezekiel *600 BC*

25 Thus saith the Lord GOD; When I shall have gathered the house of Israel from the people among whom they are scattered, and shall be sanctified in them in the sight of the heathen, then shall they dwell in their land that I have given to my servant Jacob.
26 And they shall dwell safely therein, and shall build houses, and plant vineyards; yea, they shall dwell with confidence, when I have executed judgments upon all those that despise them round about them; and they shall know that I am the LORD their God.

ZECHARIAH 2

Zechariah *520 BC*

4 And said unto him, Run, speak to this young man, saying, Jerusalem shall be inhabited as towns without walls for the multitude of men and cattle therein:
5 For I, saith the LORD, will be unto her a wall of fire round about, and will be the glory in the midst of her.

6 Ho, ho, come forth, and flee from the land of the north, saith the LORD: for I have spread you abroad as the four winds of the heaven, saith the LORD.
10 Sing and rejoice, O daughter of Zion: for, lo, I come, and I will dwell in the midst of thee, saith the LORD.
11 And many nations shall be joined to the LORD in that day, and shall be my people: and I will dwell in the midst of thee, and thou shalt know that the LORD of hosts hath sent me unto thee.
12 And the LORD shall inherit Judah his portion in the holy land, and shall choose Jerusalem again.
13 Be silent, O all flesh, before the LORD: for he is raised up out of his holy habitation.

ZECHARIAH 8

Zechariah *520 BC*

3 Thus saith the LORD; I am returned unto Zion, and will dwell in the midst of Jerusalem: and Jerusalem shall be called a city of truth; and the mountain of the LORD of hosts the holy mountain.
4 Thus saith the LORD of hosts; There shall yet old men and old women dwell in the streets of Jerusalem, and every man with his staff in his hand for very age.
5 And the streets of the city shall be full of boys and girls playing in the streets thereof.
6 Thus saith the LORD of hosts; If it be marvellous in the eyes of the remnant of this people in these days, should it also be marvellous in mine eyes? saith the LORD of hosts.
7 Thus saith the LORD of hosts; Behold, I will *gather* my people from the east country, and from the west country; [JST]
8 And I will bring them, and they shall dwell in the midst of Jerusalem: and they shall be my people, and I will be their God, in truth and in righteousness.
9 Thus saith the LORD of hosts; Let your hands be strong, ye that hear in these days these words by the mouth of the prophets, which were in the day that the foundation of the house of the LORD of hosts was laid, that the temple might be built.
10 For before these days there was no hire for man, nor any hire for beast; neither was there any peace to him that went out or came in because of the affliction: for I set all men every one against his neighbour.
11 But now I will not be unto the residue of this people as in the former days, saith the LORD of hosts.
12 For the seed shall be prosperous; the vine shall give her fruit, and the ground shall give her increase, and the heavens shall give their dew; and I will cause the remnant of this people to possess all these things.
13 And it shall come to pass, that as ye were a curse among the heathen, O house of Judah, and house of Israel; so will I save you, and ye shall be a blessing: fear not, but let your hands be strong.
20 Thus saith the LORD of hosts; It shall yet come to pass, that there shall come people, and the inhabitants of many cities:
21 And the inhabitants of one city shall go to another, saying, Let us go speedily to pray before the LORD, and to seek the LORD of hosts: I will go also.
22 Yea, many people and strong nations shall come to seek the LORD of hosts in Jerusalem, and to pray before the LORD.
23 Thus saith the LORD of hosts; In those days it shall come to pass, that ten men shall take hold out of all languages of the nations, even shall take hold of the skirt of him that is a Jew, saying, We will go with you: for we have heard that God is with you.

43

THE JERUSALEM TEMPLE

+++

A temple of the Church of Jesus Christ of Latter-day Saints will be built in Jerusalem. The Lord rules from the temple. The saints are purified and sanctified by living the laws and ordinances of the temple.

EZEKIEL 37

Ezekiel *600 BC*

21 And say unto them, Thus saith the Lord GOD; Behold, I will take the children of Israel from among the heathen, whither they be gone, and will gather them on every side, and bring them into their own land:

22 And I will make them one nation in the land upon the mountains of Israel; and one king shall be king to them all: and they shall be no more two nations, neither shall they be divided into two kingdoms any more at all:

23 Neither shall they defile themselves any more with their idols, nor with their detestable things, nor with any of their transgressions: but I will save them out of all their dwelling places, wherein they have sinned, and will cleanse them: so shall they be my people, and I will be their God.

24 And David my servant shall be king over them; and they all shall have one shepherd: they shall also walk in my judgments, and observe my statutes, and do them.

25 And they shall dwell in the land that I have given unto Jacob my servant, wherein your fathers have dwelt; and they shall dwell therein, even they, and their children, and their children's children for ever: and my servant David shall be their prince forever.

26 Moreover I will make a covenant of peace with them; it shall be an everlasting covenant with them: and I will place them, and multiply them, and will set my sanctuary in the midst of them for evermore.

27 My tabernacle also shall be with them: yea, I will be their God, and they shall be my people.

28 And the heathen shall know that I the LORD do sanctify Israel, when my sanctuary shall be in the midst of them for evermore.

ISAIAH 66

Isaiah *740 BC*

5 Hear the word of the LORD, ye that tremble at his word; Your brethren that hated you, that cast you out for my name's sake, said, Let the LORD be glorified: but he shall appear to your joy, and they shall be ashamed.

6 A voice of noise from the city, a voice from the temple, a voice of the LORD that rendereth recompence to his enemies.

DOCTRINE AND COVENANTS 133

Joseph Smith *November 1831*

13 And let them who be of Judah flee unto Jerusalem, unto the mountains of the Lord's house.

AMOS 9

Amos *792 BC*

11 In that day will I raise up the tabernacle of David that is fallen, and close up the breaches thereof; and I will raise up his ruins, and I will build it as in the days of old:

12 That they may possess the remnant of Edom, and of all the heathen, which are called by my name, saith the LORD that doeth this.

13 Behold, the days come, saith the LORD, that the plowman shall overtake the reaper, and the treader of grapes him that soweth seed; and the mountains shall drop sweet wine, and all the hills shall melt.

14 And I will bring again the captivity of my people of Israel, and they shall build the waste cities, and inhabit them; and

Rome Italy Temple, Dedicated March 10, 2020, currently the closest temple to Jerusalem.

they shall plant vineyards, and drink the wine thereof; they shall also make gardens, and eat the fruit of them.
15 And I will plant them upon their land, and they shall no more be pulled up out of their land which I have given them, saith the LORD thy God.

EZEKIEL 43

Ezekiel 600 BC

4 And the glory of the LORD came into the house by the way of the gate whose prospect is toward the east.
5 So the spirit took me up, and brought me into the inner court; and, behold, the glory of the LORD filled the house.
6 And I heard him speaking unto me out of the house; and the man stood by me.
7 And he said unto me, Son of man, the place of my throne, and the place of the soles of my feet, where I will dwell in the midst of the children of Israel forever, and my holy name, shall the house of Israel no more defile, neither they, nor their kings, by their whoredom, nor by the carcasses of their kings in their high places.
8 In their setting of their threshold by my thresholds, and their post by my posts, and the wall between me and them, they have even defiled my holy name by their abominations that they have committed: wherefore I have consumed them in mine anger.
9 Now let them put away their whoredom, and the carcasses of their kings, far from me, and I will dwell in the midst of them forever.
10 Thou son of man, shew the house to the house of Israel, that they may be ashamed of their iniquities: and let them measure the pattern.
11 And if they be ashamed of all that they have done, shew them the form of the house, and the fashion thereof, and the goings out thereof, and the comings in thereof, and all the forms thereof, and all the ordinances thereof, and all the forms thereof, and all the laws thereof: and write it in their sight, that they may keep the whole form thereof, and all the ordinances thereof, and do them.
12 This is the law of the house; Upon the top of the mountain the whole limit thereof round about shall be most holy. Behold, this is the law of the house.

By obeying temple covenants and ordinances the Jewish saints in Jerusalem are sanctified, refined, purified, and given a new name.

3 NEPHI 24 (see also MALACHI 3)

Malachi 432 BC

3 And he shall sit as a refiner and purifier of silver; and he shall purify the sons of Levi, and purge them as gold and silver, that they may offer unto the Lord an offering in righteousness.
4 Then shall the offering of Judah and Jerusalem be pleasant unto the Lord, as in the days of old, and as in former years.

EZEKIEL 11

Ezekiel 600 BC

16 Therefore say, Thus saith the Lord GOD; Although I have cast them far off among the heathen, and although I have scattered them among the countries, yet will I be to them as a little sanctuary in the countries where they shall come.
17 Therefore say, Thus saith the Lord GOD; I will even gather you from the people, and assemble you out of the countries where ye have been scattered, and I will give you the land of Israel.

18 And they shall come thither, and they
shall take away all the detestable things
thereof and all the abominations thereof
from thence.
19 And I will give them one heart, and I
will put a new spirit within you; and I will
take the stony heart out of their flesh, and
will give them an heart of flesh:
20 That they may walk in my statutes, and
keep mine ordinances, and do them: and
they shall be my people, and I will be their
God.
21 But as for them whose heart walketh
after the heart of their detestable things
and their abominations, I will recompense
their way upon their own heads, saith the
Lord GOD.
22 Then did the cherubims lift up their
wings, and the wheels beside them; and
the glory of the God of Israel was over
them above.
23 And the glory of the LORD went up
from the midst of the city, and stood upon
the mountain which is on the east side of
the city.

EZEKIEL 36

Ezekiel *600 BC*

21 But I had pity for mine holy name,
which the house of Israel had profaned
among the heathen, whither they went.
22 Therefore say unto the house of Israel,
Thus saith the Lord GOD; I do not this for
your sakes, O house of Israel, but for mine
holy name's sake, which ye have profaned
among the heathen, whither ye went.
23 And I will sanctify my great name,
which was profaned among the heathen,
which ye have profaned in the midst of
them; and the heathen shall know that I
am the LORD, saith the Lord GOD, when
I shall be sanctified in you before their
eyes.
24 For I will take you from among the
heathen, and gather you out of all countries, and will bring you into your own
land.
25 Then will I sprinkle clean water upon
you, and ye shall be clean: from all your
filthiness, and from all your idols, will I
cleanse you.
26 A new heart also will I give you, and a
new spirit will I put within you: and I will
take away the stony heart out of your
flesh, and I will give you an heart of flesh.
27 And I will put my spirit within you,
and cause you to walk in my statutes, and
ye shall keep my judgments, and do them.
28 And ye shall dwell in the land that I
gave to your fathers; and ye shall be my
people, and I will be your God.
29 I will also save you from all your
uncleannesses: and I will call for the corn,
and will increase it, and lay no famine
upon you.
30 And I will multiply the fruit of the tree,
and the increase of the field, that ye shall
receive no more reproach of famine
among the heathen.
31 Then shall ye remember your own evil
ways, and your doings that were not good,
and shall loathe yourselves in your own
sight for your iniquities and for your
abominations.
32 Not for your sakes do I this, saith the
Lord GOD, be it known unto you: be
ashamed and confounded for your own
ways, O house of Israel.
33 Thus saith the Lord GOD; In the day
that I shall have cleansed you from all
your iniquities I will also cause you to
dwell in the cities, and the wastes shall be
builded.
34 And the desolate land shall be tilled,
whereas it lay desolate in the sight of all
that passed by.
35 And they shall say, This land that was
desolate is become like the garden of
Eden; and the waste and desolate and
ruined cities are become fenced, and are
inhabited.
36 Then the heathen that are left round
about you shall know that I the LORD
build the ruined places, and plant that that
was desolate: I the LORD have spoken it,
and I will do it.
37 Thus saith the Lord GOD; I will yet for
this be inquired of by the house of Israel,
to do it for them; I will increase them with
men like a flock.
38 As the holy flock, as the flock of
Jerusalem in her solemn feasts; so shall the
waste cities be filled with flocks of men:
and they shall know that I am the LORD.

EZEKIEL 20

Ezekiel *600 BC*

33 As I live, saith the Lord GOD, surely
with a mighty hand, and with a stretched
out arm, and with fury poured out, will I
rule over you:

34 And I will bring you out from the people, and will gather you out of the countries wherein ye are scattered, with a mighty hand, and with a stretched out arm, and with fury poured out.

35 And I will bring you into the wilderness of the people, and there will I plead with you face to face.

36 Like as I pleaded with your fathers in the wilderness of the land of Egypt, so will I plead with you, saith the Lord GOD.

37 And I will cause you to pass under the rod, and I will bring you into the bond of the covenant:

38 And I will purge out from among you the rebels, and them that transgress against me: I will bring them forth out of the country where they sojourn, and they shall not enter into the land of Israel: and ye shall know that I am the LORD.

39 As for you, O house of Israel, thus saith the Lord GOD; Go ye, serve ye everyone his idols, and hereafter also, if ye will not hearken unto me: but pollute ye my holy name no more with your gifts, and with your idols.

40 For in mine holy mountain, in the mountain of the height of Israel, saith the Lord GOD, there shall all the house of Israel, all of them in the land, serve me: there will I accept them, and there will I require your offerings, and the first fruits of your oblations, with all your holy things.

41 I will accept you with your sweet savour, when I bring you out from the people, and gather you out of the countries wherein ye have been scattered; and I will be sanctified in you before the heathen.

42 And ye shall know that I am the LORD, when I shall bring you into the land of Israel, into the country for the which I lifted up mine hand to give it to your fathers.

43 And there shall ye remember your ways, and all your doings, wherein ye have been defiled; and ye shall loathe yourselves in your own sight for all your evils that ye have committed.

44 And ye shall know that I am the LORD, when I have wrought with you for my name's sake, not according to your wicked ways, nor according to your corrupt doings, O ye house of Israel, saith the Lord GOD.

ISAIAH 62

Isaiah *740 BC*

1 For Zion's sake will I not hold my peace, and for Jerusalem's sake I will not rest, until the righteousness thereof go forth as brightness, and the salvation thereof as a lamp that burneth.

2 And the Gentiles shall see thy righteousness, and all kings thy glory: and thou shalt be called by a new name, which the mouth of the LORD shall name.

3 Thou shalt also be a crown of glory in the hand of the LORD, and a royal diadem in the hand of thy God.

4 Thou shalt no more be termed Forsaken; neither shall thy land any more be termed Desolate: but thou shalt be called Hephzibah, and thy land Beulah: for the LORD delighteth in thee, and thy land shall be married.

5 For as a young man marrieth a virgin, so shall thy sons marry thee: and as the bridegroom rejoiceth over the bride, so shall thy God rejoice over thee.

6 I have set watchmen upon thy walls, O Jerusalem, which shall never hold their peace day nor night: ye that make mention of the LORD, keep not silence,

7 And give him no rest, till he establish, and till he make Jerusalem a praise in the Earth.

8 The LORD hath sworn by his right hand, and by the arm of his strength, Surely I will no more give thy corn to be meat for thine enemies; and the sons of the stranger shall not drink thy wine, for the which thou hast laboured:

9 But they that have gathered it shall eat it, and praise the LORD; and they that have brought it together shall drink it in the courts of my holiness.

10 Go through, go through the gates; prepare ye the way of the people; cast up, cast up the highway; gather out the stones; lift up a standard for the people.

11 Behold, the LORD hath proclaimed unto the end of the world, Say ye to the daughter of Zion, Behold, thy salvation cometh; behold, his reward is with him, and his work before him.

12 And they shall call them, The holy people, The redeemed of the LORD: and thou shalt be called, Sought out, A city not forsaken.

JEREMIAH 33

Jeremiah — *620 BC*

7 And I will cause the captivity of Judah
and the captivity of Israel to return, and
will build them, as at the first.
8 And I will cleanse them from all their
iniquity, whereby they have sinned
against me; and I will pardon all their
iniquities, whereby they have sinned, and
whereby they have transgressed against
me.
9 And it shall be to me a name of joy, a
praise and an honour before all the nations
of the Earth, which shall hear all the good
that I do unto them: and they shall fear
and tremble for all the goodness and for all
the prosperity that I procure unto it.
10 Thus saith the LORD; Again there shall
be heard in this place, which ye say shall
be desolate without man and without
beast, even in the cities of Judah, and in
the streets of Jerusalem, that are desolate,
without man, and without inhabitant, and
without beast,
11 The voice of joy, and the voice of glad-
ness, the voice of the bridegroom, and the
voice of the bride, the voice of them that
shall say, Praise the LORD of hosts: for the
LORD is good; for his mercy endureth for
ever: and of them that shall bring the
sacrifice of praise into the house of the
LORD. For I will cause to return the
captivity of the land, as at the first, saith
the LORD.
12 Thus saith the LORD of hosts; Again in
this place, which is desolate without man
and without beast, and in all the cities
thereof, shall be an habitation of shep-
herds causing their flocks to lie down.
13 In the cities of the mountains, in the
cities of the vale, and in the cities of the
south, and in the land of Benjamin, and in
the places about Jerusalem, and in the
cities of Judah, shall the flocks pass again
under the hands of him that telleth them,
saith the LORD.
14 Behold, the days come, saith the
LORD, that I will perform that good thing
which I have promised unto the house of
Israel and to the house of Judah.
15 In those days, and at that time, will I
cause the Branch of righteousness to grow
up unto David; and he shall execute judg-
ment and righteousness in the land.
16 In those days shall Judah be saved, and
Jerusalem shall dwell safely: and this is the
name wherewith she shall be called, The
LORD our righteousness.
17 For thus saith the LORD; David shall
never want a man to sit upon the throne
of the house of Israel;
18 Neither shall the priests the Levites
want a man before me to offer burnt offer-
ings, and to kindle meat offerings, and to
do sacrifice continually.
19 And the word of the LORD came unto
Jeremiah, saying,
20 Thus saith the LORD; If ye can break
my covenant of the day, and my covenant
of the night, and that there should not be
day and night in their season;
21 Then may also my covenant be broken
with David my servant, that he should not
have a son to reign upon his throne; and
with the Levites the priests, my ministers.
22 As the host of heaven cannot be
numbered, neither the sand of the sea
measured: so will I multiply the seed of
David my servant, and the Levites that
minister unto me.

A fountain of water from under the temple forms a river that heals the Dead Sea.

EZEKIEL 47

Ezekiel — *600 BC*

1 Afterward he brought me again unto the
door of the house; and, behold, waters
issued out from under the threshold of the
house eastward: for the forefront of the
house stood toward the east, and the
waters came down from under from the
right side of the house, at the south side of
the altar.
2 Then brought he me out of the way of
the gate northward, and led me about the
way without unto the utter gate by the
way that looketh eastward; and, behold,
there ran out waters on the right side.
3 And when the man that had the line in
his hand went forth eastward, he
measured a thousand cubits, and he
brought me through the waters; the
waters were to the ankles.
4 Again he measured a thousand, and
brought me through the waters; the
waters were to the knees. Again he
measured a thousand, and brought me
through; the waters were to the loins.

5 Afterward he measured a thousand; and
it was a river that I could not pass over: for
the waters were risen, waters to swim in,
a river that could not be passed over.
6 And he said unto me, Son of man, hast
thou seen this? Then he brought me, and
caused me to return to the brink of the
river.
7 Now when I had returned, behold, at the
bank of the river were very many trees on
the one side and on the other.
8 Then said he unto me, These waters
issue out toward the east country, and go
down into the desert, and go into the sea:
which being brought forth into the sea,
the waters shall be healed.
9 And it shall come to pass, that every-
thing that liveth, which moveth, whither-
soever the rivers shall come, shall live: and
there shall be a very great multitude of
fish, because these waters shall come
thither: for they shall be healed; and
everything shall live whither the river
cometh.
10 And it shall come to pass, that the
fishers shall stand upon it from En-gedi
even unto En-eglaim; they shall be a place
to spread forth nets; their fish shall be
according to their kinds, as the fish of the
great sea, exceeding many.
11 But the miry places thereof and the
marshes thereof shall not be healed; they
shall be given to salt.
12 And by the river upon the bank
thereof, on this side and on that side, shall
grow all trees for meat, whose leaf shall
not fade, neither shall the fruit thereof be
consumed: it shall bring forth new fruit
according to his months, because their
waters they issued out of the sanctuary:
and the fruit thereof shall be for meat, and
the leaf thereof for medicine.

JOEL 3

Joel *856 BC*

18 And it shall come to pass in that day,
that the mountains shall drop down new
wine, and the hills shall flow with milk,
and all the rivers of Judah shall flow with
waters, and a fountain shall come forth of
the house of the LORD, and shall water
the valley of Shittim.
20 ...Judah shall dwell forever, and
Jerusalem from generation to generation.
21 For I will cleanse their blood that I
have not cleansed: for the LORD dwelleth
in Zion.

44

THE SEVEN ANGELS OF DEATH

Seven Angels Pouring Vials of the Wrath of God Upon the Earth.

✦✦✦

The seven angels that were being held back until the saints were sealed with the sacred covenants of the temple are now released to pour out their destruction upon the wicked. This will happen at the beginning of the 7th thousand year period, or sometime after the year 2000.

MOSES 7

Enoch *1450 BC*

60 And the Lord said unto Enoch: As I
live, even so will I come in the last days,
in the days of wickedness and vengeance
to fulfil the oath which I have made unto
you concerning the children of Noah;
61 And the day shall come that the Earth
shall rest, but before that day the heavens
shall be darkened, and a veil of darkness
shall cover the Earth; and the heavens
shall shake, and also the Earth; and great
tribulations shall be among the children of
men, but my people will I preserve;
66 But before that day he saw great trib-
ulations among the wicked; and he also
saw the sea, that it was troubled, and
men's hearts failing them, looking forth
with fear for the judgments of the
Almighty God, which should come upon
the wicked.

REVELATION 15

John *95 AD*

1 And I saw another sign in heaven, great
and marvellous, seven angels having the
seven last plagues; for in them is filled up
the wrath of God.
2 And I saw as it were a sea of glass
mingled with fire: and them that had
gotten the victory over the beast, and over
his image, and over his mark, and over the
number of his name, stand on the sea of
glass, having the harps of God.

3 And they sing the song of Moses the servant of God, and the song of the Lamb, saying, Great and marvellous are thy works, Lord God Almighty; just and true are thy ways, thou King of saints.
4 Who shall not fear thee, O Lord, and glorify thy name? for thou only art holy: for all nations shall come and worship before thee; for thy judgments are made manifest.
5 And after that I looked, and, behold, the temple of the tabernacle of the testimony in heaven was opened:
6 And the seven angels came out of the temple, having the seven plagues, clothed in pure and white linen, and having their breasts girded with golden girdles.
7 And one of the four beasts gave unto the seven angels seven golden vials full of the wrath of God, who liveth for ever and ever.
8 And the temple was filled with smoke from the glory of God, and from his power; and no man was able to enter into the temple, till the seven plagues of the seven angels were fulfilled.

DOCTRINE AND COVENANTS 77

Joseph Smith — *March 1832*

12 Q. What are we to understand by the sounding of the trumpets, mentioned in the 8th chapter of Revelation?
A. We are to understand that as God made the world in six days, and on the seventh day he finished his work, and sanctified it, and also formed man out of the dust of the Earth, even so, in the beginning of the seventh thousand years will the Lord God sanctify the Earth, and complete the salvation of man, and judge all things, and shall redeem all things, except that which he hath not put into his power, when he shall have sealed all things, unto the end of all things; and the sounding of the trumpets of the seven angels are the preparing and finishing of his work, in the beginning of the seventh thousand years—the preparing of the way before the time of his coming.

FIRST ANGEL of DEATH

REVELATION 8

John — *95 AD*

7 The first angel sounded, and there followed hail and fire mingled with blood, and they were cast upon the Earth: and the third part of trees was burnt up, and all green grass was burnt up.

REVELATION 16

John — *95 AD*

1 And I heard a great voice out of the temple saying to the seven angels, Go your ways, and pour out the vials of the wrath of God upon the Earth.
2 And the first went, and poured out his vial upon the Earth; and there fell a noisome and grievous sore upon the men which had the mark of the beast, and upon them which worshipped his image.

DOCTRINE AND COVENANTS 29

Joseph Smith — *September 1830*

15 And there shall be weeping and wailing among the hosts of men;
16 And there shall be a great hailstorm sent forth to destroy the crops of the Earth.
17 And it shall come to pass, because of the wickedness of the world, that I will take vengeance upon the wicked, for they will not repent; for the cup of mine indignation is full; for behold, my blood shall not cleanse them if they hear me not.
18 Wherefore, I the Lord God will send forth flies upon the face of the Earth, which shall take hold of the inhabitants thereof, and shall eat their flesh, and shall cause maggots to come in upon them;
19 And their tongues shall be stayed that they shall not utter against me; and their flesh shall fall from off their bones, and their eyes from their sockets;
20 And it shall come to pass that the beasts of the forest and the fowls of the air shall devour them up.

SECOND ANGEL of DEATH

REVELATION 8

John — *95 AD*

8 And the second angel sounded, and as it were a great mountain burning with fire was cast into the sea: and the third part of the sea became blood;
9 And the third part of the creatures which were in the sea, and had life, died; and the third part of the ships were destroyed.

REVELATION 16
John *95 AD*
3 And the second angel poured out his vial
upon the sea; and it became as the blood
of a dead man: and every living soul died
in the sea.

DOCTRINE AND COVENANTS 61
Joseph Smith *August 1831*
4 Nevertheless, I suffered it that ye might
bear record; behold, there are many dan-
gers upon the waters, and more especially
hereafter;
5 For I, the Lord, have decreed in mine
anger many destructions upon the waters;
yea, and especially upon these waters.
6 Nevertheless, all flesh is in mine hand,
and he that is faithful among you shall not
perish by the waters.
13 And now, behold, for your good I gave
unto you a commandment concerning
these things; and I, the Lord, will reason
with you as with men in days of old.
14 Behold, I, the Lord, in the beginning
blessed the waters; but in the last days, by
the mouth of my servant John, I cursed
the waters.
15 Wherefore, the days will come that no
flesh shall be safe upon the waters.
16 And it shall be said in days to come that
none is able to go up to the land of Zion
upon the waters, but he that is upright in
heart.
18 And now I give unto you a command-
ment that what I say unto one I say unto
all, that you shall forewarn your brethren
concerning these waters, that they come
not in journeying upon them, lest their
faith fail and they are caught in snares;
19 I, the Lord, have decreed, and the
destroyer rideth upon the face thereof,
and I revoke not the decree.

THIRD ANGEL of DEATH

REVELATION 8
John *95 AD*
10 And the third angel sounded, and there
fell a great star from heaven, burning as it
were a lamp, and it fell upon the third part
of the rivers, and upon the fountains of
waters;
11 And the name of the star is called
Wormwood: and the third part of the
waters became wormwood; and many
men died of the waters, because they were
made bitter.

REVELATION 16
John *95 AD*
4 And the third angel poured out his vial
upon the rivers and fountains of waters;
and they became blood.
5 And I heard the angel of the waters say,
Thou art righteous, O Lord, which art, and
wast, and shalt be, because thou hast
judged thus.
6 For they have shed the blood of saints
and prophets, and thou hast given them
blood to drink; for they are worthy.
7 And I heard another out of the altar say,
Even so, Lord God Almighty, true and
righteous are thy judgments.

FOURTH ANGEL of DEATH

REVELATION 8
John *95 AD*
12 And the fourth angel sounded, and the
third part of the sun was smitten, and the
third part of the moon, and the third part
of the stars; so as the third part of them
was darkened, and the day shone not for a
third part of it, and the night likewise.
13 And I beheld, and heard an angel flying
through the midst of heaven, saying with
a loud voice, Woe, woe, woe, to the
inhabiters of the Earth by reason of the
other voices of the trumpet of the three
angels, which are yet to sound!

REVELATION 16
John *95 AD*
8 And the fourth angel poured out his vial
upon the sun; and power was given unto
him to scorch men with fire.
9 And men were scorched with great heat,
and blasphemed the name of God, which
hath power over these plagues: and they
repented not to give him glory.

FIFTH ANGEL of DEATH

DOCTRINE AND COVENANTS 77
Joseph Smith *March 1832*
13 Q. When are the things to be accom-
plished, which are written in the 9th
chapter of Revelation?
A. They are to be accomplished after the
opening of the seventh seal, before the
coming of Christ.

REVELATION 9

John *95 AD*

1 And the fifth angel sounded, and I saw a star fall from heaven unto the Earth: and to an angel was given the key of the bottomless pit.
2 And he opened the bottomless pit; and there arose a smoke out of the pit, as the smoke of a great furnace; and the sun and the air were darkened by reason of the smoke of the pit.
3 And there came out of the smoke locusts upon the Earth: and unto them was given power, as the scorpions of the Earth have power.
4 And it was commanded them that they should not hurt the grass of the Earth, neither any green thing, neither any tree; but only those men which have not the seal of God in their foreheads.
5 And to them it was given that they should not kill them, but that they should be tormented five months: and their torment was as the torment of a scorpion, when he striketh a man.
6 And in those days shall men seek death, and shall not find it; and shall desire to die, and death shall flee from them.
7 And the shapes of the locusts were like unto horses prepared unto battle; and on their heads were as it were crowns like gold, and their faces were as the faces of men.
8 And they had hair as the hair of women, and their teeth were as the teeth of lions.
9 And they had breastplates, as it were breastplates of iron; and the sound of their wings was as the sound of chariots of many horses running to battle.
10 And they had tails like unto scorpions, and there were stings in their tails: and their power was to hurt men five months.
11 And they had a king over them, which is the angel of the bottomless pit, whose name in the Hebrew tongue is Abaddon, but in the Greek tongue hath his name Apollyon.
12 One woe is past; and, behold, there come two woes more hereafter.

JOEL 2

Joel *856 BC*

1 Blow ye the trumpet in Zion, and sound an alarm in my holy mountain: let all the inhabitants of the land tremble: for the day of the LORD cometh, for it is nigh at hand;
2 A day of darkness and of gloominess, a day of clouds and of thick darkness, as the morning spread upon the mountains: a great people and a strong; there hath not been ever the like, neither shall be any more after it, even to the years of many generations.
3 A fire devoureth before them; and behind them a flame burneth: the land is as the garden of Eden before them, and behind them a desolate wilder-ness; yea, and nothing shall escape them.
4 The appearance of them is as the appearance of horses; and as horsemen, so shall they run.
5 Like the noise of chariots on the tops of mountains shall they leap, like the noise of a flame of fire that devoureth the stubble, as a strong people set in battle array.
6 Before their face the people shall be much pained: all faces shall gather blackness.
7 They shall run like mighty men; they shall climb the wall like men of war; and they shall march everyone on his ways, and they shall not break their ranks:
8 Neither shall one thrust another; they shall walk everyone in his path: and when they fall upon the

Apache attack helicopter launching its Hellfire missiles over Afghanistan, 2008. John and Joel use the best imagery they can to describe the ferocious sound and power of modern warfare.

sword, they shall not be wounded.
9 They shall run to and fro in the city; they shall run upon the wall, they shall climb up upon the houses; they shall enter in at the windows like a thief.
10 The Earth shall quake before them; the heavens shall tremble: the sun and the moon shall be dark, and the stars shall withdraw their shining:
11 And the LORD shall utter his voice before his army: for his camp is very great: for he is strong that executeth his word: for the day of the LORD is great and very terrible; and who can abide it?

REVELATION 16

John *95 AD*

10 And the fifth angel poured out his vial upon the seat of the beast; and his kingdom was full of darkness; and they gnawed their tongues for pain,
11 And blasphemed the God of heaven because of their pains and their sores, and repented not of their deeds.

SIXTH ANGEL of DEATH

REVELATION 9

John *95 AD*

13 And the sixth angel sounded, and I heard a voice from the four horns of the golden altar which is before God,
14 Saying to the sixth angel which had the trumpet, Loose the four angels which are bound in the *bottomless pit.* [JST]
15 And the four angels were loosed, which were prepared for an hour, and a day, and a month, and a year, for to slay the third part of men.
16 And the number of the army of the horsemen were two hundred thousand thousand: and I heard the number of them.
17 And thus I saw the horses in the vision, and them that sat on them, having breastplates of fire, and of jacinth, and brimstone: and the heads of the horses were as the heads of lions; and out of their mouths issued fire and smoke and brimstone.
18 By these three was the third part of men killed, by the fire, and by the smoke, and by the brimstone, which issued out of their mouths.
19 For their power is in their mouth, and in their tails: for their tails were like unto serpents, and had heads, and with them they do hurt.
20 And the rest of the men which were not killed by these plagues yet repented not of the works of their hands, that they should not worship devils, and idols of gold, and silver, and brass, and stone, and of wood: which neither can see, nor hear, nor walk:
21 Neither repented they of their murders, nor of their sorceries, nor of their fornication, nor of their thefts.

REVELATION 16

John *95 AD*

12 And the sixth angel poured out his vial upon the great river Euphrates; and the water thereof was dried up, that the way of the kings of the east might be prepared.
13 And I saw three unclean spirits like frogs come out of the mouth of the dragon, and out of the mouth of the beast, and out of the mouth of the false prophet.
14 For they are the spirits of devils, working miracles, which go forth unto the kings of the Earth and of the whole world, to gather them to the battle of that great day of God Almighty.
15 Behold, I come as a thief. Blessed is he that watcheth, and keepeth his garments, lest he walk naked, and they see his shame.
16 And he gathered them together into a place called in the Hebrew tongue Armageddon.

JOEL 1

Joel *856 BC*

6 For a nation is come up upon my land, strong, and without number, whose teeth are the teeth of a lion, and he hath the cheek teeth of a great lion.
7 He hath laid my vine waste, and barked my fig tree: he hath made it clean bare, and cast it away; the branches thereof are made white.
8 Lament like a virgin girded with sackcloth for the husband of her youth.
9 The meat offering and the drink offering is cut off from the house of the LORD; the priests, the LORD's ministers, mourn.
10 The field is wasted, the land mourneth; for the corn is wasted: the new wine is dried up, the oil languisheth.
11 Be ye ashamed, O ye husbandmen; howl, O ye vinedressers, for the wheat and

Gog and Magog, by Matthias Gerung, 1500-1570.

for the barley; because the harvest of the field is perished.
12 The vine is dried up, and the fig tree languisheth; the pomegranate tree, the palm tree also, and the apple tree, even all the trees of the field, are withered: because joy is withered away from the sons of men.
13 Gird yourselves, and lament, ye priests: howl, ye ministers of the altar: come, lie all night in sackcloth, ye ministers of my God: for the meat offering and the drink offering is withholden from the house of your God.
16 Is not the meat cut off before our eyes, yea, joy and gladness from the house of our God?
17 The seed is rotten under their clods, the garners are laid desolate, the barns are broken down; for the corn is withered.
18 How do the beasts groan! the herds of cattle are perplexed, because they have no pasture; yea, the flocks of sheep are made desolate.
19 O LORD, to thee will I cry: for the fire hath devoured the pastures of the wilderness, and the flame hath burned all the trees of the field.
20 The beasts of the field cry also unto thee: for the rivers of waters are dried up, and the fire hath devoured the pastures of the wilderness.

JOEL 3

Joel 856 BC

1 For, behold, in those days, and in that time, when I shall bring again the captivity of Judah and Jerusalem,
2 I will also gather all nations, and will bring them down into the valley of Jehoshaphat, and will plead with them there for my people and for my heritage Israel, whom they have scattered among the nations, and parted my land.
3 And they have cast lots for my people; and have given a boy for an harlot, and sold a girl for wine, that they might drink.
9 Proclaim ye this among the Gentiles; Prepare war, wake up the mighty men, let all the men of war draw near; let them come up:
10 Beat your plowshares into swords, and your pruninghooks into spears: let the weak say, I am strong.
11 Assemble yourselves, and come, all ye heathen, and gather yourselves together round about: thither cause thy mighty ones to come down, O LORD.
12 Let the heathen be wakened, and come up to the valley of Jehoshaphat: for there will I sit to judge all the heathen round about.
13 Put ye in the sickle, for the harvest is ripe: come, get you down; for the press is full, the fats overflow; for their wickedness is great.
14 Multitudes, multitudes in the valley of decision: for the day of the LORD is near in the valley of decision.
15 The sun and the moon shall be darkened, and the stars shall withdraw their shining.

EZEKIEL 38

Ezekiel 600 BC

1 And the word of the LORD came unto me, saying,
2 Son of man, set thy face against Gog, the land of Magog, the chief prince of Meshech and Tubal, and prophesy against him,
3 And say, Thus saith the Lord GOD; Behold, I am against thee, O Gog, the chief prince of Meshech and Tubal:

4 And I will turn thee back, and put hooks into thy jaws, and I will bring thee forth, and all thine army, horses and horsemen, all of them clothed with all sorts of armour, even a great company with bucklers and shields, all of them handling swords:
5 Persia, Ethiopia, and Libya with them; all of them with shield and helmet:
6 Gomer, and all his bands; the house of Togarmah of the north quarters, and all his bands: and many people with thee.
7 Be thou prepared, and prepare for thyself, thou, and all thy company that are assembled unto thee, and be thou a guard unto them.
8 After many days thou shalt be visited: in the latter-years thou shalt come into the land that is brought back from the sword, and is gathered out of many people, against the mountains of Israel, which have been always waste: but it is brought forth out of the nations, and they shall dwell safely all of them.
9 Thou shalt ascend and come like a storm, thou shalt be like a cloud to cover the land, thou, and all thy bands, and many people with thee.
10 Thus saith the Lord GOD; It shall also come to pass, that at the same time shall things come into thy mind, and thou shalt think an evil thought:
11 And thou shalt say, I will go up to the land of unwalled villages; I will go to them that are at rest, that dwell safely, all of them dwelling without walls, and having neither bars nor gates,
12 To take a spoil, and to take a prey; to turn thine hand upon the desolate places that are now inhabited, and upon the people that are gathered out of the nations, which have gotten cattle and goods, that dwell in the midst of the land.
13 Sheba, and Dedan, and the merchants of Tarshish, with all the young lions thereof, shall say unto thee, Art thou come to take a spoil? hast thou gathered thy company to take a prey? to carry away silver and gold, to take away cattle and goods, to take a great spoil?
14 Therefore, son of man, prophesy and say unto Gog, Thus saith the Lord GOD; In that day when my people of Israel dwelleth safely, shalt thou not know it?
15 And thou shalt come from thy place out of the north parts, thou, and many people with thee, all of them riding upon horses, a great company, and a mighty army:
16 And thou shalt come up against my people of Israel, as a cloud to cover the land; it shall be in the latter-days, and I will bring thee against my land, that the heathen may know me, when I shall be sanctified in thee, O Gog, before their eyes.
17 Thus saith the Lord GOD; Art thou he of whom I have spoken in old time by my servants the prophets of Israel, which prophesied in those days many years that I would bring thee against them?

JEREMIAH 25

Jeremiah *620 BC*

15 For thus saith the LORD God of Israel unto me; Take the wine cup of this fury at my hand, and cause all the nations, to whom I send thee, to drink it.
16 And they shall drink, and be moved, and be mad, because of the sword that I will send among them.
17 Then took I the cup at the LORD's hand, and made all the nations to drink, unto whom the LORD had sent me:
18 To wit, Jerusalem, and the cities of Judah, and the kings thereof, and the princes thereof, to make them a desolation, an astonishment, an hissing, and a curse; as it is this day;
19 Pharaoh king of Egypt, and his servants, and his princes, and all his people;
20 And all the mingled people, and all the kings of the land of Uz, and all the kings of the land of the Philistines, and Ashkelon, and Azzah, and Ekron, and the remnant of Ashdod,
21 Edom, and Moab, and the children of Ammon,
22 And all the kings of Tyrus, and all the kings of Zidon, and the kings of the isles which are beyond the sea,
23 Dedan, and Tema, and Buz, and all that are in the utmost corners,
24 And all the kings of Arabia, and all the kings of the mingled people that dwell in the desert,
25 And all the kings of Zimri, and all the kings of Elam, and all the kings of the Medes,
26 And all the kings of the north, far and near, one with another, and all the kingdoms of the world, which are upon

the face of the Earth: and the king of Sheshach shall drink after them.
27 Therefore thou shalt say unto them, Thus saith the LORD of hosts, the God of Israel; Drink ye, and be drunken, and spue, and fall, and rise no more, because of the sword which I will send among you.
28 And it shall be, if they refuse to take the cup at thine hand to drink, then shalt thou say unto them, Thus saith the LORD of hosts; Ye shall certainly drink.
29 For, lo, I begin to bring evil on the city which is called by my name, and should ye be utterly unpunished? Ye shall not be unpunished: for I will call for a sword upon all the inhabitants of the Earth, saith the LORD of hosts.

REVELATION 17

John 95 AD

7 And the angel said unto me, Wherefore didst thou marvel? I will tell thee the mystery of the woman, and of the beast that carrieth her, which hath the seven heads and ten horns.
8 The beast that thou sawest was, and is not; and shall ascend out of the bottomless pit, and go into perdition: and they that dwell on the Earth shall wonder, whose names were not written in the book of life from the foundation of the world, when they behold the beast that was, and is not, and yet is.
9 And here is the mind which hath wisdom. The seven heads are seven mountains, on which the woman sitteth.
10 And there are seven kings: five are fallen, and one is, and the other is not yet come; and when he cometh, he must continue a short space.
11 And the beast that was, and is not, even he is the eighth, and is of the seven, and goeth into perdition.
12 And the ten horns which thou sawest are ten kings, which have received no kingdom as yet; but receive power as kings one hour with the beast.
13 These have one mind and shall give their power and strength unto the beast.
14 These shall make war with the Lamb, and the Lamb shall overcome them: for he is Lord of lords, and King of kings: and they that are with him are called, and chosen, and faithful.
15 And he saith unto me, the waters which thou sawest, where the whore sitteth, are peoples, and multitudes, and nations, and tongues.
16 And the ten horns which thou sawest upon the beast, these shall hate the whore, and shall make her desolate and naked, and shall eat her flesh, and burn her with fire.
17 For God hath put in their hearts to fulfil his will, and to agree, and give their kingdom unto the beast, until the words of God shall be fulfilled.
18 And the woman which thou sawest is that great city, which reigneth over the kings of the Earth.

1 NEPHI 22

Nephi, Son of Lehi 580 BC

13 And the blood of that great and abominable church, which is the whore of all the Earth, shall turn upon their own heads; for they shall war among themselves, and the sword of their own hands shall fall upon their own heads, and they shall be drunken with their own blood.
14 And every nation which shall war against thee, O house of Israel, shall be turned one against another, and they shall fall into the pit which they digged to ensnare the people of the Lord. And all that fight against Zion shall be destroyed, and that great whore, who hath perverted the right ways of the Lord, yea, that great and abominable church, shall tumble to the dust and great shall be the fall of it.

ZECHARIAH 14

Zechariah 520 BC

1 Behold, the day of the LORD cometh, and thy spoil shall be divided in the midst of thee.
2 For I will gather all nations against Jerusalem to battle; and the city shall be taken, and the houses rifled, and the women ravished; and half of the city shall go forth into captivity, and the residue of the people shall not be cut off from the city.

DOCTRINE AND COVENANTS 77

Joseph Smith March 1832

15 Q. What is to be understood by the two witnesses, in the eleventh chapter of Revelation?
A. They are two prophets that are to be raised up to the Jewish nation in the last days, at the time of the restoration, and to

prophesy to the Jews after they are gathered and have built the city of Jerusalem in the land of their fathers.

REVELATION 11

John *95 AD*

1 And there was given me a reed like unto a rod: and the angel stood, saying, Rise, and measure the temple of God, and the altar, and them that worship therein.
2 But the court which is without the temple leave out, and measure it not; for it is given unto the Gentiles: and the holy city shall they tread under foot forty and two months.
3 And I will give power unto my two witnesses, and they shall prophesy a thousand two hundred and threescore days, clothed in sackcloth.
4 These are the two olive trees, and the two candlesticks standing before the God of the Earth.
5 And if any man will hurt them, fire proceedeth out of their mouth, and devoureth their enemies: and if any man will hurt them, he must in this manner be killed.
6 These have power to shut heaven, that it rain not in the days of their prophecy: and have power over waters to turn them to blood, and to smite the Earth with all plagues, as often as they will.

ZECHARIAH 4

Zechariah *520 BC*

11 Then answered I, and said unto him, What are these two olive trees upon the right side of the candlestick and upon the left side thereof?
12 And I answered again, and said unto him, What be these two olive branches which through the two golden pipes empty the golden oil out of themselves?
13 And he answered me and said, Knowest thou not what these be? And I said, No, my lord.
14 Then said he, These are the two anointed ones, that stand by the Lord of the whole Earth.

2 NEPHI 8 (see also ISAIAH 51)

Isaiah *740 BC*

18 And none to guide her among all the sons she hath brought forth; neither that taketh her by the hand, of all the sons she hath brought up.
19 These two sons are come unto thee, who shall be sorry for thee—thy desolation and destruction, and the famine and the sword—and by whom shall I comfort thee?
20 Thy sons have fainted, save these two; they lie at the head of all the streets; as a wild bull in a net, they are full of the fury of the Lord, the rebuke of thy God.

Prior to the birth of Christ, the prophet Nephi, son of Helaman, was given the power to command the elements, just as the two prophets will have prior to the Second Coming of Christ in the last days.

HELAMAN 10

Nephi, son of Helaman *22 BC*

4 Blessed art thou, Nephi, for those things which thou hast done; for I have beheld how thou hast with unwearyingness declared the word, which I have given unto thee, unto this people. And thou hast not feared them, and hast not sought thine own life, but hast sought my will, and to keep my commandments.
5 And now, because thou hast done this with such unwearyingness, behold, I will bless thee forever; and I will make thee mighty in word and in deed, in faith and in works; yea, even that all things shall be done unto thee according to thy word, for thou shalt not ask that which is contrary to my will.
6 Behold, thou art Nephi, and I am God. Behold, I declare it unto thee in the presence of mine angels, that ye shall have power over this people, and shall smite the Earth with famine, and with pestilence, and destruction, according to the wickedness of this people.
7 Behold, I give unto you power, that whatsoever ye shall seal on Earth shall be sealed in heaven; and whatsoever ye shall loose on Earth shall be loosed in heaven; and thus shall ye have power among this people.
8 And thus, if ye shall say unto this temple it shall be rent in twain, it shall be done.
9 And if ye shall say unto this mountain, Be thou cast down and become smooth, it shall be done.
10 And behold, if ye shall say that God shall smite this people, it shall come to pass.

11 And now behold, I command you, that ye shall go and declare unto this people, that thus saith the Lord God, who is the Almighty: Except ye repent ye shall be smitten, even unto destruction.

12 And behold, now it came to pass that when the Lord had spoken these words unto Nephi, he did stop and did not go unto his own house, but did return unto the multitudes who were scattered about upon the face of the land, and began to declare unto them the word of the Lord which had been spoken unto him, concerning their destruction if they did not repent.

13 Now behold, notwithstanding that great miracle which Nephi had done in telling them concerning the death of the chief judge, they did harden their hearts and did not hearken unto the words of the Lord.

14 Therefore Nephi did declare unto them the word of the Lord, saying: Except ye repent, thus saith the Lord, ye shall be smitten even unto destruction.

15 And it came to pass that when Nephi had declared unto them the word, behold, they did still harden their hearts and would not hearken unto his words; therefore they did revile against him, and did seek to lay their hands upon him that they might cast him into prison.

16 But behold, the power of God was with him, and they could not take him to cast him into prison, for he was taken by the Spirit and conveyed away out of the midst of them.

17 And it came to pass that thus he did go forth in the Spirit, from multitude to multitude, declaring the word of God, even until he had declared it unto them all, or sent it forth among all the people.

18 And it came to pass that they would not hearken unto his words; and there began to be contentions, insomuch that they were divided against themselves and began to slay one another with the sword.

REVELATION 11

John — *95 AD*

7 And when they shall have finished their testimony, the beast that ascendeth out of the bottomless pit shall make war against them, and shall overcome them, and kill them.

8 And their dead bodies shall lie in the street of the great city, which spiritually is called Sodom and Egypt, where also our Lord was crucified.

9 And they of the people and kindreds and tongues and nations shall see their dead bodies three days and an half, and shall not suffer their dead bodies to be put in graves.

10 And they that dwell upon the Earth shall rejoice over them, and make merry, and shall send gifts one to another; because these two prophets tormented them that dwelt on the Earth.

11 And after three days and an half the Spirit of life from God entered into them, and they stood upon their feet; and great fear fell upon them which saw them.

12 And they heard a great voice from heaven saying unto them, Come up hither. And they ascended up to heaven in a cloud; and their enemies beheld them.

13 And the same hour was there a great earthquake, and the tenth part of the city fell, and in the earthquake were slain of men seven thousand: and the remnant were affrighted, and gave glory to the God of heaven.

14 The second woe is past; and, behold, the third woe cometh quickly.

SEVENTH ANGEL of DEATH

REVELATION 10

John — *95 AD*

1 And I saw another mighty angel come down from heaven, clothed with a cloud: and a rainbow was upon his head, and his face was as it were the sun, and his feet as pillars of fire:

2 And he had in his hand a little book open: and he set his right foot upon the sea, and his left foot on the Earth,

3 And cried with a loud voice, as when a lion roareth: and when he had cried, seven thunders uttered their voices.

4 And when the seven thunders had uttered their voices, I was about to write: and I heard a voice from heaven saying unto me, "Seal up those things which the seven thunders uttered, and write them not."

5 And the angel which I saw stand upon the sea and upon the Earth lifted up his hand to heaven,

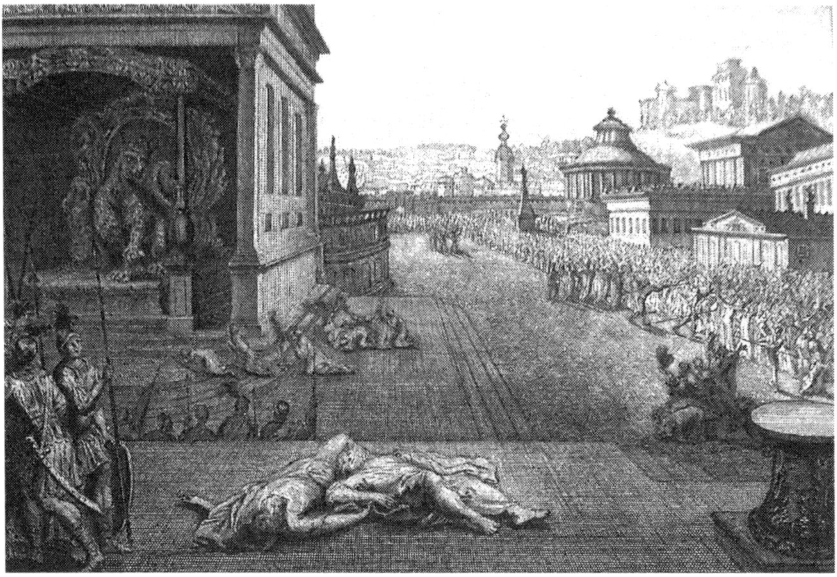

Two Prophets Lie Dead in the Streets of Jerusalem.

6 And sware by him that liveth for ever
and ever, who created heaven, and the
things that therein are, and the Earth, and
the things that therein are, and the sea,
and the things which are therein, that
there should be time no longer:
7 But in the days of the voice of the
seventh angel, when he shall begin to
sound, the mystery of God should be
finished, as he hath declared to his
servants the prophets.

REVELATION 16

John *95 AD*

17 And the seventh angel poured out his
vial into the air; and there came a great
voice out of the temple of heaven, from
the throne, saying, It is done.
18 And there were voices, and thunders,
and lightnings; and there was a great
earthquake, such as was not since men
were upon the Earth, so mighty an
earthquake, and so great.
19 And the great city was divided into
three parts, and the cities of the nations
fell: and great Babylon came in remem-
brance before God, to give unto her the
cup of the wine of the fierceness of his
wrath.
20 And every island fled away, and the
mountains were not found.
21 And there fell upon men a great hail
out of heaven, every stone about the
weight of a talent: and men blasphemed
God because of the plague of the hail; for
the plague thereof was exceeding great.

DOCTRINE AND COVENANTS 49

Joseph Smith *March 1831*

22 And again, verily I say unto you, that
the Son of Man cometh not in the form of
a woman, neither of a man traveling on
the Earth.
23 Wherefore, be not deceived, but con-
tinue in steadfastness, looking forth for
the heavens to be shaken, and the Earth to
tremble and to reel to and fro as a drunken
man, and for the valleys to be exalted, and
for the mountains to be made low, and for
the rough places to become smooth—and
all this when the angel shall sound his
trumpet.

REVELATION 11

John *95 AD*

15 And the seventh angel sounded; and
there were great voices in heaven, saying,
The kingdoms of this world are become

the kingdoms of our Lord, and of his Christ; and he shall reign for ever and ever.

16 And the four and twenty elders, which sat before God on their seats, fell upon their faces, and worshipped God,

17 Saying, We give thee thanks, O Lord God Almighty, which art, and wast, and art to come; because thou hast taken to thee thy great power, and hast reigned.

18 And the nations were angry, and thy wrath is come, and the time of the dead, that they should be judged, and that thou shouldest give reward unto thy servants the prophets, and to the saints, and them that fear thy name, small and great; and shouldest destroy them which destroy the Earth.

19 And the temple of God was opened in heaven, and there was seen in his temple the ark of his testament: and there were lightnings, and voices, and thunderings, and an earthquake, and great hail.

45

CHRIST DESCENDS ON MOUNT ZION

+++

Jerusalem is besieged by a world army of 200 million; the two prophets that vexed this army for 3½ years have been killed and resurrected; a massive earthquake and hailstorm devastates the Earth.

Christ comes in a cloud with the 144,000 high priests and all the holy angels and stands on Mount Zion in Jerusalem. The mountain splits in half and the Saints and Jews escape through the valley. The Jews recognize him as their promised Messiah and Deliverer and inquire about the scars on his hands and feet.

DOCTRINE AND COVENANTS 130
Joseph Smith — April 1843
1 When the Savior shall appear we shall see him as he is. We shall see that he is a man like ourselves.

DOCTRINE AND COVENANTS 34
Joseph Smith — November 1830
7 For behold, verily, verily, I say unto you, the time is soon at hand that I shall come in a cloud with power and great glory.
8 And it shall be a great day at the time of my coming, for all nations shall tremble.

ISAIAH 59
Isaiah — 740 BC
16 And he saw that there was no man, and wondered that there was no intercessor: therefore his arm brought salvation unto him; and his righteousness, it sustained him.
17 For he put on righteousness as a breastplate, and an helmet of salvation upon his head; and he put on the garments of vengeance for clothing, and was clad with zeal as a cloak.
18 According to their deeds, accordingly he will repay, fury to his adversaries, recompence to his enemies; to the islands he will repay recompence.
19 So shall they fear the name of the LORD from the west, and his glory from the rising of the sun. When the enemy shall come in like a flood, the Spirit of the LORD shall lift up a standard against him.
20 And the Redeemer shall come to Zion, and unto them that turn from transgression in Jacob, saith the LORD.
21 As for me, this is my covenant with them, saith the LORD; My spirit that is upon thee, and my words which I have put in thy mouth, shall not depart out of thy mouth, nor out of the mouth of thy seed, nor out of the mouth of thy seed's seed, saith the LORD, from henceforth and forever.

JOSEPH SMITH - MATTHEW 24
Jesus Christ — 33 AD
36 And, as I said before, after the tribulation of those days, and the powers of the heavens shall be shaken, then shall appear the sign of the Son of Man in heaven, and then shall all the tribes of the Earth mourn; and they shall see the Son of Man coming in the clouds of heaven, with power and great glory;
37 And whoso treasureth up my word, shall not be deceived, for the Son of Man shall come, and he shall send his angels before him with the great sound of a trumpet, and they shall gather together the remainder of his elect from the four winds, from one end of heaven to the other.

MARK 13
Jesus Christ — 33 AD
24 But in those days, after that tribulation, the sun shall be darkened, and the moon shall not give her light,
25 And the stars of heaven shall fall, and the powers that are in heaven shall be shaken.

Christ Coming in Glory, by William A Spicer, 1821.

26 And then shall they see the Son of man coming in the clouds with great power and glory.
27 And then shall he send his angels, and shall gather together his elect from the four winds, from the uttermost part of the Earth to the uttermost part of heaven.

LUKE 21

Jesus Christ *33 AD*

27 And then shall they see the Son of man coming in a cloud with power and great glory.
28 And when these things begin to come to pass, then look up, and lift up your heads; for your redemption draweth nigh.
36 Watch ye therefore, and pray always, that ye may be accounted worthy to escape all these things that shall come to pass, and to stand before the Son of man.

MATTHEW 23

Jesus Christ *33 AD*

37 O Jerusalem, Jerusalem, thou that killest the prophets, and stonest them which are sent unto thee, how often would I have gathered thy children together, even as a hen gathereth her

chickens under her wings, and ye would not!
38 Behold, your house is left unto you desolate.
39 For I say unto you, *that* ye shall not see me henceforth *and know that I am he of whom it is written by the prophets, until* ye shall say: Blessed is he who cometh in the name of the Lord, *in the clouds of heaven, and all the holy angels with him. Then understood his disciples that he should come again on the Earth, after that he was glorified and crowned on the right hand of God.* [JST]

REVELATION 14
John — *95 AD*
1 And I looked, and, lo, a Lamb stood on the mount Sion, and with him an hundred forty and four thousand, having his Father's name written in their foreheads.
14 And I looked, and behold a white cloud, and upon the cloud one sat like unto the Son of man, having on his head a golden crown, and in his hand a sharp sickle.

ISAIAH 40
Isaiah — *740 BC*
9 O Zion, that bringest good tidings, get thee up into the high mountain; O Jerusalem, that bringest good tidings, lift up thy voice with strength; lift it up, be not afraid; say unto the cities of Judah, Behold your God!
10 Behold, the Lord GOD will come with strong hand, and his arm shall rule for him: behold, his reward is with him, and his work before him.
11 He shall feed his flock like a shepherd: he shall gather the lambs with his arm, and carry them in his bosom, and shall gently lead those that are with young.

DOCTRINE AND COVENANTS 133
Joseph Smith — *November 1831*
18 When the Lamb shall stand upon Mount Zion, and with him a hundred and forty-four thousand, having his Father's name written on their foreheads.
19 Wherefore, prepare ye for the coming of the Bridegroom; go ye, go ye out to meet him.
20 For behold, he shall stand upon the mount of Olivet, and upon the mighty ocean, even the great deep, and upon the islands of the sea, and upon the land of Zion.

ZECHARIAH 14
Zechariah — *520 BC*
3 Then shall the Lord go forth, and fight against those nations, as when he fought in the day of battle.
4 And his feet shall stand in that day upon the mount of Olives, which is before Jerusalem on the east, and the mount of Olives shall cleave in the midst thereof toward the east and toward the west, and there shall be a very great valley; and half of the mountain shall remove toward the north, and half of it toward the south.
5 And ye shall flee to the valley of the mountains; for the valley of the mountains shall reach unto Azal: yea, ye shall flee, like as ye fled from before the earthquake in the days of Uzziah king of Judah: and the Lord my God shall come, and all the saints with thee.

DOCTRINE AND COVENANTS 45
Joseph Smith — *March 1831*
44 And then they shall look for me, and, behold, I will come; and they shall see me in the clouds of heaven, clothed with power and great glory; with all the holy angels; and he that watches not for me shall be cut off.
48 And then shall the Lord set his foot upon this mount, and it shall cleave in twain, and the Earth shall tremble, and reel to and fro, and the heavens also shall shake.
51 And then shall the Jews look upon me and say: What are these wounds in thine hands and in thy feet?
52 Then shall they know that I am the Lord; for I will say unto them: These wounds are the wounds with which I was wounded in the house of my friends. I am he who was lifted up. I am Jesus that was crucified. I am the Son of God.
53 And then shall they weep because of their iniquities; then shall they lament because they persecuted their king.

ZECHARIAH 13
Zechariah — *520 BC*
1 In that day there shall be a fountain opened to the house of David and to the inhabitants of Jerusalem for sin and for uncleanness.

The Jews are stunned to find their long awaited Messiah is Jesus Christ whom they crucified. The Doubting Thomas, by Carl Bloch.

2 And it shall come to pass in that day, saith the LORD of hosts, that I will cut off the names of the idols out of the land, and they shall no more be remembered: and also I will cause the prophets and the unclean spirit to pass out of the land.
3 And it shall come to pass, that when any shall yet prophesy, then his father and his mother that begat him shall say unto him, Thou shalt not live; for thou speakest lies in the name of the LORD: and his father and his mother that begat him shall thrust him through when he prophesieth.
4 And it shall come to pass in that day, that the prophets shall be ashamed every one of his vision, when he hath prophesied; neither shall they wear a rough garment to deceive:
5 But he shall say, I am no prophet, I am an husbandman; for man taught me to keep cattle from my youth.
6 And one shall say unto him, What are these wounds in thine hands? Then he shall answer, Those with which I was wounded in the house of my friends.

ZECHARIAH 12

Zechariah — *520 BC*

10 And I will pour upon the house of David, and upon the inhabitants of Jerusalem, the spirit of grace and of supplications: and they shall look upon me whom they have pierced, and they shall mourn for him, as one mourneth for his only son, and shall be in bitterness for him, as one that is in bitterness for his firstborn.
11 In that day shall there be a great mourning in Jerusalem, as the mourning of Hadadrimmon in the valley of Megiddon.

REVELATION 1

John — *95 AD*

7 Behold, he cometh with clouds; and every eye shall see him, and they also which pierced him: and all kindreds of the Earth shall wail because of him. Even so, Amen.
8 I am Alpha and Omega, the beginning and the ending, saith the Lord, which is, and which was, and which is to come, the Almighty.

46

CHRIST ENDS THE BATTLE OF ARMAGEDDON

+++

Christ fights for his people and destroys the heathen army with fire, tempest, earthquakes, pestilence, famine, rain, hail, and bloodshed. Birds and other beasts feast on the dead. Burying the dead takes seven months. The weapons of war are burned for seven years.

2 NEPHI 6

Jacob, Son of Lehi — *550 BC*

14 And behold, according to the words of
the prophet, the Messiah will set himself
again the second time to recover them;
wherefore, he will manifest himself unto
them in power and great glory, unto the
destruction of their enemies, when that
day cometh when they shall believe in
him; and none will he destroy that believe
in him.
15 And they that believe not in him shall
be destroyed, both by fire, and by tempest,
and by earthquakes, and by bloodsheds,
and by pestilence, and by famine. And
they shall know that the Lord is God, the
Holy One of Israel.
16 For shall the prey be taken from the
mighty, or the lawful captive delivered?
17 But thus saith the Lord: Even the
captives of the mighty shall be taken
away, and the prey of the terrible shall be
delivered; for the Mighty God shall
deliver his covenant people. For thus saith
the Lord: I will contend with them that
contendeth with thee—
18 And I will feed them that oppress thee,
with their own flesh; and they shall be
drunken with their own blood as with
sweet wine; and all flesh shall know that I
the Lord am thy Savior and thy Redeemer,
the Mighty One of Jacob.

EZEKIEL 38

Ezekiel — *600 BC*

18 And it shall come to pass at the same
time when Gog shall come against the
land of Israel, saith the Lord GOD, that my
fury shall come up in my face.
19 For in my jealousy and in the fire of my
wrath have I spoken, Surely in that day
there shall be a great shaking in the land
of Israel;
20 So that the fishes of the sea, and the
fowls of the heaven, and the beasts of the
field, and all creeping things that creep
upon the Earth, and all the men that are
upon the face of the Earth, shall shake at
my presence, and the mountains shall be
thrown down, and the steep places shall
fall, and every wall shall fall to the ground.
21 And I will call for a sword against him
throughout all my mountains, saith the
Lord GOD: every man's sword shall be
against his brother.
22 And I will plead against him with
pestilence and with blood; and I will rain
upon him, and upon his bands, and upon
the many people that are with him, an
overflowing rain, and great hailstones,
fire, and brimstone.
23 Thus will I magnify myself, and
sanctify myself; and I will be known in the
eyes of many nations, and they shall know
that I am the LORD.

REVELATION 14

John — *95 AD*

9 And the third angel followed them,
saying with a loud voice, If any man
worship the beast and his image, and
receive his mark in his forehead, or in his
hand,
10 The same shall drink of the wine of the
wrath of God, which is poured out with-
out mixture into the cup of his indig-
nation; and he shall be tormented with
fire and brimstone in the presence of the

holy angels, and in the presence of the Lamb:

11 And the smoke of their torment ascendeth up for ever and ever: and they have no rest day nor night, who worship the beast and his image, and whosoever receiveth the mark of his name.

12 Here is the patience of the saints: here are they that keep the commandments of God, and the faith of Jesus.

15 And another angel came out of the temple, crying with a loud voice to him that sat on the cloud, Thrust in thy sickle, and reap: for the time is come for thee to reap; for the harvest of the Earth is ripe.

16 And he that sat on the cloud thrust in his sickle on the Earth; and the Earth was reaped.

17 And another angel came out of the temple, which is in heaven, he also having a sharp sickle.

18 And another angel came out from the altar, which had power over fire; and cried with a loud cry to him that had the sharp sickle, saying, Thrust in thy sharp sickle, and gather the clusters of the vine of the Earth; for her grapes are fully ripe.

19 And the angel thrust in his sickle into the Earth, and gathered the vine of the Earth, and cast it into the great winepress of the wrath of God.

20 And the winepress was trodden without the city, and blood came out of the winepress, even unto the horse bridles, by the space of a thousand and six hundred furlongs.

ISAIAH 30

Isaiah — 740 BC

27 Behold, the name of the LORD cometh from far, burning with his anger, and the burden thereof is heavy: his lips are full of indignation, and his tongue as a devouring fire:

28 And his breath, as an overflowing stream, shall reach to the midst of the neck, to sift the nations with the sieve of vanity: and there shall be a bridle in the jaws of the people, causing them to err.

29 Ye shall have a song, as in the night when a holy solemnity is kept; and gladness of heart, as when one goeth with a pipe to come into the mountain of the LORD, to the mighty One of Israel.

30 And the LORD shall cause his glorious voice to be heard, and shall shew the lighting down of his arm, with the indignation of his anger, and with the flame of a devouring fire, with scattering, and tempest, and hailstones.

ZECHARIAH 12

Zechariah — 520 BC

1 The burden of the word of the LORD for Israel, saith the LORD, which stretcheth forth the heavens, and layeth the foundation of the Earth, and formeth the spirit of man within him.

2 Behold, I will make Jerusalem a cup of trembling unto all the people round about, when they shall be in the siege both against Judah and against Jerusalem.

3 And in that day will I make Jerusalem a burdensome stone for all people: all that burden themselves with it shall be cut in pieces, though all the people of the Earth be gathered together against it.

4 In that day, saith the LORD, I will smite every horse with astonishment, and his rider with madness: and I will open mine eyes upon the house of Judah, and will smite every horse of the people with blindness.

5 And the governors of Judah shall say in their heart, The inhabitants of Jerusalem shall be my strength in the LORD of hosts their God.

6 In that day will I make the governors of Judah like an Earth of fire among the wood, and like a torch of fire in a sheaf; and they shall devour all the people round about, on the right hand and on the left: and Jerusalem shall be inhabited again in her own place, even in Jerusalem.

7 The LORD also shall save the tents of Judah first, that the glory of the house of David and the glory of the inhabitants of Jerusalem do not magnify themselves against Judah.

8 In that day shall the LORD defend the inhabitants of Jerusalem; and he that is feeble among them at that day shall be as David; and the house of David shall be as God, as the angel of the LORD before them.

9 And it shall come to pass in that day, that I will seek to destroy all the nations that come against Jerusalem.

OBADIAH 1

Obadiah 610 BC

17 But upon mount Zion shall be deliverance, and there shall be holiness; and the house of Jacob shall possess their possessions.
18 And the house of Jacob shall be a fire, and the house of Joseph a flame, and the house of Esau for stubble, and they shall kindle in them, and devour them; and there shall not be any remaining of the house of Esau; for the LORD hath spoken it.
19 And they of the south shall possess the mount of Esau; and they of the plain the Philistines: and they shall possess the fields of Ephraim, and the fields of Samaria: and Benjamin shall possess Gilead.
20 And the captivity of this host of the children of Israel shall possess that of the Canaanites, even unto Zarephath; and the captivity of Jerusalem, which is in Sepharad, shall possess the cities of the south.
21 And saviours shall come up on mount Zion to judge the mount of Esau; and the kingdom shall be the LORD's.

ISAIAH 31

Isaiah 740 BC

4 For thus hath the LORD spoken unto me, Like as the lion and the young lion roaring on his prey, when a multitude of shepherds is called forth against him, he will not be afraid of their voice, nor abase himself for the noise of them: so shall the LORD of hosts come down to fight for mount Zion, and for the hill thereof.
5 As birds flying, so will the LORD of hosts defend Jerusalem; defending also he will deliver it; and passing over he will preserve it.

JOEL 3

Joel 856 BC

16 The LORD also shall roar out of Zion, and utter his voice from Jerusalem; and the heavens and the Earth shall shake: but the LORD will be the hope of his people, and the strength of the children of Israel.
17 So shall ye know that I am the LORD your God dwelling in Zion, my holy mountain: then shall Jerusalem be holy, and there shall no strangers pass through her anymore.

2 NEPHI 23 (see also ISAIAH 24)

Isaiah 740 BC

1 The burden of Babylon, which Isaiah the son of Amoz did see.
2 Lift ye up a banner upon the high mountain, exalt the voice unto them, shake the hand, that they may go into the gates of the nobles.
3 I have commanded my sanctified ones, I have also called my mighty ones, for mine anger is not upon them that rejoice in my highness.
4 The noise of the multitude in the mountains like as of a great people, a tumultuous noise of the kingdoms of nations gathered together, the Lord of Hosts mustereth the hosts of the battle.
5 They come from a far country, from the end of heaven, yea, the Lord, and the weapons of his indignation, to destroy the whole land.
6 Howl ye, for the day of the Lord is at hand; it shall come as a destruction from the Almighty.
7 Therefore shall all hands be faint, every man's heart shall melt;
8 And they shall be afraid; pangs and sorrows shall take hold of them; they shall be amazed one at another; their faces shall be as flames.
9 Behold, the day of the Lord cometh, cruel both with wrath and fierce anger, to lay the land desolate; and he shall destroy the sinners thereof out of it.
10 For the stars of heaven and the constellations thereof shall not give their light; the sun shall be darkened in his going forth, and the moon shall not cause her light to shine.
11 And I will punish the world for evil, and the wicked for their iniquity; I will cause the arrogancy of the proud to cease, and will lay down the haughtiness of the terrible.
12 I will make a man more precious than fine gold; even a man than the golden wedge of Ophir.
13 Therefore, I will shake the heavens, and the Earth shall remove out of her place, in the wrath of the Lord of Hosts, and in the day of his fierce anger.
14 And it shall be as the chased roe, and as a sheep that no man taketh up; and they shall every man turn to his own people, and flee every one into his own land.

15 Every one that is proud shall be thrust through; yea, and every one that is joined to the wicked shall fall by the sword.
16 Their children also shall be dashed to pieces before their eyes; their houses shall be spoiled and their wives ravished.
17 Behold, I will stir up the Medes against them, which shall not regard silver and gold, nor shall they delight in it.
18 Their bows shall also dash the young men to pieces; and they shall have no pity on the fruit of the womb; their eyes shall not spare children.
19 And Babylon, the glory of kingdoms, the beauty of the Chaldees' excellency, shall be as when God overthrew Sodom and Gomorrah.
20 It shall never be inhabited, neither shall it be dwelt in from generation to generation: neither shall the Arabian pitch tent there; neither shall the shepherds make their fold there.
21 But wild beasts of the desert shall lie there; and their houses shall be full of doleful creatures; and owls shall dwell there, and satyrs shall dance there.
22 And the wild beasts of the islands shall cry in their desolate houses, and dragons in their pleasant palaces; and her time is near to come, and her day shall not be prolonged. For I will destroy her speedily; yea, for I will be merciful unto my people, but the wicked shall perish.

Battlefield of Gettysburg, Bodies of dead Union soldiers on the field of the first day's battle, 1863. A prelude of more terrible wars to come.

JEREMIAH 25

Jeremiah *620 BC*

30 Therefore prophesy thou against them all these words, and say unto them, The LORD shall roar from on high, and utter his voice from his holy habitation; he shall mightily roar upon his habitation; he shall give a shout, as they that tread the grapes, against all the inhabitants of the Earth.
31 A noise shall come even to the ends of the Earth; for the LORD hath a controversy with the nations, he will plead with all flesh; he will give them that are wicked to the sword, saith the LORD.
32 Thus saith the LORD of hosts, Behold, evil shall go forth from nation to nation, and a great whirlwind shall be raised up from the coasts of the Earth.
33 And the slain of the LORD shall be at that day from one end of the Earth even unto the other end of the Earth: they shall not be lamented, neither gathered, nor buried; they shall be dung upon the ground.

ISAIAH 34

Isaiah *740 BC*

1 Come near, ye nations, to hear; and hearken, ye people: let the Earth hear, and all that is therein; the world, and all things that come forth of it.
2 For the indignation of the LORD is upon all nations, and his fury upon all their armies: he hath utterly destroyed them, he hath delivered them to the slaughter.
3 Their slain also shall be cast out, and their stink shall come up out of their carcasses, and the mountains shall be melted with their blood.
4 And all the host of heaven shall be dissolved, and the heavens shall be rolled together as a scroll: and all their host shall fall down, as the leaf falleth off from the fig tree, and as a falling fig from the fig tree.
5 For my sword shall be bathed in heaven: behold, it shall come down upon Idumea, and upon the people of my curse, to judgment.

EZEKIEL 39

Ezekiel *600 BC*

1 Therefore, thou son of man, prophesy against Gog, and say, Thus saith the Lord GOD; Behold, I am against thee, O Gog, the chief prince of Meshech and Tubal:
2 And I will turn thee back, and leave but the sixth part of thee, and will cause thee to come up from the north parts, and will bring thee upon the mountains of Israel:
3 And I will smite thy bow out of thy left hand, and will cause thine arrows to fall out of thy right hand.
4 Thou shalt fall upon the mountains of Israel, thou, and all thy bands, and the people that is with thee: I will give thee unto the ravenous birds of every sort, and to the beasts of the field to be devoured.
5 Thou shalt fall upon the open field: for I have spoken it, saith the Lord GOD.
6 And I will send a fire on Magog, and among them that dwell carelessly in the isles: and they shall know that I am the LORD.
7 So will I make my holy name known in the midst of my people Israel; and I will not let them pollute my holy name any more: and the heathen shall know that I am the LORD, the Holy One in Israel.
8 Behold, it is come, and it is done, saith the Lord GOD; this is the day whereof I have spoken.
9 And they that dwell in the cities of Israel shall go forth, and shall set on fire and burn the weapons, both the shields and the bucklers, the bows and the arrows, and the handstaves, and the spears, and they shall burn them with fire seven years:
10 So that they shall take no wood out of the field, neither cut down any out of the forests; for they shall burn the weapons with fire: and they shall spoil those that spoiled them, and rob those that robbed them, saith the Lord GOD.
11 And it shall come to pass in that day, that I will give unto Gog a place there of graves in Israel, the valley of the passengers on the east of the sea: and it shall stop the noses of the passengers: and there shall they bury Gog and all his multitude: and they shall call it The valley of Hamon-gog.
12 And seven months shall the house of Israel be burying of them, that they may cleanse the land.
13 Yea, all the people of the land shall bury them; and it shall be to them a renown the day that I shall be glorified, saith the Lord GOD.
14 And they shall sever out men of continual employment, passing through the land to bury with the passengers those that remain upon the face of the Earth, to cleanse it: after the end of seven months shall they search.
15 And the passengers that pass through the land, when any seeth a man's bone, then shall he set up a sign by it, till the buriers have buried it in the valley of Hamon-gog.
16 And also the name of the city shall be Hamonah. Thus shall they cleanse the land.
17 And, thou son of man, thus saith the Lord GOD; Speak unto every feathered fowl, and to every beast of the field, Assemble yourselves, and come; gather yourselves on every side to my sacrifice that I do sacrifice for you, even a great sacrifice upon the mountains of Israel, that ye may eat flesh, and drink blood.
18 Ye shall eat the flesh of the mighty, and drink the blood of the princes of the Earth, of rams, of lambs, and of goats, of bullocks, all of them fatlings of Bashan.
19 And ye shall eat fat till ye be full, and drink blood till ye be drunken, of my sacrifice which I have sacrificed for you.
20 Thus ye shall be filled at my table with horses and chariots, with mighty men, and with all men of war, saith the Lord GOD.
21 And I will set my glory among the heathen, and all the heathen shall see my judgment that I have executed, and my hand that I have laid upon them.
22 So the house of Israel shall know that I am the LORD their God from that day and forward.

47

THE WICKED MOURN FOR BABYLON

+++

Angels announce the fall of Babylon—the whore of the Earth—the great and spacious building—the pride of the Earth. The wicked mourn and are stricken with fear.

REVELATION 18

John *95 AD*

1 And after these things I saw another angel come down from heaven, having great power; and the Earth was lightened with his glory.
2 And he cried mightily with a strong voice, saying, Babylon the great is fallen, is fallen, and is become the habitation of devils, and the hold of every foul spirit, and a cage of every unclean and hateful bird.
3 For all nations have drunk of the wine of the wrath of her fornication, and the kings of the Earth have committed fornication with her, and the merchants of the Earth are waxed rich through the abundance of her delicacies.
4 And I heard another voice from heaven, saying, Come out of her, my people, that ye be not partakers of her sins, and that ye receive not of her plagues.
5 For her sins have reached unto heaven, and God hath remembered her iniquities.
6 Reward her even as she rewarded you, and double unto her double according to her works: in the cup which she hath filled fill to her double.
7 How much she hath glorified herself, and lived deliciously, so much torment and sorrow give her: for she saith in her heart, I sit a queen, and am no widow, and shall see no sorrow.
8 Therefore shall her plagues come in one day, death, and mourning, and famine; and she shall be utterly burned with fire: for strong is the Lord God who judgeth her.

Destruction, by Thomas Cole.

9 And the kings of the Earth, who have committed fornication and lived deliciously with her, shall bewail her, and lament for her, when they shall see the smoke of her burning,
10 Standing afar off for the fear of her torment, saying, Alas, alas, that great city Babylon, that mighty city! for in one hour is thy judgment come.
11 And the merchants of the Earth shall weep and mourn over her; for no man buyeth their merchandise anymore:
12 The merchandise of gold, and silver, and precious stones, and of pearls, and fine linen, and purple, and silk, and scarlet, and all thyine wood, and all manner vessels of ivory, and all manner vessels of most precious wood, and of brass, and iron, and marble,
13 And cinnamon, and odours, and ointments, and frankincense, and wine, and oil, and fine flour, and wheat, and beasts, and sheep, and horses, and chariots, and slaves, and souls of men.
14 And the fruits that thy soul lusted after are departed from thee, and all things which were dainty and goodly are departed from thee, and thou shalt find them no more at all.
15 The merchants of these things, which were made rich by her, shall stand afar off for the fear of her torment, weeping and wailing,
16 And saying, Alas, alas, that great city, that was clothed in fine linen, and purple, and scarlet, and decked with gold, and precious stones, and pearls!
17 For in one hour so great riches is come to nought. And every shipmaster, and all the company in ships, and sailors, and as many as trade by sea, stood afar off,
18 And cried when they saw the smoke of her burning, saying, What city is like unto this great city!
19 And they cast dust on their heads, and cried, weeping and wailing, saying, Alas, alas, that great city, wherein were made rich all that had ships in the sea by reason of her costliness! for in one hour is she made desolate.
20 Rejoice over her, thou heaven, and ye holy apostles and prophets; for God hath avenged you on her.
21 And a mighty angel took up a stone like a great millstone, and cast it into the sea, saying, Thus with violence shall that great city Babylon be thrown down, and shall be found no more at all.
22 And the voice of harpers, and musicians, and of pipers, and trumpeters, shall be heard no more at all in thee; and no craftsman, of whatsoever craft he be, shall be found any more in thee; and the sound of a millstone shall be heard no more at all in thee;
23 And the light of a candle shall shine no more at all in thee; and the voice of the bridegroom and of the bride shall be heard no more at all in thee: for thy merchants were the great men of the Earth; for by thy sorceries were all nations deceived.
24 And in her was found the blood of prophets, and of saints, and of all that were slain upon the Earth.

1 NEPHI 11

Nephi, Son of Lehi — *595 BC*

36 And it came to pass that I saw and bear record, that the great and spacious building was the pride of the world; and it fell, and the fall thereof was exceedingly great. And the angel of the Lord spake unto me again, saying: Thus shall be the destruction of all nations, kindreds, tongues, and people, that shall fight against the twelve apostles of the Lamb.

DOCTRINE AND COVENANTS 45

Joseph Smith — *March 1831*

49 And the Lord shall utter his voice, and all the ends of the Earth shall hear it; and the nations of the Earth shall mourn, and they that have laughed shall see their folly.
50 And calamity shall cover the mocker, and the scorner shall be consumed; and they that have watched for iniquity shall be hewn down and cast into the fire.
74 For when the Lord shall appear he shall be terrible unto them, [enemies of the Saints] that fear may seize upon them, and they shall stand afar off and tremble.
75 And all nations shall be afraid because of the terror of the Lord, and the power of his might. Even so. Amen.

REVELATION 14

John — *95 AD*

8 And there followed another angel, saying, Babylon is fallen, is fallen, that great city, because she made all nations drink of the wine of the wrath of her fornication.

The Whore of Babylon, Lucas Cranach, illustration in Martin Luther's 1534 translation of the Bible.

DOCTRINE AND COVENANTS 88

Joseph Smith *December 1832*

105 And again, another angel shall sound his trump, which is the sixth angel, saying: She is fallen who made all nations drink of the wine of the wrath of her fornication; she is fallen, is fallen!

DOCTRINE AND COVENANTS 29

Joseph Smith *September 1830*

21 And the great and abominable church, which is the whore of all the Earth, shall be cast down by devouring fire, according as it is spoken by the mouth of Ezekiel the prophet, who spoke of these things, which have not come to pass but surely must, as I live, for abominations shall not reign.

REVELATION 19

John *95 AD*

1 And after these things I heard a great voice of much people in heaven, saying, Alleluia; Salvation, and glory, and honour, and power, unto the Lord our God:
2 For true and righteous are his judgments: for he hath judged the great whore, which did corrupt the Earth with her fornication, and hath avenged the blood of his servants at her hand.
3 And again they said, Alleluia. And her smoke rose up for ever and ever.

48

RESURRECTION AND JUDGMENT DAY

+++

Shortly after the battle of Armageddon, and before the total destruction of the wicked and cleansing of the Earth, all who have died that have lived either a celestial or terrestrial law will be resurrected and become immortal. In this resurrected state they will come before God to be judged according to their works during the time of their probation.

JOB 14

Job *600 BC*

1 Man that is born of a woman is of few days, and full of trouble.
2 He cometh forth like a flower, and is cut down: he fleeth also as a shadow, and continueth not.
3 And dost thou open thine eyes upon such an one, and bringest me into judgment with thee?
4 Who can bring a clean thing out of an unclean? not one.
5 Seeing his days are determined, the number of his months are with thee, thou hast appointed his bounds that he cannot pass;
6 Turn from him, that he may rest, till he shall accomplish, as an hireling, his day.
7 For there is hope of a tree, if it be cut down, that it will sprout again, and that the tender branch thereof will not cease.
8 Though the root thereof wax old in the Earth, and the stock thereof die in the ground;
9 Yet through the scent of water it will bud, and bring forth boughs like a plant.
10 But man dieth, and wasteth away: yea, man giveth up the ghost, and where is he?
11 As the waters fail from the sea, and the flood decayeth and drieth up:
12 So man lieth down, and riseth not: till the heavens be no more, they shall not awake, nor be raised out of their sleep.
13 O that thou wouldest hide me in the grave, that thou wouldest keep me secret, until thy wrath be past, that thou wouldest appoint me a set time, and remember me!
14 If a man die, shall he live again? all the days of my appointed time will I wait, till my change come.
15 Thou shalt call, and I will answer thee: thou wilt have a desire to the work of thine hands.

ALMA 40

Alma the Younger *73 BC*

4 Behold, there is a time appointed that all shall come forth from the dead. Now when this time cometh no one knows; but God knoweth the time which is appointed.
5 Now, whether there shall be one time, or a second time, or a third time, that men shall come forth from the dead, it mattereth not; for God knoweth all these things; and it sufficeth me to know that this is the case—that there is a time appointed that all shall rise from the dead.
6 Now there must needs be a space betwixt the time of death and the time of the resurrection.
7 And now I would inquire what becometh of the souls of men from this time of death to the time appointed for the resurrection?
8 Now whether there is more than one time appointed for men to rise it mattereth not; for all do not die at once, and this mattereth not; all is as one day with God, and time only is measured unto men.
9 Therefore, there is a time appointed unto men that they shall rise from the dead; and there is a space between the time of death and the resurrection. And now, concerning this space of time, what becometh of the souls of men is the thing which I have inquired diligently of the Lord to know; and this is the thing of which I do know.
10 And when the time cometh when all shall rise, then shall they know that God

The Resurrection, by Sebastiano Ricci, 1715.

knoweth all the times which are appointed unto man

ALMA 11

Amulek *82 BC*

41 Therefore the wicked remain as though there had been no redemption made, except it be the loosing of the bands of death; for behold, the day cometh that all shall rise from the dead and stand before God, and be judged according to their works.
42 Now, there is a death which is called a temporal death; and the death of Christ shall loose the bands of this temporal death, that all shall be raised from this temporal death.
43 The spirit and the body shall be reunited again in its perfect form; both limb and joint shall be restored to its proper frame, even as we now are at this time; and we shall be brought to stand before God, knowing even as we know now, and have a bright recollection of all our guilt.
44 Now, this restoration shall come to all, both old and young, both bond and free, both male and female, both the wicked and the righteous; and even there shall not so much as a hair of their heads be lost; but everything shall be restored to its perfect frame, as it is now, or in the body, and shall be brought and be arraigned before the bar of Christ the Son, and God the Father, and the Holy Spirit, which is one Eternal God, to be judged according to their works, whether they be good or whether they be evil.
45 Now, behold, I have spoken unto you concerning the death of the mortal body, and also concerning the resurrection of the mortal body. I say unto you that this mortal body is raised to an immortal body, that is from death, even from the first death unto life, that they can die no more; their spirits uniting with their bodies, never to be divided; thus the whole becoming spiritual and immortal, that they can no more see corruption.

ALMA 12

Alma the Younger *82 BC*

12 And Amulek hath spoken plainly concerning death, and being raised from this

mortality to a state of immortality, and being brought before the bar of God, to be judged according to our works.

13 Then if our hearts have been hardened, yea, if we have hardened our hearts against the word, insomuch that it has not been found in us, then will our state be awful, for then we shall be condemned.

14 For our words will condemn us, yea, all our works will condemn us; we shall not be found spotless; and our thoughts will also condemn us; and in this awful state we shall not dare to look up to our God; and we would fain be glad if we could command the rocks and the mountains to fall upon us to hide us from his presence.

15 But this cannot be; we must come forth and stand before him in his glory, and in his power, and in his might, majesty, and dominion, and acknowledge to our everlasting shame that all his judgments are just; that he is just in all his works, and that he is merciful unto the children of men, and that he has all power to save every man that believeth on his name and bringeth forth fruit meet for repentance.

24 And we see that death comes upon mankind, yea, the death which has been spoken of by Amulek, which is the temporal death; nevertheless there was a space granted unto man in which he might repent; therefore this life became a probationary state; a time to prepare to meet God; a time to prepare for that endless state which has been spoken of by us, which is after the resurrection of the dead.

2 NEPHI 9

Jacob, Son of Lehi — *550 BC*

11 And because of the way of deliverance of our God, the Holy One of Israel, this death, of which I have spoken, which is the temporal, shall deliver up its dead; which death is the grave.

12 And this death of which I have spoken, which is the spiritual death, shall deliver up its dead; which spiritual death is hell; wherefore, death and hell must deliver up their dead, and hell must deliver up its captive spirits, and the grave must deliver up its captive bodies, and the bodies and the spirits of men will be restored one to the other; and it is by the power of the resurrection of the Holy One of Israel.

13 O how great the plan of our God! For on the other hand, the paradise of God must deliver up the spirits of the righteous, and the grave deliver up the body of the righteous; and the spirit and the body is restored to itself again, and all men become incorruptible, and immortal, and they are living souls, having a perfect knowledge like unto us in the flesh, save it be that our knowledge shall be perfect.

14 Wherefore, we shall have a perfect knowledge of all our guilt, and our uncleanness, and our nakedness; and the righteous shall have a perfect knowledge of their enjoyment, and their righteousness, being clothed with purity, yea, even with the robe of righteousness.

15 And it shall come to pass that when all men shall have passed from this first death unto life, insomuch as they have become immortal, they must appear before the judgment-seat of the Holy One of Israel; and then cometh the judgment, and then must they be judged according to the holy judgment of God.

18 But, behold, the righteous, the saints of the Holy One of Israel, they who have believed in the Holy One of Israel, they who have endured the crosses of the world, and despised the shame of it, they shall inherit the kingdom of God, which was prepared for them from the foundation of the world, and their joy shall be full forever.

19 O the greatness of the mercy of our God, the Holy One of Israel! For he delivereth his saints from that awful monster the devil, and death, and hell, and that lake of fire and brimstone, which is endless torment.

1 CORINTHIANS 15

Paul — *54 AD*

50 Now this I say, brethren, that flesh and blood cannot inherit the kingdom of God; neither doth corruption inherit incorruption.

51 Behold, I shew you a mystery; We shall not all sleep, but we shall all be changed,

52 In a moment, in the twinkling of an eye, at the last trump: for the trumpet

shall sound, and the dead shall be raised incorruptible, and we shall be changed.
53 For this corruptible must put on incorruption, and this mortal must put on immortality.
54 So when this corruptible shall have put on incorruption, and this mortal shall have put on immortality, then shall be brought to pass the saying that is written, Death is swallowed up in victory.
55 O death, where is thy sting? O grave, where is thy victory?
56 The sting of death is sin; and the strength of sin is the law.
57 But thanks be to God, which giveth us the victory through our Lord Jesus Christ.

MORMON 6

Mormon — *385 AD*

21 And the day soon cometh that your mortal must put on immortality, and these bodies which are now moldering in corruption must soon become incorruptible bodies; and then ye must stand before the judgment-seat of Christ, to be judged according to your works; and if it so be that ye are righteous, then are ye blessed with your fathers who have gone before you.

MORMON 7

Mormon — *385 AD*

5 Know ye that ye must come to the knowledge of your fathers, and repent of all your sins and iniquities, and believe in Jesus Christ, that he is the Son of God, and that he was slain by the Jews, and by the power of the Father he hath risen again, whereby he hath gained the victory over the grave; and also in him is the sting of death swallowed up.
6 And he bringeth to pass the resurrection of the dead, whereby man must be raised to stand before his judgment-seat.
7 And he hath brought to pass the redemption of the world, whereby he that is found guiltless before him at the judgment day hath it given unto him to dwell in the presence of God in his kingdom, to sing ceaseless praises with the choirs above, unto the Father, and unto the Son, and unto the Holy Ghost, which are one God, in a state of happiness which hath no end.

MORMON 9

Moroni — *400 AD*

11 But behold, I will show unto you a God of miracles, even the God of Abraham, and the God of Isaac, and the God of Jacob; and it is that same God who created the heavens and the Earth, and all things that in them are.
12 Behold, he created Adam, and by Adam came the fall of man. And because of the fall of man came Jesus Christ, even the Father and the Son; and because of Jesus Christ came the redemption of man.
13 And because of the redemption of man, which came by Jesus Christ, they are brought back into the presence of the Lord; yea, this is wherein all men are redeemed, because the death of Christ bringeth to pass the resurrection, which bringeth to pass a redemption from an endless sleep, from which sleep all men shall be awakened by the power of God when the trump shall sound; and they shall come forth, both small and great, and all shall stand before his bar, being redeemed and loosed from this eternal band of death, which death is a temporal death.
14 And then cometh the judgment of the Holy One upon them...and he that is righteous shall be righteous still; he that is happy shall be happy still;

ISAIAH 26

Isaiah — *740 BC*

19 Thy dead men shall live, together with my dead body shall they arise. Awake and sing, ye that dwell in dust: for thy dew is as the dew of herbs, and the Earth shall cast out the dead.

MORMON 3

Mormon — *362 AD*

17 Therefore I write unto you, Gentiles, and also unto you, house of Israel, when the work shall commence, that ye shall be about to prepare to return to the land of your inheritance;
18 Yea, behold, I write unto all the ends of the Earth; yea, unto you, twelve tribes of Israel, who shall be judged according to your works by the twelve whom Jesus chose to be his disciples in the land of Jerusalem.

The Resurrection of the Mortals, by Victor Mottez, 1870.

19 And I write also unto the remnant of
this people, who shall also be judged by
the twelve whom Jesus chose in this land;
and they shall be judged by the other
twelve whom Jesus chose in the land of
Jerusalem.
20 And these things doth the Spirit manifest unto me; therefore I write unto you all. And for this cause I write unto you, that ye may know that ye must all stand before the judgment-seat of Christ, yea, every soul who belongs to the whole human family of Adam; and ye must stand to be judged of your works, whether they be good or evil;
21 And also that ye may believe the gospel of Jesus Christ, which ye shall have among you; and also that the Jews, the covenant people of the Lord, shall have other witness besides him whom they saw and heard, that Jesus, whom they slew, was the very Christ and the very God.
22 And I would that I could persuade all ye ends of the Earth to repent and prepare to stand before the judgment-seat of Christ.

REVELATION 14

John *95 AD*

13 And I heard a voice from heaven saying unto me, Write, Blessed are the dead which die in the Lord from henceforth: Yea, saith the Spirit, that they may rest from their labours; and their works do follow them.

DOCTRINE AND COVENANTS 88

Joseph Smith *December 1832*

14 Now, verily I say unto you, that through the redemption which is made for you is brought to pass the resurrection from the dead.
15 And the spirit and the body are the soul of man.
16 And the resurrection from the dead is the redemption of the soul.
17 And the redemption of the soul is through him that quickeneth all things, in

whose bosom it is decreed that the poor
and the meek of the Earth shall inherit it.
27 For notwithstanding they die, they also
shall rise again, a spiritual body.
28 They who are of a celestial spirit shall
receive the same body which was a
natural body; even ye shall receive your
bodies, and your glory shall be that glory
by which your bodies are quickened.
29 Ye who are quickened by a portion of
the celestial glory shall then receive of the
same, even a fulness.

At the day of judgment Christ will advocate for the righteous before the Father.

DOCTRINE AND COVENANTS 45

Joseph Smith — *March 1831*

3 Listen to him who is the advocate with
the Father, who is pleading your cause
before him—
4 Saying: Father, behold the sufferings and
death of him who did no sin, in whom
thou wast well pleased; behold the blood
of thy Son which was shed, the blood of
him whom thou gavest that thyself might
be glorified;
5 Wherefore, Father, spare these my
brethren that believe on my name, that
they may come unto me and have
everlasting life.
6 Hearken, O ye people of my church, and
ye elders listen together, and hear my
voice while it is called today, and harden
not your hearts;
7 For verily I say unto you that I am Alpha
and Omega, the beginning and the end,
the light and the life of the world—a light
that shineth in darkness and the darkness
comprehendeth it not.
8 I came unto mine own, and mine own
received me not; but unto as many as
received me gave I power to do many mir-
acles, and to become the sons of God; and
even unto them that believed on my name
gave I power to obtain eternal life.

DOCTRINE AND COVENANTS 38

Joseph Smith — *January 1831*

4 I am the same which have taken the
Zion of Enoch into mine own bosom; and
verily, I say, even as many as have
believed in my name, for I am Christ, and
in mine own name, by the virtue of the
blood which I have spilt, have I pleaded
before the Father for them.

1 CORINTHIANS 1

Paul — *54 AD*

4 I thank my God always on your behalf,
for the grace of God which is given you by
Jesus Christ;
5 That in everything ye are enriched by
him, in all utterance, and in all know-
ledge;
6 Even as the testimony of Christ was
confirmed in you:
7 So that ye come behind in no gift;
waiting for the coming of our Lord Jesus
Christ:
8 Who shall also confirm you unto the
end, that ye may be blameless in the day
of our Lord Jesus Christ.

3 NEPHI 27

Jesus Christ — *34 AD*

13 Behold I have given unto you my
gospel, and this is the gospel which I have
given unto you—that I came into the
world to do the will of my Father, because
my Father sent me.
14 And my Father sent me that I might be
lifted up upon the cross; and after that I
had been lifted up upon the cross, that I
might draw all men unto me, that as I have
been lifted up by men even so should men
be lifted up by the Father, to stand before
me, to be judged of their works, whether
they be good or whether they be evil—

3 NEPHI 26

Mormon — *34 AD*

3 And he [Jesus Christ] did expound all
things...
4 And even unto the great and last day,
when all people, and all kindreds, and all
nations and tongues shall stand before
God, to be judged of their works, whether
they be good or whether they be evil—
5 If they be good, to the resurrection of
everlasting life; according to the mercy,
and the justice, and the holiness which is
in Christ, who was before the world
began.

MATTHEW 10

Jesus Christ — *32 AD*

32 Whosoever therefore shall confess me
before men, him will I confess also before
my Father which is in heaven.

JOHN 5

John *30 AD*

21 For as the Father raiseth up the dead, and quickeneth them; even so the Son quickeneth whom he will.
22 For the Father judgeth no man, but hath committed all judgment unto the Son:
23 That all men should honour the Son, even as they honour the Father. He that honoureth not the Son honoureth not the Father which hath sent him.
24 Verily, verily, I say unto you, He that heareth my word, and believeth on him that sent me, hath everlasting life, and shall not come into condemnation; but is passed from death unto life.
26 For as the Father hath life in himself; so hath he given to the Son to have life in himself;
27 And hath given him authority to execute judgment also, because he is the Son of man.

49

MY FATHER'S HOUSE HAS MANY MANSIONS

The relative glory of the Sun, Moon, and Stars are comparable to the relative glory of the physical resurrected bodies of those who have lived a celestial, terrestrial, or telestial law.

+++

There are many mansions in the kingdom of heaven. There will be four separate Resurrections and Judgments of the dead. Each Resurrection is based on the law those spirits lived by during the time of their probation, which is their life on Earth and the time they spent in the spirit world after they died up to the Day of Judgment.

JOHN 14

John — *33 AD*

2 In my Father's house are many mansions: if it were not so, I would have told you. I go to prepare a place for you.
3 And if I go and prepare a place for you, I will come again, and receive you unto myself; that where I am, there ye may be also.

DOCTRINE AND COVENANTS 98

Joseph Smith — *August 1833*

18 Let not your hearts be troubled; for in my Father's house are many mansions, and I have prepared a place for you; and where my Father and I am, there ye shall be also.

1 CORINTHIANS 15

Paul — *54 AD*

20 But now is Christ risen from the dead, and become the first fruits of them that slept.
21 For since by man came death, by man came also the resurrection of the dead.
22 For as in Adam all die, even so in Christ shall all be made alive.
23 But every man in his own order: Christ the first fruits; afterward they that are Christ's at his coming.
24 Then cometh the end, when he shall have delivered up the kingdom to God, even the Father; when he shall have put down all rule and all authority and power.
25 For he must reign, till he hath put all enemies under his feet.
26 The last enemy that shall be destroyed is death.
35 But some man will say, How are the dead raised up? and with what body do they come?
36 Thou fool, that which thou sowest is not quickened, except it die:
37 And that which thou sowest, thou sowest not that body that shall be, but bare grain, it may chance of wheat, or of some other grain:

38 But God giveth it a body as it hath pleased him, and to every seed his own body.
39 All flesh is not the same flesh: but there is one kind of flesh of men, another flesh of beasts, another of fishes, and another of birds.
40 Also celestial bodies, and bodies terrestrial, *and bodies telestial*; but the glory of the celestial, one; and the terrestrial, another; *and the telestial, another.* [JST]
41 There is one glory of the sun, and another glory of the moon, and another glory of the stars: for one star differeth from another star in glory.
42 So also is the resurrection of the dead. It is sown in corruption; it is raised in incorruption:
43 It is sown in dishonour; it is raised in glory: it is sown in weakness; it is raised in power:
44 It is sown a natural body; it is raised a spiritual body. There is a natural body, and there is a spiritual body.
45 And so it is written, The first man Adam was made a living soul; the last Adam was made a quickening spirit.
46 Howbeit that was not first which is spiritual, but that which is natural; and afterward that which is spiritual.
47 The first man is of the Earth, Earthy: the second man is the Lord from heaven.
48 As is the Earthy, such are they also that are Earthy: and as is the heavenly, such are they also that are heavenly.
49 And as we have borne the image of the Earthy, we shall also bear the image of the heavenly.

DOCTRINE AND COVENANTS 129

Joseph Smith — *February 1843*

1 There are two kinds of beings in heaven, namely: Angels, who are resurrected personages, having bodies of flesh and bones—
2 For instance, Jesus said: Handle me and see, for a spirit hath not flesh and bones, as ye see me have.
3 Secondly: the spirits of just men made perfect, they who are not resurrected, but inherit the same glory.

DOCTRINE AND COVENANTS 88

Joseph Smith — *December 1832*

36 All kingdoms have a law given;
37 And there are many kingdoms; for there is no space in the which there is no kingdom; and there is no kingdom in which there is no space, either a greater or a lesser kingdom.
38 And unto every kingdom is given a law; and unto every law there are certain bounds also and conditions.
39 All beings who abide not in those conditions are not justified.
40 For intelligence cleaveth unto intelligence; wisdom receiveth wisdom; truth embraceth truth; virtue loveth virtue; light cleaveth unto light; mercy hath compassion on mercy and claimeth her own; justice continueth its course and claimeth its own; judgment goeth before the face of him who sitteth upon the throne and governeth and executeth all things.
41 He comprehendeth all things, and all things are before him, and all things are round about him; and he is above all things, and in all things, and is through all things, and is round about all things; and all things are by him, and of him, even God, forever and ever.
42 And again, verily I say unto you, he hath given a law unto all things, by which they move in their times and their seasons;

DOCTRINE AND COVENANTS 130

Joseph Smith — *April 1843*

18 Whatever principle of intelligence we attain unto in this life, it will rise with us in the resurrection.
19 And if a person gains more knowledge and intelligence in this life through his diligence and obedience than another, he will have so much the advantage in the world to come.
20 There is a law, irrevocably decreed in heaven before the foundations of this world, upon which all blessings are predicated—
21 And when we obtain any blessing from God, it is by obedience to that law upon which it is predicated.

THE KING FOLLETT DISCOURSE

Joseph Smith — *April 7, 1844*

I could go back and trace every object of interest concerning the relationship of man to God, if I had time. I can enter into the mysteries; I can enter largely into the eternal worlds; for Jesus said, "In my Father's house are many mansions; if it were not so, I would have told you. I go to prepare a place for you." [John 14:2.] Paul says, "There is one glory of the sun, and another glory of the moon, and another glory of the stars; for one star differeth from another star in glory. So also is the resurrection of the dead." [1 Cor. 15:41] What have we to console us in relation to the dead? We have reason to have the greatest hope and consolation for our dead of any people on the Earth; for we have seen them walk worthily in our midst, and seen them sink asleep in the arms of Jesus; and those who have died in the faith are now in the celestial kingdom of God. And hence is the glory of the sun.

You mourners have occasion to rejoice, speaking of the death of Elder King Follett; for your husband and father is gone to wait until the resurrection of the dead—until the perfection of the remainder; for at the resurrection your friend will rise in perfect felicity and go to celestial glory, while many must wait myriads of years before they can receive the like blessings; and your expectations and hopes are far above what man can conceive; for why has God revealed it to us?

I am authorized to say, by the authority of the Holy Ghost, that you have no occasion to fear; for he [Brother Follett] is gone to the home of the just. Don't mourn, don't weep. I know it by the testimony of the Holy Ghost that is within me; and you may wait for your friends to come forth to meet you in the morn of the celestial world.

Rejoice, O Israel! Your friends who have been murdered for the truth's sake in the persecutions shall triumph gloriously in the celestial world, while their murderers shall welter for ages in torment, even until they shall have paid the uttermost farthing. I say this for the benefit of strangers.

I have a father, brothers, children, and friends who have gone to a world of spirits. They are only absent for a moment. They are in the spirit, and we shall soon meet again. The time will soon arrive when the trumpet shall sound. When we depart, we shall hail our mothers, fathers, friends, and all whom we love, who have fallen asleep in Jesus. There will be no fear of mobs, persecutions, or malicious lawsuits and arrests; but it will be an eternity of felicity.

50

THE FIRST RESURRECTION

CELESTIAL SPIRITS

+++

The celestial spirits will be resurrected and judged just prior to the Second Coming of Christ and the cleansing of the Earth. They will meet him along with the living saints as he descends on that glorious day. (The celestial spirits who lived before Christ's earthly ministry were resurrected just after Christ was resurrected.)

DOCTRINE AND COVENANTS 45
Joseph Smith — *March 1831*
45 But before the arm of the Lord shall fall, an angel shall sound his trump, and the saints that have slept shall come forth to meet me in the cloud.
46 Wherefore, if ye have slept in peace blessed are you; for as you now behold me and know that I am, even so shall ye come unto me and your souls shall live, and your redemption shall be perfected; and the saints shall come forth from the four quarters of the Earth.
47 Then shall the arm of the Lord fall upon the nations.

DOCTRINE AND COVENANTS 88
Joseph Smith — *December 1832*
97 And they who have slept in their graves shall come forth, for their graves shall be opened; and they also shall be caught up to meet him in the midst of the pillar of heaven—
98 They are Christ's, the first fruits, they who shall descend with him first, and they who are on the Earth and in their graves, who are first caught up to meet him; and all this by the voice of the sounding of the trump of the angel of God.

EZEKIEL 37
Ezekiel — *600 BC*
1 The hand of the LORD was upon me, and carried me out in the spirit of the LORD, and set me down in the midst of the valley which was full of bones,
2 And caused me to pass by them round about: and, behold, there were very many in the open valley; and, lo, they were very dry.
3 And he said unto me, Son of man, can these bones live? And I answered, O Lord GOD, thou knowest.
4 Again he said unto me, Prophesy upon these bones, and say unto them, O ye dry bones, hear the word of the LORD.
5 Thus saith the Lord GOD unto these bones; Behold, I will cause breath to enter into you, and ye shall live:
6 And I will lay sinews upon you, and will bring up flesh upon you, and cover you with skin, and put breath in you, and ye shall live; and ye shall know that I am the LORD.
7 So I prophesied as I was commanded: and as I prophesied, there was a noise, and behold a shaking, and the bones came together, bone to his bone.
8 And when I beheld, lo, the sinews and the flesh came up upon them, and the skin covered them above: but there was no breath in them.
9 Then said he unto me, Prophesy unto the wind, prophesy, son of man, and say to the wind, Thus saith the Lord GOD; Come from the four winds, O breath, and breathe upon these slain, that they may live.
10 So I prophesied as he commanded me, and the breath came into them, and they lived, and stood up upon their feet, an exceeding great army.

The righteous dead come forth in the First Resurrection of the just. By Andrea da Firenze, 1366, Santa Maria Novella, Florence, Italy.

11 Then he said unto me, Son of man, these bones are the whole house of Israel: behold, they say, Our bones are dried, and our hope is lost: we are cut off for our parts.
12 Therefore prophesy and say unto them, Thus saith the Lord GOD; Behold, O my people, I will open your graves, and cause you to come up out of your graves, and bring you into the land of Israel.
13 And ye shall know that I am the LORD, when I have opened your graves, O my people, and brought you up out of your graves,
14 And shall put my spirit in you, and ye shall live, and I shall place you in your own land: then shall ye know that I the LORD have spoken it, and performed it, saith the LORD.

DOCTRINE AND COVENANTS 76

Joseph Smith *February 1832*

50 And again we bear record—for we saw and heard, and this is the testimony of the gospel of Christ concerning them who shall come forth in the resurrection of the just—
51 They are they who received the testimony of Jesus, and believed on his name and were baptized after the manner of his burial, being buried in the water in his name, and this according to the commandment which he has given—
52 That by keeping the commandments they might be washed and cleansed from all their sins, and receive the Holy Spirit by the laying on of the hands of him who is ordained and sealed unto this power;
53 And who overcome by faith, and are sealed by the Holy Spirit of promise, which the Father sheds forth upon all those who are just and true.
54 They are they who are the church of the Firstborn.
55 They are they into whose hands the Father has given all things—
56 They are they who are priests and kings, who have received of his fulness, and of his glory;

57 And are priests of the Most High, after
the order of Melchizedek, which was after
the order of Enoch, which was after the
order of the Only Begotten Son.
58 Wherefore, as it is written, they are
gods, even the sons of God—
59 Wherefore, all things are theirs,
whether life or death, or things present, or
things to come, all are theirs and they are
Christ's, and Christ is God's.
60 And they shall overcome all things.
61 Wherefore, let no man glory in man,
but rather let him glory in God, who shall
subdue all enemies under his feet.
62 These shall dwell in the presence of
God and his Christ forever and ever.
63 These are they whom he shall bring
with him, when he shall come in the
clouds of heaven to reign on the Earth
over his people.
64 These are they who shall have part in
the first resurrection.
65 These are they who shall come forth in
the resurrection of the just.
66 These are they who are come unto
Mount Zion, and unto the city of the
living God, the heavenly place, the holiest
of all.
67 These are they who have come to an
innumerable company of angels, to the
general assembly and church of Enoch,
and of the Firstborn.
68 These are they whose names are
written in heaven, where God and Christ
are the judge of all.
69 These are they who are just men made
perfect through Jesus the mediator of the
new covenant, who wrought out this per-
fect atonement through the shedding of
his own blood.
70 These are they whose bodies are
celestial, whose glory is that of the sun,
even the glory of God, the highest of all,
whose glory the sun of the firmament is
written of as being typical.
92 And thus we saw the glory of the
celestial, which excels in all things—
where God, even the Father, reigns upon
his throne forever and ever;
93 Before whose throne all things bow in
humble reverence, and give him glory
forever and ever.
94 They who dwell in his presence are the
church of the Firstborn; and they see as
they are seen, and know as they are
known, having received of his fulness and
of his grace;
95 And he makes them equal in power,
and in might, and in dominion.
96 And the glory of the celestial is one,
even as the glory of the sun is one.

HEBREWS 12

Paul *68 AD*

22 But ye are come unto mount Sion, and
unto the city of the living God, the
heavenly Jerusalem, and to an innum-
erable company of angels,
23 To the general assembly and church of
the firstborn, which are written in
heaven, and to God the Judge of all, and to
the spirits of just men made perfect...

DOCTRINE AND COVENANTS 133

Joseph Smith *November 1831*

52 And now the year of my redeemed is
come; and they shall mention the loving
kindness of their Lord, and all that he has
bestowed upon them according to his
goodness, and according to his loving
kindness, forever and ever.
53 In all their afflictions he was afflicted.
And the angel of his presence saved them;
and in his love, and in his pity, he
redeemed them, and bore them, and
carried them all the days of old;
54 Yea, and Enoch also, and they who
were with him; the prophets who were
before him; and Noah also, and they who
were before him; and Moses also, and they
who were before him;
55 And from Moses to Elijah, and from
Elijah to John, who were with Christ in
his resurrection, and the holy apostles,
with Abraham, Isaac, and Jacob, shall be
in the presence of the Lamb.
56 And the graves of the saints shall be
opened; and they shall come forth and
stand on the right hand of the Lamb, when
he shall stand upon Mount Zion, and upon
the holy city, the New Jerusalem; and they
shall sing the song of the Lamb, day and
night forever and ever.

DOCTRINE AND COVENANTS 29

Joseph Smith *September 1830*

12 And again, verily, verily, I say unto
you, and it hath gone forth in a firm
decree, by the will of the Father, that mine
apostles, the Twelve which were with me
in my ministry at Jerusalem, shall stand at

my right hand at the day of my coming in a pillar of fire, being clothed with robes of righteousness, with crowns upon their heads, in glory even as I am, to judge the whole house of Israel, even as many as have loved me and kept my commandments, and none else.
13 For a trump shall sound both long and loud, even as upon Mount Sinai, and all the Earth shall quake, and they shall come forth—yea, even the dead which died in me, to receive a crown of righteousness, and to be clothed upon, even as I am, to be with me, that we may be one.

MATTHEW 19
Jesus Christ — *32 AD*

27 Then answered Peter and said unto him, Behold, we have forsaken all, and followed thee; what shall we have therefore?
28 And Jesus said unto them, Verily I say unto you, That ye which have followed me, in the *resurrection* when the Son of man shall sit in the throne of his glory, ye also shall sit upon twelve thrones, judging the twelve tribes of Israel. [JST]
29 And everyone that hath forsaken houses, or brethren, or sisters, or father, or mother, or wife, or children, or lands, for my name's sake, shall receive an hundredfold, and shall inherit everlasting life.

COLOSSIANS 3
Paul — *62 AD*

4 When Christ, who is our life, shall appear, then shall ye also appear with him in glory.

1 THESSALONIANS 4
Paul — *51 AD*

14 For if we believe that Jesus died and rose again, even so them also which asleep in Jesus will God bring with him.
15 For this we say unto you by the word of the Lord, that *they who* are alive *at* the coming of the Lord, shall not prevent them *who remain unto the coming of the Lord, who are asleep.*
16 For the Lord himself shall descend from heaven with a shout, with the voice of the archangel, and with the trump of God: and the dead in Christ shall rise first:
17 Then *they who* are alive, shall be caught up together *into* the clouds *with them who remain,* to meet the Lord in the air; and so shall we be ever with the Lord. [JST]

1 PETER 5
Peter — *64 AD*

4 And when the chief Shepherd shall appear, ye shall receive a crown of glory that fadeth not away.

1 THESSALONIANS 2
Paul — *51 AD*

19 For what is our hope, or joy, or crown of rejoicing? Are not even ye in the presence of our Lord Jesus Christ at his coming?
20 For ye are our glory and joy.

1 THESSALONIANS 3
Paul — *51 AD*

13 To the end he may stablish your hearts unblameable in holiness before God, even our Father, at the coming of our Lord Jesus Christ with all his saints.

2 THESSALONIANS 1
Paul — *52 AD*

10 When he shall come to be glorified in his saints, and to be admired in all them that believe (because our testimony among you was believed) in that day.

JOB 19
Job — *600 BC*

25 For I know that my redeemer liveth, and that he shall stand at the latter-day upon the Earth:
26 And though after my skin worms destroy this body, yet in my flesh shall I see God:
27 Whom I shall see for myself, and mine eyes shall behold, and not another; though my reins be consumed within me.

REVELATION 20
John — *95 AD*

4 And I saw thrones, and they sat upon them, and judgment was given unto them: and I saw the souls of them that were beheaded for the witness of Jesus, and for the word of God, and which had not worshipped the beast, neither his image, neither had received his mark upon their foreheads, or in their hands; and they lived and reigned with Christ a thousand years.
5 … This is the first resurrection.

6 Blessed and holy is he that hath part in the first resurrection: on such the second death hath no power, but they shall be priests of God and of Christ, and shall reign with him a thousand years.

REVELATION 14

John — *95 AD*

2 And I heard a voice from heaven, as the voice of many waters, and as the voice of a great thunder: and I heard the voice of harpers harping with their harps:
3 And they sung as it were a new song before the throne, and before the four beasts, and the elders: and no man could learn that song but the hundred and forty and four thousand, which were redeemed from the Earth.
4 These are they which were not defiled with women; for they are virgins. These are they which follow the Lamb whithersoever he goeth. These were redeemed from among men, being the first fruits unto God and to the Lamb.
5 And in their mouth was found no guile: for they are without fault before the throne of God.

MATTHEW 25

Jesus Christ — *33 AD*

31 When the Son of man shall come in his glory, and all the holy angels with him, then shall he sit upon the throne of his glory:
32 And before him shall be gathered all nations: and he shall separate them one from another, as a shepherd divideth his sheep from the goats:
33 And he shall set the sheep on his right hand, but the goats on the left.
34 Then shall the King say unto them on his right hand, Come, ye blessed of my Father, inherit the kingdom prepared for you from the foundation of the world:
35 For I was an hungred, and ye gave me meat: I was thirsty, and ye gave me drink: I was a stranger, and ye took me in:
36 Naked, and ye clothed me: I was sick, and ye visited me: I was in prison, and ye came unto me.
37 Then shall the righteous answer him, saying, Lord, when saw we thee an hungred, and fed thee? or thirsty, and gave thee drink?
38 When saw we thee a stranger, and took thee in? or naked, and clothed thee?
39 Or when saw we thee sick, or in prison, and came unto thee?
40 And the King shall answer and say unto them, Verily I say unto you, Inasmuch as ye have done it unto one of the least of these my brethren, ye have done it unto me.
46 And [the righteous] shall go ... into life eternal.

MOSIAH 15

Alma the Elder — *147 BC*

1 And now, it came to pass that Alma, who had fled from the servants of king Noah, repented of his sins and iniquities, and went about privately among the people, and began to teach the words of Abinadi—
2 Yea, concerning that which was to come, and also concerning the resurrection of the dead, and the redemption of the people, which was to be brought to pass through the power, and sufferings, and death of Christ, and his resurrection and ascension into heaven.
8 And it came to pass that he said unto them: Behold, here are the waters of Mormon (for thus were they called) and now, as ye are desirous to come into the fold of God, and to be called his people, and are willing to bear one another's burdens, that they may be light;
9 Yea, and are willing to mourn with those that mourn; yea, and comfort those that stand in need of comfort, and to stand as witnesses of God at all times and in all things, and in all places that ye may be in, even until death, that ye may be redeemed of God, and be numbered with those of the first resurrection, that ye may have eternal life—
10 Now I say unto you, if this be the desire of your hearts, what have you against being baptized in the name of the Lord, as a witness before him that ye have entered into a covenant with him, that ye will serve him and keep his commandments, that he may pour out his Spirit more abundantly upon you?
11 And now when the people had heard these words, they clapped their hands for joy, and exclaimed: This is the desire of our hearts.

PSALM 16

David — *1000 BC*

10 For thou wilt not leave my soul
in hell; neither wilt thou suffer
thine Holy One to see corruption.
11 Thou wilt shew me the path of
life: in thy presence is fulness of
joy; at thy right hand there are
pleasures for evermore.

JOHN 5

Jesus Christ — *31 AD*

21 For as the Father raiseth up the
dead, and quickeneth them; even
so the Son quickeneth whom he
will.
24 Verily, verily, I say unto you, He
that heareth my word, and
believeth on him that sent me,
hath everlasting life, and shall not
come into condemnation; but is
passed from death unto life.

JOHN 6

Jesus Christ — *31 AD*

40 And this is the will of him that
sent me, that everyone which seeth
the Son, and believeth on him, may
have everlasting life: and I will
raise him up *in the resurrection of
the just* at the last day. [JST]
47 Verily, verily, I say unto you, He
that believeth on me hath ever-
lasting life.
54 Whoso eateth my flesh, and drinketh
my blood, hath eternal life; and I will raise
him up and I will raise him up *in the
resurrection of the just* at the last day.
[JST]

Figure of Christ, by Heinrich Hoffman, 1884.

3 NEPHI 27

Jesus Christ — *34 AD*

15 And for this cause have I been lifted up;
therefore, according to the power of the
Father I will draw all men unto me, that
they may be judged according to their
works.
16 And it shall come to pass, that whoso
repenteth and is baptized in my name
shall be filled; and if he endureth to the
end, behold, him will I hold guiltless
before my Father at that day when I shall
stand to judge the world.
20 Now this is the commandment: Repent,
all ye ends of the Earth, and come unto me
and be baptized in my name, that ye may
be sanctified by the reception of the Holy
Ghost, that ye may stand spotless before
me at the last day.
21 Verily, verily, I say unto you, this is my
gospel; and ye know the things that ye
must do in my church; for the works
which ye have seen me do that shall ye
also do; for that which ye have seen me do
even that shall ye do;
22 Therefore, if ye do these things blessed
are ye, for ye shall be lifted up at the last
day.

51

THE FIRST RESURRECTION

THOSE CONVERTED AFTER DEATH

The Valley of Tears, by Gustave Dore, 1883

+++

After Christ's Resurrection, he visited the spirits of the righteous in the spirit world and organized a missionary effort there where all spirits would have the opportunity to learn of and to accept Christ as their Lord and Savior. Those spirits who accepted Christ in the spirit world and are living a celestial law will also rise in the First Resurrection.

JOHN 5

John *30 AD*

25 Verily, verily, I say unto you, The hour is coming, and now is, when the dead shall hear the voice of the Son of God: and they that hear shall live.
28 Marvel not at this: for the hour is coming, in the which all that are in the graves shall hear his voice,
29 And shall come forth; they that have done good, unto the resurrection of life;

1 PETER 3

Peter *64 AD*

18 For Christ also hath once suffered for sins, the just for the unjust, that he might bring us to God, being put to death in the flesh, but quickened by the Spirit:
19 By which also he went and preached unto the spirits in prison;
20 *Some of whom* were disobedient *in the days of Noah, while* the longsuffering of God waited in the days of Noah, while the ark was a preparing, wherein few, that is, eight souls were saved by water. [JST]
21 The like figure whereunto even baptism doth also now save us (not the putting away of the filth of the flesh, but the answer of a good conscience toward God,) by the resurrection of Jesus Christ:
22 Who is gone into heaven, and is on the right hand of God; angels and authorities and powers being made subject unto him.

1 PETER 4

Peter *64 AD*

5 Who shall give account to him that is ready to judge the quick and the dead.
6 *Because of this, is* the gospel preached to them *who* are dead, that they might be judged according to men in the flesh, but live *in the spirit* according to *the will of* God. [JST]

1 CORINTHIANS 15

Paul *54 AD*

29 Else what shall they do which are baptized for the dead, if the dead rise not at all? why are they then baptized for the dead?

DOCTRINE AND COVENANTS 138

Joseph F. Smith *October 1918*

6 I opened the Bible and read the third and fourth chapters of the first epistle of Peter,
11 As I pondered over these things which are written, the eyes of my understanding were opened, and the Spirit of the Lord rested upon me, and I saw the hosts of the dead, both small and great.
12 And there were gathered together in one place an innumerable company of the spirits of the just, who had been faithful in the testimony of Jesus while they lived in mortality;
13 And who had offered sacrifice in the similitude of the great sacrifice of the Son of God, and had suffered tribulation in their Redeemer's name.
14 All these had departed the mortal life, firm in the hope of a glorious resurrection, through the grace of God the Father and his Only Begotten Son, Jesus Christ.
15 I beheld that they were filled with joy and gladness, and were rejoicing together because the day of their deliverance was at hand.
16 They were assembled awaiting the advent of the Son of God into the spirit world, to declare their redemption from the bands of death.
17 Their sleeping dust was to be restored unto its perfect frame, bone to his bone, and the sinews and the flesh upon them, the spirit and the body to be united never again to be divided, that they might receive a fulness of joy.
18 While this vast multitude waited and conversed, rejoicing in the hour of their deliverance from the chains of death, the Son of God appeared, declaring liberty to the captives who had been faithful;
19 And there he preached to them the everlasting gospel, the doctrine of the resurrection and the redemption of mankind from the fall, and from individual sins on conditions of repentance.
20 But unto the wicked he did not go, and among the ungodly and the unrepentant who had defiled themselves while in the flesh, his voice was not raised;
21 Neither did the rebellious who rejected the testimonies and the warnings of the ancient prophets behold his presence, nor look upon his face.
22 Where these were, darkness reigned, but among the righteous there was peace;
23 And the saints rejoiced in their redemption, and bowed the knee and acknowledged the Son of God as their Redeemer and Deliverer from death and the chains of hell.
24 Their countenances shone, and the radiance from the presence of the Lord rested upon them, and they sang praises unto his holy name.
29 And as I wondered, my eyes were opened, and my understanding quickened, and I perceived that the Lord went not in person among the wicked and the disobedient who had rejected the truth, to teach them;
30 But behold, from among the righteous, he organized his forces and appointed messengers, clothed with power and authority, and commissioned them to go forth and carry the light of the gospel to them that were in darkness, even to all the spirits of men; and thus was the gospel preached to the dead.
31 And the chosen messengers went forth to declare the acceptable day of the Lord and proclaim liberty to the captives who were bound, even unto all who would repent of their sins and receive the gospel.
32 Thus was the gospel preached to those who had died in their sins, without a knowledge of the truth, or in transgression, having rejected the prophets.
33 These were taught faith in God, repentance from sin, vicarious baptism for the remission of sins, the gift of the Holy Ghost by the laying on of hands,
34 And all other principles of the gospel that were necessary for them to know in order to qualify themselves that they

might be judged according to men in the flesh, but live according to God in the spirit.

35 And so it was made known among the dead, both small and great, the unrighteous as well as the faithful, that redemption had been wrought through the sacrifice of the Son of God upon the cross.

36 Thus was it made known that our Redeemer spent his time during his sojourn in the world of spirits, instructing and preparing the faithful spirits of the prophets who had testified of him in the flesh;

37 That they might carry the message of redemption unto all the dead, unto whom he could not go personally, because of their rebellion and transgression, that they through the ministration of his servants might also hear his words.

38 Among the great and mighty ones who were assembled in this vast congregation of the righteous were Father Adam, the Ancient of Days and father of all,

39 And our glorious Mother Eve, with many of her faithful daughters who had lived through the ages and worshiped the true and living God.

40 Abel, the first martyr, was there, and his brother Seth, one of the mighty ones, who was in the express image of his father, Adam.

41 Noah, who gave warning of the flood; Shem, the great high priest; Abraham, the father of the faithful; Isaac, Jacob, and Moses, the great law-giver of Israel;

42 And Isaiah, who declared by prophecy that the Redeemer was anointed to bind up the broken-hearted, to proclaim liberty to the captives, and the opening of the prison to them that were bound, were also there.

43 Moreover, Ezekiel, who was shown in vision the great valley of dry bones, which were to be clothed upon with flesh, to come forth again in the resurrection of the dead, living souls;

44 Daniel, who foresaw and foretold the establishment of the kingdom of God in the latter-days, never again to be destroyed nor given to other people;

45 Elias, who was with Moses on the Mount of Transfiguration;

46 And Malachi, the prophet who testified of the coming of Elijah—of whom also Moroni spake to the Prophet Joseph Smith, declaring that he should come before the ushering in of the great and dreadful day of the Lord—were also there.

47 The Prophet Elijah was to plant in the hearts of the children the promises made to their fathers,

48 Foreshadowing the great work to be done in the temples of the Lord in the dispensation of the fulness of times, for the redemption of the dead, and the sealing of the children to their parents, lest the whole Earth be smitten with a curse and utterly wasted at his coming.

49 All these and many more, even the prophets who dwelt among the Nephites and testified of the coming of the Son of God, mingled in the vast assembly and waited for their deliverance,

50 For the dead had looked upon the long absence of their spirits from their bodies as a bondage.

51 These the Lord taught, and gave them power to come forth, after his resurrection from the dead, to enter into his Father's kingdom, there to be crowned with immortality and eternal life,

52 And continue thenceforth their labor as had been promised by the Lord, and be partakers of all blessings which were held in reserve for them that love him.

53 The Prophet Joseph Smith, and my father, Hyrum Smith, Brigham Young, John Taylor, Wilford Woodruff, and other choice spirits who were reserved to come forth in the fulness of times to take part in laying the foundations of the great latter-day work,

54 Including the building of the temples and the performance of ordinances therein for the redemption of the dead, were also in the spirit world.

55 I observed that they were also among the noble and great ones who were chosen in the beginning to be rulers in the Church of God.

56 Even before they were born, they, with many others, received their first lessons in the world of spirits and were prepared to come forth in the due time of the Lord to labor in his vineyard for the salvation of the souls of men.

57 I beheld that the faithful elders of this dispensation, when they depart from mortal life, continue their labors in the preaching of the gospel of repentance and redemption, through the sacrifice of the

Only Begotten Son of God, among those who are in darkness and under the bondage of sin in the great world of the spirits of the dead.
58 The dead who repent will be redeemed, through obedience to the ordinances of the house of God,
59 And after they have paid the penalty of their transgressions, and are washed clean, shall receive a reward according to their works, for they are heirs of salvation.
60 Thus was the vision of the redemption of the dead revealed to me, and I bear record, and I know that this record is true, through the blessing of our Lord and Savior, Jesus Christ, even so. Amen.

All spirits who died without a knowledge of Christ, who ignorantly sinned without the law, or who died as children, and who have accepted Jesus Christ in the spirit world will come forth in the First Resurrection.

DOCTRINE AND COVENANTS 88
Joseph Smith *December 1832*
99 And after this another angel shall sound, which is the second trump; and then cometh the redemption of those who are Christ's at his coming; who have received their part in that prison which is prepared for them, that they might receive the gospel, and be judged according to men in the flesh.

ROMANS 5
Paul *57 AD*
13 (For until the law sin was in the world: but sin is not imputed when there is no law.

DOCTRINE AND COVENANTS 45
Joseph Smith *March 1831*
54 And then shall the heathen nations be redeemed, and they that knew no law shall have part in the first resurrection; and it shall be tolerable for them.

ROMANS 2
Paul *57 AD*
12 For as many as have sinned without law shall also perish without law: and as many as have sinned in the law shall be judged by the law;
13 (For not the hearers of the law are just before God, but the doers of the law shall be justified.
14 For when the Gentiles, which have not the law, do by nature the things contained in the law, these, having not the law, are a law unto themselves:
15 Which shew the work of the law written in their hearts, their conscience also bearing witness, and their thoughts the mean while accusing or else excusing one another;)
16 In the day when God shall judge the secrets of men by Jesus Christ according to my gospel.

ROMANS 4
Paul *57 AD*
15 Because the law worketh wrath: for where no law is, there is no transgression.

2 NEPHI 9
Jacob, Son of Lehi *550 BC*
25 Wherefore, he has given a law; and where there is no law given there is no punishment; and where there is no punishment there is no condemnation; and where there is no condemnation the mercies of the Holy One of Israel have claim upon them, because of the atonement; for they are delivered by the power of him.
26 For the atonement satisfieth the demands of his justice upon all those who have not the law given to them, that they are delivered from that awful monster, death and hell, and the devil, and the lake of fire and brimstone, which is endless torment; and they are restored to that God who gave them breath, which is the Holy One of Israel.

DOCTRINE AND COVENANTS 131
Joseph Smith *May 1843*
6 It is impossible for a man to be saved in ignorance.

MOSIAH 15
Abinadi *148 BC*
23 They are raised to dwell with God who has redeemed them; thus they have eternal life through Christ, who has broken the bands of death.
24 And these are those who have part in the first resurrection; and these are they that have died before Christ came, in their

ignorance, not having salvation declared unto them. And thus the Lord bringeth about the restoration of these; and they have a part in the first resurrection, or have eternal life, being redeemed by the Lord.
25 And little children also have eternal life.

DOCTRINE AND COVENANTS 74

Joseph Smith — *January 1832*

7 But little children are holy, being sanctified through the atonement of Jesus Christ; and this is what the scriptures mean.

DOCTRINE AND COVENANTS 29

Joseph Smith — *September 1830*

46 But behold, I say unto you, that little children are redeemed from the foundation of the world through mine Only Begotten;
47 Wherefore, they cannot sin, for power is not given unto Satan to tempt little children, until they begin to become accountable before me;

MATTHEW 18

Jesus Christ — *32 AD*

1 At the same time came the disciples unto Jesus, saying, Who is the greatest in the kingdom of heaven?
2 And Jesus called a little child unto him, and set him in the midst of them,
3 And said, Verily I say unto you, Except ye be converted, and become as little children, ye shall not enter into the kingdom of heaven.
4 Whosoever therefore shall humble himself as this little child, the same is greatest in the kingdom of heaven.
5 And whoso shall receive one such little child in my name receiveth me.

Suffer the Children, by Carl Bloch.

6 But whoso shall offend one of these little ones which believe in me, it were better for him that a millstone were hanged about his neck, and that he were drowned in the depth of the sea.
10 Take heed that ye despise not one of these little ones; for I say unto you, That in heaven their angels do always behold the face of my Father which is in heaven.
11 For the Son of man is come to save that which was lost *and to call sinners to repentance; but these little ones have no need of repentance, and I will save them.* [JST]
14 Even so it is not the will of your Father which is in heaven, that one of these little ones should perish.

MATTHEW 19

Jesus Christ — *32 AD*

13 Then were there brought unto him little children, that he should put his hands on them, and pray: and the disciples rebuked them *saying, There is no need, for Jesus hath said, Such shall be saved.* [JST]
14 But Jesus said, Suffer little children, and forbid them not, to come unto me: for of such is the kingdom of heaven.
15 And he laid his hands on them, and departed thence.

THE KING FOLLETT DISCOURSE

Joseph Smith — *April 7, 1844*

A question may be asked—"Will mothers have their children in eternity?" Yes! Yes! Mothers, you shall have your children; for they shall have eternal life, for their debt is paid. There is no damnation awaiting them for they are in the spirit. But as the child dies, so shall it rise from the dead, and be forever living in the learning of God. It will never grow [in the grave]; it will still be the child, in the same precise form [when it rises] as it appeared before it died out of its mother's arms, but possessing all the intelligence of a God. …

DOCTRINE AND COVENANTS 137

Joseph Smith — *January 1836*

1 The heavens were opened upon us, and I beheld the Celestial kingdom of God, and the glory thereof, whether in the body or out I cannot tell.
2 I saw the transcendent beauty of the gate through which the heirs of that kingdom will enter, which was like unto circling flames of fire;
3 Also the blazing throne of God, whereon was seated the Father and the Son.
4 I saw the beautiful streets of that kingdom, which had the appearance of being paved with gold.
5 I saw Father Adam and Abraham; and my father and my mother; my brother Alvin, that has long since slept;
6 And marveled how it was that he had obtained an inheritance in that kingdom, seeing that he had departed this life before the Lord had set his hand to gather Israel the second time, and had not been baptized for the remission of sins.
7 Thus came the voice of the Lord unto me, saying: All who have died without a knowledge of this gospel, who would have received it if they had been permitted to tarry, shall be heirs of the Celestial kingdom of God;
8 Also all that shall die henceforth without a knowledge of it, who would have received it with all their hearts, shall be heirs of that kingdom;
9 For I, the Lord, will judge all men according to their works, according to the desire of their hearts.
10 And I also beheld that all children who die before they arrive at the years of

Mother Mourning the Death of Her Child, by Giuseppe Molteni, 1845.

accountability are saved in the celestial kingdom of heaven.

DOCTRINE AND COVENANTS 29

Joseph Smith *September 1830*

26 But, behold, verily I say unto you, before the Earth shall pass away, Michael, mine archangel, shall sound his trump, and then shall all the dead awake, for their graves shall be opened, and they shall come forth—yea, even all.
27 And the righteous shall be gathered on my right hand unto eternal life;

DANIEL 12

Daniel *606 BC*

2 And many of them that sleep in the dust of the Earth shall awake, some to everlasting life…
3 And they that be wise shall shine as the brightness of the firmament; and they that turn many to righteousness as the stars for ever and ever.

DOCTRINE AND COVENANTS 132

Joseph Smith *July 1843*

26 Verily, verily, I say unto you, if a man marry a wife according to my word, and they are sealed by the Holy Spirit of promise, according to mine appointment, and he or she shall commit any sin or transgression of the new and everlasting covenant whatever, and all manner of blasphemies, and if they commit no murder wherein they shed innocent blood, yet they shall come forth in the first resurrection, and enter into their exaltation; but they shall be destroyed in the flesh, and shall be delivered unto the buffetings of Satan unto the day of redemption, saith the Lord God.

1 PETER 4

Peter *64 AD*

17 For the time is come that judgment must begin at the house of God: and if it first begin at us, what shall the end be of them that obey not the gospel of God?
18 And if the righteous scarcely be saved, where shall the ungodly and the sinner appear?

52

THE SECOND RESURRECTION

TERRESTRIAL SPIRITS

+++

Description and qualifications of those spirits who will come forth in the Second Resurrection and who are judged to inherit the terrestrial Kingdom. These souls will live with Christ on Earth during the 1,000-year Millennium when the Earth is transfigured into a terrestrial Kingdom at Christ's coming.

DOCTRINE AND COVENANTS 76

Joseph Smith *February 1832*

71 And again, we saw the terrestrial world, and behold and lo, these are they who are of the terrestrial, whose glory differs from that of the church of the Firstborn who have received the fulness of the Father, even as that of the moon differs from the sun in the firmament.
72 Behold, these are they who died without law;
73 And also they who are the spirits of men kept in prison, whom the Son visited, and preached the gospel unto them, that they might be judged according to men in the flesh;
74 Who received not the testimony of Jesus in the flesh, but afterwards received it.
75 These are they who are honorable men of the Earth, who were blinded by the craftiness of men.
76 These are they who receive of his glory, but not of his fulness.
77 These are they who receive of the presence of the Son, but not of the fulness of the Father.
78 Wherefore, they are bodies terrestrial, and not bodies celestial, and differ in glory as the moon differs from the sun.
79 These are they who are not valiant in the testimony of Jesus; wherefore, they obtain not the crown over the kingdom of our God.
80 And now this is the end of the vision which we saw of the terrestrial, that the Lord commanded us to write while we were yet in the Spirit.
86 These are they who receive not of his fulness in the eternal world, but of the Holy Spirit through the ministration of the celestial;
91 And thus we saw the glory of the terrestrial which excels in all things the glory of the telestial, even in glory, and in power, and in might, and in dominion.
97 And the glory of the terrestrial is one, even as the glory of the moon is one.

DOCTRINE AND COVENANTS 88

Joseph Smith *December 1832*

21 And they who are not sanctified through the law which I have given unto you, even the law of Christ, must inherit another kingdom, even that of a terrestrial kingdom...
22 For he who is not able to abide the law of a celestial kingdom cannot abide a celestial glory.
30 And they who are quickened by a portion of the terrestrial glory shall then receive of the same, even a fulness.

DOCTRINE AND COVENANTS 132

Joseph Smith *July 1843*

15 Therefore, if a man marry him a wife in the world, and he marry her not by me nor by my word, and he covenant with her so long as he is in the world and she with him, their covenant and marriage are not of force when they are dead, and when they are out of the world; therefore, they are not bound by any law when they are out of the world.
16 Therefore, when they are out of the world they neither marry nor are given in

marriage; but are appointed angels in heaven, which angels are ministering servants, to minister for those who are worthy of a far more, and an exceeding, and an eternal weight of glory.
17 For these angels did not abide my law; therefore, they cannot be enlarged, but remain separately and singly, without exaltation, in their saved condition, to all eternity; and from henceforth are not gods, but are angels of God forever and ever.
18 And again, verily I say unto you, if a man marry a wife, and make a covenant with her for time and for all eternity, if that covenant is not by me or by my word, which is my law, and is not sealed by the Holy Spirit of promise, through him whom I have anointed and appointed unto this power, then it is not valid neither of force when they are out of the world, because they are not joined by me, saith the Lord, neither by my word; when they are out of the world it cannot be received there, because the angels and the gods are appointed there, by whom they cannot pass; they cannot, therefore, inherit my glory; for my house is a house of order, saith the Lord God.

LUKE 20

Jesus Christ — *33 AD*

34 And Jesus answering said unto them, The children of this world marry, and are given in marriage:
35 But they which shall be accounted worthy to obtain that world, *through* resurrection from the dead, neither marry, nor are given in marriage: [JST]
36 Neither can they die any more: for they are equal unto the angels; and are the children of God, being the children of the resurrection.
37 Now that the dead are raised, even Moses shewed at the bush, when he calleth the Lord the God of Abraham, and the God of Isaac, and the God of Jacob.
38 For he is not a God of the dead, but of the living: for all live unto him.

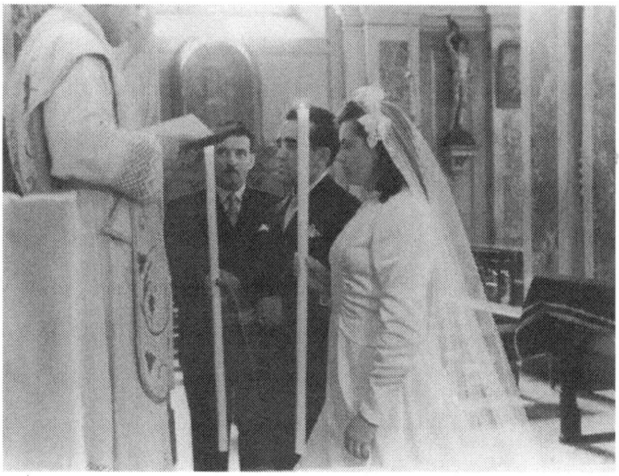

Traditional Christian marriage vows date to the medieval church and to this day contain phrases such as "till death do us part" or "so long as you both shall live." The idea that marriage was for this life only is based on an interpretation of Luke 20:34-38. The prophet Joseph Smith clarified that marriages will exist in the next life, but they must be performed by the proper priesthood authority in mortality, or by proxy in a temple for those who have died. Individuals who do not marry in this life are assured that no blessings will be withheld from them as long as they remain faithful to their covenants. Catholic marriage of Giuseppe Pietro Arosio and Adriana Agostoni in San Fruttuoso, Monza, Italy, 5 May 1951.

53

THE RIGHTEOUS NEED NOT FEAR

Prior to the great Day of Judgment, when the wicked will be burned as stubble, missionaries from the restored Church of Jesus Christ will have been sent throughout the world to preach the gospel and warn the nations of the Earth to repent. Because of this, when the great and dreadful day comes, all will have knowledge of the Savior and none shall be found blameless or ignorant. Jesus Christ will save his people at his coming.

DOCTRINE AND COVENANTS 88

Joseph Smith — *December 1832*

103 And another trump shall sound, which is the fifth trump, which is the fifth angel who committeth the everlasting gospel—flying through the midst of heaven, unto all nations, kindreds, tongues, and people;

104 And this shall be the sound of his trump, saying to all people, both in heaven and in Earth, and that are under the Earth—for every ear shall hear it, and every knee shall bow, and every tongue shall confess, while they hear the sound of the trump, saying: Fear God, and give glory to him who sitteth upon the throne, forever and ever; for the hour of his judgment is come.

REVELATION 14

John — *95 AD*

6 And I saw another angel fly in the midst of heaven, having the everlasting gospel to preach unto them that dwell on the Earth, and to every nation, and kindred, and tongue, and people,

7 Saying with a loud voice, Fear God, and give glory to him; for the hour of his judgment is come: and worship him that made heaven, and Earth, and the sea, and the fountains of waters.

DOCTRINE AND COVENANTS 133

Joseph Smith — *November 1831*

16 Hearken and hear, O ye inhabitants of the Earth. Listen, ye elders of my church together, and hear the voice of the Lord; for he calleth upon all men, and he commandeth all men everywhere to repent.

17 For behold, the Lord God hath sent forth the angel crying through the midst of heaven, saying: Prepare ye the way of the Lord, and make his paths straight, for the hour of his coming is nigh...

57 And for this cause, that men might be made partakers of the glories which were to be revealed, the Lord sent forth the fulness of his gospel, his everlasting covenant, reasoning in plainness and simplicity—

58 To prepare the weak for those things which are coming on the Earth, and for the Lord's errand in the day when the weak shall confound the wise, and the little one become a strong nation, and two shall put their tens of thousands to flight.

59 And by the weak things of the Earth the Lord shall thresh the nations by the power of his Spirit.

60 And for this cause these commandments were given; they were commanded to be kept from the world in the day that they were given, but now are to go forth unto all flesh—

61 And this according to the mind and will of the Lord, who ruleth over all flesh.

62 And unto him that repenteth and sanctifieth himself before the Lord shall be given eternal life.

DOCTRINE AND COVENANTS 1

Joseph Smith — *November 1831*

1 Hearken, O ye people of my church, saith the voice of him who dwells on high, and whose eyes are upon all men; yea, verily I say: Hearken ye people from afar; and ye that are upon the islands of the sea, listen together.

Two missionaries from the Church of Jesus Christ of Latter-day Saints in Jerusalem in 1903.

2 For verily the voice of the Lord is unto
all men, and there is none to escape; and
there is no eye that shall not see, neither
ear that shall not hear, neither heart that
shall not be penetrated.
3 And the rebellious shall be pierced with
much sorrow; for their iniquities shall be
spoken upon the housetops, and their
secret acts shall be revealed.
4 And the voice of warning shall be unto
all people, by the mouths of my disciples,
whom I have chosen in these last days.
5 And they shall go forth and none shall
stay them, for I the Lord have commanded
them.
6 Behold, this is mine authority, and the
authority of my servants, and my preface
unto the book of my commandments,
which I have given them to publish unto
you, O inhabitants of the Earth.
7 Wherefore, fear and tremble, O ye
people, for what I the Lord have decreed
in them shall be fulfilled.
8 And verily I say unto you, that they who
go forth, bearing these tidings unto the
inhabitants of the Earth, to them is power
given to seal both on Earth and in heaven,
the unbelieving and rebellious;
9 Yea, verily, to seal them up unto the day
when the wrath of God shall be poured
out upon the wicked without measure—
10 Unto the day when the Lord shall come
to recompense unto every man according
to his work, and measure to every man
according to the measure which he has
measured to his fellow man.
11 Wherefore the voice of the Lord is unto
the ends of the Earth, that all that will
hear may hear:
12 Prepare ye, prepare ye for that which is
to come, for the Lord is nigh;
13 And the anger of the Lord is kindled,
and his sword is bathed in heaven, and it
shall fall upon the inhabitants of the
Earth.
14 And the arm of the Lord shall be
revealed; and the day cometh that they
who will not hear the voice of the Lord,
neither the voice of his servants, neither
give heed to the words of the prophets and
apostles, shall be cut off from among the
people;
15 For they have strayed from mine
ordinances, and have broken mine ever-
lasting covenant;
16 They seek not the Lord to establish his
righteousness, but every man walketh in
his own way, and after the image of his
own god, whose image is in the likeness of
the world, and whose substance is that of
an idol, which waxeth old and shall perish
in Babylon, even Babylon the great, which
shall fall.

1 NEPHI 22

Nephi, Son of Lehi *580 BC*

17 Wherefore, he will preserve the right-
eous by his power, even if it so be that the
fulness of his wrath must come, and the
righteous be preserved, even unto the
destruction of their enemies by fire.
Wherefore, the righteous need not fear;
for thus saith the prophet, they shall be
saved, even if it so be as by fire.
19 For behold, the righteous shall not
perish; for the time surely must come that
all they who fight against Zion shall be cut
off.
20 And the Lord will surely prepare a way
for his people, unto the fulfilling of the
words of Moses, which he spake, saying: A
prophet shall the Lord your God raise up
unto you, like unto me; him shall ye hear
in all things whatsoever he shall say unto
you. And it shall come to pass that all
those who will not hear that prophet shall
be cut off from among the people.

21 And now I, Nephi, declare unto you, that this prophet of whom Moses spake was the Holy One of Israel; wherefore, he shall execute judgment in righteousness.

22 And the righteous need not fear, for they are those who shall not be confounded...

28 But, behold, all nations, kindreds, tongues, and people shall dwell safely in the Holy One of Israel if it so be that they will repent.

29 And now I, Nephi, make an end; for I durst not speak further as yet concerning these things.

30 Wherefore, my brethren, I would that ye should consider that the things which have been written upon the plates of brass are true; and they testify that a man must be obedient to the commandments of God.

31 Wherefore, ye need not suppose that I and my father are the only ones that have testified, and also taught them. Wherefore, if ye shall be obedient to the commandments, and endure to the end, ye shall be saved at the last day. And thus it is. Amen.

MOSIAH 3

King Benjamin — *124 BC*

20 And moreover, I say unto you, that the time shall come when the knowledge of a Savior shall spread throughout every nation, kindred, tongue, and people.

21 And behold, when that time cometh, none shall be found blameless before God, except it be little children, only through repentance and faith on the name of the Lord God Omnipotent.

22 And even at this time, when thou shalt have taught thy people the things which the Lord thy God hath commanded thee, even then are they found no more blameless in the sight of God, only according to the words which I have spoken unto thee.

23 And now I have spoken the words which the Lord God hath commanded me.

ISAIAH 45

Isaiah — *740 BC*

5 I am the LORD, and there is none else, there is no God beside me: I girded thee, though thou hast not known me:

6 That they may know from the rising of the sun, and from the west, that there is none beside me. I am the LORD, and there is none else.

7 I form the light, and create darkness: I make peace, and create evil: I the LORD do all these things.

8 Drop down, ye heavens, from above, and let the skies pour down righteousness: let the Earth open, and let them bring forth salvation, and let righteousness spring up together; I the LORD have created it.

11 Thus saith the LORD, the Holy One of Israel, and his Maker, Ask me of things to come concerning my sons, and concerning the work of my hands command ye me.

12 I have made the Earth, and created man upon it: I, even my hands, have stretched out the heavens, and all their host have I commanded.

13 I have raised him up in righteousness, and I will direct all his ways: he shall build my city, and he shall let go my captives, not for price nor reward, saith the LORD of hosts.

14 Thus saith the LORD, The labour of Egypt, and merchandise of Ethiopia and of the Sabeans, men of stature, shall come over unto thee, and they shall be thine: they shall come after thee; in chains they shall come over, and they shall fall down unto thee, they shall make supplication unto thee, saying, Surely God is in thee; and there is none else, there is no God.

17 But Israel shall be saved in the LORD with an everlasting salvation: ye shall not be ashamed nor confounded world without end.

18 For thus saith the LORD that created the heavens; God himself that formed the Earth and made it; he hath established it, he created it not in vain, he formed it to be inhabited: I am the LORD; and there is none else.

20 Assemble yourselves and come; draw near together, ye that are escaped of the nations: they have no knowledge that set up the wood of their graven image, and pray unto a god that cannot save.

21 Tell ye, and bring them near; yea, let them take counsel together: who hath declared this from ancient time? who hath told it from that time? have not I the LORD? and there is no God else beside me; a just God and a Saviour; there is none beside me.

22 Look unto me, and be ye saved, all the ends of the Earth: for I am God, and there is none else.

Christ the Redeemer Statue, Rio De Janeiro, Brazil, 2019.

23 I have sworn by myself, the word is
gone out of my mouth in righteousness,
and shall not return, That unto me every
knee shall bow, every tongue shall swear.
24 Surely, shall one say, in the LORD have
I righteousness and strength: even to him
shall men come; and all that are incensed
against him shall be ashamed.
25 In the LORD shall all the seed of Israel
be justified, and shall glory.

ISAIAH 63

Isaiah *740 BC*

7 I will mention the lovingkindnesses of
the LORD, and the praises of the LORD,
according to all that the LORD hath
bestowed on us, and the great goodness
toward the house of Israel, which he hath
bestowed on them according to his mer-
cies, and according to the multitude of his
lovingkindnesses.
8 For he said, Surely they are my people,
children that will not lie: so he was their
Saviour.
9 In all their affliction he was afflicted,
and the angel of his presence saved them:
in his love and in his pity he redeemed
them; and he bare them, and carried them
all the days of old.
10 But they rebelled, and vexed his holy
Spirit: therefore he was turned to be their
enemy, and he fought against them.
11 Then he remembered the days of old,
Moses, and his people, saying, Where is he
that brought them up out of the sea with
the shepherd of his flock? where is he that
put his holy Spirit within him?
12 That led them by the right hand of
Moses with his glorious arm, dividing the
water before them, to make himself an
everlasting name?
13 That led them through the deep, as an
horse in the wilderness, that they should
not stumble?
14 As a beast goeth down into the valley,
the Spirit of the LORD caused him to rest:
so didst thou lead thy people, to make
thyself a glorious name.
15 Look down from heaven, and behold
from the habitation of thy holiness and of
thy glory: where is thy zeal and thy
strength, the sounding of thy bowels and
of thy mercies toward me? are they
restrained?
16 Doubtless thou art our father, though
Abraham be ignorant of us, and Israel
acknowledge us not: thou, O LORD, art

our father, our redeemer; thy name is
from everlasting.
17 O LORD, why hast thou made us to err
from thy ways, and hardened our heart
from thy fear? Return for thy servants'
sake, the tribes of thine inheritance.
18 The people of thy holiness have
possessed it but a little while: our adver-
saries have trodden down thy sanctuary.
19 We are thine: thou never barest rule
over them; they were not called by thy
name.

DANIEL 12

Daniel — *600 BC*

1 And at that time shall Michael stand up,
the great prince which standeth for the
children of thy people: and there shall be
a time of trouble, such as never was since
there was a nation even to that same time:
and at that time thy people shall be
delivered, every one that shall be found
written in the book.

ISAIAH 33

Isaiah — *740 BC*

14 The sinners in Zion are afraid; fear-
fulness hath surprised the hypocrites.
Who among us shall dwell with the
devouring fire? who among us shall dwell
with everlasting burnings?
15 He that walketh righteously, and
speaketh uprightly; he that despiseth the
gain of oppressions, that shaketh his hands
from holding of bribes, that stoppeth his
ears from hearing of blood, and shutteth
his eyes from seeing evil;
16 He shall dwell on high: his place of
defence shall be the munitions of rocks:
bread shall be given him; his waters shall
be sure.
17 Thine eyes shall see the king in his
beauty: they shall behold the land that is
very far off.
20 Look upon Zion, the city of our
solemnities: thine eyes shall see Jerusalem
a quiet habitation, a tabernacle that shall
not be taken down; not one of the stakes
thereof shall ever be removed, neither
shall any of the cords thereof be broken.
21 But there the glorious LORD will be
unto us a place of broad rivers and streams;
wherein shall go no galley with oars,
neither shall gallant ship pass thereby.
22 For the LORD is our judge, the LORD
is our lawgiver, the LORD is our king; he
will save us.

2 NEPHI 8 (see also ISAIAH 51)

Isaiah — *740 BC*

3 For the Lord shall comfort Zion, he will
comfort all her waste places; and he will
make her wilderness like Eden, and her
desert like the garden of the Lord. Joy and
gladness shall be found therein, thanks-
giving and the voice of melody.
4 Hearken unto me, my people; and give
ear unto me, O my nation; for a law shall
proceed from me, and I will make my
judgment to rest for a light for the people.
5 My righteousness is near; my salvation is
gone forth, and mine arm shall judge the
people. The isles shall wait upon me, and
on mine arm shall they trust.
6 Lift up your eyes to the heavens, and
look upon the Earth beneath; for the
heavens shall vanish away like smoke, and
the Earth shall wax old like a garment; and
they that dwell therein shall die in like
manner. But my salvation shall be forever,
and my righteousness shall not be
abolished.
7 Hearken unto me, ye that know
righteousness, the people in whose heart I
have written my law, fear ye not the
reproach of men, neither be ye afraid of
their revilings.
8 For the moth shall eat them up like a
garment, and the worm shall eat them like
wool. But my righteousness shall be
forever, and my salvation from generation
to generation.

54

TO BEHOLD THE FACE OF GOD AND LIVE

Just as Shadrach, Meshach and Abednego were not burned in the flames, so shall the righteous not be burned when the Earth is purified of all unrighteousness. Image depicts Babylonian King Nebuchadnezzar seeing the three Jews unhurt by the flames, by Philip Galle of Holland, 1565.

+++

By faith in and obedience to the principles and sacred ordinances of the gospel of Jesus Christ, and by the power of the Melchizedek Priesthood, those alive at Christ's coming will be purified, sanctified, quickened and then caught up to meet him when he comes. This process of purification will allow the living saints to stand in the glorious presence of Jesus Christ and not be burned as stubble when he comes in all his glory.

DOCTRINE AND COVENANTS 101

Joseph Smith — *December 1833*

5 For all those who will not endure chastening, but deny me, cannot be sanctified.

22 Behold, it is my will, that all they who call on my name, and worship me according to mine everlasting gospel, should gather together, and stand in holy places;
23 And prepare for the revelation which is to come, when the veil of the covering of my temple, in my tabernacle, which hideth the Earth, shall be taken off, and all flesh shall see me together.

DOCTRINE AND COVENANTS 67

Joseph Smith — *November 1831*

10 And again, verily I say unto you that it is your privilege, and a promise I give unto you that have been ordained unto this ministry, that inasmuch as you strip yourselves from jealousies and fears, and humble yourselves before me, for ye are not sufficiently humble, the veil shall be

rent and you shall see me and know that I am—not with the carnal neither natural mind, but with the spiritual.
11 For no man has seen God at any time in the flesh, except quickened by the Spirit of God.
12 Neither can any natural man abide the presence of God, neither after the carnal mind.
13 Ye are not able to abide the presence of God now, neither the ministering of angels; wherefore, continue in patience until ye are perfected.
14 Let not your minds turn back; and when ye are worthy, in mine own due time, ye shall see and know that which was conferred upon you by the hands of my servant Joseph Smith, Jun. Amen.

1 TIMOTHY 6

Paul *63 AD*

13 I give thee charge in the sight of God, who quickeneth all things, and before Christ Jesus, who before Pontius Pilate witnessed a good confession;
14 That thou keep this commandment without spot, unrebukable, until the appearing of our Lord Jesus Christ:
15 Which in his times he shall *show*, who is the blessed and only Potentate, the King of kings, and Lord of lords, *to whom be honor and power everlasting;*
16 *Whom no man hath seen, nor can see, unto whom no man can approach, only he who hath the light and the hope of immortality dwelling in him.* [JST]

DOCTRINE AND COVENANTS 38

Joseph Smith *January 1831*

8 But the day soon cometh that ye shall see me, and know that I am; for the veil of darkness shall soon be rent, and he that is not purified shall not abide the day.
9 Wherefore, gird up your loins and be prepared. Behold, the kingdom is yours, and the enemy shall not overcome.

TITUS 2

Paul *66 AD*

11 For the grace of God *which* bringeth salvation *to all men hath appeared,* [JST]
12 Teaching us that, denying ungodliness and worldly lusts, we should live soberly, righteously, and godly, in this present world;
13 Looking for that blessed hope, and the glorious appearing of the great God and our Saviour Jesus Christ;
14 Who gave himself for us, that he might redeem us from all iniquity, and purify unto himself a peculiar people, zealous of good works.

DOCTRINE AND COVENANTS 128

Joseph Smith *September 1842*

24 Behold, the great day of the Lord is at hand; and who can abide the day of his coming, and who can stand when he appeareth? For he is like a refiner's fire, and like fuller's soap; and he shall sit as a refiner and purifier of silver, and he shall purify the sons of Levi, and purge them as gold and silver, that they may offer unto the Lord an offering in righteousness. Let us, therefore, as a church and a people, and as Latter-day Saints, offer unto the Lord an offering in righteousness; and let us present in his holy temple, when it is finished, a book containing the records of our dead, which shall be worthy of all acceptation.

DOCTRINE AND COVENANTS 35

Joseph Smith *December 1830*

19 Wherefore, watch over him that his faith fail not, and it shall be given by the Comforter, the Holy Ghost, that knoweth all things.
20 And a commandment I give unto thee—that thou shalt write for him; and the scriptures shall be given, even as they are in mine own bosom, to the salvation of mine own elect;
21 For they will hear my voice, and shall see me, and shall not be asleep, and shall abide the day of my coming; for they shall be purified, even as I am pure.

DOCTRINE AND COVENANTS 76

Joseph Smith *February 1832*

113 This is the end of the vision which we saw, which we were commanded to write while we were yet in the Spirit.
114 But great and marvelous are the works of the Lord, and the mysteries of his kingdom which he showed unto us, which surpass all understanding in glory, and in might, and in dominion;
115 Which he commanded us we should not write while we were yet in the Spirit, and are not lawful for man to utter;

116 Neither is man capable to make them known, for they are only to be seen and understood by the power of the Holy Spirit, which God bestows on those who love him, and purify themselves before him;
117 To whom he grants this privilege of seeing and knowing for themselves;
118 That through the power and manifestation of the Spirit, while in the flesh, they may be able to bear his presence in the world of glory.

DOCTRINE AND COVENANTS 45

Joseph Smith — *March 1831*

56 And at that day, when I shall come in my glory, shall the parable be fulfilled which I spake concerning the ten virgins.
57 For they that are wise and have received the truth, and have taken the Holy Spirit for their guide, and have not been deceived—verily I say unto you, they shall not be hewn down and cast into the fire, but shall abide the day.

DOCTRINE AND COVENANTS 88

Joseph Smith — *December 1832*

95 And there shall be silence in heaven for the space of half an hour; and immediately after shall the curtain of heaven be unfolded, as a scroll is unfolded after it is rolled up, and the face of the Lord shall be unveiled;
96 And the saints that are upon the Earth, who are alive, shall be quickened and be caught up to meet him.

MOSES 1

Moses — *1500 BC*

1 The words of God, which he spake unto Moses at a time when Moses was caught up into an exceedingly high mountain,
2 And he saw God face to face, and he talked with him, and the glory of God was upon Moses; therefore Moses could endure his presence.
5 Wherefore, no man can behold all my works, except he behold all my glory; and no man can behold all my glory, and afterwards remain in the flesh on the Earth.
9 And the presence of God withdrew from Moses, that his glory was not upon Moses; and Moses was left unto himself. And as he was left unto himself, he fell unto the Earth.
10 And it came to pass that it was for the space of many hours before Moses did again receive his natural strength like unto man; and he said unto himself: Now, for this cause I know that man is nothing, which thing I never had supposed.
11 But now mine own eyes have beheld God; but not my natural, but my spiritual eyes, for my natural eyes could not have beheld; for I should have withered and died in his presence; but his glory was upon me; and I beheld his face, for I was transfigured before him.

2 CORINTHIANS 3

Paul — *57 AD*

7 But if the ministration of death, written and engraven in stones, was glorious, so that the children of Israel could not steadfastly behold the face of Moses for the glory of his countenance; which glory was to be done away:
8 How shall not the ministration of the spirit be rather glorious?
9 For if the ministration of condemnation be glory, much more doth the ministration of righteousness exceed in glory.
10 For even that which was made glorious had no glory in this respect, by reason of the glory that excelleth.
11 For if that which is done away was glorious, much more that which remaineth is glorious.
12 Seeing then that we have such hope, we use great plainness of speech:
13 And not as Moses, which put a veil over his face, that the children of Israel could not steadfastly look to the end of that which is abolished:

MATTHEW 17

Matthew — *32 AD*

1 And after six days Jesus taketh Peter, James, and John his brother, and bringeth them up into an high mountain apart,
2 And was transfigured before them: and his face did shine as the sun, and his raiment was white as the light.
3 And, behold, there appeared unto them Moses and Elias talking with him.
4 Then answered Peter, and said unto Jesus, Lord, it is good for us to be here: if thou wilt, let us make here three tabernacles; one for thee, and one for Moses, and one for Elias.

The Transfiguration of Christ, by Carl Bloch, 1865.

5 While he yet spake, behold, a bright cloud overshadowed them: and behold a voice out of the cloud, which said, This is my beloved Son, in whom I am well pleased; hear ye him.
6 And when the disciples heard it, they fell on their face, and were sore afraid.
7 And Jesus came and touched them, and said, Arise, and be not afraid.
8 And when they had lifted up their eyes, they saw no man, save Jesus only.
9 And as they came down from the mountain, Jesus charged them, saying, Tell the vision to no man, until the Son of man be risen again from the dead.

MARK 9

<u>*Mark* 32 *AD*</u>

2 And after six days Jesus taketh with him Peter, and James, and John, and leadeth them up into an high mountain apart by themselves: and he was transfigured before them.
3 And his raiment became shining, exceeding white as snow; so as no fuller on Earth can white them.
4 And there appeared unto them Elias with Moses *or in other words, John the Baptist and Moses*: and they were talking with Jesus. [JST]
5 And Peter answered and said to Jesus, Master, it is good for us to be here: and let

us make three tabernacles; one for thee,
and one for Moses, and one for Elias.
6 For he wist not what to say; for they
were sore afraid.
7 And there was a cloud that over-
shadowed them: and a voice came out of
the cloud, saying, This is my beloved Son:
hear him.
8 And suddenly, when they had looked
round about, they saw no man any more,
save Jesus only with themselves.
9 And as they came down from the
mountain, he charged them that they
should tell no man what things they had
seen, till the Son of man were risen from
the dead.

LUKE 9

Luke — *32 AD*

28 And it came to pass about an eight days
after these sayings, he took Peter and John
and James, and went up into a mountain
to pray.
29 And as he prayed, the fashion of his
countenance was altered, and his raiment
was white and glistering.
30 And, behold, there talked with him
two men, which were Moses and Elias:
31 Who appeared in glory, and spake of
his *death, and also his resurrection*, which
he should accomplish at Jerusalem. [JST]
32 But Peter and they that were with him
were heavy with sleep: and when they
were awake, they saw his glory, and the
two men that stood with him.
33 And it came to pass, as they departed
from him, Peter said unto Jesus, Master, it
is good for us to be here: and let us make
three tabernacles; one for thee, and one
for Moses, and one for Elias: not knowing
what he said.
34 While he thus spake, there came a
cloud, and overshadowed them: and they
feared as they entered into the cloud.
35 And there came a voice out of the
cloud, saying, This is my beloved Son:
hear him.
36 And when the voice was past, Jesus was
found alone. And they kept it close, and
told no man in those days any of those
things which they had seen.

ACTS 6

Luke — *34 AD*

8 And Stephen, full of faith and power, did
great wonders and miracles among the
people...
15 And all that sat in the council, looking
steadfastly on him, saw his face as it had
been the face of an angel.

ACTS 7

Luke — *34 AD*

55 But he [Stephen], being full of the Holy
Ghost, looked up steadfastly into heaven,
and saw the glory of God, and Jesus
standing on the right hand of God,
56 And said, Behold, I see the heavens
opened, and the Son of man standing on
the right hand of God.

DOCTRINE AND COVENANTS 107

Joseph Smith — *March 1835*

18 The power and authority of the higher,
or Melchizedek Priesthood, is to hold the
keys of all the spiritual blessings of the
church—
19 To have the privilege of receiving the
mysteries of the kingdom of heaven, to
have the heavens opened unto them, to
commune with the general assembly and
church of the Firstborn, and to enjoy the
communion and presence of God the
Father, and Jesus the mediator of the new
covenant.

DOCTRINE AND COVENANTS 66

Joseph Smith — *October 1831*

2 Verily I say unto you, blessed are you for
receiving mine everlasting covenant, even
the fulness of my gospel, sent forth unto
the children of men, that they might have
life and be made partakers of the glories
which are to be revealed in the last days,
as it was written by the prophets and
apostles in days of old.

DOCTRINE AND COVENANTS 84

Joseph Smith — *September 1832*

19 And this greater priesthood admin-
istereth the gospel and holdeth the key of
the mysteries of the kingdom, even the
key of the knowledge of God.
20 Therefore, in the ordinances thereof,
the power of godliness is manifest.
21 And without the ordinances thereof,
and the authority of the priesthood, the

power of godliness is not manifest unto
men in the flesh;
22 For without this no man can see the
face of God, even the Father, and live.
23 Now this Moses plainly taught to the
children of Israel in the wilderness, and
sought diligently to sanctify his people
that they might behold the face of God;
24 But they hardened their hearts and
could not endure his presence; therefore,
the Lord in his wrath, for his anger was
kindled against them, swore that they
should not enter into his rest while in the
wilderness, which rest is the fulness of his
glory.
33 For whoso is faithful unto the obtain-
ing these two priesthoods of which I have
spoken, and the magnifying their calling,
are sanctified by the Spirit unto the
renewing of their bodies.
34 They become the sons of Moses and of
Aaron and the seed of Abraham, and the
church and kingdom, and the elect of God.
35 And also all they who receive this
priesthood receive me, saith the Lord;
36 For he that receiveth my servants
receiveth me;
37 And he that receiveth me receiveth my
Father;
38 And he that receiveth my Father
receiveth my Father's kingdom; therefore
all that my Father hath shall be given unto
him.
39 And this is according to the oath and
covenant which belongeth to the priest-
hood.
40 Therefore, all those who receive the
priesthood, receive this oath and covenant
of my Father, which he cannot break,
neither can it be moved.

PSALM 110

David *1000 BC*

1 The Lord said unto my Lord, Sit thou at
my right hand, until I make thine enemies
thy footstool.
2 The Lord shall send the rod of thy
strength out of Zion: rule thou in the
midst of thine enemies.
4 The Lord hath sworn, and will not
repent, Thou art a priest for ever after the
order of Melchizedek.
5 The Lord at thy right hand shall strike
through kings in the day of his wrath.
6 He shall judge among the heathen, he
shall fill the places with the dead bodies;

Melchizedek offers bread and wine to the Patriarch Abraham, in similitude of the sacrifice that would be offered by Jesus Christ. Painting by Moretto da Brescia, ca 1530.

he shall wound the heads over many
countries.

HEBREWS 6

Paul *68 AD*

11 And we desire that every one of you do
shew the same diligence to the full assur-
ance of hope unto the end:
12 That ye be not slothful, but followers of
them who through faith and patience
inherit the promises.
13 For when God made promise to Abra-
ham, because he could swear by no
greater, he sware by himself,
14 Saying, Surely blessing I will bless thee,
and multiplying I will multiply thee.
15 And so, after he had patiently endured,
he obtained the promise.
16 For men verily swear by the greater:
and an oath for confirmation is to them an
end of all strife.
17 Wherein God, willing more abun-
dantly to shew unto the heirs of promise

the immutability of his counsel, con-
firmed it by an oath:
18 That by two immutable things, in
which it was impossible for God to lie, we
might have a strong consolation, who
have fled for refuge to lay hold upon the
hope set before us:
19 Which hope we have as an anchor of
the soul, both sure and steadfast, and
which entereth into that within the veil;
20 Whither the forerunner is for us
entered, even Jesus, made an high priest
for ever after the order of Melchisedec.

HEBREWS 7

Paul *68 AD*

14 For it is evident that our Lord sprang
out of Juda; of which tribe Moses spake
nothing concerning priesthood.
15 And it is yet far more evident: for that
after the similitude of Melchisedec there
ariseth another priest,
16 Who is made, not after the law of a
carnal commandment, but after the power
of an endless life.
17 For he testifieth, Thou art a priest for
ever after the order of Melchisedec.
18 For there is verily a disannulling of the
commandment going before for the weak-
ness and unprofitableness thereof.
19 For the law *was administered without
an oath and* made nothing perfect, but *was
only* the bringing in of a better hope; by
the which we draw nigh unto God. [JST]
20 Inasmuch as *this high priest was* not
without an oath, *by so much was Jesus
made the surety of a better testament.*
[JST]
21 (For those priests were made without
an oath; but this with an oath by him that
said unto him, The Lord sware and will
not repent, Thou art a priest for ever after
the order of Melchisedec:)
22 By so much was Jesus made a surety of
a better testament.
23 And they truly were many priests,
because they were not suffered to
continue by reason of death:
24 But this man, because he continueth
ever, hath an unchangeable priesthood.
25 Wherefore he is able also to save them
to the uttermost that come unto God by
him, seeing he ever liveth to make inter-
cession for them.
26 For such an high priest became us, who
is holy, harmless, undefiled, separate from
sinners, and made *ruler over* the heavens;
[JST]
27 *And not* as those high priests *who*
offered up sacrifice *daily*, first for *their*
own sins, and then for the *sins of the
people*; for *he needeth not offer sacrifice
for his own sins, for he knew no sins; but
for the sins of the people. And* this he did
once, when he offered up himself. [JST]
28 For the law maketh men high priests
which have infirmity; but the word of the
oath, which was since the law, maketh the
Son, who is consecrated for evermore.

3 NEPHI 28

Jesus Christ *34 AD*

7 Therefore, more blessed are ye [the
three Nephites disciples], for ye shall
never taste of death; but ye shall live to
behold all the doings of the Father unto
the children of men, even until all things
shall be fulfilled according to the will of
the Father, when I shall come in my glory
with the powers of heaven.
8 And ye shall never endure the pains of
death; but when I shall come in my glory
ye shall be changed in the twinkling of an
eye from mortality to immortality; and
then shall ye be blessed in the kingdom of
my Father.
9 And again, ye shall not have pain while
ye shall dwell in the flesh, neither sorrow
save it be for the sins of the world; and all
this will I do because of the thing which
ye have desired of me, for ye have desired
that ye might bring the souls of men unto
me, while the world shall stand.
13 And behold, the heavens were opened,
and they were caught up into heaven, and
saw and heard unspeakable things.
14 And it was forbidden them that they
should utter; neither was it given unto
them power that they could utter the
things which they saw and heard;
15 And whether they were in the body or
out of the body, they could not tell; for it
did seem unto them like a transfiguration
of them, that they were changed from this
body of flesh into an immortal state, that
they could behold the things of God.
17 And now, whether they were mortal or
immortal, from the day of their trans-
figuration, I know not;
36 And now behold, as I spake concerning
those whom the Lord hath chosen, yea,
even three who were caught up into the

heavens, that I knew not whether they were cleansed from mortality to immortality—
37 But behold, since I wrote, I have inquired of the Lord, and he hath made it manifest unto me that there must needs be a change wrought upon their bodies, or else it needs be that they must taste of death;
38 Therefore, that they might not taste of death there was a change wrought upon their bodies, that they might not suffer pain nor sorrow save it were for the sins of the world.
39 Now this change was not equal to that which shall take place at the last day; but there was a change wrought upon them, insomuch that Satan could have no power over them, that he could not tempt them; and they were sanctified in the flesh, that they were holy, and that the powers of the Earth could not hold them.
40 And in this state they were to remain until the judgment day of Christ; and at that day they were to receive a greater change, and to be received into the kingdom of the Father to go no more out, but to dwell with God eternally in the heavens.

ISAIAH 26

Isaiah *740 BC*

20 Come, my people, enter thou into thy chambers, and shut thy doors about thee: hide thyself as it were for a little moment, until the indignation be overpast.

MORONI 10

Moroni *425 AD*

30 And again I would exhort you that ye would come unto Christ, and lay hold upon every good gift, and touch not the evil gift, nor the unclean thing.
31 And awake, and arise from the dust, O Jerusalem; yea, and put on thy beautiful garments, O daughter of Zion; and strengthen thy stakes and enlarge thy borders forever, that thou mayest no more be confounded, that the covenants of the Eternal Father which he hath made unto thee, O house of Israel, may be fulfilled.
32 Yea, come unto Christ, and be perfected in him, and deny yourselves of all ungodliness; and if ye shall deny yourselves of all ungodliness, and love God with all your might, mind and strength, then is his grace sufficient for you, that by his grace ye may be perfect in Christ; and if by the grace of God ye are perfect in Christ, ye can in nowise deny the power of God.
33 And again, if ye by the grace of God are perfect in Christ, and deny not his power, then are ye sanctified in Christ by the grace of God, through the shedding of the blood of Christ, which is in the covenant of the Father unto the remission of your sins, that ye become holy, without spot.

55

BE PREPARED FOR HIS COMING

+++

Christ will come unexpectedly, as a thief in the night, as people are going about their business. No one knows the exact time of his coming. Zechariah says only one third of those present will survive the great day of burning.

DOCTRINE AND COVENANTS 49

Joseph Smith — *March 1831*

5 Thus saith the Lord; for I am God, and have sent mine Only Begotten Son into the world for the redemption of the world, and have decreed that he that receiveth him shall be saved, and he that receiveth him not shall be damned—
6 And they have done unto the Son of Man even as they listed; and he has taken his power on the right hand of his glory, and now reigneth in the heavens, and will reign till he descends on the Earth to put all enemies under his feet, which time is nigh at hand—
7 I, the Lord God, have spoken it; but the hour and the day no man knoweth, neither the angels in heaven, nor shall they know until he comes.

JOSEPH SMITH – MATTHEW 24

Jesus Christ — *33 AD*

38 Now learn a parable of the fig tree—
When its branches are yet tender, and it begins to put forth leaves, you know that summer is nigh at hand;
39 So likewise, mine elect, when they shall see all these things, they shall know that he is near, even at the doors;
40 But of that day, and hour, no one knoweth; no, not the angels of God in heaven, but my Father only.
41 But as it was in the days of Noah, so it shall be also at the coming of the Son of Man;
42 For it shall be with them, as it was in the days which were before the flood; for until the day that Noah entered into the ark they were eating and drinking, marrying and giving in marriage;
43 And knew not until the flood came, and took them all away; so shall also the coming of the Son of Man be.
44 Then shall be fulfilled that which is written, that in the last days, two shall be in the field, the one shall be taken, and the other left;
45 Two shall be grinding at the mill, the one shall be taken, and the other left;
46 And what I say unto one, I say unto all men; watch, therefore, for you know not at what hour your Lord doth come.
47 But know this, if the good man of the house had known in what watch the thief would come, he would have watched, and would not have suffered his house to have been broken up, but would have been ready.
48 Therefore be ye also ready, for in such an hour as ye think not, the Son of Man cometh.
49 Who, then, is a faithful and wise servant, whom his lord hath made ruler over his household, to give them meat in due season?
50 Blessed is that servant whom his lord, when he cometh, shall find so doing; and verily I say unto you, he shall make him ruler over all his goods.
51 But if that evil servant shall say in his heart: My lord delayeth his coming,
52 And shall begin to smite his fellow-servants, and to eat and drink with the drunken,
53 The lord of that servant shall come in a day when he looketh not for him, and in an hour that he is not aware of,
54 And shall cut him asunder, and shall appoint him his portion with the hypocrites; there shall be weeping and gnashing of teeth.
55 And thus cometh the end of the wicked, according to the prophecy of Moses, saying: They shall be cut off from

among the people; but the end of the Earth is not yet, but by and by.

ZECHARIAH 13

Zechariah *520 BC*

7 Awake, O sword, against my shepherd, and against the man that is my fellow, saith the LORD of hosts: smite the shepherd, and the sheep shall be scattered: and I will turn mine hand upon the little ones.
8 And it shall come to pass, that in all the land, saith the LORD, two parts therein shall be cut off and die; but the third shall be left therein.
9 And I will bring the third part through the fire, and will refine them as silver is refined, and will try them as gold is tried: they shall call on my name, and I will hear them: I will say, It is my people: and they shall say, The LORD is my God.

LUKE 17

Jesus Christ *33 AD*

26 And as it was in the days of Noe, so shall it be also in the days of the Son of man.
27 They did eat, they drank, they married wives, they were given in marriage, until the day that Noe entered into the ark, and the flood came, and destroyed them all.
28 Likewise also as it was in the days of Lot; they did eat, they drank, they bought, they sold, they planted, they builded;
29 But the same day that Lot went out of Sodom it rained fire and brimstone from heaven, and destroyed them all.
30 Even thus shall it be in the day when the Son of man is revealed.
31 In that day, he which shall be upon the housetop, and his stuff in the house, let him not come down to take it away: and he that is in the field, let him likewise not return back.
32 Remember Lot's wife.
33 Whosoever shall seek to save his life shall lose it; and whosoever shall lose his life shall preserve it.
34 I tell you, in that night there shall be two men in one bed; the one shall be taken, and the other shall be left.
35 Two women shall be grinding together; the one shall be taken, and the other left.
36 Two men shall be in the field; the one shall be taken, and the other left. And they answered and said unto him, Where, Lord, *shall they be taken*?
37 And he said unto them, Wheresoever the body is *gathered*; *or, in other words, whithersoever the saints are gathered,* thither will the eagles be gathered together*; or, thither will the remainder be gathered together.*
38 *This he spake, signifying the gathering of his saints; and of angels descending and gathering the remainder unto them; the one from the bed, the other from the grinding, and the other from the field, whithersoever he listeth.* [JST]

1 THESSALONIANS 5

Paul *52 AD*

1 But of the times and the seasons, brethren, ye have no need that I write unto you.
2 For yourselves know perfectly that the day of the Lord so cometh as a thief in the night.
3 For when they shall say, Peace and safety; then sudden destruction cometh upon them, as travail upon a woman with child; and they shall not escape.
4 But ye, brethren, are not in darkness, that that day should overtake you as a thief.
5 Ye are all the children of light, and the children of the day: we are not of the night, nor of darkness.
6 Therefore let us not sleep, as do others; but let us watch and be sober.
7 For they that sleep sleep in the night; and they that be drunken are drunken in the night.

DOCTRINE AND COVENANTS 130

Joseph Smith *April 1843*

14 I was once praying very earnestly to know the time of the coming of the Son of Man, when I heard a voice repeat the following:
15 Joseph, my son, if thou livest until thou art eighty-five years old, thou shalt see the face of the Son of Man; therefore let this suffice, and trouble me no more on this matter.
16 I was left thus, without being able to decide whether this coming referred to the beginning of the millennium or to some previous appearing, or whether I should die and thus see his face.
17 I believe the coming of the Son of Man will not be any sooner than that time.

DOCTRINE AND COVENANTS 61

Joseph Smith *August 1831*

38 Gird up your loins and be watchful and be sober, looking forth for the coming of the Son of Man, for he cometh in an hour you think not.

DOCTRINE AND COVENANTS 106

Joseph Smith *November 1834*

4 And again, verily I say unto you, the coming of the Lord draweth nigh, and it overtaketh the world as a thief in the night—
5 Therefore, gird up your loins, that you may be the children of light, and that day shall not overtake you as a thief.

56

THE SECOND COMING

THE EARTH IS SANCTIFIED

The Second Coming of Christ

+++

The Second Coming of Jesus Christ—the marriage of the Bridegroom. Members of his church will have been gathered, sanctified, and purified through obedience to the ordinances of the gospel and by the power of the Melchizedek Priesthood and temple covenants. Christ descends on a white horse, clothed in red, and commands the Earth to be cleansed, purified, and sanctified. The mountains melt and the oceans boil as the Earth is purified and transfigured into a terrestrial kingdom.

PSALM 102
David — *1000 BC*
16 When the Lord shall build up Zion, he shall appear in his glory.

DOCTRINE AND COVENANTS 82
Joseph Smith — *April 1832*
14 For Zion must increase in beauty, and in holiness; her borders must be enlarged; her stakes must be strengthened; yea, verily I say unto you, Zion must arise and put on her beautiful garments.

REVELATION 19
John — *95 AD*
4 And the four and twenty elders and the four beasts fell down and worshipped God that sat on the throne, saying, Amen; Alleluia.
5 And a voice came out of the throne, saying, Praise our God, all ye his servants, and ye that fear him, both small and great.
6 And I heard as it were the voice of a great multitude, and as the voice of many waters, and as the voice of mighty thunderings, saying, Alleluia: for the Lord God omnipotent reigneth.

7 Let us be glad and rejoice, and give honour to him: for the marriage of the Lamb is come, and his wife hath made herself ready.
8 And to her was granted that she should be arrayed in fine linen, clean and white: for the fine linen is the righteousness of saints.
9 And he saith unto me, Write, Blessed are they which are called unto the marriage supper of the Lamb. And he saith unto me, These are the true sayings of God.
10 And I fell at his feet to worship him. And he said unto me, See thou do it not: I am thy fellow servant, and of thy brethren that have the testimony of Jesus: worship God: for the testimony of Jesus is the spirit of prophecy.
11 And I saw heaven opened, and behold a white horse; and he that sat upon him was called Faithful and True, and in righteousness he doth judge and make war.
12 His eyes were as a flame of fire, and on his head were many crowns; and he had a name written, that no man knew, but he himself.
13 And he was clothed with a vesture dipped in blood: and his name is called The Word of God.
14 And the armies which were in heaven followed him upon white horses, clothed in fine linen, white and clean.
15 And out of his mouth *proceedeth the word of God, and* with it he *will* smite the nations: and he *will* rule them with *the word of his mouth*; and he treadeth the winepress *in* the fierceness and wrath of Almighty God. [JST]
16 And he hath on his vesture and on his thigh a name written, KING OF KINGS, AND LORD OF LORDS.

ISAIAH 63

Isaiah — *740 BC*

1 Who is this that cometh from Edom, with dyed garments from Bozrah? this that is glorious in his apparel, travelling in the greatness of his strength? I that speak in righteousness, mighty to save.
2 Wherefore art thou red in thine apparel, and thy garments like him that treadeth in the winefat?
3 I have trodden the winepress alone; and of the people there was none with me: for I will tread them in mine anger, and trample them in my fury; and their blood shall be sprinkled upon my garments, and I will stain all my raiment.
4 For the day of vengeance is in mine heart, and the year of my redeemed is come.
5 And I looked, and there was none to help; and I wondered that there was none to uphold: therefore mine own arm brought salvation unto me; and my fury, it upheld me.
6 And I will tread down the people in mine anger, and make them drunk in my fury, and I will bring down their strength to the Earth.

Christ was given a scarlet or purple robe, the colors worn by kings of the day, to mock him at his Crucifixion. But the robe was also symbolic of the blood he would shed for all mankind.

MATTHEW 27

Matthew — *33 AD*

26 Then released he Barabbas unto them: and when he had scourged Jesus, he delivered him to be crucified.
27 Then the soldiers of the governor took Jesus into the common hall, and gathered unto him the whole band of soldiers.
28 And they stripped him, and put on him a scarlet robe.
29 And when they had plaited a crown of thorns, they put it upon his head, and a reed in his right hand: and they bowed the knee before him, and mocked him, saying, Hail, King of the Jews!
30 And they spit upon him, and took the reed, and smote him on the head.
31 And after that they had mocked him, they took the robe off from him, and put his own raiment on him, and led him away to crucify him.

MARK 15

Mark — *33 AD*

15 And so Pilate, willing to content the people, released Barabbas unto them, and delivered Jesus, when he had scourged him, to be crucified.
16 And the soldiers led him away into the hall, called Prætorium; and they call together the whole band.
17 And they clothed him with purple, and plaited a crown of thorns, and put it about his head,

Christ the Redeemer, , by Titian, 1533, wearing a red robe, stained with the blood of all mankind.

18 And began to salute him, Hail, King of
the Jews!
19 And they smote him on the head with
a reed, and did spit upon him, and bowing
their knees worshipped him.
20 And when they had mocked him, they
took off the purple from him, and put his
own clothes on him, and led him out to
crucify him.

JOHN 19

John *33 AD*

4 Pilate therefore went forth again, and
saith unto them, Behold, I bring him forth
to you, that ye may know that I find no
fault in him.
5 Then came Jesus forth, wearing the
crown of thorns, and the purple robe. And
Pilate saith unto them, Behold the man!

DOCTRINE AND COVENANTS 133

Joseph Smith *November 1831*

10 Yea, let the cry go forth among all
people: Awake and arise and go forth to
meet the Bridegroom; behold and lo, the
Bridegroom cometh; go ye out to meet
him. Prepare yourselves for the great day
of the Lord.
19 Wherefore, prepare ye for the coming
of the Bridegroom; go ye, go ye out to
meet him.
21 And he shall utter his voice out of Zion,
and he shall speak from Jerusalem, and his
voice shall be heard among all people;
22 And it shall be a voice as the voice of
many waters, and as the voice of a great
thunder, which shall break down the
mountains, and the valleys shall not be
found.
23 He shall command the great deep, and
it shall be driven back into the north
countries, and the islands shall become
one land;
24 And the land of Jerusalem and the land
of Zion shall be turned back into their
own place, and the Earth shall be like as it
was in the days before it was divided.
25 And the Lord, even the Savior, shall
stand in the midst of his people, and shall
reign over all flesh.
26 And they who are in the north coun-
tries shall come in remembrance before
the Lord; and their prophets shall hear his
voice, and shall no longer stay themselves;
and they shall smite the rocks, and the ice
shall flow down at their presence.
27 And an highway shall be cast up in the
midst of the great deep.
28 Their enemies shall become a prey unto
them,
29 And in the barren deserts there shall
come forth pools of living water; and the
parched ground shall no longer be a
thirsty land.
30 And they shall bring forth their rich
treasures unto the children of Ephraim,
my servants.
31 And the boundaries of the everlasting
hills shall tremble at their presence.
32 And there shall they fall down and be
crowned with glory, even in Zion, by the
hands of the servants of the Lord, even the
children of Ephraim.
33 And they shall be filled with songs of
everlasting joy.
34 Behold, this is the blessing of the ever-
lasting God upon the tribes of Israel, and
the richer blessing upon the head of
Ephraim and his fellows.
35 And they also of the tribe of Judah,
after their pain, shall be sanctified in holi-
ness before the Lord, to dwell in his
presence day and night, forever and ever.
36 And now, verily saith the Lord, that
these things might be known among you,
O inhabitants of the Earth, I have sent
forth mine angel flying through the midst

of heaven, having the ever-
lasting gospel, who hath
appeared unto some and hath
committed it unto man, who
shall appear unto many that
dwell on the Earth.
37 And this gospel shall be
preached unto every nation, and
kindred, and tongue, and people.
38 And the servants of God shall
go forth, saying with a loud
voice: Fear God and give glory to
him, for the hour of his judgment
is come;
39 And worship him that made
heaven, and Earth, and the sea,
and the fountains of waters—
40 Calling upon the name of the
Lord day and night, saying: O
that thou wouldst rend the
heavens, that thou wouldst come
down, that the mountains might
flow down at thy presence.
41 And it shall be answered upon
their heads; for the presence of
the Lord shall be as the melting
fire that burneth, and as the fire
which causeth the waters to boil.
42 O Lord, thou shalt come down
to make thy name known to
thine adversaries, and all nations shall
tremble at thy presence—
43 When thou doest terrible things, things
they look not for;
44 Yea, when thou comest down, and the
mountains flow down at thy presence,
thou shalt meet him who rejoiceth and
worketh righteousness, who remember-
eth thee in thy ways.
45 For since the beginning of the world
have not men heard nor perceived by the
ear, neither hath any eye seen, O God,
besides thee, how great things thou hast
prepared for him that waiteth for thee.
46 And it shall be said: Who is this that
cometh down from God in heaven with
dyed garments; yea, from the regions
which are not known, clothed in his glor-
ious apparel, traveling in the greatness of
his strength?
47 And he shall say: I am he who spake in
righteousness, mighty to save.
48 And the Lord shall be red in his
apparel, and his garments like him that
treadeth in the wine-vat.

Christ in a winepress. He bows under the pressure of a cross and blood pours from his wounds into a pool. Anonymous artist, 1568.

49 And so great shall be the glory of his
presence that the sun shall hide his face in
shame, and the moon shall withhold its
light, and the stars shall be hurled from
their places.
50 And his voice shall be heard: I have
trodden the wine-press alone, and have
brought judgment upon all people; and
none were with me;
51 And I have trampled them in my fury,
and I did tread upon them in mine anger,
and their blood have I sprinkled upon my
garments, and stained all my raiment; for
this was the day of vengeance which was
in my heart.

DOCTRINE AND COVENANTS 88

Joseph Smith *December 1832*

106 And again, another angel shall sound
his trump, which is the seventh angel,
saying: It is finished; it is finished! The
Lamb of God hath overcome and trodden
the wine-press alone, even the wine-press
of the fierceness of the wrath of Almighty
God.

PSALM 50

David *1000 BC*

3 Our God shall come, and shall not keep silence: a fire shall devour before him, and it shall be very tempestuous round about him.
4 He shall call to the heavens from above, and to the Earth, that he may judge his people.
5 Gather my saints together unto me; those that have made a covenant with me by sacrifice.
6 And the heavens shall declare his righteousness: for God is judge himself. Selah.

ISAIAH 64

Isaiah *740 BC*

1 Oh that thou wouldest rend the heavens, that thou wouldest come down, that the mountains might flow down at thy presence,
2 As when the melting fire burneth, the fire causeth the waters to boil, to make thy name known to thine adversaries, that the nations may tremble at thy presence!
3 When thou didst terrible things which we looked not for, thou camest down, the mountains flowed down at thy presence.
4 For since the beginning of the world men have not heard, nor perceived by the ear, neither hath the eye seen, O God, beside thee, what he hath prepared for him that waiteth for him.
8 But now, O LORD, thou art our father; we are the clay, and thou our potter; and we all are the work of thy hand.

PSALM 97

David *1000 BC*

1 The Lord reigneth; let the Earth rejoice; let the multitude of isles be glad thereof.
2 Clouds and darkness are round about him: righteousness and judgment are the habitation of his throne.
3 A fire goeth before him, and burneth up his enemies round about.
4 His lightnings enlightened the world: the Earth saw, and trembled.
5 The hills melted like wax at the presence of the Lord, at the presence of the Lord of the whole Earth.
6 The heavens declare his righteousness, and all the people see his glory.
7 Confounded be all they that serve graven images, that boast themselves of idols: worship him, all ye gods.
8 Zion heard, and was glad; and the daughters of Judah rejoiced because of thy judgments, O Lord.
9 For thou, Lord, art high above all the Earth: thou art exalted far above all gods.
10 Ye that love the Lord, hate evil: he preserveth the souls of his saints; he delivereth them out of the hand of the wicked.
11 Light is sown for the righteous, and gladness for the upright in heart.
12 Rejoice in the Lord, ye righteous; and give thanks at the remembrance of his holiness.

ISAIAH 24

Isaiah *740 BC*

19 The Earth is utterly broken down, the Earth is clean dissolved, the Earth is moved exceedingly.
20 The Earth shall reel to and fro like a drunkard, and shall be removed like a cottage; and the transgression thereof shall be heavy upon it; and it shall fall, and not rise again.
23 Then the moon shall be confounded, and the sun ashamed, when the LORD of hosts shall reign in mount Zion, and in Jerusalem, and before his ancients gloriously.

NAHUM 1

Nahum *642 BC*

2 God is jealous, and the LORD revengeth; the LORD revengeth, and is furious; the LORD will take vengeance on his adversaries, and he reserveth wrath for his enemies.
3 The LORD is slow to anger, and great in power, and will not at all acquit the wicked: the LORD hath his way in the whirlwind and in the storm, and the clouds are the dust of his feet.
4 He rebuketh the sea, and maketh it dry, and drieth up all the rivers: Bashan languisheth, and Carmel, and the flower of Lebanon languisheth.
5 The mountains quake at him, and the hills melt, and the Earth is burned at his presence, yea, the world, and all that dwell therein.
6 Who can stand before his indignation? and who can abide in the fierceness of his anger? his fury is poured out like fire, and the rocks are thrown down by him.

7 The LORD is good, a strong hold in the day of trouble; and he knoweth them that trust in him.
8 But with an overrunning flood he will make an utter end of the place thereof, and darkness shall pursue his enemies.
9 What do ye imagine against the LORD? he will make an utter end: affliction shall not rise up the second time.
10 For while they be folden together as thorns, and while they are drunken as drunkards, they shall be devoured as stubble fully dry.
11 There is one come out of thee, that imagineth evil against the LORD, a wicked counsellor.
12 Thus saith the LORD; Though they be quiet, and likewise many, yet thus shall they be cut down, when he shall pass through. Though I have afflicted thee, I will afflict thee no more.
13 For now will I break his yoke from off thee, and will burst thy bonds in sunder.
14 And the LORD hath given a commandment concerning thee, that no more of thy name be sown: out of the house of thy gods will I cut off the graven image and the molten image: I will make thy grave; for thou art vile.
15 Behold upon the mountains the feet of him that bringeth good tidings, that publisheth peace! O Judah, keep thy solemn feasts, perform thy vows: for the wicked shall no more pass through thee; he is utterly cut off.

2 PETER 3

Peter — *67 AD*

7 But the heavens, and the Earth which are now, are kept in store *by the same word*, reserved unto fire against the day of judgment and perdition of ungodly men.
9 The Lord is not slack concerning his promise *and coming*, as some men count slackness; but long-suffering *toward us*, not willing that any should perish, but that all should come to repentance.
10 But the day of the Lord will come as a thief in the night, in the which the heavens shall *shake, and the Earth also shall tremble, and the mountains shall melt, and* pass away with a great noise, and the elements shall *be filled* with fervent heat; the Earth also *shall be filled*,

A New Heaven and a New Earth. Christ ushering in the kingdom of God to the Earth as the wicked are burned.

and the *corruptible* works which *are* therein shall be burned up.
11 *If* then all these things shall be *destroyed*, what manner of persons ought ye to be in holy *conduct* and godliness,
12 Looking *unto*, and *preparing for the day* of the coming of the Lord wherein the *corruptible things of the heavens* being on fire, shall be dissolved, and the *mountains* shall melt with fervent heat?
13 Nevertheless, *if we shall endure*, we *shall be kept* according to his promise. *And we* look for a new heavens, and a new Earth wherein dwelleth righteousness. [JST]

DOCTRINE AND COVENANTS 101
Joseph Smith *December 1833*
24 And every corruptible thing, both of man, or of the beasts of the field, or of the fowls of the heavens, or of the fish of the sea, that dwells upon all the face of the Earth, shall be consumed;
25 And also that of element shall melt with fervent heat; and all things shall become new, that my knowledge and glory may dwell upon all the Earth.

DOCTRINE AND COVENANTS 63
Joseph Smith *August 1831*
20 Nevertheless, he that endureth in faith and doeth my will, the same shall overcome, and shall receive an inheritance upon the Earth when the day of transfiguration shall come;
21 When the Earth shall be transfigured, even according to the pattern which was shown unto mine apostles upon the mount; of which account the fulness ye have not yet received.

LUKE 17
Jesus Christ *33 AD*
39 For verily there shall be new heavens, and a new Earth, wherein dwelleth righteousness.
40 And there shall be no unclean thing; for the Earth becoming old, even as a garment, having waxed in corruption, wherefore it vanisheth away, and the footstool remaineth sanctified, cleansed from all sin. [JST]

ISAIAH 66
Isaiah *740 BC*
22 For as the new heavens and the new Earth, which I will make, shall remain before me, saith the LORD, so shall your seed and your name remain.
23 And it shall come to pass, that from one new moon to another, and from one sabbath to another, shall all flesh come to worship before me, saith the LORD.
24 And they shall go forth, and look upon the carcasses of the men that have transgressed against me: for their worm shall not die, neither shall their fire be quenched; and they shall be an abhorring unto all flesh.

REVELATION 21
John *95 AD*
1 And I saw a new heaven and a new Earth: for the first heaven and the first Earth were passed away; and there was no more sea.

ISAIAH 65
Isaiah *740 BC*
17 For, behold, I create new heavens and a new Earth: and the former shall not be remembered, nor come into mind.

ETHER 13
Ether *600 BC*
9 And there shall be a new heaven and a new Earth; and they shall be like unto the old save the old have passed away, and all things have become new.

57

THE WICKED AND REBELLIOUS ARE BURNED AT CHRIST'S COMING

Judgment Day, by Raphael Coxie, 1588.

+++

The wicked and the rebellious are burned as stubble in an instant when Christ appears in all his glory. In their unsanctified state, they cannot abide Christ's presence or the Earth in its terrestrial glory. Their souls are cast out into outer darkness where they will suffer the buffetings of Satan until they are called forth to be resurrected at the end of the Millennium.

PSALM 58

David *1000 BC*

10 The righteous shall rejoice when he seeth the vengeance: he shall wash his feet in the blood of the wicked.
11 So that a man shall say, Verily there is a reward for the righteous: verily he is a God that judgeth in the Earth.

REVELATION 19

John *95 AD*

17 And I saw an angel standing in the sun; and he cried with a loud voice, saying to all the fowls that fly in the midst of heaven, Come and gather yourselves together unto the supper of the great God;
18 That ye may eat the flesh of kings, and the flesh of captains, and the flesh of mighty men, and the flesh of horses, and of them that sit on them, and the flesh of all men *who fight against the Lamb*, both *bond and* free, both small and great. [JST]

19 And I saw the beast, and the kings of the Earth, and their armies, gathered together to make war against him that sat on the horse, and against his army.

DOCTRINE AND COVENANTS 112

Joseph Smith — *July 1837*

23 Verily, verily, I say unto you, darkness covereth the Earth, and gross darkness the minds of the people, and all flesh has become corrupt before my face.
24 Behold, vengeance cometh speedily upon the inhabitants of the Earth, a day of wrath, a day of burning, a day of desolation, of weeping, of mourning, and of lamentation; and as a whirlwind it shall come upon all the face of the Earth, saith the Lord.

DOCTRINE AND COVENANTS 63

Joseph Smith — *August 1831*

54 And until that hour there will be foolish virgins among the wise; and at that hour cometh an entire separation of the righteous and the wicked;

MATTHEW 13

Jesus Christ — *32 AD*

36 Then Jesus sent the multitude away, and went into the house: and his disciples came unto him, saying, Declare unto us the parable of the tares of the field.
37 He answered and said unto them, He that soweth the good seed is the Son of man;
38 The field is the world; the good seed are the children of the kingdom; but the tares are the children of the wicked one;
39 The harvest is the end of the world, *or the destruction of the wicked.*
40 The reapers are the angels, *or the messengers sent of heaven.*
41 As, therefore, the tares are gathered and burned in the fire, so shall it be in the end of this world, *or the destruction of the wicked.*
42 *For in that day, before* the Son of man shall *come, he* shall send forth his angels *and messengers of heaven.*
43 And they shall gather out of his kingdom all things that offend, and them which do iniquity, and shall cast them *out among the wicked; and* there shall be wailing and gnashing of teeth.
44 *For the world shall be burned with fire.*
45 Then shall the righteous shine forth as the sun in the kingdom of their Father. Who hath ears to hear, let him hear.
47 Again, the kingdom of heaven is like unto a net, that was cast into the sea, and gathered of every kind:
48 Which, when it was full, they drew to shore, and sat down, and gathered the good into vessels, but cast the bad away.
49 So shall it be at the end of the world: *And the world is the children of the wicked.* the angels shall come forth, and sever the wicked from among the just,
50 And shall cast them *out into the world to be burned*: there shall be wailing and gnashing of teeth. [JST]

2 NEPHI 30

Nephi, Son of Lehi — *550 BC*

9 And with righteousness shall the Lord God judge the poor, and reprove with equity for the meek of the Earth. And he shall smite the Earth with the rod of his mouth; and with the breath of his lips shall he slay the wicked.
10 For the time speedily cometh that the Lord God shall cause a great division among the people, and the wicked will he destroy; and he will spare his people, yea, even if it so be that he must destroy the wicked by fire.

2 NEPHI 21 (see also ISAIAH 11)

Isaiah — *740 BC*

1 And there shall come forth a rod out of the stem of Jesse, and a branch shall grow out of his roots.
2 And the Spirit of the Lord shall rest upon him, the spirit of wisdom and understanding, the spirit of counsel and might, the spirit of knowledge and of the fear of the Lord;
3 And shall make him of quick understanding in the fear of the Lord; and he shall not judge after the sight of his eyes, neither reprove after the hearing of his ears.
4 But with righteousness shall he judge the poor, and reprove with equity for the meek of the Earth; and he shall smite the Earth with the rod of his mouth, and with the breath of his lips shall he slay the wicked.
5 And righteousness shall be the girdle of his loins, and faithfulness the girdle of his reins.

DOCTRINE AND COVENANTS 113
Joseph Smith *March 1838*
1 Who is the Stem of Jesse spoken of in the 1st, 2d, 3d, 4th, and 5th verses of the 11th chapter of Isaiah?
2 Verily thus saith the Lord: It is Christ.
3 What is the rod spoken of in the first verse of the 11th chapter of Isaiah, that should come of the Stem of Jesse?
4 Behold, thus saith the Lord: It is a servant in the hands of Christ, who is partly a descendant of Jesse as well as of Ephraim, or of the house of Joseph, on whom there is laid much power.

3 NEPHI 24 (see also MALACHI 3)
Malachi *432 BC*
2 But who may abide the day of his coming, and who shall stand when he appeareth? For he is like a refiner's fire, and like fuller's soap.
5 And I will come near to you to judgment; and I will be a swift witness against the sorcerers, and against the adulterers, and against false swearers, and against those that oppress the hireling in his wages, the widow and the fatherless, and that turn aside the stranger, and fear not me, saith the Lord of Hosts.
6 For I am the Lord, I change not; therefore ye sons of Jacob are not consumed.
11 And I will rebuke the devourer for your sakes, and he shall not destroy the fruits of your ground; neither shall your vine cast her fruit before the time in the fields, saith the Lord of Hosts.
12 And all nations shall call you blessed, for ye shall be a delightsome land, saith the Lord of Hosts.
16 Then they that feared the Lord spake often one to another, and the Lord hearkened and heard; and a book of remembrance was written before him for them that feared the Lord, and that thought upon his name.
17 And they shall be mine, saith the Lord of Hosts, in that day when I make up my jewels; and I will spare them as a man spareth his own son that serveth him.
18 Then shall ye return and discern between the righteous and the wicked, between him that serveth God and him that serveth him not.

ZEPHANIAH 3
Zephaniah *640 BC*
6 I have cut off the nations: their towers are desolate; I made their streets waste, that none passeth by: their cities are destroyed, so that there is no man, that there is none inhabitant.
7 I said, Surely thou wilt fear me, thou wilt receive instruction; so their dwelling should not be cut off, howsoever I punished them: but they rose early, and corrupted all their doings.
8 Therefore wait ye upon me, saith the LORD, until the day that I rise up to the prey: for my determination is to gather the nations, that I may assemble the kingdoms, to pour upon them mine indignation, even all my fierce anger: for all the Earth shall be devoured with the fire of my jealousy.

ISAIAH 26
Isaiah *740 BC*
21 For, behold, the LORD cometh out of his place to punish the inhabitants of the Earth for their iniquity: the Earth also shall disclose her blood, and shall no more cover her slain.

HEBREWS 12
Paul *68 AD*
29 For our God is a consuming fire.

DOCTRINE AND COVENANTS 63
Joseph Smith *August 1831*
54 … and in that day will I send mine angels to pluck out the wicked and cast them into unquenchable fire.

ISAIAH 66
Isaiah *740 BC*
15 For, behold, the LORD will come with fire, and with his chariots like a whirlwind, to render his anger with fury, and his rebuke with flames of fire.
16 For by fire and by his sword will the LORD plead with all flesh: and the slain of the LORD shall be many.
17 They that sanctify themselves, and purify themselves in the gardens behind one tree in the midst, eating swine's flesh, and the abomination, and the mouse, shall be consumed together, saith the LORD.

Last Judgment, by Stephan Lochner, 1435.

ISAIAH 1

Isaiah *740 BC*

24 Therefore saith the Lord, the LORD of hosts, the mighty One of Israel, Ah, I will ease me of mine adversaries, and avenge me of mine enemies:
25 And I will turn my hand upon thee, and purely purge away thy dross, and take away all thy tin:
28 And the destruction of the transgressors and of the sinners shall be together, and they that forsake the LORD shall be consumed.
29 For they shall be ashamed of the oaks which ye have desired, and ye shall be confounded for the gardens that ye have chosen.
30 For ye shall be as an oak whose leaf fadeth, and as a garden that hath no water.
31 And the strong shall be as tow, and the maker of it as a spark, and they shall both burn together, and none shall quench them.

3 NEPHI 25 (see also MALACHI 4)

Malachi *432 BC*

1 For behold, the day cometh that shall burn as an oven; and all the proud, yea, and all that do wickedly, shall be stubble; and the day that cometh shall burn them up, saith the Lord of Hosts, that it shall leave them neither root nor branch.
2 But unto you that fear my name, shall the Son of Righteousness arise with healing in his wings; and ye shall go forth and grow up as calves in the stall.
3 And ye shall tread down the wicked; for they shall be ashes under the soles of your feet in the day that I shall do this, saith the Lord of Hosts.

DOCTRINE AND COVENANTS 133

Joseph Smith *November 1831*

63 And upon them that hearken not to the voice of the Lord shall be fulfilled that which was written by the prophet Moses, that they should be cut off from among the people.
64 And also that which was written by the prophet Malachi: For, behold, the day cometh that shall burn as an oven, and all the proud, yea, and all that do wickedly, shall be stubble; and the day that cometh shall burn them up, saith the Lord of hosts, that it shall leave them neither root nor branch.

DOCTRINE AND COVENANTS 64

Joseph Smith — *September 1831*

23 Behold, now it is called today until the coming of the Son of Man, and verily it is a day of sacrifice, and a day for the tithing of my people; for he that is tithed shall not be burned at his coming.
24 For after today cometh the burning—this is speaking after the manner of the Lord—for verily I say, tomorrow all the proud and they that do wickedly shall be as stubble; and I will burn them up, for I am the Lord of Hosts; and I will not spare any that remain in Babylon.
25 Wherefore, if ye believe me, ye will labor while it is called today.

DOCTRINE AND COVENANTS 29

Joseph Smith — *September 1830*

9 For the hour is nigh and the day soon at hand when the Earth is ripe; and all the proud and they that do wickedly shall be as stubble; and I will burn them up, saith the Lord of Hosts, that wickedness shall not be upon the Earth;

2 THESSALONIANS 1

Paul — *52 AD*

7 And to you who are troubled rest with us, when the Lord Jesus shall be revealed from heaven with his mighty angels,
8 In flaming fire taking vengeance on them that know not God, and that obey not the gospel of our Lord Jesus Christ:
9 Who shall be punished with everlasting destruction from the presence of the Lord, and from the glory of his power;

DOCTRINE AND COVENANTS 63

Joseph Smith — *August 1831*

1 Hearken, O ye people, and open your hearts and give ear from afar; and listen, you that call yourselves the people of the Lord, and hear the word of the Lord and his will concerning you.
2 Yea, verily, I say, hear the word of him whose anger is kindled against the wicked and rebellious;
3 Who willeth to take even them whom he will take, and preserveth in life them whom he will preserve;
4 Who buildeth up at his own will and pleasure; and destroyeth when he pleases, and is able to cast the soul down to hell.
5 Behold, I, the Lord, utter my voice, and it shall be obeyed.
6 Wherefore, verily I say, let the wicked take heed, and let the rebellious fear and tremble; and let the unbelieving hold their lips, for the day of wrath shall come upon them as a whirlwind, and all flesh shall know that I am God.
34...nevertheless, I, the Lord, am with them [Saints], and will come down in heaven from the presence of my Father and consume the wicked with unquenchable fire.

MATTHEW 3

John the Baptist — *30 AD*

12 *And it is he of whom I shall bear record,* whose fan shall be in his hand, and he will thoroughly purge his floor, and gather his wheat into the garner*; but in the fullness of his own time* will burn up the chaff with unquenchable fire. [JST]

2 THESSALONIANS 2

Paul — *52 AD*

8 And then shall that Wicked be revealed, whom the Lord shall consume with the spirit of his mouth, and shall destroy with the brightness of his coming:
9 Even him, whose coming is after the working of Satan with all power and signs and lying wonders,
10 And with all deceivableness of unrighteousness in them that perish; because they received not the love of the truth, that they might be saved.
11 And for this cause God shall send them strong delusion, that they should believe a lie:
12 That they all might be damned who believed not the truth, but had pleasure in unrighteousness.

HEBREWS 6

Paul — *68 AD*

4 For *he hath made it* impossible for those who were once enlightened, and have tasted of the heavenly gift, and were made partakers of the Holy Ghost,
5 And have tasted the good word of God, and the powers of the world to come,
6 If they shall fall away, to *be renewed* again unto repentance; seeing they crucify unto themselves the Son of God afresh, and put him to an open shame.
7 For *the day cometh that* the Earth which drinketh in the rain that cometh oft upon it, and bringeth forth herbs meet for them

who dwelleth thereon, by whom it is dressed, *who now* receiveth blessings from God, *shall be cleansed with fire*.
8 *For* that which beareth thorns and briers is rejected, and is nigh unto cursing; *therefore they who bring not forth good fruits, shall be cast into the fire; for their* end is to be burned. [JST]

1 NEPHI 22

Nephi, Son of Lehi — *580 BC*

15 ...for the day soon cometh that all the proud and they who do wickedly shall be as stubble; and the day cometh that they must be burned.
16 For the time soon cometh that the fulness of the wrath of God shall be poured out upon all the children of men; for he will not suffer that the wicked shall destroy the righteous.
18 Behold, my brethren, I say unto you, that these things must shortly come; yea, even blood, and fire, and vapor of smoke must come; and it must needs be upon the face of this Earth; and it cometh unto men according to the flesh if it so be that they will harden their hearts against the Holy One of Israel.
22 But it is the kingdom of the devil, which shall be built up among the children of men, which kingdom is established among them which are in the flesh—
23 For the time speedily shall come that all churches which are built up to get gain, and all those who are built up to get power over the flesh, and those who are built up to become popular in the eyes of the world, and those who seek the lusts of the flesh and the things of the world, and to do all manner of iniquity; yea, in fine, all those who belong to the kingdom of the devil are they who need fear, and tremble, and quake; they are those who must be brought low in the dust; they are those who must be consumed as stubble; and this is according to the words of the prophet.

ZEPHANIAH 1

Zephaniah — *630 BC*

1 The word of the LORD which came unto Zephaniah...
2 I will utterly consume all things from off the land, saith the LORD.
3 I will consume man and beast; I will consume the fowls of the heaven, and the fishes of the sea, and the stumbling blocks with the wicked; and I will cut off man from off the land, saith the LORD.
4 I will also stretch out mine hand upon Judah, and upon all the inhabitants of Jerusalem; and I will cut off the remnant of Baal from this place, and the name of the Chemarims with the priests;
5 And them that worship the host of heaven upon the housetops; and them that worship and that swear by the LORD, and that swear by Malcham;
6 And them that are turned back from the LORD; and those that have not sought the LORD, nor inquired for him.
7 Hold thy peace at the presence of the Lord GOD: for the day of the LORD is at hand: for the LORD hath prepared a sacrifice, he hath bid his guests.
8 And it shall come to pass in the day of the LORD's sacrifice, that I will punish the princes, and the king's children, and all such as are clothed with strange apparel.
9 In the same day also will I punish all those that leap on the threshold, which fill their masters' houses with violence and deceit.
10 And it shall come to pass in that day, saith the LORD, that there shall be the noise of a cry from the fish gate, and an howling from the second, and a great crashing from the hills.
11 Howl, ye inhabitants of Maktesh, for all the merchant people are cut down; all they that bear silver are cut off.
12 And it shall come to pass at that time, that I will search Jerusalem with candles, and punish the men that are settled on their blees: that say in their heart, The LORD will not do good, neither will he do evil.
13 Therefore their goods shall become a booty, and their houses a desolation: they shall also build houses, but not inhabit them; and they shall plant vineyards, but not drink the wine thereof.
14 The great day of the LORD is near, it is near, and hasteth greatly, even the voice of the day of the LORD: the mighty man shall cry there bitterly.
15 That day is a day of wrath, a day of trouble and distress, a day of wasteness and desolation, a day of darkness and gloominess, a day of clouds and thick darkness,

16 A day of the trumpet and alarm against the fenced cities, and against the high towers.
17 And I will bring distress upon men, that they shall walk like blind men, because they have sinned against the LORD: and their blood shall be poured out as dust, and their flesh as the dung.
18 Neither their silver nor their gold shall be able to deliver them in the day of the LORD's wrath; but the whole land shall be devoured by the fire of his jealousy: for he shall make even a speedy riddance of all them that dwell in the land.

2 NEPHI 7 (see also ISAIAH 50)

Isaiah 740 BC

8 And the Lord is near, and he justifieth me. Who will contend with me? Let us stand together. Who is mine adversary? Let him come near me, and I will smite him with the strength of my mouth.
9 For the Lord God will help me. And all they who shall condemn me, behold, all they shall wax old as a garment, and the moth shall eat them up.

2 NEPHI 20 (see also ISAIAH 10)

Isaiah 740 BC

16 Therefore shall the Lord, the Lord of Hosts, send among his fat ones, leanness; and under his glory he shall kindle a burning like the burning of a fire.
17 And the light of Israel shall be for a fire, and his Holy One for a flame, and shall burn and shall devour his thorns and his briers in one day;
18 And shall consume the glory of his forest, and of his fruitful field, both soul and body; and they shall be as when a standard-bearer fainteth.
19 And the rest of the trees of his forest shall be few, that a child may write them.
22 ...the consumption decreed shall overflow with righteousness.
23 For the Lord God of Hosts shall make a consumption, even determined in all the land.

ISAIAH 24

Isaiah 740 BC

5 The Earth also is defiled under the inhabitants thereof; because they have transgressed the laws, changed the ordinance, broken the everlasting covenant.
6 Therefore hath the curse devoured the Earth, and they that dwell therein are desolate: therefore the inhabitants of the Earth are burned, and few men left.

ZECHARIAH 13

Zechariah 520 BC

7 Awake, O sword, against my shepherd, and against the man that is my fellow, saith the LORD of hosts: smite the shepherd, and the sheep shall be scattered: and I will turn mine hand upon the little ones.
8 And it shall come to pass, that in all the land, saith the LORD, two parts therein shall be cut off and die; but the third shall be left therein.
9 And I will bring the third part through the fire, and will refine them as silver is refined, and will try them as gold is tried: they shall call on my name, and I will hear them: I will say, It is my people: and they shall say, The LORD is my God.

DOCTRINE AND COVENANTS 5

Joseph Smith March 1829

19 For a desolating scourge shall go forth among the inhabitants of the Earth, and shall continue to be poured out from time to time, if they repent not, until the Earth is empty, and the inhabitants thereof are consumed away and utterly destroyed by the brightness of my coming.

58

SATAN AND THE WICKED ARE CAST OUT

+++

Satan is bound and cast into outer darkness, along with the spirits of the wicked and rebellious, for 1,000 years. Because of the righteousness of the Lord's people, Satan has no power over them.

REVELATION 19

John 95 AD

20 And the beast was taken, and with him the false prophet that wrought miracles before him, with which he deceived them that had received the mark of the beast, and them that worshipped his image. These both were cast alive into a lake of fire burning with brimstone.
21 And the remnant were slain with the *word* of him that sat upon the horse, which *word* proceeded out of his mouth: and all the fowls were filled with their flesh.

REVELATION 20

John 95 AD

1 And I saw an angel come down from heaven, having the key of the bottomless pit and a great chain in his hand.
2 And he laid hold on the dragon, that old serpent, which is the Devil, and Satan, and bound him a thousand years,
3 And cast him into the bottomless pit, and shut him up, and set a seal upon him, that he should deceive the nations no more, till the thousand years should be fulfilled: and after that he must be loosed a little season.

DANIEL 7

Daniel 600 BC

11 I beheld then because of the voice of the great words which the horn spake: I

Satan Bound for 1000 Years, Illustration in Peiter Mortier's Bible, 1700.

beheld even till the beast was slain, and his body destroyed, and given to the burning flame.

ISAIAH 27

Isaiah *740 BC*

1 In that day the LORD with his sore and great and strong sword shall punish leviathan the piercing serpent, even leviathan that crooked serpent; and he shall slay the dragon that is in the sea.

2 NEPHI 24 (see also ISAIAH 14)

Isaiah *740 BC*

4 And it shall come to pass in that day, that thou shalt take up this proverb against the king of Babylon, and say: How hath the oppressor ceased, the golden city ceased!
5 The Lord hath broken the staff of the wicked, the scepters of the rulers.
6 He who smote the people in wrath with a continual stroke, he that ruled the nations in anger, is persecuted, and none hindereth.
9 Hell from beneath is moved for thee to meet thee at thy coming; it stirreth up the dead for thee, even all the chief ones of the Earth; it hath raised up from their thrones all the kings of the nations.
10 All they shall speak and say unto thee: Art thou also become weak as we? Art thou become like unto us?
11 Thy pomp is brought down to the grave; the noise of thy viols is not heard; the worm is spread under thee, and the worms cover thee.
12 How art thou fallen from heaven, O Lucifer, son of the morning! Art thou cut down to the ground, which did weaken the nations!
13 For thou hast said in thy heart: I will ascend into heaven, I will exalt my throne above the stars of God; I will sit also upon the mount of the congregation, in the sides of the north;
14 I will ascend above the heights of the clouds; I will be like the Most High.
15 Yet thou shalt be brought down to hell, to the sides of the pit.
16 They that see thee shall narrowly look upon thee, and shall consider thee, and shall say: Is this the man that made the Earth to tremble, that did shake kingdoms?
17 And made the world as a wilderness, and destroyed the cities thereof, and opened not the house of his prisoners?

ISAIAH 24

Isaiah *740 BC*

21 And it shall come to pass in that day, that the LORD shall punish the host of the high ones that are on high, and the kings of the Earth upon the Earth.
22 And they shall be gathered together, as prisoners are gathered in the pit, and shall be shut up in the prison, and after many days shall they be visited.

DOCTRINE AND COVENANTS 133

Joseph Smith *November 1831*

65 Wherefore, this shall be the answer of the Lord unto them:
66 In that day when I came unto mine own, no man among you received me, and you were driven out.
67 When I called again there was none of you to answer; yet my arm was not shortened at all that I could not redeem, neither my power to deliver.
68 Behold, at my rebuke I dry up the sea. I make the rivers a wilderness; their fish stink, and die for thirst.
69 I clothe the heavens with blackness, and make sackcloth their covering.
70 And this shall ye have of my hand—ye shall lie down in sorrow.
71 Behold, and lo, there are none to deliver you; for ye obeyed not my voice when I called to you out of the heavens; ye believed not my servants, and when they were sent unto you ye received them not.
72 Wherefore, they sealed up the testimony and bound up the law, and ye were delivered over unto darkness.
73 These shall go away into outer darkness, where there is weeping, and wailing, and gnashing of teeth.
74 Behold the Lord your God hath spoken it. Amen.

ALMA 40

Alma the Younger *73 BC*

11 Now, concerning the state of the soul between death and the resurrection—Behold, it has been made known unto me by an angel, that the spirits of all men, as soon as they are departed from this mortal body, yea, the spirits of all men, whether

The Heavenly Jerusalem / The Bound Devil, by Matthias Gerung, 1530.

they be good or evil, are taken home to that God who gave them life.
12 And then shall it come to pass, that the spirits of those who are righteous are received into a state of happiness, which is called paradise, a state of rest, a state of peace, where they shall rest from all their troubles and from all care, and sorrow.
13 And then shall it come to pass, that the spirits of the wicked, yea, who are evil—for behold, they have no part nor portion of the Spirit of the Lord; for behold, they chose evil works rather than good; therefore the spirit of the devil did enter into them, and take possession of their house—and these shall be cast out into outer darkness; there shall be weeping, and wailing, and gnashing of teeth, and this because of their own iniquity, being led captive by the will of the devil.
14 Now this is the state of the souls of the wicked, yea, in darkness, and a state of awful, fearful looking for the fiery indignation of the wrath of God upon them; thus they remain in this state, as well as the righteous in paradise, until the time of their resurrection.

1 NEPHI 22
Nephi, Son of Lehi — *580 BC*

15 For behold, saith the prophet, the time cometh speedily that Satan shall have no more power over the hearts of the children of men;
24 And the time cometh speedily that the righteous must be led up as calves of the stall, and the Holy One of Israel must reign in dominion, and might, and power, and great glory.
25 And he gathereth his children from the four quarters of the Earth; and he numbereth his sheep, and they know him; and there shall be one fold and one shepherd; and he shall feed his sheep, and in him they shall find pasture.
26 And because of the righteousness of his people, Satan has no power; wherefore, he cannot be loosed for the space of many years; for he hath no power over the hearts of the people, for they dwell in righteousness, and the Holy One of Israel reigneth.

DOCTRINE AND COVENANTS 45
Joseph Smith — *March 1831*

55 And Satan shall be bound, that he shall have no place in the hearts of the children of men.

DOCTRINE AND COVENANTS 101
Joseph Smith — *December 1833*

28 And in that day Satan shall not have power to tempt any man.

DOCTRINE AND COVENANTS 43
Joseph Smith — *February 1831*

29 For in mine own due time will I come upon the Earth in judgment, and my people shall be redeemed and shall reign with me on Earth.
30 For the great millennium, of which I have spoken by the mouth of my servants, shall come.
31 For Satan shall be bound,

2 NEPHI 30
Nephi, Son of Lehi — *550 BC*

18 ...and Satan shall have power over the hearts of the children of men no more, for a long time. And now, my beloved brethren, I make an end of my sayings.

DOCTRINE AND COVENANTS 88
Joseph Smith — *December 1832*

108 And then shall the first angel again sound his trump in the ears of all living, and reveal the secret acts of men, and the mighty works of God in the first thousand years.
109 And then shall the second angel sound his trump, and reveal the secret acts of men, and the thoughts and intents of their hearts, and the mighty works of God in the second thousand years—
110 And so on, until the seventh angel shall sound his trump; and he shall stand forth upon the land and upon the sea, and swear in the name of him who sitteth upon the throne, that there shall be time no longer; and Satan shall be bound, that old serpent, who is called the devil, and shall not be loosed for the space of a thousand years.

DOCTRINE AND COVENANTS 29
Joseph Smith — *September 1830*

11 For I will reveal myself from heaven with power and great glory, with all the hosts thereof, and dwell in righteousness with men on Earth a thousand years, and the wicked shall not stand.

59

CHRIST REIGNS ON EARTH

+++

Jesus reigns on Earth for 1,000 years. The veil is lifted. Peace is proclaimed. The marriage of the Bridegroom. The city of Enoch—The New Jerusalem—descends from heaven to Earth. Christ reigns on Earth as king and lawgiver.

MOSES 7

Enoch *3000 BC*

60 And the Lord said unto Enoch: As I live, even so will I come in the last days, in the days of wickedness and vengeance, to fulfil then oath which I have made unto you concerning the children of Noah;
65 And it came to pass that Enoch saw the day of the coming of the Son of Man, in the last days, to dwell on the Earth in righteousness for the space of a thousand years;

2 NEPHI 22 (see also ISAIAH 12)

Isaiah *740 BC*

1 And in that day thou shalt say: O Lord, I will praise thee; though thou wast angry with me thine anger is turned away, and thou comfortedst me.
2 Behold, God is my salvation; I will trust, and not be afraid; for the Lord Jehovah is my strength and my song; he also has become my salvation.
3 Therefore, with joy shall ye draw water out of the wells of salvation.
4 And in that day shall ye say: Praise the Lord, call upon his name, declare his doings among the people, make mention that his name is exalted.
5 Sing unto the Lord; for he hath done excellent things; this is known in all the Earth.
6 Cry out and shout, thou inhabitant of Zion; for great is the Holy One of Israel in the midst of thee.

JACOB 5

Zenos *~700-800 BC*

74 And thus they labored, with all diligence, according to the commandments of the Lord of the vineyard, even until the bad had been cast away out of the vineyard, and the Lord had preserved unto himself that the trees had become again the natural fruit; and they became like unto one body; and the fruits were equal; and the Lord of the vineyard had preserved unto himself the natural fruit, which was most precious unto him from the beginning.
75 And it came to pass that when the Lord of the vineyard saw that his fruit was good, and that his vineyard was no more corrupt, he called up his servants, and said unto them: Behold, for this last time have we nourished my vineyard; and thou beholdest that I have done according to my will; and I have preserved the natural fruit, that it is good, even like as it was in the beginning. And blessed art thou; for because ye have been diligent in laboring with me in my vineyard, and have kept my commandments, and have brought unto me again the natural fruit, that my vineyard is no more corrupted, and the bad is cast away, behold ye shall have joy with me because of the fruit of my vineyard.
76 For behold, for a long time will I lay up of the fruit of my vineyard unto mine own self against the season, which speedily cometh; and for the last time have I nourished my vineyard, and pruned it, and dug about it, and dunged it; wherefore I will lay up unto mine own self of the fruit, for a long time, according to that which I have spoken.

ISAIAH 25

Isaiah *740 BC*

6 And in this mountain shall the LORD of hosts make unto all people a feast of fat things, a feast of wines on the lees, of fat

things full of marrow, of wines on the lees well refined.
7 And he will destroy in this mountain the face of the covering cast over all people, and the veil that is spread over all nations.
8 He will swallow up death in victory; and the Lord GOD will wipe away tears from off all faces; and the rebuke of his people shall he take away from off all the Earth: for the LORD hath spoken it.
9 And it shall be said in that day, Lo, this is our God; we have waited for him, and he will save us: this is the LORD; we have waited for him, we will be glad and rejoice in his salvation.

HOSEA 2

Hosea — *790 BC*

18 And in that day will I make a covenant for them with the beasts of the field, and with the fowls of heaven, and with the creeping things of the ground: and I will break the bow and the sword and the battle out of the Earth, and will make them to lie down safely.
19 And I will betroth thee unto me for ever; yea, I will betroth thee unto me in righteousness, and in judgment, and in lovingkindness, and in mercies.
20 I will even betroth thee unto me in faithfulness: and thou shalt know the LORD.
21 And it shall come to pass in that day, I will hear, saith the LORD, I will hear the heavens, and they shall hear the Earth;
22 And the Earth shall hear the corn, and the wine, and the oil; and they shall hear Jezreel.
23 And I will sow her unto me in the Earth; and I will have mercy upon her that had not obtained mercy; and I will say to them which were not my people, Thou art my people; and they shall say, Thou art my God.

ISAIAH 66

Isaiah — *740 BC*

18 For I know their works and their thoughts: it shall come, that I will gather all nations and tongues; and they shall come, and see my glory.
19 And I will set a sign among them, and I will send those that escape of them unto the nations, to Tarshish, Pul, and Lud, that draw the bow, to Tubal, and Javan, to the isles afar off, that have not heard my fame, neither have seen my glory; and they shall declare my glory among the Gentiles.
20 And they shall bring all your brethren for an offering unto the LORD out of all nations upon horses, and in chariots, and in litters, and upon mules, and upon swift beasts, to my holy mountain Jerusalem, saith the LORD, as the children of Israel bring an offering in a clean vessel into the house of the LORD.
21 And I will also take of them for priests and for Levites, saith the LORD.

PSALM 98

David — *1000 BC*

1 O sing unto the Lord a new song; for he hath done marvellous things: his right hand, and his holy arm, hath gotten him the victory.
2 The Lord hath made known his salvation: his righteousness hath he openly shewed in the sight of the heathen.
3 He hath remembered his mercy and his truth toward the house of Israel: all the ends of the Earth have seen the salvation of our God.
4 Make a joyful noise unto the Lord, all the Earth: make a loud noise, and rejoice, and sing praise.
5 Sing unto the Lord with the harp; with the harp, and the voice of a psalm.
6 With trumpets and sound of cornet make a joyful noise before the Lord, the King.
7 Let the sea roar, and the fulness thereof; the world, and they that dwell therein.
8 Let the floods clap their hands: let the hills be joyful together
9 Before the Lord; for he cometh to judge the Earth: with righteousness shall he judge the world, and the people with equity.

CITY OF ENOCH RETURNS

REVELATION 21

John — *95 AD*

2 And I John saw the holy city, new Jerusalem, coming down from God out of heaven, prepared as a bride adorned for her husband.
3 And I heard a great voice out of heaven saying, Behold, the tabernacle of God is with men, and he will dwell with them,

John Watches the New Jerusalem Descend, 14th Century Tapestry.

and they shall be his people, and God himself shall be with them, and be their God.
4 And God shall wipe away all tears from their eyes; and there shall be no more death, neither sorrow, nor crying, neither shall there be any more pain: for the former things are passed away.
5 And he that sat upon the throne said, Behold, I make all things new. And he said unto me, Write: for these words are true and faithful.
6 And he said unto me, It is done. I am Alpha and Omega, the beginning and the end. I will give unto him that is athirst of the fountain of the water of life freely.
7 He that overcometh shall inherit all things; and I will be his God, and he shall be my son.
9 And there came unto me one of the seven angels which had the seven vials full of the seven last plagues, and talked with me, saying, Come hither, I will shew thee the bride, the Lamb's wife.
10 And he carried me away in the spirit to a great and high mountain, and shewed me that great city, the holy Jerusalem, descending out of heaven from God,
11 Having the glory of God: and her light was like unto a stone most precious, even like a jasper stone, clear as crystal;
12 And had a wall great and high, and had twelve gates, and at the gates twelve angels, and names written thereon, which are the names of the twelve tribes of the children of Israel:
13 On the east three gates; on the north three gates; on the south three gates; and on the west three gates.
14 And the wall of the city had twelve foundations, and in them the names of the twelve apostles of the Lamb.
15 And he that talked with me had a golden reed to measure the city, and the gates thereof, and the wall thereof.
16 And the city lieth foursquare, and the length is as large as the breadth: and he measured the city with the reed, twelve thousand furlongs. The length and the breadth and the height of it are equal.
17 And he measured the wall thereof, an hundred and forty and four cubits, according to the measure of a man, that is, of the angel.
18 And the building of the wall of it was of jasper: and the city was pure gold, like unto clear glass.
19 And the foundations of the wall of the city were garnished with all manner of precious stones. The first foundation was jasper; the second, sapphire; the third, a chalcedony; the fourth, an emerald;

20 The fifth, sardonyx; the sixth, sardius; the seventh, chrysolite; the eighth, beryl; the ninth, a topaz; the tenth, a chrysoprasus; the eleventh, a jacinth; the twelfth, an amethyst.
21 And the twelve gates were twelve pearls; every several gate was of one pearl: and the street of the city was pure gold, as it were transparent glass.
22 And I saw no temple therein: for the Lord God Almighty and the Lamb are the temple of it.
23 And the city had no need of the sun, neither of the moon, to shine in it: for the glory of God did lighten it, and the Lamb is the light thereof.
24 And the nations of them which are saved shall walk in the light of it: and the kings of the Earth do bring their glory and honour into it.
25 And the gates of it shall not be shut at all by day: for there shall be no night there.
26 And they shall bring the glory and honour of the nations into it.
27 And there shall in no wise enter into it anything that defileth, neither whatsoever worketh abomination, or maketh a lie: but they which are written in the Lamb's book of life.

ETHER 13

Ether — *600 BC*

10 And then cometh the New Jerusalem; and blessed are they who dwell therein, for it is they whose garments are white through the blood of the Lamb; and they are they who are numbered among the remnant of the seed of Joseph, who were of the house of Israel.

MOSES 7

Enoch — *3000 BC*

61 And the day shall come that the Earth shall rest…
63 And the Lord said unto Enoch: Then shalt thou and all thy city meet them there, and we will receive them into our bosom, and they shall see us; and we will fall upon their necks, and they shall fall upon our necks, and we will kiss each other;
64 And there shall be mine abode, and it shall be Zion, which shall come forth out of all the creations which I have made; and for the space of a thousand years the Earth shall rest.
67 And the Lord showed Enoch all things, even unto the end of the world; and he saw the day of the righteous, the hour of their redemption, and received a fulness of joy;

GENESIS 9

Noah — *2400 BC*

21 And the bow shall be in the cloud; and I will look upon it, that I may remember the everlasting covenant, *which I made unto thy father Enoch; that, when men should keep all my commandments, Zion should again come on the Earth, the city of Enoch which I have caught up unto myself.*
22 *And this is mine everlasting covenant, that when thy posterity shall embrace the truth, and look upward, then shall Zion look downward, and all the heavens shall shake with gladness, and the Earth shall tremble with joy;*
23 *And the general assembly of the church of the firstborn shall come down out of heaven, and possess the Earth, and shall have place until the end come. And this is mine everlasting covenant, which I made with thy father Enoch.* [JST]

GENESIS 14

Moses — *2100 BC*

33 *And now, Melchizedek was a priest of this order; therefore he obtained peace in Salem, and was called the Prince of peace.*
34 *And his people wrought righteousness, and obtained heaven, and sought for the city of Enoch which God had before taken, separating it from the Earth, having reserved it unto the latter-days, or the end of the world;*
35 *And hath said, and sworn with an oath, that the heavens and the Earth should come together; and the sons of God should be tried so as by fire.* [JST]

MATTHEW 6

Jesus Christ — *30 AD*

10 Thy kingdom come. Thy will be done in Earth, as it is in heaven.

DOCTRINE AND COVENANTS 45

Joseph Smith — *March 1831*

11 Wherefore, hearken ye together and let me show unto you even my wisdom—the

wisdom of him whom ye say is the God of
Enoch, and his brethren,
12 Who were separated from the Earth,
and were received unto myself—a city
reserved until a day of righteousness shall
come—a day which was sought for by all
holy men, and they found it not because
of wickedness and abominations;
13 And confessed they were strangers and
pilgrims on the Earth;
14 But obtained a promise that they
should find it and see it in their flesh.

ETHER 13
Ether *600 BC*

11 And then also cometh the Jerusalem of
old; and the inhabitants thereof, blessed
are they, for they have been washed in the
blood of the Lamb; and they are they who
were scattered and gathered in from the
four quarters of the Earth, and from the
north countries, and are partakers of the
fulfilling of the covenant which God made
with their father, Abraham.
12 And when these things come, bringeth
to pass the scripture which saith, there are
they who were first, who shall be last; and
there are they who were last, who shall be
first.

JESUS CHRIST IS KING

ISAIAH 32
Isaiah *740 BC*

1 Behold, a king shall reign in righteousness, and princes shall rule in judgment.

DOCTRINE AND COVENANTS 65
Joseph Smith *October 1831*

5...the Son of Man shall come down in heaven, clothed in the brightness of his glory, to meet the kingdom of God which is set up on the Earth.

ISAIAH 1
Isaiah *740 BC*

26 And I will restore thy judges as at the
first, and thy counsellors as at the beginning: afterward thou shalt be called, The
city of righteousness, the faithful city.
27 Zion shall be redeemed with judgment,
and her converts with righteousness.

DOCTRINE AND COVENANTS 38
Joseph Smith *January 1831*

21 But, verily I say unto you that in time
ye shall have no king nor ruler, for I will
be your king and watch over you.
22 Wherefore, hear my voice and follow
me, and you shall be a free people, and ye
shall have no laws but my laws when I
come, for I am your lawgiver, and what
can stay my hand?

DOCTRINE AND COVENANTS 45
Joseph Smith *March 1831*

58 And the Earth shall be given unto them
for an inheritance; and they shall multiply
and wax strong, and their children shall
grow up without sin unto salvation.
59 For the Lord shall be in their midst, and
his glory shall be upon them, and he will
be their king and their lawgiver.

DANIEL 7
Daniel *610 BC*

22 Until the Ancient of days came, and
judgment was given to the saints of the
most High; and the time came that the
saints possessed the kingdom.
9 I beheld till the thrones were cast down,
and the Ancient of days did sit, whose
garment was white as snow, and the hair
of his head like the pure wool: his throne
was like the fiery flame, and his wheels as
burning fire.
10 A fiery stream issued and came forth
from before him: thousand thousands
ministered unto him, and ten thousand
times ten thousand stood before him: the
judgment was set, and the books were
opened.
13 I saw in the night visions, and, behold,
one like the Son of man came with the
clouds of heaven, and came to the Ancient
of days, and they brought him near before
him.
14 And there was given him dominion,
and glory, and a kingdom, that all people,
nations, and languages, should serve him:
his dominion is an everlasting dominion,
which shall not pass away, and his
kingdom that which shall not be
destroyed.
18 But the saints of the most High shall
take the kingdom, and possess the kingdom forever, even for ever and ever.

Christ Reigns as King, stained glass panel in the transept of St. John's Anglican Church, Ashfield, New South Wales.

26 But the judgment shall sit, and they shall take away his dominion, to consume and to destroy it unto the end.
27 And the kingdom and dominion, and the greatness of the kingdom under the whole heaven, shall be given to the people of the saints of the most High, whose kingdom is an everlasting kingdom, and all dominions shall serve and obey him.
28 Hitherto is the end of the matter. As for me Daniel, my cogitations much troubled me, and my countenance changed in me: but I kept the matter in my heart.

DOCTRINE AND COVENANTS 58

Joseph Smith — *August 1831*

22 Wherefore, be subject to the powers that be, until he reigns whose right it is to reign, and subdues all enemies under his feet.

DOCTRINE AND COVENANTS 84

Joseph Smith — *September 1832*

118 For, with you saith the Lord Almighty, I will rend their kingdoms; I will not only shake the Earth, but the starry heavens shall tremble.
119 For I, the Lord, have put forth my hand to exert the powers of heaven; ye cannot see it now, yet a little while and ye shall see it, and know that I am, and that I will come and reign with my people.
120 I am Alpha and Omega, the beginning and the end. Amen.

60

LIFE IN THE KINGDOM OF GOD

Then Shall the Wolf Dwell With the Lamb.

✦✦✦

All of the spirits of the dead, except the wicked and rebellious, have been resurrected. Mortals have been transfigured physically and live alongside the resurrected saints from the past. Peace and safety prevail. Christ provides light, there will no longer be day and night. One language is spoken. Children are born but there is no death. People will live to the age of a tree, then be instantly resurrected. Animals will no longer be dangerous or deadly.

DOCTRINE AND COVENANTS 84
Joseph Smith *September 1832*
98 Until all shall know me, who remain, even from the least unto the greatest, and shall be filled with the knowledge of the Lord, and shall see eye to eye, and shall lift up their voice, and with the voice together sing this new song, saying:
99 The Lord hath brought again Zion; The Lord hath redeemed his people, Israel, according to the election of grace, which was brought to pass by the faith and covenant of their fathers.
100 The Lord hath redeemed his people; And Satan is bound and time is no longer. The Lord hath gathered all things in one. The Lord hath brought down Zion from above. The Lord hath brought up Zion from beneath.
101 The Earth hath travailed and brought forth her strength; And truth is established in her bowels; And the heavens have smiled upon her; And she is clothed with the glory of her God; For he stands in the midst of his people.
102 Glory, and honor, and power, and might, Be ascribed to our God; for he is full of mercy, Justice, grace and truth, and peace, Forever and ever, Amen.

DOCTRINE AND COVENANTS 130
Joseph Smith *April 1843*
2 And that same sociality which exists among us here will exist among us there, only it will be coupled with eternal glory, which glory we do not now enjoy.

REVELATION 22

John 95 AD

1 And he shewed me a pure river of water of life, clear as crystal, proceeding out of the throne of God and of the Lamb.
2 In the midst of the street of it, and on either side of the river, was there the tree of life, which bare twelve manner of fruits, and yielded her fruit every month: and the leaves of the tree were for the healing of the nations.
3 And there shall be no more curse: but the throne of God and of the Lamb shall be in it; and his servants shall serve him:
4 And they shall see his face; and his name shall be in their foreheads.
5 And there shall be no night there; and they need no candle, neither light of the sun; for the Lord God giveth them light: and they shall reign for ever and ever.

ZECHARIAH 14

Zechariah 520 BC

6 And it shall come to pass in that day, that the light shall not be clear, nor dark:
7 But it shall be one day which shall be known to the LORD, not day, nor night: but it shall come to pass, that at evening time it shall be light.
8 And it shall be in that day, that living waters shall go out from Jerusalem; half of them toward the former sea, and half of them toward the hinder sea: in summer and in winter shall it be.
9 And the LORD shall be king over all the Earth: in that day shall there be one LORD, and his name one.
10 All the land shall be turned as a plain from Geba to Rimmon south of Jerusalem: and it shall be lifted up, and inhabited in her place, from Benjamin's gate unto the place of the first gate, unto the corner gate, and from the tower of Hananeel unto the king's winepresses.
11 And men shall dwell in it, and there shall be no more utter destruction; but Jerusalem shall be safely inhabited.

ISAIAH 60

Isaiah 740 BC

18 Violence shall no more be heard in thy land, wasting nor destruction within thy borders; but thou shalt call thy walls Salvation, and thy gates Praise.
19 The sun shall be no more thy light by day; neither for brightness shall the moon give light unto thee: but the LORD shall be unto thee an everlasting light, and thy God thy glory.
20 Thy sun shall no more go down; neither shall thy moon withdraw itself: for the LORD shall be thine everlasting light, and the days of thy mourning shall be ended.
21 Thy people also shall be all righteous: they shall inherit the land for ever, the branch of my planting, the work of my hands, that I may be glorified.
22 A little one shall become a thousand, and a small one a strong nation: I the LORD will hasten it in his time.

ZEPHANIAH 3

Zephaniah 640 BC

9 For then will I turn to the people a pure language, that they may all call upon the name of the LORD, to serve him with one consent.
10 From beyond the rivers of Ethiopia my suppliants, even the daughter of my dispersed, shall bring mine offering.
11 In that day shalt thou not be ashamed for all thy doings, wherein thou hast transgressed against me: for then I will take away out of the midst of thee them that rejoice in thy pride, and thou shalt no more be haughty because of my holy mountain.
12 I will also leave in the midst of thee an afflicted and poor people, and they shall trust in the name of the LORD.
13 The remnant of Israel shall not do iniquity, nor speak lies; neither shall a deceitful tongue be found in their mouth: for they shall feed and lie down, and none shall make them afraid.
14 Sing, O daughter of Zion; shout, O Israel; be glad and rejoice with all the heart, O daughter of Jerusalem.
15 The LORD hath taken away thy judgments, he hath cast out thine enemy: the king of Israel, even the LORD, is in the midst of thee: thou shalt not see evil anymore.
16 In that day it shall be said to Jerusalem, Fear thou not: and to Zion, Let not thine hands be slack.
17 The LORD thy God in the midst of thee is mighty; he will save, he will rejoice over thee with joy; he will rest in his love, he will joy over thee with singing.

18 I will gather them that are sorrowful for the solemn assembly, who are of thee, to whom the reproach of it was a burden.
19 Behold, at that time I will undo all that afflict thee: and I will save her that halteth, and gather her that was driven out; and I will get them praise and fame in every land where they have been put to shame.
20 At that time will I bring you again, even in the time that I gather you: for I will make you a name and a praise among all people of the Earth, when I turn back your captivity before your eyes, saith the LORD.

2 NEPHI 21 (see also ISAIAH 11)

Isaiah 740 BC

6 The wolf also shall dwell with the lamb, and the leopard shall lie down with the kid, and the calf and the young lion and fatling together; and a little child shall lead them.
7 And the cow and the bear shall feed; their young ones shall lie down together; and the lion shall eat straw like the ox.
8 And the sucking child shall play on the hole of the asp, and the weaned child shall put his hand on the cockatrice's den.
9 They shall not hurt nor destroy in all my holy mountain, for the Earth shall be full of the knowledge of the Lord, as the waters cover the sea.

ISAIAH 65

Isaiah 740 BC

18 But be ye glad and rejoice forever in that which I create: for, behold, I create Jerusalem a rejoicing, and her people a joy.
19 And I will rejoice in Jerusalem, and joy in my people: and the voice of weeping shall be no more heard in her, nor the voice of crying.
20 There shall be no more thence an infant of days, nor an old man that hath not filled his days: for the child shall die an hundred years old; but the sinner being an hundred years old shall be accursed.
21 And they shall build houses, and inhabit them; and they shall plant vineyards, and eat the fruit of them.
22 They shall not build, and another inhabit; they shall not plant, and another eat: for as the days of a tree are the days of my people, and mine elect shall long enjoy the work of their hands.
23 They shall not labour in vain, nor bring forth for trouble; for they are the seed of the blessed of the LORD, and their offspring with them.
24 And it shall come to pass, that before they call, I will answer; and while they are yet speaking, I will hear.
25 The wolf and the lamb shall feed together, and the lion shall eat straw like the bullock: and dust shall be the serpent's meat. They shall not hurt nor destroy in all my holy mountain, saith the LORD.

DOCTRINE AND COVENANTS 101

Joseph Smith *December 1833*

26 And in that day the enmity of man, and the enmity of beasts, yea, the enmity of all flesh, shall cease from before my face.
29 And there shall be no sorrow because there is no death.
30 In that day an infant shall not die until he is old; and his life shall be as the age of a tree;
31 And when he dies he shall not sleep, that is to say in the Earth, but shall be changed in the twinkling of an eye, and shall be caught up, and his rest shall be glorious.
35 And all they who suffer persecution for my name, and endure in faith, though they are called to lay down their lives for my sake yet shall they partake of all this glory.
36 Wherefore, fear not even unto death; for in this world your joy is not full, but in me your joy is full.
37 Therefore, care not for the body, neither the life of the body; but care for the soul, and for the life of the soul.
38 And seek the face of the Lord always, that in patience ye may possess your souls, and ye shall have eternal life.

DOCTRINE AND COVENANTS 63

Joseph Smith *August 1831*

49 Yea, and blessed are the dead that die in the Lord, from henceforth, when the Lord shall come, and old things shall pass away, and all things become new, they shall rise from the dead and shall not die after, and shall receive an inheritance before the Lord, in the holy city.
50 And he that liveth when the Lord shall come, and hath kept the faith, blessed is he; nevertheless, it is appointed to him to die at the age of man.

51 Wherefore, children shall grow up
until they become old; old men shall die;
but they shall not sleep in the dust, but
they shall be changed in the twinkling of
an eye.
52 Wherefore, for this cause preached the
apostles unto the world the resurrection of
the dead.

3 NEPHI 28

Jesus Christ — *34 AD*

7 Therefore, more blessed are ye [three
Nephite disciples], for ye shall never taste
of death; but ye shall live to behold all the
doings of the Father unto the children of
men, even until all things shall be fulfilled
according to the will of the Father, when
I shall come in my glory with the powers
of heaven.
8 And ye shall never endure the pains of
death; but when I shall come in my glory
ye shall be changed in the twinkling of an
eye from mortality to immortality; and
then shall ye be blessed in the kingdom of
my Father.
9 And again, ye shall not have pain while
ye shall dwell in the flesh, neither sorrow
save it be for the sins of the world; and all
this will I do because of the thing which
ye have desired of me, for ye have desired
that ye might bring the souls of men unto
me, while the world shall stand.
13 And behold, the heavens were opened,
and they were caught up into heaven, and
saw and heard unspeakable things.
14 And it was forbidden them that they
should utter; neither was it given unto
them power that they could utter the
things which they saw and heard;
15 And whether they were in the body or
out of the body, they could not tell; for it
did seem unto them like a transfiguration
of them, that they were changed from this
body of flesh into an immortal state, that
they could behold the things of God.
17 And now, whether they were mortal or
immortal, from the day of their trans-
figuration, I know not;
36 And now behold, as I spake concerning
those whom the Lord hath chosen, yea,
even three who were caught up into the
heavens, that I knew not whether they
were cleansed from mortality to immor-
tality—
37 But behold, since I wrote, I have
inquired of the Lord, and he hath made it
manifest unto me that there must needs be
a change wrought upon their bodies, or
else it needs be that they must taste of
death;
38 Therefore, that they might not taste of
death there was a change wrought upon
their bodies, that they might not suffer
pain nor sorrow save it were for the sins of
the world.
39 Now this change was not equal to that
which shall take place at the last day; but
there was a change wrought upon them,
insomuch that Satan could have no power
over them, that he could not tempt them;
and they were sanctified in the flesh, that
they were holy, and that the powers of the
Earth could not hold them.
40 And in this state they were to remain
until the judgment day of Christ; and at
that day they were to receive a greater
change, and to be received into the
kingdom of the Father to go no more out,
but to dwell with God eternally in the
heavens.

MICAH 4

Micah — *722 BC*

3 And he shall judge among many people,
and rebuke strong nations afar off; and
they shall beat their swords into plow-
shares, and their spears into pruning-
hooks: nation shall not lift up a sword
against nation, neither shall they learn
war anymore.
4 But they shall sit every man under his
vine and under his fig tree; and none shall
make them afraid: for the mouth of the
LORD of hosts hath spoken it.
5 For all people will walk everyone in the
name of his god, and we will walk in the
name of the LORD our God for ever and
ever.

61

ALL THINGS ARE REVEALED

+++

All things will be revealed. When people fully receive and accept the Book of Mormon, then the Lord will reveal the full record of those ancient prophets. This includes the vision of the Brother of Jared, which comprised the sealed portion of the gold plates that the Lord did not allow Joseph Smith to translate.

HABAKKUK 2

Habakkuk *600 BC*

14 For the Earth shall be filled with the knowledge of the glory of the LORD, as the waters cover the sea.

DOCTRINE AND COVENANTS 101

Joseph Smith *December 1833*

27 And in that day whatsoever any man shall ask, it shall be given unto him.
32 Yea, verily I say unto you, in that day when the Lord shall come, he shall reveal all things—
33 Things which have passed, and hidden things which no man knew, things of the Earth, by which it was made, and the purpose and the end thereof—
34 Things most precious, things that are above, and things that are beneath, things that are in the Earth, and upon the Earth, and in heaven.

DOCTRINE AND COVENANTS 121

Joseph Smith *March 1839*

26 God shall give unto you knowledge by his Holy Spirit, yea, by the unspeakable gift of the Holy Ghost, that has not been revealed since the world was until now;
27 Which our forefathers have awaited with anxious expectation to be revealed in the last times, which their minds were pointed to by the angels, as held in reserve for the fulness of their glory;
28 A time to come in the which nothing shall be withheld, whether there be one God or many gods, they shall be manifest.
29 All thrones and dominions, principalities and powers, shall be revealed and set forth upon all who have endured valiantly for the gospel of Jesus Christ.
30 And also, if there be bounds set to the heavens or to the seas, or to the dry land, or to the sun, moon, or stars—
31 All the times of their revolutions, all the appointed days, months, and years, and all the days of their days, months, and years, and all their glories, laws, and set times, shall be revealed in the days of the dispensation of the fulness of times—
32 According to that which was ordained in the midst of the Council of the Eternal God of all other gods before this world was, that should be reserved unto the finishing and the end thereof, when every man shall enter into his eternal presence and into his immortal rest.

DOCTRINE AND COVENANTS 76

Joseph Smith *February 1832*

5 For thus saith the Lord—I, the Lord, am merciful and gracious unto those who fear me, and delight to honor those who serve me in righteousness and in truth unto the end.
6 Great shall be their reward and eternal shall be their glory.
7 And to them will I reveal all mysteries, yea, all the hidden mysteries of my kingdom from days of old, and for ages to come, will I make known unto them the good pleasure of my will concerning all things pertaining to my kingdom.
8 Yea, even the wonders of eternity shall they know, and things to come will I show them, even the things of many generations.
9 And their wisdom shall be great, and their understanding reach to heaven; and before them the wisdom of the wise shall perish, and the understanding of the prudent shall come to naught.
10 For by my Spirit will I enlighten them, and by my power will I make known unto

Spiral Galaxy NGC 4414 imaged by the Hubble Space Telescope 1995.

them the secrets of my will—yea, even those things which eye has not seen, nor ear heard, nor yet entered into the heart of man.

2 NEPHI 30

Nephi, Son of Lehi 550 BC

15 They shall not hurt nor destroy in all my holy mountain; for the Earth shall be full of the knowledge of the Lord as the waters cover the sea.

16 Wherefore, the things of all nations shall be made known; yea, all things shall be made known unto the children of men.

17 There is nothing which is secret save it shall be revealed; there is no work of darkness save it shall be made manifest in the light; and there is nothing which is sealed upon the Earth save it shall be loosed.

18 Wherefore, all things which have been revealed unto the children of men shall at that day be revealed;

3 NEPHI 26

Mormon 385 AD

6 And now there cannot be written in this book even a hundredth part of the things which Jesus did truly teach unto the people;

7 But behold the plates of Nephi do contain the more part of the things which he taught the people.

8 And these things have I written, which are a lesser part of the things which he taught the people; and I have written them to the intent that they may be brought again unto this people, from the Gentiles, according to the words which Jesus hath spoken.

9 And when they shall have received this, which is expedient that they should have first, to try their faith, and if it shall so be that they shall believe these things then shall the greater things be made manifest unto them.

10 And if it so be that they will not believe these things, then shall the greater things be withheld from them, unto their condemnation.
11 Behold, I was about to write them, all which were engraven upon the plates of Nephi, but the Lord forbade it, saying: I will try the faith of my people.

MORMON 8

Moroni — *401 AD*

12 And whoso receiveth this record, and shall not condemn it because of the imperfections which are in it, the same shall know of greater things than these. Behold, I am Moroni; and were it possible, I would make all things known unto you.

ETHER 3

The Brother of Jared — *2200 BC*

21 And it came to pass that the Lord said unto the brother of Jared: Behold, thou shalt not suffer these things which ye have seen and heard to go forth unto the world, until the time cometh that I shall glorify my name in the flesh; wherefore, ye shall treasure up the things which ye have seen and heard, and show it to no man.
22 And behold, when ye shall come unto me, ye shall write them and shall seal them up, that no one can interpret them; for ye shall write them in a language that they cannot be read.
23 And behold, these two stones will I give unto thee, and ye shall seal them up also with the things which ye shall write.
24 For behold, the language which ye shall write I have confounded; wherefore I will cause in my own due time that these stones shall magnify to the eyes of men these things which ye shall write.
25 And when the Lord had said these words, he showed unto the brother of Jared all the inhabitants of the Earth which had been, and also all that would be; and he withheld them not from his sight, even unto the ends of the Earth.
26 For he had said unto him in times before, that if he would believe in him that he could show unto him all things—it should be shown unto him; therefore the Lord could not withhold anything from him, for he knew that the Lord could show him all things.
27 And the Lord said unto him: Write these things and seal them up; and I will show them in mine own due time unto the children of men.
28 And it came to pass that the Lord commanded him that he should seal up the two stones which he had received, and show them not, until the Lord should show them unto the children of men.

ETHER 4

Moroni — *400 AD*

1 And the Lord commanded the brother of Jared to go down out of the mount from the presence of the Lord, and write the things which he had seen; and they were forbidden to come unto the children of men until after that he should be lifted up upon the cross; and for this cause did king Mosiah keep them, that they should not come unto the world until after Christ should show himself unto his people.
2 And after Christ truly had showed himself unto his people he commanded that they should be made manifest.
3 And now, after that, they have all dwindled in unbelief; and there is none save it be the Lamanites, and they have rejected the gospel of Christ; therefore I am commanded that I should hide them up again in the Earth.
4 Behold, I have written upon these plates the very things which the brother of Jared saw; and there never were greater things made manifest than those which were made manifest unto the brother of Jared.
5 Wherefore the Lord hath commanded me to write them; and I have written them. And he commanded me that I should seal them up; and he also hath commanded that I should seal up the interpretation thereof; wherefore I have sealed up the interpreters, according to the commandment of the Lord.
6 For the Lord said unto me: They shall not go forth unto the Gentiles until the day that they shall repent of their iniquity, and become clean before the Lord.
7 And in that day that they shall exercise faith in me, saith the Lord, even as the brother of Jared did, that they may become sanctified in me, then will I manifest unto them the things which the brother of Jared saw, even to the unfolding unto them all my revelations, saith Jesus Christ, the Son of God, the Father of the heavens and of the Earth, and all things that in them are.

8 And he that will contend against the word of the Lord, let him be accursed; and he that shall deny these things, let him be accursed; for unto them will I show no greater things, saith Jesus Christ; for I am he who speaketh.
9 And at my command the heavens are opened and are shut; and at my word the Earth shall shake; and at my command the inhabitants thereof shall pass away, even so as by fire.
10 And he that believeth not my words believeth not my disciples; and if it so be that I do not speak, judge ye; for ye shall know that it is I that speaketh, at the last day.
11 But he that believeth these things which I have spoken, him will I visit with the manifestations of my Spirit, and he shall know and bear record. For because of my Spirit he shall know that these things are true; for it persuadeth men to do good.
12 And whatsoever thing persuadeth men to do good is of me; for good cometh of none save it be of me. I am the same that leadeth men to all good; he that will not believe my words will not believe me—that I am; and he that will not believe me will not believe the Father who sent me. For behold, I am the Father, I am the light, and the life, and the truth of the world.
13 Come unto me, O ye Gentiles, and I will show unto you the greater things, the knowledge which is hid up because of unbelief.
14 Come unto me, O ye house of Israel, and it shall be made manifest unto you how great things the Father hath laid up for you, from the foundation of the world; and it hath not come unto you, because of unbelief.
15 Behold, when ye shall rend that veil of unbelief which doth cause you to remain in your awful state of wickedness, and hardness of heart, and blindness of mind, then shall the great and marvelous things which have been hid up from the foundation of the world from you—yea, when ye shall call upon the Father in my name, with a broken heart and a contrite spirit, then shall ye know that the Father hath remembered the covenant which he made unto your fathers, O house of Israel.
16 And then shall my revelations which I have caused to be written by my servant John be unfolded in the eyes of all the people. Remember, when ye see these things, ye shall know that the time is at hand that they shall be made manifest in very deed.
17 Therefore, when ye shall receive this record ye may know that the work of the Father has commenced upon all the face of the land.
18 Therefore, repent all ye ends of the Earth, and come unto me, and believe in my gospel, and be baptized in my name; for he that believeth and is baptized shall be saved; but he that believeth not shall be damned; and signs shall follow them that believe in my name.
19 And blessed is he that is found faithful unto my name at the last day, for he shall be lifted up to dwell in the kingdom prepared for him from the foundation of the world. And behold it is I that hath spoken it. Amen.

ETHER 12
Moroni — *400 AD*

24 And thou hast made us that we could write but little, because of the awkwardness of our hands. Behold, thou hast not made us mighty in writing like unto the brother of Jared, for thou madest him that the things which he wrote were mighty even as thou art, unto the overpowering of man to read them.

DOCTRINE AND COVENANTS 63
Joseph Smith — *August 1831*

23 But unto him that keepeth my commandments I will give the mysteries of my kingdom, and the same shall be in him a well of living water, springing up unto everlasting life.

2 NEPHI 27 (see also ISAIAH 29)
Isaiah — *740 BC*

7 And behold the book shall be sealed; and in the book shall be a revelation from God, from the beginning of the world to the ending thereof.
8 Wherefore, because of the things which are sealed up, the things which are sealed shall not be delivered in the day of the wickedness and abominations of the people. Wherefore the book shall be kept from them.
10 But the words which are sealed he shall not deliver, neither shall he deliver the book. For the book shall be sealed by the

power of God, and the revelation which was sealed shall be kept in the book until the own due time of the Lord, that they may come forth; for behold, they reveal all things from the foundation of the world unto the end thereof.
11 And the day cometh that the words of the book which were sealed shall be read upon the house tops; and they shall be read by the power of Christ; and all things shall be revealed unto the children of men which ever have been among the children of men, and which ever will be even unto the end of the Earth.
21 Touch not the things which are sealed, for I will bring them forth in mine own due time; for I will show unto the children of men that I am able to do mine own work.
22 Wherefore, when thou hast read the words which I have commanded thee, and obtained the witnesses which I have promised unto thee, then shalt thou seal up the book again, and hide it up unto me, that I may preserve the words which thou hast not read, until I shall see fit in mine own wisdom to reveal all things unto the children of men.

1 NEPHI 14

Nephi, Son of Lehi *595 BC*

20 And the angel said unto me: Behold one of the twelve apostles of the Lamb.
21 Behold, he shall see and write the remainder of these things; yea, and also many things which have been.
22 And he shall also write concerning the end of the world.
26 And also others who have been, to them hath he shown all things, and they have written them; and they are sealed up to come forth in their purity, according to the truth which is in the Lamb, in the own due time of the Lord, unto the house of Israel.

DOCTRINE AND COVENANTS 5

Joseph Smith *March 1829*

9 Behold, verily I say unto you, I have reserved those things which I have entrusted unto you, my servant Joseph, for a wise purpose in me, and it shall be made known unto future generations;

DANIEL 12

Daniel *600 BC*

4 But thou, O Daniel, shut up the words, and seal the book, even to the time of the end: many shall run to and fro, and knowledge shall be increased.

DOCTRINE AND COVENANTS 107

Joseph Smith *March 1835*

53 Three years previous to the death of Adam, he called Seth, Enos, Cainan, Mahalaleel, Jared, Enoch, and Methuselah, who were all high priests, with the residue of his posterity who were righteous, into the valley of Adam-ondi-Ahman, and there bestowed upon them his last blessing.
54 And the Lord appeared unto them, and they rose up and blessed Adam, and called him Michael, the prince, the archangel.
55 And the Lord administered comfort unto Adam, and said unto him: I have set thee to be at the head; a multitude of nations shall come of thee, and thou art a prince over them forever.
56 And Adam stood up in the midst of the congregation; and, notwithstanding he was bowed down with age, being full of the Holy Ghost, predicted whatsoever should befall his posterity unto the latest generation.
57 These things were all written in the book of Enoch, and are to be testified of in due time.

62

THE ABRAHAMIC COVENANT IS FULFILLED

✦✦✦

During the 1,000 year Millennium, the sacred covenant made to Abraham, Isaac, and Jacob, which God long promised he would not forget, will be fulfilled. Specifically, God promised that their posterity would be innumerable and would continue both in life and in death; and that they would inherit a specific area of the newly transfigured Earth for an everlasting inheritance. This chapter will revisit the covenant's origins and then outline how it is to be fulfilled.

GENESIS 13

Abraham *1950 BC*

14 And the LORD said unto Abram, after that Lot was separated from him, Lift up now thine eyes, and look from the place where thou art northward, and southward, and eastward, and westward: and remember the covenant which I make with thee; for it shall be an everlasting covenant; and thou shalt remember the days of Enoch thy father;
15 For all the land which thou seest, to thee will I give it, and to thy seed forever.
16 And I will make thy seed as the dust of the Earth: so that if a man can number the dust of the Earth, then shall thy seed also be numbered.
17 Arise, walk through the land in the length of it and in the breadth of it; for I will give it unto thee.

GENESIS 15

Abraham *1950 BC*

5 And he brought him forth abroad, and said, Look now toward heaven, and tell the stars, if thou be able to number them: and he said unto him, So shall thy seed be.
6 And he believed in the LORD; and he counted it to him for righteousness.
9 And Abram said, Lord God, how wilt thou give me this land for an everlasting inheritance?
10 And the Lord said, Though thou wast dead, yet am I not able to give it thee?
11 And if thou shalt die, yet thou shalt possess it, for the day cometh, that the Son of Man shall live; but how can he live if he be not dead? he must first be quickened.
12 And it came to pass, that Abram looked forth and saw the days of the Son of Man, and was glad, and his soul found rest, and he believed in the Lord; and the Lord counted it unto him for righteousness. [JST]
18 In the same day the LORD made a covenant with Abram, saying, Unto thy seed have I given this land, from the river of Egypt unto the great river, the river Euphrates:

GENESIS 17

Abraham *1950 BC*

1 And when Abram was ninety years old and nine, the LORD appeared to Abram, and said unto him, I am the Almighty God; walk before me, and be thou perfect.
2 And I will make my covenant between me and thee, and will multiply thee exceedingly.
3 And *it came to pass, that* Abram fell on his face, *and called upon the name of the Lord.*
4 And God talked with him, saying, *My people have gone astray from my precepts, and have not kept mine ordinances, which I gave unto their fathers;*
5 *And they have not observed mine anointing, and the burial, or baptism wherewith I commanded them;*
6 *But have turned from the commandment, and taken unto themselves the washing of children, and the blood of sprinkling;*
7 *And have said that the blood of the righteous Abel was shed for sins; and have*

All the Land Which Thou Seest, to Thee Will I Give It, and to Thy Seed Forever. Illustration from Old Testament Bible Primer, 1919.

not known wherein they are accountable before me.

8 *But* as for *thee*, behold, *I will make* my covenant with thee, and thou shalt be a father of many nations.

9 *And this covenant I make, that thy children may be known among all nations.* Neither shall thy name any more be called Abram, but thy name shall be called Abraham; for, a father of many nations have I made thee.

10 And I will make thee exceedingly fruitful, and I will make nations of thee, and kings shall come of thee, *and of thy seed.*

11 And I will establish *a covenant of circumcision with thee, and it shall be* my covenant between me and thee, and thy seed after thee, in their generations; *that thou mayest know forever that children are not accountable before me until they are eight years old.*

12 *And thou shalt observe to keep all my covenants wherein I covenanted with thy fathers; and thou shalt keep the commandments which I have given thee with mine own mouth, and I will be a God unto thee and thy seed after thee.*

13 And I will give unto thee, and to thy seed after thee, the land wherein thou art a stranger, all the land of Canaan, for an everlasting possession; and I will be their God.

20 And God said unto Abraham, As for Sarai thy wife, thou shalt not call her name Sarai, but Sarah shall her name be.

21 And I will bless her, and give thee a son also of her: yea, I will bless her, and she shall be a mother of nations; kings of people shall be of her.

GENESIS 22

Abraham — *1950 BC*

15 And the angel of the LORD called unto Abraham out of heaven the second time,
16 And said, By myself have I sworn, saith the LORD, for because thou hast done this thing, and hast not withheld thy son, thine only son:
17 That in blessing I will bless thee, and in multiplying I will multiply thy seed as the stars of the heaven, and as the sand which is upon the sea shore; and thy seed shall possess the gate of his enemies;
18 And in thy seed shall all the nations of the Earth be blessed; because thou hast obeyed my voice.

GENESIS 24

Isaac — *1850 BC*

60 And they [Rebekah's brother Laban and mother Bethuel] blessed Rebekah, and said unto her, Thou art our sister, be thou the mother of thousands of millions, and let thy seed possess the gate of those which hate them.

GENESIS 26

Isaac — *1850 BC*

2 And the LORD appeared unto him [Isaac], and said, Go not down into Egypt; dwell in the land which I shall tell thee of:
3 Sojourn in this land, and I will be with thee, and will bless thee; for unto thee, and unto thy seed, I will give all these countries, and I will perform the oath which I sware unto Abraham thy father;
4 And I will make thy seed to multiply as the stars of heaven, and will give unto thy seed all these countries; and in thy seed shall all the nations of the Earth be blessed;
5 Because that Abraham obeyed my voice, and kept my charge, my commandments, my statutes, and my laws.
24 And the LORD appeared unto him the same night, and said, I am the God of Abraham thy father: fear not, for I am with thee, and will bless thee, and multiply thy seed for my servant Abraham's sake.

GENESIS 28

Isaac and Jacob — *1800 BC*

1 And Isaac called Jacob, and blessed him, and charged him, and said unto him, ...
3 And God Almighty bless thee, and make thee fruitful, and multiply thee, that thou mayest be a multitude of people;
4 And give thee the blessing of Abraham, to thee, and to thy seed with thee; that thou mayest inherit the land wherein thou art a stranger, which God gave unto Abraham.
12 And he [Jacob] dreamed, and behold a ladder set up on the Earth, and the top of it reached to heaven: and behold the angels of God ascending and descending on it.
13 And, behold, the LORD stood above it, and said, I am the LORD God of Abraham thy father, and the God of Isaac: the land whereon thou liest, to thee will I give it, and to thy seed;
14 And thy seed shall be as the dust of the Earth, and thou shalt spread abroad to the west, and to the east, and to the north, and to the south: and in thee and in thy seed shall all the families of the Earth be blessed.
15 And, behold, I am with thee, and will keep thee in all places whither thou goest, and will bring thee again into this land; for I will not leave thee, until I have done that which I have spoken to thee of.

GENESIS 35

Jacob — *1800 BC*

9 And God appeared unto Jacob again, when he came out of Padan-aram, and blessed him.
10 And God said unto him, Thy name is Jacob: thy name shall not be called any more Jacob, but Israel shall be thy name: and he called his name Israel.
11 And God said unto him, I am God Almighty: be fruitful and multiply; a nation and a company of nations shall be of thee, and kings shall come out of thy loins;
12 And the land which I gave Abraham and Isaac, to thee I will give it, and to thy seed after thee will I give the land.

GENESIS 48

Jacob and Joseph — *1700 BC*

3 And Jacob said unto Joseph, God Almighty appeared unto me at Luz in the land of Canaan, and blessed me,
4 And said unto me, Behold, I will make thee fruitful, and multiply thee, and I will make of thee a multitude of people; and

will give this land to thy seed after thee for
an everlasting possession.

HOSEA 1

Hosea 826 BC

10 Yet the number of the children of Israel
shall be as the sand of the sea, which can-
not be measured nor numbered; and it
shall come to pass, that in the place where
it was said unto them, Ye are not my
people, there it shall be said unto them, Ye
are the sons of the living God.
11 Then shall the children of Judah and
the children of Israel be gathered
together, and appoint themselves one
head, and they shall come up out of the
land: for great shall be the day of Jezreel.

ETERNAL INCREASE

DOCTRINE AND COVENANTS 131

Joseph Smith May 1843

1 In the celestial glory there are three
heavens or degrees;
2 And in order to obtain the highest, a
man must enter into this order of the
priesthood [meaning the new and ever-
lasting covenant of marriage];
3 And if he does not, he cannot obtain it.
4 He may enter into the other, but that is
the end of his kingdom; he cannot have an
increase.

DOCTRINE AND COVENANTS 132

Joseph Smith July 1843

19 And again, verily I say unto you, if a
man marry a wife by my word, which is
my law, and by the new and everlasting
covenant, and it is sealed unto them by the
Holy Spirit of promise, by him who is
anointed, unto whom I have appointed
this power and the keys of this priesthood;
and it shall be said unto them—Ye shall
come forth in the first resurrection; and if
it be after the first resurrection, in the next
resurrection; and shall inherit thrones,
kingdoms, principalities, and powers,
dominions, all heights and depths—then
shall it be written in the Lamb's Book of
Life, that he shall commit no murder
whereby to shed innocent blood, and if ye
abide in my covenant, and commit no
murder whereby to shed innocent blood,
it shall be done unto them in all things
whatsoever my servant hath put upon

Couples are married and sealed to each other for time and all eternity in temples. Salt Lake City, UT Temple.

them, in time, and through all eternity;
and shall be of full force when they are out
of the world; and they shall pass by the
angels, and the gods, which are set there,
to their exaltation and glory in all things,
as hath been sealed upon their heads,
which glory shall be a fulness and a
continuation of the seeds forever and ever.
20 Then shall they be gods, because they
have no end; therefore shall they be from
everlasting to everlasting, because they
continue; then shall they be above all,
because all things are subject unto them.
Then shall they be gods, because they
have all power, and the angels are subject
unto them.
21 Verily, verily, I say unto you, except ye
abide my law ye cannot attain to this
glory.
22 For strait is the gate, and narrow the
way that leadeth unto the exaltation and
continuation of the lives, and few there be
that find it, because ye receive me not in
the world neither do ye know me.
23 But if ye receive me in the world, then
shall ye know me, and shall receive your
exaltation; that where I am ye shall be
also.
24 This is eternal lives—to know the only
wise and true God, and Jesus Christ,

whom he hath sent. I am he. Receive ye, therefore, my law.

28 I am the Lord thy God, and will give unto thee the law of my Holy Priesthood, as was ordained by me and my Father before the world was.

29 Abraham received all things, whatsoever he received, by revelation and commandment, by my word, saith the Lord, and hath entered into his exaltation and sitteth upon his throne.

30 Abraham received promises concerning his seed, and of the fruit of his loins—from whose loins ye are, namely, my servant Joseph—which were to continue so long as they were in the world; and as touching Abraham and his seed, out of the world they should continue; both in the world and out of the world should they continue as innumerable as the stars; or, if ye were to count the sand upon the seashore ye could not number them.

31 This promise is yours also, because ye are of Abraham, and the promise was made unto Abraham; and by this law is the continuation of the works of my Father, wherein he glorifieth himself.

32 Go ye, therefore, and do the works of Abraham; enter ye into my law and ye shall be saved.

INHERIT THE EARTH

DOCTRINE AND COVENANTS 38

Joseph Smith — *January 1831*

17 And I have made the Earth rich, and behold it is my footstool, wherefore, again I will stand upon it.

18 And I hold forth and deign to give unto you greater riches, even a land of promise, a land flowing with milk and honey, upon which there shall be no curse when the Lord cometh;

19 And I will give it unto you for the land of your inheritance, if you seek it with all your hearts.

20 And this shall be my covenant with you, ye shall have it for the land of your inheritance, and for the inheritance of your children forever, while the Earth shall stand, and ye shall possess it again in eternity, no more to pass away.

DOCTRINE AND COVENANTS 85

Joseph Smith — *November 1832*

7 And it shall come to pass that I, the Lord God, will send one mighty and strong, holding the scepter of power in his hand, clothed with light for a covering, whose mouth shall utter words, eternal words; while his bowels shall be a fountain of truth, to set in order the house of God, and to arrange by lot the inheritances of the saints whose names are found, and the names of their fathers, and of their children, enrolled in the book of the law of God;

DOCTRINE AND COVENANTS 84

Joseph Smith — *September 1832*

33 For whoso is faithful unto the obtaining these two priesthoods of which I have spoken, and the magnifying their calling, are sanctified by the Spirit unto the renewing of their bodies.

34 They become the sons of Moses and of Aaron and the seed of Abraham, and the church and kingdom, and the elect of God.

35 And also all they who receive this priesthood receive me, saith the Lord;

36 For he that receiveth my servants receiveth me;

37 And he that receiveth me receiveth my Father;

38 And he that receiveth my Father receiveth my Father's kingdom; therefore all that my Father hath shall be given unto him.

39 And this is according to the oath and covenant which belongeth to the priesthood.

DOCTRINE AND COVENANTS 88

Joseph Smith — *December 1832*

107 And then shall the angels be crowned with the glory of his might, and the saints shall be filled with his glory, and receive their inheritance and be made equal with him.

PSALM 37

David — *1000 BC*

9 For evildoers shall be cut off: but those that wait upon the Lord, they shall inherit the Earth.

10 For yet a little while, and the wicked shall not be: yea, thou shalt diligently consider his place, and it shall not be.

11 But the meek shall inherit the Earth; and shall delight themselves in the abundance of peace.
18 The Lord knoweth the days of the upright: and their inheritance shall be forever.
22 For such as be blessed of him shall inherit the Earth; and they that be cursed of him shall be cut off.
29 The righteous shall inherit the land, and dwell therein forever.
34 Wait on the Lord, and keep his way, and he shall exalt thee to inherit the land: when the wicked are cut off, thou shalt see it.

PSALM 76

David — *1000 BC*

8 Thou didst cause judgment to be heard from heaven; the Earth feared, and was still,
9 When God arose to judgment, to save all the meek of the Earth. Selah.

MATTHEW 5

Jesus Christ — *30 AD*

3 Blessed are the poor in spirit: for theirs is the kingdom of heaven.
4 Blessed are they that mourn: for they shall be comforted.
5 Blessed are the meek: for they shall inherit the Earth.
6 Blessed are they which do hunger and thirst after righteousness: for they shall be filled.
7 Blessed are the merciful: for they shall obtain mercy.
8 Blessed are the pure in heart: for they shall see God.
9 Blessed are the peacemakers: for they shall be called the children of God.
10 Blessed are they which are persecuted for righteousness' sake: for theirs is the kingdom of heaven.

DOCTRINE AND COVENANTS 56

Joseph Smith — *July 1831*

18 But blessed are the poor who are pure in heart, whose hearts are broken, and whose spirits are contrite, for they shall see the kingdom of God coming in power and great glory unto their deliverance; for the fatness of the Earth shall be theirs.
19 For behold, the Lord shall come, and his recompense shall be with him, and he shall reward every man, and the poor shall rejoice;
20 And their generations shall inherit the Earth from generation to generation, forever and ever…

DOCTRINE AND COVENANTS 81

Joseph Smith — *March 1832*

6 And if thou art faithful unto the end thou shalt have a crown of immortality, and eternal life in the mansions which I have prepared in the house of my Father.

DOCTRINE AND COVENANTS 72

Joseph Smith — *December 1831*

4 For he who is faithful and wise in time is accounted worthy to inherit the mansions prepared for him of my Father.

DOCTRINE AND COVENANTS 78

Joseph Smith — *March 1832*

15 That you may come up unto the crown prepared for you, and be made rulers over many kingdoms, saith the Lord God, the Holy One of Zion, who hath established the foundations of Adam-ondi-Ahman;
16 Who hath appointed Michael your prince, and established his feet, and set him upon high, and given unto him the keys of salvation under the counsel and direction of the Holy One, who is without beginning of days or end of life.
17 Verily, verily, I say unto you, ye are little children, and ye have not as yet understood how great blessings the Father hath in his own hands and prepared for you;
18 And ye cannot bear all things now; nevertheless, be of good cheer, for I will lead you along. The kingdom is yours and the blessings thereof are yours, and the riches of eternity are yours.
19 And he who receiveth all things with thankfulness shall be made glorious; and the things of this Earth shall be added unto him, even an hundred fold, yea, more.
20 Wherefore, do the things which I have commanded you, saith your Redeemer, even the Son Ahman, who prepareth all things before he taketh you;
21 For ye are the church of the Firstborn, and he will take you up in a cloud, and appoint every man his portion.
22 And he that is a faithful and wise steward shall inherit all things. Amen.

1 CORINTHIANS 2

Paul *54 AD*

7 But we speak the wisdom of God in a mystery, even the hidden wisdom, which God ordained before the world unto our glory:
8 Which none of the princes of this world knew: for had they known it, they would not have crucified the Lord of glory.
9 But as it is written, Eye hath not seen, nor ear heard, neither have entered into the heart of man, the things which God hath prepared for them that love him.

ISAIAH 64

Isaiah *740 BC*

4 For since the beginning of the world men have not heard, nor perceived by the ear, neither hath the eye seen, O God, beside thee, what he hath prepared for him that waiteth for him.

ISAIAH 57

Isaiah *740 BC*

13 When thou criest, let thy companies deliver thee; but the wind shall carry them all away; vanity shall take them: but he that putteth his trust in me shall possess the land, and shall inherit my holy mountain;
14 And shall say, Cast ye up, cast ye up, prepare the way, take up the stumbling block out of the way of my people.
15 For thus saith the high and lofty One that inhabiteth eternity, whose name is Holy; I dwell in the high and holy place, with him also that is of a contrite and humble spirit, to revive the spirit of the humble, and to revive the heart of the contrite ones.

EZEKIEL 47

Ezekiel *600 BC*

13 Thus saith the Lord GOD; This shall be the border, whereby ye shall inherit the land according to the twelve tribes of Israel: Joseph shall have two portions.
14 And ye shall inherit it, one as well as another: concerning the which I lifted up mine hand to give it unto your fathers: and this land shall fall unto you for inheritance.
15 And this shall be the border of the land toward the north side, from the great sea, the way of Hethlon, as men go to Zedad;
16 Hamath, Berothah, Sibraim, which is between the border of Damascus and the border of Hamath; Hazar-hatticon, which is by the coast of Hauran.
17 And the border from the sea shall be Hazar-enan, the border of Damascus, and the north northward, and the border of Hamath. And this is the north side.
18 And the east side ye shall measure from Hauran, and from Damascus, and from Gilead, and from the land of Israel by Jordan, from the border unto the east sea. And this is the east side.
19 And the south side southward, from Tamar even to the waters of strife in Kadesh, the river to the great sea. And this is the south side southward.
20 The west side also shall be the great sea from the border, till a man come over against Hamath. This is the west side.
21 So shall ye divide this land unto you according to the tribes of Israel.
22 And it shall come to pass, that ye shall divide it by lot for an inheritance unto you, and to the strangers that sojourn among you, which shall beget children among you: and they shall be unto you as born in the country among the children of Israel; they shall have inheritance with you among the tribes of Israel.
23 And it shall come to pass, that in what tribe the stranger sojourneth, there shall ye give him his inheritance, saith the Lord GOD.

EZEKIEL 48

Ezekiel *600 BC*

1 Now these are the names of the tribes. From the north end to the coast of the way of Hethlon, as one goeth to Hamath, Hazar-enan, the border of Damascus northward, to the coast of Hamath; for these are his sides east and west; a portion for Dan.
2 And by the border of Dan, from the east side unto the west side, a portion for Asher.
3 And by the border of Asher, from the east side even unto the west side, a portion for Naphtali.
4 And by the border of Naphtali, from the east side unto the west side, a portion for Manasseh.
5 And by the border of Manasseh, from the east side unto the west side, a portion for Ephraim.

The tribes of Israel are all given their inheritance in the kingdom of God on Earth.

6 And by the border of Ephraim, from the east side even unto the west side, a portion for Reuben.
7 And by the border of Reuben, from the east side unto the west side, a portion for Judah.
8 And by the border of Judah, from the east side unto the west side, shall be the offering which ye shall offer of five and twenty thousand reeds in breadth, and in length as one of the other parts, from the east side unto the west side: and the sanctuary shall be in the midst of it.
9 The oblation that ye shall offer unto the LORD shall be of five and twenty thousand in length, and of ten thousand in breadth.
10 And for them, even for the priests, shall be this holy oblation; toward the north five and twenty thousand in length, and toward the west ten thousand in breadth, and toward the east ten thousand in breadth, and toward the south five and twenty thousand in length: and the sanctuary of the LORD shall be in the midst thereof.
11 It shall be for the priests that are sanctified of the sons of Zadok; which have kept my charge, which went not astray when the children of Israel went astray, as the Levites went astray.
12 And this oblation of the land that is offered shall be unto them a thing most holy by the border of the Levites.
13 And over against the border of the priests the Levites shall have five and twenty thousand in length, and ten thousand in breadth: all the length shall be five and twenty thousand, and the breadth ten thousand.
14 And they shall not sell of it, neither exchange, nor alienate the first fruits of the land: for it is holy unto the LORD.
15 And the five thousand, that are left in the breadth over against the five and twenty thousand, shall be a profane place for the city, for dwelling, and for suburbs: and the city shall be in the midst thereof.
16 And these shall be the measures thereof; the north side four thousand and five hundred, and the south side four thousand and five hundred, and on the east side four thousand and five hundred, and the west side four thousand and five hundred.
17 And the suburbs of the city shall be toward the north two hundred and fifty, and toward the south two hundred and fifty, and toward the east two hundred

and fifty, and toward the west two hundred and fifty.
18 And the residue in length over against the oblation of the holy portion shall be ten thousand eastward, and ten thousand westward: and it shall be over against the oblation of the holy portion; and the increase thereof shall be for food unto them that serve the city.
19 And they that serve the city shall serve it out of all the tribes of Israel.
20 All the oblation shall be five and twenty thousand by five and twenty thousand: ye shall offer the holy oblation foursquare, with the possession of the city.
21 And the residue shall be for the prince, on the one side and on the other of the holy oblation, and of the possession of the city, over against the five and twenty thousand of the oblation toward the east border, and westward over against the five and twenty thousand toward the west border, over against the portions for the prince: and it shall be the holy oblation; and the sanctuary of the house shall be in the midst thereof.
22 Moreover from the possession of the Levites, and from the possession of the city, being in the midst of that which is the prince's, between the border of Judah and the border of Benjamin, shall be for the prince.
23 As for the rest of the tribes, from the east side unto the west side, Benjamin shall have a portion.
24 And by the border of Benjamin, from the east side unto the west side, Simeon shall have a portion.
25 And by the border of Simeon, from the east side unto the west side, Issachar a portion.
26 And by the border of Issachar, from the east side unto the west side, Zebulun a portion.
27 And by the border of Zebulun, from the east side unto the west side, Gad a portion.
28 And by the border of Gad, at the south side southward, the border shall be even from Tamar unto the waters of strife in Kadesh, and to the river toward the great sea.
29 This is the land which ye shall divide by lot unto the tribes of Israel for inheritance, and these are their portions, saith the Lord GOD.
30 And these are the goings out of the city on the north side, four thousand and five hundred measures.
31 And the gates of the city shall be after the names of the tribes of Israel: three gates northward; one gate of Reuben, one gate of Judah, one gate of Levi.
32 And at the east side four thousand and five hundred: and three gates; and one gate of Joseph, one gate of Benjamin, one gate of Dan.
33 And at the south side four thousand and five hundred measures: and three gates; one gate of Simeon, one gate of Issachar, one gate of Zebulun.
34 At the west side four thousand and five hundred, with their three gates; one gate of Gad, one gate of Asher, one gate of Naphtali.
35 It was round about eighteen thousand measures: and the name of the city from that day shall be, The LORD is there.

PART 5

PROPHECIES OF EVENTS AT THE END OF THE MILLENNIUM

ABOUT 3000 AD

63

SATAN IS CAST OUT FOREVER

Satan Cast Out For the Last Time, painting by Phillip Medhurst.

+++

At the close of the Millennium people begin to sin again and Satan is loosed from his prison. There is a final battle between good and evil where Michael (Adam) overcomes Satan and his armies and casts them out forever.

REVELATION 20

John — *95 AD*

7 And when the thousand years are expired, Satan shall be loosed out of his prison,
8 And shall go out to deceive the nations which are in the four quarters of the Earth, Gog and Magog, to gather them together to battle: the number of whom is as the sand of the sea.
9 And they went up on the breadth of the Earth, and compassed the camp of the saints about, and the beloved city: and fire came down from God out of heaven, and devoured them.

DOCTRINE AND COVENANTS 29

Joseph Smith — *September 1830*

22 And again, verily, verily, I say unto you that when the thousand years are ended, and men again begin to deny their God, then will I spare the Earth but for a little season;

DOCTRINE AND COVENANTS 43

Joseph Smith — *February 1831*

31... and when he [Satan] is loosed again he shall only reign for a little season,

JACOB 5

Zenos — *~700-800 BC*

77 And when the time cometh that evil fruit shall again come into my vineyard, then will I cause the good and the bad to be gathered; and the good will I preserve unto myself, and the bad will I cast away into its own place. And then cometh the season and the end; and my vineyard will I cause to be burned with fire.

DOCTRINE AND COVENANTS 88

Joseph Smith — *December 1832*

111 And then he [Satan] shall be loosed for a little season, that he may gather together his armies.
112 And Michael, the seventh angel, even the archangel, shall gather together his armies, even the hosts of heaven.
113 And the devil shall gather together his armies; even the hosts of hell, and shall come up to battle against Michael and his armies.
114 And then cometh the battle of the great God; and the devil and his armies shall be cast away into their own place, that they shall not have power over the saints any more at all.
115 For Michael shall fight their battles, and shall overcome him who seeketh the throne of him who sitteth upon the throne, even the Lamb.
116 This is the glory of God, and the sanctified; and they shall not anymore see death.

64

THE RESURRECTION OF THE WICKED

+++

The wicked come forth to be resurrected – those that have been held in the prison of outer darkness, the lake of fire and brimstone. These souls will have had the gospel preached to them in the spirit and will have had time to accept it. This is the last Resurrection of the just, or the last Resurrection of those who will avail themselves of the Atonement of Jesus Christ and inherit a kingdom of glory.

DOCTRINE AND COVENANTS 88
Joseph Smith *December 1832*
100 And again, another trump shall sound, which is the third trump; and then come the spirits of men who are to be judged, and are found under condemnation;
101 And these are the rest of the dead; and they live not again until the thousand years are ended, neither again, until the end of the Earth.

REVELATION 20
John *95 AD*
5 But the rest of the dead lived not again until the thousand years were finished.

DOCTRINE AND COVENANTS 38
Joseph Smith *January 1831*
5 But behold, the residue of the wicked have I kept in chains of darkness until the judgment of the great day, which shall come at the end of the Earth;
6 And even so will I cause the wicked to be kept, that will not hear my voice but harden their hearts, and wo, wo, wo, is their doom.

DOCTRINE AND COVENANTS 43
Joseph Smith *February 1831*
33 And the wicked shall go away into unquenchable fire, and their end no man knoweth on Earth, nor ever shall know, until they come before me in judgment.

1 NEPHI 14
Nephi, Son of Lehi *595 BC*
3 And that great pit, which hath been digged for them by that great and abominable church, which was founded by the devil and his children, that he might lead away the souls of men down to hell—yea, that great pit which hath been digged for the destruction of men shall be filled by those who digged it, unto their utter destruction, saith the Lamb of God; not the destruction of the soul, save it be the casting of it into that hell which hath no end.
4 For behold, this is according to the captivity of the devil, and also according to the justice of God, upon all those who will work wickedness and abomination before him.

REVELATION 21
John *95 AD*
8 But the fearful, and unbelieving, and the abominable, and murderers, and whoremongers, and sorcerers, and idolaters, and all liars, shall have their part in the lake which burneth with fire and brimstone: which is the second death.

1 CORINTHIANS 6
Paul *54 AD*
9 Know ye not that the unrighteous shall not inherit the kingdom of God? Be not deceived: neither fornicators, nor idolaters, nor adulterers, nor effeminate, nor abusers of themselves with mankind,
10 Nor thieves, nor covetous, nor drunkards, nor revilers, nor extortioners, shall inherit the kingdom of God.

DOCTRINE AND COVENANTS 63
Joseph Smith *August 1831*
16 And verily I say unto you, as I have said before, he that looketh on a woman to lust after her, or if any shall commit adultery in their hearts, they shall not have the

Spirit, but shall deny the faith and shall fear.
17 Wherefore, I, the Lord, have said that the fearful, and the unbelieving, and all liars, and whosoever loveth and maketh a lie, and the whoremonger, and the sorcerer, shall have their part in that lake which burneth with fire and brimstone, which is the second death.
18 Verily I say, that they shall not have part in the first resurrection.

MATTHEW 7

Jesus Christ *30 AD*

13 Enter ye in at the strait gate: for wide is the gate, and broad is the way, that leadeth to destruction, and many there be which go in thereat:

EPHESIANS 5

Paul *62 AD*

3 But fornication, and all uncleanness, or covetousness, let it not be once named among you, as becometh saints;
4 Neither filthiness, nor foolish talking, nor jesting, which are not convenient: but rather giving of thanks.
5 For this ye know, that no whoremonger, nor unclean person, nor covetous man, who is an idolater, hath any inheritance in the kingdom of Christ and of God.

GALATIANS 5

Paul *58 AD*

19 Now the works of the flesh are manifest, which are these; Adultery, fornication, uncleanness, lasciviousness,
20 Idolatry, witchcraft, hatred, variance, emulations, wrath, strife, seditions, heresies,
21 Envyings, murders, drunkenness, revellings, and such like: of the which I tell you before, as I have also told you in time past, that they which do such things shall not inherit the kingdom of God.

DOCTRINE AND COVENANTS 138

Joseph F. Smith *October 1918*

20 But unto the wicked he [Christ] did not go, and among the ungodly and the unrepentant who had defiled themselves while in the flesh, his voice was not raised;
21 Neither did the rebellious who rejected the testimonies and the warnings of the ancient prophets behold his presence, nor look upon his face.
22 Where these were, darkness reigned...

DOCTRINE AND COVENANTS 76

Joseph Smith *February 1832*

81 And again, we saw the glory of the telestial, which glory is that of the lesser, even as the glory of the stars differs from that of the glory of the moon in the firmament.
82 These are they who received not the gospel of Christ, neither the testimony of Jesus.
83 These are they who deny not the Holy Spirit.
84 These are they who are thrust down to hell.
85 These are they who shall not be redeemed from the devil until the last resurrection, until the Lord, even Christ the Lamb, shall have finished his work.
86 These are they who receive not of his fulness in the eternal world, but of the Holy Spirit through the ministration of the terrestrial;
88 And also the telestial receive it of the administering of angels who are appointed to minister for them, or who are appointed to be ministering spirits for them; for they shall be heirs of salvation.
89 And thus we saw, in the heavenly vision, the glory of the telestial, which surpasses all understanding;
90 And no man knows it except him to whom God has revealed it.
98 And the glory of the telestial is one, even as the glory of the stars is one; for as one star differs from another star in glory, even so differs one from another in glory in the telestial world;
99 For these are they who are of Paul, and of Apollos, and of Cephas.
100 These are they who say they are some of one and some of another—some of Christ and some of John, and some of Moses, and some of Elias, and some of Esaias, and some of Isaiah, and some of Enoch;
101 But received not the gospel, neither the testimony of Jesus, neither the prophets, neither the everlasting covenant.
102 Last of all, these all are they who will not be gathered with the saints, to be caught up unto the church of the Firstborn, and received into the cloud.

103 These are they who are liars, and sorcerers, and adulterers, and whore-mongers, and whosoever loves and makes a lie.
104 These are they who suffer the wrath of God on Earth.
105 These are they who suffer the vengeance of eternal fire.
106 These are they who are cast down to hell and suffer the wrath of Almighty God, until the fulness of times, when Christ shall have subdued all enemies under his feet, and shall have perfected his work;
107 When he shall deliver up the kingdom, and present it unto the Father, spotless, saying: I have overcome and have trodden the winepress alone, even the winepress of the fierceness of the wrath of Almighty God.
108 Then shall he be crowned with the crown of his glory, to sit on the throne of his power to reign forever and ever.
109 But behold, and lo, we saw the glory and the inhabitants of the telestial world, that they were as innumerable as the stars in the firmament of heaven, or as the sand upon the seashore;
110 And heard the voice of the Lord saying: These all shall bow the knee, and every tongue shall confess to him who sits upon the throne forever and ever;
111 For they shall be judged according to their works, and every man shall receive according to his own works, his own dominion, in the mansions which are prepared;
112 And they shall be servants of the Most High; but where God and Christ dwell they cannot come, worlds without end.

DOCTRINE AND COVENANTS 88

Joseph Smith — *December 1832*

21 And they who are not sanctified through the law...of a terrestrial kingdom...must inherit another kingdom...or that of a telestial kingdom.
23 And he who cannot abide the law of a terrestrial kingdom cannot abide a terrestrial glory.
31 And also they who are quickened by a portion of the telestial glory shall then receive of the same, even a fulness.

Sepp Dietrich, Colonel-General of the Waffen SS; Adolf Hitler, Reich's Chancellor; and Heinrich Himmler, Reichsführer SS. 1937. Should they choose to repent and follow the commandments while in the lake of fire and brimstone, then even they can be forgiven and inherit a Telestial glory—a testament to the immense power of the Atonement of Jesus Christ.

DOCTRINE AND COVENANTS 104

Joseph Smith — *April 1834*

8 Therefore, inasmuch as you are found transgressors, you cannot escape my wrath in your lives.
9 Inasmuch as ye are cut off for transgression, ye cannot escape the buffetings of Satan until the day of redemption.

65

THE RESURRECTION OF THE REBELLIOUS

+++

The final group to be resurrected will be that of the unjust, those who refuse to repent, who deny the Holy Ghost and Jesus Christ to the last day, who break the oath and covenant of the priesthood, and whose names are not written in the Book of Life. All will kneel and confess that Jesus is the Christ, and will suffer for their own sins, as the Atonement of Christ does not apply to them. They are then resurrected, and in their filthy state, they are cast into outer darkness where they will remain forever and ever.

The rebellious will get what they want. No one can be compelled to worship Christ. No unclean thing can inherit the kingdom of heaven.

DOCTRINE AND COVENANTS 88
Joseph Smith *December 1832*
102 And another trump shall sound, which is the fourth trump, saying: There are found among those who are to remain until that great and last day, even the end, who shall remain filthy still.

DOCTRINE AND COVENANTS 88
Joseph Smith *December 1832*
24 And he who cannot abide the law of a telestial kingdom cannot abide a telestial glory; therefore he is not meet for a kingdom of glory. Therefore he must abide a kingdom which is not a kingdom of glory.
32 And they who remain shall also be quickened; nevertheless, they shall return again to their own place, to enjoy that which they are willing to receive, because they were not willing to enjoy that which they might have received.
33 For what doth it profit a man if a gift is bestowed upon him, and he receive not the gift? Behold, he rejoices not in that which is given unto him, neither rejoices in him who is the giver of the gift.
34 And again, verily I say unto you, that which is governed by law is also preserved by law and perfected and sanctified by the same.
35 That which breaketh a law, and abideth not by law, but seeketh to become a law unto itself, and willeth to abide in sin, and altogether abideth in sin, cannot be sanctified by law, neither by mercy, justice, nor judgment. Therefore, they must remain filthy still.

HELAMAN 14
Samuel the Lamanite *6 BC*
30 And now remember, remember, my brethren, that whosoever perisheth, perisheth unto himself; and whosoever doeth iniquity, doeth it unto himself; for behold, ye are free; ye are permitted to act for yourselves; for behold, God hath given unto you a knowledge and he hath made you free.
31 He hath given unto you that ye might know good from evil, and he hath given unto you that ye might choose life or death; and ye can do good and be restored unto that which is good, or have that which is good restored unto you; or ye can do evil, and have that which is evil restored unto you.

ALMA 42
Alma the Younger *73 BC*
27 Therefore, O my son, whosoever will come may come and partake of the waters of life freely; and whosoever will not come the same is not compelled to come; but in the last day it shall be restored unto him according to his deeds.
28 If he has desired to do evil, and has not repented in his days, behold, evil shall be done unto him, according to the restoration of God.

The rebellious are resurrected and cast into outer darkness. The Last Judgment, by Gustave Dore, 1866.

ALMA 41

Alma the Younger *73 BC*

3 And it is requisite with the justice of God
that men should be judged according to
their works; and if their works were good
in this life, and the desires of their hearts
were good, that they should also, at the
last day, be restored unto that which is
good.
4 And if their works are evil they shall be
restored unto them for evil. Therefore, all
things shall be restored to their proper
order, everything to its natural frame—
mortality raised to immortality, corrupt-
ion to incorruption—raised to endless
happiness to inherit the kingdom of God,
or to endless misery to inherit the king-
dom of the devil, the one on one hand, the
other on the other—
5 The one raised to happiness according to
his desires of happiness, or good according
to his desires of good; and the other to evil

according to his desires of evil; for as he has desired to do evil all the day long even so shall he have his reward of evil when the night cometh.
6 And so it is on the other hand. If he hath repented of his sins, and desired righteousness until the end of his days, even so he shall be rewarded unto righteousness.
7 These are they that are redeemed of the Lord; yea, these are they that are taken out, that are delivered from that endless night of darkness; and thus they stand or fall; for behold, they are their own judges, whether to do good or do evil.

ALMA 9
Alma the Younger *82 BC*
28 Therefore, prepare ye the way of the Lord, for the time is at hand that all men shall reap a reward of their works, according to that which they have been—if they have been righteous they shall reap the salvation of their souls, according to the power and deliverance of Jesus Christ; and if they have been evil they shall reap the damnation of their souls, according to the power and captivation of the devil.

MORMON 9
Moroni *421 AD*
14 And then cometh the judgment of the Holy One upon them; and then cometh the time that he that is filthy shall be filthy still...and he that is unhappy shall be unhappy still.

ALMA 7
Alma the Younger *83 BC*
21 And he doth not dwell in unholy temples; neither can filthiness or anything which is unclean be received into the kingdom of God; therefore I say unto you the time shall come, yea, and it shall be at the last day, that he who is filthy shall remain in his filthiness.

ALMA 11
Amulek *82 BC*
37 And I say unto you again that he cannot save them in their sins; for I cannot deny his word, and he hath said that no unclean thing can inherit the kingdom of heaven; therefore, how can ye be saved, except ye inherit the kingdom of heaven? Therefore, ye cannot be saved in your sins.

JOHN 5
Jesus Christ *30 BC*
29 … and they that have done evil, unto the resurrection of damnation.

DANIEL 12
Daniel *600 BC*
2 And many of them that sleep in the dust of the Earth shall awake, some to shame and everlasting contempt.

DOCTRINE AND COVENANTS 29
Joseph Smith *September 1830*
26 But, behold, verily I say unto you, before the Earth shall pass away, Michael, mine archangel, shall sound his trump, and then shall all the dead awake, for their graves shall be opened, and they shall come forth—yea, even all.
27 … and the wicked on my left hand will I be ashamed to own before the Father;
28 Wherefore I will say unto them—Depart from me, ye cursed, into everlasting fire, prepared for the devil and his angels.
29 And now, behold, I say unto you, never at any time have I declared from mine own mouth that they should return, for where I am they cannot come, for they have no power.

MOSIAH 26
Jesus Christ (to Alma the Elder) *120 BC*
25 And it shall come to pass that when the second trump shall sound then shall they that never knew me come forth and shall stand before me.
26 And then shall they know that I am the Lord their God, that I am their Redeemer; but they would not be redeemed.
27 And then I will confess unto them that I never knew them; and they shall depart into everlasting fire prepared for the devil and his angels.
28 Therefore I say unto you, that he that will not hear my voice, the same shall ye not receive into my church, for him I will not receive at the last day.

3 NEPHI 14 (see also MATTHEW 7)
Jesus Christ *34 AD*
21 Not everyone that saith unto me, Lord, Lord, shall enter into the kingdom of heaven; but he that doeth the will of my Father who is in heaven.

22 Many will say to me in that day: Lord, Lord, have we not prophesied in thy name, and in thy name have cast out devils, and in thy name done many wonderful works?
23 And then will I profess unto them: I never knew you; depart from me, ye that work iniquity.

MATTHEW 25

Jesus Christ *33 AD*

24 Then he which had received the one talent came and said, Lord, I knew thee that thou art an hard man, reaping where thou hast not sown, and gathering where thou hast not strawed:
25 And I was afraid, and went and hid thy talent in the Earth: lo, there thou hast that is thine.
26 His lord answered and said unto him, Thou wicked and slothful servant, thou knewest that I reap where I sowed not, and gather where I have not strawed:
27 Thou oughtest therefore to have put my money to the exchangers, and then at my coming I should have received mine own with usury.
28 Take therefore the talent from him, and give it unto him which hath ten talents.
29 For unto everyone that hath shall be given, and he shall have abundance: but from him that hath not shall be taken away even that which he hath.
30 And cast ye the unprofitable servant into outer darkness: there shall be weeping and gnashing of teeth.
32 And before him shall be gathered all nations: and he shall separate them one from another, as a shepherd divideth his sheep from the goats:
33 And he shall set the sheep on his right hand, but the goats on the left.
41 Then shall he say also unto them on the left hand, Depart from me, ye cursed, into everlasting fire, prepared for the devil and his angels:
42 For I was an hungred, and ye gave me no meat: I was thirsty, and ye gave me no drink:
43 I was a stranger, and ye took me not in: naked, and ye clothed me not: sick, and in prison, and ye visited me not.
44 Then shall they also answer him, saying, Lord, when saw we thee an hungred, or athirst, or a stranger, or naked, or sick, or in prison, and did not minister unto thee?
45 Then shall he answer them, saying, Verily I say unto you, Inasmuch as ye did it not to one of the least of these, ye did it not to me.
46 And these shall go away into everlasting punishment:

2 NEPHI 9

Jacob, Son of Lehi *550 BC*

16 And assuredly, as the Lord liveth, for the Lord God hath spoken it, and it is his eternal word, which cannot pass away, that they who are righteous shall be righteous still, and they who are filthy shall be filthy still; wherefore, they who are filthy are the devil and his angels; and they shall go away into everlasting fire, prepared for them; and their torment is as a lake of fire and brimstone, whose flame ascendeth up forever and ever and has no end.
17 O the greatness and the justice of our God! For he executeth all his words, and they have gone forth out of his mouth, and his law must be fulfilled.

1 NEPHI 15

Nephi, Son of Lehi *595 BC*

26 And they said unto me: What meaneth the river of water which our father saw?
27 And I said unto them that the water which my father saw was filthiness; and so much was his mind swallowed up in other things that he beheld not the filthiness of the water.
28 And I said unto them that it was an awful gulf, which separated the wicked from the tree of life, and also from the saints of God.
29 And I said unto them that it was a representation of that awful hell, which the angel said unto me was prepared for the wicked.
30 And I said unto them that our father also saw that the justice of God did also divide the wicked from the righteous; and the brightness thereof was like unto the brightness of a flaming fire, which ascendeth up unto God forever and ever, and hath no end.
31 And they said unto me: Doth this thing mean the torment of the body in the days of probation, or doth it mean the final state of the soul after the death of the

temporal body, or doth it speak of the things which are temporal?
32 And it came to pass that I said unto them that it was a representation of things both temporal and spiritual; for the day should come that they must be judged of their works, yea, even the works which were done by the temporal body in their days of probation.
33 Wherefore, if they should die in their wickedness they must be cast off also, as to the things which are spiritual, which are pertaining to righteousness; wherefore, they must be brought to stand before God, to be judged of their works; and if their works have been filthiness they must needs be filthy; and if they be filthy it must needs be that they cannot dwell in the kingdom of God; if so, the kingdom of God must be filthy also.
34 But behold, I say unto you, the kingdom of God is not filthy, and there cannot any unclean thing enter into the kingdom of God; wherefore there must needs be a place of filthiness prepared for that which is filthy.
35 And there is a place prepared, yea, even that awful hell of which I have spoken, and the devil is the preparator of it; wherefore the final state of the souls of men is to dwell in the kingdom of God, or to be cast out because of that justice of which I have spoken.
36 Wherefore, the wicked are rejected from the righteous, and also from that tree of life, whose fruit is most precious and most desirable above all other fruits; yea, and it is the greatest of all the gifts of God. And thus I spake unto my brethren. Amen

Those that come forth in the last resurrection are those who choose not to repent, not to believe in Christ, and willingly remain in their sins despite many warnings to change course. But in the end every knee will bow, and every tongue will confess that Jesus is the Christ, and that his judgments on are just.

DOCTRINE AND COVENANTS 56
Joseph Smith — *June 1831*

1 Hearken, O ye people who profess my name, saith the Lord your God; for behold, mine anger is kindled against the rebellious, and they shall know mine arm and mine indignation, in the day of visitation and of wrath upon the nations.
2 And he that will not take up his cross and follow me, and keep my commandments, the same shall not be saved.
3 Behold, I, the Lord, command; and he that will not obey shall be cut off in mine own due time, after I have commanded and the commandment is broken.
4 Wherefore I, the Lord, command and revoke, as it seemeth me good; and all this to be answered upon the heads of the rebellious, saith the Lord.

ISAIAH 45
Isaiah — *740 BC*

23 I have sworn by myself, the word is gone out of my mouth in righteousness, and shall not return, That unto me every knee shall bow, every tongue shall swear.

ROMANS 14
Paul — *57 BC*

11 For it is written, As I live, saith the Lord, every knee shall bow to me, and every tongue shall confess to God.

2 NEPHI 9
Jacob, Son of Lehi — *550 BC*

46 Prepare your souls for that glorious day when justice shall be administered unto the righteous, even the day of judgment, that ye may not shrink with awful fear; that ye may not remember your awful guilt in perfectness, and be constrained to exclaim: Holy, holy are thy judgments, O Lord God Almighty—but I know my guilt; I transgressed thy law, and my transgressions are mine; and the devil hath obtained me, that I am a prey to his awful misery.

PHILIPPIANS 2
Paul — *62 AD*

10 That at the name of Jesus every knee should bow, of things in heaven, and things in Earth, and things under the Earth;

MOSIAH 27
Alma the Younger — *95 BC*

31 Yea, every knee shall bow, and every tongue confess before him. Yea, even at the last day, when all men shall stand to be judged of him, then shall they confess that he is God; then shall they confess,

Cain and Abel, by Titian, 1542.

who live without God in the world, that the judgment of an everlasting punishment is just upon them; and they shall quake, and tremble, and shrink beneath the glance of his all-searching eye.

MOSIAH 16

Abinadi *148 BC*

1 And now, it came to pass that after Abinadi had spoken these words he stretched forth his hand and said: The time shall come when all shall see the salvation of the Lord; when every nation, kindred, tongue, and people shall see eye to eye and shall confess before God that his judgments are just.
2 And then shall the wicked be cast out, and they shall have cause to howl, and weep, and wail, and gnash their teeth; and this because they would not hearken unto the voice of the Lord; therefore the Lord redeemeth them not.
3 For they are carnal and devilish, and the devil has power over them; yea, even that old serpent that did beguile our first parents, which was the cause of their fall; which was the cause of all mankind becoming carnal, sensual, devilish, knowing evil from good, subjecting themselves to the devil.
4 Thus all mankind were lost; and behold, they would have been endlessly lost were

it not that God redeemed his people from their lost and fallen state.
5 But remember that he that persists in his own carnal nature, and goes on in the ways of sin and rebellion against God, remaineth in his fallen state and the devil hath all power over him. Therefore he is as though there was no redemption made, being an enemy to God; and also is the devil an enemy to God.
6 And now if Christ had not come into the world, speaking of things to come as though they had already come, there could have been no redemption.
7 And if Christ had not risen from the dead, or have broken the bands of death that the grave should have no victory, and that death should have no sting, there could have been no resurrection.
8 But there is a resurrection, therefore the grave hath no victory, and the sting of death is swallowed up in Christ.
9 He is the light and the life of the world; yea, a light that is endless, that can never be darkened; yea, and also a life which is endless, that there can be no more death.
10 Even this mortal shall put on immortality, and this corruption shall put on incorruption, and shall be brought to stand before the bar of God, to be judged of him according to their works whether they be good or whether they be evil—
11 If they be good, to the resurrection of endless life and happiness; and if they be evil, to the resurrection of endless damnation, being delivered up to the devil, who hath subjected them, which is damnation—
12 Having gone according to their own carnal wills and desires; having never called upon the Lord while the arms of mercy were extended towards them; for the arms of mercy were extended towards them, and they would not; they being warned of their iniquities and yet they would not depart from them; and they were commanded to repent and yet they would not repent.
13 And now, ought ye not to tremble and repent of your sins, and remember that only in and through Christ ye can be saved?
14 Therefore, if ye teach the law of Moses, also teach that it is a shadow of those things which are to come—
15 Teach them that redemption cometh through Christ the Lord, who is the very Eternal Father. Amen.

Those who do not repent will not be forgiven and will be cast off forever. Do not procrastinate the day of your repentance to the end.

DOCTRINE AND COVENANTS 29

Joseph Smith — *September 1830*

43 And thus did I, the Lord God, appoint unto man the days of his probation—that by his natural death he might be raised in immortality unto eternal life, even as many as would believe;
44 And they that believe not unto eternal damnation; for they cannot be redeemed from their spiritual fall, because they repent not;
45 For they love darkness rather than light, and their deeds are evil, and they receive their wages of whom they list to obey.

ALMA 34

Amulek — *74 BC*

15 And thus he shall bring salvation to all those who shall believe on his name; this being the intent of this last sacrifice, to bring about the bowels of mercy, which overpowereth justice, and bringeth about means unto men that they may have faith unto repentance.
16 And thus mercy can satisfy the demands of justice, and encircles them in the arms of safety, while he that exercises no faith unto repentance is exposed to the whole law of the demands of justice; therefore only unto him that has faith unto repentance is brought about the great and eternal plan of redemption.
32 For behold, this life is the time for men to prepare to meet God; yea, behold the day of this life is the day for men to perform their labors.
33 And now, as I said unto you before, as ye have had so many witnesses, therefore, I beseech of you that ye do not procrastinate the day of your repentance until the end; for after this day of life, which is given us to prepare for eternity, behold, if we do not improve our time while in this life, then cometh the night of

darkness wherein there can be no labor performed.
34 Ye cannot say, when ye are brought to that awful crisis, that I will repent, that I will return to my God. Nay, ye cannot say this; for that same spirit which doth possess your bodies at the time that ye go out of this life, that same spirit will have power to possess your body in that eternal world.
35 For behold, if ye have procrastinated the day of your repentance even until death, behold, ye have become subjected to the spirit of the devil, and he doth seal you his; therefore, the Spirit of the Lord hath withdrawn from you, and hath no place in you, and the devil hath all power over you; and this is the final state of the wicked.

ALMA 12

Alma the Younger — *82 BC*

31 Wherefore, he gave commandments unto men, they having first transgressed the first commandments as to things which were temporal, and becoming as gods, knowing good from evil, placing themselves in a state to act, or being placed in a state to act according to their wills and pleasures, whether to do evil or to do good—
32 Therefore God gave unto them commandments, after having made known unto them the plan of redemption, that they should not do evil, the penalty thereof being a second death, which was an everlasting death as to things pertaining unto righteousness; for on such the plan of redemption could have no power, for the works of justice could not be destroyed, according to the supreme goodness of God.
35 And whosoever will harden his heart and will do iniquity, behold, I swear in my wrath that he shall not enter into my rest.
36 And now, my brethren, behold I say unto you, that if ye will harden your hearts ye shall not enter into the rest of the Lord; therefore your iniquity provoketh him that he sendeth down his wrath upon you as in the first provocation, yea, according to his word in the last provocation as well as the first, to the everlasting destruction of your souls; therefore, according to his word, unto the last death, as well as the first.
37 And now, my brethren, seeing we know these things, and they are true, let us repent, and harden not our hearts, that we provoke not the Lord our God to pull down his wrath upon us in these his second commandments which he has given unto us; but let us enter into the rest of God, which is prepared according to his word.

HELAMAN 13

Samuel the Lamanite — *6 BC*

38 But behold, your days of probation are past; ye have procrastinated the day of your salvation until it is everlastingly too late, and your destruction is made sure; yea, for ye have sought all the days of your lives for that which ye could not obtain; and ye have sought for happiness in doing iniquity, which thing is contrary to the nature of that righteousness which is in our great and Eternal Head.

3 NEPHI 27

Jesus Christ — *34 AD*

17 And he that endureth not unto the end, the same is he that is also hewn down and cast into the fire, from whence they can no more return, because of the justice of the Father.
18 And this is the word which he hath given unto the children of men. And for this cause he fulfilleth the words which he hath given, and he lieth not, but fulfilleth all his words.
19 And no unclean thing can enter into his kingdom; therefore nothing entereth into his rest save it be those who have washed their garments in my blood, because of their faith, and the repentance of all their sins, and their faithfulness unto the end.

HELAMAN 12

Samuel the Lamanite — *6 BC*

20 And behold, if the Lord shall say unto a man—Because of thine iniquities, thou shalt be accursed forever—it shall be done.
21 And if the Lord shall say—Because of thine iniquities thou shalt be cut off from my presence—he will cause that it shall be so.
22 And wo unto him to whom he shall say this, for it shall be unto him that will do iniquity, and he cannot be saved; there-

fore, for this cause, that men might be saved, hath repentance been declared.
23 Therefore, blessed are they who will repent and hearken unto the voice of the Lord their God; for these are they that shall be saved.
24 And may God grant, in his great fulness, that men might be brought unto repentance and good works, that they might be restored unto grace for grace, according to their works.
25 And I would that all men might be saved. But we read that in the great and last day there are some who shall be cast out, yea, who shall be cast off from the presence of the Lord;
26 Yea, who shall be consigned to a state of endless misery, fulfilling the words which say: They that have done good shall have everlasting life; and they that have done evil shall have everlasting damnation. And thus it is. Amen.

MATTHEW 22

Jesus Christ — *33 AD*

11 And when the king came in to see the guests, he saw there a man which had not on a wedding garment:
12 And he saith unto him, Friend, how camest thou in hither not having a wedding garment? And he was speechless.
13 Then said the king to the servants, Bind him hand and foot, and take him away, and cast him into outer darkness; there shall be weeping and gnashing of teeth.
14 For many are called, but few are chosen; *wherefore all do not have on the wedding garment.* [JST]

JOHN 3

John the Baptist — *30 AD*

36 ...*but* he *who* believeth not the Son shall not *receive of his fulness*; *for* the wrath of God *is upon* him. [JST]

DOCTRINE AND COVENANTS 18

Joseph Smith — *June 1829*

23 Behold, Jesus Christ is the name which is given of the Father, and there is none other name given whereby man can be saved;
24 Wherefore, all men must take upon them the name which is given of the Father, for in that name shall they be called at the last day;
25 Wherefore, if they know not the name by which they are called, they cannot have place in the kingdom of my Father.

2 NEPHI 9

Jacob, Son of Lehi — *550 BC*

27 But wo unto him that has the law given, yea, that has all the commandments of God, like unto us, and that transgresseth them, and that wasteth the days of his probation, for awful is his state!
28 O that cunning plan of the evil one! O the vainness, and the frailties, and the foolishness of men! When they are learned they think they are wise, and they hearken not unto the counsel of God, for they set it aside, supposing they know of themselves, wherefore, their wisdom is foolishness and it profiteth them not. And they shall perish.
29 But to be learned is good if they hearken unto the counsels of God.
30 But wo unto the rich, who are rich as to the things of the world. For because they are rich they despise the poor, and they persecute the meek, and their hearts are upon their treasures; wherefore, their treasure is their god. And behold, their treasure shall perish with them also.
31 And wo unto the deaf that will not hear; for they shall perish.
32 Wo unto the blind that will not see; for they shall perish also.
33 Wo unto the uncircumcised of heart, for a knowledge of their iniquities shall smite them at the last day.
34 Wo unto the liar, for he shall be thrust down to hell.
35 Wo unto the murderer who deliberately killeth, for he shall die.
36 Wo unto them who commit whoredoms, for they shall be thrust down to hell.
37 Yea, wo unto those that worship idols, for the devil of all devils delighteth in them.
38 And, in fine, wo unto all those who die in their sins; for they shall return to God, and behold his face, and remain in their sins.
39 O, my beloved brethren, remember the awfulness in transgressing against that Holy God, and also the awfulness of yielding to the enticings of that cunning one. Remember, to be carnally-minded is

death, and to be spiritually-minded is life eternal.
42 And whoso knocketh, to him will he open; and the wise, and the learned, and they that are rich, who are puffed up because of their learning, and their wisdom, and their riches—yea, they are they whom he despiseth; and save they shall cast these things away, and consider themselves fools before God, and come down in the depths of humility, he will not open unto them.
43 But the things of the wise and the prudent shall be hid from them forever—yea, that happiness which is prepared for the saints.

The rebellious are those that knew the power of God and were members of his church and willingly rebelled against him, defied his power, and sided with Satan. They are the only ones who shall suffer a second death. The Atonement of Jesus Christ does not apply to them. They suffer eternal punishment.

DOCTRINE AND COVENANTS 64

Joseph Smith — *September 1831*

35 And the rebellious shall be cut off out of the land of Zion, and shall be sent away, and shall not inherit the land.
36 For, verily I say that the rebellious are not of the blood of Ephraim, wherefore they shall be plucked out.

DOCTRINE AND COVENANTS 76

Joseph Smith — *February 1832*

25 And this we saw also, and bear record, that an angel of God who was in authority in the presence of God, who rebelled against the Only Begotten Son whom the Father loved and who was in the bosom of the Father, was thrust down from the presence of God and the Son,
26 And was called Perdition, for the heavens wept over him—he was Lucifer, a son of the morning.
27 And we beheld, and lo, he is fallen! is fallen, even a son of the morning!
28 And while we were yet in the Spirit, the Lord commanded us that we should write the vision; for we beheld Satan, that old serpent, even the devil, who rebelled against God, and sought to take the kingdom of our God and his Christ—

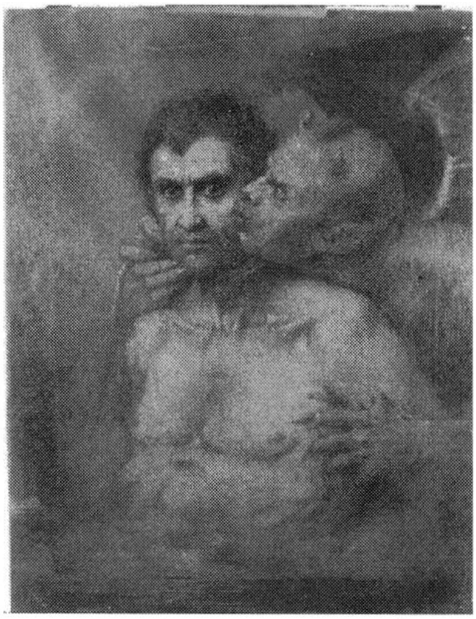

Judas and Satan, by Benoit-Hermogaste Molin, 1840s.

29 Wherefore, he maketh war with the saints of God, and encompasseth them round about.
30 And we saw a vision of the sufferings of those with whom he made war and overcame, for thus came the voice of the Lord unto us:
31 Thus saith the Lord concerning all those who know my power, and have been made partakers thereof, and suffered themselves through the power of the devil to be overcome, and to deny the truth and defy my power—
32 They are they who are the sons of perdition, of whom I say that it had been better for them never to have been born;
33 For they are vessels of wrath, doomed to suffer the wrath of God, with the devil and his angels in eternity;
34 Concerning whom I have said there is no forgiveness in this world nor in the world to come—
35 Having denied the Holy Spirit after having received it, and having denied the Only Begotten Son of the Father, having crucified him unto themselves and put him to an open shame.
36 These are they who shall go away into the lake of fire and brimstone, with the devil and his angels—

37 And the only ones on whom the second
death shall have any power;
38 Yea, verily, the only ones who shall not
be redeemed in the due time of the Lord,
after the sufferings of his wrath.
39 For all the rest shall be brought forth
by the resurrection of the dead, through
the triumph and the glory of the Lamb,
who was slain, who was in the bosom of
the Father before the worlds were made.
40 And this is the gospel, the glad tidings,
which the voice out of the heavens bore
record unto us—
41 That he came into the world, even
Jesus, to be crucified for the world, and to
bear the sins of the world, and to sanctify
the world, and to cleanse it from all
unrighteousness;
42 That through him all might be saved
whom the Father had put into his power
and made by him;
43 Who glorifies the Father, and saves all
the works of his hands, except those sons
of perdition who deny the Son after the
Father has revealed him.
44 Wherefore, he saves all except them—
they shall go away into everlasting punishment, which is endless punishment,
which is eternal punishment, to reign
with the devil and his angels in eternity,
where their worm dieth not, and the fire
is not quenched, which is their torment—
45 And the end thereof, neither the place
thereof, nor their torment, no man knows;
46 Neither was it revealed, neither is,
neither will be revealed unto man, except
to them who are made partakers thereof;
47 Nevertheless, I, the Lord, show it by
vision unto many, but straightway shut it
up again;
48 Wherefore, the end, the width, the
height, the depth, and the misery thereof,
they understand not, neither any man
except those who are ordained unto this
condemnation.
49 And we heard the voice, saying: Write
the vision, for lo, this is the end of the
vision of the sufferings of the ungodly.

DOCTRINE AND COVENANTS 82

Joseph Smith — *April 1832*

3 For of him unto whom much is given
much is required; and he who sins against
the greater light shall receive the greater
condemnation.
10 I, the Lord, am bound when ye do what
I say; but when ye do not what I say, ye
have no promise.

2 NEPHI 31

Nephi, Son of Lehi — *550 BC*

14 But, behold, my beloved brethren, thus
came the voice of the Son unto me, saying:
After ye have repented of your sins, and
witnessed unto the Father that ye are
willing to keep my commandments, by
the baptism of water, and have received
the baptism of fire and of the Holy Ghost,
and can speak with a new tongue, yea,
even with the tongue of angels, and after
this should deny me, it would have been
better for you that ye had not known me.
16 And now, my beloved brethren, I know
by this that unless a man shall endure to
the end, in following the example of the
Son of the living God, he cannot be saved.

REVELATION 20

John — *95 AD*

10 And the devil that deceived them was
cast into the lake of fire and brimstone,
where the beast and the false prophet are,
and shall be tormented day and night for
ever and ever.
11 And I saw a great white throne, and
him that sat on it, from whose face the
Earth and the heaven fled away; and there
was found no place for them.
12 And I saw the dead, small and great,
stand before God; and the books were
opened: and another book was opened,
which is the book of life: and the dead
were judged out of those things which
were written in the books, according to
their works.
13 And the sea gave up the dead which
were in it; and death and hell delivered up
the dead which were in them: and they
were judged every man according to their
works.
14 And death and hell were cast into the
lake of fire. This is the second death.
15 And whosoever was not found written
in the book of life was cast into the lake of
fire.

DOCTRINE AND COVENANTS 20

Joseph Smith — *April 1830*

32 But there is a possibility that man may
fall from grace and depart from the living
God;

DOCTRINE AND COVENANTS 18
Joseph Smith *June 1829*

45 Wherefore, the blessings which I give
unto you are above all things.
46 And after that you have received this,
if you keep not my commandments you
cannot be saved in the kingdom of my
Father.

ALMA 12
Alma the Younger *82 BC*

16 And now behold, I say unto you then
cometh a death, even a second death,
which is a spiritual death; then is a time
that whosoever dieth in his sins, as to a
temporal death, shall also die a spiritual
death; yea, he shall die as to things pertaining unto righteousness.
17 Then is the time when their torments
shall be as a lake of fire and brimstone,
whose flame ascendeth up forever and
ever; and then is the time that they shall
be chained down to an everlasting destruction, according to the power and
captivity of Satan, he having subjected
them according to his will.
18 Then, I say unto you, they shall be as
though there had been no redemption
made; for they cannot be redeemed
according to God's justice; and they
cannot die, seeing there is no more
corruption.

ALMA 13
Alma the Younger *82 BC*

30 And may the Lord grant unto you
repentance, that ye may not bring down
his wrath upon you, that ye may not be
bound down by the chains of hell, that ye
may not suffer the second death.

MATTHEW 8
Jesus Christ *30 AD*

12 But the children of the kingdom shall
be cast out into outer darkness: there shall
be weeping and gnashing of teeth.

DOCTRINE AND COVENANTS 19
Joseph Smith *March 1830*

1 I am Alpha and Omega, Christ the Lord;
yea, even I am he, the beginning and the
end, the Redeemer of the world.
2 I, having accomplished and finished the
will of him whose I am, even the Father,
concerning me—having done this that I
might subdue all things unto myself—
3 Retaining all power, even to the
destroying of Satan and his works at the
end of the world, and the last great day of
judgment, which I shall pass upon the
inhabitants thereof, judging every man
according to his works and the deeds
which he hath done.
4 And surely every man must repent or
suffer, for I, God, am endless.
5 Wherefore, I revoke not the judgments
which I shall pass, but woes shall go forth,
weeping, wailing and gnashing of teeth,
yea, to those who are found on my left
hand.
6 Nevertheless, it is not written that there
shall be no end to this torment, but it is
written endless torment.
7 Again, it is written eternal damnation;
wherefore it is more express than other
scriptures, that it might work upon the
hearts of the children of men, altogether
for my name's glory.
8 Wherefore, I will explain unto you this
mystery, for it is meet unto you to know
even as mine apostles.
9 I speak unto you that are chosen in this
thing, even as one, that you may enter into
my rest.
10 For, behold, the mystery of godliness,
how great is it! For, behold, I am endless,
and the punishment which is given from
my hand is endless punishment, for Endless is my name. Wherefore—
11 Eternal punishment is God's punishment.
12 Endless punishment is God's punishment.
13 Wherefore, I command you to repent,
and keep the commandments which you
have received by the hand of my servant
Joseph Smith, Jun., in my name;
14 And it is by my almighty power that
you have received them;
15 Therefore I command you to repent—
repent, lest I smite you by the rod of my
mouth, and by my wrath, and by my
anger, and your sufferings be sore—how
sore you know not, how exquisite you
know not, yea, how hard to bear you
know not.
16 For behold, I, God, have suffered these
things for all, that they might not suffer if
they would repent;
17 But if they would not repent they must
suffer even as I;

18 Which suffering caused myself, even God, the greatest of all, to tremble because of pain, and to bleed at every pore, and to suffer both body and spirit—and would that I might not drink the bitter cup, and shrink—
19 Nevertheless, glory be to the Father, and I partook and finished my preparations unto the children of men.
20 Wherefore, I command you again to repent, lest I humble you with my almighty power; and that you confess your sins, lest you suffer these punishments of which I have spoken, of which in the smallest, yea, even in the least degree you have tasted at the time I withdrew my Spirit.

PSALM 75

David *1000 BC*

7 But God is the judge: he putteth down one, and setteth up another.
8 For in the hand of the Lord there is a cup, and the wine is red; it is full of mixture; and he poureth out of the same: but the dregs thereof, all the wicked of the Earth shall wring them out, and drink them.

ALMA 40

Alma the Younger *73 BC*

26 But behold, an awful death cometh upon the wicked; for they die as to things pertaining to things of righteousness; for they are unclean, and no unclean thing can inherit the kingdom of God; but they are cast out, and consigned to partake of the fruits of their labors or their works, which have been evil; and they drink the dregs of a bitter cup.

MOSIAH 3

King Benjamin *124 BC*

23 And now I have spoken the words which the Lord God hath commanded me.
24 And thus saith the Lord: They shall stand as a bright testimony against this people, at the judgment day; whereof they shall be judged, every man according to his works, whether they be good, or whether they be evil.
25 And if they be evil they are consigned to an awful view of their own guilt and abominations, which doth cause them to shrink from the presence of the Lord into a state of misery and endless torment,

Christ in Gethsemane, by Heinrich Hofmann.

from whence they can no more return; therefore they have drunk damnation to their own souls.
26 Therefore, they have drunk out of the cup of the wrath of God, which justice could no more deny unto them than it could deny that Adam should fall because of his partaking of the forbidden fruit; therefore, mercy could have claim on them no more forever.
27 And their torment is as a lake of fire and brimstone, whose flames are unquenchable, and whose smoke ascendeth up forever and ever. Thus hath the Lord commanded me. Amen.

HEBREWS 10

Paul *68 AD*

26 For if we sin wilfully after that we have received the knowledge of the truth, there remaineth no more sacrifice for sins,
27 But a certain fearful looking for of judgment and fiery indignation, which shall devour the adversaries.
28 He that despised Moses' law died without mercy under two or three witnesses:
29 Of how much sorer punishment, suppose ye, shall he be thought worthy, who hath trodden under foot the Son of God,

and hath counted the blood of the covenant, wherewith he was sanctified, an unholy thing, and hath done despite unto the Spirit of grace?
30 For we know him that hath said, Vengeance belongeth unto me, I will recompense, saith the Lord. And again, The Lord shall judge his people.
31 It is a fearful thing to fall into the hands of the living God.

MOSIAH 3
King Benjamin *124 BC*
12 But wo, wo unto him who knoweth that he rebelleth against God! For salvation cometh to none such except it be through repentance and faith on the Lord Jesus Christ.

HEBREWS 6
Paul *68 AD*
4 For *he hath made* it impossible for those who were once enlightened, and have tasted of the heavenly gift, and were made partakers of the Holy Ghost,
5 And have tasted the good word of God, and the powers of the world to come,
6 If they shall fall away, to be *renewed* again unto repentance; seeing they crucify *unto* themselves the Son of God afresh, and put him to an open shame. [JST]

MOSIAH 2
King Benjamin *124 BC*
32 But, O my people, beware lest there shall arise contentions among you, and ye list to obey the evil spirit, which was spoken of by my father Mosiah.
33 For behold, there is a wo pronounced upon him who listeth to obey that spirit; for if he listeth to obey him, and remaineth and dieth in his sins, the same drinketh damnation to his own soul; for he receiveth for his wages an everlasting punishment, having transgressed the law of God contrary to his own knowledge.
36 And now, I say unto you, my brethren, that after ye have known and have been taught all these things, if ye should transgress and go contrary to that which has been spoken, that ye do withdraw yourselves from the Spirit of the Lord, that it may have no place in you to guide you in wisdom's paths that ye may be blessed, prospered, and preserved—
37 I say unto you, that the man that doeth this, the same cometh out in open rebellion against God; therefore he listeth to obey the evil spirit, and becometh an enemy to all righteousness; therefore, the Lord has no place in him, for he dwelleth not in unholy temples.
38 Therefore if that man repenteth not, and remaineth and dieth an enemy to God, the demands of divine justice do awaken his immortal soul to a lively sense of his own guilt, which doth cause him to shrink from the presence of the Lord, and doth fill his breast with guilt, and pain, and anguish, which is like an unquenchable fire, whose flame ascendeth up forever and ever.
39 And now I say unto you, that mercy hath no claim on that man; therefore his final doom is to endure a never-ending torment.

ALMA 36
Alma the Younger *73 BC*
6 For I went about with the sons of Mosiah, seeking to destroy the church of God; but behold, God sent his holy angel to stop us by the way.
7 And behold, he spake unto us, as it were the voice of thunder, and the whole Earth did tremble beneath our feet; and we all fell to the Earth, for the fear of the Lord came upon us.
8 But behold, the voice said unto me: Arise. And I arose and stood up, and beheld the angel.
9 And he said unto me: If thou wilt of thyself be destroyed, seek no more to destroy the church of God.
10 And it came to pass that I fell to the Earth; and it was for the space of three days and three nights that I could not open my mouth, neither had I the use of my limbs.
11 And the angel spake more things unto me, which were heard by my brethren, but I did not hear them; for when I heard the words—If thou wilt be destroyed of thyself, seek no more to destroy the church of God—I was struck with such great fear and amazement lest perhaps I should be destroyed, that I fell to the Earth and I did hear no more.
12 But I was racked with eternal torment, for my soul was harrowed up to the greatest degree and racked with all my sins.

13 Yea, I did remember all my sins and iniquities, for which I was tormented with the pains of hell; yea, I saw that I had rebelled against my God, and that I had not kept his holy commandments.

14 Yea, and I had murdered many of his children, or rather led them away unto destruction; yea, and in fine so great had been my iniquities, that the very thought of coming into the presence of my God did rack my soul with inexpressible horror.

15 Oh, thought I, that I could be banished and become extinct both soul and body, that I might not be brought to stand in the presence of my God, to be judged of my deeds.

16 And now, for three days and for three nights was I racked, even with the pains of a damned soul.

ROMANS 1

Paul — *57 AD*

18 For the wrath of God is revealed from heaven against all ungodliness and unrighteousness of men, who hold the truth in unrighteousness;

19 Because that which may be known of God is manifest in them; for God hath shewed it unto them.

20 For the invisible things of him from the creation of the world are clearly seen, being understood by the things that are made, even his eternal power and God-head; so that they are without excuse:

21 Because that, when they knew God, they glorified him not as God, neither were thankful; but became vain in their imaginations, and their foolish heart was darkened.

22 Professing themselves to be wise, they became fools,

23 And changed the glory of the uncorruptible God into an image made like to corruptible man, and to birds, and fourfooted beasts, and creeping things.

24 Wherefore God also agave them up to uncleanness through the lusts of their own hearts, to dishonour their own bodies between themselves:

25 Who changed the truth of God into a lie, and worshipped and served the creature more than the Creator, who is blessed forever. Amen.

26 For this cause God agave them up unto vile affections: for even their women did change the natural use into that which is against nature:

27 And likewise also the men, leaving the natural use of the woman, burned in their lust one toward another; men with men working that which is unseemly, and receiving in themselves that recompence of their error which was meet.

28 And even as they did not like to retain God in their knowledge, God gave them over to a reprobate mind, to do those things which are not convenient;

29 Being filled with all unrighteousness, fornication, wickedness, covetousness, maliciousness; full of envy, murder, debate, deceit, malignity; whisperers,

30 Backbiters, haters of God, despiteful, proud, boasters, inventors of evil things, disobedient to parents,

31 Without understanding, covenant breakers, without natural affection, implacable, unmerciful:

32 Who knowing the judgment of God, that they which commit such things are worthy of death, not only do the same, but have pleasure in them that do them.

MOSIAH 15

Abinadi — *148 BC*

26 But behold, and fear, and tremble before God, for ye ought to tremble; for the Lord redeemeth none such that rebel against him and die in their sins; yea, even all those that have perished in their sins ever since the world began, that have wilfully rebelled against God, that have known the commandments of God, and would not keep them; these are they that have no part in the first resurrection.

27 Therefore ought ye not to tremble? For salvation cometh to none such; for the Lord hath redeemed none such; yea, neither can the Lord redeem such; for he cannot deny himself; for he cannot deny justice when it has its claim.

HELAMAN 8

Nephi, Son of Helaman — *20 BC*

25 But behold, ye have rejected the truth, and rebelled against your holy God; and even at this time, instead of laying up for yourselves treasures in heaven, where nothing doth corrupt, and where nothing can come which is unclean, ye are heaping up for yourselves wrath against the day of judgment.

26 Yea, even at this time ye are ripening, because of your murders and your fornication and wickedness, for everlasting destruction; yea, and except ye repent it will come unto you soon.

Those who break the oath and covenant of the holy priesthood shall not have forgiveness.

DOCTRINE AND COVENANTS 84
Joseph Smith — September 1832
40 Therefore, all those who receive the priesthood, receive this oath and covenant of my Father, which he cannot break, neither can it be moved.
41 But whoso breaketh this covenant after he hath received it, and altogether turneth therefrom, shall not have forgiveness of sins in this world nor in the world to come.

Blasphemy against the Holy Ghost is the unpardonable sin.

DOCTRINE AND COVENANTS 132
Joseph Smith — July 1843
27 The blasphemy against the Holy Ghost, which shall not be forgiven in the world nor out of the world, is in that ye commit murder wherein ye shed innocent blood, and assent unto my death, after ye have received my new and everlasting covenant, saith the Lord God; and he that abideth not this law can in nowise enter into my glory, but shall be damned, saith the Lord.

MARK 3
Jesus Christ — 30 AD
21 *And then came certain men unto him, accusing him, saying, Why do ye receive sinners, seeing thou makest thyself the Son of God?*
22 *But he answered them and said,* Verily I say unto you, All sins *which men have committed, when they repent,* shall be forgiven *them; for I came to preach repentance* unto the sons of men.
23 And blasphemies, wherewith soever they shall blaspheme, *shall be forgiven them that come unto me, and do the works which they see me do.*
24 *But there is a sin which shall not be forgiven.* He that shall blaspheme against the Holy Ghost, hath never forgiveness; but is in danger of *being cut down out of the world. And they shall inherit* eternal damnation. [JST]

MATTHEW 12
Jesus Christ — 30 AD
31 Wherefore I say unto you, All manner of sin and blasphemy shall be forgiven unto men *who receive me and repent*; but the blasphemy against the Holy Ghost shall not be forgiven unto men. [JST]
32 And whosoever speaketh a word against the Son of man, it shall be forgiven him: but whosoever speaketh against the Holy Ghost, it shall not be forgiven him, neither in this world, neither in the world to come.

LUKE 12
Jesus Christ — 30 AD
9 But he *who* denieth me before men, shall be denied before the angels of God.
10 *Now his disciples knew that he said this, because they had spoken evil against him before the people; for they were afraid to confess him before men.*
11 *And they reasoned among themselves, saying, He knoweth our hearts, and he speaketh to our condemnation, and we shall not be forgiven. But he answered them, and said unto them,*
12 Whosoever shall speak a word against the Son of man, *and repenteth*, it shall be forgiven him; but unto him *who* blasphemeth against the Holy Ghost, it shall not be forgiven him. [JST]

ALMA 39
Alma the Younger — 73 BC
5 Know ye not, my son, that these things [fornication] are an abomination in the sight of the Lord; yea, most abominable above all sins save it be the shedding of innocent blood or denying the Holy Ghost?
6 For behold, if ye deny the Holy Ghost when it once has had place in you, and ye know that ye deny it, behold, this is a sin which is unpardonable; yea, and whosoever murdereth against the light and knowledge of God, it is not easy for him to obtain forgiveness; yea, I say unto you, my

son, that it is not easy for him to obtain a forgiveness.

THE KING FOLLETT DISCOURSE

Joseph Smith *April 7, 1844*

I have a declaration to make as to the provisions which God hath made to suit the conditions of man—made from before the foundation of the world. What has Jesus said? All sins, and all blasphemies, and every transgression, except one, that man can be guilty of, may be forgiven; and there is a salvation for all men, either in this world or the world to come, who have not committed the unpardonable sin, there being a provision either in this world or the world of spirits. Hence God hath made a provision that every spirit in the eternal world can be ferreted out and saved unless he has committed that unpardonable sin which cannot be remitted to him either in this world or the world of spirits. God has wrought out a salvation for all men, unless they have committed a certain sin; and every man who has a friend in the eternal world can save him, unless he has committed the unpardonable sin. And so you can see how far you can be a savior.

A man cannot commit the unpardonable sin after the dissolution of the body, and there is a way possible for escape. Knowledge saves a man; and in the world of spirits no man can be exalted but by knowledge. So long as a man will not give heed to the commandments, he must abide without salvation. If a man has knowledge, he can be saved; although, if he has been guilty of great sins, he will be punished for them. But when he consents to obey the gospel, whether here or in the world of spirits, he is saved.

A man is his own tormentor and his own condemner. Hence the saying, They shall go into the lake that burns with fire and brimstone. The torment of disappointment in the mind is as exquisite as a lake burning with fire and brimstone. I say, so is the torment of man.

I know the scriptures and understand them. I said, no man can commit the unpardonable sin after the dissolution of the body, nor in this life, until he receives the Holy Ghost; but they must do it in this world. Hence the salvation of Jesus Christ was wrought out for all men, in order to triumph over the devil; for if it did not catch him in one place, it would in another; for he stood up as a Savior. All will suffer until they obey Christ himself. The contention in heaven was—Jesus said there would be certain souls that would not be saved; and the devil said he would save them all, and laid his plans before the grand council, who gave their vote in favor of Jesus Christ. So the devil rose up in rebellion against God, and was cast down, with all who put up their heads for him.

All sins shall be forgiven, except the sin against the Holy Ghost; for Jesus will save all except the sons of perdition. What must a man do to commit the unpardonable sin? He must receive the Holy Ghost, have the heavens opened unto him, and know God, and then sin against him. After a man has sinned against the Holy Ghost, there is no repentance for him. He has got to say that the sun does not shine while he sees it; he has got to deny Jesus Christ when the heavens have been opened unto him, and to deny the plan of salvation with his eyes open to the truth of it; and from that time he begins to be an enemy. This is the case with many apostates of The Church of Jesus Christ of Latter-day Saints.

When a man begins to be an enemy to this work, he hunts me, he seeks to kill me, and never ceases to thirst for my blood. He gets the spirit of the devil—the same spirit that sins against the Holy Ghost. You cannot save such persons; you cannot bring them to repentance; they make open war, like the devil, and awful is the consequence.

I advise all of you to be careful what you do, or you may by-and-by find out that you have been deceived. Stay yourselves; do not give way; don't make any hasty moves, you may be saved. If a spirit of bitterness is in you, don't be in haste. You may say, that man is a sinner. Well, if he repents, he shall be forgiven. Be cautious: await. When you find a spirit that wants bloodshed,—murder, the same is not of

God, but is of the devil. Out of the abundance of the heart of man the mouth speaketh.

The best men bring forth the best works. The man who tells you words of life is the man who can save you. I warn you against all evil characters who sin against the Holy Ghost; for there is no redemption for them in this world nor in the world to come…

Hear it, all ye ends of the Earth —all ye priests, all ye sinners, and all men. Repent! Repent! Obey the gospel. Turn to God; for your religion won't save you, and you will be damned. I do not say how long. There have been remarks made concerning all men being redeemed from hell; but I say that those who sin against the Holy Ghost cannot be forgiven in this world or in the world to come; they shall die the second death. Those who commit the unpardonable sin are doomed to Gnolom—to dwell in hell, worlds without end. As they concocted scenes of bloodshed in this world, so they shall rise to that resurrection which is as the lake of fire and brimstone. Some shall rise to the everlasting burnings of God; for God dwells in everlasting burnings and some shall rise to the damnation of their own filthiness, which is as exquisite a torment as the lake of fire and brimstone.

Those who reject the Savior Jesus Christ shall not obtain forgiveness.

JACOB 6

Jacob, Son of Lehi — *500 BC*

5 Wherefore, my beloved brethren, I beseech of you in words of soberness that ye would repent, and come with full purpose of heart, and cleave unto God as he cleaveth unto you. And while his arm of mercy is extended towards you in the light of the day, harden not your hearts.
6 Yea, today, if ye will hear his voice, harden not your hearts; for why will ye die?
7 For behold, after ye have been nourished by the good word of God all the day long, will ye bring forth evil fruit, that ye must be hewn down and cast into the fire?
8 Behold, will ye reject these words? Will ye reject the words of the prophets; and will ye reject all the words which have been spoken concerning Christ, after so many have spoken concerning him; and deny the good word of Christ, and the power of God, and the gift of the Holy Ghost, and quench the Holy Spirit, and make a mock of the great plan of redemption, which hath been laid for you?
9 Know ye not that if ye will do these things, that the power of the redemption and the resurrection, which is in Christ, will bring you to stand with shame and awful guilt before the bar of God?
10 And according to the power of justice, for justice cannot be denied, ye must go away into that lake of fire and brimstone, whose flames are unquenchable, and whose smoke ascendeth up forever and ever, which lake of fire and brimstone is endless torment.
11 O then, my beloved brethren, repent ye, and enter in at the strait gate, and continue in the way which is narrow, until ye shall obtain eternal life.
12 O be wise; what can I say more?
13 Finally, I bid you farewell, until I shall meet you before the pleasing bar of God, which bar striketh the wicked with awful dread and fear. Amen.

JOHN 3

Jesus Christ — *30 AD*

18 … he that believeth not is condemned already, because he hath not believed in the name of the only begotten Son of God.
19 And this is the condemnation, that light is come into the world, and men loved darkness rather than light, because their deeds were evil.
20 For everyone that doeth evil hateth the light, neither cometh to the light, lest his deeds should be reproved.
36 … he that believeth not the Son shall not see life; but the wrath of God abideth on him.

MATTHEW 10

Jesus Christ — *31 AD*

28 And fear not them which kill the body, but are not able to kill the soul: but rather fear him which is able to destroy both soul and body in hell.

33 But whosoever shall deny me before men, him will I also deny before my Father which is in heaven.

3 NEPHI 28

Mormon *385 AD*

34 And wo be unto him that will not hearken unto the words of Jesus, and also to them whom he hath chosen and sent among them; for whoso receiveth not the words of Jesus and the words of those whom he hath sent receiveth not him; and therefore he will not receive them at the last day;

35 And it would be better for them if they had not been born. For do ye suppose that ye can get rid of the justice of an offended God, who hath been trampled under feet of men, that thereby salvation might come?

Those whose names are not written in the book of remembrance—that have apostatized and have been cut off from the church—shall have no inheritance in the kingdom of God.

DOCTRINE AND COVENANTS 85

Joseph Smith *November 1832*

1 It is the duty of the Lord's clerk, whom he has appointed, to keep a history, and a general church record of all things that transpire in Zion, and of all those who consecrate properties, and receive inheritances legally from the bishop;

2 And also their manner of life, their faith, and works; and also of the apostates who apostatize after receiving their inheritances.

3 It is contrary to the will and commandment of God that those who receive not their inheritance by consecration, agreeable to his law, which he has given, that he may tithe his people, to prepare them against the day of vengeance and burning, should have their names enrolled with the people of God.

4 Neither is their genealogy to be kept, or to be had where it may be found on any of the records or history of the church.

5 Their names shall not be found, neither the names of the fathers, nor the names of the children written in the book of the law of God, saith the Lord of Hosts.

8 While that man, who was called of God and appointed, that putteth forth his hand to steady the ark of God, shall fall by the shaft of death, like as a tree that is smitten by the vivid shaft of lightning.

9 And all they who are not found written in the book of remembrance shall find none inheritance in that day, but they shall be cut asunder, and their portion shall be appointed them among unbelievers, where are wailing and gnashing of teeth.

10 These things I say not of myself; therefore, as the Lord speaketh, he will also fulfil.

11 And they who are of the High Priesthood, whose names are not found written in the book of the law, or that are found to have apostatized, or to have been cut off from the church, as well as the lesser priesthood, or the members, in that day shall not find an inheritance among the saints of the Most High;

12 Therefore, it shall be done unto them as unto the children of the priest, as will be found recorded in the second chapter and sixty-first and second verses of Ezra.

EZRA 2

Ezra *458 BC*

61 And of the children of the priests: the children of Habaiah, the children of Koz, the children of Barzillai; which took a wife of the daughters of Barzillai the Gileadite, and was called after their name:

62 These sought their register among those that were reckoned by genealogy, but they were not found: therefore were they, as polluted, put from the priesthood.

ALMA 5

Alma the Younger *83 BC*

15 Do ye exercise faith in the redemption of him who created you? Do you look forward with an eye of faith, and view this mortal body raised in immortality, and this corruption raised in incorruption, to stand before God to be judged according to the deeds which have been done in the mortal body?

16 I say unto you, can you imagine to yourselves that ye hear the voice of the Lord, saying unto you, in that day: Come unto me ye blessed, for behold, your works have been the works of righteousness upon the face of the Earth?

17 Or do ye imagine to yourselves that ye can lie unto the Lord in that day, and say—Lord, our works have been righteous works upon the face of the Earth—and that he will save you?
18 Or otherwise, can ye imagine yourselves brought before the tribunal of God with your souls filled with guilt and remorse, having a remembrance of all your guilt, yea, a perfect remembrance of all your wickedness, yea, a remembrance that ye have set at defiance the commandments of God?
19 I say unto you, can ye look up to God at that day with a pure heart and clean hands? I say unto you, can you look up, having the image of God engraven upon your countenances?
20 I say unto you, can ye think of being saved when you have yielded yourselves to become subjects to the devil?
21 I say unto you, ye will know at that day that ye cannot be saved; for there can no man be saved except his garments are washed white; yea, his garments must be purified until they are cleansed from all stain, through the blood of him of whom it has been spoken by our fathers, who should come to redeem his people from their sins.
22 And now I ask of you, my brethren, how will any of you feel, if ye shall stand before the bar of God, having your garments stained with blood and all manner of filthiness? Behold, what will these things testify against you?
23 Behold will they not testify that ye are murderers, yea, and also that ye are guilty of all manner of wickedness?
24 Behold, my brethren, do ye suppose that such an one can have a place to sit down in the kingdom of God, with Abraham, with Isaac, and with Jacob, and also all the holy prophets, whose garments are cleansed and are spotless, pure and white?
25 I say unto you, Nay; except ye make our Creator a liar from the beginning, or suppose that he is a liar from the beginning, ye cannot suppose that such can have place in the kingdom of heaven; but they shall be cast out for they are the children of the kingdom of the devil.
26 And now behold, I say unto you, my brethren, if ye have experienced a change of heart, and if ye have felt to sing the song of redeeming love, I would ask, can ye feel so now?
27 Have ye walked, keeping yourselves blameless before God? Could ye say, if ye were called to die at this time, within yourselves, that ye have been sufficiently humble? That your garments have been cleansed and made white through the blood of Christ, who will come to redeem his people from their sins?
28 Behold, are ye stripped of pride? I say unto you, if ye are not ye are not prepared to meet God. Behold ye must prepare quickly; for the kingdom of heaven is soon at hand, and such an one hath not eternal life.
29 Behold, I say, is there one among you who is not stripped of envy? I say unto you that such an one is not prepared; and I would that he should prepare quickly, for the hour is close at hand, and he knoweth not when the time shall come; for such an one is not found guiltless.
30 And again I say unto you, is there one among you that doth make a mock of his brother, or that heapeth upon him persecutions?
31 Wo unto such an one, for he is not prepared, and the time is at hand that he must repent or he cannot be saved!
32 Yea, even wo unto all ye workers of iniquity; repent, repent, for the Lord God hath spoken it!
33 Behold, he sendeth an invitation unto all men, for the arms of mercy are extended towards them, and he saith: Repent, and I will receive you.
34 Yea, he saith: Come unto me and ye shall partake of the fruit of the tree of life; yea, ye shall eat and drink of the bread and the waters of life freely;
35 Yea, come unto me and bring forth works of righteousness, and ye shall not be hewn down and cast into the fire—
36 For behold, the time is at hand that whosoever bringeth forth not good fruit, or whosoever doeth not the works of righteousness, the same have cause to wail and mourn.
37 O ye workers of iniquity; ye that are puffed up in the vain things of the world, ye that have professed to have known the ways of righteousness nevertheless have gone astray, as sheep having no shepherd, notwithstanding a shepherd hath called

after you and is still calling after you, but
ye will not hearken unto his voice!
38 Behold, I say unto you, that the good
shepherd doth call you; yea, and in his
own name he doth call you, which is the
name of Christ; and if ye will not hearken
unto the voice of the good shepherd, to
the name by which ye are called, behold,
ye are not the sheep of the good shepherd.
39 And now if ye are not the sheep of the
good shepherd, of what fold are ye?
Behold, I say unto you, that the devil is
your shepherd, and ye are of his fold; and
now, who can deny this? Behold, I say
unto you, whosoever denieth this is a liar
and a child of the devil.
40 For I say unto you that whatsoever is
good cometh from God, and whatsoever is
evil cometh from the devil.
41 Therefore, if a man bringeth forth good
works he hearkeneth unto the voice of the
good shepherd, and he doth follow him;
but whosoever bringeth forth evil works,
the same becometh a child of the devil, for
he hearkeneth unto his voice, and doth
follow him.
42 And whosoever doeth this must receive
his wages of him; therefore, for his wages
he receiveth death, as to things pertaining
unto righteousness, being dead unto all
good works.
51 And also the Spirit saith unto me, yea,
crieth unto me with a mighty voice,
saying: Go forth and say unto this
people—Repent, for except ye repent ye
can in nowise inherit the kingdom of
heaven.
52 And again I say unto you, the Spirit
saith: Behold, the ax is laid at the root of
the tree; therefore every tree that bringeth
not forth good fruit shall be hewn down
and cast into the fire, yea, a fire which
cannot be consumed, even an unquench-
able fire. Behold, and remember, the Holy
One hath spoken it.
56 And finally, all ye that will persist in
your wickedness, I say unto you that these
are they who shall be hewn down and cast
into the fire except they speedily repent.
57 And now I say unto you, all you that
are desirous to follow the voice of the
good shepherd, come ye out from the
wicked, and be ye separate, and touch not
their unclean things; and behold, their
names shall be blotted out, that the names
of the wicked shall not be numbered
among the names of the righteous, that
the word of God may be fulfilled, which
saith: The names of the wicked shall not
be mingled with the names of my people;

MARK 9

Jesus Christ — *32 AD*

42 And whosoever shall offend one of
these little ones that believe in me, it is
better for him that a millstone were
hanged about his neck, and he were cast
into the sea.
43 And if thy hand offend thee, cut it off:
it is better for thee to enter into life
maimed, than having two hands to go into
hell, into the fire that never shall be
quenched:
44 Where their worm dieth not, and the
fire is not quenched.
45 And if thy foot offend thee, cut it off: it
is better for thee to enter halt into life,
than having two feet to be cast into hell,
into the fire that never shall be quenched:
46 Where their worm dieth not, and the
fire is not quenched.
47 And if thine eye offend thee, pluck it
out: it is better for thee to enter into the
kingdom of God with one eye, than hav-
ing two eyes to be cast into hell fire:
48 Where their worm dieth not, and the
fire is not quenched.

2 PETER 2

Peter — *67 AD*

9 The Lord knoweth how to deliver the
godly out of temptations, and to reserve
the unjust unto the day of judgment to be
punished:
10 But chiefly them that walk after the
flesh in the lust of uncleanness, and
despise government. Presumptuous are
they, self-willed, they are not afraid to
speak evil of dignities.
11 Whereas angels, which are greater in
power and might, bring not railing accus-
ation against them before the Lord.
12 But these, as natural brute beasts, made
to be taken and destroyed, speak evil of
the things that they understand not; and
shall utterly perish in their own corrupt-
tion;
13 And shall receive the reward of
unrighteousness, as they that count it
pleasure to riot in the day time. Spots they
are and blemishes, sporting themselves

with their own deceivings while they feast with you;
14 Having eyes full of adultery, and that cannot cease from sin; beguiling unstable souls: an heart they have exercised with covetous practices; cursed children:
15 Which have forsaken the right way, and are gone astray, following the way of Balaam the son of Bosor, who loved the wages of unrighteousness;
16 But was rebuked for his iniquity: the dumb ass speaking with man's voice forbad the madness of the prophet.
17 These are wells without water, clouds that are carried with a tempest; to whom the mist of darkness is reserved for ever.
18 For when they speak great swelling words of vanity, they allure through the lusts of the flesh, through much wantonness, those that were clean escaped from them who live in error.
19 While they promise them liberty, they themselves are the servants of corruption: for of whom a man is overcome, of the same is he brought in bondage.
20 For if after they have escaped the pollutions of the world through the knowledge of the Lord and Saviour Jesus Christ, they are again entangled therein, and overcome, the latter end is worse with them than the beginning.
21 For it had been better for them not to have known the way of righteousness, than, after they have known it, to turn from the holy commandment delivered unto them.
22 But it is happened unto them according to the true proverb, The dog is turned to his own vomit again; and the sow that was washed to her wallowing in the mire.

German steel engraving of Jesus Christ knocking at the door, by Peter Carl Geissler, 1802-1872. Will you let him in?

MOSIAH 5

King Benjamin *124 BC*

10 And now it shall come to pass, that whosoever shall not take upon him the name of Christ must be called by some other name; therefore, he findeth himself on the left hand of God.
11 And I would that ye should remember also, that this is the name that I said I should give unto you that never should be blotted out, except it be through transgression; therefore, take heed that ye do not transgress, that the name be not blotted out of your hearts.
12 I say unto you, I would that ye should remember to retain the name written always in your hearts, that ye are not found on the left hand of God, but that ye hear and know the voice by which ye shall be called, and also, the name by which he shall call you.
13 For how knoweth a man the master whom he has not served, and who is a stranger unto him, and is far from the thoughts and intents of his heart?
14 And again, doth a man take an ass which belongeth to his neighbor, and

keep him? I say unto you, Nay; he will not even suffer that he shall feed among his flocks, but will drive him away, and cast him out. I say unto you, that even so shall it be among you if ye know not the name by which ye are called.

MORMON 9

Moroni *400 AD*

1 And now, I speak also concerning those
who do not believe in Christ.
2 Behold, will ye believe in the day of your
visitation—behold, when the Lord shall
come, yea, even that great day when the
Earth shall be rolled together as a scroll,
and the elements shall melt with fervent
heat, yea, in that great day when ye shall
be brought to stand before the Lamb of
God—then will ye say that there is no
God?
3 Then will ye longer deny the Christ, or
can ye behold the Lamb of God? Do ye
suppose that ye shall dwell with him
under a consciousness of your guilt? Do ye
suppose that ye could be happy to dwell
with that holy Being, when your souls are
racked with a consciousness of guilt that
ye have ever abused his laws?
4 Behold, I say unto you that ye would be
more miserable to dwell with a holy and
just God, under a consciousness of your
filthiness before him, than ye would to
dwell with the damned souls in hell.
5 For behold, when ye shall be brought to
see your nakedness before God, and also
the glory of God, and the holiness of Jesus
Christ, it will kindle a flame of unquench-
able fire upon you.

66

THE EARTH IS TRANSFIGURED INTO A CELESTIAL KINGDOM

+++

The Earth will become sanctified and transfigured into a celestial kingdom.

DOCTRINE AND COVENANTS 29
Joseph Smith — *September 1830*
23 And the end shall come, and the heaven and the Earth shall be consumed and pass away, and there shall be a new heaven and a new Earth.
24 For all old things shall pass away, and all things shall become new, even the heaven and the Earth, and all the fulness thereof, both men and beasts, the fowls of the air, and the fishes of the sea;
25 And not one hair, neither mote, shall be lost, for it is the workmanship of mine hand.

DOCTRINE AND COVENANTS 43
Joseph Smith — *February 1831*
31 ... and then cometh the end of the Earth.
32 And he that liveth in righteousness shall be changed in the twinkling of an eye, and the Earth shall pass away so as by fire.

DOCTRINE AND COVENANTS 88
Joseph Smith — *December 1832*
18 Therefore, it [the Earth] must needs be sanctified from all unrighteousness, that it may be prepared for the celestial glory;
19 For after it hath filled the measure of its creation, it shall be crowned with glory, even with the presence of God the Father;
20 That bodies who are of the celestial kingdom may possess it forever and ever; for, for this intent was it made and created, and for this intent are they sanctified.
25 And again, verily I say unto you, the Earth abideth the law of a celestial kingdom, for it filleth the measure of its creation, and transgresseth not the law—
26 Wherefore, it shall be sanctified; yea, notwithstanding it shall die, it shall be quickened again, and shall abide the power by which it is quickened, and the righteous shall inherit it.

3 NEPHI 26
Jesus Christ — *34 AD*
3 And he did expound all things...even until the elements should melt with fervent heat, and the Earth should be wrapt together as a scroll, and the heavens and the Earth should pass away;

1 JOHN 2
John — *90 AD*
17 And the world passeth away, and the lust thereof: but he that doeth the will of God abideth forever.

HEBREWS 1
Paul — *68 AD*
10 And, Thou, Lord, in the beginning hast laid the foundation of the Earth; and the heavens are the works of thine hands:
11 They shall perish; but thou remainest; and they all shall wax old as doth a garment;
12 And as a vesture shalt thou fold them up, and they shall be changed: but thou art the same, and thy years shall not fail.

DOCTRINE AND COVENANTS 130
Joseph Smith — *April 1843*
4 In answer to the question—Is not the reckoning of God's time, angel's time, prophet's time, and man's time, according to the planet on which they reside?
5 I answer, Yes. But there are no angels who minister to this Earth but those who do belong or have belonged to it.

6 The angels do not reside on a planet like this Earth;
7 But they reside in the presence of God, on a globe like a sea of glass and fire, where all things for their glory are manifest, past, present, and future, and are continually before the Lord.
8 The place where God resides is a great Urim and Thummim.
9 This Earth, in its sanctified and immortal state, will be made like unto crystal and will be a Urim and Thummim to the inhabitants who dwell thereon, whereby all things pertaining to an inferior kingdom, or all kingdoms of a lower order, will be manifest to those who dwell on it; and this Earth will be Christ's.

67

THEN SHALL THEY BE GODS

God the Father Inviting Christ to Sit on the Throne at His Right Hand, by Pieter de Grebber, 1645.

+++

Jesus Christ, the first begotten spirit child of the Father, does not think it robbery to be equal with God. He does not receive of the Father's fulness at first but progresses from grace to grace until he is exalted and made heir of all things.

PHILIPPIANS 2

Paul *62 AD*

5 Let this mind be in you, which was also in Christ Jesus:
6 Who, being in the form of God, thought it not robbery to be equal with God:
7 But made himself of no reputation, and took upon him the form of a servant, and was made in the likeness of men:
8 And being found in fashion as a man, he humbled himself, and became obedient unto death, even the death of the cross.
9 Wherefore God also hath highly exalted him, and given him a name which is above every name.

HEBREWS 10

Paul *68 AD*

10 By the which will we are sanctified through the offering of the body of Jesus Christ once for all.

11 And every priest standeth daily ministering and offering oftentimes the same sacrifices, which can never take away sins:

12 But this man, after he had offered one sacrifice for sins forever, sat down on the right hand of God;

HEBREWS 1

Paul *68 AD*

1 God, who at sundry times and in divers manners spake in time past unto the fathers by the prophets,

2 Hath in these last days spoken unto us by his Son, whom he hath appointed heir of all things, by whom also he made the worlds;

3 Who being the brightness of his glory, and the express image of his person, and upholding all things by the word of his power, when he had by himself purged our sins, sat down on the right hand of the Majesty on high;

4 Being made so much better than the angels, as he hath by inheritance obtained a more excellent name than they.

5 For unto which of the angels said he at any time, Thou art my Son, this day have I begotten thee? And again, I will be to him a Father, and he shall be to me a Son?

6 And again, when he bringeth in the first begotten into the world, he saith, And let all the angels of God worship him *who maketh his ministers as a flame of fire..*

7 And of the angels he saith, *Angels are ministering spirits.* [JST]

8 But unto the Son he saith, Thy throne, O God, is for ever and ever: a scepter of righteousness is the scepter of thy kingdom.

9 Thou hast loved righteousness, and hated iniquity; therefore God, even thy God, hath anointed thee with the oil of gladness above thy fellows.

13 But to which of the angels said he at any time, Sit on my right hand, until I make thine enemies thy footstool?

14 Are they not all ministering spirits, sent forth to minister for them who shall be heirs of salvation?

DOCTRINE AND COVENANTS 93

Joseph Smith *May 1833*

1 Verily, thus saith the Lord: It shall come to pass that every soul who forsaketh his sins and cometh unto me, and calleth on my name, and obeyeth my voice, and keepeth my commandments, shall see my face and know that I am;

2 And that I am the true light that lighteth every man that cometh into the world;

3 And that I am in the Father, and the Father in me, and the Father and I are one—

4 The Father because he gave me of his fulness, and the Son because I was in the world and made flesh my tabernacle, and dwelt among the sons of men.

5 I was in the world and received of my Father, and the works of him were plainly manifest.

6 And John saw and bore record of the fulness of my glory, and the fulness of John's record is hereafter to be revealed.

7 And he bore record, saying: I saw his glory, that he was in the beginning, before the world was;

8 Therefore, in the beginning the Word was, for he was the Word, even the messenger of salvation—

9 The light and the Redeemer of the world; the Spirit of truth, who came into the world, because the world was made by him, and in him was the life of men and the light of men.

10 The worlds were made by him; men were made by him; all things were made by him, and through him, and of him.

11 And I, John, bear record that I beheld his glory, as the glory of the Only Begotten of the Father, full of grace and truth, even the Spirit of truth, which came and dwelt in the flesh, and dwelt among us.

12 And I, John, saw that he received not of the fulness at the first, but received grace for grace;

13 And he received not of the fulness at first, but continued from grace to grace, until he received a fulness;

14 And thus he was called the Son of God, because he received not of the fulness at the first.

15 And I, John, bear record, and lo, the heavens were opened, and the Holy Ghost descended upon him in the form of a dove, and sat upon him, and there came a voice out of heaven saying: This is my beloved Son.

16 And I, John, bear record that he received a fulness of the glory of the Father;

Jesus Christ Receiving the World from the Hands of God the Father, by Antonio Arias Fernandez, 1657.

17 And he received all power, both in heaven and on Earth, and the glory of the Father was with him, for he dwelt in him.
18 And it shall come to pass, that if you are faithful you shall receive the fulness of the record of John.

Salvation and exaltation through Christ's Atonement is conditioned on faith, hope, charity, love, repentance, baptism, receiving the gift of the Holy Ghost, obedience to the commandments, and enduring to the end.

MOSES 1

Moses 1500 BC

39 For behold, this is my work and my glory – to bring to pass the immortality and eternal life of man.

JOHN 15

Jesus Christ 33 AD

1 I am the true vine, and my Father is the husbandman.
4 Abide in me, and I in you. As the branch cannot bear fruit of itself, except it abide in the vine; no more can ye, except ye abide in me.
5 I am the vine, ye are the branches: He that abideth in me, and I in him, the same bringeth forth much fruit: for without me ye can do nothing.
8 Herein is my Father glorified, that ye bear much fruit; so shall ye be my disciples.
9 As the Father hath loved me, so have I loved you: continue ye in my love.
10 If ye keep my commandments, ye shall abide in my love; even as I have kept my Father's commandments, and abide in his love.
11 These things have I spoken unto you, that my joy might remain in you, and that your joy might be full.
12 This is my commandment, That ye love one another, as I have loved you.
13 Greater love hath no man than this, that a man lay down his life for his friends.
14 Ye are my friends, if ye do whatsoever I command you.
15 Henceforth I call you not servants; for the servant knoweth not what his lord doeth: but I have called you friends; for all things that I have heard of my Father I have made known unto you.
16 Ye have not chosen me, but I have chosen you, and ordained you, that ye should go and bring forth fruit, and that your fruit should remain: that whatsoever ye shall ask of the Father in my name, he may give it you.
17 These things I command you, that ye love one another.

JOHN 3

John 30 AD

15 That whosoever believeth in him should not perish but have eternal life.
16 For God so loved the world, that he gave his only begotten Son, that whosoever believeth in him should not perish, but have everlasting life.
17 For God sent not his Son into the world to condemn the world; but that the world through him might be saved.

2 NEPHI 9
Jacob, Son of Lehi — *550 BC*
41 O then, my beloved brethren, come unto the Lord, the Holy One. Remember that his paths are righteous. Behold, the way for man is narrow, but it lieth in a straight course before him, and the keeper of the gate is the Holy One of Israel; and he employeth no servant there; and there is none other way save it be by the gate; for he cannot be deceived, for the Lord God is his name.

JOHN 3
John the Baptist — *30 AD*
35 The Father loveth the Son, and hath given all things into his hand.
36 *And* he *who* believeth on the Son hath everlasting life; *and shall receive of his fulness.*

3 NEPHI 14 (see also MATTHEW 7)
Jesus Christ — *34 AD*
13 Enter ye in at the strait gate; for wide is the gate, and broad is the way, which leadeth to destruction, and many there be who go in thereat;
14 Because strait is the gate, and narrow is the way, which leadeth unto life, and few there be that find it.

3 NEPHI 27
Jesus Christ — *34 AD*
33 And it came to pass that when Jesus had ended these sayings he said unto his disciples: Enter ye in at the strait gate; for strait is the gate, and narrow is the way that leads to life, and few there be that find it; but wide is the gate, and broad the way which leads to death, and many there be that travel therein, until the night cometh, wherein no man can work.

2 NEPHI 31
Nephi, Son of Lehi — *550 BC*
13 Wherefore, my beloved brethren, I know that if ye shall follow the Son, with full purpose of heart, acting no hypocrisy and no deception before God, but with real intent, repenting of your sins, witnessing unto the Father that ye are willing to take upon you the name of Christ, by baptism—yea, by following your Lord and your Savior down into the water, according to his word, behold, then shall ye receive the Holy Ghost; yea, then cometh the baptism of fire and of the Holy Ghost; and then can ye speak with the tongue of angels, and shout praises unto the Holy One of Israel.
15 And I heard a voice from the Father, saying: Yea, the words of my Beloved are true and faithful. He that endureth to the end, the same shall be saved.
17 Wherefore, do the things which I have told you I have seen that your Lord and your Redeemer should do; for, for this cause have they been shown unto me, that ye might know the gate by which ye should enter. For the gate by which ye should enter is repentance and baptism by water; and then cometh a remission of your sins by fire and by the Holy Ghost.
18 And then are ye in this strait and narrow path which leads to eternal life; yea, ye have entered in by the gate; ye have done according to the commandments of the Father and the Son; and ye have received the Holy Ghost, which witnesses of the Father and the Son, unto the fulfilling of the promise which he hath made, that if ye entered in by the way ye should receive.
19 And now, my beloved brethren, after ye have gotten into this strait and narrow path, I would ask if all is done? Behold, I say unto you, Nay; for ye have not come thus far save it were by the word of Christ with unshaken faith in him, relying wholly upon the merits of him who is mighty to save.
20 Wherefore, ye must press forward with a steadfastness in Christ, having a perfect brightness of hope, and a love of God and of all men. Wherefore, if ye shall press forward, feasting upon the word of Christ, and endure to the end, behold, thus saith the Father: Ye shall have eternal life.
21 And now, behold, my beloved brethren, this is the way; and there is none other way nor name given under heaven whereby man can be saved in the kingdom of God. And now, behold, this is the doctrine of Christ, and the only and true doctrine of the Father, and of the Son, and of the Holy Ghost, which is one God, without end. Amen.

JOHN 3
Jesus Christ — *30 AD*
3 Jesus answered and said unto him, Verily, verily, I say unto thee, Except a

man be born again, he cannot see the kingdom of God.
4 Nicodemus saith unto him, How can a man be born when he is old? can he enter the second time into his mother's womb, and be born?
5 Jesus answered, Verily, verily, I say unto thee, Except a man be born of water and of the Spirit, he cannot enter into the kingdom of God.

THE KING FOLLETT DISCOURSE

Joseph Smith *April 7, 1844*

I will leave this subject here, and make a few remarks on the subject of baptism. The baptism of water, without the baptism of fire and the Holy Ghost attending it, is of no use; they are necessarily and inseparably connected. An individual must be born of water and the spirit in order to get into the kingdom of God. In the German, the text bears me out the same as the revelations which I have given and taught for the past fourteen years on that subject. I have the testimony to put in their teeth. My testimony has been true all the time. You will find it in the declaration of John the Baptist. (Reads from the German.) John says, "I baptize you with water, but when Jesus comes, who has the power (or keys) He shall administer the baptism of fire and the Holy Ghost." Great God! Where is now all the sectarian world? And if this testimony is true, they are all damned as clearly as anathema can do it. I know the text is true. I call upon all you Germans who know that it is true to say, Eye. (Loud shouts of "Aye.")

Alexander Campbell, how are you going to save people with water alone? For John said his baptism was good for nothing without the baptism of Jesus Christ. "Therefore, not leaving the principles of the doctrine of Christ, let us go on unto perfection; not laying again the foundation of repentance from dead works, and of faith towards God, of the doctrine of baptism, and of laying on of hands, and of resurrection of the dead, and of eternal judgment. And this will we do, if God permit." [Heb. 6:1–3]

There is one God, one Father, one Jesus, one hope of our calling, one baptism. All these three baptisms only make one. Many talk of baptism not being essential to salvation; but this kind of teaching would lay the foundation of their damnation. I have the truth, and am at the defiance of the world to contradict me, if they can.

MOSIAH 26

Jesus Christ (to Alma the Elder) *120 BC*

22 For behold, this is my church; whosoever is baptized shall be baptized unto repentance. And whomsoever ye receive shall believe in my name; and him will I freely forgive.
23 For it is I that taketh upon me the sins of the world; for it is I that hath created them; and it is I that granteth unto him that believeth unto the end a place at my right hand.
24 For behold, in my name are they called; and if they know me they shall come forth, and shall have a place eternally at my right hand.

ALMA 5

Alma the Younger *83 BC*

58 For the names of the righteous shall be written in the book of life, and unto them will I grant an inheritance at my right hand. And now, my brethren, what have ye to say against this? I say unto you, if ye speak against it, it matters not, for the word of God must be fulfilled.

MOSIAH 2

King Benjamin *124 BC*

41 And moreover, I would desire that ye should consider on the blessed and happy state of those that keep the commandments of God. For behold, they are blessed in all things, both temporal and spiritual; and if they hold out faithful to the end they are received into heaven, that thereby they may dwell with God in a state of never-ending happiness. O remember, remember that these things are true; for the Lord God hath spoken it.

MATTHEW 19

Jesus Christ *32 AD*

16 And, behold, one came and said unto him, Good Master, what good thing shall I do, that I may have eternal life?
17 And he said unto him, Why callest thou me good? there is none good but one,

that is, God: but if thou wilt enter into life, keep the commandments.

18 He saith unto him, Which? Jesus said, Thou shalt do no murder, Thou shalt not commit adultery, Thou shalt not steal, Thou shalt not bear false witness,

19 Honour thy father and thy mother: and, Thou shalt love thy neighbour as thyself.

20 The young man saith unto him, All these things have I kept from my youth up: what lack I yet?

21 Jesus said unto him, If thou wilt be perfect, go and sell that thou hast, and give to the poor, and thou shalt have treasure in heaven: and come and follow me.

22 But when the young man heard that saying, he went away sorrowful: for he had great possessions.

23 Then said Jesus unto his disciples, Verily I say unto you, That a rich man shall hardly enter into the kingdom of heaven.

24 And again I say unto you, It is easier for a camel to go through the eye of a needle, than for a rich man to enter into the kingdom of God.

25 When his disciples heard it, they were exceedingly amazed, saying, Who then can be saved?

26 But Jesus beheld *their thoughts*, and said unto them, With men this is impossible; but *if they will forsake all things for my sake,* with God *whatsoever things I speak* are possible. [JST]

MOSIAH 4

King Benjamin — *124 BC*

5 For behold, if the knowledge of the goodness of God at this time has awakened you to a sense of your nothingness, and your worthless and fallen state—

6 I say unto you, if ye have come to a knowledge of the goodness of God, and his matchless power, and his wisdom, and his patience, and his long-suffering towards the children of men; and also, the atonement which has been prepared from the foundation of the world, that thereby salvation might come to him that should put his trust in the Lord, and should be diligent in keeping his commandments, and continue in the faith even unto the end of his life, I mean the life of the mortal body—

7 I say, that this is the man who receiveth salvation, through the atonement which was prepared from the foundation of the world for all mankind, which ever were since the fall of Adam, or who are, or whoever shall be, even unto the end of the world.

8 And this is the means whereby salvation cometh. And there is none other salvation save this which hath been spoken of; neither are there any conditions whereby man can be saved except the conditions which I have told you.

9 Believe in God; believe that he is, and that he created all things, both in heaven and in Earth; believe that he has all wisdom, and all power, both in heaven and in Earth; believe that man doth not comprehend all the things which the Lord can comprehend.

10 And again, believe that ye must repent of your sins and forsake them, and humble yourselves before God; and ask in sincerity of heart that he would forgive you; and now, if you believe all these things see that ye do them.

11 And again I say unto you as I have said before, that as ye have come to the knowledge of the glory of God, or if ye have known of his goodness and have tasted of his love, and have received a remission of your sins, which causeth such exceedingly great joy in your souls, even so I would that ye should remember, and always retain in remembrance, the greatness of God, and your own nothingness, and his goodness and longsuffering towards you, unworthy creatures, and humble yourselves even in the depths of humility, calling on the name of the Lord daily, and standing steadfastly in the faith of that which is to come, which was spoken by the mouth of the angel.

12 And behold, I say unto you that if ye do this ye shall always rejoice, and be filled with the love of God, and always retain a remission of your sins; and ye shall grow in the knowledge of the glory of him that created you, or in the knowledge of that which is just and true.

13 And ye will not have a mind to injure one another, but to live peaceably, and to render to every man according to that which is his due.

14 And ye will not suffer your children that they go hungry, or naked; neither

will ye suffer that they transgress the laws of God, and fight and quarrel one with another, and serve the devil, who is the master of sin, or who is the devil spirit which hath been spoken of by our fathers, he being an enemy to all righteousness.

15 But ye will teach them to walk in the ways of truth and soberness; ye will teach them to love one another, and to serve one another.

16 And also, ye yourselves will succor those that stand in need of your succor; ye will administer of your substance unto him that standeth in need; and ye will not suffer that the beggar putteth up his petition to you in vain, and turn him out to perish.

17 Perhaps thou shalt say: The man has brought upon himself his misery; therefore I will stay my hand, and will not give unto him of my food, nor impart unto him of my substance that he may not suffer, for his punishments are just—

18 But I say unto you, O man, whosoever doeth this the same hath great cause to repent; and except he repenteth of that which he hath done he perisheth forever, and hath no interest in the kingdom of God.

19 For behold, are we not all beggars? Do we not all depend upon the same Being, even God, for all the substance which we have, for both food and raiment, and for gold, and for silver, and for all the riches which we have of every kind?

20 And behold, even at this time, ye have been calling on his name, and begging for a remission of your sins. And has he suffered that ye have begged in vain? Nay; he has poured out his Spirit upon you, and has caused that your hearts should be filled with joy, and has caused that your mouths should be stopped that ye could not find utterance, so exceedingly great was your joy.

21 And now, if God, who has created you, on whom you are dependent for your lives and for all that ye have and are, doth grant unto you whatsoever ye ask that is right, in faith, believing that ye shall receive, O then, how ye ought to impart of the substance that ye have one to another.

22 And if ye judge the man who putteth up his petition to you for your substance that he perish not, and condemn him, how much more just will be your condemnation for withholding your substance, which doth not belong to you but to God, to whom also your life belongeth; and yet ye put up no petition, nor repent of the thing which thou hast done.

23 I say unto you, wo be unto that man, for his substance shall perish with him; and now, I say these things unto those who are rich as pertaining to the things of this world.

24 And again, I say unto the poor, ye who have not and yet have sufficient, that ye remain from day to day; I mean all you who deny the beggar, because ye have not; I would that ye say in your hearts that: I give not because I have not, but if I had I would give.

25 And now, if ye say this in your hearts ye remain guiltless, otherwise ye are condemned; and your condemnation is just for ye covet that which ye have not received.

26 And now, for the sake of these things which I have spoken unto you—that is, for the sake of retaining a remission of your sins from day to day, that ye may walk guiltless before God—I would that ye should impart of your substance to the poor, every man according to that which he hath, such as feeding the hungry, clothing the naked, visiting the sick and administering to their relief, both spiritually and temporally, according to their wants.

27 And see that all these things are done in wisdom and order; for it is not requisite that a man should run faster than he has strength. And again, it is expedient that he should be diligent, that thereby he might win the prize; therefore, all things must be done in order.

28 And I would that ye should remember, that whosoever among you borroweth of his neighbor should return the thing that he borroweth, according as he doth agree, or else thou shalt commit sin; and perhaps thou shalt cause thy neighbor to commit sin also.

29 And finally, I cannot tell you all the things whereby ye may commit sin; for there are divers ways and means, even so many that I cannot number them.

30 But this much I can tell you, that if ye do not watch yourselves, and your thoughts, and your words, and your deeds, and observe the commandments of God,

Allegory of Salvation by Antonius Heusler 1525. John the Baptist makes a man, Adam, clothed only in a loin cloth, aware of the great and last sacrifice of Jesus Christ. Behind the man stand Isaiah and an Apostle. In the background are the brazen serpent, the Annunciation to the Virgin Mary, and Christ triumphing over Death and the Devil.

and continue in the faith of what ye have heard concerning the coming of our Lord, even unto the end of your lives, ye must perish. And now, O man, remember, and perish not.

JAMES 1

James 62 AD

22 But be ye doers of the word, and not hearers only, deceiving your own selves.

27 Pure religion and undefiled before God and the Father is this, To visit the fatherless and widows in their affliction, and to keep himself unspotted from the world.

MORONI 7

Moroni 421 AD

26 And after that he came men also were saved by faith in his name; and by faith, they become the sons of God. And as surely as Christ liveth he spake these words unto our fathers, saying: Whatsoever thing ye shall ask the Father in my name, which is good, in faith believing that ye shall receive, behold, it shall be done unto you.

34 And he hath said: Repent all ye ends of the Earth, and come unto me, and be baptized in my name, and have faith in me, that ye may be saved.

40 And again, my beloved brethren, I would speak unto you concerning hope. How is it that ye can attain unto faith, save ye shall have hope?

41 And what is it that ye shall hope for? Behold I say unto you that ye shall have hope through the atonement of Christ and the power of his resurrection, to be raised unto life eternal, and this because of your faith in him according to the promise.

42 Wherefore, if a man have faith he must needs have hope; for without faith there cannot be any hope.

43 And again, behold I say unto you that he cannot have faith and hope, save he shall be meek, and lowly of heart.

44 If so, his faith and hope is vain, for none is acceptable before God, save the meek and lowly in heart; and if a man be meek and lowly in heart, and confesses by the power of the Holy Ghost that Jesus is the Christ, he must needs have charity; for if he have not charity he is nothing; wherefore he must needs have charity.

45 And charity suffereth long, and is kind, and envieth not, and is not puffed up, seeketh not her own, is not easily provoked, thinketh no evil, and rejoiceth not in iniquity but rejoiceth in the truth, beareth all things, believeth all things, hopeth all things, endureth all things.

46 Wherefore, my beloved brethren, if ye have not charity, ye are nothing, for charity never faileth. Wherefore, cleave unto charity, which is the greatest of all, for all things must fail—

47 But charity is the pure love of Christ, and it endureth forever; and whoso is found possessed of it at the last day, it shall be well with him.

48 Wherefore, my beloved brethren, pray unto the Father with all the energy of heart, that ye may be filled with this love, which he hath bestowed upon all who are true followers of his Son, Jesus Christ; that ye may become the sons of God; that when he shall appear we shall be like him, for we shall see him as he is; that we may have this hope; that we may be purified even as he is pure. Amen.

MORONI 10

Moroni 421 AD

20 Wherefore, there must be faith; and if there must be faith there must also be hope; and if there must be hope there must also be charity.

21 And except ye have charity ye can in nowise be saved in the kingdom of God; neither can ye be saved in the kingdom of God if ye have not faith; neither can ye if ye have no hope.

22 And if ye have no hope ye must needs be in despair; and despair cometh because of iniquity.

32 Yea, come unto Christ, and be perfected in him, and deny yourselves of all ungodliness; and if ye shall deny yourselves of all ungodliness, and love God with all your might, mind and strength, then is his grace sufficient for you, that by his grace ye may be perfect in Christ; and if by the grace of God ye are perfect in Christ, ye can in nowise deny the power of God.

33 And again, if ye by the grace of God are perfect in Christ, and deny not his power, then are ye sanctified in Christ by the grace of God, through the shedding of the blood of Christ, which is in the covenant of the Father unto the remission of your sins, that ye become holy, without spot.

ALMA 14
Alma the Younger *83 BC*

14 Now I say unto you that ye must repent, and be born again; for the Spirit saith if ye are not born again ye cannot inherit the kingdom of heaven; therefore come and be baptized unto repentance, that ye may be washed from your sins, that ye may have faith on the Lamb of God, who taketh away the sins of the world, who is mighty to save and to cleanse from all unrighteousness.
15 Yea, I say unto you come and fear not, and lay aside every sin, which easily doth beset you, which doth bind you down to destruction, yea, come and go forth, and show unto your God that ye are willing to repent of your sins and enter into a covenant with him to keep his commandments, and witness it unto him this day by going into the waters of baptism.
16 And whosoever doeth this, and keepeth the commandments of God from thenceforth, the same will remember that I say unto him, yea, he will remember that I have said unto him, he shall have eternal life, according to the testimony of the Holy Spirit, which testifieth in me.
22 And now my beloved brethren, I have said these things unto you that I might awaken you to a sense of your duty to God, that ye may walk blameless before him, that ye may walk after the holy order of God, after which ye have been received.
23 And now I would that ye should be humble, and be submissive and gentle; easy to be entreated; full of patience and longsuffering; being temperate in all things; being diligent in keeping the commandments of God at all times; asking for whatsoever things ye stand in need, both spiritual and temporal; always returning thanks unto God for whatsoever things ye do receive.
24 And see that ye have faith, hope, and charity, and then ye will always abound in good works.
25 And may the Lord bless you, and keep your garments spotless, that ye may at last be brought to sit down with Abraham, Isaac, and Jacob, and the holy prophets who have been ever since the world began, having your garments spotless even as their garments are spotless, in the kingdom of heaven to go no more out.

HELAMAN 3
Mormon *385 AD*

27 Thus we may see that the Lord is merciful unto all who will, in the sincerity of their hearts, call upon his holy name.
28 Yea, thus we see that the gate of heaven is open unto all, even to those who will believe on the name of Jesus Christ, who is the Son of God.
29 Yea, we see that whosoever will may lay hold upon the word of God, which is quick and powerful, which shall divide asunder all the cunning and the snares and the wiles of the devil, and lead the man of Christ in a strait and narrow course across that everlasting gulf of misery which is prepared to engulf the wicked—
30 And land their souls, yea, their immortal souls, at the right hand of God in the kingdom of heaven, to sit down with Abraham, and Isaac, and with Jacob, and with all our holy fathers, to go no more out.

PSALM 84
David *1000 BC*

10 For a day in thy courts is better than a thousand. I had rather be a doorkeeper in the house of my God, than to dwell in the tents of wickedness.
11 For the Lord God is a sun and shield: the Lord will give grace and glory: no good thing will he withhold from them that walk uprightly.

Because we love him, Christ promises to send us the Second Comforter, or the promise of eternal life, even the glory of the celestial kingdom.

JOHN 14
Jesus Christ *33 AD*

15 If ye love me, keep my commandments.
16 And I will pray the Father, and he shall give you another Comforter, that he may abide with you forever;
17 Even the Spirit of truth; whom the world cannot receive, because it seeth him not, neither knoweth him: but ye know him; for he dwelleth with you, and shall be in you.
18 I will not leave you comfortless: I will come to you.

19 Yet a little while, and the world seeth
me no more; but ye see me: because I live,
ye shall live also.
20 At that day ye shall know that I am in
my Father, and ye in me, and I in you.

DOCTRINE AND COVENANTS 88

Joseph Smith *December 1832*

1 Verily, thus saith the Lord unto you who
have assembled yourselves together to
receive his will concerning you:
2 Behold, this is pleasing unto your Lord,
and the angels rejoice over you; the alms
of your prayers have come up into the ears
of the Lord of Sabaoth, and are recorded
in the book of the names of the sanctified,
even them of the celestial world.
3 Wherefore, I now send upon you
another Comforter, even upon you my
friends, that it may abide in your hearts,
even the Holy Spirit of promise; which
other Comforter is the same that I
promised unto my disciples, as is recorded
in the testimony of John.
4 This Comforter is the promise which I
give unto you of eternal life, even the
glory of the celestial kingdom;
5 Which glory is that of the church of the
Firstborn, even of God, the holiest of all,
through Jesus Christ his Son—
6 He that ascended up on high, as also he
descended below all things, in that he
comprehended all things, that he might be
in all and through all things, the light of
truth;
7 Which truth shineth. This is the light of
Christ. As also he is in the sun, and the
light of the sun, and the power thereof by
which it was made.
8 As also he is in the moon, and is the light
of the moon, and the power thereof by
which it was made;
9 As also the light of the stars, and the
power thereof by which they were made;
10 And the Earth also, and the power
thereof, even the Earth upon which you
stand.
11 And the light which shineth, which
giveth you light, is through him who
enlighteneth your eyes, which is the same
light that quickeneth your under-
standings;
12 Which light proceedeth forth from the
presence of God to fill the immensity of
space—
13 The light which is in all things, which
giveth life to all things, which is the law
by which all things are governed, even the
power of God who sitteth upon his throne,
who is in the bosom of eternity, who is in
the midst of all things.

2 PETER 1

Peter *67 AD*

10 Wherefore the rather, brethren, give
diligence to make your calling and
election sure: for if ye do these things, ye
shall never fall:
11 For so an entrance shall be ministered
unto you abundantly into the everlasting
kingdom of our Lord and Saviour Jesus
Christ.

Jesus Christ calls the faithful saints his offspring, his sons and daughters, and his heirs. He is the father of the faithful.

ACTS 17

Paul *49 AD*

28 For in him we live, and move, and have
our being; as certain also of your own
poets have said, For we are also his
offspring.
29 Forasmuch then as we are the offspring
of God, we ought not to think that the
Godhead is like unto gold, or silver, or
stone, graven by art and man's device.

1 JOHN 3

John *90 AD*

1 Behold, what manner of love the Father
hath bestowed upon us, that we should be
called the sons of God: therefore the world
knoweth us not, because it knew him not.
2 Beloved, now are we the sons of God,
and it doth not yet appear what we shall
be: but we know that, when he shall
appear, we shall be like him; for we shall
see him as he is.
3 And every man that hath this hope in
him purifieth himself, even as he is pure.

DOCTRINE AND COVENANTS 11

Joseph Smith *May 1829*

30 But verily, verily, I say unto you, that
as many as receive me, to them will I give
power to become the sons of God, even to
them that believe on my name. Amen.

DOCTRINE AND COVENANTS 34

Joseph Smith — *November 1830*

1 My son Orson, hearken and hear and behold what I, the Lord God, shall say unto you, even Jesus Christ your Redeemer;
2 The light and the life of the world, a light which shineth in darkness and the darkness comprehendeth it not;
3 Who so loved the world that he gave his own life, that as many as would believe might become the sons of God. Wherefore you are my son;

DOCTRINE AND COVENANTS 35

Joseph Smith — *December 1830*

2 I am Jesus Christ, the Son of God, who was crucified for the sins of the world, even as many as will believe on my name, that they may become the sons of God, even one in me as I am one in the Father, as the Father is one in me, that we may be one.

EPHESIANS 1

Paul — *62 AD*

4 According as he hath chosen us in him before the foundation of the world, that we should be holy and without blame before him in love:
5 Having predestinated us unto the adoption of children by Jesus Christ to himself, according to the good pleasure of his will,
6 To the praise of the glory of his grace, wherein he hath made us accepted in the beloved.
7 In whom we have redemption through his blood, the forgiveness of sins, according to the riches of his grace;
8 Wherein he hath abounded toward us in all wisdom and prudence;
9 Having made known unto us the mystery of his will, according to his good pleasure which he hath purposed in himself:
10 That in the dispensation of the fulness of times he might gather together in one all things in Christ, both which are in heaven, and which are on Earth; even in him:
11 In whom also we have obtained an inheritance, being predestinated according to the purpose of him who worketh all things after the counsel of his own will:
12 That we should be to the praise of his glory, who first trusted in Christ.
13 In whom ye also trusted, after that ye heard the word of truth, the gospel of your salvation: in whom also after that ye believed, ye were sealed with that holy Spirit of promise,
14 Which is the earnest of our inheritance until the redemption of the purchased possession, unto the praise of his glory.
18 The eyes of your understanding being enlightened; that ye may know what is the hope of his calling, and what the riches of the glory of his inheritance in the saints,
19 And what is the exceeding greatness of his power to us-ward who believe, according to the working of his mighty power,
20 Which he wrought in Christ, when he raised him from the dead, and set him at his own right hand in the heavenly places,
21 Far above all principality, and power, and might, and dominion, and every name that is named, not only in this world, but also in that which is to come:
22 And hath put all things under his feet, and gave him to be the head over all things to the church,
23 Which is his body, the fulness of him that filleth all in all.

HEBREWS 2

Paul — *68 AD*

8 Thou [Father] hast put all things in subjection under his [the Son's] feet. For in that he put all in subjection under him, he left nothing that is not put under him. But now we see not yet all things put under him.
9 But we see Jesus, who was made a little lower than the angels for the suffering of death, crowned with glory and honour; that he by the grace of God should taste death for every man.
10 For it became him, for whom are all things, and by whom are all things, in bringing many sons unto glory, to make the captain of their salvation perfect through sufferings.
11 For both he that sanctifieth and they who are sanctified are all of one: for which cause he is not ashamed to call them brethren,
12 Saying, I will declare thy name unto my brethren, in the midst of the church will I sing praise unto thee.

13 And again, I will put my trust in him. And again, Behold I and the children which God hath given me.
14 Forasmuch then as the children are partakers of flesh and blood, he also himself likewise took part of the same; that through death he might destroy him that had the power of death, that is, the devil;
15 And deliver them who through fear of death were all their lifetime subject to bondage.
16 For verily he took not on him the nature of angels; but he took on him the seed of Abraham.
17 Wherefore in all things it behooved him to be made like unto his brethren, that he might be a merciful and faithful high priest in things pertaining to God, to make reconciliation for the sins of the people.
18 For in that he himself hath suffered being tempted, he is able to succor them that are tempted.

GALATIANS 3

Paul — *54 AD*

24 Wherefore the law was our schoolmaster *until* Christ, that we might be justified by faith. [JST]
25 But after that faith is come, we are no longer under a schoolmaster.
26 For ye are all the children of God by faith in Christ Jesus.
27 For as many of you as have been baptized into Christ have put on Christ.
28 There is neither Jew nor Greek, there is neither bond nor free, there is neither male nor female: for ye are all one in Christ Jesus.
29 And if ye be Christ's, then are ye Abraham's seed, and heirs according to the promise.

JOHN 1

John — *30 AD*

12 But as many as received him, to them gave he power to become the sons of God; *only* to them who believe on his name…
16 *For in the beginning was the Word, even the Son, who is made flesh, and sent unto us by the will of the Fathe*r. *And as many as believe on his name shall receive of his fullness.* And of his fullness have all we received, *even immortality and eternal life, through his grace.* [JST]

TITUS 3

Paul — *66 AD*

4 But after that the kindness and love of God our Saviour toward man appeared,
5 Not by works of righteousness which we have done, but according to his mercy he saved us, by the washing of regeneration, and renewing of the Holy Ghost;
6 Which he shed on us abundantly through Jesus Christ our Saviour;
7 That being justified by his grace, we should be made heirs according to the hope of eternal life.

GALATIANS 4

Paul — *54 AD*

4 But when the fulness of the time was come, God sent forth his Son, made of a woman, made under the law,
5 To redeem them that were under the law, that we might receive the adoption of sons.
6 And because ye are sons, God hath sent forth the Spirit of his Son into your hearts, crying, Abba, Father.
7 Wherefore thou art no more a servant, but a son; and if a son, then an heir of God through Christ.

MOSIAH 15

Abinadi — *148 BC*

10 And now I say unto you, who shall declare his generation? Behold, I say unto you, that when his soul has been made an offering for sin he shall see his seed. And now what say ye? And who shall be his seed?
11 Behold I say unto you, that whosoever has heard the words of the prophets, yea, all the holy prophets who have prophesied concerning the coming of the Lord—I say unto you, that all those who have hearkened unto their words, and believed that the Lord would redeem his people, and have looked forward to that day for a remission of their sins, I say unto you, that these are his seed, or they are the heirs of the kingdom of God.
12 For these are they whose sins he has borne; these are they for whom he has died, to redeem them from their transgressions. And now, are they not his seed?
13 Yea, and are not the prophets, every one that has opened his mouth to prophesy, that has not fallen into transgression, I mean all the holy prophets ever since the

world began? I say unto you that they are his seed.

14 And these are they who have published peace, who have brought good tidings of good, who have published salvation; and said unto Zion: Thy God reigneth!

15 And O how beautiful upon the mountains were their feet!

16 And again, how beautiful upon the mountains are the feet of those that are still publishing peace!

17 And again, how beautiful upon the mountains are the feet of those who shall hereafter publish peace, yea, from this time henceforth and forever!

18 And behold, I say unto you, this is not all. For O how beautiful upon the mountains are the feet of him that bringeth good tidings, that is the founder of peace, yea, even the Lord, who has redeemed his people; yea, him who has granted salvation unto his people;

MOSIAH 27

Alma the Younger — *100 BC*

24 For, said he, I have repented of my sins, and have been redeemed of the Lord; behold I am born of the Spirit.

25 And the Lord said unto me: Marvel not that all mankind, yea, men and women, all nations, kindreds, tongues and people, must be born again; yea, born of God, changed from their carnal and fallen state, to a state of righteousness, being redeemed of God, becoming his sons and daughters;

26 And thus they become new creatures; and unless they do this, they can in nowise inherit the kingdom of God.

MOSIAH 5

King Benjamin — *124 BC*

6 And now, these are the words which king Benjamin desired of them; and therefore he said unto them: Ye have spoken the words that I desired; and the covenant which ye have made is a righteous covenant.

7 And now, because of the covenant which ye have made ye shall be called the children of Christ, his sons, and his daughters; for behold, this day he hath spiritually begotten you; for ye say that your hearts are changed through faith on his name; therefore, ye are born of him and have become his sons and his daughters.

8 And under this head ye are made free, and there is no other head whereby ye can be made free. There is no other name given whereby salvation cometh; therefore, I would that ye should take upon you the name of Christ, all you that have entered into the covenant with God that ye should be obedient unto the end of your lives.

9 And it shall come to pass that whosoever doeth this shall be found at the right hand of God, for he shall know the name by which he is called; for he shall be called by the name of Christ.

15 Therefore, I would that ye should be steadfast and immovable, always abounding in good works, that Christ, the Lord God Omnipotent, may seal you his, that you may be brought to heaven, that ye may have everlasting salvation and eternal life, through the wisdom, and power, and justice, and mercy of him who created all things, in heaven and in Earth, who is God above all. Amen.

ROMANS 8

Paul — *57 AD*

14 For as many as are led by the Spirit of God, they are the sons of God.

15 For ye have not received the spirit of bondage again to fear; but ye have received the Spirit of adoption, whereby we cry, Abba, Father.

16 The Spirit itself beareth witness with our spirit, that we are the children of God:

17 And if children, then heirs; heirs of God, and joint-heirs with Christ; if so be that we suffer with him, that we may be also glorified together.

29 For whom he did foreknow, he also did predestinate to be conformed to the image of his Son, that he might be the firstborn among many brethren.

30 Moreover whom he did predestinate, them he also called: and whom he called, them he also justified: and whom he justified, them he also glorified.

31 What shall we then say to these things? If God be for us, who can be against us?

32 He that spared not his own Son, but delivered him up for us all, how shall he not with him also freely give us all things?

We were in the beginning with Christ. Through faith and obedience to the laws and ordinances of the gospel we will progress from grace to grace until we are perfected. We become one with Jesus Christ and Heavenly Father, and we will inherit all things.

DOCTRINE AND COVENANTS 93

Joseph Smith *May 1833*

19 I give unto you these sayings that you may understand and know how to worship, and know what you worship, that you may come unto the Father in my name, and in due time receive of his fulness.
20 For if you keep my commandments you shall receive of his fulness, and be glorified in me as I am in the Father; therefore, I say unto you, you shall receive grace for grace.
21 And now, verily I say unto you, I was in the beginning with the Father, and am the Firstborn;
22 And all those who are begotten through me are partakers of the glory of the same, and are the church of the Firstborn.
23 Ye were also in the beginning with the Father; that which is Spirit, even the Spirit of truth;
24 And truth is knowledge of things as they are, and as they were, and as they are to come;
25 And whatsoever is more or less than this is the spirit of that wicked one who was a liar from the beginning.
26 The Spirit of truth is of God. I am the Spirit of truth, and John bore record of me, saying: He received a fulness of truth, yea, even of all truth;
27 And no man receiveth a fulness unless he keepeth his commandments.
28 He that keepeth his commandments receiveth truth and light, until he is glorified in truth and knoweth all things.
29 Man was also in the beginning with God. Intelligence, or the light of truth, was not created or made, neither indeed can be.
30 All truth is independent in that sphere in which God has placed it, to act for itself, as all intelligence also; otherwise there is no existence.
31 Behold, here is the agency of man, and here is the condemnation of man; because that which was from the beginning is plainly manifest unto them, and they receive not the light.

The Transfiguration of Christ, by Alexandr Ivanov, 1824.

32 And every man whose spirit receiveth not the light is under condemnation.
33 For man is spirit. The elements are eternal, and spirit and element, inseparably connected, receive a fulness of joy;
34 And when separated, man cannot receive a fulness of joy.
35 The elements are the tabernacle of God; yea, man is the tabernacle of God, even temples; and whatsoever temple is defiled, God shall destroy that temple.
36 The glory of God is intelligence, or, in other words, light and truth.
37 Light and truth forsake that evil one.
38 Every spirit of man was innocent in the beginning; and God having redeemed man from the fall, men became again, in their infant state, innocent before God.
39 And that wicked one cometh and taketh away light and truth, through disobedience, from the children of men, and because of the tradition of their fathers.
40 But I have commanded you to bring up your children in light and truth.

DOCTRINE AND COVENANTS 131

Joseph Smith — *May 1843*

7 There is no such thing as immaterial matter. All spirit is matter, but it is more fine or pure, and can only be discerned by purer eyes;
8 We cannot see it; but when our bodies are purified we shall see that it is all matter.

DOCTRINE AND COVENANTS 50

Joseph Smith — *May 1831*

24 That which is of God is light; and he that receiveth light, and continueth in God, receiveth more light; and that light groweth brighter and brighter until the perfect day.
25 And again, verily I say unto you, and I say it that you may know the truth, that you may chase darkness from among you;
26 He that is ordained of God and sent forth, the same is appointed to be the greatest, notwithstanding he is the least and the servant of all.
27 Wherefore, he is possessor of all things; for all things are subject unto him, both in heaven and on the Earth, the life and the light, the Spirit and the power, sent forth by the will of the Father through Jesus Christ, his Son.
28 But no man is possessor of all things except he be purified and cleansed from all sin.
29 And if ye are purified and cleansed from all sin, ye shall ask whatsoever you will in the name of Jesus and it shall be done.
35 And by giving heed and doing these things which ye have received, and which ye shall hereafter receive—and the kingdom is given you of the Father, and power to overcome all things which are not ordained of him—
40 Behold, ye are little children and ye cannot bear all things now; ye must grow in grace and in the knowledge of the truth.
41 Fear not, little children, for you are mine, and I have overcome the world, and you are of them that my Father hath given me;
42 And none of them that my Father hath given me shall be lost.
43 And the Father and I are one. I am in the Father and the Father in me; and inasmuch as ye have received me, ye are in me and I in you.
44 Wherefore, I am in your midst, and I am the good shepherd, and the stone of Israel. He that buildeth upon this rock shall never fall.
45 And the day cometh that you shall hear my voice and see me, and know that I am.
46 Watch, therefore, that ye may be ready. Even so. Amen.

2 CORINTHIANS 3

Paul — *57 AD*

17 Now the Lord is that Spirit: and where the Spirit of the Lord is, there is liberty.
18 But we all, with open face beholding as in a glass the glory of the Lord, are changed into the same image from glory to glory, even as by the Spirit of the Lord.

DOCTRINE AND COVENANTS 88

Joseph Smith — *December 1832*

67 And if your eye be single to my glory, your whole bodies shall be filled with light, and there shall be no darkness in you; and that body which is filled with light comprehendeth all things.
68 Therefore, sanctify yourselves that your minds become single to God, and the days will come that you shall see him; for he will unveil his face unto you, and it

shall be in his own time, and in his own way, and according to his own will.

1 PETER 1

Peter — *64 AD*

1 Peter, an apostle of Jesus Christ, to the strangers scattered throughout Pontus, Galatia, Cappadocia, Asia, and Bithynia,
2 Elect according to the foreknowledge of God the Father, through sanctification of the Spirit, unto obedience and sprinkling of the blood of Jesus Christ: Grace unto you, and peace, be multiplied.
3 Blessed be the God and Father of our Lord Jesus Christ, which according to his abundant mercy hath begotten us again unto a lively hope by the resurrection of Jesus Christ from the dead,
4 To an inheritance incorruptible, and undefiled, and that fadeth not away, reserved in heaven for you,
5 Who are kept by the power of God through faith unto salvation ready to be revealed in the last time.
6 Wherein ye greatly rejoice, though now for a season, if need be, ye are in heaviness through manifold temptations:
7 That the trial of your faith, being much more precious than of gold that perisheth, though it be tried with fire, might be found unto praise and honour and glory at the appearing of Jesus Christ:
8 Whom having not seen, ye love; in whom, though now ye see him not, yet believing, ye rejoice with joy unspeakable and full of glory:
9 Receiving the *object* of your faith, even the salvation of your souls. [JST]
10 Of which salvation the prophets have inquired and searched diligently, who prophesied of the grace that should come unto you:
11 Searching what, or what manner of time the Spirit of Christ which was in them did signify, when it testified beforehand the sufferings of Christ, and the glory that should follow.
12 Unto whom it was revealed, that not unto themselves, but unto us they did minister the things, which are now reported unto you by them that have preached the gospel unto you with the Holy Ghost sent down from heaven; which things the angels desire to look into.
13 Wherefore gird up the loins of your mind, be sober, and hope to the end for the grace that is to be brought unto you at the revelation of Jesus Christ;
14 As obedient children, not fashioning yourselves according to the former lusts in your ignorance:
15 But as he which hath called you is holy, so be ye holy in all manner of conversation;
16 Because it is written, Be ye holy; for I am holy.
17 And if ye call on the Father, who without respect of persons judgeth according to every man's work, pass the time of your sojourning here in fear:
18 Forasmuch as ye know that ye were not redeemed with corruptible things, as silver and gold, from your vain conversation received by tradition from your fathers;
19 But with the precious blood of Christ, as of a lamb without blemish and without spot:
20 Who verily was foreordained before the foundation of the world, but was manifest in these last times for you,
21 Who by him do believe in God, that raised him up from the dead, and gave him glory; that your faith and hope might be in God.
22 Seeing ye have purified your souls in obeying the truth through the Spirit unto unfeigned love of the brethren, see that ye love one another with a pure heart fervently:
23 Being born again, not of corruptible seed, but of incorruptible, by the word of God, which liveth and abideth forever.

ROMANS 15

Paul — *57 AD*

6 That ye may with one mind and one mouth glorify God, even the Father of our Lord Jesus Christ.
7 Wherefore receive ye one another, as Christ also received us to the glory of God.

MATTHEW 5

Jesus Christ — *31 AD*

48 *Ye are* therefore *commanded to be* perfect even as your Father which is in heaven is perfect. [JST]

COLOSSIANS 1

Paul *62 AD*

12 Giving thanks unto the Father, which hath made us meet to be partakers of the inheritance of the saints in light:
13 Who hath delivered us from the power of darkness, and hath translated us into the kingdom of his dear Son:
14 In whom we have redemption through his blood, even the forgiveness of sins:
25 Whereof I am made a minister, according to the dispensation of God which is given to me for you, to fulfil the word of God;
26 Even the mystery which hath been hid from ages and from generations, but now is made manifest to his saints:
27 To whom God would make known what is the riches of the glory of this mystery among the Gentiles; which is Christ in you, the hope of glory:
28 Whom we preach, warning every man, and teaching every man in all wisdom; that we may present every man perfect in Christ Jesus:

EPHESIANS 4

Paul *62 AD*

11 And he gave some, apostles; and some, prophets; and some, evangelists; and some, pastors and teachers;
12 For the perfecting of the saints, for the work of the ministry, for the edifying of the body of Christ:
13 Till we all come in the unity of the faith, and of the knowledge of the Son of God, unto a perfect man, unto the measure of the stature of the fulness of Christ:
14 That we henceforth be no more children, tossed to and fro, and carried about with every wind of doctrine, by the sleight of men, and cunning craftiness, whereby they lie in wait to deceive;
15 But speaking the truth in love, may grow up into him in all things, which is the head, even Christ:

HEBREWS 6

Paul *68 AD*

1 Therefore *not* leaving the principles of the doctrine of Christ, let us go on unto perfection; not laying again the foundation of repentance from dead works, and of faith toward God,
2 Of the doctrine of baptisms, and of laying on of hands, and of resurrection of the dead, and of eternal judgment.
3 And *we will go on unto perfection* if God permit. [JST]

3 NEPHI 28

Jesus Christ *34 AD*

37 But behold, since I wrote, I have inquired of the Lord, and he hath made it manifest unto me that there must needs be a change wrought upon their [three Nephite disciples] bodies, or else it needs be that they must taste of death;
38 Therefore, that they might not taste of death there was a change wrought upon their bodies, that they might not suffer pain nor sorrow save it were for the sins of the world.
39 Now this change was not equal to that which shall take place at the last day; but there was a change wrought upon them, insomuch that Satan could have no power over them, that he could not tempt them; and they were sanctified in the flesh, that they were holy, and that the powers of the Earth could not hold them.
40 And in this state they were to remain until the judgment day of Christ; and at that day they were to receive a greater change, and to be received into the kingdom of the Father to go no more out, but to dwell with God eternally in the heavens.

PHILIPPIANS 3

Paul *62 AD*

8 Yea doubtless, and I count all things but loss for the excellency of the knowledge of Christ Jesus my Lord: for whom I have suffered the loss of all things, and do count them but dung, that I may win Christ,
9 And be found in him, not having mine own righteousness, which is of the law, but that which is through the faith of Christ, the righteousness which is of God by faith:
10 That I may know him, and the power of his resurrection, and the fellowship of his sufferings, being made conformable unto his death;
11 If by any means I might attain unto the resurrection of the dead.
12 Not as though I had already attained, either were already perfect: but I follow after, if that I may apprehend that for

which also I am apprehended of Christ Jesus.
13 Brethren, I count not myself to have apprehended: but this one thing I do, forgetting those things which are behind, and reaching forth unto those things which are before,
14 I press toward the mark for the prize of the high calling of God in Christ Jesus.
15 Let us therefore, as many as be perfect, be thus minded: and if in anything ye be otherwise minded, God shall reveal even this unto you.
20 For our conversation is in heaven; from whence also we look for the Saviour, the Lord Jesus Christ:
21 Who shall change our vile body, that it may be fashioned like unto his glorious body, according to the working whereby he is able even to subdue all things unto himself.

The saints who overcome and endure to the end will receive a white stone, a new name, eternal life, and exaltation. They will sit in God's throne and be partakers of his divine nature, and will become kings and priests, queens, and priestesses.

REVELATION 2
John *95 AD*
7 ...To him that overcometh will I give to eat of the tree of life, which is in the midst of the paradise of God.
11 ...He that overcometh shall not be hurt of the second death.
17 ...To him that overcometh will I give to eat of the hidden manna, and will give him a white stone, and in the stone a new name written, which no man knoweth saving he that receiveth it.
26 And he that overcometh, and keepeth my works unto the end, to him will I give power over the nations:
27 And he shall rule them with a rod of iron; as the vessels of a potter shall they be broken to shivers: even as I received of my Father.
28 And I will give him the morning star.

DOCTRINE AND COVENANTS 130
Joseph Smith *April 1843*
10 Then the white stone mentioned in Revelation 2:17, will become a Urim and Thummim to each individual who receives one, whereby things pertaining to a higher order of kingdoms will be made known;
11 And a white stone is given to each of those who come into the celestial kingdom, whereon is a new name written, which no man knoweth save he that receiveth it. The new name is the key word.

REVELATION 3
John *95 AD*
5 He that overcometh, the same shall be clothed in white raiment; and I will not blot out his name out of the book of life, but I will confess his name before my Father, and before his angels.
12 Him that overcometh will I make a pillar in the temple of my God, and he shall go no more out: and I will write upon him the name of my God, and the name of the city of my God, which is new Jerusalem, which cometh down out of heaven from my God: and I will write upon him my new name.
21 To him that overcometh will I grant to sit with me in my throne, even as I also overcame, and am set down with my Father in his throne.

3 NEPHI 15
Jesus Christ *34 AD*
9 Behold, I am the law, and the light. Look unto me, and endure to the end, and ye shall live; for unto him that endureth to the end will I give eternal life.

DOCTRINE AND COVENANTS 5
Joseph Smith *March 1829*
35 And if thou art faithful in keeping my commandments, thou shalt be lifted up at the last day. Amen.

DOCTRINE AND COVENANTS 6
Joseph Smith *April 1829*
13 If thou wilt do good, yea, and hold out faithful to the end, thou shalt be saved in the kingdom of God, which is the greatest of all the gifts of God; for there is no gift greater than the gift of salvation.

DOCTRINE AND COVENANTS 14
Joseph Smith *June 1829*
7 And, if you keep my commandments and endure to the end you shall have

eternal life, which gift is the greatest of all the gifts of God.

DOCTRINE AND COVENANTS 25
Joseph Smith — June 1830
15 Keep my commandments continually, and a crown of righteousness thou shalt receive. And except thou do this, where I am you cannot come.

DOCTRINE AND COVENANTS 10
Joseph Smith — 1828
69 And now, behold, whosoever is of my church, and endureth of my church to the end, him will I establish upon my rock, and the gates of hell shall not prevail against them.

DOCTRINE AND COVENANTS 18
Joseph Smith — June 1829
22 And as many as repent and are baptized in my name, which is Jesus Christ, and endure to the end, the same shall be saved.

PSALM 103
David — 1000 BC
17 But the mercy of the Lord is from everlasting to everlasting upon them that fear him, and his righteousness unto children's children;
18 To such as keep his covenant, and to those that remember his commandments to do them.
19 The Lord hath prepared his throne in the heavens; and his kingdom ruleth over all.
20 Bless the Lord, ye his angels, that excel in strength, that do his commandments, hearkening unto the voice of his word.
21 Bless ye the Lord, all ye his hosts; ye ministers of his, that do his pleasure.
22 Bless the Lord, all his works in all places of his dominion: bless the Lord, O my soul.

DOCTRINE AND COVENANTS 20
Joseph Smith — April 1830
29 And we know that all men must repent and believe on the name of Jesus Christ, and worship the Father in his name, and endure in faith on his name to the end, or they cannot be saved in the kingdom of God.

DOCTRINE AND COVENANTS 103
Joseph Smith — February 1834
7 And by hearkening to observe all the words which I, the Lord their God, shall speak unto them, they shall never cease to prevail until the kingdoms of the world are subdued under my feet, and the Earth is given unto the saints, to possess it forever and ever.

DOCTRINE AND COVENANTS 78
Joseph Smith — March 1832
7 For if you will that I give unto you a place in the Celestial world, you must prepare yourselves by doing the things which I have commanded you and required of you.

2 CORINTHIANS 4
Paul — 57 AD
17 For our light affliction, which is but for a moment, worketh for us a far more exceeding and eternal weight of glory;

ALMA 13
Alma the Younger — 82 BC
10 Now, as I said concerning the holy order, or this high priesthood, there were many who were ordained and became high priests of God; and it was on account of their exceeding faith and repentance, and their righteousness before God, they choosing to repent and work righteousness rather than to perish;
11 Therefore they were called after this holy order, and were sanctified, and their garments were washed white through the blood of the Lamb.
12 Now they, after being sanctified by the Holy Ghost, having their garments made white, being pure and spotless before God, could not look upon sin save it were with abhorrence; and there were many, exceedingly great many, who were made pure and entered into the rest of the Lord their God.

ALMA 34
Amulek — 74 BC
36 And this I know, because the Lord hath said he dwelleth not in unholy temples, but in the hearts of the righteous doth he dwell; yea, and he has also said that the righteous shall sit down in his kingdom, to go no more out; but their garments should

be made white through the blood of the Lamb.

DOCTRINE AND COVENANTS 88

Joseph Smith *December 1832*

49 The light shineth in darkness, and the darkness comprehendeth it not; nevertheless, the day shall come when you shall comprehend even God, being quickened in him and by him.
50 Then shall ye know that ye have seen me, that I am, and that I am the true light that is in you, and that you are in me; otherwise ye could not abound.

2 PETER 1

Peter *67 AD*

1 Simon Peter, a servant and an apostle of Jesus Christ, to them that have obtained like precious faith with us through the righteousness of God and our Saviour Jesus Christ:
2 Grace and peace be multiplied unto you through the knowledge of God, and of Jesus our Lord,
3 According as his divine power hath given unto us all things that pertain unto life and godliness, through the knowledge of him that hath called us to glory and virtue:
4 Whereby are given unto us exceeding great and precious promises: that by these ye might be partakers of the divine nature, having escaped the corruption that is in the world through lust.

EPHESIANS 2

Paul *62 AD*

4 But God, who is rich in mercy, for his great love wherewith he loved us,
5 Even when we were dead in sins, hath quickened us together with Christ, (by grace ye are saved;)
6 And hath raised us up together, and made us sit together in heavenly places in Christ Jesus:
7 That in the ages to come he might shew the exceeding riches of his grace in his kindness toward us through Christ Jesus.
8 For by grace are ye saved through faith; and that not of yourselves: it is the gift of God:
9 Not of works, lest any man should boast.

REVELATION 1

John *95 AD*

5 And from Jesus Christ, who is the faithful witness, and the first begotten of the dead, and the prince of the kings of the Earth. Unto him that loved us, and washed us from our sins in his own blood,
6 And hath made us kings and priests unto God and his Father; to him be glory and dominion for ever and ever. Amen.

REVELATION 5

John *95 AD*

8 And when he had taken the book, the four beasts and four and twenty elders fell down before the Lamb, having every one of them harps, and golden vials full of odours, which are the prayers of saints.
9 And they sung a new song, saying, Thou art worthy to take the book, and to open the seals thereof: for thou wast slain, and hast redeemed us to God by thy blood out of every kindred, and tongue, and people, and nation;
10 And hast made us unto our God kings and priests: and we shall reign on the Earth.

The Saints who enter the new and everlasting covenant of marriage may, if they remain faithful, attain the highest level of the celestial kingdom and become Gods, having eternal increase with all things subject unto them. God the Father was once a man like we are now and progressed from grace to grace until he became exalted.

2 CORINTHIANS 12

Paul *57 AD*

1 It is not expedient for me doubtless to glory. I will come to visions and revelations of the Lord.
2 I knew a man in Christ above fourteen years ago, (whether in the body, I cannot tell; or whether out of the body, I cannot tell: God knoweth;) such an one caught up to the third heaven.
3 And I knew such a man, (whether in the body, or out of the body, I cannot tell: God knoweth;)
4 How that he was caught up into paradise, and heard unspeakable words, which it is not lawful for a man to utter.

DOCTRINE AND COVENANTS 131

Joseph Smith *May 1843*

1 In the celestial glory there are three heavens or degrees;
2 And in order to obtain the highest, a man must enter into this order of the priesthood [meaning the new and everlasting covenant of marriage];
3 And if he does not, he cannot obtain it.
4 He may enter into the other, but that is the end of his kingdom; he cannot have an increase.

1 PETER 3

Peter *64 AD*

7 Likewise, ye husbands, dwell with them according to knowledge, giving honour unto the wife, as unto the weaker vessel, and as being heirs together of the grace of life; that your prayers be not hindered.

DOCTRINE AND COVENANTS 132

Joseph Smith *July 1843*

19 And again, verily I say unto you, if a man marry a wife by my word, which is my law, and by the new and everlasting covenant, and it is sealed unto them by the Holy Spirit of promise, by him who is anointed, unto whom I have appointed this power and the keys of this priesthood; and it shall be said unto them—Ye shall come forth in the first resurrection; and if it be after the first resurrection, in the next resurrection; and shall inherit thrones, kingdoms, principalities, and powers, dominions, all heights and depths—then shall it be written in the Lamb's Book of Life, that he shall commit no murder whereby to shed innocent blood, and if ye abide in my covenant, and commit no murder whereby to shed innocent blood, it shall be done unto them in all things whatsoever my servant hath put upon them, in time, and through all eternity; and shall be of full force when they are out of the world; and they shall pass by the angels, and the gods, which are set there, to their exaltation and glory in all things, as hath been sealed upon their heads, which glory shall be a fulness and a continuation of the seeds forever and ever.
20 Then shall they be gods, because they have no end; therefore shall they be from everlasting to everlasting, because they continue; then shall they be above all, because all things are subject unto them. Then shall they be gods, because they have all power, and the angels are subject unto them.
21 Verily, verily, I say unto you, except ye abide my law ye cannot attain to this glory.
22 For strait is the gate, and narrow the way that leadeth unto the exaltation and continuation of the lives, and few there be that find it, because ye receive me not in the world neither do ye know me.
23 But if ye receive me in the world, then shall ye know me, and shall receive your exaltation; that where I am ye shall be also.
24 This is eternal lives—to know the only wise and true God, and Jesus Christ, whom he hath sent. I am he. Receive ye, therefore, my law.
28 I am the Lord thy God, and will give unto thee the law of my Holy Priesthood, as was ordained by me and my Father before the world was.
29 Abraham received all things, whatsoever he received, by revelation and commandment, by my word, saith the Lord, and hath entered into his exaltation and sitteth upon his throne.
30 Abraham received promises concerning his seed, and of the fruit of his loins—from whose loins ye are, namely, my servant Joseph—which were to continue so long as they were in the world; and as touching Abraham and his seed, out of the world they should continue; both in the world and out of the world should they continue as innumerable as the stars; or, if ye were to count the sand upon the seashore ye could not number them.
31 This promise is yours also, because ye are of Abraham, and the promise was made unto Abraham; and by this law is the continuation of the works of my Father, wherein he glorifieth himself.
32 Go ye, therefore, and do the works of Abraham; enter ye into my law and ye shall be saved.

JOHN 5

John *31 AD*

18 Therefore the Jews sought the more to kill him, because he not only had broken the sabbath, but said also that God was his Father, making himself equal with God.
19 Then answered Jesus and said unto them, Verily, verily, I say unto you, The

Son can do nothing of himself, but what he seeth the Father do: for what things soever he doeth, these also doeth the Son likewise.

PSALM 82

David — *1000 BC*

6 I have said, Ye are gods; and all of you are children of the most High.

JOHN 16

John — *33 AD*

15 All things that the Father hath are mine:

JOHN 15

John — *33 AD*

8 Herein is my Father glorified, that ye bear much fruit; so shall ye be my disciples.

JOHN 17

Jesus Christ — *33 AD*

1 These words spake Jesus, and lifted up his eyes to heaven, and said, Father, the hour is come; glorify thy Son, that thy Son also may glorify thee:
2 As thou hast given him power over all flesh, that he should give eternal life to as many as thou hast given him.
3 And this is life eternal, that they might know thee the only true God, and Jesus Christ, whom thou hast sent.
4 I have glorified thee on the Earth: I have finished the work which thou gavest me to do.
5 And now, O Father, glorify thou me with thine own self with the glory which I had with thee before the world was.
6 I have manifested thy name unto the men which thou gavest me out of the world: thine they were, and thou gavest them me; and they have kept thy word.
7 Now they have known that all things whatsoever thou hast given me are of thee.
8 For I have given unto them the words which thou gavest me; and they have received them, and have known surely that I came out from thee, and they have believed that thou didst send me.
9 I pray for them: I pray not for the world, but for them which thou hast given me; for they are thine.
10 And all mine are thine, and thine are mine; and I am glorified in them.
11 And now I am no more in the world, but these are in the world, and I come to thee. Holy Father, keep through thine own name those whom thou hast given me, that they may be one, as we are.
17 Sanctify them through thy truth: thy word is truth.
18 As thou hast sent me into the world, even so have I also sent them into the world.
19 And for their sakes I sanctify myself, that they also might be sanctified through the truth.
20 Neither pray I for these alone, but for them also which shall believe on me through their word;
21 That they all may be one; as thou, Father, art in me, and I in thee, that they also may be one in us: that the world may believe that thou hast sent me.
22 And the glory which thou gavest me I have given them; that they may be one, even as we are one:
23 I in them, and thou in me, that they may be made perfect in one; and that the world may know that thou hast sent me, and hast loved them, as thou hast loved me.

DOCTRINE AND COVENANTS 76

Joseph Smith — *February 1832*

92 And thus we saw the glory of the celestial, which excels in all things—where God, even the Father, reigns upon his throne forever and ever;
93 Before whose throne all things bow in humble reverence, and give him glory forever and ever.
94 They who dwell in his presence are the church of the Firstborn; and they see as they are seen, and know as they are known, having received of his fulness and of his grace;
95 And he makes them equal in power, and in might, and in dominion.
96 And the glory of the celestial is one, even as the glory of the sun is one.

THE KING FOLLETT DISCOURSE

Joseph Smith — *April 7, 1844*

In the first place, I wish to go back to the beginning—to the morn of creation. There is the starting point for us to look to, in order to understand and be fully acquainted with the mind, purposes and decrees of the Great Eloheim, who sits in yonder heavens as he did at the creation of the world. It is necessary for us to have an understanding of God himself in the beginning. If we start right, it is easy to go right all the time; but if we start wrong we may go wrong, and it will be a hard matter to get right...

If men do not comprehend the character of God, they do not comprehend themselves. I want to go back to the beginning, and so lift your minds into more lofty spheres and a more exalted understanding than what the human mind generally aspires to.

I want to ask this congregation, every man, woman and child, to answer the question in their own hearts, what kind of a being God is? Ask yourselves; turn your thoughts into your hearts, and say if any of you have seen, heard, or communed with Him? This is a question that may occupy your attention for a long time. I again repeat the question—What kind of being is God? Does any man or woman know? Have any of you seen Him, heard Him, or communed with Him? Here is the question that will, peradventure, from this time henceforth occupy your attention. The scriptures inform us that "this is life eternal, that they might know thee the only true God, and Jesus Christ, whom thou hast sent."

If any man does not know God, and inquires what kind of a being He is—if he will search diligently his own heart—if the declaration of Jesus and the apostles be true, he will realize that he has not eternal life; for there can be eternal life on no other principle.

My first object is to find out the character of the only wise and true God, and what kind of a being He is...

I will prove that the world is wrong, by showing what God is. I am going to inquire after God; for I want you all to know Him, and to be familiar with Him; and if I am bringing you to a knowledge of Him, all persecutions against me ought to cease. You will then know that I am His servant; for I speak as one having authority.

I will go back to the beginning before the world was, to show what kind of a being God is. What sort of a being was God in the beginning? Open your ears and hear, all ye ends of the Earth, for I am going to prove it to you by the Bible, and to tell you the designs of God in relation to the human race, and why He interferes with the affairs of man.

God himself was once as we are now, and is an exalted man, and sits enthroned in yonder heavens! That is the great secret. If the veil were rent today, and the great God who holds this world in its orbit, and who upholds all worlds and all things by His power, was to make himself visible—I say, if you were to see him today, you would see him like a man in form—like yourselves in all the person, image, and very form as a man; for Adam was created in the very fashion, image and likeness of God, and received instruction from, and walked, talked and conversed with Him, as one man talks and communes with another.

In order to understand the subject of the dead, for consolation of those who mourn for the loss of their friends, it is necessary we should understand the character and being of God and how He came to be so; for I am going to tell you how God came to be God. We have imagined and supposed that God was God from all eternity. I will refute that idea, and take away the veil, so that you may see.

These ideas are incomprehensible to some, but they are simple. It is the first principle of the gospel to know for a certainty the character of God, and to know that we may converse with Him as one man converses with another, and that He was once a man like us; yea, that God himself, the Father of us all, dwelt on an Earth, the same as Jesus Christ Himself did; and I will show it from the Bible.

I wish I was in a suitable place to tell it, and that I had the trump of an archangel, so that I could tell the story in such a manner that persecution would cease forever. What did Jesus say? The scriptures inform us that Jesus said, as the Father hath power in himself, even so hath the

Son power—to do what? Why, what the Father did. The answer is obvious—in a manner to lay down his body and take it up again. Jesus, what are you going to do? To lay down my life as my Father did, and take it up again. Do you believe it? If you do not believe it you do not believe the Bible. The scriptures say it, and I defy all the learning and wisdom and all the combined powers of Earth and hell together to refute it. Here, then, is eternal life—to know the only wise and true God; and you have got to learn how to be gods yourselves, and to be kings and priests to God, the same as all gods have done before you, namely, by going from one small degree to another, and from a small capacity to a great one; from grace to grace, from exaltation to exaltation, until you attain to the resurrection of the dead, and are able to dwell in everlasting burnings, and to sit in glory, as do those who sit enthroned in everlasting power. And I want you to know that God, in the last days, while certain individuals are proclaiming His name, is not trifling with you or me.

These are the first principles of consolation. How consoling to the mourners when they are called to part with a husband, wife, father, mother, child, or dear relative, to know that, although the Earthly tabernacle is laid down and dissolved, they shall rise again to dwell in everlasting burnings in immortal glory, not to sorrow, suffer, or die any more, but they shall be heirs of God and joint heirs with Jesus Christ. What is it? To inherit the same power, the same glory and the same exaltation, until you arrive at the station of a god, and ascend the throne of eternal power, the same as those who have gone before. What did Jesus do? Why, I do the things I saw my Father do when worlds came rolling into existence. My Father worked out His kingdom with fear and trembling, and I must do the same; and when I get my kingdom, I shall present it to My Father, so that He may obtain kingdom upon kingdom, and it will exalt Him in glory. He will then take a higher exaltation, and I will take His place, and thereby become exalted myself. So that Jesus treads in the tracks of His Father, and inherits what God did before; and God is thus glorified and exalted in the salvation and exaltation of all His children. It is plain beyond disputation, and you thus learn some of the first principles of the gospel, about which so much hath been said.

When you climb up a ladder, you must begin at the bottom, and ascend step by step, until you arrive at the top; and so it is with the principles of the gospel—you must begin with the first, and go on until you learn all the principles of exaltation. But it will be a great while after you have passed through the veil before you will have learned them. It is not all to be comprehended in this world; it will be a great work to learn our salvation and exaltation even beyond the grave.

I have another subject to dwell upon, which is calculated to exalt man; but it is impossible for me to say much on this subject. I shall therefore just touch upon it, for time will not permit me to say all. It is associated with the subject of the resurrection of the dead—namely, the soul—the mind of man —the immortal spirit. Where did it come from? All learned men and doctors of divinity say that God created it in the beginning; but it is not so: the very idea lessens man in my estimation. I do not believe the doctrine; I know better. Hear it, all ye ends of the world; for God has told me so; and if you don't believe me, it will not make the truth without effect. I will make a man appear a fool before I get through; if he does not believe it. I am going to tell of things more noble.

We say that God Himself is a self-existing being. Who told you so? It is correct enough; but how did it get into your heads? Who told you that man did not exist in like manner upon the same principles? Man does exist upon the same principles. God made a tabernacle and put a spirit into it, and it became a living soul. (Refers to the Bible.) How does it read in the Hebrew? It does not say in the Hebrew that God created the spirit of man. It says, "God made man out of the Earth and put

Jacob's Dream, by William Blake, 1805.

into him Adam's spirit, and so became a living body."

The mind or the intelligence which man possesses is co-equal [co-eternal] with God himself. I know that my testimony is true; hence, when I talk to these mourners, what have they lost? Their relatives and friends are only separated from their bodies for a short season: their spirits which existed with God have left the tabernacle of clay only for a little moment, as it were; and they now exist in a place where they converse together the same as we do on the Earth.

I am dwelling on the immortality of the spirit of man. Is it logical to say that the intelligence of spirits is immortal, and yet that it has a beginning? The intelligence of spirits had no beginning, neither will it have an end. That is good logic. That which has a beginning may have an end. There never was a time when there were not spirits; for they are co-equal [co-eternal] with our Father in heaven.

I want to reason more on the spirit of man; for I am dwelling on the body and spirit of man—on the subject of the dead. I take my ring from my finger and liken it unto the mind of man—the immortal part, because it had no beginning. Suppose you cut it in two; then it has a beginning and an end; but join it again, and it continues one eternal round. So with the spirit of man. As the Lord liveth, if it had a beginning, it will have an end. All the fools and learned and wise men from the beginning of creation, who say that the spirit of man had a beginning, prove that it must have an end; and if that doctrine is true, then the doctrine of annihilation would be true. But if I am right, I might with boldness proclaim from the housetops that God never had the power to create the spirit of man at all. God himself could not create himself.

Intelligence is eternal and exists upon a self-existent principle. It is a spirit from age to age and there is no creation about it. All the minds and spirits that God ever sent into the world are susceptible of enlargement.

The first principles of man are self-existent with God. God himself, finding he was in the midst of spirits and glory, because he was more intelligent, saw proper to institute laws whereby the rest could have a privilege to advance like himself. The relationship we have with God places us in a situation to advance in knowledge. He has power to institute laws to instruct the weaker intelligences, that they may be exalted with Himself, so that they might have one glory upon another, and all that knowledge, power, glory, and intelligence, which is requisite in order to save them in the world of spirits.

This is good doctrine. It tastes good. I can taste the principles of eternal life, and so can you. They are given to me by the revelations of Jesus Christ; and I know that when I tell you these words of eternal life as they are given to me, you taste them, and I know that you believe them. You say honey is sweet, and so do I. I can also taste the spirit of eternal life. I know that it is good; and when I tell you of these things which were given me by inspiration of the Holy Spirit, you are bound to receive them as sweet, and rejoice more and more.

SOURCES

These works are in the public domain in the United States because they were published before January 1, 1926.

The King James Version of the Bible

- Originally published in 1611
- https://en.wikisource.org/wiki/Bible_(King_James_Version,_1611)

The Book of Mormon

- Originally published in 1830, the text of this version is from the 1981 edition published by the Church of Jesus Christ of Latter-day Saints. No additions in the 1981 edition are included in this book such as chapter headings, footnotes, etc.…only the text.
- https://en.wikisource.org/wiki/Book_of_Mormon_(1981)

The Doctrine and Covenants of the Church of Jesus Christ of Latter-day Saints

- Originally published 1835 as *Doctrine and Covenants of the Church of the Latter-day Saints: Carefully Selected from the Revelations of God.*
- https://en.wikisource.org/wiki/The_Doctrine_and_Covenants

Recommendation for Orson Hyde

- General Conference address by Joseph Smith in Nauvoo, Hancock Co., IL, 6 April 1840
- Published in Times and Seasons, April 1840 on page 86, 87.

Orson Hyde's Dedicatory Prayer

- Originally recorded Nov. 22, 1841, and reprinted in Chapter 26, Volume 4 of History of the Church.
- http://www.vibrationdata.com/Orson_Hyde.htm

The Pearl of Great Price (1913)

- Originally published in 1851, the text of this version was published in 1913 by the Church of Jesus Christ of Latter-day Saints.
- https://en.wikisource.org/wiki/The_Pearl_of_Great_Price_(1913)

King Follett Discourse

- Originally delivered by Joseph Smith, Jr., on April 7, 1844, to a general conference of approximately 10,000 church members that took place after the funeral service of church Elder, King Follett, who had died on March 9, 1844, by accidentally falling down a well.
- The notes from the speech were published in a church paper, Times and Seasons, on August 15, 1844.
- https://en.wikisource.org/wiki/King_Follett_Discourse

The Joseph Smith Translation of the Bible

- Originally published in 1867 under the title *The Holy Scriptures, Translated and Corrected by the Spirit of Revelation*, by the Reorganized Church of Jesus Christ of Latter-day Saints

SCRIPTURE INDEX

OLD TESTAMENT

BOOK OF MORMON

DOCTRINE AND COVENANTS

PEARL OF GREAT PRICE

OTHER DOCUMENTS

IMAGE CREDITS and PERMISSIONS

Cover: Portrait of Christ, by Heinrich Hoffman, 1889 [Public Domain], via Wikimedia Commons. / **Page 13**: The Hubble Ultra Deep Field, photo by the Hubble Space Telescope, between 2003-2004, courtesy of NASA and the European Space Agency [Public Domain], via Wikimedia Commons. / **Page 19**: Artist's Impression of the Hadean Eon, courtesy of Tim Bertelink, [CC BY-SA 4.0], via Wikimedia Commons. / **Page 21**: Thunderstorms Over the Pacific Seen From Earth's Orbit on STS-64, courtesy of NASA [Public Domain], via Wikimedia Commons. / **Page 22**: Fagus Sylvatica Pliocenica MHNT.PAL.VEG.2002.31.jpg, photograph courtesy of Didier Descouens, [CC BY-SA 4.0], via Wikimedia Commons. / **Page 23**: Artist's Concept of Collision at HD, courtesy NASA/JPL-Caltech [Public Domain], via Wikimedia Commons. / **Page 24**: Cheirurus Ingricus – Trilobite, photograph courtesy of Tim Evanson [CC BY-SA 2.0], via Wikimedia Commons. / **Page 25**: The Garden of Eden and the Creation of Eve, by Jan Brueghel the Younger, 1630s [Public Domain], via Wikimedia Commons. / **Page 29**: Satan, by Gustave Doré, as illustrated in John Milton's Paradise Lost, 1866 [Public Domain], via Wikimedia Commons. / **Page 32**: The Spiritual Descent of Lucifer Into Satan, by Gustave Doré, as illustrated in John Milton's Paradise Lost, 1866 [Public Domain], via Wikimedia Commons. / **Page 35**: Adam Names the Animals in the Garden of Eden, photograph of etching courtesy of the Science Museum Group in the United Kingdom [CC BY-SA 4.0], via Wikimedia Commons. / **Page 39**: The Explusion of Adam and Eve from Paradise, by Benjamin West, 1791, courtesy of the National Gallery of Art, [Public Domain], via Wikimedia Commons. / **Page 40**: Adam and Eve are Driven Out of Eden, by Gustave Doré, as illustrated in John Milton's Paradise Lost, 1866, [Public Domain], via Wikimedia Commons. / **Page 49**: The Brazen Serpent, as illustrated in the Holman Bible, 1890, [Public Domain], via Wikimedia Commons. / **Page 52**: The Face of Jesus Reconstructed From Turin Shroud, courtesy of Monozigote [CC BY-SA 4.0], via Wikimedia Commons. / **Page 55:** Le Sacrifice d'Isaac, by Philippe de Champaigne, 1602-1674, courtesy of The Bridgeman Art Gallery [Public Domain], via Wikimedia Commons. / **Page 62**: The Nativity, attributed to Jacobo Bussano, 1510-1592, courtesy of the Royal Collection of the British Royal Family [Public Domain], via Wikimedia Commons. / **Page 63**: The Prophet Isaiah, by Raphael, 1511, courtesy of the Sant' Agostino Collection,

Rome, Italy [Public Domain], via Wikimedia Commons. / **Page 64**: The Nativity with the Infant John the Baptist and Shepherds, by a follower of II Sodoma, ca 1550 [Public Domain], via Wikimedia Commons. / **Page 65**: Saint John the Baptist Bearing Witness, by Annibale Carracci, circa 1600, courtesy of the Metropolitan Museum of Art [Public Domain], via Wikimedia Commons. / **Page 68**: John the Baptist Baptizing Jesus, from the Life on Earth of our Blessed Lord, by Grace Wallace Doonan, 1913 [Public Domain], via Wikimedia Commons. / **Page 70**: The Baptism of Christ, by Grigory Gaagarin, ca. 1840-50 [Public Domain], via Wikimedia Commons. / **Page 71**: Christ and the Rich Young Ruler, by Heinrich Hoffman, 1889, courtesy of the Riverside Church, New York City [Public Domain], via Wikimedia Commons. / **Page 72**: Christ Healing the Sick at Bethesda, by Carl Heinrich Bloch, 1883 [Public Domain], via Wikimedia Commons. / **Page 73**: The Mocking of Christ, by Carl Heinrich Bloch, 1880, courtesy of Brigham Young University Museum of Art [Public Domain], via Wikimedia Commons. / **Page 77**: Christ in Gethsemane, by Carl Heinrich Bloch, 1873, courtesy of the Chapel at Frederiksborg Palace in Copenhagen [Public Domain], via Wikimedia Commons. / **Page 79**: Christ at the Cross, by Carl Heinrich Bloch, 1870, courtesy of the Museum of National History Frederiksborg Castle, Copenhagen, Denmark [Public Domain], via Wikimedia Commons. / **Page 81**: The Resurrection, by Carl Heinrich Bloch, 1881, courtesy of Brigham Young University Museum of Art [Public Domain], via Wikimedia Commons. / **Page 84**: Christ's Appearance to Mary Magdalene After the Resurrection, by Alexander Ivanov, 1835, courtesy of the Russian Museum [Public Domain], via Wikimedia Commons. / **Page 86:** Temple of the Feathered Serpent, photograph courtesy of JK23JK23, [CC BY-SA 3.0], via Wikimedia Commons. / **Page 90**: Christ in the Land Bountiful, by Simon Dewey, 2010, [CC BY-SA 4.0], via Wikimedia Commons. / **Page 91**: Christ Appears to the Nephites, from The Story of the Book of Mormon, by George Reynolds, 1888 [Public Domain], via Wikimedia Commons. / **Page 93**: The Destruction of the Temple of Jerusalem, by Francesco Hayez, 1867, courtesy of the Gallerie dell'Accademia [Public Domain], via Wikimedia Commons. / **Page 96**: Rome, Arch of Titus, Triumphal Procession, courtesy of Dnalor_01, [CC BY-SA 3.0], via Wikimedia Commons. / **Page 100**: Vision of Cornelius the Centurion, by Gerbrand van den Eeckhout, 1664, courtesy of the Walters Art Museum [Public Domain], via Wikimedia Commons. / **Page 102**: De Bekering Van Saulus (Paulus), 1696 – 1748, courtesy of Riksmuseum [CC BY-SA 1.0 Public Domain], via Wikimedia Commons. / **Page 108**: Triumph of Faith,

Christian Martyrs in the Time of Nero, by Eugene Thirion, ca 19th Century [Public Domain], via Wikimedia Commons. / **Page 109**: Painting of Pope Boniface VIII, medieval origin, painter unknown [Public Domain], via Wikimedia Commons. / **Page 112**: Saint Paul, by Bartolomeo Montagna, 1482, courtesy of the Museo Poldi Pezzoli [Public Domain], via Wikimedia Commons. / **Page 114**: Parting of St Peter and Paul – Being Led to Martyrdom, by Giovanni Serodine, 1625, courtesy of the Galleria Nazionale d'Arte Antica [Public Domain], via Wikimedia Commons. / **Page 116**: Map of Western Anatolia, Seven Churches of Asia [Public Domain], via Wikimedia Commons. / **Page 119**: Bonampak Bloodletting Mural Scene, photograph courtesy of Emma Shavrick, [CC BY-SA 4.0], via Wikimedia Commons. / **Page 121**: War Scene, from a vase depicting warfare between two Maya forces, photograph courtesy of Justin Kerr, [CC BY-SA 4.0], via Wikimedia Commons. / **Page 125**: Mayan Ruins, Yucatan, by Robert Scott Duncanson, 1848. Courtesy of the Dayton Art Institute [Public Domain], via Wikimedia Commons. / **Page 129**: The Baptism, by Pietro Longhi, 1755, courtesy of the Fondazione Querini Stampalia Collection [Public Domain], via Wikimedia Commons. / **Page 133**: The Whore of Babylon, woodcut by Lucas Cranach, 1472-1553 [Public Domain], via Wikimedia Commons. / **Page 138**: Taking of Jerusalem by the Crusaders, 15th July 1099, by Emile Signol, 1847, courtesy of the Palace of Versailles [Public Domain], via Wikimedia Commons. / **Page 141**: Portrait of a Man, said to be Christopher Columbus, by Sebastiano del Piombo, 1519, courtesy of the Metropolitan Museum of Art [Public Domain], via Wikimedia Commons. / **Page 142:** John Wesley Preaching to Native American Indians, courtesy of Wellcome Images [CC BY-SA 4.0], via Wikimedia Commons. / **Page 144**: Surrender of Lord Cornwallis, by John Trumbull, 1820, courtesy of the Rotunda of the US Capitol [Public Domain], via Wikimedia Commons. / **Page 146**: George Washington at the Constitutional Convention, by Junius Brutus Stearns, 1856, [Public Domain], via Wikimedia Commons. / **Page 149**: The Statue of Liberty National Monument, photograph courtesy of Sujal Wattamwar, [CC BY-SA 4.0], via Wikimedia Commons. / **Page 154**: Joseph Smith's First Vision, by unknown artist, 1913, courtesy of the Museum of Church History and Art, Salt Lake City, Utah [Public Domain], via Wikimedia Commons. / **Page 156**: Joseph Smith, Jr., by unknown artist, 1842, courtesy of the Community of Christ Headquarters, Independence, Missouri [Public Domain], via Wikimedia Commons. / **Page 159**: The Angel Moroni Delivering the Plates of the Book of Mormon to Joseph Smith, Jun., 1886 [Public Domain], via Wikimedia Commons. / **Page 162**: Joseph Smith Receiving the Golden Plates, engraving by Edward Stevenson, taken from Reminiscences of Joseph, the Prophet, 1893 [Public Domain], via Wikimedia Commons. / **Page 164**: The Hill Cumorah, by C.C.A. Christensen, 19th century [Public Domain], via Wikimedia Commons. / **Page 166**: Dr Charles Anthon, photograph by Mathew Brady, 1822-1896 [Public Domain], via Wikimedia Commons. / **Page 166**: Dr Samuel Latham Mitchill, artist unknown, [Public Domain], via Wikimedia Commons. / **Page 167**: Caracters Large, copied by John Whitmer, ca 1829–1831, courtesy of the Community of Christ [Public Domain], via Wikimedia Commons. / **Page 170**: The Three Witnesses of the Book of Mormon, by Edward Hart, as depicted in the front piece of the 1883 Contributor magazine [Public Domain], via Wikimedia Commons. / **Page 171**: Hyrum Smith, drawing ca 1880 – 1920, courtesy of The George Edward Anderson Collection, Brigham Young University [Public Domain], via Wikimedia Commons. / **Page 171**: Joseph Smith Sen., portrait by unknown artist, prior to 1856, courtesy of the Joseph Smith Birthplace Memorial [Public Domain], via Wikimedia Commons. / **Page 171**: Samuel H Smith, unknown artist, prior to 1844, courtesy of The Joseph Smith Sr. Genealogical Website [Public Domain], via Wikimedia Commons. / **Page 171**: Jacob Whitmer, unknown artist, prior to 1856, courtesy of Find a Grave – Jacob Whitmer [Public Domain], via Wikimedia Commons. / **Page 171**: John Whitmer, unknown photographer, prior to 1878, courtesy of LDS Church History Library [Public Domain], via Wikimedia Commons. / **Page 172**: Portrait of John Calvin, by anonymous artist, ca 1550, courtesy of the Museum Catharijneconvent [Public Domain], via Wikimedia Commons. / **Page 174**: Assertion of Liberty of Conscience by the Independents of the Westminster Assembly of Divines, by John Rogers Herbert, 1847, courtesy of the Palace of Westminster [Public Domain], via Wikimedia Commons. / **Page 176**: Sentinel and Democrat, Burlington, VT 4 June 1830, Page 1. / **Page 179**: Latter-day Saint Scripture Quadruple Combination, unknown photographer [Public Domain], via Wikimedia Commons. / **Page 183**: Priesthood Restoration, by George W. Crocheron, 1898 [Public Domain], via Wikimedia Commons. / **Page 184**: 1830 Edition of the Book of Mormon, photograph courtesy of Troy DeSpain [CC BY-SA 4.0], via Wikimedia Commons. / **Page 187:** Dan Jones, photographer unknown [Public Domain], via Wikimedia Commons. / **Page 196**: Hedrickite Temple Lot with Church of Christ Buildings Nearby, photograph courtesy of EGDJ, 2010, [CC BY-SA 3.0], via Wikimedia Commons. / **Page 199**: Saints Driven from Jackson

County Missouri, by C.C.A. Christensen, ca 19th century, courtesy of the Brigham Young University Museum of Art [Public Domain], via Wikimedia Commons. / **Page 202**: The Kirtland Temple, image from The House of the Lord: A Study of Holy Sanctuaries, Ancient and Modern, by C.R. Savage Co., 1912 [Public Domain], via Wikimedia Commons. / **Page 206**: Interior Detail of Kirtland Temple (looking west), April 1934, photograph courtesy of Carl F. Waite, [Public Domain], via Wikimedia Commons. / **Page 207**: The Nauvoo Temple, daguerreotype, photograph by Louis C. Chaffin, 1847, courtesy of Cedar City Chapter of the Daughters of the Utah Pioneers [Public Domain], via Wikimedia Commons. / **Page 208**: Baptismal Font in the Salt Lake Temple, photograph courtesy of James Roscoe Savage, 1909 [Public Domain], via Wikimedia Commons. / **Page 210**: The Nauvoo Temple, unknown photographer, prior to 1850 [Public Domain], via Wikimedia Commons. / **Page 213**: John W Hess' Wives, image courtesy of Greg Hammond. / **Page 215**: Ira Eldredge and His Three Wives, unknown photographer, 1864 [Public Domain], via Wikimedia Commons. / **Page 217**: Elder James L. Ray with the Incas, 1967, photograph courtesy of James L. Ray. / **Page 224**: Baptism of Sister Desiraa Nkohla, 1993, photograph courtesy of Clint Bennion. / **Page 228**: Baptism of Vietnamese Saints, Burlington, VT, 1992, photograph courtesy of Greg Hammond. / **Page 233**: Palmach, Immigration to Israel, unknown photographer, 1947, courtesy of the Palmach Archive via the PikiWiki – Israel free image collection project [Public Domain], via Wikimedia Commons. / **Page 234**: Orson Hyde, original member of the Quorum of the Twelve Apostles (1835-1878) [Public Domain], via Wikimedia Commons. / **Page 235**: Orson Hyde Memorial Park in Jerusalem, Israel, photograph by Tamarah [CC BY-SA 3.0], via Wikimedia Commons. / **Page 239**: Karl Marx, photograph by John Jabez Edwin Mayal, pre-1875 [Public Domain], via Wikimedia Commons. / **Page 241**: Battle of Gettysburg, by Thure de Thulstrup, 1887, restoration by Adam Cuerden [Public Domain], via Wikimedia Commons. / **Page 247**: Palmyra New York Temple, 2006, photograph courtesy of Runt35 [CC BY-SA 3.0], via Wikimedia Commons. / **Page 248**: Parable of the Wise and Foolish Virgins, by Ernest Karlovich Lipgart, 1886 [Public Domain], via Wikimedia Commons. / **Page 249**: Polarlicht, the aurora borealis shines above Bear Lake, AK, Eielson Air Force Base, 2005 [Public Domain], via Wikimedia Commons. / **Page 254**: Total Solar Eclipse, photograph courtesy of O'Dea, 2017 [CC BY-SA 4.0], via Wikimedia Commons. / **Page 256**: WTC smoking on 9-11, photograph courtesy of Michael Foran [CC BY-SA 2.0], via Wikimedia

Commons. / **Page 257**: Blood Moon Eclipse, photograph courtesy of Andrew00111, 2015 [CC BY-SA 3.0], via Wikimedia Commons. / **Page 259**: Jews Praying in the Synagogue on Yom Kippur, by Maurycy Gottlieb, 1878, courtesy of the Tel Aviv Museum of Art [Public Domain], via Wikimedia Commons. / **Page 268**: Rome Temple at Sunset, photograph courtesy of Mbattista22 [CC BY-SA 4.0], via Wikimedia Commons. / **Page 273**: Seven Angels Pouring Vials of the Wrath of God Upon the Earth, by a British School Painter influenced by William Blake, 19th Century [Public Domain], via Wikimedia Commons. / **Page 276**: Apache Firing Rockets, photograph courtesy of MOD [CC BY-SA 4.0], via Wikimedia Commons. / **Page 278**: Holzschnitte zur Apokalypse, by Mattias Gerung, ca 1544-58 [Public Domain], via Wikimedia Commons. / **Page 283**: Apocalypse 15. Two Witnesses to be Unbound. Revelation Chapter 11 verse 3. Mortimer's Bible. Courtesy of Phillip Medhurst Collection [CC BY-SA 3.0], via Wikimedia Commons. / **Page 286**: Christ Coming in Glory, illustration from the book "Our Day in the Light of Prophecy and Providence," page 58, by William A Spicer, 1821 [Public Domain], via Wikimedia Commons. / **Page 288**: The Doubting Thomas, by unknown Carl Heinrich Bloch [Public Domain], via Wikimedia Commons. / **Page 292**: Battle of Gettysburg, Bodies of Dead Federal Soldiers on the Field of the First Day's Battle, 1863, photograph courtesy of the Civil War Glass Negatives [Public Domain], via Wikimedia Commons. / **Page 294**: Destruction, by Thomas Cole, 1836, courtesy of the New York Historical Society [Public Domain], via Wikimedia Commons. / **Page 296**: The Whore of Babylon, by Lucas Cranach, illustration in Martin Luther's translation of the Bible, 1534 [Public Domain], via Wikimedia Commons. / **Page 298**: The Resurrection, by Sebastiano Ricci, 1715, courtesy of Chelsea College [Public Domain], via Wikimedia Commons. / **Page 301**: The Resurrection of the Mortals, by Victor Mottez, 1870, courtesy of the Palais des Beaux-Arts de Lille (Nord) [Public Domain], via Wikimedia Commons. / **Page 304**: Bright Red Sun, photograph courtesy of Hell Rider [CC BY-SA 4.0], via Wikimedia Commons. / **Page 304**: Moon, photograph courtesy of Takeshi Kuboki [CC BY-SA 2.0], via Wikimedia Commons. / **Page 304**: Night Sky Full of Stars, photograph courtesy of Alessandro Caproni [CC BY-SA 2.0], via Wikimedia Commons. / **Page 308**: Descent Into Hell, by Andrea di Bonaiuto da Firenze, 1366, fresco, courtesy of Cappellone degli Spagnoli, Santa Maria Novella, Florence, Italy [Public Domain], via Wikimedia Commons. / **Page 312**: Figure of Christ, by Heinrich Hoffman, 1884 [Public Domain], via Wikimedia Commons. / **Page 313**: The

Valley of Tears, by Gustave Doré, 1883 [Public Domain], via Wikimedia Commons. / **Page 317**: Jesus Christ With the Children, by Carl Heinrich Bloch, ca 1800s, courtesy of The Museum of Natural History [Public Domain], via Wikimedia Commons. **Page 318**: Mother Mourning the Death of her Child, by Giuseppe Molteni, 1845, courtesy of Brera Pinacoteca [Public Domain], via Wikimedia Commons. / **Page 321**: Catholic Marriage of Giuseppe Pietro Arosio and Adriana Agostoni, San Fruttuoso, Monza, Italy, 5 May 1951 [Public Domain], via Wikimedia Commons. / **Page 323**: Two Mormon Missionaries in Jerusalem in 1903, photograph courtesy of Charles Ellis Johnson [Public Domain], via Wikimedia Commons. / **Page 325**: Unique Moment with the Sun and Christ the Redeemer, photograph courtesy of Donatas Dabravolskas, [CC BY-SA 4.0], via Wikimedia Commons. / **Page 327**: Nebuchadnezzar Seeing the Three Jews Unhurt in the Flames, by Philip Galle, 1565, courtesy of the Los Angeles County Museum of Art [Public Domain], via Wikimedia Commons. / **Page 330**: The Transfiguration of Jesus, by Carl Heinrich Bloch, 1865 [Public Domain], via Wikimedia Commons. / **Page 332**: Melchisedec Offers Bread and Wine to the Patriarch Abraham, by Moretto da Brescia, 1498-1554 [Public Domain], via Wikimedia Commons. / **Page 338**: The Second Coming Jesus in Red on a White Horse, unknown artist. / **Page 340**: Christ the Redeemer, by Titian, 1533, courtesy of the Pitti Palace [Public Domain], via Wikimedia Commons. / **Page 341**: The Fall and Salvation of Mankind Through the Life and Passion of Christ, by anonymous artist, 1568, courtesy of the British Museum [Public Domain], via Wikimedia Commons. / **Page 343**: Apocalypse 36. A New Heaven and New Earth. Revelation cap 21, courtesy of the De Vos. Phillip Medhurst Collection [CC BY-SA 3.0], via Wikimedia Commons. / **Page 345**: Het Lasstste Oordeel, by Raphael Coxie, ca 1588, courtesy of the Museum of Fine Arts, Ghent [Public Domain], via Wikimedia Commons. / **Page 348**: Last Judgment, by Stefan Lochner, ca 1435 [Public Domain], via Wikimedia Commons. / **Page 352**: Satan is Bound for 1000 Years, illustration on Rev 20:1 in The Great Bible of Pieter Mortier [Public Domain], via Wikimedia Commons. / **Page 354**: The Heavenly Jerusalem / The Bound Devil, by Matthias Gerung, ca 1530-32, illustration in the Ottheinrich-Bibel [Public Domain], via Wikimedia Commons. / **Page 358**: La Jerusalem Celeste, extraite de la Tapisserie de l'Apocalypse du Chateau d'Angers, France, photograph courtesy of Octave 444 [CC BY-SA 4.0], via Wikimedia Commons. / **Page 361**: St. Johns Ashfield Stained Glass King, photograph courtesy of Toby Hudson [CC BY-SA 3.0], via Wikimedia Commons. / **Page 362**: The Wolf and the Lamb, photograph courtesy of Pixabay License [Public Domain], via Wikimedia Commons. / **Page 367**: Spiral Galaxy NGC 4414, photograph by Hubble Space Telescope, courtesy of NASA and the Hubble Heritage Team [Public Domain], via Wikimedia Commons. / **Page 372**: Bible Primer, Old Testament, by Adolf Hult, 1919 [Public Domain], via Wikimedia Commons. / **Page 374**: Salt Lake City Temple, photograph by Carol M. Highsmith, courtesy of the US Library of Congress's Prints and Photographs Division [Public Domain], via Wikimedia Commons. / **Page 378**: Apocalypse 39, A New Heaven and New Earth, Revelation 21:2, by Phillip Medhurst, 2008, Phillip Medhurst Collection [CC BY-SA 3.0], via Wikimedia Commons. / **Page 383**: Satan Bound for 1000 Years, by Phillip Medhurst, 2008 [CC BY-SA 3.0], via Wikimedia Commons. / **Page 387**: Berlin: Sepp Dietrich, Adolf Hitler and Heinrich Himmler, by unknown photographer, 1937, courtesy of the German Federal Archives [CC BY-SA 3.0] Germany license, Bundesarchiv, Bild 183-C05557, via Wikimedia Commons. / **Page 389**: The Last Judgment, by Gustave Doré, 1866, illustration from John Milton's Paradise Lost [Public Domain], via Wikimedia Commons. / **Page 393**: Cain and Abel, by Titian, ca 1542-44, courtesy of the Santa Maria della Salute [Public Domain], via Wikimedia Commons. / **Page 397**: Judas and Satan, by Benoit-Hermogaste Molin, ca 1840s, courtesy of the Chambrey Musee des Beaux-arts [Public Domain], via Wikimedia Commons. / **Page 400**: Christ in Gethsemane, by Heinrich Hofmann, 1886, courtesy of the Riverside Church, New York City [Public Domain], via Wikimedia Commons. / **Page 409**: German steel engraving of Jesus Christ knocking at the door, by Peter Carl Geissler, 1802-1872 [Public Domain], via Wikimedia Commons. / **Page 413** : God Inviting Christ to Sit on the Throne at His Right Hand, by Pieter de Grebber, 1645, courtesy of the Museum Catharijneconvent [Public Domain], via Wikimedia Commons. / **Page 415**: Jesus Christ Receiving the World from the Hands of God the Father, by Antonio Arias Fernandez, 1657, courtesy of the Museo del Prado [Public Domain], via Wikimedia Commons. / **Page 420**: Allegory of Salvation, by Antonius Heusler, ca 1525, courtesy of the Museumslandschaft Hessen Kassel [Public Domain], via Wikimedia Commons. / **Page 427**: The Transfiguration, by Alexandr Andreyevich Ivanov, 1824 [Public Domain], via Wikimedia Commons. / **Page 438**: Jacob's Dream, by William Blake, 1805, courtesy of the British Museum [Public Domain], via Wikimedia Commons.